WIERSBE'S
EXPOSITORY
OUTLINES
ON THE
NEW TESTAMENT

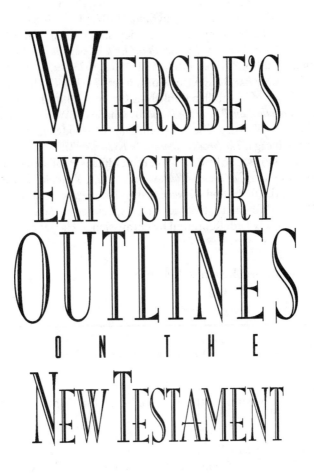

WIERSBE'S EXPOSITORY OUTLINES ON THE NEW TESTAMENT

WARREN W. WIERSBE

VICTOR BOOKS

A DIVISION OF SCRIPTURE PRESS PUBLICATIONS INC.
USA CANADA ENGLAND

Copyediting: Michael Kendrick, Robert N. Hosack
Cover Design: Scott Rattray

Library of Congress Cataloging-in-Publication Data

Wiersbe, Warren W.
    Wiersbe's expository outlines on the New Testament / by Warren Wiersbe.
      p.   cm.
    ISBN 0-89693-848-4
    1. Bible. N.T.—Commentaries. 2. Bible. N.T.—Outlines, syllabi, etc. 3. Bible. N.T.—Homiletical use. I. Title.
BS2341.2.W543   1992
225.7—dc20

                92-5611
                CIP

---

1 2 3 4 5 6 7 8 9 10 Printing/Year 96 95 94 93 92

CONTENTS

DEDICATED WITH GRATEFUL APPRECIATION
TO THE MEMORY OF DR. D.B. EASTEP (1900–1962),
A LOVING AND FAITHFUL PASTOR,
A GIFTED EXPOSITOR OF THE WORD,
A GODLY MENTOR TO ALL PASTORS.

PREFACE

The purpose of this book is to take you chapter-by-chapter through the New Testament and give you the opportunity to study each book and chapter and learn how they fit into the total revelation God has given us of Christ and His redemptive work. The studies are concise and practical and are especially suitable for Sunday School classes and Bible study groups that want to examine God's Word in a systematic manner.

These studies grew out of the lessons I prepared for the Calvary Baptist Church, Covington, Kentucky, when I ministered there from 1961 to 1971. My godly predecessor, Dr. D.B. Eastep, had devised "The Whole Bible Study Course" which took the student through the Bible in seven years, three years in the Old Testament and four years in the New Testament. The lessons were duplicated and distributed week by week to the Bible School students. When requests began to come from other churches that wanted to follow the same study schedule, eventually the lessons were assembled in notebook form and published by the Calvary Book Room, the literature ministry of the church. Thousands of sets of these outlines have been distributed throughout the world and the Lord has seen fit to bless them in a singular way.

When I decided it was time to publish the studies in a more permanent form, I approached Mark Sweeney at Victor Books; and he was more than glad to work with me on the project. I have revised and updated the material and added outlines on Mark and Luke, which were not in the original studies; but there has been no change in the theological position or the basic interpretations.

If you have used any of the volumes in my *BE* series, you will recognize a similar approach in these studies. However, there is material in this volume that is not found in the *BE* series; and the approach here is chapter-by-chapter rather than verse-by-verse. Even if you have my *Bible Exposition Commentary*, you will find this new volume helpful in your studies.

I want to record my deep appreciation to Mrs. D.B. Eastep, for many years manager of the Calvary Book Room, who supervised the publishing and distributing of the original *Expository Outlines on the New Testament*. She and her staff accepted this difficult task as a ministry of love for which the Lord will abundantly reward them. I can't begin to name individually all the dear people at Calvary Baptist Church who have had a part in producing the original lesson sheets and then the notebooks, but they know who they are and that I love them and appreciate their sacrificial ministries. Some of them are in heaven and know firsthand how God has used these simple studies around the world to win the lost and build His church.

My editor at Victor Books, Robert Hosack, deserves special thanks for his patience and encouragement, particularly when I was struggling to get the computer program working right so I could edit the material quickly.

Finally, my wife Betty is surely being measured for a special crown to reward her for all the hours she gave me for Bible study and writing while these studies were in preparation. It wasn't easy for the pastor of a large and growing church, and the father of four active children, to carve out time to write these lessons; but Betty was always there to keep the household running smoothly, handle the phone calls and interruptions, and encourage me to practice Paul's philosophy of "this one thing I do."

My prayer is that this new edition of *Expository Outlines on the New Testament* will have a wide and fruitful ministry to the glory of God.

Warren W. Wiersbe

MATTHEW

A Suggested Outline of Matthew

I. The Revelation of the King (1–10)

    A. The person of the King (1–4)
        1. His ancestry and birth (1–2)
        2. His messenger (3)
        3. His temptation and early ministry (4)
    B. The principles of the King (5–7)
    C. The power of the King (8–10)

II. The Rebellion Against the King (11–13)

    A. His messenger rejected (11:1-19)
    B. His works denied (11:20-30)
    C. His principles refused (12:1-21)
    D. His person attacked (12:22-50)
    E. Result: the parables of the kingdom (13)

III. The Retirement of the King (14–20)

    A. Before Peter's confession (14:1–16:12)
    B. Peter's confession: the church (16:13-28)
       First mention of the crucifixion (16:21)
    C. After Peter's confession (17–20)
       Second mention of the crucifixion (17:22-23)
       Third mention of the crucifixion (20:17-19)

IV. The Rejection of the King (21–27)

    A. His public presentation to the Jews (21:1-16)
    B. His conflict with the religious leaders (21:17–23:39)
    C. His prophecies of the future kingdom (24–25)
    D. His suffering and death (26–27)

V. The Resurrection of the King (28)

Introductory Notes to Matthew

I. The Relationship to the Other Gospels

A. Matthew is primarily Jewish and presents Christ as the King (1:1: "the Son of David").

B. Mark is primarily Roman and presents Christ as the Servant.

C. Luke is primarily for the Greeks and presents Christ as the perfect Son of Man.

D. John is universal in appeal and presents Christ as the eternal Son of God.

II. The Jewish Character of Matthew's Gospel

A. It was written by a Jewish tax collector named Levi (Matt. 9:9-13; Luke 5:27-32; Mark 2:13-17).

B. Because of its position, it is the bridge between the OT and the NT.

C. It abounds in OT quotations and references.

According to W. Graham Scroggie's *Guide to the Gospels* there are 53 quotations from the OT and 76 references to OT passages, a total of 129 references or allusions. Matthew refers to 25 of the 39 OT books. The word "fulfilled" is used at least 12 times (see 1:22; 2:15, 17, 23, etc.).

D. Christ is spoken of often as the Son of David (1:1; 9:27; 12:23, etc.)

E. It is filled with references to "the kingdom of heaven," basically a Jewish concept, and can rightly be termed "The Kingdom Gospel."

F. The Jewish character of Matthew's Gospel is found in the material unique to it.

This includes Christ's genealogy to Abraham (1:1-17); the information about Joseph (1:18-25); the mission of the disciples to the lost sheep of the Children of Israel (chap. 10); Christ's denunciation of the Pharisees (chap. 23); and several parables in chapters 20–22 and 25.

III. The Basic Theme of Matthew

A. *Matthew is not chronological, as are Mark and Luke.*

Matthew has selected material from Christ's life and arranged it to convey one specific truth: Christ is the King of the Jews, rejected by His people, crucified for the whole world, and now alive in heaven.

B. *In chapters 1–10, Christ reveals Himself as the long-awaited King of the Jews.*

He was born as predicted, announced by the messenger God promised, and proved His messiahship by doing the very works the prophets said He would do. In chapters 11–13, the Jewish leaders rebel against Him and claim Christ's works are of the devil. They insisted on their man-made traditions and religious customs instead of His principles. Though He did many mighty works, the nation rejected Him; and the result was that Jesus turned to the Gentiles ("Come unto Me *all* you that labor," 11:28, italics mine) and gave the parables of the kingdom (chap. 13). He described in these parables what the kingdom would be like on earth during this present age.

C. *In chapters 14–20 Christ retires with His disciples to prepare them for the events of the Cross.*

Of course, He is still carrying on a public ministry, but during this time He is specifically teaching the disciples new truths concerning His death and resurrection. Here we have Peter's great confession of faith, the first prediction of Christ's death, and the first mention of the church.

D. *In 21–27, the King is openly rejected.*

What began as rebellion now becomes open hostility and leads to His crucifixion. During this time He is in open conflict with the religious leaders. He teaches His disciples what the future will be like (chaps. 26–27) and willingly dies on the cross as "the King of the Jews" (27:29).

E. *The final chapter gives His resurrection and ascension as a King with all authority over all things.*

IV. The Kingdom of Heaven

A. The kingdom of heaven refers to the rule of God on the earth.

It takes different forms at different times. In the beginning, God ruled on earth through Adam, whom He appointed to have dominion. During the days of Israel, He ruled through judges and kings. When Israel went into captivity, God even ruled through Gentile monarchs (Dan. 2:37). Christ offered Himself to the Jews when He came (see Matt. 4:17), but they did not receive Him. "He came unto His own [world], and His own [people] received Him not" (John 1:11). The Jews rejected the kingdom when they rejected the King.

In Matt. 13, He described the kingdom of heaven in this age. It is a mixture of good and bad, true and false. At the end of the age, the good will be separated from the evil, and the kingdom will be established on the earth in purity and righteousness. The church is in the kingdom of heaven, but it is not the kingdom of heaven. To apply Matt. 13 to the church is to create confusion. Perhaps the best equivalent for "the kingdom of heaven" in today's vocabulary is the word "Christendom," the "professed church" as seen in the world, a mixture of the true and the false.

MATTHEW 1

In the first ten chapters of Matthew, we have "The Revelation of the King." He reveals Himself to the Jews as to His Person (1–4), His principles (5–7), and His power (8–10). Remember that Matthew is seeking to prove that Jesus Christ is the King, "the Son of David." In this first chapter, he gives the human ancestry of Christ (vv. 1-17), then describes the birth of Christ (vv. 18-25). Thus, Jesus is the "root and the offspring of David" (Rev. 22:16). He is "the root" in that He is eternal God and brought David into being; He is the "offspring" in that His humanity is linked to David in His birth (Rom. 1:1-4).

I. The Faithful Providence of God (1:1-17)

Providence is God's control of circumstances so that His will prevails and His purposes are fulfilled. Think of Satan's attacks against Israel and how he sought to prevent Christ from coming! Because of Abraham's disobedience, Sarah was almost lost and the promised seed ruined (Gen. 12:10-20). At one time, the royal seed was all slain, except for young Joash (2 Kings 11). This genealogy is not a dull list of names. It is a record of the faithfulness of God in preserving the children of Abraham as a channel through whom Christ could come into the world.

Matthew's genealogy is of Joseph, Jesus' father in the eyes of the law. Luke gives Mary's genealogy. Mary and Joseph were both descendants of David.

You can see the grace of God in this list of names. Note the four women mentioned: Tamar (v. 3, see Gen. 38); Rahab (v. 5, see Josh. 2; Heb. 11:31); Ruth (v. 5, see the Book of Ruth); and Bathsheba (v. 6, see 2 Sam. 12). Mary is also mentioned. These women illustrate the grace of God. Tamar was guilty of whoredom, yet God permitted her to be listed in the ancestry of Christ. Rahab was both a harlot and a foreigner. She was saved by her faith. Ruth was a Moabitess; and according to Deut. 23:3-6, she was excluded from the nation of Israel. Bathsheba was partner to David's awful sin, yet God forgave her and permitted her to be one of Christ's ancestors through Solomon. "Where sin abounded, grace did much more abound" (Rom. 5:20).

This genealogy is not complete, of course. Several names are left out. It was common among the Jews to leave out unimportant

15

names to help the children remember the lists. Three sets of fourteen names would be easy to remember. In 1:8, Ahaziah, Joash, and Amaziah are omitted, probably because of their relationship to Ahab's wicked daughter, Athaliah. No Jew today has his *legal* genealogy. All the records were destroyed in A.D. 70 when the temple was ruined. Jesus Christ is the only Jew alive today who can prove His rights to the throne of David.

II. The Fulfilled Promise of God (1:18-25)

"Betrothal" (engagement) among the Jews was as binding as marriage. When Joseph discovered Mary's condition, he naturally assumed she had been unfaithful to him. Note his prudence: "While he thought on these things" (v. 20). How important it is to be "slow to wrath" and to consider matters thoughtfully! (see Prov. 21:5)

According to Deut. 22:23-24, Mary could have been stoned. Indications are that the Jews did not obey this law but rather allowed the innocent party to divorce the unfaithful mate. It took great faith for Joseph to believe God's message in the dream. His love for God and for Mary made him willing to "bear reproach" for Christ. Imagine how the neighbors must have talked! In John 8:41, there is a suggestion that the Jews slandered Christ's birth, intimating that He was born of fornication. Satan has always attacked the truth of the Virgin Birth, for when he does, he denies the Person and work of Christ and the truth of the Bible.

The name Jesus means "Savior" and is a Gk. version of the Heb. name "Joshua." In the OT, there are two well-known Joshuas: the soldier who led Israel into Canaan (see the Book of Joshua), and the high priest mentioned in Zech. 3. Christ is our Captain of Salvation, leading us to victory. He is our Great High Priest, representing us before the throne of God.

Christ's birth fulfills the prophecy of Isa. 7:14. Read Isa. 7 very carefully. Ahaz was about to be attacked by Rezin, King of Syria, and Pekah, King of Israel. The Lord sent Isaiah to encourage Ahaz (7:1-9) and to give Ahaz a sign. Ahaz acted very pious and refused the sign. So, God gave the sign to the whole house of David, not just to Ahaz (see 7:13). The sign is the birth of Immanuel ("God with us") to the virgin mother. This sign had nothing to do with Ahaz at that time. In Isa. 8, God gave Ahaz His sign, using the child of Isaiah to do this. (Note: the Heb. word in Isa. 7:14, and the Gk. word in Matt. 1:23, can only mean virgin.)

We must admire Joseph's immediate obedience (v. 24). He was careful to keep his relationship with Mary pure. In the Bible, only four ways are noted to get a body: (1) without a man or a woman—as Adam did, made from the dust of the earth; (2) with a man, but no woman—as Eve did, made from Adam's side; (3) with a man and a woman—as all humans are born; or (4) with a woman, but no man—as Jesus was born, having an earthly mother but no biological father. It was important that Jesus be born of a virgin that He might have a sinless human nature, conceived by the Holy Spirit (see Luke 1). Since He existed before the creation of man, how could He ever be born of a human father and mother? Every new baby is a being that has never existed before. The modernist who denies Christ's virgin birth denies His eternal Godhead and deity. Either He is God, or He is an imposter.

"Fulfilled" (v. 22) is a favorite word of Matthew's. He uses it at least twelve times to show that Jesus completed the prophecies given in the OT Scriptures.

MATTHEW 2

I. The Homage Shown to the King (2:1-12)

These "wise men" were Magi, Oriental astrologers who studied the stars and sought to understand the times. They were Gentiles who had been especially called of God to come and pay homage to the newborn King. There may be a reference to the miraculous star in Balaam's prophecy in Num. 24:17. We do not know how many Magi there were, where they came from, or what their names were. Familiar Christmas traditions do not always have scriptural support.

Jesus' title, "King of the Jews," raised suspicion because Herod feared anyone who threatened his throne. He was a ruthless monster who even killed his own children to protect his throne. He had nine (or ten) wives and was known for his treachery and lust. An Edomite, he had a natural hatred for the Jews. Herod did not know God's Word, but had to ask the scribes. The scribes knew the Word, but did not act upon it. The wise men were both hearers and doers of the Word! How close the priests were to the Messiah, yet they did not go.

The visit of the Magi is an indication that the Gentiles will someday worship the King when the kingdom is set up on earth

(Isa. 60:6). Their experience is a good lesson in finding the will of God: (1) they followed the light God gave them; (2) they confirmed their steps by the Word of God; and (3) they obeyed God without question and He led them each step of the way. Note that they went home by "another way" (v. 12). Anyone who comes to Christ will go home another way and be a new creature (2 Cor. 5:17).

Matthew cites Micah 5:2 to show that Christ was born where the prophet had predicted. God bypassed proud Jerusalem and chose humble Bethlehem. King David had come from Bethlehem, and Christ is David's Son (1:1). For comparisons between David and Christ, see the outline for chapter 4.

II. The Hatred Against the King (2:13-18)

Just as Satan had tried to keep Christ from being born, now he tried to destroy Him after He was born (see Rev. 12:1-4). The flesh wars against the Spirit, and Herod (an Edomite) warred against Christ. We cannot help but admire Joseph for his faithfulness in obeying God and caring for both Mary and Jesus. Matthew quoted Hosea 11:1 to show that Christ would come out of Egypt. Herod slew not more than twenty infants, since there could not have been too many babies of that age in the town. Matthew saw in this a fulfillment of Jer. 31:15.

III. The Humility of the King (2:19-23)

Joseph used his "sanctified common sense" and did not return to Judea. God affirmed the decision, and the family moved to Nazareth. Matthew refers to what "was spoken by the prophets" (v. 23, note the plural) but does not give any specific references. The word "Nazarene" may relate to the Heb. word *netzer* which means "branch," a name for Jesus. This is why Matthew wrote "prophets" (plural) since Christ is called "the Branch" in Isa. 11:1 and 4:2; also Jer. 23:5 and 33:15, and Zech. 3:8 and 6:12. Because He lived in a despised place, Jesus was like a lowly branch; but the Branch would one day blossom with beauty and great glory.

Nazareth was an ignoble town. "Can anything good come from there?" asked Nathanael (John 1:46, NIV). Jesus was a humble King. He emptied and humbled Himself even unto death to save us (see Phil. 2:1-11).

MATTHEW 3

In the first ten chapters, Matthew is recording the revelation of the King to the nation Israel. In chapters 1 and 2 he gave the ancestry and birth of the King, showing from the prophets that Jesus Christ is the King of Israel. In chapter 3 he introduces Jesus through His "forerunner" John the Baptist.

I. John the Baptist Came (3:1-6)

A. His messsage (vv. 1-2).

Keep in mind that the kingdom is being offered to the Jews. As the forerunner of the King, John is asking the people to repent (change their minds) and prepare for the King. Jesus preached this message (4:17) and so did the disciples (10:7). When the nation rejected the King, the kingdom was taken from them (21:42-43).

B. His authority (v. 3).

John fulfilled the prophecy of Isa. 40:3. He was the last of the OT prophets (Luke 16:16). No prophet had been heard for 400 years!

C. His person (v. 4).

He was humble and rustic in manner and dress. His dress reminds one of Elijah (2 Kings 1:8). In Mal. 4:5-6, God promised that Elijah would come before the dreadful Day of the Lord. The Jews asked John if he was Elijah and he denied it (John 1:21). Yet, if the Jews had received their King, John would have been that Elijah (see 11:14). John came in the spirit and power of Elijah (Luke 1:17).

D. His baptism (vv. 5-6).

This was not Christian baptism (see Acts 19:1-7), but rather baptism unto repentance (see v. 11). His baptism was from heaven (21:25-27) for two purposes: (1) to introduce Christ to the nation (John 1:31) and (2) to prepare their hearts for the coming of the King. The Jews baptized Gentiles who became Jewish proselytes, but John baptized Jews!

II. The Pharisees and Sadducees Came (3:7-12)

A. Their character (vv. 7-8).

The Pharisees were legal literalists who turned the law into a burden; the Sadducees were "liberals" who denied much of the OT (see Acts 23:8). On three occasions, the Pharisees were called "generation of vipers": by John the Baptist, and by Jesus (12:34 and 23:33). Satan is a serpent, and these men were children of Satan (John 8:44). The Pharisees were Christ's enemies and appear often in Matthew. You find them united again in 16:1 and 22:23 and 34.

B. Their need (vv. 9-12).

They depended on their human relationship to Abraham to save them (see Rom. 9:6ff and Gal. 3:7). Like Nicodemus in John 3, they stumbled at the truth that they needed to be born again. God gets to the root of our lives (v. 10), for the root determines the fruit (v. 8). Note how John points them to Jesus and magnifies Him alone! Two "baptisms" are mentioned in v. 11—with the Holy Spirit (fulfilled at Pentecost, Acts 1:5, and to the Gentiles in Acts 11:16); and with fire, to be fulfilled at His second coming (see Mal. 3:1-2 with Luke 7:27). The little "and" covers a long period of time! The fire speaks of judgment.

III. Jesus Came (3:13-17)

A. Jesus and John (vv. 13-15).

Why was the sinless Son of God baptized? We suggest six reasons:

1. Obligation—"to fulfill all righteousness" (cf. John 8:29).

2. Consecration—the OT priest was washed, then anointed. Jesus submitted to water baptism, then the Holy Spirit came as a dove. See Ex. 29.

3. Commendation—Jesus gave His approval of John's ministry and thus obligated the people to listen to John and obey him. Instead, the religious leaders rejected John's baptism (21:23-27).

4. Proclamation—this was John's official introduction of Jesus to the Jewish nation. See John 1:31.

5. Anticipation—this water baptism looked forward to His baptism of suffering for us on the cross (Luke 12:50). Jesus fulfilled all righteousness through His sacrificial death on Calvary.

6. Identification—Jesus identified Himself with sinful men. Immediately after, the Spirit drove Him into the wilderness. There may be here a picture of the "scapegoat" that symbolically carried the nation's sins into the wilderness (Lev. 16:1-10).

The Gk. word *baptizo* means "to dip, to immerse," and John required "much water" for his baptism (John 3:23). All the waves and billows of God's wrath were experienced by Jesus on the cross.

B. Jesus and the Spirit (v. 16).

This was the sign God had promised to give John to identify Christ (John 1:31-34). Though Jesus and John were related (Luke 1:36), it is likely they had not seen each other for years. Even if John did know Jesus in the flesh, he would want the divine assurance from heaven. The symbol of the Spirit as a dove is important: the dove is a clean bird; it is faithful to its mate in love; it is peaceful and gentle. Christ was born through the power of the Spirit (Luke 1:34-35) and was also empowered by the Spirit for His life and ministry.

C. Jesus and the Father (v. 17).

This is the first of three occasions when the Father spoke to the Son from heaven (see Matt. 17:5 and John 12:28). We have the Trinity revealed here: the Son is baptized, the Spirit descends like a dove, and the Father speaks from heaven. As He entered His ministry, the Son was approved by the Father; as He approached the cross (17:5), He received that commendation again.

MATTHEW 4

Before a king can rule others, he must prove that he can rule himself. This is why King Saul lost his kingship—he was unable to control himself and obey God. This chapter shows the King meeting His enemy, "the prince of this world" (John 14:30), and defeating him.

I. The Temptation of Jesus (4:1-11)

A. The first temptation (vv. 3-4).

Satan appealed to the body, the desires of the flesh. There was no sin in being hungry. Yet Satan suggested that, if Christ were God's Son, He should not let Him hunger. Satan always wants us to think that God is "holding out on us" (see Gen. 3:5). The suggestion is, "God must not love you. If He did, He would take better care of you!" For Christ to use His divine powers out of the will of God would be defeat. He always did what pleased God (John 8:29).

Christ met this temptation with Deut. 8:3. Feeding the inner spiritual person is far more important than feeding the physical. Read Deut. 8:1-6 and note that God tests us and proves us in the ordinary things of life, like eating and drinking. Jesus lived under the authority of God's Word; so should we.

Note that Jesus had the Word "hidden in His heart" (Ps. 119:11) and was able to quote it and apply it at the right time.

B. The second temptation (vv. 5-7).

Satan "dares" Jesus to prove the faithfulness of God. "Since You believe the Word of God," implies Satan, "then why not prove one of God's promises?" Satan then quotes—or misquotes—Ps. 91:11-12. "If You really believe in God's care, then throw Yourself off the temple and let the angels catch You!" Christ answered him from Deut. 6:16.

Satan left out the important phrase "in all Your ways" (Ps. 91:11, NKJV). God keeps His promises when we keep His ways. Jesus said we should live by every word that God utters, but Satan adds to the Bible or takes from it. He can twist the Bible and give carnal Christians biblical reasons to support their foolish actions. Beware of taking promises out of their context, or claiming promises when you have not met the conditions.

To do something without the Bible's authority is to sin, "for whatsoever is not of faith is sin" (Rom. 14:23). This is to tempt God—to "dare Him" to intervene and rescue us when we are in trouble. Deliberate disobedience is an invitation for chastening.

C. The third temptation (vv. 8-10).

Satan offers Christ an "easy way" to become King. As the prince of this world (John 14:30), Satan is permitted by God to have a certain amount of control over its kingdoms. According to Ps. 2:6-9, God had already promised these kingdoms to Christ. (Note how Ps. 2:6-7, NKJV, takes you back to Christ's baptism, "You art My Son.") But He would have to die on the cross to gain this kingdom. Satan was trying to tempt Him away from the cross.

Christ defeated Satan with Deut. 6:13. Whatever we worship is the god we serve. If a person worships money, he or she lives for money and obeys it. If we worship God, we live for God and obey Him. We cannot do both (Matt. 6:24). One day in the future, Satan will hand over the kingdoms to the Antichrist (Rev. 13). But Christ will come to take these kingdoms (Rev. 19:11-21) and set up His own kingdom for 1,000 years.

II. OT Temptation Types

In His temptation, Christ appears to fulfill two OT types: Adam and David.

A. The last Adam (1 Cor. 15:45).

1. Adam was tempted in a beautiful garden; Christ struggled in a lonely wilderness.
2. Adam was at his best when tempted; Christ was hungry.
3. Adam was the king of the old creation (Gen. 1:26); Christ is King of the new (spiritual) creation (2 Cor. 5:17).
4. Adam sinned and lost his dominion (Heb. 2:6-9); Christ obeyed and regained what Adam lost and more (Rom. 5:12-21).
5. Adam was defeated and brought death to humanity; Christ was victorious and brought life to all who will trust Him.

B. The Son of David (Matt. 1:1).

1. Both David and Christ came from Bethlehem.
2. Both were chosen and anointed by God.
3. Both were "exiles" and persecuted before being crowned.
4. Goliath dared Israel for forty days; Satan attacked Christ forty days.
5. David used one stone from five to slay the giant; Christ used one book (Deut.) from five (the Law of Moses) to defeat Satan.
6. Goliath was a strong man; Satan is compared to a strong man (Matt. 12:22-30).
7. David cut off the giant's head with his sword; Christ overcame Satan with the sword of the Spirit, the Word of God (Heb. 4:12).

The Sermon on the Mount (Matthew 5–7)

I. Suggested Outline of the Sermon

A. True righteousness pictured by Christ (5:1-48).

Key verse: 5:48
1. Positive — righteousness is inward (5:1-16)
2. Negative — sin is inward (5:17-48)
   Murder * adultery * swearing * retaliation

B. True righteousness practiced by believers (6:1–7:12).

Key verses: 6:1; 6:33; 7:12

1. In worship, relationship to God (6:1-18)
   Giving * praying * fasting
2. In wealth, relationship to the world (6:19-34)
3. In walk, relationship to others (7:1-12)

C. True righteousness proved by tests (7:13-29).

Key verse: 7:20
1. The test of self-denial: "Will I walk the narrow way?" (7:13-14)
2. The test of fruit-bearing: "What comes from my life?" (7:15-20)
3. The test of obedience: "Am I doing as well as saying?" (7:21-29)

II. Survey of the Sermon

Few passages in the Bible are more misunderstood and misapplied than the Sermon on the Mount. Often people will take single verses or phrases from Matt. 5–7 and disregard the context. It's important that we have a total view of this important sermon before we attempt to study the various divisions of this passage.

A. Theme.

Christ gives the theme in 5:17-20 — true righteousness as opposed to the false righteousness of the scribes and Pharisees. It's important to remember that the people looked to the scribes and Pharisees as their models and teachers in the things of God. They set the rules and determined what was holy and unholy. One reason why the scribes and Pharisees hated Jesus is because He exposed their shallowness and deceit in this sermon. See also Matt. 23.

B. Purposes.

There are three basic purposes for Christ giving this sermon: (1) to tell His followers what true righteousness is, as opposed to the false righteousness of the scribes and Pharisees; (2) to describe the laws of His kingdom, the spiritual principles He uses to govern the lives of men; and (3) to relate His message to the OT law and the traditions of the scribes and Pharisees.

C. Three mistakes.

Many people make one (or all) of three mistakes when studying the Sermon on the Mount: (1) They apply it to nations when it is for individuals. (2) They apply it to the unsaved when it is for believers. (3) They make it into a "Christian law" to be obeyed, when it is really a description of what a Christian is like when the Holy Spirit is working through our lives (Rom. 8:1-4).

D. Is it for us today?

Since Matthew is the "kingdom Gospel" and at this stage the King has not been rejected, some students say that the Sermon on the Mount applies only to God's people during the kingdom age. If Israel had received Christ, then these laws would have been put into practice; but, since they rejected Him, Matthew 5–7 must await the Millennium for their fulfillment. One may hold to the dispensational character of Matthew without losing the Sermon on the Mount for today. In fact, if the Sermon on the Mount applies only to the Kingdom Age, then will there be thieves in the Millennium? (6:19) Will there be Pharisees? (5:17-20) Will there be false prophets? (7:15) If Satan is bound during the Millennium, then why pray in 6:13, "Deliver us from the evil one"? Will there be fasting in the Millennium? (6:16-18) And why pray, "Thy kingdom come" (6:10) if we are already in the kingdom?

The Jews (led by the scribes and Pharisees) were expecting a political kingdom and had forgotten the spiritual element. Jesus upset their thinking in this sermon by announcing the spiritual basis for His kingdom. These principles will apply in every age. In fact, most of the material in the Sermon on the Mount is repeated in one way or another in the NT epistles to the church. So, while Matt. 5–7 *may* have a dispensational meaning, we dare not say that these chapters are not for the church today.

The following chart shows the contrast between the righteousness that Christ gives and the righteousness of the scribes and Pharisees.

Sermon on the Mount	Pharisees
1. Righteousness is first inward, then outward (5:1-16)	1. Righteousness a matter of outward acts (Matt. 23:23-28; Luke 11:37-41)
2. Sin is a matter of the heart, not only the actions (5:17-48)	2. Sin is mainly in outward actions only (Luke 18:9-14; Mark 2:13-28)
3. Righteousness is for God to see, not for men to praise (6:1-18)	3. Want to be seen of men (Matt. 23:2-12)

| 4. God first; money second (6:19-31) | 4. Covetous (Luke 16:14ff) |
| 5. Not to judge (7:1-12) | 5. Harsh in judging (Luke 18:9ff; Matt. 12:22ff) |

III. The Sermon and Salvation

Millions of people think they can be saved by obeying the Sermon on the Mount. They think it is easier than trying to obey the Ten Commandments. How foolish! Nobody was ever saved by obeying any law (Gal. 2:16; 3:10-11), and the Sermon on the Mount is much more strict than Moses' Law! Under his Law, if a man murdered another, he was guilty, but Jesus says that hatred in the heart is the moral equivalent of murder. Lust is adultery in the heart. Please keep in mind that the Beatitudes come first. They describe the kind of person who, under the power of the Spirit, can live the way Matt. 5–7 describes. Note the progression in the Beatitudes:

poor in spirit—this means humble before God

mourn—this means sorrow for sin, repentance

meek—waiting before God for His mercy

hunger and thirst—asking for God's righteousness

merciful—condemning self, not others

pure in heart—this is the result!

peacemakers—trying to win others to Christ

persecuted—this happens to all who live godly lives

The Sermon on the Mount does not mention the Holy Spirit or the blood of Christ, yet the basis for it is Calvary, and the power to live it is by the Holy Spirit. Again, keep in mind that these are not commandments to obey—a "Christian Law." The Sermon on the Mount describes the character of the truly righteous person, character that comes from a walk with the Lord. It's the spirit of this

Sermon that is important. Keeping it according to its letter is going back to the very Pharisaic righteousness that Jesus is condemning!

MATTHEW 5

The first sixteen verses of Matthew 5 describe the true Christian and deal with character. The rest of the Sermon on the Mount deals with conduct that grows out of character. Character always comes before conduct, because what we are determines what we do. In Matt. 5:1-16, Jesus shows us that true righteousness is inward, and in 5:17-48, He points out that sin is also inward. Thus, He exposed the false righteousness of the Pharisees, who taught that holiness consisted in religious actions, and that sin was what you did outwardly. How many people make these mistakes today! God looks upon the heart, for there is life's destiny decided.

I. The Beatitudes Collectively (5:1-12)

The word *beatitude* is not found in your Bible. It simply means blessing and comes from the Latin word for blessed.

There is definite progression in these verses. They show how the person begins with his or her own sense of sin and finally becomes a child of God and the results that then follow. Note that these verses deal with attitudes—what we think in our hearts, our outlook on life. "Beatitudes"—the *attitudes* that ought to *be* in our lives if we are true Christians.

A. "Poor in spirit" (v. 3).

Our attitude toward ourselves in which we feel our need and admit it.

B. "Mourn" (v. 4).

Our attitude toward sin, a true sorrow for sin.

C. "Meek" (v. 5).

Our attitude toward others; we are teachable; we do not defend ourselves when we are wrong.

D. "Hunger and thirst" (v. 6).

Here our attitude toward God is expressed; we receive His righteousness by faith because we ask for it.

The rest of the Beatitudes show the results of the new life in the believer:

E. "Merciful" (v. 7).

We have a forgiving spirit and love others.

F. "Pure in heart" (v. 8).

We keep our lives clean; holiness is happiness to us, and we want no substitutes.

G. "Peacemakers" (v. 9).

Christians should bring peace, between people and God and between those who are at odds with each other. We share the Gospel of peace.

H. "Persecuted" (v. 10).

All who live godly lives will suffer persecution.

II. The Beatitudes Individually (5:1-12)

A. "Poor in spirit" (v. 3).

We must be empty before we can be full. The opposite of this is self-sufficiency. Our sufficiency is not of ourselves (2 Cor. 3:5). The world promotes self-sufficiency, yet God dwells with the person whose heart is broken (Isa. 57:15). This does not mean false humility or cowardice; it means a proper attitude toward self, realizing how weak and sinful we are apart from Christ. Compare the two men in Luke 18:9-14.

B. "Mourn" (v. 4).

This is sincere sorrow for sin, our sin and the sins of others. How careless we are about sin! We excuse it, yet God hates it, and sin breaks God's heart. Beware of the sorrow of this world (2 Cor. 7:8-10). Peter mourned with godly sorrow and was forgiven; Judas had remorse—the sorrow of this world—and he took his life.

C. "Meek" (v. 5).

Meekness is not weakness! Jesus was meek (Matt. 11:29), yet He drove the changers from the temple. Moses was meek (Num. 12:3), yet he judged sinners and even faced Aaron with his sin.

Meekness means not asserting my own rights, but living for the glory of God. Christians are to show meekness (Eph. 4:1-2; Titus 3:2). We are prone to be self-willed.

D. "Hunger and thirst" (v. 6).

A true Christian has an appetite for spiritual things. Ask people what they desire and you will know what they are like.

E. "Merciful" (v. 7).

This is not legalism, but merely the working of the biblical principle of sowing and reaping. If we show mercy, because Christ has been merciful to us, then mercy will come back to us (see Luke 16:1-13; James 2:13; Prov. 11:17). We do not earn mercy, but we must have hearts prepared to receive it.

F. "Pure in heart" (v. 8).

Not sinlessness (1 John 1:8) but the truth within (Ps. 51:6). It means a single heart, not divided between God and the world.

G. "Peacemakers" (v. 9).

Titus 3:3 describes this world at war. Christians have the Gospel of peace on their feet (Eph. 6:15), so that wherever they go, they bring peace. This is not "peace at any price," for holiness is more important than a peace based on sin (see James 3:17; Heb. 12:14). Compromise is not peace, but Christians should not be contentious as they contend for the faith.

H. "Persecuted" (v. 10).

See 2 Tim. 3:12 and 1 Peter 4:15. Note that we should be accused "falsely." We should never be guilty of deliberately asking for persecution. If we live godly lives, suffering will come! Note the rewards: we are in the same company as Christ and the prophets, and we shall be rewarded in heaven.

III. Salt and Light (5:13-16)

There are two pictures of the Christian in closing: salt and the light. Salt speaks of inward character that influences a decaying world; light speaks of the outward testimony of good works that points to God. Our task is to keep our lives pure that we might "salt" this earth and hold back corruption so that the Gospel can get out. Our good works must accompany our dedicated lives as we let our lights shine.

IV. The Old and the New (5:17-48)

Having declared the meaning of true righteousness, the Lord then explained the meaning of sin. He pointed out that He was not abandoning or nullifying the law but fulfilling it. The OT law dealt only with outward actions; but in the kingdom, we must beware of sinful inward attitudes. Jesus fulfilled the law in His life, for nobody could accuse Him of sin; and He fulfilled it in His death and resurrection. God's people do not obey Him because of outward constraint but because of an inward life, the power of the Spirit of God. While the Holy Spirit is not mentioned in the Sermon on the Mount, it is clear that we cannot practice what Jesus teaches here apart from the Spirit's help (Rom. 8:1-13). Jesus deals with several sins and explains how we must overcome them.

A. Anger (vv. 21-26).

The law said, "You shalt not kill [murder]" (Ex. 20:13, NKJV); but Jesus said, "Don't be angry with others." Anger is like murder in the heart and it can lead to evil words and actual murder. "The judgment" refers to a local court and "the council" to the Jewish Sanhedrin, the highest court of the land. Don't wait for your angry brother or sister to take the first step; you do it, and do it quickly before things get worse!

B. Lust (vv. 27-32).

While actual adultery is far worse than inward lustful fantasies, the inner desires can quickly lead to this forbidden sin (Ex. 20:14). We must deal ruthlessly with ourselves and not encourage the imagination to "feed on" these sins. The eyes and the hands (seeing and touching) must be kept under control. For Christ's teachings on marriage and divorce, see Matt. 19:1-11.

C. Deception (vv. 33-37).

For the law of Moses, see Lev. 19:12 and Deut. 23:23. The Jewish legal experts had many ways to get around the law and break oaths, so that a person's promises might mean nothing. Jesus does not forbid us to take a legal oath, but He warns us to speak the truth and not embellish our conversation with oaths that are supposed to strengthen our words. Have such integrity that people will believe what you say.

D. Retaliation (vv. 38-48).

The law of Moses (Lev. 24:19-24) prevented offended people from taking the law into their own hands and seeking private revenge against an enemy. It also kept magistrates from issuing exorbitant sentences that did not fit the offenses. But Jesus asks His people to suffer rather than cause others to suffer (1 Cor. 6:1-8). Keep in mind that this has to do with private offenses; the courts must still deal with people who break the law and must be punished accordingly. Christians may sacrifice and suffer as the Lord leads them, but they have no right to ask others to join them. Verse 42 does not command us to give to everybody who asks whatever they desire, for in so doing we might do them harm. We must give them *what they need the most* and not what they want the most.

Leviticus 19:17-18 deals with the treatment of enemies, and see Ex. 23:4-5. Nowhere does the law command people to hate their enemies. Jesus advised us to pray for them and do them good, just as the Father does to us. If we treat our enemies as they treat us, we are stooping to their low level. Nor should we be satisfied to do what the average Christian does. "What do you more than others?" We must go higher and imitate the Heavenly Father. The word "perfect" in v. 48 points the way to maturity of character, the kind of qualities described in 2 Peter 1 and Gal. 5:22-23.

MATTHEW 6

Matthew 6 deals with true righteousness practiced in the believer's life. This section actually continues through 7:12, and contains three sections: the believer and worship (6:1-18), the believer and wealth (6:19-34), and the believer and his or her walk (7:1-12). The first involves relationship to God, the second to the world, and the third to humankind.

I. The Believer and Worship (6:1-18)

Christ puts worship first since one's relationship to God determines his or her relationship to the world and other people. The key is v. 1, where "alms" should be translated "righteousnesses."

The main thought is that our relationship to God must be secret, for God to see and not for people to applaud. God will not allow two rewards, one from humans and one from heaven!

A. Giving (vv. 2-4).

The Pharisees loved to advertise their giving (Mark 12:38-40). How people today love to tell others how much they have given! If this is their motive for giving, then they have their reward — the praise of people. But they have no reward from the Father.

B. Praying (vv. 5-15).

Jesus says, "When you pray" (NIV) not "If you pray"; He expects us to pray. The first thing that characterized Paul after his conversion was his praying (Acts 22:17). Jesus emphasizes that it is a sin to pray to be seen and heard by others. Prayer is secret fellowship with God, although public prayer is certainly authorized in the Bible. However, nobody should pray in public who does not pray in private; for that would be hypocrisy. Jesus points out three common errors concerning prayer: (1) praying to be heard by others (vv. 5-6); (2) praying mere words, empty repetition (vv. 7-8); and (3) praying with sin in the heart (vv. 14-15). God does not forgive us because we forgive others but on the basis of the blood of Christ (1 John 1:9). However, an unforgiving spirit will hinder a prayer life and show that a person has no understanding of the grace of God.

The so-called "Lord's Prayer" of vv. 9-13 is not given to be recited thoughtlessly. Rather, it is a model for us to use to learn to pray. It is a "family prayer" — note the repeated "our" and "us." It puts God's name, God's kingdom, and God's will before the earthly needs of people. It cautions us against selfish praying.

C. Fasting (vv. 16-18).

True fasting is of the heart, not just the body (see Joel 2:13; Isa. 58:5). Fasting for the Christian is preparation for praying and other spiritual exercises. It means giving up a lesser thing to gain a greater, and this could involve food, sleep, or even sex (1 Cor. 7:1-6).

II. The Believer and Wealth (6:19-34)

The key in this section is v. 33, "But seek first the kingdom of God and His righteousness; and all these things shall be added to you"

(NKJV). Put God first and material things will be taken care of by God.

A. The basic principle (vv. 19-24).

Christ states several reasons why living for material things is foolish. For one thing, material things do not last. Fabrics were treasured by Jews, yet moths ruin them. Rust ruins metal; thieves steal riches. But treasure used for God's glory is invested in heaven where it lasts eternally. The way people use wealth is an indication of the condition of their hearts. If we spend our time and money only on business, and neglect God, then our hearts are in business and not fixed on God. Compare Abraham and Lot in Gen. 13:5-18 for an illustration of the "single eye." The eye here speaks of the outlook of the heart. A single eye means one that is fixed on the spiritual. It is the opposite of the double-minded person in James 1:8; 4:4, 8. "Evil" in v. 23 means the opposite of simple; it suggests a sinful outlook, a double vision. In v. 24 Jesus clearly tells us that we cannot look in two directions at one time, serve two masters, and live for God and material wealth. The Bible does not condemn the possession of wealth, but it does warn against the love of money and the wrong use of wealth (see 1 Tim. 6:9-10, 17-18; Heb. 13:5; Luke 16:1-31).

B. The daily practice (vv. 25-34).

Christ's "therefore" suggests that now He is going to apply this principle to our lives. He shows that worrying about material things is foolish because it accomplishes nothing! He reminds us to have our values straight—life consists of far more than food and clothing. Jesus was poor, yet how happy and peaceful He was! Paul said he was "poor, yet making many rich" (2 Cor. 6:10). Luke 12:13-21 tells us to distinguish between the true riches (spiritual) and uncertain riches (the material).

Christ points to God's care of nature—the flowers, grass, and birds. "You are of more value than they. Certainly God will care for you!" The Father knows our needs, and if we put Him first, He will meet every need. How do believers today practice Matt. 6:33? We will start with our time, and put God first in every day. This means time for prayer and reading the Word. We will put God first in every week, attending the house of God faithfully. We will put God first every payday, paying the tithe to the Lord. We will put God first in our choices, making no decision that would leave God out. Lot left God out of his decisions and ended up in the darkness of a cave, practicing terrible sin! He did not put God first in his selection of a place to live and raise his family.

There are spiritual parallels for the material things people seek today. We should seek to feed the hidden person of the heart with spiritual food just as we seek to feed the body (Matt. 4:4; 1 Peter 3:4). We should see that our spiritual garments are in order (Col. 3:7-15) just as we fret over the physical garments that clothe our body. We drink physical water, but we should also drink the spiritual water of life that Christ offers (John 4:13-14; 7:37-39).

MATTHEW 7

The first part of chapter 7 completes the second section of the Sermon on the Mount—"True Righteousness Practiced by the Believer" (6:1–7:12). In 6:1-18 the emphasis was on worship; in 6:19-34, it is on wealth; and 7:1-12 deals with the walk of the Christian in relationship to other people. The final section of the Sermon on the Mount (7:13-29) is titled "True Righteousness Proved by Tests."

I. The Believer's Walk (7:1-12)

The key verse for this section is 12, "So in everything, do to others what you would have them do to you" (NIV). This is the Golden Rule that governs a believer's relationship to other people. While other religions have sayings similar to this, the Golden Rule is strictly Christian because it is positive. It does not say, "Don't do to others what you don't want them to do to you." It lays the responsibility on the believer to act so that others will imitate the deeds and in the end glorify God (5:16). This section has three parts, each related to the other.

A. Judging (7:1-5).

Christ is not telling us to avoid evaluating people or not to use our God-given wisdom (see 1 John 4:1-6). The world is full of false Christians and even ministers of Satan (2 Cor. 11:13-15). As never before, Christians must be alert and must "try the spirits" (1 John 4:1). What Christ is condemning is harsh judgment and unjust criticism of others' motives. Note that He uses the symbol of the eye. In 6:22-23, Christ defined "the eye" as the spiritual outlook of a person, that which motivates one's life. Every believer has the obligation to test others by their fruits (vv. 15-20), but no Christian should ever judge motives (see Rom. 14 and 1 Cor. 4:5).

This command of Christ does not prohibit church discipline. He tells us to face disobedient Christians honestly and humbly, examine the evidence, and deal with sin decisively (see 18:15-18; 1 Cor. 5). The Christian who says that church discipline is not biblical should read 2 Thes. 3:11-15 and Gal. 6:1-5.

Christ gives us the right to help others after we have straightened out our own lives. He did not say that it was wrong for you to help your brothers or sisters get rid of their sins; but He did say that first you should take care of your own sin. In other words, we should be as severe with ourselves as we are with others. Christ points out two dangers in the lives of Christians who judge others: (1) that judgment will come back on them, and (2) they will become blind to their own needs and eventually need help themselves.

B. Discriminating (7:6).

This command balances the one previously given. We are not to judge others, but we must also be careful how we distribute holy things. "That which is holy" refers to the meat the priest takes off the altar; "pearls" typify Bible truths, the "precious promises" of the Word. The Gospel is to be preached in all the world, but we must not carelessly preach the deeper truths—the "family jewels"—lest we cheapen them. The "dogs and swine" are professors of the faith who have never really been saved (2 Peter 2:19-22)."

C. Praying (7:7-12).

Why does Christ include this exhortation on prayer at this point in the sermon? Because it is so difficult for us, in our own power and wisdom, to obey the commands He has given. "If any of you lack wisdom, let him ask of God," says James 1:5, echoing what Jesus says here. The believer who seeks to obey the Word of God must constantly ask for strength, seek wisdom, and knock at God's door for the supply of grace needed. Note that Christ bases prayer on the fatherhood of God (vv. 9-11). As God's children, we may expect God to care for us and meet our needs.

III. True Righteousness Proved by Tests (7:13-29)

Christ outlines three tests that will prove our righteousness is truly from God. False Christianity, a counterfeit, will fail these tests.

A. The test of self-denial (vv. 13-14).

The two ways refer to two types of life-style: the easy, comfortable, popular life, or the difficult way of self-denial. These ways are entered by two gates: a narrow gate of surrender or a broad gate of self-sufficiency. True righteousness leads to self-denial. Note in Matt. 8:18-22 that two men turned from Christ because they failed this test. Demas also failed this test (2 Tim. 4:10).

B. The test of spiritual fruit (vv. 15-23).

"False prophets" does not only mean false preachers who proclaim a false gospel, but primarily false professors of faith in Christ. Their inward nature has not changed (see 2 Peter 1:4); they merely wear the outward guise of a sheep. They call Christ "Lord" and even do religious deeds, but they have not been saved! How do we detect these false believers? "You will know them by their fruits" (v. 16, NKJV). What fruits does Christ seek? He seeks: (1) the fruit of the Spirit, or Christian character as described in the Beatitudes and Gal. 5:22-23; (2) the fruit of the lips, testimony and praise to God (Heb. 13:15); (3) holy living (Rom. 6:22); (4) good works (Col. 1:10); (5) lost souls won to Christ (Rom. 1:13). Professing Christians may be involved in religious activities and pretend to be saved, but if they are honestly born again, they will reveal these fruits in daily life.

Note that these "counterfeits" are surprised at the judgment! It is possible to fool ourselves! Satan blinds the mind (2 Cor. 4:3-4) and deceives people into thinking they are saved. When Christ returns, millions of professing Christians will be surprised to find out they were never saved at all!

C. The test of permanence or obedience (vv. 24-29).

The two builders represent two men in this life. They both use the same material and the same plans, and the world cannot tell the difference in their two houses. But when the storm comes—the time of testing—the house not founded on the rock crumbles and falls. The true Christian is founded on the Rock, Christ Jesus (1 Cor. 3:11). Righteousness is not based on a church, a creed, or a "good life" but on Jesus Christ who died for the believer. A child of God is proven by lasting through the storms that test him or her. A true Christian is proven by obeying Christ. One is not merely a hearer of the Word, but is also a doer (James 1:22-25).

Go through your Bible and note how false believers always fall away in the time of testing. The mixed multitude in Israel wanted to go back to Egypt when things became difficult in their journey. Many of the so-called Christians in Rome deserted Paul at his time of need (2 Tim. 4:9-18). Yet, note how the true believers stand regardless of the test. Abraham, Moses, Joshua, David, Isaiah, Jeremiah, Daniel, Peter, Paul, and many others proved the reality of their faith by standing through the storm. They were built on the Rock!

MATTHEW 8

We move now into a new section of Matt., in which the King reveals His power (chaps. 8–10). Matthew groups together ten miracles to prove to his readers that Jesus Christ possessed the powers of the King that the OT promised the Messiah would have. In His first "sermon" (Luke 4:18-19) He had announced that He would prove that the Spirit was upon Him by healing and helping the multitudes. Isaiah 35 promised that in the Kingdom Age the blind would see, the lame walk, etc. (vv. 5-6). These miracles were Christ's credentials, proving that He was sent of God. These chapters take us back to 4:23-25.

I. Power over Disease (8:1-17)

A. Leprosy (vv. 1-4).
This was the most dreaded disease in Jesus' day, a disease for which there was no cure. Jesus touched the leper, thus defiling Himself; yet His touch meant healing. He also healed through His word, "Be clean!" (v. 3, NIV) Leviticus 13 describes the priests' test for leprosy and shows how leprosy is a picture of sin: it lies deeper than the skin (v. 3); it spreads (v. 7); it defiles (vv. 44-45); it isolates from God and man (v. 46); and it is dealt with by fire (v. 52). The nation of Israel was pictured as defiled with leprosy (Isa. 1:5-6). Leviticus 14 describes the ceremony the healed leper went through when declared clean. It describes the work of the Cross.

B. Palsy (vv. 5-13).
Here we have a Gentile coming to Christ for help. There are two instances in Matt. of Gentiles coming to Christ, here and in 15:21-28. Note that in both cases Christ healed at a distance. This paral-

lels Eph. 2:12-13 where the Gentiles are said to be "far off" spiritually speaking. In both cases it was faith that Christ honored, and it was by the power of His word that the miracles took place. Christ offers a stern warning to the Jews (vv. 10-12) that because of their unbelief, they will lose the kingdom and the Gentiles will receive it instead.

C. Fever (vv. 14-17).

We have moved from a terrible disease, leprosy, to a common ailment, a fever; yet Christ has power over both. Peter was married (1 Cor. 9:5) and perhaps his mother-in-law lived with her daughter and Peter. She served Christ after He healed her, which shows how complete the cure was, and how grateful she was for what He had done. We should do likewise.

Note that Matthew quotes Isa. 53:4 to give scriptural proof for Christ's ministry. Some interpreters take this passage to mean that there is "healing in the atonement" and that the death of Christ gives us the privilege of physical healing today. But notice that Matthew is not referring to His death, but His life! Isaiah 53:4 does not refer to Calvary, but to Christ's earthly ministry of healing. First Peter 2:24 applies Isa. 53:4 to the healing of our sins. Certainly God has the power to heal today, and because of the death of Christ we shall have physical redemption someday (Rom. 8:18-24); but let us not apply this verse to healing today. Matthew did not, nor should we.

II. Power over Nature (8:18-27)

Instead of "playing up" to the crowds, Jesus left them! How different from some Christian celebrities today who appeal to the crowd and love the praise of people. Verses 19-22 show why Jesus was not impressed with the great crowds: the people were not willing to forsake all to follow Christ. They were interested in seeing the miracles, but not interested in giving their all for Christ.

Some believe that this storm was satanic in origin, since the disciples (some of whom were expert seamen) were terrified. Perhaps it was a satanic attack to destroy Christ. We do know that sudden storms are common on the Sea of Galilee. See the peace Christ displayed—able to sleep in a dangerous storm. This is the peace we can have when we know we are in the center of God's will. Again, by His word He controls the wind and the sea, and there is an immediate calm. We go from a "great tempest" (v. 24) to a "great calm" (v. 26) because of a great Savior! How thankful we should be that Christ calms the storms of life (see Ps. 107:23-31).

III. Power over Satan (8:28-34)

Christ now meets His enemy again, this time in a graveyard. What an illustration this is of Eph. 2:1-3! We see death (the graveyard), satanic possession, the filthiness of the flesh, and an awful display of enmity against God. While Matthew speaks of two men, the other Gospels speak of one, perhaps the one who was the most prominent. Matthew does not contradict Mark and Luke; he supplements their account.

We must admit the reality of demonic powers in our world today (Eph. 6:12) and the desire of Satan to destroy human bodies and condemn their souls to hell. The fear of the demons that Christ would torment them "before the time" (v. 29) indicates that there is a future judgment for Satan and his armies. Demons must have bodies to do their work in this world, just as the Spirit needs the Christian's body (Rom. 12:1-2). This is why the demons begged to enter the swine. A pig is as good as a man in Satan's eyes! (See where the prodigal son ended up—with the swine, Luke 15:15-16.)

Demons must obey His Word, and His one word "Go!" expelled them from the men. The swine perished because Satan is a murderer (John 8:44). This is what the demons would have done to the men had Christ not intervened in His love and grace. Jesus was willing to go through a storm to save these men from Satan! Yes, and He was willing to go through the storms of men's hatred and the storms of Calvary to save our souls!

How foolish the citizens were to ask Jesus to leave. If you compare this with the Gospels of Luke and Mark, you discover that there were three "prayers" in that graveyard: the demons prayed for permission to enter the swine; one of the healed men prayed for the privilege of following Jesus; and the citizens prayed that Jesus would leave them.

Jesus Christ today has power over Satan (John 12:31; 14:30; Col. 2:15). The devil's demonic powers may work in different ways from when the Lord was on earth, but they are at work just the same. One man is beset with pride; another, with lust; a third with a love for money. Christ alone can deliver the captives and set them free.

Note the power of God's Word in chapter 8 (vv. 8, 16, 26, 32). It is the Word of God, not our word, that is powerful (Heb. 4:12). We must major on the Bible in our preaching, our personal witnessing, and our daily living.

MATTHEW 9

This chapter continues in the presentation of the power of the King (chaps. 8–10). Previously we have seen Christ's power over disease (8:1-17), over nature (8:18-27), and over Satan (8:28-34).

I. Power over Sin (9:1-17)

A. The miracle (vv. 1-8).

Palsy was a type of paralysis, leaving the man helpless. He was brought to Jesus by believing friends, and Christ answered their faith by healing the man. But He did far more: He also forgave his sins! "The Son of Man has power on earth to forgive sins" (v. 6). Christ's critics accused Him of blasphemy, thus proving they did not accept His kingship and His sonship.

B. The results (vv. 9-17).

The scribes and Pharisees were starting to look for reasons to accuse and oppose Christ (see vv. 3, 11, 34). Thus when Matthew held a dinner for Christ and invited his "sinner friends," the Pharisees attended to cause trouble. In this passage, Christ pictures Himself as a physician to heal sinful hearts (v. 12) and a bridegroom to bring joy to people's lives (v. 15). Many Christians today think that our task is to open the church doors and invite sinners to come to us, but Jesus instructs us to go to lost men with the message of the Gospel. There is a danger that "separation" becomes "isolation" and we fail to contact lost sinners.

John was in prison and his disciples were confused. Later on (11:1-6) John himself expressed his desire to know more about what Christ was doing. Jesus' ministry was different from that of the Pharisees, who fasted often (Luke 18:12), and they wanted an explanation. Jesus told them He was introducing a new thing, and He spoke of new cloth and new wine. You cannot pour the new message of the Gospel into the old container of the law. To mix law and grace is to cause confusion and destroy both. The new life in Christ must take new forms. Mixing the Old and New Covenant leads to religious confusion.

II. Power over Death (9:18-26)

A. The desire (9:18-19).

This man was religious and obedient to the law, yet when death came, his religion was powerless to help. The law kills; the Spirit makes alive. For further details see Luke 8:40-56 and Matt. 5:21-43.

B. The delay (9:20-22).

The woman with the issue of blood had faith and was willing to humble herself at His feet. The physicians of the world could not heal her (Mark 5:26) so she came to the Great Physician. But this delayed the Lord as He went to the home of Jairus, and how Jairus must have fretted! Yet, Christ's delays always lead to greater blessing. (See the case of Lazarus in John 11.) Instead of merely healing the girl, He raised her from the dead!

C. The derision (9:23-24).

Imagine, sinners laughing at Jesus! This proves that the girl really was dead, otherwise they would not have laughed at Christ. We can expect the world to laugh at us as we seek to raise sinners from the dead (Eph. 2:1-10).

D. The demonstration (9:25-26).

He touches and speaks to her and she comes back to life. Christ raised three people from the dead, about whom we have full accounts in the Bible: a little girl (here), a young man (Luke 7:11-16), and an older man (John 11). Death is a picture of spiritual death (Eph. 2:1; John 5:24-25). Thus, sin reaches all ages; but though all sinners are dead spiritually, there are different degrees of decay. The little girl had just died, the young man was dead perhaps a day, and Lazarus had been entombed four days! The "moral sinner" is like the little girl: there is no decay, but there is still death. The "immoral sinner" is like Lazarus: his sin smells. All three were raised by the power of the Word, a picture of John 5:24.

III. Power over Darkness (9:27-31)

How these men came to be blind, we do not know. It may have been from disease, sin, or an accident. They acknowledged Jesus as the Son of David (cf. 1:1) and followed Him into the house. Jesus asked if they had faith, and because they did, He healed them. Note how faith shows up in chapters 8 and 9. The centurion had great faith (8:10), but the disciples in the storm had little faith (8:26). The faith of his friends helped the palsied man (9:2), and the faith of the woman healed her (9:22). Jairus' faith was tested by the delay along the road, and the blind men had their faith rewarded. The healing of the blind was a proof of Christ's messiahship according to Luke 4:18 and Isa. 61:1-2.

IV. Power over Demons (9:32-38)

This miracle caused a great stir: "It was never so seen in Israel!" (v. 33) Thus, Christ presented Himself and proved His kingship. Yet, the religious leaders rejected Him and even accused Him of being in league with Satan! One day in the future, Israel will receive a false Christ who will be empowered by Satan (John 5:43). It was this accusation of the enemy that eventually grew into open rebellion in 12:22-37.

Note that Jesus did not argue with people, but rather went to help those who would receive Him. He preached "the Gospel of the kingdom" (v. 35), which means He was still offering Himself to the nation as their King. Later, He sent His disciples out to preach the same Gospel, and perform the same miracles (10:5-8). This commission is not our commission today, nor do we dare to claim the power to perform miracles. All of this relates to Israel as a nation, not the church, "for the Jews require a sign" (1 Cor. 1:22).

The multitudes today are still in need of the Shepherd. Only Christ can lead them and feed them (see Ezek. 34). Christ pictures Himself as a shepherd and as a harvester, the Lord of the Harvest. The harvest is His (v. 38) and we must obey Him if the souls are going to be won. See John 4:31-38 for a parallel teaching.

MATTHEW 10

This chapter brings us to the end of the first section of Matthew, "The Revelation of the King" (1–10). In 1–4, He has revealed His person, in 5–7 His principles, and in 8–10 His power. In chapters 8–9 Christ revealed His power through a series of miracles which He performed; in this chapter He sends His ambassadors to perform miracles and carry the message of the kingdom. Keep in mind that wherever you have signs, you are dealing with the Jews and the message of the kingdom (1 Cor. 1:22).

As you read this chapter you will note that there is a change in the instructions at vv. 16 and 24. If you apply all of this chapter to the 12 Apostles, you will have confusion, for in vv. 15-23, Jesus leaps over the centuries and deals with the message of the kingdom during the Tribulation. This chapter gives instructions to the apostles in the past (vv. 1-15), the apostles of the future Tribulation period (vv. 16-23), and God's servants today (vv. 24-42).

I. Instructions to the Past Apostles (10:1-15)

Christ had asked them to pray about the harvest in 9:36-38; now He sends them into the harvest to serve. It is a serious thing to pray for the lost, because God will want to use you to help answer those prayers.

Note the change from "disciples" (those who learn) in v. 1 to "apostles" (those who are sent) in v. 2. These twelve were the first missionaries. Christ gave them the divine power they needed to do His work, for He always equips those whom He calls into service. God uses a variety of people to accomplish His work.

Their commission was clear: preach the kingdom of heaven and go only to the Jews. John the Baptist had done this (3:2), Jesus had done this (4:17), and now His disciples were to spread the message across the nation. The miracles they would perform would be their credentials that they represented the King (Heb. 2:1-4).

This commission is not for the church or for individual missionaries today. We don't have these miraculous powers since they were given especially to His apostles (Mark 16:17-18; Rom. 15:18-19; 2 Cor. 12:12). While the servant of God is not to depend on material things, he still must prepare and provide for himself and his family if he is to carry the message today (1 Tim. 5:8). Today's missionaries are not to follow the instruction of vv. 9-10. Paul appreciated the support of the churches, as do missionaries throughout the world today.

Finally, we do not preach the Gospel of the kingdom to those "who are worthy." We announce the Gospel of God's grace to all people and invite sinners to come to Christ. While the spiritual principles of this section may apply to us today, the specific instructions do not.

II. Instructions to Future Apostles (10:16-23)

It is not unusual for Bible writers to leap from one period to another without warning. Here Jesus looks down through history and sees those who will be His witnesses during the Tribulation period. These verses do not apply to the 12 Apostles for several reasons: (1) Verse 1 forbids them to go to the Gentiles, while v. 18 says they will be witnesses to the Gentiles. (2) The Spirit could not speak in them until after Christ had been crucified and raised from the dead (see John 14:17). (3) There is no evidence that the twelve apostles were persecuted. Luke 9:10 and Mark 6:30 indicate that they had a most successful ministry and were happy with it. (4) Verses 22-23 parallel 24:9, 13, where they definitely apply to the end time. There is a sense in which this section could apply to the ministry of the apostles during the Book of Acts, especially the Apostle Paul. However, the true application is for the Tribulation period. Note that v. 22 has nothing to do with salvation from sin. It is talking about the faithful endurance of His ambassadors during the time of persecution in the Tribulation. This will end with the return of the Lord (v. 23).

III. Instructions for Present Disciples (10:24-42)

Note that He returns to the word disciple and that He does not limit it to the Jew only. This passage contains encouragement and instruction for His followers today. We are learners (disciples) and laborers (servants). He warns against the fear of man (vv. 25-31). He assures us that men treated Him the same way and that it is a privilege for us to suffer for His sake (see Phil. 1:29; Acts 5:41). Verse 28 is not talking about Satan, for he does not have the power to destroy body and soul in hell. God does, and Christ tells us to fear Him and Him alone. When you fear God, you need fear nothing else. Christ assures them of the Father's care, for God cares even for the hungry sparrows. In vv. 31-33 He states the importance of open confession of Jesus Christ. This would apply to the servants and to their converts (see Rom. 10:9-10; 2 Tim. 2:12). Confession does not save, but it's the natural result of salvation.

Verses 34-39 indicate clearly that the Gospel is a divider of people. Christ is the Prince of Peace, and the Gospel is the message of peace, but when people confess Christ, they usually make enemies. Christ separates and makes the strongest natural ties of family and friends seem less important. Christians cannot serve

Christ without taking up the cross; this means being crucified to self and bearing His reproach. To save our lives means to lose them but to lose our lives for His sake means to save them.

The closing verses (40-42) indicate the importance of the servant of Christ. He is the representative of Christ. To reject the servant is to reject Christ, as Paul states in 2 Cor. 5:20. What an encouragement it is to know that we represent the King of kings and that He is right with us as we serve Him.

In this section, Christ outlines the servant's position (vv. 24-25), protection (vv. 26-32), privilege (vv. 33-38), promise (v. 39), and practice (vv. 40-42).

MATTHEW 11

We have reached a turning point in the ministry of Christ as presented by Matthew. "The Revelation of the King" is now complete (chaps. 1–10); now "Rebellion against the King" begins to appear (chaps. 11–13). In this section, the Jews rebel against every revelation Christ gave of Himself:

He was announced by John	They allowed John to be arrested (11:1-19)
He performed many miracles	The cities refused to repent (11:20-30)
He announced His principles	They argued with Him about them (12:1-21)
He revealed His Person	They said He worked with Satan (12:22-50)

The result, of course, is that Jesus turns from the nation (chaps. 14–20) and looks toward the cross. What began as rebellion will later on become open rejection.

I. Explanation Concerning John the Baptist (11:1-19)

A. The request (vv. 1-3).

John had been in prison a long time now (see 4:12). Why did John doubt Christ's kingship when he had been told by the Spirit who Christ was? (John 1:29-34) The answer is in the word "another" in John's question, "Or, do we look for another?" (v. 3) There are two words in the Gk. for "another." One means "another of the same kind," as when Jesus said, "He shall give you another Comforter" (John 14:16). The word used in Matt. 11:3 is "another of a different kind." John had announced the coming of the King and had promised a time of judgment and purging (Matt. 3:7-12); yet Jesus was having a ministry of mercy. John asked, "Are You the Messiah, or do we look for another of a different kind—one who will purge the nation and judge sin?" Long months in prison undoubtedly had dimmed John's vision, not unlike the OT Elijah in whose spirit John came (1 Kings 19:1-4).

B. The reply (vv. 4-6).

Jesus tenderly assures His servant and encourages his faith. If you compare this with Luke 7:18, you will see that John's disciples were giving him reports of Christ's healing ministry. This is why Jesus said, "Go and show John again" (11:4). In other words, Jesus was assuring John that He was the King, for He was performing the very miracles that the Scriptures said He would perform (see Isa. 35:5-6 and 61:1). "Don't stumble over Me," Jesus said to John, referring probably to Isa. 8:14-15. Christ uses the Word to encourage John, a good lesson for us in times of doubt and discouragement.

C. The recognition (vv. 7-15).

What a tremendous recognition Christ gave to John in this passage! This is His "Well done!" to a good and faithful servant who would give his life for Christ. John was not a reed, easily swayed; he was a man with convictions. He was not a celebrity, enjoying fame and luxury; he was a servant willing to suffer for Christ. Christ states that John's ministry was the fulfillment of Malachi 3:1. Had the nation received Jesus, John would have been the Elijah promised by God (v. 14, and see 17:10-13). Because they rejected both John and Jesus, the literal and final fulfillment of Malachi 3:1-3 will not come until the end times. John was the last of the OT prophets. Because he only announced the kingdom, he was not as great as the humblest person in the kingdom (v. 11).

D. The rebuke (vv. 16-19).

Christ rebuked the people of that generation for their childishness. Nothing pleased them! John and Jesus were opposites in their lives and ministries, yet neither one could satisfy the childish crowd.

There is a difference between being childish and childlike. In vv. 25-26, Jesus says that only the childlike can understand His Word. The world today is like spoiled children who demand entertainment and something new all the time. They refuse to be serious about life or death.

II. Condemnation of the Cities (11:20-24)

This is the first time we find Jesus uttering words of condemnation. He had done many mighty works, and His disciples had performed miracles too, yet the cities rejected Him. Capernaum had been especially blessed, since this was Christ's "headquarters" for the early part of His ministry (see Matt. 8:5-17; 9:1ff). Where the light shines the brightest, people have the greatest responsibility. There will be degrees of judgment according to the amount of light a person had. It is a serious thing to know the truth and turn from it!

III. Invitation to the Burdened (11:25-30)

This is a crucial moment in His ministry. The rebellion against the King has already set in and will culminate in open rejection. Christ turns to His Father and gives thanks! What an example for us when we come to times of difficulty.

The Father's will should always govern our lives. God bypassed the wise and prudent scribes and Pharisees and chose the simple but believing common people for salvation (see 1 Cor. 1). We cannot explain the mystery of the Father's will, but we can adore and obey Him. Christ's invitation here is for all to come to Him. It is no longer a message limited to the Jews, as it was in 10:5-6. Christ now opens the door to all who will come and believe and take His yoke.

The Pharisees had laid many burdens on the people (Matt. 23:4), and their religion did not give rest and peace. No human religion can give peace to the heart. Christ offers a yoke that is easy in contrast to the grinding, binding yoke of the law (Acts 15:10). Note the double use of the word "rest" (NKJV). "I will give you rest"—this is the peace with God that comes with salvation. "You will find rest"—this is the peace of God that comes with surrender (see Phil. 4:6-9). To be yoked to Christ is the greatest blessing possible.

MATTHEW 12

The events in chapters 12–13 took place on one crucial day in our Lord's ministry. We see the rebellion against the King getting more and more fierce. The Pharisees have rejected His messenger, John the Baptist (11:1-19) and have not repented though Jesus has done mighty works (11:20-30). Now they argue with Christ concerning His principles (the Sabbath question) and even accuse Him of being in league with Satan! This is a chapter filled with conflict.

I. Conflict over the Sabbath (12:1-21)

A. Their accusation (vv. 1-2).

The Sabbath was dear to the Jews, since it was God's special covenant sign to the nation (Ex. 31:12-17). However, the religious leaders had turned this day of spiritual blessing and joy into a day of legal observances, and the rules made their Sabbath a burden, not a blessing. Keep in mind that the Sabbath was never given to the church. Our covenant day is the first day of the week, the Lord's Day, the day of resurrection.

B. Christ's answer (vv. 3-8).

Jesus used the Word to answer His enemies. He referred them to David (1 Sam. 21:1ff), who hungered on the Sabbath and ate the sacred shewbread from the tabernacle. At that time, David was a rejected king, just as Jesus was, but he had not yet been crowned. Christ also referred to the Law (Num. 28:9-10) which permitted the priest to labor on the Sabbath and offer sacrifices. Finally, He quoted from the prophets (Hosea 6:6) to show that God is more interested in the heart than in empty outward observances. Christ boldly stated that He, not the Pharisees, was the Lord of the Sabbath, which was another way of claiming to be God, since God had ordained the Sabbath.

C. Their second accusation (vv. 9-21).

The Pharisees had made the "no-work" rule so strict that they even claimed it was a sin to heal on the Sabbath! Jesus used plain logic to show that their regulations were wrong. They helped their cattle on the Sabbath Day; is not a man worth more than a sheep? Thus, Jesus was affirming the value of the human soul to God. Verse 14 relates the beginning of the plan of the Pharisees to destroy Jesus. How did Christ respond? He withdrew from there. This fulfilled Isaiah's prophecy (see Isa. 42:1-3) describing the ministry of the Messiah. He would not argue with His enemies (v. 19), nor would He bring judgment upon them (v. 20). Some students say that the "bruised reed" and "smoking flax" of v. 20 refer to weak and needy sinners; but it is likely these are pictures of Christ's enemies, people whom Christ would not judge until the right time. Note that the word "Gentiles" appears in vv. 18 and 21, another indication that the King has been rejected by His nation and will turn to the Gentiles. You will meet Gentiles again in vv. 41-42, when He talks about Nineveh and the Queen of Sheba.

II. Conflict over Satan (12:22-37)

The Pharisees, like worldly people today, were always looking for something to criticize. Instead of rejoicing over the healing of the man, they accused Christ of being in league with Satan. Christ points out that this argument is not logical, since it would mean Satan is fighting against himself! Even unbelieving Jews were able to cast out demons (v. 27, and see Acts 19:13ff); does this mean they are in league with Satan too? Christ's final argument (v. 29) is that He could never cast out the demons unless first He had overcome their leader, Satan, which He did in chapter 4. This leads to the awful statement about the unpardonable sin. Keep these things in mind when you consider the unpardonable sin:

A. It is a sin of the heart, not the lips (vv. 34-35).

The words from the lips are the evidence of the condition of the heart; and evil words indicate an evil heart.

B. It is a sin committed in the light of great evidence.

These men had seen Christ's miracles and yet hardened their hearts against Him.

C. It is the sin of willful, persistent unbelief and final rejection of Jesus Christ.

Adultery is not unpardonable (see John 8:1-11), nor is murder (God forgave David). But when a person persists in rejecting Christ and comes to the place where his heart is so calloused he has no concern for his eternal destiny, then it is too late.

Jesus is preaching John the Baptist's message here (see 3:7). He calls the Pharisees a "generation of vipers" because they were children of that old serpent, the devil (see 23:33). They had a form of godliness, but they did not know God. Like Satan, they were imitators of true godliness (2 Cor. 11:13-15).

III. Conflict over Signs (12:38-50)

Christ had performed many miracles, yet they asked for a sign (John 12:35-43). Christ promises only one sign: His death, burial, and resurrection, as pictured by Jonah. Keep in mind that Jonah was a messenger to the Gentiles, another indication that Israel would reject Christ. How is Christ "greater than Jonah"? (v. 41) He is greater in His ministry, since Jonah disobeyed God. He is greater in His message, since He preached salvation and not coming judgment.

The parable in vv. 43-45 might be termed "reformation without inward regeneration." The Jews came back from captivity purged from their sin of idolatry. The "house" had been swept clean, but it was still empty. They had religion and outward morality, but their hearts were empty and their religion was vain. Consequently, Satan was able to reenter the house with other sins, and the latter end of the nation was worse than the first! In the OT, the Jews worshiped idols, but in the Gospels they killed their own Messiah!

This same thing happens to individuals. How easy it is to "reform," join a church, and live respectably, without Jesus Christ dwelling in the heart. This "false righteousness" will last only for a time; then Satan will get hold of that empty life and ruin it. Religion means cleaning up the outside; salvation means new life and holiness on the inside. See 2 Peter 2:20-22.

At the end of chapter 11, Jesus gave an invitation to "all who are weary and heavy laden" (v. 28, author's trans.). Here (vv. 46-50) He uses that wonderful word "whosoever." He was breaking all natural ties. The nation had rebelled against His message and ministry. Now He speaks of a worldwide family of God, to "whosoever" will do the will of God.

MATTHEW 13

This is a crucial chapter in the Bible, one that every believer should seek to understand thoroughly. The rebellion against Christ reached its peak, and He turned from the nation to all who will come to Him (Matt. 11:28-30). The big question now is, "What about the kingdom, now that the King has been refused?" The answer to that question is in Matt. 13. In this chapter, Christ outlines the "mysteries of the kingdom" and explains what the "kingdom of heaven" is like during this present age.

I. The Setting of the Parables

A. "Out of the house" (v. 1).

"The house" here refers to the literal house in which Jesus had been teaching, but it can symbolize the house of Israel (10:6). By leaving the house, He was saying (symbolically) that He had left the nation and would now turn to the Gentiles.

B. "By the seaside" (v. 1).

The sea in Scripture stands for the Gentile nations of the world (Rev. 17:15; Isa. 60:5). Christ now goes to the Gentiles and begins a new phase of His ministry (see 10:5-6; 12:17-21, 39-42).

II. The Reason for Parables

A. The human reason (vv. 10-17).

The condition of the people's hearts made it necessary for Christ to use parables. (A parable is a story in which something familiar explains something unfamiliar.) Christ quotes Isa. 6:9-10 to explain why He was using parables: the hearts, ears, and eyes of the people had become dull, hard, and blind. By using parables, He was exciting the curiosity of the concerned, those who really wanted to know the truth. But He was also hiding the truth from the rebellious; He would not cast these pearls of truth before swine (7:6). The parables did not keep people from learning the truth; rather, the parables excited their interest and encouraged them to learn. This is a fulfillment of 11:25 — the proud will not see, but the babes will learn the truth and be saved.

B. The divine reason (vv. 34-35).

Christ fulfilled the prophecy in Ps. 78:2. The truths given in Matt. 13 had been kept secret from the foundation of the world; they were a "mystery" hidden from people, but now revealed. For this reason, do not look for these truths in the OT. A "mystery" in the

Bible is a truth hidden in ages past, but now revealed by God through His servants. It is not to be found in the OT, except in type or symbol. See Eph. 3.

III. The Mysteries of the Kingdom of Heaven

A. The term.

Please keep in mind that the "kingdom of heaven" in Matt. 13 is in "mystery" form. That is, it does not refer to the earthly kingdom of Messiah but rather to the kingdom here on earth during the King's absence. The "kingdom of heaven" is a mixture of good and evil, true and false. It is not the church. The church is in the kingdom of heaven, but distinct from it. The kingdom of heaven is equivalent to our term "Christendom." It is made up of all who profess allegiance to the King, whether in truth or pretense.

B. The time.

You will note in the analysis of Matt. 13 that the kingdom begins with the sowing of the Word in Christ's day and continues to the end of this age. These parables outline God's program and Satan's opposition during this age.

The Parable of the Tares (Matt. 13:24-30, 36-43)

I. The Symbols Used

A. An explanation.

Jesus explains the symbols for us.
1. The man is Christ (v. 37).
2. The seed is believers, children of the kingdom (v. 38).
3. The field is the world (v. 38).
4. The enemy is Satan (v. 39).
5. The tares are the children of the devil (v. 38).
6. The reapers are angels (v. 39).
7. The harvest is the end of the age (v. 39).

B. A word of warning.

Be careful in interpretation here. Don't confuse these symbols with those used in the Parable of the Sower. In the Parable of the Sower, the seed represents the Word of God, and the soil represents different kinds of hearts.

ANALYSIS OF MATTHEW 13

Introduction — 1–2

In the
INDIVIDUAL

"Behold a
sower went
out to
sow . . ."

B E G A G E I E N S

THE SOWER 3-9

Explanation: Why parables?
HUMAN REASON 10-17

Explanation: The Sower 18-23

PUBLIC
"by the
seaside"

Man's view
—*Failure*

In the
WORLD

"The kingdom
of heaven
is like . . ."

"The field
is the
world . . ."

O P P O S E D

TARES 24-30 — False Christians

MUSTARD SEED 31-32 — False Growth

LEAVEN 33 — False Doctrine

Explanation: Why parables?
DIVINE REASON 34-35

R E S U L T S

Explanation: The Tares 36-43

TREASURE 44 Israel

PEARL 45-46 Church

DRAG-NET 47-50 Gentile Nations
Conclusion — 51–52

PRIVATE

"in the
house"

God's view
—*Success*

SATAN'S OPPOSITION

IN THE INDIVIDUAL	Point of attack	IN THE WORLD
Parable of Sower		Tares, Mustard Seed, Leaven
	THE SEED	
1. Snatches the seed		1. Plants counterfeit seed — TARES
2. Starves the plant — it cannot grow	THE GROWTH	2. Allows the plant to grow out of measure — MUSTARD SEED
3. Smothers the fruit — "becomes unfruitful"	THE FRUIT	3. Injects false doctrine — LEAVEN within the meal — made from seed

C. The main lesson.

Wherever Christ "plants" true believers to bear fruit for His glory, Satan plants false Christians who oppose the work and hinder the harvest. Christians are seeds, and the kingdom of heaven is a mixture of the true seed (Christians) and the counterfeit (children of the devil).

II. The Two "Seeds" in the Bible

A. Gen. 3:15.

This is the first mention of the two seeds in the Bible. God said that the woman would have a seed (Christ) (Gal. 3:16; 4:4), and the serpent (Satan) would have a seed. It also states that there would be constant enmity between the serpent's seed and the woman's seed.

B. Cain and Abel.

When Cain murdered Abel (Gen. 4:1-16) he started this enmity between the two seeds. First John 3:12 states that Cain was "of that wicked one"—a child of the devil! This conflict continues throughout the entire OT.

C. The Pharisees and Jesus.

Satan's seed ("children of the devil") opposed John the Baptist (3:7) and did nothing when he was killed by Herod. They opposed Christ (12:34; 23:33) and asked to have Him crucified. At the cross, Satan bruised Christ's heel but Christ bruised Satan's head and defeated him forever.

D. The Apostle Paul.

Satan's seed opposed Paul when he first started his missionary work (Acts 13:10) and all through his life. Satan opposed Paul (as he does the church today) with a false gospel (Gal. 1:6-9), false ministers (2 Cor. 11:13-26), false righteousness (Rom. 10:1-3), and false brethren (2 Cor. 11:26).

E. The final result.

This enmity between the two seeds will finally culminate in a false Christ (2 Thes. 2). The "son of perdition" will oppose the Son of God, the "mystery of lawlessness" will oppose the mystery of godliness. The harlot religious system (Rev. 17) will fight the bride (the true church), and there will be a satanic trinity—the devil, the beast, the false prophet (Rev. 19:20; 20:1-3)—to oppose the Father, Son, and Holy Spirit. In the end, all satanic forces will be defeated by the Son of God.

III. The Lessons We Should Learn

A. The hindrance.

Satan opposes the work of God in several ways:
1. He snatches the Word of God from hearts, smothers the seed with worldliness, or scorches the shoots with persecution.
2. If he cannot overcome the Word, he plants false Christians ("children of the devil") wherever the Lord plants true believers. Many people are going to hell, not because of gross overt sins, but because they have a "false righteousness" apart from faith in Jesus Christ.
3. He sits in the branches of "Christendom" and influences what goes on.
4. He plants false doctrine that deceives people.

B. The method.

Satan's chief method of opposing God is through imitation. He preaches an imitation gospel, establishes imitation churches, plants imitation Christians, etc.

C. The task.

True and false will grow together until the end, and God will separate them. Our job is not to try to "clean up" the world, although we should do all we can to better society. This does not mean we should not use discipline in the local church. The church is not the kingdom of heaven. God commands us to judge sin and discipline Christians who would hinder the growth of the church by godless living (see 1 Cor. 5 and Matt. 18:15-18). Our job is to plant the Word in hearts and let God "plant" us in places where we can bear fruit for His glory.

D. The climate.

The "tares" will be bound together at the end of the age. In these last days, we see many organizations and even nations uniting for one purpose or another. We have world church organizations, world banks, world labor movements, world trade organizations, etc. In the religious world, denominations are getting together, organizations are merging for mutual protection. Some of these cooperative efforts may be profitable, but we wonder how many tares are being bundled for the burning?

E. Stay awake.

While we sleep, Satan works. A sleeping church is an opportunity for Satan to plant false Christians (see Prov. 24:30-34). It is important that we stay awake (Rom. 13:11-14).

F. Be discerning.

We must "try the spirits" to detect when Satan is at work (1 John 4:1-6). This is not judging (Matt. 7:1-5), but rather exercising our spiritual senses to see if people really belong to Christ (Heb. 5:14).

MATTHEW 14

We now move into a new and important section of the Gospel of Matthew, "The Retirement of the King" (chaps. 14–20). In this section, we see Jesus "withdrawing" from the multitudes and spending time alone with His disciples, preparing them for the coming crisis in Jerusalem. Keep in mind that even the disciples, at this stage, thought in terms of an earthly kingdom; and His teaching about a cross perplexed them. It was necessary that He prepare them for this faith-testing experience. The three events in this chapter illustrate the characteristics of this present age, when the King is rejected:

> Persecution (1–12): Christ's servants will suffer and die for Him
> Provision (13–21): Christ's servants will minister the bread of
> life to man
> Protection (22–36): Christ will pray for His servants and rescue
> them.

I. Persecution (14:1-12)

John had been in prison for several months (see 4:12), and undoubtedly was martyred a few weeks prior to the events recorded here. (Note that vv. 3-12 are a flashback.) Matthew puts John's death at this point in his Gospel because it illustrates the attitude of men toward the King; for, by slaying His messenger, they were rejecting the King Himself! "He who receives you receives Me," said Jesus in 10:40 (NKJV), and the reverse is also true: to reject the messenger is to reject Christ. John's death is a prediction, so to speak, of Christ's own death, a topic He discusses with His disciples in this period of retirement.

The name "Herod" was a family name, and it is easy to confuse the different Herods of the NT. "Herod the Great" was the Herod who slew the children (2:16-18). "Herod Antipas" was a younger son of Herod the Great. He was not really a king, but merely a tetrarch—the ruler over a fourth of the kingdom. He is the Herod who had John the Baptist killed and before whom Jesus was silent (Luke 23:5-12). "Herod Agrippa" is the Herod who slew James and imprisoned Peter (Acts 12). He was a grandson of Herod the Great. Finally, "Herod Agrippa II" was the Herod before whom Paul was tried (Acts 25:13ff). He was a great-grandson of Herod the Great. All the Herods had Edomite blood in their veins and hated the Jews. They were treacherous rulers who in the Bible typify the "god of this age" and the spirit of Antichrist. Like Satan, all of them were liars and murderers (John 8:44).

John's ministry was now completed. He had heralded the coming of the King and had faithfully preached God's truth. Christ must increase, and he must decrease (John 3:30). Any Christian who is faithful to the Word of God, as John was, will suffer persecution. The world is not the friend of the Christian. The world has rejected the King and will also reject His messengers.

II. Provision (14:13-21)

Jesus now withdraws (v. 13). There were several reasons for this withdrawing: (1) the report of John's death, (2) the growing antagonism of Herod, (3) the disciples' need for rest after their preaching tour (see Mark 6:31), and (4) His need to get alone with His disciples to teach them. It is important that we get alone from time to time to hear God's voice and refresh ourselves physically and mentally. "If we don't come apart and rest—we'll come apart!" said Vance Havner.

John 6 makes it clear that the miracle of the feeding of the 5,000 was a sermon in action. Christ, through His Word, is the Bread of Life on whom we feed. It is the privilege—and responsibility—of His servants to give this bread to the hungry multitudes. The servants receive that bread personally from Christ, then pass it on to others.

There are other lessons from this miracle: (1) Christ can take our little and make it much. (2) Whatever He blesses, He breaks. Are we willing to be broken? (3) People today are in the wilderness of sin (v. 15) and need Christ. (4) Christ can overcome every difficulty and feed the multitudes. The disciples had many excuses — not enough money, the wrong place, the wrong time — but Christ took what they had and met the need. He will do this today!

III. Protection (14:22-36)

John 6:15 tells us why Christ was so anxious to dismiss the crowds: they had been filled with bread and wanted to make Him king! Men will follow anyone who promises them the material things of life, but Jesus will not have "bread-and-butter" disciples.

We have here a beautiful picture of the church today. Christ is on the mountain praying while the disciples are battling the storm on the lake. Today, Jesus is in heaven interceding for us while we fight the storms of sin on this earth. His coming seems a long way off, yet just at the darkest hour (the fourth watch — 3-6 A.M.) He came to them! He stilled the storm and took His own safely to their destination (John 6:21).

Peter's experience gives us the personal application. Peter could walk on the water because he had faith in Christ's word, "Come" (v. 29). "Faith comes by hearing and hearing by the Word of God" (Rom. 10:17, NKJV). But when he forgot the source and stopped looking unto Jesus (Heb. 12:1-2), he began to sink. The secret of overcoming the storm and doing the impossible is simply to believe the Word of God and keep looking to the Son of God. Yet, even when we fail, Jesus graciously helps us! How well-prepared Peter was to write, "Casting all your care upon Him, for He cares for you" (1 Peter 5:7, NKJV).

This present age will be one of storms for the church. Keep in mind that the disciples were in the storm, not because they disobeyed Christ (as Jonah did), but because they obeyed Him. If we obey the Word of God, there will be suffering and persecution, but Christ is praying for us and will soon come to take us home. The secret is faith. Doubt and fear always go together, and faith and peace always go together. May we not be "little-faith" Christians!

This entire chapter, then, shows the course of this age. The King withdraws and there is persecution against His servants. Through His servants He distributes the precious Bread of Life to a hungry world. His servants go through storms and testing, but Christ returns to give them peace and rescue them from the enemy. Hallelujah, what a Savior!

MATTHEW 15

In this chapter we see Christ withdrawing from the Pharisees (v. 21) into the region of Tyre and Sidon, from there into Galilee (v. 29), and finally from Galilee into the coasts of Magadan (v. 39). Keep in mind that during this period He is avoiding open confrontation with the Jewish leaders and also teaching His disciples and preparing them for His death on the cross.

I. Jesus and the Jewish Leaders: Truth Vs. Tradition (15:1-20)

A. *Their accusation (vv. 1-2).*

These religious leaders were constantly looking for some charge to bring against Christ. This apparently was an official committee from the Council at Jerusalem. They accused Christ's disciples of violating the traditions of the Jewish elders by not going through the ceremonial washings when they ate. Keep in mind that the Pharisees honored their traditions above the written Word of God. "It is a greater offense to teach anything contrary to the voice of the Rabbis, than to contradict Scripture itself," says the *Mishna* (a collection of Jewish traditions). Rabbi Eleazer said, "He who expounds the Scriptures in opposition to the tradition has no share in the world to come." Christ condemns their washings in Matt. 23:25-26.

B. *Christ's reply (vv. 3-9).*

Note how Christ always uses the Word to silence His accusers. He points out their own disobedience to Ex. 20:12 and 21:17. By "dedicating" their possessions to God, the Pharisees released themselves from any obligation to care for their parents. How many "religious" people there are even today who carefully keep traditions, yet openly disobey the Word of God! Christ quoted Isa. 29:13 to show that their religion was not of the heart, but was merely external actions. They missed the main lesson of the Sermon on the Mount: true righteousness comes from within.

C. Christ's announcement (vv. 10-11).

Christ addresses the entire multitude and openly declares the Pharisees' traditions null and void. Previously He had referred to Scripture; now He uses plain logic to show their errors. How can foods defile a man when they do not go into his heart? The Pharisees saw in this a declaration of war.

D. Christ's explanation (vv. 12-20).

Even the disciples were astounded! Peter called His plain teaching "a parable." How hard it is for men to break away from men's traditions and believe God's simple truth! Holiness, Christ explains, is a matter of what comes out of the heart. People often blame the devil for the sins listed here, but Christ blames the wickedness of the human heart. This is why people must be born again and get new hearts. Note the contrast between God's truth and human traditions:

Human traditions	God's truth
Outward forms that bring bondage	Inward faith that brings liberty
Trifling rules, the letter of the law	Basic principles, the spirit of the Law
Man-made laws that exalt men	God-breathed words that humble men
Produces "religious piety"— death	Results in true holiness—life

We must constantly remind ourselves that true religion comes from the heart. We believe with the heart (Rom. 10:9-10); love from the heart (Matt. 22:37); sing from the heart (Col. 3:16); obey from the heart (Rom. 6:17); give from the heart (2 Cor. 9:7); and pray from the heart (Ps. 51:10, 17).

II. Jesus and the Gentiles (15:21-39)

It is significant that Jesus now departs for Gentile territory. This woman's spiritual condition is pictured in Eph. 2:11-12. It is worthy of note that the two cases of Gentile healing were both from a distance (here and 8:5-13), because the Gentiles were "far off" spiritually speaking. That the Christ would go to the Gentiles was no secret (see Matt. 12:17-21). Christ responded to this woman's plea in four different ways: first, He was silent; then He refused; then He seemed to rebuke her; and finally He rewarded her faith. Why did He not answer her plea immediately? One reason is that she, a Gentile, approached Him on Jewish terms, calling Him "Son of David." Gentiles are not saved by first becoming Jews! When she called Him "Lord" He answered her plea (see Rom. 10:12-13). Of course, His delay also tested her faith. She knew that the Gentiles were saved through the Jewish nation (John 4:22) and was willing to take even the crumbs from their table. What an indictment against the Jews that the two people Christ commended for their great faith were both Gentiles (Matt. 8:10; 15:28).

The multitudes in vv. 32-39 were predominantly Gentile. Because of Christ's ministry, they glorified the God of Israel. Do not confuse the feeding of the 4,000 with the previous miracle of feeding the 5,000. This chart shows the contrast:

The 5,000 (Matt. 14:15-21)	The 4,000 (Matt. 15:32-39)
Predominantly Jews	Predominantly Gentiles
Took place in Galilee, Bethsaida	Took place at Decapolis (Mark 8:31ff)
5 loaves, 2 fish	7 loaves, "a few fish"
12 baskets left over	7 baskets left over
In the spring of the year	In the summer
Crowd with Him one day	Crowd with Him three days

How slow were the disciples to understand His power! Their unbelief in v. 33 shows they had not learned the lesson from the previous miracle of feeding 5,000. It may be that they thought He would not feed the Gentiles, and thus this was another lesson for them in Christ's changing ministry. Christ not only wants to save and satisfy the Jews, but also the Gentiles. Check the notes on Matt. 14 for the spiritual lessons involved in this miracle.

MATTHEW 16

While the key lesson in this chapter is Peter's confession of faith, we must consider the entire chapter to get the proper setting.

Christ and His disciples have been in "retirement," and He has been preparing them for His approaching suffering and death. Peter's confession of faith at this point is the climax of the months of instruction. From that point on, Christ *openly* taught them about His crucifixion, and they began to make their way to Jerusalem. There are four outstanding movements in the chapter.

I. Conflict: Christ Tempted by the Enemy (16:1-5)

Note how the Pharisees and Sadducees, who were enemies, united to tempt Christ. Pilate and Herod were "made friends" for the same reason (Luke 23:6-12). In asking for "a sign from heaven" (v. 1) they were discrediting His miracles, which they considered signs upon earth. Perhaps they wanted fire from heaven, as Elijah had done, or bread from heaven, as Moses had done. Jesus described their spiritual condition: (1) they could interpret things physical and earthly, but not things spiritual; (2) they were wicked, in that they tempted God; and (3) they were adulterous in that they had forsaken the true God for their empty religion. He pointed to His death, burial, and resurrection, and to His ministry to the Gentiles, by referring to the Prophet Jonah.

II. Confusion: The Unbelief of the Disciples (16:6-12)

The disciples were apparently more concerned about physical things than spiritual, for while Christ was considering the sad state of the Pharisees, the disciples were irritated because they had forgotten to bring bread with them. The seven baskets left over from the feeding of the 4,000 (Matt. 15:37) were probably given to the poor. When Jesus spoke of spiritual things — the leaven of the Pharisees and Sadducees — the disciples thought only of physical bread. This is an illustration of Matt. 13:22 — the cares of this world choking out the seed of the Word. Christ rebukes them for their "little faith," for if they needed bread, could they not trust Him to provide it? He had just fed 4,000 people with a few loaves and fishes! Luke 12:1 names hypocrisy too as the leaven of the Pharisees. The leaven of hypocrisy corrupts the church.

III. Confession: Peter's Confession of the Christ (16:13-20)

How confused the multitudes were about Christ! They held Him in high esteem, ranking Him with the great prophets, but they lacked the perception to see Him as the Son of the living God. They even compared Him with John the Baptist, yet these two were dissimilar in their ministries (Matt. 11:18-19). But no man can confess Christ apart from the revelation of the Father (Matt. 11:27ff) and the witness of the Spirit (1 Cor. 12:3). A right confession about Christ is important to salvation (1 John 2:22-23; 5:10).

Verses 18-19 have been a battleground for centuries, the Romanists claiming from them the office of the Pope and the power of the church to dispense grace; and the Protestants seeing in them something entirely different. We will let the Bible speak for itself as we consider the symbols in these verses.

A. The rock is Jesus Christ.

Christ said so (Matt. 21:42) referring to Isa. 28:16. Peter himself said so (1 Peter 2:4-8; Acts 4:11-12 with Ps. 118:22). Paul names Christ as the Rock in 1 Cor. 10:4 and calls Christ the Head of the church (Eph. 1:20-23; 4:8-16; 5:23; Col. 1:18). Throughout the OT, the rock speaks of God and not man (Deut. 32:4, 15; Dan. 2:45; Ps. 18:2). Jesus said, "You are Peter (*petros*, a small rock), and on this rock (*petra*, a large rock foundation) I will build My church" (v. 18, NIV; see 1 Cor. 3:1).

B. The keys.

The keys mentioned here refer to Peter's stewardship in the kingdom. These are not the keys to the church, but the keys of the kingdom. They are not the keys to death or eternity, for Christ holds those (Rev. 1:18). In the Bible, "keys" stand for authority and stewardship (Isa. 22:22; Luke 11:52). Peter used these keys when he "opened the door of faith" (Acts 14:27) to the Jews (Acts 2), the Samaritans (Acts 8), and the Gentiles (Acts 10). This is stewardship, not lordship.

C. Binding and loosing.

This implies applying God's Word to people. In 18:18 this is used of church discipline, and the power is given to all the disciples, not Peter alone. In Jesus' day, the Jews spoke of "binding and loosing" when a rabbi would forbid something or permit something. The more accurate translation is in the Williams translation of the NT: "Whatsoever you forbid on earth must be what is already forbidden in heaven, and whatsoever you permit on earth must be what is already permitted in heaven" (v. 19, WMS). The church does not tell heaven what to do, but obeys on earth what heaven commands the church to do!

Peter never claimed to be a Pope (see 1 Peter 5:1-4). Note that Christ, not Peter, builds the church. This is the first mention of "church" in the NT.

IV. Correction: Peter the Stumbling Block (16:21-28)

Christ now openly announced His coming suffering and death. He had intimated His death in various symbols in John 2:19, 3:14, 6:51, and Matt. 9:15 and 12:40-41; but now He spoke of it openly (Mark 8:32). Of course, the disciples were shocked at the news, especially Peter, who repeated Satan's temptation of Matt. 4:8-10 by trying to detour Christ from the cross. Satan was obviously using Peter to be a stumbling block in Christ's path of obedience. Satan was to use Peter again to hinder Christ's work (Luke 22:31ff). Christ rebuked Peter and then taught the disciples the importance of the Cross in the life of the believer. "Bearing the cross" means dying to self, bearing Christ's reproach, and crucifying the world and the flesh as we follow Him in obedience. Peter was to learn that suffering and glory always go together (1 Peter 4:12-19; 5:1, 10).

MATTHEW 17

I. The King in His Glory (17:1-13)

The transfiguration of Christ is one of the key events in His earthly ministry. This was the only time His glory, veiled in human flesh, was allowed to shine forth (see John 1:14). "Transfigure" is the same as our English word metamorphosis and means "a change from within." This glory was not the reflection of outward light; it was the revelation of inward glory. The same word is used in Rom. 12:2 ("transformed") and 2 Cor. 3:18 ("changed") referring to the Christian's growth in holiness.

A. The participants.

There were seven: Christ, Peter, James, John, Moses, Elijah, and God the Father. Peter, James, and John had three special experiences with Christ—here on the mount of transfiguration, in the home of Jairus (Mark 5:37ff), and in the Garden of Gethsemane

(26:36-46). In each instance, Jesus taught them a new lesson about Himself.

B. The purposes.

The Transfiguration was, first of all, a picture of the coming kingdom. Jesus promised that some of the disciples would not see death until they had seen His kingdom (16:28). Read carefully 2 Peter 1:16-20 for Peter's explanation, and you will see that it has to do with the promised kingdom. Peter had just recently confessed Christ as the Son of God (16:16) and had learned the truth about His coming death (16:21-23). He and the other disciples were probably asking, "If He is going to die on the cross, what about all the promises of the kingdom? Will they be fulfilled?" Christ in His transfiguration assured them that the Word would stand and the kingdom would come. The scene is actually a picture of the kingdom: Christ glorified, the three apostles representing the redeemed Israel, Moses representing saints who died in Christ, Elijah representing saints who were raptured (for Elijah did not die), and the multitudes at the foot of the mountain representing the other nations.

Another purpose was to strengthen Christ for His suffering. Moses and Elijah talked with Him about His coming "decease" ("exodus") at Jerusalem (Luke 9:30-31), and the voice of the Father came as another encouragement to the Son. It was also an encouragement to the disciples as they faced separation from the Lord as He experienced His suffering and death. Had they remembered this scene, they would not have failed Him or lost hope when He died.

C. The peril.

Again Peter speaks with a carnal viewpoint and tempts Jesus from the cross! The Father rebukes him. "Hear Him!" (v. 5, NKJV) is still God's message, for Christ is God's "last word" to men (Heb. 1:1-3). The law (Moses) and the prophets (Elijah) witness to Christ (Luke 24:27, 44), but Christ is superior to Moses and Elijah (see Rom. 10:4; Acts 10:43.) "Jesus only" (v. 8) is the only safe attitude for the Christian to have.

D. The perplexity.

Coming down the mountain, the disciples asked about Elijah, referring to the promises in Mal. 3:1; 4:5-6. Christ states that John the

Baptist fulfilled these promises in spirit (Luke 1:17), but that Elijah himself would come.

II. The King in His Power (17:14-21)

We cannot always stay on the mount of glory with the King; we must descend with Him into the valley of need where Satan is at work. "Through the veil" and "without the camp" are two essentials for victory (Heb. 10:19-22; 13:13). The nine disciples left at the foot of the mountain were embarrassed by failure; they had lost the power over demons Christ had given them (10:8). The cause was their unbelief and lack of devotion. Perhaps they had become envious because the other three disciples had gone up to the mount with Jesus.

Secret sin robs us of power. Unbelief also robs us of power. When the King comes again, He will bind Satan and set the world free from demonic powers (Rev. 19:11–20:3).

III. The King in His Humility (17:22-27)

What a paradox: the King is too poverty-stricken to pay His temple dues! Truly, He became poor that we might be made rich (2 Cor. 8:9). There are four distinctive characteristics of this miracle that must be noted.

A. It is the only miracle Christ performed to meet His own needs.

The temple tax of a half-shekel was paid by every Jewish male (Ex. 30:11ff). Jesus was so poor that He did not have this small amount. How humble Jesus was! (Phil. 2:5-8)

B. The miracle is recorded only by Matthew.

This is the Gospel of the King, and this miracle has to do with Christ's kingship. Jesus affirms here that He is the "Child of the King" and therefore need not pay the tax. Christ proved His kingship by performing a complicated miracle. A coin had to be lost in the sea, a fish had to take it in its mouth — and then the fish had to bite on Peter's hook! Christ has dominion over the fish of the sea (Ps. 8:6-8; Heb. 2:6ff).

C. It is the only miracle using money.

This tax was a reminder of the Jews' redemption from Egyptian slavery. They were redeemed by the blood of the lamb (Ex. 12), not by silver and gold. But the silver shekel was a token of that redemption. Peter caught this lesson (1 Peter 1:18-19).

D. *It was performed especially for Peter.*

Jesus performed many miracles for Peter: healing his mother-in-law, helping him walk on the sea, saving him when he began to sink, giving him great catches of fish. Even in the Book of Acts, Christ delivered Peter several times. Why did Jesus do all this for Peter? For Peter's good and God's glory. Whatever the need, Christ can meet it. See 1 Peter 5:7.

MATTHEW 18

I. Lessons on Greatness (18:1-14)

A. *The disciples' question (v. 1).*

This may have been prompted by the recent experience of Peter, James, and John on the mount of transfiguration, or Peter's experience with the temple tax. The other disciples may have thought that Christ was "playing favorites" and neglecting them. Of course, we do want to commend the disciples for having faith in His word that there would be a kingdom and that they would be in it. But it is not spiritual to be seeking for position and greatness (see Rom. 12:10, 16).

B. *The object lesson (vv. 2-6).*

A child is Christ's illustration of greatness. Honor comes from humility; we must go down before God will lift us up (1 Peter 5:5-6). All great saints have been humble saints. While children aren't sinless or perfect, they do have the characteristics that ought to be in every Christian's life: they are teachable, simple in their wants, have expectant attitudes, and depend on their fathers to meet their needs. Of course, the only way we can become children is to be born again (John 3).

C. *The warning (vv. 7-10).*

By "these little ones" (v. 10) Jesus means not only children, but the children of God who are God's "little children" (see 1 John 2:1, 12, 18, 28; 3:7, 18; 4:4; 5:21). It is tragic when we cause another believer to stumble (Rom. 14:1-23; 1 Cor. 8:1-13). Christ is not speaking literally when He commands us to "cut off" (v. 8) the members of the body that cause us to sin, for sin comes from the heart, not the hands and feet. He is telling us to deal with our sins drastically, completely, and mercilessly, the way a surgeon deals with a cancerous growth. We must not "play with" sin or delay getting rid of it. We must face our sins honestly, confess and forsake them.

D. The parable (vv. 11-14).

If you compare v. 11 with Luke 19:10, you will note that the phrase "to seek" is missing. Christ is talking about "the children"; and children, though lost after reaching the age of accountability, may not be as prone to wander away as are adults. But they still must be saved by the Good Shepherd. This entire passage warns us not to offend children (v. 6), despise the children (v. 10), or allow them to perish without Christ (v. 14). He gives several reasons why the children are important: they are examples of true greatness (v. 4); they represent Christ (v. 5); the angels represent them before the Father (v. 10); Christ wants to save them (v. 11); and it is the will of the Father that they be saved (v. 14).

It is a dangerous thing for parents (or other adults) to cause children to stumble and miss the way of salvation. How important it is to have a good example at home. Many backslidden parents and worldly minded adults will have much to answer for at the judgment!

II. Lessons on Forgiveness (18:15-35)

Christ is dealing with "family matters" and He moves now from children to the relationship between brethren. If all Christians were perfect, there would be no need for these instructions, but because we fail and sin, we need to know how to keep the church family happy and holy.

A. Church discipline (vv. 15-20).

The pattern is clear: first a private interview, then bring two or three witnesses, then take it to the church. Note the purpose: "You have gained a brother" (v. 15, NKJV). The motive for church discipline is love: we are seeking to help a sinning brother. Since Christ is in the midst of the church (v. 20), it is also important that the church be obedient and pure. Our attitude should not be that of a policeman out to arrest a criminal, but rather that of a physician seeking to heal a wound in the body of Christ, a wound that will spread sickness and death if left alone.

Verse 18 indicates that the "binding and loosing" ministry has to do with applying the Word of God in matters of discipline. Paul "bound" the offending brother in Corinth in 1 Cor. 5 and "loosed him" after he had confessed (2 Cor. 2). This has nothing to do with the eternal destiny of a soul. Verse 19 suggests that prayer is an important factor in church discipline. Certainly we want to pray for the offender and for ourselves that we might be spiritually able to minister (Gal. 6:1). For other passages on church discipline, see Rom. 16:17, 2 Thes. 3:14, and 1 Cor. 5.

B. Forgiving from the heart (vv. 21-35).

Peter thought he was "extra-spiritual" for offering to forgive seven times, because the Jewish rabbis said that three times was enough. Jesus put no limit on forgiveness, for true forgiveness comes from a heart of love, and love keeps no record of wrongs (1 Cor. 13:5).

The lesson of the parable is obvious: if the king could forgive the servant's debt of $12,000,000, certainly the servant could forgive his friend's debt of about $15! We forgive others because Christ has forgiven us (Eph. 4:32; Col. 3:13). Keep in mind that this has nothing to do with salvation; it is a matter of "family forgiveness" between siblings in Christ, not between God and the sinner; so do not read eternal judgment into v. 34. God will certainly deal with a believer who harbors an unforgiving spirit.

One of the evidences that a person is saved is love for the brethren (1 John 3:10-17). Christians who cannot forgive others have forgotten what Christ has done for them on the cross. The church must beware of "the leaven of malice and wickedness" (1 Cor. 5:6-8) that will silently grow and corrupt the entire fellowship.

MATTHEW 19

I. Marriage and Divorce (19:1-15)

The Pharisees asked the question about marriage because it was one of the "burning issues" of that day, and they wanted Christ to commit Himself and thus divide the people against Him. The followers of Rabbi Hillel interpreted Deut. 24:1 to mean that a man could divorce his wife for any cause, while the followers of Rabbi Shammai held to a strict interpretation, that marriage could be broken only by adultery. Jesus went beyond the rabbis, and even beyond the Law, and reminded the people of the original law of marriage established in Eden. In this passage, there are three "laws" of marriage discussed.

A. The original Edenic law (vv. 4-6; Gen. 1:27-28; 2:18-25).

God instituted marriage in Eden, long before the Mosaic Law. The Bible gives at least four purposes for marriage: (1) to continue the race (Gen. 1:28); (2) for companionship and enjoyment (Gen. 2:18); (3) to avoid fornication (1 Cor. 7:1-6); and (4) to show the relationship between Christ and His church (Eph. 5:22-23). God's original purpose was that one man should wed one woman, and only death should break that union (Rom. 7:1-3). Marriage is basically a physical union (v. 5), although it ought to be a union of minds and hearts too. The marriage union is even stronger than family ties, for a man is to leave father and mother and cleave to his wife. It is a sacred union, for Jesus said that God joins a man and woman together.

B. The temporary Mosaic Law (vv. 7-8; Deut. 24:1-4).

Sinners are always looking for excuses, and the Pharisees appealed to Deut. 24:1, trying to show that Christ and Moses were in conflict. It is important that we realize why Moses gave this law and what the law really stated. Moses did not *command* divorce; Christ said that God *permitted* it, "because of the hardness of your hearts" (v. 8). Moses did command that the divorced woman be given a bill of divorcement, to protect her and to make it more difficult for the man to divorce her in the heat of anger. The woman was forbidden to return to her first husband, but she could marry another man. The phrase "some uncleanness" literally means "a matter of nakedness" and suggests immorality on the part of the woman (Lev. 18). This divorce law was a temporary one for Israel and not permanent for all people.

C. Christ's law for marriage (vv. 9-12).

Christ clearly states that divorce is permitted for only one cause, fornication. This is a sin against the body (1 Cor. 6:15-18) and thus a sin against the marriage union, which is a physical union. The word "fornication" as used in the Bible seems to include a number of sexual sins. Mark 7:21 speaks of "fornications" (plural), while

Acts 15:20, Rom. 1:29, and 1 Cor. 6:13 indicate that "fornication" covers sexual sins in general. It is commonly agreed that fornication is used of sins committed by the unmarried, adultery by the married. In any case, Jesus states that divorce for any other reason makes the parties guilty of adultery if they remarry (see 5:27-31; Luke 16:18; Mark 10:1-2). Thus, there are but two physical causes that can break the marriage union: death and fornication.

The response of the disciples (vv. 10-12) indicates they didn't understand God's will regarding marriage. While the Bible does not exalt celibacy, it does recognize that not everybody is supposed to be married. Paul indicates this in 1 Cor. 7:7. Paul himself refrained from marriage that he might better serve God, but this is not the will of God for all His servants. A person must find God's will for his life and be sure to marry "in the Lord" (1 Cor. 7:39).

II. Riches and Salvation (19:16-30)

This passage revolves around five questions and the answers Christ gave.

A. "What good thing shall I do?" (vv. 16-17)

We must admire the rich ruler for his courtesy, earnestness, desire for spiritual truth, and courage. Christ's reply was intended to emphasize His own deity. "Either I am good, or I am not God," is what He implied. He wanted the young man to realize he was dealing with God and not a mere human teacher of the Law.

B. "Which commandments?" (vv. 18-19)

Christ told him to keep the Law, not because the Law saves, but because we must be convicted by the Law before we feel the need to be saved by grace. This young man knew the Law, and the Law had served as a schoolmaster to bring him to Christ (Gal. 3:24). Now the Law was serving as a mirror (James 1:22-25) to show the young man his real need. If he really tried to obey God's Law, the man would discover how sinful he was!

C. "What lack I yet?" (vv. 20-22)

We have no reason to doubt that the young man had kept all the commandments, at least outwardly. But as he faced the perfect Law of God, he should have thought of the one that said, "You shall not covet" (Ex. 20:17, NKJV) and that great command, "You

71

shall have no other gods before Me" (Ex. 20:3, NKJV). His wealth was his god, but he would not admit it. Why did Jesus tell him to sell all and give to the poor? This is not how a man is saved! No, but this commandment pointed up his real problem: he was covetous. Christ told the sinful woman at the well to call her husband, and this command brought her to the place of confession and repentance. Sad to say, the young ruler would not confess his sin or change his mind. He went away sad; the woman in John 4 went away rejoicing.

D. "Who can be saved?" (vv. 23-26)

The disciples were amazed: if a rich man can't be saved, then who can be saved? They were still under the OT Jewish idea that riches meant the blessing of God on your life. Mark 10:24 indicates that the rich have a hard time being saved because they trust in their riches. See Paul's admonitions in 1 Tim. 6:6-10.

E. "What shall we have?" (vv. 27-30)

Peter was quick to contrast himself with the rich ruler and point to his own self-sacrifice. Jesus tenderly assured His own that they will get their rewards in the kingdom age. ("Regeneration" means when earth shall be "born again.") However, he cautions them not to make themselves "first" because the first shall be last. He illustrated this with the parable in the next chapter and shows that motive for service is most important. If Peter served Christ only because of the promised reward, then he needed to examine his heart and motives. Fortunately, Peter grew from the "How much will I get?" attitude of Matt. 19 to the "Such as I have give I thee" attitude of Acts 3:6, and so must we.

MATTHEW 20

This parable and the events that followed grew out of the meeting with the rich young man in 19:16-30. The parable is Christ's explanation of His paradoxical statement about the first and the last (19:30 and 20:16).

I. The Parable of the Vineyard (20:1-16)

A. The setting.

The rich ruler had refused to give up his possessions and follow

Christ, and the Lord warned His disciples about the dangers of riches. Peter boasted that he and his friends had left all to follow Him, and he boldly asked, "Therefore what shall we have?" (19:27, NKJV) His question revealed a wrong motive: he was serving Christ for what he could get and not out of loyalty and love. Christ warned them that some who were "first" in the eyes of men would be "last" when it came to the final reckoning, and some whom the disciples might think "last" would instead be first.

B. The meaning.

Don't try to make everything in this parable mean something. The main spiritual truth Christ brings out is that God has a right to deal with His servants as He will, according to their motives for service.

The parable is not about salvation but service. The "penny" does not stand for salvation or eternal life, because salvation is not by good works (Eph. 2:8-9; Titus 3:5-6).

Christ is not talking about rewards for service. God will reward His own differently according to their service (1 Cor. 3:8; John 4:36). If the "penny" stands for rewards, then God is not fair, for every worker got the same reward!

If you connect 20:10 with Peter's remarks in 19:27, you will get the lesson. "When the first came, they supposed that they should have received." Isn't this what Peter was doing? "We have left all," he said. "What will we get?" He was thinking to himself, "Surely we will get more!" Christ teaches him that God has a right to do what He pleases with His servants, and that to have a wrong motive ("eye evil" in v. 15) is sinful. Note also that the 6 A.M. workers demanded a contract; they wanted to know what they would get!

C. The living.

Christ has summoned us to labor for Him. It is too bad that there are Christians standing around idle all the day, when there is so much work to be done! This parable reminds us that we should serve Christ out of love and loyalty, and not just for rewards. It is not sinful to earn rewards, and God in His grace will give rewards to faithful servants (1 Cor. 3:12-15). But the Rewarder should fill our hearts, not the reward.

We must watch our motives for Christian service. The right work done with the wrong motive dishonors God and robs us of the blessing. It is a solemn thing to realize that Christians whom we may admire today will be "last" at the final reckoning at the Judgment Seat of Christ because their motives were wrong. We cannot judge motives (7:1-3), but we can judge our own hearts. Let's do all for the glory of God because we love Him.

II. The Prayer for Glory (20:17-28)

A. The announcement (vv. 17-19).

This is Christ's third announcement of the cross to His disciples (see Matt. 16:21; 17:22-23). He was preparing them for the crisis He would face in Jerusalem. The first time He spoke of the cross, Peter rebuked Him; and on this occasion, the mother of James and John came with a selfish prayer. How slow we are to grasp the message of the Cross!

B. The request (vv. 20-21).

Her faith in Christ must be admired; also her trust in His promise of the kingdom (19:28). But her motive was not right, since she was asking not for God's glory but for her own.

C. The reply (vv. 22-23).

Jesus speaks to the disciples (James and John) and not to the mother, suggesting that perhaps they had encouraged her to ask on their behalf. Of course, they were ignorant of what He meant by the "cup" and the "baptism," both of which pointed to His suffering and death on Calvary (see 26:39-42 and Luke 12:50). Jesus promised that they would indeed taste of His cup and baptism. James was the first disciple martyred (Acts 12), and John suffered greatly, exiled on the Isle of Patmos (Rev. 1). We must be careful how we pray and how we answer the Lord; for He will hold us to what we say (Ecc. 5:1-6).

D. The result (vv. 24-25).

"How great a forest a little fire kindles" (James 3:5, NKJV). Selfishness on the part of one believer can cause trouble in the lives of others. Jesus used this as an opportunity to teach the disciples a lesson on humility. The truly great person is one who serves others. Christ Himself is the example of this (see Phil. 2). To "exercise lordship" as the people of the world do is foreign to the spirit of the Christian life. While Christian leaders are to "shepherd the flock" (1 Peter 5:2; see Acts 20:28), they are not to govern in self-will and pride, but humbly as "undershepherds."

III. The Miracle of Healing (20:29-34)

Mark 10:46-52 indicates only one blind man, but Matthew states there were two. It is likely that Bartimaeus (mentioned by Mark) was the better known of the two and the one who took the lead in coming to Jesus. This miracle is a picture of salvation. The two men were blind, and every lost sinner is blind (2 Cor. 4:1-6). They were poor beggars, and the lost sinner is poverty-stricken apart from Christ (Luke 7:40-50). They cried out to Jesus, who alone can open men's eyes. He showed them mercy; they were not healed by their praying or their crying. The crowd tried to stop them, and the world today tries to keep sinners from coming to Christ. The touch of Christ healed them, and they proved that their lives had changed by following Him.

The Rejection of the King

Matthew 21–27 records "The Rejection of the King," and it is important that we understand their scope. Christ meets His enemies in that final conflict that led to His crucifixion. The chapters may be outlined as follows:

I. Three Signs (21:1-22)

A. The presentation of the king (vv. 1-11).
Israel's spiritual blindness.

B. The purifying of the temple (vv. 12-16).
Israel's inward corruption.

C. The cursing of the fig tree (vv. 17-22).
Israel's outward fruitlessness.

II. Three Parables (21:23–22:14)

A. The two sons (vv. 23-32).
They rejected the Father.

B. The vineyard (vv. 33-46).
They rejected the Son.

C. The wedding (vv. 1-14).
They rejected the Spirit.

III. Three Questions (22:15-46)

A. Tribute to Caesar (vv. 15-22).
Political question from Herodians.

B. The resurrection (vv. 23-33).
Doctrinal question from Sadducees.

C. The great commandment (vv. 34-46).
Legal question from Pharisees.

IV. Three Discourses (23:1–26:46)

A. Condemnation of the Pharisees (chap. 23).

B. Explanation of the future kingdom (chaps. 24–25).

C. Preparation of the disciples for the cross (26:1-46).

V. Three Trials (26:47–27:66)

A. Before Caiaphas and the council (vv. 47-75).

B. Before the council in the morning (vv. 1-10).

C. Before Pilate, leading to Christ's death (vv. 11-66).

Of course, this outline shows only the broad sweep of the events and not the details. Matthew does not record all the events of the final week of our Lord's ministry, so you will want to read the other Gospels and consult a Gospel Harmony for the sequence of events.

The traditional chronology of the Passion Week is as follows:
Sunday: The entry into Jerusalem.
Monday: Cleansing the temple; cursing of the fig tree.
Tuesday: Conflicts with the leaders; parables; condemnation of Pharisees; discourse on the kingdom (Matt. 24–25).
Wednesday: No recorded words or deeds; a day of rest.
Thursday: Last Supper; discourses in the Upper Room.
Friday: Arrest and trial; crucifixion and entombment.
Saturday: In the tomb.
Sunday: Resurrection.

Some Bible scholars believe that Christ could have been cruci-fied on Thursday or possibly even Wednesday. This would make it possible for Him to spend exactly three days and three nights in the tomb (Matt. 12:40) and rise from the dead "after three days" (Mark 8:31; 9:31). The phrase "three days and three nights" can be interpreted as a popular expression that would include even the part of a day or night. Thus, if Christ was buried about 3 o'clock on Friday afternoon, you could include Friday, all of Saturday and whatever hours He was in the tomb before His resurrection on Sunday.

Fortunately, it is not necessary to agree on these details. The fact of His death, burial, and resurrection is the important thing; and we must not use these matters to divide the church.

MATTHEW 21

You will note that chapter 21 begins with three definite signs to the nation of Israel; these are followed by three parables (including 21:1-14 where the chapter break is unfortunate). The parables grew out of the antagonism of the scribes and Pharisees over His cleansing of the temple.

I. Three Signs Concerning Israel (21:1-22)

A. Presentation of the King (vv. 1-11).

This was in fulfillment of Zech. 9:9. Matthew omitted "just and having salvation" when he quoted Zechariah, because Christ will not come with justice and salvation (victory) for Israel until He returns in Rev. 19:11-21, riding a white horse. John 12:17-18 indicates that many in the great crowd were there because of the raising of Lazarus. The crowd quoted Ps. 118:26 in its praises; later (v. 42) Christ would quote from that same psalm to refute the leaders. Note in v. 11 that the city called Him "the prophet" but not the King! Unfortunately, the Jews "did not know the time of your visitation" (Luke 19:41-44, NKJV) and rejected their King.

B. Purifying of the temple (vv. 12-16).

Israel's inward corruption is seen by the way the temple had become a house of merchandise. The first cleansing at the start of Christ's ministry (John 2) did not last, for the leaders' hearts were not changed. Christ quoted Isa. 56:7 and called the temple "My house" (v. 13), thus claiming to be God. He also referred to Jer. 7:11. Later, Christ would say, "Your house is left unto you *desolate*"

(Matt. 23:38; emphasis mine); for having rejected their King, Israel now had an empty temple. When accused by the leaders, Christ quoted Ps. 8:2, which is a messianic psalm (see Heb. 2:5-9) pointing to the time when Christ will reign on earth as the King.

C. Cursing the fig tree (vv. 17-22).

Matthew 24:32-33 and Luke 13:6-10 suggest that the fig tree pictures Israel. This tree had leaves but not fruit, picturing Israel with its outward "show of religion" but its fruitlessness. Luke 13:6-10 indicates that God gave Israel three years in which to bring forth fruit, but the nation failed. Christ uses the miracle as a lesson in faith, suggesting that it was Israel's unbelief that brought about her judgment. How easy it is to have "a form of godliness" (2 Tim. 3:5) but never bear any fruit! Many counterfeit Christians will hear Christ's "Depart from Me, you cursed" (Matt. 25:41) because they had "nothing . . . but leaves" (v. 19).

In these three signs, then, Christ reveals Israel's spiritual blindness, her inward corruption, and her outward fruitlessness.

II. Three Parables Concerning Israel (21:23–22:14)

From 21:23 to 23:39, Christ is in the temple contending with leaders. In 24:1 He departs from the temple and never again entered it! "Ichabod" was now written over the temple: "The glory is departed" (1 Sam. 4:19-22). Of course, the Jews questioned His authority, and He took them back to the ministry of John the Baptist. Why? Because they knew John told the truth, yet they rejected him. God does not reveal new truth until we obey what He has already revealed. Having rejected John, the Jews did not deserve an answer from Jesus.

Jesus told three parables concerning the nation of Israel.

A. The two sons (vv. 28-32).

Here we see Israel as a son disobedient to his Father. The vineyard speaks of Israel (Isa. 5:1-7; Ps. 80:8-16). By rejecting John the Baptist, the Jews disobeyed the Father who sent him. The sinners, however, heeded John and entered into the kingdom of God!

B. The vineyard and husbandmen (vv. 33-46).

God did much for Israel, expecting the nation to bear fruit for His glory, but the nation rebelled against God and refused to bear fruit.

God sent many prophets and other servants to deal with them, but Israel mistreated and even killed them. Then God sent His Son—and they killed Him! They even "cast Him out of the vineyard" (v. 39; see Heb. 13:11-13). The Jews themselves spoke their own sentence in v. 41, and God did just what they said. He took their spiritual privileges away, destroyed Jerusalem, and gave their blessings to the Gentiles.

Christ quoted Ps. 118:22-23, calling Himself "the stone which the builders rejected" (v. 42; see Isa. 28:16). Peter called the leaders of Israel "you builders" (Acts 4:11), and Rom. 9:33 and 1 Peter 2:4-8 point to Christ as the stumbling stone to Israel, but the foundation stone to the church. The sinner who "falls on the stone" in humility will be broken but saved, but the rebel who resists Christ will be crushed by the stone in judgment.

C. The marriage feast (vv. 1-14).

The Father invited the guests (Israel) to enjoy blessings because of His Son. However, the nation spurned the invitations given: v. 3 probably indicates the invitation from the apostles when the Lord was on earth; and vv. 4-6 the invitation during the early chapters of Acts, when the message was again offered to the Jews. Israel resisted the Spirit (Acts 7:51-52) and this brought national judgment, including the ruin of Jerusalem (v. 7). Then the King turned to the Gentiles, as was done in Acts 10 after the nation had sealed its decision by killing Stephen and persecuting the church.

The closing verses of the parable (11-14) emphasize the fact that the guests must receive a covering from the King to be accepted. The King called "both bad and good" (v. 10), but provided a garment to make them acceptable. This speaks of the gift of righteousness that God provides through Christ for all who believe (2 Cor. 5:20). Do not put this scene in heaven, for certainly no one will enter heaven without Christ's righteousness. These verses warn false professors not to respond to the invitation outwardly, without receiving the Lord inwardly.

These three parables show the spiritual history of Israel. She was chosen of God to be fruitful (the vineyard and the fig tree), and she failed to bear fruit. She disobeyed the Father (Parable of the Two Sons), crucified the Son (Parable of the Vineyard), and resisted the Spirit (Parable of the Marriage Feast). She is today set aside and the blessings of Christ have been given to the church until the fullness of the Gentiles comes in (Rom. 11:25ff).

MATTHEW 22

We considered the first fourteen verses in the previous section. The rest of the chapter deals with questions that the scribes and Pharisees asked Jesus as they tried to "trap Him in His words" (v. 15, NIV).

I. A Question about Tribute (22:15-22)

This was asked by the Herodians, a religious group with political ambitions. While the NT does not give us much information about them, it appears that they were in league with the Herods in cooperating with Rome. They were opposed to the Pharisees who hated Roman rule, but these two enemies got together to oppose Christ.

The question of tribute was a delicate one. If Christ opposed tribute to Rome, then He could be arrested as a traitor; but if He favored tribute to Caesar, He would lose the hearts of the Jews who despised their Roman rulers. Christ's reply shows that the true child of God has obligations both to God and to his country. As D. L. Moody used to say, "A Christian should not be so heavenly minded [that] he is no earthly good." Romans 13 and 1 Peter 2:13-18 teach that Christians should obey the law and honor their leaders. The best citizen is a Christian citizen.

Just as Caesar stamped his image on the coin, so God has stamped His image on man (Gen. 1:26-27). Sin has marred that image, but through Christ that image is restored (Eph. 4:24; Col. 3:10). The Parable of the Lost Coin in Luke 15:8-10 suggests that man, made in the image of God, is lost and must be found before that true image can be seen.

II. A Question about the Resurrection (22:23-33)

Now the Sadducees enter the picture with a doctrinal question. Again see how the Pharisees and Sadducees, who were enemies, unite to oppose Christ. They present a hypothetical question about marriage in the next life, based on the OT law that a man marry his brother's widow to perpetuate the family (see Gen. 38:8; Deut. 25:5-10). They were ignorant, said Jesus, of God's power and God's Word. He explained that human marriage as we know it will not exist in the next life, but that people will be as the angels, that is, living in a spiritual world not controlled by human laws. (This does not mean that we shall be angels, but that we shall be like them in regards to marriage. Saints will always reign as children of God, and not as servants like the angels.)

Christ answered His critics from the Bible, referring to Ex. 3:6, 15-16. God said, "I am the God of Abraham, and the God of Isaac, and the God of Jacob" (v. 32), not "I was the God. . . . " This means that these men are still alive and with God. Death does not destroy the person, although the body may turn to dust. Thus, Jesus teaches that the soul exists after death and that those who have faith go to be with God. But God saves the total person, including the body, which shall be glorified (Phil. 3:20-21). Therefore, the continuation of life after death (something the Sadducees denied) is in itself proof of a future resurrection. God's power is great enough to raise the dead!

III. A Question about the Great Commandment (22:34-46)

Now the Pharisees appear openly to ask a legal question about the OT law. (The word "put . . . to silence" in v. 34 literally means "muzzled." This shows how completely Christ silenced His enemies!) The doctors of the law debated over which of the many commandments was the greatest. They divided the commandments into "heavy" and "light" and separated the "ritual laws" and the "moral laws." It got to the place that the smallest detail of the ritual law was as binding as the great moral laws of God! The Pharisees thought they could trap Jesus by forcing Him to take sides on this controversial theological issue.

Again, Jesus appealed to the Scriptures and quoted Deut. 6:5 and Lev. 19:18. Love for God and love for one's neighbor: these two commandments sum up the entire Law (see Rom. 13:8-10). Instead of debating, we should be obeying and making sure we love God and others. This is the true heart of religion. Of course, no one can love God apart from knowing Jesus Christ as Savior (John 8:42). And when you know and love God, the love of God will be shared with others (Rom. 5:5).

Having silenced the Herodians, Sadducees, and Pharisees, Christ asked a question Himself (vv. 41-42), and no one was able to answer it! He referred to Ps. 110:1 where David calls Him "Lord." Note that Christ states that David wrote the psalm, wrote it inspired by the Spirit (v. 43), and wrote it concerning Christ, the Son of David. His question was, "If David then calls Him "Lord" [meaning He is God], how is He his Son?" (v. 45) The answer is given in Matt. 1–2 — the virgin birth of Christ. As eternal God, Christ is David's Lord, but as the God-man, come in the flesh, He is David's Son.

If the scribes and Pharisees had answered this question honestly and correctly, they would have had to acknowledge the messiahship of Christ. But in their hardness of heart, they rejected the truth and turned to more devilish ways of silencing Him. They were the children of the devil (John 8:44); they had tried lies and had failed, so now they would try to murder Him.

If you will read all of Ps. 110, you will note that it deals with the high priesthood of Jesus Christ, as well as His conquest of His enemies. Peter quoted it at Pentecost (Acts 2:32-36) to prove the resurrection of Christ, and it is also quoted in Heb. 10:13. Rejected as King by the Jews, Christ turns to the Gentiles and becomes the High Priest of all who trust Him. When He returns to the earth, He will make His enemies the footstool of His feet. Meanwhile, He is patiently waiting ("expecting," Heb. 10:13) until that day of judgment and triumph.

MATTHEW 23

Having silenced His enemies, Christ proceeded to expose them openly. In the Sermon on the Mount, He said that our righteousness had to exceed that of the scribes and Pharisees, if we ever hoped to enter the kingdom of heaven (Matt. 5:20). He exposed their hypocrisy and showed conclusively that mere "religion" can never make people holy. This public exposure certainly angered the Pharisees and had much to do with their final crucifixion of Christ.

I. Explanation to the Multitudes and Disciples (23:1-12)

The Pharisees appeared as a group during the time in Israel's history when the nation was pressured by the Greeks to forsake their law and become liberal. Men like Ezra (Ezra 7:10) remained true to the faith, protected the Law, and separated themselves from pagan defilement. They became the official interpreters of the Law when Israel had no prophet or teaching priests. In this sense, the Pharisees "sat in Moses' seat." Jesus did not tell the people to observe everything the Pharisees taught, but only those teachings that were true to the Law of Moses. Christ Himself had rejected many of the

Pharisees' teachings (see Matt. 5:21–6:18; 12:1ff).

The great sin of the Pharisees was hypocrisy based on pride. Their religion was external, not internal; it was to impress people, not to please God. They bound people with heavy burdens, while Christ came to set people free (Luke 4:18-19). They loved titles and public recognition and exalted themselves at the expense of others. They wore boxes containing the Scriptures ("phylacteries"—supposedly based on Ex. 13:16; Deut. 6:8; 11:18) and made the hems of their garments wide (Num. 15:38) to advertise their religious zeal. They had a "form of godliness" but no power (2 Tim. 3:5), while the borders of Christ's garments gave forth power to change lives (Matt. 9:20; 14:36).

We see the Trinity in vv. 8-10. We have one "Master" (meaning teacher), the Holy Spirit (v. 8; "even Christ" should be omitted); we have one Father (v. 9); and we have one Leader ("Master" here means leader), that is Christ (v. 10). For men to take the place of the Father, or the Son, or the Spirit, is to disobey the Word of God and lead people astray.

II. Condemnation of the Pharisees (23:13-36)

There are eight "woes" here, and you can contrast them with the eight "blesseds" (Beatitudes) of Matt. 5:3-12. "The poor in spirit" inherit the kingdom (5:3), while the proud "shut up the kingdom" (v. 13). Mourners are comforted (5:4) while the devourers receive damnation (v. 14). The meek "inherit the earth" (5:5) but the proud send people to hell (v. 15). God fills those who are hungry for holiness (5:6), but those who are greedy for material gain go away empty (vv. 16-22). The merciful "obtain mercy" (5:7), but the Pharisees rejected mercy as they majored in trivialities (vv. 23-24). "The pure in heart" see God (5:8), while the outwardly religious are inwardly corrupt (vv. 25-28). The peacemakers and persecuted are the "children of God" (5:9-12), but the murderers and persecutors are called "children of the devil" (vv. 29-33).

Jesus did not utter these "woes" with a feeling of hatred or malice in His heart. There is a sense of "pitying sorrow" in these verses, as the loving heart of Christ reveals the wicked hearts of His enemies. It was anguish that He revealed, not anger.

How did they "shut up the kingdom"? (v. 13) First, by refusing to receive the message of John the Baptist (21:25-27; 11:16-19). Second, by refusing to acknowledge Christ Himself (John 7:47ff).

Third, by keeping the true meaning of the Scriptures from the people (Luke 11:52). By hiding "the key of knowledge" (Christ as seen in the Scriptures) behind their man-made traditions, the scribes and Pharisees actually locked the door to the kingdom of heaven! How tragic when "religious leaders" today shut people out of heaven by rejecting Christ, resisting His Spirit, and refusing to preach and teach His Word.

The Pharisees preyed upon poor widows and took their possessions under the pretense of using them for God (v. 14). They were covetous liars and "religious racketeers."

Their values were confused (vv. 16-22). They were interested in the gold and the gifts but not the spiritual worship in the temple (see Luke 16:14ff).

"Whited sepulchers" (v. 27) refers to the practice of whitewashing tombs so that the Jews would not accidentally defile themselves (see Num. 19:16).

"The measure of your fathers" (v. 32) refers to the increasing sin of the nation from OT days to Acts 7, when they finally "resisted the Spirit" (7:51; read all of Stephen's speech for details) and God set Israel aside. They had killed the prophets; they had permitted John to be murdered; they would crucify Christ; they would imprison the apostles and slay Stephen and "fill up the measure." When we sin, we write our own sentence of judgment.

"Generation of vipers" (v. 33) means "children of the devil" (see 3:7; 12:34; John 8:44 and review the Parable of the Tares found in Matt. 13).

Children of the devil are persecutors of the children of God (v. 35). Cain was a child of the devil (1 John 3:12).

III. Lamentation over Jerusalem (23:37-39)

This final word of sorrow from Christ indicates that God had given the people many opportunities to be saved, but they would not receive His offer. God does not send people to hell; they send themselves there by their own stubbornness.

"Your house" (v. 38) probably refers to the house of Israel, as pictured by the temple. In 24:1, Christ left the temple and never returned to it, thus symbolically saying, "You have rejected Me, therefore your temple is empty." (See Matt. 13:1 where He left the house — Israel — to go by the seaside — the Gentiles.) He called the temple "My house" in 21:13; but now it is "your house."

Israel will receive her Messiah when He returns to establish the kingdom on earth (see Zech. 12:10). Between the "Blessed is He who comes" of Matt. 21:9 (NKJV) and the "Blessed is He who comes" of Matt. 23:39 (still future) lies the Church Age which was not yet revealed. Believers today do not look for an earthly king, but for the heavenly Bridegroom who will return in the twinkling of an eye!

Christ's Prophecy on the Mount (Matthew 24–25)

Next to the Sermon on the Mount and the parables in Matt. 13, no part of Matthew has suffered more misinterpretation than His discourse on the Mount of Olives. Many cults use Matt. 24:1-41, along with Dan. 9:20-27, to "prove" that Christ has already returned! Even well-meaning evangelicals confuse the issue by applying this section to the church in this age. It is important that we get an overall view of the Olivet Discourse before we examine the details.

There are three major divisions in the discourse; 24:1-44, which is primarily Jewish; 24:45–25:30, which deals with Christendom, the professing church as seen in the world; and 25:31-46, which deals with the Gentiles. You have, then, the threefold division of humanity today—the Jews, the Gentiles, and the church (see 1 Cor. 10:32). The Jewish character of 24:1-44 is seen in the following:

1. The discourse grew out of a discussion about the Jewish temple (v. 2).

2. The disciples asked Him concerning His return and the end of the age. This could not mean His return for the church, or the end of the Church Age, because these truths were still hidden from the Twelve (see Eph. 3).

3. He discusses the land of Judea, not the whole earth (v. 16).

4. He mentions the Sabbath, a Jewish institution (v. 20).

5. He refers them to Daniel the prophet (v. 15), who prophesied concerning the Jews and the city of Jerusalem (Dan. 9:24ff).

6. He warns about false Christs (vv. 3-5) and false prophets (v. 11). This is a warning to Jews, for true believers would not follow a false Christ. We are to watch out for false teachers and false spirits (1 John 4:1-3; 2 Peter 2:1ff).

7. He gave the message on the Mount of Olives, which in Zech. 14:4 is associated with His return to earth to establish the promised Jewish kingdom.

The second section (24:45–25:30) has a different "atmosphere" from the first. For one thing, each of these parables presents Christ as delaying His return (24:48; 25:5, 19). Since the events of the previous section will take place during the seven year tribulation period (see analysis of Matt. 24–25), you cannot put these parables in that same time period; for seven years can hardly be called "delaying His coming" or "after a long time." Matt. 24:1-44 speaks of a Christ — a King — who will return at a definite time according to given signs, but this second section pictures a Lord, a Bridegroom, and a Rich Master who delays His return and comes when He is not expected. The three parables picture the condition of "Christendom" when Christ returns for His church. It is a mixture of true and false, good and bad, as found in Matt. 13. These verses refer to the situation today.

The final section (25:31-46) presents the judgment of the Gentiles before the kingdom is set up.

Keep in mind, then, that the first section is Jewish, future, and applies to the tribulation period which will take place after the rapture of the church. The second section applies to Christendom today and looks forward to the coming of Jesus Christ for His own. The third section deals with the Gentiles and looks ahead to the end of the tribulation and the establishing of the kingdom of God on earth.

A Suggested Analysis of Matthew 24–25

I. Introduction (24:1-3)

A. Jesus predicts the destruction of the temple (vv. 1-2).

B. The disciples ask Him three questions (v. 3).

1. When will the temple be destroyed? Answer: Luke 21:20-24. This question is not answered in Matt.
2. What is the sign of His coming? Answer: Matt. 24:29-44.
3. What is the sign of the end of the age? Answer: Matt. 24:4-28.

C. Jesus also discusses two matters about which the disciples did not ask:

1. Christ's coming for the church — Matt. 24:45–25:30
2. Christ's judgment of the Gentiles — Matt. 25:31-46

II. Christ's Coming and Israel (24:4-44)

First	1. "The Beginning of sorrows"—4-8	
3¹/₂ years	(1) False Christs, 4-5	Rev. 6:1-2 (Antichrist)
of the	(2) Wars, 6	Rev. 6:3-4
70th week	(3) Famines, 7a	Rev. 6:5-6
of Daniel	(4) Death, 7b-8	Rev. 6:7-8
	2. Events leading up to "The End"—9-14	
	(1) Martyrs, 9	Rev. 6:9-11
	(2) Worldwide chaos, 10-13	Rev. 6:12-17
	(3) Worldwide preaching, 14	Rev. 7—144,000 JEWS
	"THEN COMES THE END . . ."	
	3. The Great Tribulation—15-28	
	(1) The Abomination of Desolation, 15	Rev. 13
Last	(2) Warnings to Jews to flee, 16-20	
3¹/₂ years	(3) The tribulation proper, 21-27	Rev. 16
of the	(4) Gathering of nations at Armageddon, 28	Rev. 19:17-18
70th week	4. "After the Tribulation"—29-31	Rev. 19:11-21
of Daniel	(1) Signs in heavens, 29	
	(2) Coming of Christ in power, 30	
	(3) Gathering of Israel ("elect"), 31	
	5. Three concluding exhortations—32-44	
	(1) The fig tree, 32-35	"Know it is near" 33
	(2) The days of Noah, 36-42	"Watch therefore!" 42
	(3) The Householder, 43-44	"Be ready!" 44

III. Christ's Coming and Christendom (24:45–25:30)

Note: These parables picture "Christendom" when Christ comes for His church. It is a mixture of good and bad, saved and unsaved, as the kingdom pictured in Matt. 13.

A. The faithful and evil servants (24:45-51).

B. The wise and foolish virgins (24:1-13).

C. The profitable and unprofitable servants (25:14-30).

IV. Christ's Coming and the Gentile Nations (25:31-46)

Note: This judgment must not be confused with the White Throne of Rev. 20. There are three groups here: "brethren" (the Jews), "sheep" (people who received the Jews during the Tribulation), and "goats" (the people who persecuted the Jews and rejected the message).

MATTHEW 24–25

In this discourse, Christ is answering the questions put to Him by His disciples in 24:3. They asked, "When shall these things [the destruction of the temple, v. 2] take place?" He told them (see Luke 21:20-24), but Matthew does not record the answer. It took place in A.D. 70 when Titus conquered Jerusalem and destroyed the city. "What will be the sign of Your coming?" (NIV) is answered in 24:29-44; and "What shall be the sign of the end of the (Jewish) age?" is answered in 24:4-28.

The events described in Matt. 24:4-31 will take place during the seven years of tribulation following the rapture of the church. This is the 70th week of Daniel, described in Daniel 9:20-27. This same period of time is described in Rev. 6–19. It is the time when God will pour out His wrath on a rebellious world.

I. Christ's Coming and Israel (24:4-44)

A. The beginning of sorrows (vv. 4-8).

These are the signs that tell the world that judgment is beginning. Note how they parallel the events described in Rev. 6 (see outline). We see these signs in the world today, indicating that the end is near. However, we must admit that many of these signs have always been here, but as we see them getting more intense, we know the coming of the Lord is near.

B. Events leading up to the end (vv. 9-14).

The persecution of His servants (v. 9) will increase. During the Tribulation, God will seal 144,000 Jews (Rev. 7) who will probably be missionaries to the lost world (v. 14), and through their efforts multitudes will be saved. However, many will give their lives for their faith. Do not apply vv. 13-14 to the ministry of the church today. Verse 13 has nothing to do with salvation by grace and v. 14 does not mean that the church must get the Gospel into all the world before Christ can return. Both verses apply to the tribulation period.

C. The Great Tribulation (vv. 15-18).

The Antichrist will make a covenant with the Jewish nation (still in unbelief) for seven years ("one week," Dan. 9:27), and will break it after 3 1/2 years, or at the middle of the tribulation period. He will set up his own image in the Jewish temple (Dan. 11:31 and 12:11) and force the world to worship him (see Rev. 13; 2 Thes. 2:3-4). Note Matthew's little parenthesis: "whoever reads, let him understand" (v. 15, NKJV). Jews living during this tribulation period will read Matt. 24, and understand what to do. In fact, many statements in Dan., Matt. 24–25, and Rev. that are perplexing to us will be understood then by believers. Christ warned the Jews to flee Jerusalem (vv. 16-20), for the last half of this period will be great tribulation and will end with the armies of the nations assembled against Jerusalem. "The elect" in v. 22 are the saved of Israel, not believers in the church. Empowered by Satan, the Antichrist will perform miracles (v. 24, see Rev. 13:13-14; 2 Thes. 2:8-10). The nations, deceived by Satan, will gather at Armageddon to battle Christ (v. 28, see Rev. 19:17-18) and will be defeated.

D. After the Tribulation (24:29-31).

There will be disturbances in the heavens (Joel 3:11-21) and then the sign of His coming will appear. We are not told what this sign is. Some believe it is the Shekinah glory that once abode in the tabernacle and temple. Christ will then return to earth with His saints to establish His promised kingdom. There will be great mourning (Zech. 12:10; Rev. 1:7). This is a public return, not a secret one. And He comes as King, not as Bridegroom. Israel will have been gathered together by the ministry of angels. (For Israel's regathering, see Isa. 11:11-12; 27:12-13; Deut. 30:1-5.) At this time, Christ will be received by Israel, now purged of sin and unbelief, and the nation will be the center of the kingdom. The judgment of the Gentiles (Matt. 25:31-46) also takes place.

E. Three exhortations to Israel (24:32-44).

The fig tree is a symbol of Israel (Luke 13:6-10; Joel 1:6-7; Hosea 9:10). When we see Israel "coming back to life," then we know His return is approaching. This may be happening in our day. Verse 34 teaches that the events described will cover a generation of time. ("This generation" means the generation alive at that time, not the generation alive when Christ was speaking. Some take the word "generation" to mean the nation of Israel that would never be destroyed.) Just as Noah and his family survived the flood, so Israel will survive the Tribulation. Do not make the word "taken" in vv. 40-41 mean "taken to heaven," for Jesus was not describing the rapture of the church. In Noah's day, the flood took people in judgment and left Noah and his family to dwell on the cleansed earth. When God's judgment falls in the Tribulation, one will be taken (in judgment), but another will be left on earth to enter the glorious kingdom. His final exhortation is for the believer to watch. We as Christians do not look for signs, but for Him—a Person—to return (Phil. 3:20). However, as we see world conditions shaping up, we know that His return is near.

II. Christ's Coming and Christendom (24:45–25:30)

The three parables in this section refer to Christendom when Christ returns for the church (1 Thes. 4:13-18). It covers the same mixed group as Matt. 13—true and false Christians, all professing to know Christ. This section pictures Christ as delaying His return (24:48; 25:5, 19), so it cannot fit into the seven year tribulation period in the previous section. There is no mention of signs; for if there were signs, the people would know about when He would return and would be ready! These parables describe the attitudes of professing Christians and exhort us all to be ready for His coming. Some Christians will be ashamed when He returns.

A. The faithful and evil servants (24:45-51).

The church is the household of faith (Gal. 6:10; Eph. 2:19), and the servants are those who must feed the spiritual family. When the heart grows cold, the life becomes careless. Worldly living begins when we forget Christ is coming back (1 John 3:1-3). "Cut him asunder" in v. 51 should read "scourge him severely." This speaks of the discipline Christ will exercise on unfaithful servants when He returns to give rewards. The word "hypocrites" means "unfaithful," suggesting that unfaithful Christians will have sorrow at the Judgment Seat of Christ (see 1 Cor. 3:11-18; 2 Cor. 5:9-11). No true believer will ever go to hell (John 5:24). This language suggests that loss of reward will be a difficult experience.

This parable exhorts us to serve Christ faithfully, looking for His return every day. What a wonderful motive for service—to hear His "Well done!" (25:23) If we serve to please people or to get gain, we will lose the reward. Keep looking up!

B. *The wise and foolish virgins (25:1-13).*

While the full revelation of the church and Christ as the Bridegroom was not made until later, the disciples did know that Christ's relationship to His own was that of a bridegroom. (See Matt. 9:15 and John 3:29.) In 25:1 we have separation (they were virgins); illumination or testimony (they had lamps, Phil. 2:15-16); and expectation, as they went forth to meet the bridegroom. Is this not a picture of what the church ought to be doing today? However, within the group there were those who were not prepared, just as in "the church" (Christendom) today. Of course, all believers are in the true church and are ready for heaven. However, in the professing church, as we see it, there are many who appear to be Christians but have never been born again. As in Matt. 13, there are the tares among the wheat.

It has been nearly 2,000 years since Christ promised to return, and during that time, the church has gone to sleep. In the last century, Christians have awakened to the great truth of Christ's return, and the cry has gone out, "Behold, the Bridegroom is coming"(v. 6, NKJV).

It's not necessary to make each detail of this parable mean something. The oil may speak of the Holy Spirit, whom every true believer has within (Rom. 8:9). Christ's main lesson in this parable is: stay awake and be ready! When He returns, we will be surprised to find some whom we thought were true Christians not ready at all.

C. *The profitable and unprofitable servants (vv. 14-30).*

The first parable spoke of service within the household; this parable deals with service in the world. "Talents" are different from "abilities," for in v. 15, he gave to every man "according to his own ability" (NKJV). The talents represent opportunities to use our abilities to serve Christ. We are born with various abilities, but Christ gives us opportunities to exercise our abilities. The important thing is to be faithful (see 1 Cor. 4:2).

The first two servants were both faithful and doubled their talents, so they both received the very same reward (vv. 21, 23). The Christian who is faithful in his or her sphere of service, though it be small, will get the same reward as the person who seems to have a great ministry. It is doubtful whether the third servant can be called a Christian. He called the Lord "an hard man" and said that he was "afraid" (vv. 24-25). Actually, he refused the reward by not using the opportunity Christ gave him. In v. 26, Christ repeats the servant's unjust accusation (but does not say it is true), and says, "Therefore, if these things are true, you should have worked even harder to please me!" The principle is given in v. 29: to whom much is given, much shall be required. If we fail to use what He gives us, we will lose it to another.

II. Christ's Coming and the Gentiles (25:31-46)

People confuse this passage by calling it "the General Judgment," thinking it's the same as the White Throne Judgment of Rev. 20:1-15. There is no such thing as a general judgment in the Bible. The saints have their works judged at the Judgment Seat of Christ immediately after the rapture (2 Cor. 5:1-10). The unsaved dead will be raised to face Christ at the White Throne Judgment at the close of the 1,000 year reign of Christ (Rev. 20:1-15). This judgment is that of the Gentile nations at the close of the Tribulation.

In God's covenant with Abraham, He promised that all nations of the earth would be blessed through Israel (Gen. 12:1-3). During the tribulation, God will be purging Israel, so that at the close of the seven-year period, there will be a believing remnant waiting to meet Christ. The nation of Israel will receive her King, and Christ will establish His kingdom on this earth, as promised in Luke 1:31-33, 67-80, and other places in Scripture. The question is which of the Gentiles shall enter into this kingdom.

Note the three groups of people in this scene: (1) the sheep, (2) the goats, and (3) those whom Christ calls "My brethren" (v. 40). "My brethren" are the believing Jews who witness for Christ during the Tribulation period. Since they would be enemies of the Antichrist, yet sealed and protected by God, they would suffer great persecution. They would not be able to buy or sell, and thus would be hungry. They would flee from their homes (Matt. 24:15-21) and would need places to stay. Without jobs and without the mark of the beast (Rev. 13:17), they could not secure clothing and would be naked. Many would be cast into prison.

Many Gentiles during this period will believe the message of the Jewish missionaries (Matt. 24:14; Rev. 7:9-17). They will then show love and mercy to these suffering Jews, by feeding, clothing, and visiting them in prison, etc. Just as Paul had persecuted Christ by persecuting His saints (Acts 9:4-5), these Gentiles will show love for Christ by showing love for His people. These acts of kindness are not good works that save them (Eph. 2:8-9); they are proof of their faith in the message and their love for Christ. The Gentiles who rejected the messengers, rejected Christ (see Matt. 10:16-23, 40-42). Their end is outer darkness—hell.

It's important to note that Christ will not judge the Gentile nations en masse as nations, but as individuals. The word "nations" in v. 32 is neuter in the Gk. while "them" is masculine, referring to individual persons. There will not be "sheep nations" and "goat nations," but "sheep" separated from the "goats" in every nation. While it is true that God has judged entire nations for mistreating the Jews (Egypt, Babylon, etc.), the truth here is that individuals within the nations will be judged, and only those who have evidenced faith in Christ by their love for the "brethren" will enter into the kingdom. They will have life eternal; the others will go away into eternal punishment.

MATTHEW 26

Three people stand out in the account of the last hours of the Lord before Calvary: Christ Himself, Peter, and Judas Iscariot. It is interesting to see how Peter and Judas are contrasted in this chapter, each one teaching us spiritual lessons by his failures. Judas is a warning against resisting the Word of God and rejecting Christ; Peter is an illustration of how a believer may backslide and lose his testimony. Note the different places where these events took place.

I. At Bethany (26:1-19)

This is also given in John 12, where the woman who anointed Christ is definitely called Mary. While the "religious" Jewish leaders were plotting to kill Christ, the believers at Bethany were honoring Him! We don't know who Simon the leper was, but he must have been cured by the Lord, for the Jews would never feast in the house of a leper. This was not the home of Mary and Martha, although they were there and Martha served (John 12:2).

Mary's act of love was accepted by Christ and criticized by the disciples, Judas being the chief accuser (John 12:4-6). John explains why Judas criticized her: he was a thief and wanted the money for himself! (The word "bare" in John 12:6 means he took out or stole what was in the treasury.) It is sad to see Peter agreeing with Judas and walking "in the counsel of the ungodly" (Ps. 1:1). Soon he would be standing in the way of sinners (John 18:18) and then sitting in the seat of the scornful (Luke 22:55), where he would deny his Lord three times.

It is a dangerous thing for Christians to judge one another, for that judgment always comes back on our own heads (Matt. 7:1-5). Judas called Mary's worship "waste," but Jesus said it was a lasting memorial! To this day, wherever the Gospel is preached, Mary and her loving deed are mentioned. This stinging rebuke from Christ made Judas all the more anxious to betray Him. He left Bethany and went to plot with the Jewish leaders how to arrest Christ. They agreed for thirty pieces of silver, as the Scriptures promised (Zech. 11:12). Peter, on the other hand, went with John to prepare the Passover feast for Christ (Luke 22:8). With all of his failings, Peter loved Christ and trusted Him, while Judas went out from them, because he was not of them (1 John 2:18-19).

II. In the Upper Room (26:20-35)

Here we see Judas as he deceives and Peter as he boasts. Jesus announced that one would betray Him, as Ps. 41:9 prophesied. When Judas asked, "Master [Rabbi—not Lord], is it I?" his language suggests he expected a negative reply. In other words, he was pretending that he was faithful to Christ, when he had yielded himself to the devil (John 13:2, 27).

It was after Judas left that Christ instituted the Lord's Supper. Note in v. 29 that He promised a literal kingdom. The "hymn" they sang is from Pss. 115–118; read these psalms and see the messianic teachings, especially in Ps. 118. It was as they were leaving for Gethsemane that Peter boasted and all but denied the words of Christ (and Zech. 13:7) that the disciples would forsake Him. When a Christian opposes the Word of God, he is heading for trouble.

III. In the Garden (26:36-56)

Here we see Judas pretending to honor Christ by repeatedly kissing Him, and Peter failing Christ by sleeping when he should have been praying, fighting with a sword when he should have been yielding, and fleeing when he boasted he would die for the Lord. "The cup" (v. 39) was the price Christ would pay by being made sin on the cross. His holy nature revolted at the prospect of being made sin, yet His holy will was one with the Father and He willingly laid down His life.

Peter, a fisherman, tries to be a soldier and win spiritual victories with a carnal weapon! We need to remind ourselves that Christ does not need to be defended. We fight Satan, not flesh and blood (Eph. 6:10-18); the weapons we use are spiritual, not fleshly (2 Cor. 10:3-5; Heb. 4:12). Moses made this same mistake (Acts 7:22-28), and had to spend forty years learning to let God fight his battles.

IV. In the High Priest's Home (26:57-75)

Peter should not have followed at all, let alone "afar off" (v. 58). Zechariah 13:7 (Matt. 26:31) prophesied that the sheep would scatter, and in John 18:8, Jesus plainly told the disciples to "go their way." Christ had warned Peter that Satan was after them (Luke 22:31-34) and that he would deny his Lord that night. When believers fail to heed the Word of God, they always get into trouble.

It was illegal for the Jewish council (Sanhedrin) to meet and pass sentence at night, so they met again the next morning (27:1) to make their decision "legal." Christ's silence before His accusers fulfilled Isa. 53:7. His statement in v. 64 goes back both to Dan. 7:13 and His words to the Pharisees about sitting at the Lord's right hand (22:41-46). He was claiming to be God, and this led the high priest to pronounce Him guilty of blasphemy (Lev. 24:16).

Peter now reached the end of the rope as he joined Christ's enemies and warmed himself at the fire (John 18:18). It was a cold night, yet Christ had "sweat as . . . great drops of blood" (Luke 22:44). Peter had a cold heart, and because his heart was not right, he had difficulty answering those who questioned him (see 1 Peter 3:15). When the cock began to crow, Peter remembered the Word. It was forgetting the Word that got him into sin, and now by remembering the Word, his cold heart was warmed again (Luke 24:32) and he wept in repentance. After His resurrection, Jesus met Peter and the disciple was restored to fellowship. What a contrast to Judas who confessed his sin to the priests and then went out and hanged himself! Peter's sorrow was a godly sorrow that results in repentance and forgiveness; Judas' sorrow was the "sorrow of the world [that] worketh death" (see 2 Cor. 7:10).

Peter started downward back at Bethany when he joined Judas in judging Mary. Then he boasted of his devotion and failed to pay attention to the Word of God, particularly Christ's warnings. He did not watch and pray, but went to sleep instead. Yet he tried to appear spiritual by using his sword. He followed Christ when he was told to go away, and he mingled with the enemy, seeking fleshly comfort while Christ was enduring great suffering and shame. But Peter was honest enough to admit his sin and confess it (1 John 1:9). Peter lost his discipleship, not his sonship, and his commission was restored in John 21. Judas rejected Christ and went to hell (Acts 1:18-19).

MATTHEW 27

I. Jesus and Judas (27:1-10)

Some have tried to make Judas a hero, saying that he deliberately sold Jesus to make sure the prophecies would be fulfilled. Yet, Jesus clearly stated that Judas was not a hero, but a devil (John 6:70), and that, though the prophecies would be fulfilled, Judas would still be guilty of deliberate sin (Matt. 26:24). His love of money (and probably selfish desire to be a leader in an earthly kingdom) kept him in the band of disciples, but his heart was never with Christ. He said, "I have sinned" (v. 4) because he had been caught in the act, but he did not evidence sincere repentance. He had rejected the truth and believed a lie, and Satan had taken possession of him (John 13:3, 27). Judas took his own life because Satan is a murderer (John 8:44). But note that Judas had to confess that Christ was innocent (v. 4). He would not call Him "Lord" (26:25 is "Rabbi"), but one day he will be forced to call Him Lord (Phil. 2:9-11). The purchase of the "Potter's Field" fulfilled the prophecy of Zech. 11:13. Jeremiah 18–19 also has to do with a potter's field; so it is possible that Jeremiah *spoke* the prophecy in his time but that it was *written* by Zechariah later on. Christ's death purchased the redemption of the world; Judas' death purchased a cemetery for strangers!

II. Jesus and Pilate (27:11-32)

You must read all the Gospel accounts to see the restlessness and indecision of the Roman governor. Time after time he went out to the crowd, then came in to question Jesus, all the while seeking some way to avoid making a decision. But no man can avoid making a decision about Christ! Pilate was warned by his wife and his own conscience, yet he deliberately gave Christ over to be crucified. True, this was the plan of God (Acts 2:23), but Pilate was not held guiltless. Acts 3:13 puts much of the blame on the Jews themselves. God's eternal plan never denies man's freedom of choice or subsequent guilt. Pilate thought the crowd would call for Jesus, not Barabbas, but he was mistaken. Jesus is not "The People's Choice." Men will always ask for the sinner, not the Savior. "Barabbas" means "son of the father." They rejected the Son of God for a murderer! Note that Pilate, like Judas, testified that Christ was innocent (v. 24). The request of the Jews in v. 25 was answered; Christ's blood has been upon them and their children and will be until the nation " shall look upon Me [Jesus] whom they pierced" and repents (Zech. 12:10). The ruin of Jerusalem in A.D. 70, the scattering and persecuting of the Jews, and the future wrath of God on the land of Israel during the Tribulation, are all answers to this request.

It was customary for the convicted criminal to bear his own cross as a testimony of guilt (John 19:17); but along the way, the soldiers "drafted" Simon to bear it for Him. Thus Christ was not guilty; Simon was the real sinner!

III. Jesus and the Spectators (27:33-54)

Read Ps. 22 for a graphic prophecy of the crucifixion, and notice how many of these prophecies are fulfilled in this chapter. What a picture Calvary continues to be of humanity today! While the Son of God suffers for man's sin, the soldiers gamble for His earthly possessions; the Jews revile Him; the people sit and stare at Him; yet one Roman soldier confesses, "Truly this was the Son of God" (v. 54). Christ's offices of Prophet and King were ridiculed. They denied His prophecy about the temple (v. 40, see John 2:19; Matt. 26:61) and they repeatedly laughed at His claims to Kingship (vv. 37, 42).

The darkness mentioned here (v. 45) was clearly supernatural. It could not have been an eclipse, because the Passover season was at the full moon. It was God's way of veiling the cross while His Son bore the sins of the world and tasted the wrath of God for humankind. The mystery of God the Father forsaking His only begotten

Son is too deep for us to fathom and understand.

The three events at His death are striking. The veil was torn, because His blood opened a new and living way to God (Heb. 10:19-25). It is possible that this miracle caused many of the priests to trust Christ later on (Acts 6:7). The tombs opened because His death conquered death (Heb. 2:14-18). The saints did not come out of the tombs until after His resurrection because Christ is the "firstfruits" (1 Cor. 15:20, 23). Judas and Pilate confessed Christ's innocence, as did the Roman soldier (v. 54). Even the wrath of man praises God.

IV. Jesus and His Friends (27:55-66)

Once He had finished His work of redemption, note that Jesus Christ was not again touched by enemy hands. While Christ was being made sin for us, God permitted people to do their worst. But when the work was finished, God permitted only Christ's friends to handle Him. Joseph and Nicodemus were certainly believers, otherwise they would not have defiled themselves on the Passover by burying the body of Jesus. They no longer needed a Passover lamb; they had discovered forgiveness in the Lamb of God. Nicodemus had come to Jesus by night (John 3) and had defended Him before the Council (John 7:45-53). Apparently, Nicodemus and Joseph of Arimathea had done what the Council suggested — "Search and look" (John 7:52). As they searched the Scriptures, they were enlightened by the Spirit to understand about Christ's sufferings and glory. From Daniel's prophecy they would understand when He would die and from other Scriptures why and how He would die. Thus, they had the tomb and spices prepared (John 19:38-42) and were near at hand when Jesus died. Thus did God in His providence care for the body of His Son, and thus was the prophecy of Isa. 53:9 fulfilled.

The Jewish leaders remembered what the disciples forgot: that Christ promised to come out of the tomb after three days. How unfortunate it is when Satan and his children know the Bible better than Christians do! The Jews called Christ "that deceiver" (v. 63), little realizing that one day the nation of Israel will accept the "arch-deceiver," the Antichrist, and make a covenant with him. "Make it as sure as you can" (v. 65), was all Pilate could say. But no earthly seal could hinder Christ from coming out of the tomb as He promised.

MATTHEW 28

This chapter records "The Resurrection of the King" and forms the great climax to the Gospel story.

I. The Importance of Christ's Resurrection

A. It proves He is the Son of God (John 10:17-18).

B. It attests to the truth of Scripture (cf. Acts 2:31 with Ps. 16:10).

C. It assures us of our own future resurrection when we die (1 Thes. 4:13ff).

D. It is a proof of future judgment (Acts 17:30-31).

E. It is one of the central truths in the Gospel (1 Cor. 15:1-8).

F. It is the assurance of our future inheritance (1 Peter 1:3ff).

G. It is the foundation for Christ's heavenly priesthood (Heb. 7:23-28).

H. It gives the power to the Christian life (Gal. 2:20; Eph. 1:18-20; Rom. 6:4).

II. The Empty Tomb (28:1-10)

We must admire these women for their devotion to Christ. God rewarded their love by allowing them to see the empty tomb and hear the message of the Resurrection from the angel. The stone was not rolled away to allow Christ to come out; it was rolled away to allow men to look in and see that He was gone! The true Easter message is "Come and see. . . . Go and tell!" Every Sunday is resurrection day for the believer.

The empty graveclothes lying in the tomb were in the shape of the body of Christ, like an empty cocoon. This proves His body was not stolen, but that He arose through the graveclothes and left them behind as testimonies of a miracle. If His body were stolen, it was stolen by either friends or enemies. If by enemies, they would have produced it and silenced the disciples. If by friends, they would not have willingly given their lives for a lie, and His friends did not even believe that He would rise from the dead!

III. The Proof of Christ's Resurrection (28:11-15)

A. The resurrection of Christ is an accepted historical fact, and the person who questions or denies it must offer the proof that He did not arise from the dead.

The same Satan who tried to destroy Christ on the cross now wants men to believe that He is still dead! It was Satan, the liar, who was the author of the conspiracy between the Jews and the soldiers in Matt. 28:11-15.

B. Christ's Person demands that He be raised from the dead.

As the Son of God, He could not be held by death (Acts 2:24).

C. Christ promised He would be raised from the dead.

His virtuous life proved that He always told the truth, and even His enemies could find no fault in Him. Either He came out of the tomb, or He was a liar.

D. Eyewitnesses testified that they had seen Christ (Luke 24:33-36; John 20:19, 26; Acts 1:3, 21-22).

At one time, over 500 people saw Christ alive (1 Cor. 15:6). Some unbelievers say that these early witnesses were "hypnotized" or that they suffered from "self-imposed hallucinations." But it would be impossible for 500 people at one time to be hypnotized or to suffer hallucinations.

E. The change in the early believers proves He arose from the dead.

When you stop to think that Peter and the other apostles didn't expect the Resurrection, the remarkable change in their lives proves that they must have met Christ. Peter was a frightened coward one day and a mighty preacher a few weeks later!

F. Paul's conversion (Acts 9) proves that Christ was alive.

No "delusion" or "myth" could change this dedicated Jewish rabbi into a fiery Christian preacher.

G. The existence of the NT, the continuation of the church, and the significance of the Lord's Day are all proofs that Christ is alive.

H. Of course, the best proof is the conversion of a sinner.

"You ask me how I know He lives? He lives within my heart!"

IV. The Great Commission (28:16-20)

Have you noticed the mountain scenes in Matthew? You have the Sermon on the Mount (chaps. 5–7), the Transfiguration (chap. 17), the Olivet prophecy (chaps. 24–25), the crucifixion on Mt. Calvary, and now the final meeting with the disciples on a mountain in Galilee. Note the "universals" in this passage:

A. "All power" (v. 18, authority).

This was no more the humble peasant of Galilee, but the mighty Son of God! In His death and resurrection, He had conquered Satan, sin, and death. God had given all authority into His hands. In Matt. 4:8-10, Satan had taken Christ to a mountain and offered Him all the kingdoms of the world. Here on this Galilee mount, Christ proclaimed that He now had all authority and that Satan had been defeated!

B. "All nations" (v. 19).

"Teach" is actually "make disciples." This is a commission to take the Gospel to all nations, and is a definite change from 10:5-6, where the commission was limited to the Jews only. Evangelism alone is not the commission; after people are won, they should be baptized, which suggests a local church fellowship. They should also be taught, which suggests the teaching and preaching of the Word of God. Please keep in mind that our commission is not simply "to win souls." It is to "make disciples"—which includes winning them, bringing them into a Christian fellowship, and building them up in the faith. While we thank God for every Christian ministry that is true to the Lord and His Word, whatever is done should be tied to the local church.

C. "All things" (v. 20).

A disciple is a learner, and he is to be taught "all things whatsoever I have commanded you." This includes the whole Word of God. Man is to live by every word of God (4:4). All Scripture is profitable (2 Tim. 3:16). The church that fails to teach people the whole counsel of God (Acts 20:27) is not obeying the Great Commission.

D. "Always" (v. 20).

What a tremendous assurance. "I am with you always!" In

Matt. 1:23, He was called "Immanuel" — God with us, and here He reaffirms that name. He is with us through His Spirit, in His Word, by His providential care, and with His divine presence. This is the promise that carried Livingstone into the heart of darkest Africa and that encouraged and enabled messengers of Christ down through the years.

Matthew ends his Gospel with a responsibility on the part of the Christian: to take the Gospel to all people. Not all will be saved, but all deserve a chance to hear the Gospel.

MARK

A Suggested Outline of Mark

Introduction (1:1-13)

I. The Servant's Ministry in Galilee (1:14–9:50)

   A. Initial success (1:14–6:29)
   B. Personal withdrawal (6:30–9:32)
   C. Final ministry in Galilee (9:33-50)

II. The Servant's Journey to Jerusalem (10)

III. The Servant's Last Week of Ministry (11–15)

IV. The Servant's Victory (16)

Features. Mark records about half of Christ's miracles. The healing of a deaf and dumb man (7:31-37) and the healing of a blind man (8:22-26) are found only in Mark. Of the eighteen parables he records, two are peculiar to Mark's Gospel (4:26-29; 13:34-37). Only one long discourse is included (chap. 13), for Mark focuses on action and not speeches. He often mentions our Lord's actions, such as His "looking around" and His expressions of emotion. His Gospel is indeed an exciting account of the life and works of Jesus Christ, the Servant of God.

Introductory Notes to Mark

I. Author

John Mark lived in Jerusalem with his mother Mary (Acts 12:12), who was a leader in the Jerusalem church. Some scholars think he was the young man who fled in the garden when Jesus was arrested (Mark 14:51-52), but this is only conjecture. John Mark accompanied his cousin Barnabas (Col. 4:10) and Paul on their "famine ministry" (Acts 11:27-30) and their first missionary journey (Acts 13:5), but left them at Perga and returned home (Acts 13:13). This later caused a division between Barnabas and Paul and led to Barnabas taking Mark under his wing (Acts 15:36-41). However, before he died, Paul acknowledged Mark's ministry and spoke highly of him (Col. 4:10; 2 Tim. 4:11). Peter called Mark "my son" (1 Peter 5:13), which may indicate that it was Peter who brought John Mark to faith in Christ. Tradition calls Mark "the interpreter of Peter," which suggests that the Gospel of Mark is Peter's report of the words and deeds of Jesus. (See 2 Peter 1:15.)

II. Theme

Mark wrote primarily for Roman readers, and his emphasis is on Jesus Christ as the Servant of God (Mark 10:44-45). One of his key words is "straightway" (immediately), used forty-one times in the book. Mark portrays Jesus as the Servant of God constantly on the go and meeting the needs of all kinds of people. The fact that Mark explains Jewish customs and translates Aramaic words indicates that he had Gentile readers in mind. Mark also has an emphasis on discipleship and persecution. The Gospel of Mark was undoubtedly a great encouragement to suffering Christians during the persecution under Nero (A.D. 64-67).

MARK 1

The word *gospel* means "good news" (1:14-15; 8:35; 10:29; 13:10; 14:9; 16:15). In the OT, it was used for "good news of victory" (1 Kings 1:42; Isa. 40:9; 41:27; 52:7; 61:1); and in the NT, it designates the message of Jesus Christ, the Son of God, who died for the sins of the world (1 Cor. 15:1-8; Gal. 1:6-17). Mark proceeds to give us the personal "credentials" of Jesus Christ, the Servant of God.

I. Announcement (1:1-8)

Mark declares from the outset that Jesus is the Son of God, a testimony that he gives throughout the book (1:11; 3:11; 5:7; 9:7; 12:6; 13:32; 14:61-62; 15:39). Mark quoted Mal. 3:1 in v. 2, and Isa. 40:3 in v. 3, both of which refer to John the Baptist, who prepared the way for the Lord. Whenever notable people were to come to a city, the roads were repaired so their journey would be easier. The people of Israel were at that time in a "spiritual wilderness," and John had to get them ready for the arrival of the Son of God, the Servant (Luke 1:13-17, 67-79). He wanted to lead them out of their spiritual bondage in a "second exodus" that would bring them salvation. John's ministry was effective and the people responded enthusiastically. However, the spiritual leaders did not repent and trust the Savior, and they eventually allowed John to be killed (11:27-33). John was the last of the OT prophets, and he presented the Messiah to the nation (Matt. 11:1-19).

II. Acknowledgment (1:9-13)

Jesus was not baptized because He was a repentant sinner, since He is the sinless Son of God. His baptism in water was a picture of His baptism of suffering on the cross (Luke 12:50) when the "waves and billows" of God's judgment went over Him (Ps. 42:7; Jonah 2:3). He "fulfilled all righteousness" through His death, burial, and resurrection (Matt. 3:15). The voice of the Father and the presence of the Spirit as a dove both acknowledged the deity of the Servant. His victory over Satan is further proof of His divine Sonship. The first Adam failed the test in a lovely garden (Gen. 3; 1 Cor. 15:45), while the Last Adam overcame the enemy in a terrible wilderness.

III. Authority (1:14-25)

Jesus came to Galilee as a preacher, heralding the Good News that God's kingdom had come to men in the person of the Servant of God. While He had not yet revealed the facts about His death on the cross, Jesus could still invite people to trust Him and be saved.

A. Authority over destiny (vv. 16-20).

Peter, Andrew, James, and John had met Jesus and trusted Him some months before (John 1:35-49), but this was their call to full-time ministry as disciples. Zebedee must have had a profitable business if he could afford hired workers, so the departure of his sons did not impoverish him. At least seven of our Lord's disciples were professional fishermen (John 21:1-2). Fishermen have courage and tenacity, and are willing to work hard; and they know how to work together. These are good qualities for "fishers of men."

B. Authority over demons (vv. 21-28).

Jesus made Capernaum His "headquarters" (2:1; 9:33) and went out from there to various parts of the country to minister. He often taught in the local synagogues, and on this particular Sabbath He delivered a man from the power of a demon. Even the demons must confess that Jesus is the Son of God, but their confession does not save them (James 2:19). Mark often reports the amazement of people (1:22, 27; 2:12; 5:20, 42; 6:2, 51; 7:37; 10:26; 11:18). This one work of power spread Jesus' fame to other places.

C. Authority over disease (vv. 29-34, 40-45).

Peter's house became a place of healing for the whole city! How important it is for us to "take Jesus home with us" after we have worshiped. The Lord met the need in the home and then used the home to meet the needs of others. The crowds did not come until the Sabbath had ended because religious tradition said that healing was work that must not be done on the Sabbath. But Jesus had deliberately broken that tradition already (1:21-28) and would do it again (3:1-5; John 5; John 9). Mark made a distinction between those who were diseased and those who were demon-possessed (1:32). While some physical affliction may be caused by demons (Luke 13:10-17), not every disease is demonic in origin.

It was illegal for lepers to approach others; they had to keep their distance and cry out, "Unclean, unclean!" (See Lev. 13:44-46.) But this man had heard about Jesus and was certain that He would heal him (1 Tim. 2:4; 2 Peter 3:9). Technically, Jesus was made "unclean" when He touched the man, but His touch brought immediate healing. For the ritual of restoration the healed leper had to experience, see Lev. 14; and note that the ritual is a picture of Christ's atoning work. The compassion of Jesus is mentioned three other times by Mark (6:34; 8:2; 9:22).

D. Authority in prayer (vv. 35-39).

No matter how much the Servant labored to help others, He still took time early in the morning to meet with His Father (Isa. 50:4). This was the source of His power, for Jesus served on earth just as you and I must serve: by faith, depending on the power of the Spirit. Workers who are too busy to pray are too busy, and God will not bless their efforts (John 15:5). If the Son of God had to spend time in prayer while ministering on earth, how much more do we need to pray!

MARK 2

Jesus had become a "popular" person, for the people wanted to be with Him and watch His miracles. It is unfortunate that most of them were so enthralled by His miracles that they ignored His message. Mark often mentions that great crowds followed the Lord (2:2, 13; 3:7-9, 20, 32; 4:1, 36; 5:31; 7:33; 8:1-2; 9:14, 17). Our Lord's popularity attracted the attention of the Jewish religious leaders, and this sometimes led to disagreement and questions. Mark describes four such disagreements.

I. Disagreement about Forgiveness (2:1-12)

"The house" could well have been Peter's house, for the whole city knew where it was (1:29-32). It was easy for the four friends to break up the roof, for it was composed of laths, tiles, and grass; and the men would have access to the roof by means of an outside stairway. We must commend them for their love for their friend, their concern to get him to Jesus, and their faith that Jesus would heal him (v. 5). The scribes must have arrived early, because they were near enough to Jesus to see and hear all that went on (v. 6). Of course, it would have been much easier for Jesus to say "Your sins be forgiven," for nobody could prove whether or not the man's sins were indeed forgiven. So, Jesus backed up His word of forgiveness with a word of healing, and the man went home whole. The scribes knew that Jesus was claiming to be God, and this was the beginning of their opposition to His message and ministry, opposition that led finally to Christ's arrest and crucifixion.

II. Disagreement about Fellowship (2:13-17)

The call of Levi (Matthew means "the gift of God") shocked the official religious leaders, for what rabbi would want a tax collector as a disciple? Jews who worked for Rome were looked upon as traitors both to God and to Israel, yet Jesus welcomed them and gave them new life (Luke 15:1-2). But Jesus went even further and fellowshipped with Matthew and his "sinner" friends! ("Sinners" in v. 15 refers to Jews who did not keep the Law but lived like Gentiles. To the religious Jews, they were outcasts.) Jesus sees sinners as sick people who need a physician, and He is that physician (Ps. 107:20).

III. Disagreement about Fasting (2:18-22)

Jesus answered their question about His guests, and now He had to defend the meal! In Eastern lands in that day, to eat with a person meant to seal a solemn bond of friendship. How could Jesus and His disciples enjoy feasts when other religious people were fasting? (The only fast actually required of the Jews was on the annual Day of Atonement; see Lev. 16.) Jesus had compared Himself to a physician; now He pictured Himself as a bridegroom (John 3:29; Eph. 5:32). The Christian life is a feast, not a funeral!

Now that Jesus is no longer on earth, His people may fast if they wish (Matt. 6:16-18; Acts 13:2-3; 2 Cor. 6:5; 11:27). The phrase "taken away" in v. 20 is a hint of His future death (Isa. 53:7). The religious leaders wanted Jesus to compromise and "mix" His message and ministry with theirs, but He refused to do so. He did not come to patch up the old but to bring in the new.

IV. Disagreement about Freedom (2:23-28)

By now, the religious leaders watched everything that Jesus did. They were gathering evidence they could use to discredit Him before the people and possibly to accuse Him before the authorities. Jewish tradition said that there were thirty-nine acts that must not be performed on the Sabbath, among them harvesting grain. It was legal to take grain to eat from your neighbor's field (Deut. 23:25), but not on the Sabbath. Jesus defended Himself and His disciples by referring to David's experience (1 Sam. 21:1-6) and affirming that He was Lord of the Sabbath. This was the same as claiming to be God!

In Matthew's account (12:1-8), he gives three arguments from Jesus: what David did, what the priests had to do, and what the prophet said (Hosea 6:6). Writing for Gentile readers, Mark left out the material about the priests and the prophet and focused on the person they would be interested in — a king. The shewbread was for the priests alone (Lev. 24:5-9), so David "broke the law" when he ate it and shared it with his men. But the meeting of a human need (hunger) is more important than the protecting of a religious practice, even one given by God. Jesus would use this same defense later (3:1-15).

Mark identified the high priest as Abiathar (v. 26), while 1 Sam. 21:1 named Ahimelech as high priest. He was the father of Abiathar (1 Sam. 22:20). It is possible that father and son had the same names. (See 1 Chron. 18:16 and 24:6.) Surely the Son of God would not make a mistake about a fact of history recorded in the sacred Scriptures.

MARK 3

The crowds continued to follow Jesus (vv. 7, 20, 32) and people were now having to make personal decisions about Him. Mark records five such decisions.

I. "He Is a Lawbreaker" (3:1-6)

For the third time, Jesus deliberately violated the Jewish Sabbath traditions. The man with the paralyzed hand had no idea that Jesus would come to the synagogue to heal him, so waiting one more day would not have upset him. But Jesus wanted to do more than merely heal a man; He wanted to teach the Pharisees (Luke 6:7) that God wanted His people to enjoy freedom and not suffer in religious bondage (see Acts 15:10). It is always right to do good; and if we do not do good, we do evil (James 4:17). Jesus knew what

His critics were thinking and was angry at the hardening (not "hardness") of their hearts. He saw the evil process taking place within them, and He knew where it would end. These religious men would actually become murderers of their own Messiah!

II. "He Is a Miracle Worker" (3:7-12)

Great crowds followed Jesus from all over the region so that He was unable to have any privacy. Thousands of people came from all over either to be healed or to watch Jesus heal others. When He was near the Sea of Galilee, the disciples kept a boat handy so He could preach from it (Luke 5:3). It is unfortunate that these people came only for physical help and not for spiritual blessing. The crowds created a problem for Jesus, for the Romans might think He was leading a popular uprising and interfere with His ministry.

III. "He Is Our Master" (3:13-19)

Our Lord's response was to go to a mountain alone and spend the night in prayer (Luke 6:12). When He came down the next morning, He selected twelve men and named them "apostles." The word means "one who is sent with a commission." Jesus had many followers, even fewer true disciples, but only twelve apostles. While the word "apostle" is sometimes used in the NT in the general sense of "a sent one" (Acts 14:14; Rom. 16:7), in its specific meaning, it refers to the Twelve and Paul. Ten times in his Gospel, Mark refers to "the Twelve" (3:14; 4:10; 6:7; 9:35; 10:32; 11:11; 14:10, 17, 20, 43). These men would live with Jesus, learn from Him, and go out and serve under His authority. The qualifications given in Acts 1:21-22 indicate that there can be no apostles today in the strictest meaning of the word.

The men are also named in Matt. 10:2-4, Luke 6:14-16, and Acts 1:13. Three of them had nicknames: Simon Peter ("rock"), and James and John ("sons of thunder," see Luke 9:54-55). Bartholomew is identified with Nathanael (John 1:45), and Thaddeus with Judas, son of James (not Iscariot) (John 14:22; Luke 6:16). The word "Canaanite" of v. 18 comes from the Heb. and means "a zealous one." Before his conversion, Simon belonged to a Jewish "underground" group, the Zealots, who tried to overthrow Rome (Luke 6:15). After appointing His assistants, Jesus preached the Sermon on the Mount (Matt. 5–7). It was their "ordination sermon" to let them know what God expected of them as Christ's servants.

IV. "He Is Beside Himself" (3:20-21, 31-35)

Our Lord's own friends and family did not understand Him. His friends came to "take charge of Him" because they thought He was a fanatic (see Acts 26:24-25; 2 Cor. 5:13), and His family was greatly worried about Him. The huge crowds, the miracles, and the widespread reports about Jesus convinced them that something had to be done. Verse 31 is the only mention of Mary in the Gospel of Mark. After all, who cares about the mother of a servant! Our Lord was not rude to His family; He simply used their concern as an opportunity to explain what it means to belong to the family of God. God's children are closer to Jesus than even His own earthly family, for we are "bone of His bone and flesh of His flesh" (see Eph. 5:30).

V. "He Is in League with Satan" (3:22-30)

Unwilling to submit to our Lord's authority, the religious leaders had to explain His miracles in some way; so they said He was empowered by the devil. Jesus pointed out the folly of that argument; for if He were casting out demons by Satan's power, then Satan would be fighting against himself! Satan's kingdom and house would be divided! (Note that Satan does have a kingdom, for he is the "prince of this world." See John 12:31, Eph. 6:10-20, and Col. 1:13.) The fact that Jesus cast out demons is proof that He is stronger than "the strong man" and able to deliver those who have been bound by the devil.

What is the "unpardonable sin"? (vv. 28-30) It is much more than a sin of words (v. 30); because words come from the heart, and that is where the sin lies (Matt. 12:34-37). If it is only a sin of words, then why can blasphemy against Jesus be forgiven (Matt. 12:32) but not blasphemy against the Holy Spirit? Is the Holy Spirit greater than the Son of God?

Jesus made it clear that God can and will forgive all sins (v. 28). The only "unpardonable sin" is refusal to trust in Jesus Christ (John 3:16-18, 36). When Jesus warned the Jewish leaders, He was actually warning the Jewish nation. They could reject the Son of God while He was on earth, and God would not judge them immediately (Luke 23:34: "Father, forgive them."). But when the Spirit came at Pentecost and the believers did many marvelous works, the leaders still refused to believe. This was their last opportunity: they rejected the evidence and died in unbelief. They sinned against the witness of the Spirit and could not be forgiven.

In the strictest sense, there can be no "unpardonable sin" today; for we have never seen Jesus on earth in the flesh. But the sinner who resists the witness of the Spirit and rejects Christ commits the one sin God cannot forgive. Satan uses passages like Heb. 6:1-8 and 10:26-31 to accuse and attack God's people, trying to convince them they are lost; but it is impossible for a true Christian to commit an "unpardonable sin." All of our sins have been forgiven (Eph. 1:7; Col. 2:13); and if we sin against God, we can confess that sin and He will forgive us (1 John 1:5–2:2).

MARK 4

Mark introduced the word "parable" in 3:23 and used it seven times in this chapter (4:2, 10-11, 13, 33-34). The word means "to throw alongside." Jesus used familiar images to help explain the spiritual truths in His message about "the kingdom" (vv. 11, 26, 30). He used this approach so that He could arouse the careless and instruct the concerned, and yet conceal the truth from His enemies who would use it against Him (vv. 10-12). The chapter presents four responsibilities of God's people.

I. Sowing (4:1-20, 30-34)

Jesus explained the parable and emphasized that knowing it was basic to understanding all parables (v. 13, and see Matt. 13:1-23). Unless our hearts are prepared to receive the seed of the Word, we cannot grow in grace or knowledge (2 Peter 3:18). The sower originally was Jesus, who came teaching the Word of God (the seed) and seeking a harvest. Today, anyone who shares God's Word with others is sowing the seed. Like seed, God's Word is "living and powerful" (Heb. 4:12) and, when cultivated, can produce fruit. However, there are forces that fight against the seed bearing fruit: the devil snatches the seed from hard hearts (vv. 4, 15); the flesh produces a temporary response in shallow hearts (vv. 5-6, 16-17); and the world smothers the growth in crowded hearts (vv. 7, 18-19). The good ground represents the prepared heart that receives the seed and produces a harvest in varying degrees ("fruit . . . more fruit . . . much fruit," John 15:1-8).

It is significant that three-fourths of the hearts did not produce fruit (they were never truly born again), and the hearts that were fruitful did not all produce "a hundredfold." As we sow the seed in our preaching, teaching, and witnessing, we must not become discouraged (Gal. 6:9; Ps. 126:5-6), for God will use His Word as He sees fit, and it will not be wasted (Isa. 55:8-11). Neither should we become elated over a false growth (vv. 30-34). A mustard seed is tiny but, when grown, produces a large shrub, not a tree. There is the suggestion here that Satan (the birds in the tree, v. 15) will encourage a false growth that will give opportunity for the enemy to work. In Scripture, a large tree can symbolize a great worldly kingdom (Ezek. 17:22-24; 31:3-9; Dan. 4:20-22). God's true people have always been a minority (Luke 12:32), but the professing church is very much like a great tree with many branches.

II. Shining (4:21-25)

The word "hear" is used thirteen times in this chapter and refers to the receiving of God's truth into the inner person, just the way soil receives the seed. We must be careful how we hear (Luke 8:18) and what we hear (v. 24); for this determines what we have to share with others. We do not receive the Word so we can enjoy it by ourselves. We receive that we might share, just as a lamp gives itself to provide light for the house. See Matt. 5:15-16 and Luke 11:33-36.

III. Reaping (4:26-29)

This parable can be summarized in four words: sowing (v. 26), sleeping (v. 27), growing (v. 28), reaping (v. 29). All we can do is sow the seed; God alone can give the increase (1 Cor. 3:6-7). We cannot make the seed grow; in fact, we do not fully understand how the seed grows. Our task is to sow the seed and be alert when the harvest is ready (John 4:35-38). While sleeping is sometimes a picture of sin (Rom. 13:11-14; 1 Thes. 5:1-11), here it simply reminds us that hard-working people need their rest (see Mark 6:31). If workers do not take care of themselves, they cannot do the work God has called them to do.

IV. Trusting (4:35-41)

Jesus completed the lesson and then gave His disciples an unexpected examination! They had listened to the Word of God, and that Word should have increased their faith (Rom. 10:17). Alas, they failed the test! It is not unusual for terrible storms to come suddenly on the Sea of Galilee, although this one may have been satanic in origin. The word "rebuked" in v. 39 is the same word Jesus used when dealing with the demons (1:25). Perhaps the enemy was trying to keep Jesus from arriving at Gadara, where He would deliver two demoniacs from Satan's power. "With Christ in the vessel, you can smile at the storm"—if your faith is in Him and Him alone.

MARK 5

Mark introduces us to three people who had one thing in common: they all were at the feet of Jesus (vv. 6 and 15, 22, 33).

I. A Demoniac (5:1-20)

Matthew informs us that two demonized men met Jesus (8:28), but Mark and Luke focused on the one man who was the more vocal, the man who wanted to go with Jesus and be His disciple. The narrative describes the awful plight of these men who were drawn to Jesus and yet, because of the demons, feared Him (vv. 6-7). A Roman legion could be as many as 6,000 men! Nowhere does Scripture explain either the physiology or psychology of being demonized, but it does make clear the overcoming power of the Savior. Every unsaved person is controlled to a certain extent by Satan (Eph. 2:1-3; Col. 1:13), although the awful things described here (vv. 3-5) may not be evidenced in their lives. Satan is both an angel of light (2 Cor. 11:14) and a roaring lion (1 Peter 5:8).

The demons feared that Jesus would send them into the abyss (Luke 8:31; Rev. 9:1-2, 11; 20:1-3), which for them would mean eternal torment and the end of their liberty to serve Satan on earth. They knew who Jesus was and what He could do to them. Some people have criticized Jesus for destroying 2,000 pigs, but their accusations are foolish. Jesus could have sent the demons anywhere; but when He chose to send them into the pigs, He accomplished several purposes.

First, He demonstrated that the demons were real and that the deliverance was genuine. Second, He gave vivid proof that Satan is a destroyer (Rev. 9:11; John 10:10) and that, to Satan, a pig is as good as a man! If you surrender your life to Satan and sin, you end up living and dying like an animal. What a warning this was to those who saw it; but apparently they did not take it to heart, for they asked Jesus to depart from them. As the Creator, Jesus owns all things (Ps. 50:10) and can dispose of them as He sees fit. Finally, the destruction of the pigs revealed the spiritual condition of the people of that district: they would rather have their swine than have the Savior! Money was more important than the healing of the two men or the salvation of their own souls.

One of the healed men so appreciated what Jesus had done for him that he wanted to go with Him and serve Him, but Jesus sent him home to bear witness to the Gentiles in that area. It is interesting that Jesus answered the requests of the demons and of the citizens, but He did not agree to the request of the man who wanted to be His disciple. This says to us, before you go out to serve Jesus elsewhere, be sure you have served Him faithfully at home.

II. The Ruler of a Synagogue (5:21-23, 35-43)

It took a great deal of courage for Jairus to come to Jesus, for many of the religious leaders were bent on destroying Him. But his love for his dying daughter forced him to lay aside his prejudices and go to Jesus. The ground is level at the feet of Jesus, for all who have burdens meet there. Jesus could have healed the girl from a distance (John 4:46-54; Matt. 8:5-13), but He chose to go with the worried father.

The delay caused by the anonymous woman may have irritated Jairus, for by the time Jesus was through helping her, news came that Jairus' daughter had died. Jairus' friends were sure that Jesus could do nothing more (John 11:37), but He is the only one who can conquer death (Heb. 2:14-15). Jesus encouraged Jairus with, "Be not afraid, only believe" (v. 36). When everything seems to be falling apart around us, and even our friends discourage us, all we can do is cling by faith to the promises of God.

Peter, James, and John were apparently an "inner circle" in the band of disciples, for Jesus invited them alone to share three special experiences with Him: the raising of Jairus' daughter from the dead, the Transfiguration (9:1-8), and His prayer in the Garden of Gethsemane (14:33). Each of these experiences taught them a lesson about death: Christ is victorious over death, glorified in death, and submitted to death.

The little girl was actually dead, and the mourners knew it. But for the believer, death is only sleep: the spirit leaves the body (James 2:26) and the body sleeps (1 Thes. 4:13-18). The spirit does not sleep but at death goes to be with the Lord (Phil. 1:20-23). See the tenderness and practicality of Jesus: He told them to give her something to eat!

III. A Suffering Woman (5:24-34)

This woman's affliction not only brought discomfort and discouragement, but it prevented her from worshiping at the temple (Lev. 15:19ff) and cost her all of her wealth in useless remedies. (Luke, a doctor, wrote that she "could not be healed by anyone"—Luke 8:43 [NASB]. Mark was not as easy on the doctors—he wrote that she "had endured much at the hands of many physicians" [v. 26, NASB]).

We must admire this woman's faith, for she made her way through a dense crowd in order to get to Jesus. People would open the way for an important man like Jairus, but who would step aside for a needy woman? The Gk. text of v. 28 reads, "For she kept saying." It was as though she encouraged herself as she made her way to Jesus. Her faith was rewarded!

But Jesus was unwilling for her to experience a miracle and not have opportunity to give glory to God (Ps. 107:2, 20-21). In tenderness, He encouraged her to tell what had happened; and then He sent her on her way in peace (v. 34). This suggests that she experienced much more than physical healing: she came to know Jesus as her Lord and Savior (see Luke 7:40-50). Her witness to the power of Christ should have encouraged Jairus as he stood waiting, but apparently he missed the message.

These are only three of many people who came to the feet of Jesus while He was ministering here on earth. Read the four Gospels and meet these people. They will be a blessing to you as they reveal the love and power of Jesus.

MARK 6

This is a chapter filled with opportunities, some of which were missed because of unbelief, some of which were enjoyed because of faith.

I. Opportunity to Know the Servant (6:1-6)

The people in His hometown had tried to kill Jesus a year before (Luke 4:29), but He graciously returned and gave them another opportunity to get to know Him. They thought they really knew Him because He had grown up in their city and lived there for thirty years. Yet they saw Him only as "the carpenter" (v. 3) and not as the Son of God, and they were amazed at His wisdom and works. Familiarity of the wrong kind encouraged unbelief, and unbelief robbed them of blessing. Just as He had marveled at faith (Matt. 8:10), Jesus now marveled at unbelief.

II. Opportunity to Share the Word (6:7-13)

The Twelve were Christ's ambassadors, commissioned and empowered by Him to serve wherever He sent them. If you compare Mark's count with Matthew's (10:1-42), you will see that Mark has omitted mention of the ministry to the Jews, for he wrote for Gentile readers. There was an urgency about this work, and Jesus told the men not to acquire new equipment or be encumbered with things they did not need. We must not take these orders as pertaining to all ministry, for God does expect us to use common sense as we plan our trips. Jesus encouraged them to live by faith, a lesson God's people need to learn in every age. Their main task was to preach the Word and lead people to trust the Savior.

III. Opportunity to Repent of Sin (6:14-29)

Herod Antipas was only the tetrarch of Galilee and Perea, but he liked to be known as king. He had married his niece Herodias, who had left her husband Herod Philip to form this evil alliance; and John the Baptist rebuked him (Lev. 18:16). Herodias wanted her husband to kill John, but Herod compromised by putting John in prison and occasionally listening to him preach. Herod heard the greatest prophet God ever sent and yet refused to submit to the Word of God. The phrase "did many things" (v. 20) can be translated "was in a state of perplexity" (Wuest). Herod's indecision made him a murderer, for instead of heeding the Word, he tried to silence the Word by killing John the Baptist. A year later, when Jesus stood before Herod Antipas (Luke 23:6-12), the Son of God refused to speak to him, for Herod had once and for all silenced the voice of God. Herod wasted all his God-given opportunities.

IV. Opportunity to Show Compassion (6:30-44)

The Twelve were sent out by Jesus, so they returned to report to Him and tell what God had done through them. After an intensive time of ministry, they needed rest; so Jesus and the apostles went off by themselves. It is good to minister to the needs of people, but it is also good to take care of yourself so you are strong enough to minister again. Dr. Vance Havner used to say, "If you don't come apart and rest, you will come apart!"

Jesus tried to withdraw from the crowds, but His attempt was not successful (see 7:24). God's Servant cannot even take time off to rest! The people followed Him, and He had compassion on them and taught them and then fed them. The feeding of the 5,000 is recorded in all four Gospels, so it is an important miracle. The disciples' solution to the problem was "go and buy" (v. 37), but Jesus' solution was, "Go and see" (v. 38). Always start with what you have before you ask God to give you more. The miracle of multiplication took place in the hands of Jesus: He was the manufacturer; the disciples were only the distributors. How wonderful to have a Master who can solve every problem, meet every need, and enable us to minister to others.

V. Opportunity to Grow in Faith (6:45-52)

John tells us that the crowd, amazed at His ability to feed so many people, wanted to make Jesus king (John 6:15). At this stage in their faith, the Twelve probably would have agreed with the crowd; so Jesus sent them off in the boat while He dismissed the people and then went to the mountain to pray (see 1:35). He was testing the apostles' faith, for He knew that the storm was coming. Jonah got into a storm because he disobeyed the Lord, but the Twelve got into a storm because they obeyed the Lord. The men did not want to leave Him; He had to "constrain" them to go ("to compel by force").

In the previous storm (4:35-41), Jesus was with the men in the boat; but now He was absent. When the situation was at its worst, Jesus came to them, spoke to them, and brought peace and safety. Mark does not mention Peter's walking on the water (Matt. 14:22-32); but if Mark was Peter's spokesman in his Gospel, that omission is understandable. But Mark does record the failure of all the disciples to understand the power of Jesus and learn the spiritual truths He wanted to teach them (v. 52).

VI. Opportunity to Receive the Lord's Help (6:53-56)

Their boat landed south of Capernaum. The people recognized Jesus, ran to get their sick and afflicted, and brought them to Him. They had not been expecting Him; but now that He was there, they did not want to waste their opportunity. They not only brought their own sick, but they spread the good news to other villages, so that wherever Jesus went, needy people were waiting for Him. The Servant was at the beck and call of all kinds of people, and He graciously met their needs.

It was on the next day that Jesus gave His sermon on "The Bread of Life" and lost His crowd (John 6:22-71). They wanted bread but they did not want the truth. How like many people today who want Jesus to help and heal them, but not to save and deliver them from their sins.

MARK 7

This chapter would be of special interest to Mark's readers, because in it, Jesus answers two important questions about the Gentiles.

I. Do the Gentiles Defile the Jews? (7:1-13)

The visit of the scribes and Pharisees was evidently an official inquiry from the Sanhedrin, the Jewish religious ruling council. Jesus had violated the Sabbath traditions (2:15-28; 3:22-30), and now they were watching Him closely to see what else He might do. In this case, it was a violation of their tradition about the ceremonial washing of hands. This ritual had nothing to do with hygiene; it was purely ceremonial to get rid of whatever defilement the Jews accidentally picked up from the Gentiles or Samaritans.

Tradition is not necessarily a bad thing, but when it has more authority than the Word of God, then it is wrong. Colossians 2:8 warns us against man-made traditions, but we should heed the traditions given by God and handed down to His people (1 Cor. 11:2; 2 Thes. 2:15; 2 Tim. 2:2). Jesus pointed out that the great danger was hypocrisy: we obey the traditions with words and deeds, but we fail to serve God from the heart (Isa. 29:13). Note the steps downward: first we lay aside God's Word (v. 8), then we reject the Word (v. 9), and finally we rob the Word of any power in our lives

(v. 13). Man's tradition, not God's truth, controls our lives. The Pharisees were able to rob their own parents of help by hiding behind their traditions! ("Corban" in v. 11 means "a gift [to God]" and has to do with the laws in Num. 20.)

But Jesus did not stop with exposing the Jews' hypocrisy; He also exposed their hearts (vv. 14-23). The Jews were not defiled from without by coming in contact with Gentiles, but from within because of their own sinful hearts. And no amount of washing on the outside can remove defilement on the inside (Ps. 51:6-10). The disciples were as much in the dark about this as were the common people, and Jesus had to explain the truth to them privately. How difficult it is for people to disengage themselves from religious traditions that have been so much a part of their lives! At the same time, Jesus set aside the Jewish dietary laws (Lev. 11), although it took the Jewish believers a long time to get used to their new freedom (Acts 10–11; Rom. 14–15; Gal. 2:11-17; Col. 2:20-22; 1 Tim. 4:4-5). The phrase "purging all meats" (v. 19) means "making all foods clean." These were Mark's words and should be considered a comment on our Lord's teaching.

The list in vv. 21-22 should convince any honest person that the human heart is "deceitful above all things and desperately wicked" (Jer. 17:9). See also the lists in Rom. 1:29-32, Gal. 5:19-21, 1 Tim. 1:9-10, and 2 Tim. 3:2-5. Only the blood of Jesus Christ can cleanse the heart of sin and make us new creations.

II. Are the Gentiles Less Important Than the Jews? (7:24-37)

Jesus visited two predominantly Gentile regions, Tyre and Sidon (vv. 24-30) and the Decapolis ("Ten Cities," vv. 31-37), and ministered to a woman and a man. The Jewish Law separated the Jews from the Gentiles, not because the Jews were better, but because the Jews were different in their covenant relationship with God. A wall in the temple prevented Gentiles from entering the Jewish temple courts under penalty of death. God wanted the Jews to witness to the Gentiles of the true and living God; but His people failed in their task. Jesus would break down the wall of separation and remove the "spiritual distance," thus making believing Gentiles and believing Jews one in Christ (Eph. 2:11-22). Note that Jesus healed the woman's daughter at a distance and healed the deaf-mute away from the crowd.

The woman, being a Gentile, had no covenant right to come to

Jesus and call Him "Son of David" (Matt. 15:22); but she could call Him "Lord" and have her prayer answered. Jesus was not rude to her; He was only testing and strengthening her faith. The word "dogs" in v. 27 is "puppies." Jesus was not calling her a "dog" in the manner that some of the Jews addressed the Gentiles; she was quick to pick up on this word and argue from it! Twice Jesus marveled at great faith; and in both instances, it involved Gentiles (Matt. 8:10 and 15:28).

The man (vv. 31-37) could neither hear nor speak, but the people were sure that Jesus could heal him (Isa. 35:6). Since the man could not hear the Word and thus have his faith strengthened and could not pray verbally, the Lord used spittle and touch to encourage him. Our Lord's "sigh" (groan; see 8:12) reminds us of 2 Cor. 5:2 and Rom. 8:22. How His holy soul must have grieved over the sad consequences of sin in the world! Jesus took the man away from the curious crowd and did not make a spectacle of him. Jesus did not want people to follow Him because of His miracles; but the more He told people to keep quiet, the more they talked! On the other hand, He tells us to tell everyone the Good News, and we keep quiet!

MARK 8

The Decapolis (Gk. for "ten cities") was a league of ten cities that was like a country within a country. They had their own army, court system, and currency and enjoyed a high level of Gentile culture. The events described in this chapter took place in the area of the Decapolis as Jesus ministered among the Gentiles.

I. Compassion (8:1-9)

Whenever Jesus saw the needy multitudes, He was moved with compassion and wanted to help them (Matt. 9:36; 14:14; Mark 6:34). This miracle must not be confused with one recorded in 6:32-44, for each has its own distinguishing features:

Mark 6:32-44	Mark 8:1-9
5,000+ people, mostly Jews	4,000+ people, mostly Gentiles
With Jesus one day (6:35)	With Jesus three days (8:2)
Took place in Galilee	Took place near the Decapolis

Five loaves, two fish	Seven loaves, a few fish
Twelve baskets left over	Seven baskets left over
(small lunch baskets)	(large hampers)

Why the Twelve were perplexed about feeding the crowd is difficult to understand, especially when Jesus had already fed a much larger multitude. But, like us, they were prone to forget all His benefits! (Ps. 103:1-2)

II. Concern (8:10-21)

Jesus and His disciples returned to Galilee, only to be met by the Pharisees who wanted a sign from heaven. The feeding of the 5,000 was not a great enough miracle for them, for Moses had brought bread down from heaven. (See John 6:30-33.) We once again see Jesus sighing (v. 12; 7:34), and His only response was to leave once again and go to the eastern shore of the sea. Jesus has no faith in the faith of people who depend upon signs and wonders (John 2:23-25).

Jesus commanded the disciples to depart so quickly that they did not have time to pack a lunch, and this led to an argument as to whose fault it was. Jesus used the discussion about bread to warn His disciples to avoid false teachings. He compared false teaching to yeast: it is small but powerful and can spread quickly. As Jews, the Twelve were acquainted with the symbolism of leaven at the Passover (Ex. 12:18-20), so the image was not new to them. (See Matt. 16:11; Gal. 5:1-9; 1 Cor. 5.) Hypocrisy is the leaven of the Pharisees, and worldly compromise the leaven of Herod.

Alas, the Twelve still lacked spiritual understanding! They were like the deaf man Jesus healed and the blind man He was about to heal!

III. Condemnation (8:22-26)

This is the second of two miracles recorded only by Mark; the other is the healing of the deaf mute (7:31-37). In both instances, Jesus took the person away from the crowd; here, He took him out of the town! Why? To avoid publicity, for one thing, and to let the town know it was under the judgment of God (Matt. 11:21-24). This is the only "gradual" miracle recorded in any of the four Gospels.

122

According to the Gospel record, Jesus healed at least seven blind men; and each time, the approach was different. Was the miracle hindered by the atmosphere of unbelief in the town? (6:5)

IV. Crucifixion (8:27-33)

Although He had previously hinted at His death (John 2:19; 3:14), this is the first time Jesus clearly taught His disciples that He was going to die and be raised from the dead. (See 9:30-32; 10:32-34.) Like most orthodox Jews, the Twelve believed that their Messiah would come in power and glory and defeat their enemies, not be defeated by their enemies. Peter's confession of faith came from the Father (Matt. 16:17), not from the gossip of the crowd; but Peter's confusion originated with the devil, who does not want us to understand the doctrine of the Cross. Peter wanted the glory but not the suffering that leads to glory! Read Peter's two epistles and see how much he says about suffering and glory.

V. Consecration (8:34-38)

We become children of God by trusting Christ and confessing Him to be the Son of God (1 John 4:1-3) who died for us on the cross and rose again (Rom. 10:9-10). We become disciples of Jesus Christ by surrendering our all to Him, taking up our cross, and following Him. If we live for ourselves, we lose our lives and He is ashamed of us; but if we live for Christ, we save our lives and glorify Him (John 12:23-28). Discipleship saves us from the tragedy of a wasted life. Yes, there is suffering in taking up a cross to follow Jesus; but that suffering always leads to glory.

MARK 9

Jesus was on His way to Jerusalem to die. As the Twelve walked with Him, they had a variety of experiences to prepare them for their coming ministry. Understanding the experiences recorded in this chapter can help us in our ministry today.

I. A Confirmation of Hope (9:1-13)

Verse 1 should be placed in chapter 8, for it climaxes our Lord's words about discipleship and promises His return in glory. He confirmed these words by showing that promised glory to Peter, James, and John (John 1:14; 2 Peter 1:16-18). This is the only recorded instance during our Lord's ministry of His revealing His inner glory for others to see. It was really a confirmation of the kingdom that God has promised to His people Israel (Matt. 16:28).

Moses represented the Law and Elijah the prophets, both of which are fulfilled in Jesus Christ (Heb. 1:1-2; and see Malachi 4:4-5 and Luke 24:25-27). They discussed with our Lord His decease ("departure" or "exodus": see Luke 9:31) that He would accomplish in Jerusalem. The cross is the theme of heaven's conversation and of heaven's praise (Rev. 5).

The disciples had been asleep (Luke 9:32), so Peter's words were born out of confusion and fear. (When you are confused and afraid, it is best to keep quiet! See Prov. 18:13.) In suggesting that they all remain on the mountain in the glory, Peter was once again hindering our Lord's plans to go to the cross (8:32-33). While a cloud of glory enveloped the scene, the Father's voice interrupted Peter and gently rebuked him. "Hear Him!" is a command we need to heed today. We can trust the Word of God.

Imagine having this great experience and not being able to share it! (v. 9) No doubt the other nine disciples asked them what had happened on the mountain, but they had to keep quiet. They had seen the glory of the Son and had been reminded of the dependability of the Scriptures and the reality of the kingdom. They had also had their questions answered. In a spiritual sense, John the Baptist was "the Elijah" promised to Israel (Mal. 3:1; 4:5-6; Luke 1:16-17; John 1:21; Matt. 17:13).

II. A Demonstration of Faith (9:14-29)

While Peter, James, and John were experiencing the glory of God on the mountain, the other nine disciples were involved in an embarrassing situation in the valley below. A distraught father had brought his demonized son, deaf and dumb (v. 25), for the disciples to heal, but they could not cast out the demon. Jesus had given them this power (3:15; 6:7, 13), but they were unable to deliver the boy. Of course, the religious leaders were having a good time arguing with the disciples (v. 14) and trying to discredit them before the people.

Jesus delivered the boy, but the devil made one last attempt to destroy him (v. 26; Luke 9:42). Often just before deliverance, the devil seems to get a great victory, but the Lord ultimately wins the battle. Why had the disciples failed? Because of their unbelief (vv. 19, 23; Matt. 17:20) and their lack of prayer and discipline (v. 29). Apparently, during the Lord's absence, the men had grown careless in their spiritual walk. How important it is to stay spiritually fresh; you never know when somebody may need your help. The disciples' lack of faith was a great concern to the Lord (4:40; 6:50-52; 8:17-21).

III. An Affirmation of Love (9:30-50)

A. Christ's love for sinners (vv. 30-32).

This is the second time (see 8:31) that Jesus spoke openly to the Twelve about His impending death and resurrection, but they still could not grasp what He was saying. The verb "delivered" indicates that His death was not an accident or a murder; it was the result of a divine plan (Rom. 4:25; 8:32).

B. Loving one another (vv. 33-37).

Jesus spoke about suffering and death, but the Twelve argued over who was the greatest! They misunderstood Jesus' teaching. They lived in a society in which position and power were important, and they thought that the Christian fellowship functioned the same way. Even in the Upper Room, before Jesus went to the cross, the Twelve were still debating over which of them was number one (Luke 22:24-30). God wants us to be childlike but not childish. In the Aramaic that Jesus spoke, "child" and "servant" are the same word. True greatness is found, not in rank or possessions, but in character and service (Phil. 2:1-13).

C. Loving those outside our fellowship (vv. 38-41).

John thought he would impress Jesus with his zeal, but Jesus lovingly rebuked him for his lack of love and discernment. Did the Twelve think that they were the only ones serving Jesus? And had the nine who were left behind forgotten their failure to cast the demon out of the boy? How often we criticize others for success that we cannot attain ourselves! Verse 40 and Matt. 12:30 together teach us the impossibility of neutrality when it comes to Jesus. If we are not with Him, we are against Him; if we are not against Him, we are for Him. It is dangerous to get the idea that our fellowship is the only one that is right and the only one God is blessing and using.

D. *Loving the lost (vv. 42-50).*

This is our Lord's longest and most awesome warning about future punishment. If we are not serving others (v. 35), we may cause others to stumble ("offend," v. 42); and this might lead to their eternal condemnation. We must deal drastically with sin in our lives, both for our sake and the sake of others, for the fires of hell are real and everlasting. Jesus compared hell to a furnace (Matt. 13:42) and an unquenchable fire. The image here is of the garbage dump in the Valley of Hinnom outside Jerusalem (2 Kings 23:10; Isa. 66:24), where the waste was burned by fire and eaten by worms. The Gk. word for hell ("Gehenna") comes from the Heb. "ge Hinnom" — the valley of Hinnom. Hell is a real place, and lost souls will suffer there forever. Do we have a love for the lost, or are we only concerned with being "the greatest"? God's people would indeed be "salted with fire" (suffer persecution — v. 49), and it is important that we "have salt in ourselves" (maintain true Christian character and integrity — Matt. 5:13). The believers who read Mark's Gospel during the "fiery trial" under Nero must have been encouraged by what Jesus said here (1 Peter 4:12ff).

MARK 10

The chapter presents five requests that people brought to the Servant.

I. A Request for Interpretation (10:1-12)

The rabbis did not agree in their interpretations of Deut. 24:1-4, so they kept asking (v. 2) what Jesus thought the passage taught. They were not questioning the legality of either divorce or remarriage, for Moses made it clear that God permitted both. The big question was, "For what cause may a man put his wife away and take another?" Of course, their motive was not to learn truth but to try to get Jesus into trouble. The disciples of the rabbi Shammai held to a strict interpretation (divorce only for unfaithfulness) while the disciples of Hillel held to a lenient interpretation (divorce for almost any reason). The Law commanded that those who committed adultery be stoned (Deut. 22:22; Lev. 20:10); but in Jesus' day, this law was rarely obeyed (Matt. 1:18-25).

Instead of taking sides with either Shammai or Hillel, Jesus went back to Moses and the first marriage (Gen. 1:27; 2:21-25). From the beginning, marriage meant one man and one woman becoming one flesh for one lifetime. Moses' commandment in Deut. 24:1-4 was a concession to the Jews because of their hardness of heart. It does not represent God's ideal for marriage. The parallel passage (Matt. 19:1-12) indicates that Jesus did permit divorce on the grounds of sexual immorality (12:9). Divorce for any other reason — even one permitted by the courts — leads to adultery if the parties remarry (vv. 11-12).

Marriage is fundamentally a physical relationship ("one flesh") and can be broken only by a physical cause, either death (Rom. 7:1-3) or adultery (Matt. 19:9). In the OT, the guilty party was stoned to death, thus leaving the other party free to remarry. Today, the church does not have the authority to kill people, so divorce is the NT equivalent of death, leaving the opportunity for remarriage. Of course, before getting a divorce, the husband and wife should do everything possible to rescue the marriage and rebuild the relationship. God established marriage, and He is the only one who can regulate it (v. 9). Man cannot divide that which God says is "one flesh," but God can.

II. A Request for Benediction (10:13-16)

Marriage leads to children, and children should be brought to the Lord and dedicated to Him. It was customary for rabbis to bless children, and parents brought their little ones to Jesus for His blessing. (The pronoun "those" in v. 13 is masculine, so the fathers were also there.) This was not a matter of baptism, for Jesus did not baptize even adults (John 4:1-2), and the disciples would not have hindered candidates for baptism. The parents were asking for His special blessing on their little ones, and He was pleased to grant their request. Unspoiled children are the ideal models for all who belong to Jesus: they are humble, receptive, dependent on others, and filled with potential.

III. A Request for Information (10:17-31)

This man was rich (Luke 18:23), young (Matt. 19:20, 22), and a ruler (Luke 18:18), and had everything but salvation. The Jews would not use the word "good" in addressing a rabbi, so Jesus had every right to ask the man why he used it. Did he really believe that Jesus was God? If so, would he obey what Jesus said?

Nobody is saved by keeping the Law (Gal. 3:21). Jesus held before the young man the mirror of the Law so he could see how sinful he was (James 1:22-25; Rom. 3:20). The young man had paid attention to the Law since his youth, and the Law had brought him to Christ (Gal. 3:24); but he had not yet humbled himself as a lost sinner. He wanted to have the best of both worlds!

Nobody is saved by selling everything and giving the money to the poor. We are saved by trusting the Son of God who gave everything to make us rich (2 Cor. 8:9). Jesus touched this "sore spot" in the young man's life because love of money was the great sin that was keeping him out of the kingdom (vv. 23-27). There is a principle here that must be remembered as we seek to lead lost people to Jesus: sinners cannot hang on to their sins and at the same time reach out to Jesus. There must be sincere repentance before sinners can turn to God and be saved by His grace.

Like many Jews, the disciples thought that wealth was proof of God's blessing, but Jesus corrected their wrong idea. Peter was sure that he and his friends would receive a special reward for doing what the rich young ruler did not do. God does reward faithfulness, but our motive should be love for Christ and not desire for gain. As industrialist R.G. LeTourneau used to say, "If you give because it pays, it won't pay!" (See Matt. 20:1-16 for Christ's parable of warning about bad attitudes in Christian service.) Many who are first in their own eyes will be last in God's eyes.

IV. A Request for Coronation (10:32-45)

For the third time, the Lord instructs the disciples about His coming death; now He tells them He will be crucified in Jerusalem (Matt. 20:19). You would think that this third announcement would have humbled the Twelve; but instead, James and John and their mother (Matt. 20:20) came asking Jesus for thrones! They had not yet learned the lesson that the cross must come before the crown, that suffering comes before glory.

The "cup" refers to His submission to the Father's will in becoming sin for us (14:36; John 18:11), and the "baptism" refers to His suffering on the cross for the sins of the world (Luke 12:50; Pss. 41:7 and 69:2, 15). What pride that James and John thought that they could drink His cup and experience His baptism!

James would be the first of the Twelve to be martyred (Acts

12:2), and John would experience Roman persecution at the end of his long life (Rev. 1:9). Be careful how you pray; God may give you what you ask!

Jesus used this embarrassing event as an opportunity to teach His disciples once again the importance of humble service in the name of Jesus. Verse 45 is a key verse in Mark's Gospel and summarizes the book: Christ came (chap. 1), ministered (chaps. 2–13), and gave His life as a ransom (chaps. 14–16).

V. A Request for Illumination (10:46-52)

With a great crowd following Him, Jesus was on His way to Jerusalem for that final Passover. There were two cities named Jericho: the ruined old city and the new city about a mile away, built by Herod. This helps to explain how He could depart from Jericho (Matt. 20:29), draw near to Jericho (Luke 18:35), and come and go out of Jericho all at the same time and still meet the two blind beggars (Matt. 20:30). Mark describes the healing of Bartimaeus, the more vocal of the two, just as he did the healing of one of the Gadarene demoniacs (5:2).

Bartimaeus (Aramaic for "son of Timaeus") heard the crowd and recognized that there was something different about it, so he asked who was going by. When he heard it was Jesus, he immediately cried out for mercy. He had heard about the miraculous cures Jesus had wrought, and he wanted the Master's help. Nothing could keep him from getting to Jesus!

MARK 11

I. The Triumph (11:1-11)

This description of our Lord's "Triumphal Entry" may have surprised Mark's Roman readers, who were accustomed to the glory of the "Roman Triumph." This was the official welcoming parade given to a victorious Roman general whose armies killed at least 5,000 enemy soldiers, gained new territory for Rome, and brought home rich trophies and important prisoners. The general rode in a golden chariot, surrounded by his officers; and in the parade, he displayed his treasures and prisoners. The Roman priests would be there, offering incense to their gods. Paul alludes to the Roman Triumph in 2 Cor. 2:14-17.

But our Lord's ride into Jerusalem involved a donkey, some garments and branches thrown on the ground, and the praises of some nondescript Passover pilgrims. It was the only time Jesus permitted a public demonstration on His behalf, and He did it to force the Jewish religious leaders to act during the Passover when it was ordained that He should die (Matt. 26:3-5).

Mark does not quote Zech. 9:9, but he does quote Ps. 118:25-26 (vv. 9-10), a messianic psalm. Hosanna means, "Save now, we pray!" ("God save the king!") When Jesus rode into the city, He proclaimed His Kingship, but He also signed His own death warrant.

II. The Tree (11:12-14, 20-26)

At first sight, this is a puzzling miracle. Passover was not the season for figs, yet the Son of God had hoped to find fruit on the tree. When He did not find any, He used His divine power to destroy the tree instead of helping it to become fruitful. Actually, the whole episode was a sermon in action. The tree represents the nation of Israel (Hos. 9:10, 16; Nahum 3:12), which was producing no fruit to the glory of God. Its spiritual roots were dead (v. 20; Matt. 3:10), and it could not produce fruit.

But Jesus also used the miracle to teach His disciples some practical lessons about faith and prayer. Mountains represent great difficulties that must be removed (Zech. 4:7), and it is our faith in God that enables us to overcome. But faith in God is not enough; we must also have forgiveness toward others (vv. 25-26). We do not earn God's forgiveness by forgiving others, but forgiving others shows that we have a humble heart before God.

II. The Temple (11:11, 15-19)

Jesus investigated the temple and then returned the next day to cleanse it. He had cleansed the temple early in His ministry (John 2:13-22), but the religious merchants came back again. Mere outward reformation does not last unless the heart is changed. What began as a service to foreign Jews (who needed to change money or purchase sacrifices) had become a business that had no place in the house of God. People used the temple as a shortcut from the Mount of Olives (v. 16), and the stalls and tables cluttered up the Court of the Gentiles where the Jews should have been witnessing about the true God to their Gentile neighbors.

In His indictment against the leaders (v. 17), Jesus quoted Isaiah (56:7) and Jeremiah (7:11), both of whom had condemned the nation for its sins in the temple (Isa. 1; Jer. 7). A "den of thieves" is the place thieves go to hide when they have committed a crime. The religious leaders were using the worship of God as a cover for their sins!

IV. The Test (11:27-33)

The religious leaders were angry at what Jesus did and said and were determined to destroy Him (v. 18); but first, they had to get enough evidence to bring charges against Him. It was all a question of authority (vv. 28-29, 33): What right did He have to cleanse the temple and call it His house? He was claiming to be God!

Jesus took them back three years, when John the Baptist was ministering to the people. "Where did John get the authority for his baptism?" Jesus asked. "Was it from God or from men?" (v. 30) This put the scribes, elders, and chief priests in a dilemma; no matter how they answered, they were in trouble! These leaders may have forgotten their decision about John the Baptist, but their decision did not forget them. It finally caught up with them and condemned them. They had not submitted to John's ministry (Luke 7:29-30); therefore, they were not ready to receive Jesus and trust Him. In their unbelief and cowardice, they had even allowed John to be killed by Herod Antipas; and soon they would ask Pilate to crucify Jesus.

MARK 12

God's Passover Lamb (John 1:29) was being "examined" by the Jewish leaders, and He proved to be perfect (1 Peter 1:18-19), although they did not accept Him. How tragic it is when religious people cling to their traditions and reject the living truth when it is so evident before their very eyes. In answering their many questions, the Lord Jesus was actually revealing the sins in their hearts.

I. Selfishness (12:1-12)

Jesus knew that His enemies wanted to kill Him; and in this parable, He revealed their sinful desire to destroy Him and claim the inheritance for themselves (John 11:45-53). The image of the vineyard immediately identifies the nation of Israel (Isa. 5:1-7; Ps. 80:8-16; Jer. 2:21), and the tenants are the leaders of the nation (v. 10; Acts 4:11).

See Lev. 19:23-25 for regulations about harvesting. An owner had to receive a certain amount of "token payment" in order to maintain his rights over the land. By refusing to pay him, the tenants stripped away his rights to the land. If the heir died, the land would then fall to the residents. It was a selfish scheme that put possessions ahead of people.

Jesus quoted from Ps. 118, a messianic psalm (118:22-23; and compare Mark 11:9 with Ps. 118:25-26); and He allowed His hearers to pronounce their own sentence (Matt. 21:41). By applying to Himself the image of the cornerstone, Jesus was affirming that He was indeed the Messiah (Acts 4:11; 1 Peter 2:7). This was blasphemy to the religious leaders, and they would have arrested Him then and there were it not for their fear of the people.

II. Hyprocrisy (12:13-17)

The Pharisees opposed Rome while the Herodians (a political party) cooperated with Rome. The only thing that brought them together was their common enemy, Jesus Christ (see Luke 23:12).

The Gk. word for "catch" in v. 13 conveys an image of a trap for hunting game. The committee from the Pharisees and the Herodians thought they could trap Jesus with a question that had political and religious connotations.

Knowing themselves to be God's chosen people, the orthodox Jews despised having to pay taxes to Rome. It meant acknowledging Rome's power over their nation—something they were too proud to admit (John 8:33)—as well as supporting pagan idolatry. If Jesus approved paying taxes to Rome, He would be in trouble with His own people; but if He opposed the paying of taxes, He would be in trouble with Rome.

Knowing their hypocrisy, our Lord replied in a way that not only avoided the horns of the dilemma but drove home to His questioners their responsibility to the state. Since they were using Caesar's coins, they were admitting Caesar's authority over them; and when they paid their taxes, they were only giving back to Caesar what he had first made available to them. Taxes are not a gift to the government; they are a debt we pay in return for services rendered (police and fire protection, social agencies, defense, etc.). But at the same time, the image of God is stamped on each human; and we must pay back to God the things that are God's. Since it is God who established human government for our good, we are obligated to respect officials and obey the law (Rom. 13; 1 Tim. 2:1-6; 1 Peter 2:13-17). Daniel Webster said, "Whatever makes men good Christians makes them good citizens."

III. Ignorance (12:18-27)

This is the only place where Mark mentions the Sadducees in his Gospel. They accepted the authority of only the five Books of Moses, and they did not believe in the resurrection of the body or in the existence of angels (Acts 23:8). Based on Deut. 25:7-10, their question was hypothetical, devised only for the purpose of trying to catch Jesus in His speech. Instead of revealing His ignorance, it revealed their ignorance of God's Word and power.

To Jesus, the answer to every question was in the Scriptures and not in man's own thinking (Isa. 8:20; see Mark 10:19; 12:10).

He referred them to Ex. 3:1-12 and drew the logical conclusion that since Jehovah is the God of the living, Abraham, Isaac, and Jacob were alive. There is life after death and therefore a hope of future resurrection. But resurrection is not reconstruction and the continuation of life as it now is. God's children will not become angels, for we shall be like Christ (1 John 3:1-3); but we shall be like the angels in that we will not marry or have families. It will be a whole new kind of life.

IV. Shallowness (12:28-40)

The Pharisees tried one more question, one that the rabbis had been debating for a long time. Of the 613 commandments found in the Law (365 negative, 248 positive), which one is the most important? Jesus replied with the traditional Jewish "statement of faith" (the Shema) found in Deut. 6:4. It was recited morning and evening by pious Jews. He then added Lev. 19:18; for if we love God, we will show it by loving our neighbor (Luke 10:25-37). One of the scribes got the message clearly and boldly agreed with Jesus, but the others missed the point completely. They had a shallow view of the real meaning of the Law and failed to understand the importance of obeying from the heart.

Jesus asked the final — and most important — question, and it put them to silence (Matt. 22:46; Rom. 3:19). When He rode into the city, Jesus had been called "Son of David" (Matt. 21:9) by the crowds, and the children had echoed this cry in the temple (Matt. 21:15). This was, of course, a messianic title, which explains why the Pharisees wanted to silence the people (Luke 19:39-40). Quoting from Ps. 110, Jesus asked them to explain how David's Lord could also be David's son; and they would not answer. The answer is that David's Lord had to become man, but the "theologians" refused to face the implications of both the question and the answer. Their knowledge of the Word was shallow and their submission to it very insincere.

Jesus closed this "debate" with a warning (vv. 38-40) and an example (vv. 41-44), both of which exposed the hypocrisy of the religious leaders. When you contrast the conduct of the widow and that of the scribes, you see what God values most. For a detailed exposure of the Pharisees, see Matt. 23.

MARK 13

The believers who first read Mark's Gospel were being persecuted and were tempted to give up and compromise their witness. This version of the Olivet Discourse (Matt. 24–25) was just the encouragement they needed to remain faithful to the Lord. The sermon focuses on the last days and describes the first part (13:5-13), the middle (13:14-18), and the last part of the tribulation, leading up to the Lord's return to the earth (13:19-27). But the sermon also gives us principles that apply to suffering saints in every age. Jesus issued four warnings for His people to heed in times of persecution and opposition.

I. Don't Be Deceived (13:1-8)

The beautiful temple was desolate (Matt. 23:38) and would be destroyed (v. 2). Four of the disciples asked when it would be destroyed and what sign would announce this disastrous event. They thought that the destruction of the temple, the end of the age, and the coming of the kingdom would occur at the same time; so Jesus explained to them the general course of the last days. But His greatest concern was that His people not be deceived by the false Christs that would appear and promise to lead them to victory and glory. He also pointed out the "false signs" that could lead them astray (vv. 7-8). This admonition relates primarily to the Jews, for the church must watch out for false teachers, not false Christs (2 Peter 2); and we are looking for the Savior and not for signs (Phil. 3:20-21).

II. Don't Be Afraid (13:9-13)

Times of persecution are times for proclamation, and we must not be afraid to declare the Gospel and acknowledge Jesus Christ as our Savior and Lord. The Holy Spirit helps those who walk with the Lord and sincerely want to glorify Him. This is seen many times in the Book of Acts.

Verse 10 is not a requirement for the coming of the Lord. Jesus was stating a divine determination and assurance: in spite of all that Satan does during the "time of Jacob's trouble," God's Word shall be proclaimed and His will accomplished. Nor is v. 11 an excuse for shabby ministry! Preachers and teachers should study, meditate, and pray and not "trust" the Spirit to give them their messages at the last minute. Jesus is giving us encouragement for the difficult times when we face danger and do not know what to say.

The promise in v. 13 is not a condition for salvation, for it applies primarily to believers during the tribulation. "The end" in v. 7 refers to the end of the age, not the end of one's life; and the meaning in v. 13 is the same. In every age of the church, true faith is always proved by faithfulness.

III. Don't Be Ignorant (13:14-27)

The emphasis here is on knowing what the Scriptures teach (vv. 14, 23). The "abomination of desolation" refers to the image that the Antichrist ("the Beast" of Rev. 13) will put into the Jewish temple (Dan. 9:27; 2 Thes. 2:3-10) and force the godless world to worship. This will happen in the middle of the seven-year tribulation period and will be a special warning to the Jews in Judea that it is time to get out! This warning has nothing to do with the return of Christ for His church (1 Thes. 4:13-18), for we have no idea when that event will take place. How important it is for us to study and know the prophetic Scriptures so we will not be "in the dark" and led astray (2 Peter 1:12-21).

Verses 24-27 describe the end of the Tribulation and the coming of Christ to the earth to defeat His enemies and establish His kingdom (Rev. 19:11–20:5). Once again, the emphasis is on signs; for "the Jews require a sign" (1 Cor. 1:22). See Isa. 13:10 and 34:4, and Joel 2:10, 31, and 3:15. The scattered Jewish nation will be regathered (Deut. 30:3-6; Isa. 43:6) and the nation restored.

IV. Don't Be Careless (13:28-37)

The emphasis is on knowing (vv. 28-29) and watching (vv. 33-35, 37). The Parable of the Fig Tree stresses what we know (His coming is near), and the Parable of the Servants stresses what we do not know (when He will come). "Coming events cast their shadows before"; so when we see some of the "tribulation signs" beginning in our day, we know that the time is short (Luke 21:28). But the important thing is not watching the calendar but building our character. We must be alert ("watch") and be found doing His work when He comes. See 1 Thes. 5:1-11.

"This generation" in v. 30 probably refers to the generation of people living when all these things take place. Note how Jesus used the word "generation" in 8:12, 38 and 9:19. In spite of man's wickedness and Satan's anti-Semitic programs, the nation of Israel will not be destroyed.

MARK 14

The chief priests and scribes had already determined to kill Jesus, but they wanted to do it after the Passover. Since Jesus was a popular person, and Jerusalem was filled with excited Jews, it seemed wisest to wait until after the feast; but God had other plans. Judas would make it possible for the leaders to arrest Him during the feast (vv. 10-11; Matt. 26:14-16). The Lamb of God must die on Passover. In this chapter, Mark presents Jesus in four different roles.

I. Jesus, the Honored Guest (14:1-11)

This event (Matt. 26:6-13; John 12:2-11) took place before the Triumphal Entry, but Mark placed it here without giving a time reference as John did (John 12:1). We do not know who Simon the leper was. Perhaps he was someone in Bethany whom Jesus had healed of leprosy and whose home was opened to the Master, as was the home of Mary, Martha, and Lazarus.

Mary's act of love was accepted by Jesus, criticized by Judas and the other disciples (John 12:4-6), and reported to the church throughout the world (v. 9). During Passover, the Jews did especially try to help the poor, and Jesus did not oppose this good custom. The ointment cost a year's wages for the average worker, so if it had been sold, the money would have fed a lot of poor people. But Mary wanted to anoint Jesus in preparation for His death and burial, and that was more important than feeding the poor.

Her good work glorified God and was a blessing to the whole world (vv. 6, 9; Matt. 5:14-16). The word "waste" in v. 4 is, in the Gk., the same as "perdition" in John 17:12, a verse that refers to Judas. It was Judas who was the "waster," not Mary! He wasted his God-given opportunities and eventually wasted his life, ending it by committing suicide. What a contrast between Mary the worshiper and Judas the traitor!

II. Jesus, the Gracious Host (14:12-26)

Jesus sent Peter and John (Luke 22:8) to prepare the Upper Room for the last Passover He would celebrate with His disciples. It was unusual for a man to carry a pitcher of water, for this was a task for the women. It is likely that this man, the owner of the house, was one of His disciples. Because He was being watched by His enemies, Jesus had to do things carefully so that others would not be implicated.

Jesus made two startling revelations that evening. First, He revealed that one of the Twelve was a traitor (vv. 17-21). The form of their question indicates that nobody at the table thought himself guilty: "Surely it is not I!" Jesus protected Judas until the very end and gave him every opportunity to repent. We must not think of Judas as a robot, fated to fulfill prophecy (Ps. 41:9; 55:12-14), but as a man who sinned away his opportunities.

The second revelation was that Peter would betray Him. Jesus first revealed this after Judas left the room (John 13:31-38; Luke 22:31-38), and then repeated it when He and the disciples got to the Garden of Gethsemane (vv. 26-31; Matt. 26:30-35). Of course, in his carnal self-confidence, Peter denied that such a thing could happen; but it happened just the same.

At the close of the Passover meal, Jesus took the bread and wine and gave them new meanings as He instituted the Communion

(Lord's Supper, Eucharist ["to give thanks"]). We remember people for their lives, but Jesus wants us to remember Him for His death; the spiritual blessings we have as children of God come through His death. The hymn they sang was from Pss. 115–118. Imagine Jesus singing a hymn just before being arrested and crucified!

III. Jesus, the Submissive Son (14:27-42)

When they arrived at Gethsemane (meaning "oil press"), Jesus quoted Zech. 13:7 to warn the disciples not to linger or to follow Him after His arrest. He also gave them a word of encouragement: He would rise from the dead and meet them in Galilee. This was now the fifth mention of His resurrection (8:31; 9:9, 31; 10:34), but the disciples simply did not grasp the message.

The phrases "sore amazed," "very heavy," and "exceedingly sorrowful" reveal the human suffering of our Lord in the Garden (Heb. 5:7-8). He was overwhelmed with anguish as He contemplated taking "the cup": being made sin on the cross and being separated from the Father. The presence and prayers of His friends would have meant so much to Him, but they went to sleep! "The hour had come" (John 2:4; 7:30; 8:20; 12:23; 13:1; 17:1), and He was ready to do the Father's will.

IV. Jesus, the Obedient Prisoner (14:43-72)

So ignorant was Judas of the heart of Jesus that he came with a "multitude" of armed Roman soldiers to arrest Him! So hypocritical was Judas that he used kisses, a mark of affection, to betray Jesus. So unprepared spiritually was Peter that he tried to defend Jesus with his sword! Had Peter been awake, he would have heard his Master's prayers and known that He was ready to die. Jesus had a cup in His hand and did the Father's will, for "the Scriptures must be fulfilled." Peter had a sword in his hand and opposed the Father's will, and Jesus had to repair the damage that sword did to Malchus (Luke 22:49-51).

Who was the young man in the Garden? (vv. 51-52) Some think it was John Mark, since it is mentioned only in his Gospel. Was the Upper Room near the home of John Mark, and did Judas and his band go there first? Did Mark hastily wrap a sheet around his body and follow them? We will never know unless the Lord explains it to us in heaven.

Jesus was first led to Annas, father-in-law to Caiaphas, the official high priest (John 18:13-24). Then Jesus was taken to Caiaphas and the Jewish council where people witnessed against Jesus, but their witness did not agree. When Jesus made the messianic claims of v. 62, it was more than the high priest could take; and he declared Him guilty.

Like the other disciples, Peter fled the scene (v. 50); but then he and John disobeyed the Lord's command (v. 27) and began to follow. This led Peter right into the jaws of temptation, and he denied the Lord three times. The Lord's prediction came true (v. 30), but the crowing of the cock brought Peter to repentance (Luke 22:62). If an apostle who lived with Jesus could fall into such sin, how much more do we need to take heed, watch, and pray! John 21:15-19 assures us that Peter was forgiven and restored to apostolic ministry.

MARK 15

Six times in this chapter, Jesus is called "the king" (vv. 2, 9, 12, 18, 26, 32). The Jewish leaders knew that a religious charge would not make Pilate indict Jesus, so they produced a political charge: Jesus claimed to be a king and was therefore a threat to the peace of the land and the authority of Rome.

I. The King on Trial (15:1-15)

Early in the morning, the Sanhedrin met a second time and pronounced Jesus guilty of blasphemy and therefore worthy of death (Lev. 24:16). But only Rome could put a criminal to death, so the council needed the cooperation of the governor, Pontius Pilate. The chief priests repeatedly accused Jesus before Pilate, but Jesus was silent. It was Pilate, not Jesus, who was on trial! See Isa. 53:7 and 1 Peter 2:13-25.

As the defender of the rights of the people, Pilate should have examined the facts and made a decision based on truth. But he was more interested in peace than truth, so he offered the crowd an attractive compromise: Jesus or Barabbas? By rights, Barabbas should have been slain because he was a convicted murderer (Num. 35:16-21). If Pilate thought the crowd would choose Jesus, he was certainly ignorant of the human heart!

II. The King Mocked (15:16-20)

Jesus had told His disciples that the Gentiles would mock Him (10:34), and His words came true. If a prisoner were treated that way today, what would the official consequences be? Roman soldiers could not help but be entertained by the thought of a Jewish king! Once again, prophecy was fulfilled (Isa. 50:6; 52:14; 53:5; Ps. 69:7).

III. The King Crucified (15:21-41)

Jesus started out for Golgotha carrying His own cross (John 19:17), but along the way, the Roman soldiers took it from Him and drafted Simon to carry it. The word "compel" in v. 21 means "to impress into public service," and the soldiers had the legal right to do this (Matt. 5:41). When Mark wrote his Gospel, his readers would know Simon as "the father of Alexander and Rufus" (v. 21), well-known men in the church (Rom. 16:13). Simon's humiliating experience led to his own conversion and that of his family. He came to Jerusalem for Passover and met the Lamb of God!

The narcotic drink that was provided would have deadened the pain, but Jesus refused it. He bore to the fullest the sufferings for our sins. Also, He had promised His disciples that He would not drink the fruit of the vine until He feasted with them in the kingdom (Matt. 26:29).

They crucified Jesus about 9 o'clock in the morning (v. 25) along with two thieves (Isa. 53:12; Luke 22:37). When the soldiers cast lots for His garments, they unknowingly fulfilled Ps. 22:18. When man was doing his worst, God was still in control and accomplishing His purposes. You would think that the people would have been hushed and reverent at a place like Calvary, but they were not; the mockery continued. "Save yourself!" has always been the world's cry, but "Give yourself!" is the Lord's command to us (John 12:23-28). Jesus was reviled by the passersby (v. 29), the leaders (vv. 31-32), the thieves (v. 32), and the soldiers (Luke 23:36-37). One of the thieves did trust Christ, however, and entered into His kingdom (Luke 23:39-43).

Mark records the miracles of the darkness (v. 33) and the rent veil (v. 38). The darkness reminds us of God's judgment on Egypt (Ex. 10:22ff), and the rent veil announces that the way into God's presence has been opened by the death of Christ (Heb. 10:1-25). Jesus was not murdered; He voluntarily gave up His spirit (John

10:11, 15). His cry (v. 34) echoes Ps. 22:1; in fact, Ps. 22:1-21 is a prophetic picture of our Lord's death on the cross. Jesus was forsaken of the Father that we might never be forsaken.

IV. The King Buried (15:42-47)

Faithful women were the last to be found at the cross and the first to be found at the tomb (16:1ff). Our Lord's mother was at the cross until John took her away (John 19:25-27). But it was Joseph of Arimathea and Nicodemus (John 19:38-42) that God had prepared to protect the body of Jesus and bury it (Isa. 53:9; Matt. 27:57). Nicodemus had come to Jesus by night (John 3), but now he stepped out into the light and took his stand for Christ. Had these two brave men not buried the body of Jesus, it might have been disposed of in some humiliating manner. It is important to the legitimacy of the Gospel message that the death, burial, and resurrection of Jesus Christ be authenticated as historic facts (1 Cor. 15:1-4).

MARK 16

I. An Unexpected Miracle (16:1-8)

The women came to give Jesus' body proper preparation for permanent burial, and while we admire their devotion, we wonder why they forgot His many resurrection promises. Now that the Sabbath was ended, the shops were open, and they could purchase the large amount of spices needed. Their biggest problem was getting into the tomb, for a large stone blocked the entrance. What they found in the garden was entirely unexpected: the stone rolled back, the body gone, and a messenger waiting to give them the good news of His resurrection!

It was not enough to be spectators; they had to become ambassadors and carry the word to others. "Come and see! Go and tell!" is the resurrection responsibility (Matt. 28:6-7). Note that the angel had a special word of encouragement for Peter and a word of direction for all the disciples (v. 7). Like the women, the men had forgotten His promises and instructions (14:28). Were the women emotionally fit to carry such a message? They trembled, were amazed and afraid, and fled from the place! Matthew tells us their hearts were filled with "fear and great joy" (Matt. 28:8) because the news was just too good to be true! They did tell the disciples, who doubted what they heard, but Peter and John investigated the open tomb (John 20:1-10; Luke 24:12).

II. An Unbelievable Message (16:9-14)

The emphasis in this section is on the unbelief of Christ's own disciples when confronted with the fact of His resurrection. The disciples "mourned and wept" when they should have been rejoicing and praising God. The appearance to the two men on the Emmaus road is given in detail by Luke (Luke 24:13-32), and His appearance in the Upper Room in John 20:19-25. It was a weeping church instead of a witnessing church because they did not really believe that their Master was alive. The miracle of His bodily resurrection is important to the message of the Gospel and the motivation of God's people for witness and service (Acts 1:21-22; 2:32; 4:10, 33).

III. An Unlimited Mandate (16:15-18)

Each of the four Gospels ends with a commission from Christ to His church to carry the Gospel message to the ends of the earth (Matt. 28:18-20; Luke 24:46-49; John 20:21-23; and see Acts 1:8). The emphasis in v. 16 is not on baptism but on believing. In the early church, believing on Jesus Christ led to a public declaration of faith in the ordinance of water baptism (Acts 8:36-38; 10:47-48), and being baptized sometimes cost people their family, friends, and job. If water baptism is essential to salvation, then nobody in the OT was saved; Heb. 11 tells us that OT saints were saved by faith.

The special signs described in vv. 17-18 applied primarily to the apostolic age (Heb. 2:3-4; 2 Cor. 12:12) and are recorded in the Book of Acts: speaking in tongues (Acts 2:1-4; 10:44-46), casting out demons (Acts 8:5-7; 19:12), taking up serpents (Acts 28:3-6), and healing the sick (Acts 3:1-10; 5:15-16). There are no references to people surviving after drinking poison, but not every miracle is mentioned in Acts. These "sign" miracles are given to encourage us to trust God and not to tempt Him with foolish experiments. These signs were the credentials of the apostles (v. 20), but it is not necessary to perform miracles in order to serve the Lord (John 10:39-42).

The church's mandate is still to take the Gospel to the whole world, and we have a long way to go!

IV. An Unchanging Ministry (16:19-20)

Having completed His work on earth, Jesus returned to the Father in heaven; and there He represents us as our High Priest (Heb. 4:14-16) and Advocate (1 John 2:1-2). But He does more than represent us; He also works in us and through us to accomplish the mandate He left with His church. Since the Gospel of Mark emphasizes Christ the Servant, it is only right that the book close with this reminder that God's Servant is still at work! He works in us (Heb. 13:20-21; Phil. 2:12-13), with us (v. 20), and for us (Rom. 8:28) if we will allow Him to work through us by the power of His Holy Spirit.

A. Special Note on Mark 16:9-20.

Good and godly evangelical Bible scholars do not agree on the authenticity of the closing verses of Mark's Gospel. Some believe they are a part of the original text while others think they were added by another author as a "summary" because the original text was lost. (It is difficult to believe that a part of inspired Scripture could be lost.) It must be admitted that the vocabulary and style are not Mark's and that the passage is lacking in the two oldest manuscripts. Some of the early church fathers quoted from this passage, showing that they knew it existed and that they trusted it. If these verses do not constitute the ending of Mark's Gospel, then we must accept the abrupt ending of v. 8 and with it, an incomplete record. Since there is nothing in these verses that is contrary to anything else in Scripture, it seems reasonable to accept them as historically authentic and live with the "mysteries" that surround them.

LUKE

A Suggested Outline of Luke

Introduction (1:2-4)

I. The Advent of the Son of Man (1:5–2:52)
- A. The announcement to Zacharias (1:5-25)
- B. The announcement to Mary (1:26-46)
- C. The birth of John (1:57-80)
- D. The birth of Jesus (2:1-20)
- E. The presentation of Jesus (2:21-38)
- F. The boyhood of Jesus (2:39-52)

II. The Itinerant Ministry of the Son of Man (3:1–19:27)
- A. Preparation (3:1–4:13)
  - Baptized by John the Baptist (3:1-38)
  - Tempted by Satan (4:1-13)
- B. Ministry in Galilee (4:14–9:50)
- C. Ministry in Judea (9:51–13:21)
- D. Ministry in Perea (13:22–19:27)

III. The Son of Man in Jerusalem (19:28–23:56)
- A. Entering the city (19:28-48)
- B. Debating with the leaders (20:1-47)
- C. Teaching the apostles (21:1–22:38)
- D. Suffering as a criminal (22:39–23:25)
- E. Dying on the cross (23:26-56)

IV. The Victory of the Son of Man (24:1-53)
- A. The Conqueror of death (24:1-12)
- B. The Encourager of hope (24:13-35)
- C. The Bestower of peace (24:36-43)
- D. The Master of service (24:44-53)

Introductory Notes to Luke

I. Author

Paul called Luke "the beloved physician" (Col. 4:14); and from the way Paul's coworkers were identified in Col. 4:7-14, Luke was probably a Gentile. He first appeared in Acts 16:10 (note the "we"), traveled with Paul (Acts 20:5; 21:1; 27:1), and ministered to the churches. Some students think that Luke pastored the new church in Philippi after Paul and Silas left town and was the "true companion" (NKJV) Paul addressed in Phil. 4:3. Luke also wrote the Book of Acts (compare Luke 1:1-4 with Acts 1:1-3). In his Gospel, Luke recorded what Jesus *began* to do and teach, and in the Book of Acts, he recorded what Jesus *continued* to do and teach by His Spirit through His church.

II. Theme

Luke wrote primarily for the Greeks and presented Jesus Christ as the compassionate Son of Man who came to seek and save the lost (Luke 19:10). This Gospel has a universal outlook. Our Lord's genealogy goes back to Adam (3:38), and the whole world is seen as the sphere of God's redemption (2:14, 32; 3:6). Whether they are Jews or Gentiles, Luke is concerned about sinners, and uses the word sixteen times. You would expect a doctor to have a concern for individuals, and Luke's Gospel reflects this. More than any other Gospel writer, he mentions women and children; and he gives a decided emphasis to prayer, singing, and rejoicing, as well as poverty and wealth. Six of our Lord's miracles and nineteen parables are found only in Luke. Doctor Luke gives us the most detailed account of our Lord's birth—no surprise for a physician!

III. Luke and Travel

Luke must have loved to travel, for both of his books describe journeys. The Gospel of Luke takes our Lord from His birth in Bethlehem to His death outside Jerusalem (see 9:51; 13:22; 17:11; 18:31; 19:11, 28), while Acts opens in Jerusalem and ends in Rome. Luke describes Christ's ministry in Galilee (4:14–9:50), Judea (9:51–13:21), Perea (13:22–19:27), and finally Jerusalem (19:28–24:53).

IV. Paul and Luke

Luke could not have traveled with Paul without being greatly influenced by him, and that influence is seen in his Gospel. Graham Scroggie writes in his *Guide to the Gospels,* "Luke, like Paul, emphasizes faith, and repentance, and mercy, and forgiveness." (Check your concordance.) Luke uses the word *justified* five times, a word that was important in the Apostle Paul's vocabulary. Passages like 7:36-50, 15:1-32, 18:9-14, and 19:1-10 would have pleased the heart of the Apostle Paul!

LUKE 1

Luke wrote his Gospel under the inspiration of the Holy Spirit after he had carefully researched the life of Jesus Christ (1:1-4). The phrase "from the very first" can be translated "from above" (v. 3; see John 3:31) and indicated that God guided Luke as he gathered information, organized it, and then wrote his book. His purpose was to give us an accurate and authoritative account of the birth, life, teaching, death, and resurrection of Jesus.

Theophilus ("one who loves God") may have been a Roman official ("most excellent") who, as a new believer, needed to have his faith firmly established. The Gk. word for "instructed" (v. 4) gives us our English word "catechize," so Theophilus may have been a "catechumen," a beginner in the Christian faith.

Luke opens his Gospel by recording four important visits.

I. Gabriel Visits Zacharias (1:1-25)

"The days of Herod the king" (v. 5) (Herod the Great) were not the best of days for the Jewish people, but this priest and his wife faithfully prayed and served God in spite of the discouragements. God has His faithful remnant even in the darkest days, people like Zacharias ("Jehovah has remembered"), Elizabeth ("My God is an oath"), Simeon ("hearing" — 2:25-35), and Anna ("grace" — 2:36-38). It was the providence of God that Zacharias was chosen to burn the incense, for this ministry came to a man but once in a lifetime. He had prayed all his married life for a son; and now, while he was praying, God announced the answer to his prayers.

Angels are mentioned twenty-three times in Luke, but only two are named in Scripture: Gabriel (Dan. 8:16; 9:21; Luke 1:19, 26) and Michael (Dan. 10:13, 21; 12:1; Jude 9; Rev. 12:7). How gracious that the first words from heaven are, "Fear not!" This is a phrase found often in Luke (1:13, 30; 2:10; 5:10; 8:50; 12:7, 32). "Joy" and "rejoice" are used nineteen times in Luke.

Was Zacharias asking for a sign when he said, "How shall I know this?" (See 1 Cor. 1:22.) If so, his request was answered; for he was dumb until his promised son was eight days old! Faith opens our lips in praise to God, while unbelief silences us (2 Cor. 4:13).

What an honor for this elderly couple to be the parents of the last and greatest of the prophets (7:25-28; Matt. 11:7-13), the man who would introduce the Messiah to the nation! But what a tragedy that Zacharias could not herald the good news abroad that God was about to send the Messiah to the world!

II. Gabriel Visits Mary (1:26-38)

Six months later (v. 26), Gabriel visited Mary in Nazareth and told her that she would be the mother of the Messiah. Mary was probably a teenager, for Jewish girls married young. She was engaged to a carpenter named Joseph (Matt. 13:55); she came from the line of David (Luke 3:31) and was a virgin (v. 27; Isa. 7:14). In those days, engagement was tantamount to marriage, and to break the engagement was like a divorce. This explains why Joseph was called her "husband" before they actually were wed (Matt. 1:19).

Gabriel's greeting is literally, "Grace, you who are highly graced!" Although she was a godly woman, it was God's grace, not Mary's character, that made her God's choice. The phrase "highly favored" is used of all God's people in Eph. 1:6 ("which He freely bestowed on us" [NASB]). Mary is blessed among women but not above women.

The coming of the Son of God to earth involved not only our personal salvation but also the fulfilling of God's promises to His people Israel (vv. 32-33). To "spiritualize" these promises is to rob the Jews of what God promised them (2 Sam. 7; Isa. 9:6-7; Jer. 33:14-18). If the angel's words in vv. 30-31 are to be taken literally, so should his words in vv. 32-33.

Unlike Zacharias, Mary had faith that God would do what He promised. She asked, "How shall this be?" and not "How can this be?" Since Jesus existed before His mother, He could not be conceived in the womb in the normal way. The virgin birth is a miracle of God that brought the eternal Son of God into the world without any taint of sin in His human nature (v. 35; 2 Cor. 5:21; 1 Peter 2:22; Heb. 4:15). Mary yielded herself to the Holy Spirit (Rom. 12:1) knowing full well that she would experience shame and misunderstanding.

III. Mary Visits Elizabeth (1:39-56)

Zacharias and Elizabeth lived in one of the priestly cities (Joshua 21), so Mary had to make a journey to get there. When she arrived and greeted Elizabeth, wonderful things began to happen. Elizabeth gave praise to God for what He had done for Mary, and the unborn John the Baptist leaped for joy in his mother's womb (see John 3:29-30). Note that Elizabeth called Mary "the mother of my Lord," which is a proper title. It was Mary's faith that was extolled most of all (v. 45).

Mary's song of praise is called "The Magnificat" (from the Latin word for "magnify"). Mary knew the Scriptures, for there are at least fifteen OT quotations or allusions in her song. (See 1 Sam. 2:1-10.) She praises God and eight times tells us what God has done ("He has . . . ," NKJV). Note that Mary acknowledged God as her Savior (v. 47), which indicates that she had trusted the Lord for her own salvation. She praised God for what He did for her (vv. 46-49), for all who fear Him (vv. 50-53), and for His people Israel (vv. 54-55). Mary took God's promises to Israel literally and did not explain them away.

IV. God Visits His People (1:57-80)

"He has visited and redeemed His people" (v. 68) is the major theme of this hymn of praise. The little boy being named (John means "grace of God") was the forerunner of the Messiah who would bring salvation to lost sinners and one day deliver Israel from all her enemies. God was visiting His people, but they did not know "the time of their visitation" (19:44). Zacharias took literally God's covenants and promises with Israel and expected God to fulfill them (vv. 72-73).

In this beautiful song, Zacharias gave several pictures symbolizing the salvation we have in Jesus Christ: purchase from slavery (v. 68), deliverance from danger (v. 74), forgiveness of a debt (v. 77), and the dawning of a new day (vv. 78-79; Isa. 9:2). Note the emphasis on salvation (vv. 69, 71, 77).

LUKE 2

I. Advent (2:1-7)

That Jesus would be born in Bethlehem was ordained by God long before Caesar Augustus made his decree (Micah 5:2; Acts 15:18). The difficult three-day journey from Nazareth to Bethlehem may have taken longer because of Mary's condition. Some preachers and some people who present Christmas pageants like to condemn the innkeeper because he did not give Mary a decent place to give birth to her Baby, but the Bible is silent about the matter. The "inn" was probably a typical Eastern "caravansary," a two-story structure (the lower level was for animals) built around a courtyard where travelers could camp. Jesus must have been born in one of the cattle stalls; the feeding trough was His bed. See Phil. 2:1-11 and 2 Cor. 8:9.

II. Announcement (2:8-20)

In that day, shepherds were considered to be at the lowest rung of the social ladder. Their work not only kept them away from the temple and the synagogue, but it made them ceremonially unclean. Yet in His grace, God gave the first announcement of the Savior's birth to lowly shepherds! (See 1:52.)

Was Gabriel the angel who appeared? What a privilege this messenger had to tell about the advent of the Messiah! We have the privilege of sharing the good news with the world, and angels cannot take our place. The "singing army" of angels proclaimed the glory of the Lord. Luke's Gospel is filled with praise (1:64; 2:13, 28; 5:25-26; 7:16; 13:13; 17:15, 18; 18:43; 19:37; 23:47; 24:53). Since 27 B.C., the famous "Roman peace" *(Pax Romana)* had been in effect; but there was no real peace on earth, nor can there be until the Prince of Peace reigns on David's throne.

The first human ambassadors of the Gospel were humble shepherds who hastened to see the Baby and then told everybody what they had seen and heard (Acts 4:20). The Gk. verb for "found" in v. 16 means "to find after a search." The Magi had a star to guide them (Matt. 2), but all the shepherds had was the sign given them by the angel (v. 12). The shepherds, like the angels before them, glorified and praised God (v. 20).

III. Adoration (2:21-40)

Jesus was "made under the law" (Gal. 4:4) and was therefore circumcised on the eighth day (Gen. 17:12) and given the name "Jesus," which means "Jehovah is salvation." But there were two other OT laws Mary and Joseph had to obey: the purification of the mother after forty days (Lev. 12) and the redemption of their firstborn (Ex. 13:1-12). The Redeemer was redeemed! Because Mary and Joseph were too poor to purchase a lamb, they brought two birds.

There was a remnant of believing Jews, waiting for their Redeemer (v. 38); Simeon and Anna were among them. We do not know how old Simeon was, but he was probably elderly. The Spirit both taught him and led him, so he was right there when Mary and Joseph came with their Baby. The remarkable thing about his hymn of praise is that he included the Gentiles! He was now ready to die because he had seen the Messiah with his own eyes. Simeon blessed God, and he also blessed Mary and Joseph; but he did not bless the Baby, because Jesus is the source of every blessing. Mary did feel "the sword" in her heart repeatedly as she watched her Son during His ministry and then stood at the cross where He died (John 19:25-27).

How old was Anna? It depends on how you interpret the text. Was she then eighty-four years old, or had she been a widow for eighty-four years? If the latter, then she was over a hundred years old. (Jewish girls married in their early teens.) Like Simeon, she was in the right place at the right time, and she went and told others what she had seen. Anna was one of several prophetesses found in Scripture: the others were Miriam (Ex. 15:20), Deborah (Judges 4:4), Hulduh (2 Kings 22:14), Noadiah (Neh. 6:14), the wife of Isaiah (Isa. 8:3), and Philip's daughters (Acts 21:8-9).

IV. Amazement (2:41-52)

Jewish men were required by law to go to three feasts each year in Jerusalem (Deut. 16:16), but not all of them always obeyed. The one feast they all tried to attend was Passover; and when Jesus was twelve years old (the age for becoming "a son of the law"), He went with Mary and Joseph to the feast. Friends and relatives traveled together and made it a festive time, women and children in the front of the procession and the men at the rear. Jesus was such an obedient child (vv. 40, 51-52) that Mary and Joseph had no fear that He would do anything wrong. Imagine their surprise when He could not be found!

Jesus was "filled with wisdom" (v. 40) and His questions and answers amazed the teachers in the temple. We must not assume that at the age of twelve Jesus understood as much as He did when He launched His ministry at the age of thirty (3:23); for Luke makes it clear that He "increased in wisdom" (v. 52). But He was already aware of His special mission to "be about [His] Father's business."

Nazareth was not an easy place for a lad to grow up. Mary bore other children (Matt. 13:54-58), so Jesus grew up in a crowded and probably poor home.

LUKE 3

Luke gives us five descriptions of the ministry of John the Baptist.

I. The Road-Builder (3:1-6)

God bypassed great and mighty rulers and gave His Word to a Jewish prophet in the wilderness. The nation of Israel was certainly in the wilderness spiritually, and John brought them the good news of the Messiah and His kingdom. John was not only a prophet but was himself the subject of prophecy (Isa. 40:3-5). Verses 4-5 describe the work of a road-builder who gets everything ready for the arrival of the king. In his ministry, John had to remove a great deal of "religious debris" so that the people would be ready to welcome their Messiah.

Acts 19:1-5 makes it clear that John's ministry of baptism looked forward to the coming of the Savior, while Christian baptism looks back in identification with Christ's death, burial, and resurrection (Rom. 6:1-6). The Jews baptized Gentile proselytes, but they did not baptize Jews; John, on the other hand, called for the Jews to repent and be baptized.

II. The Farmer (3:7-9)

John described himself as a farmer, chopping down a fruitless tree and watching snakes fleeing a burning field. John got to the root of things and called the people to repentance. There is a wrath to come, and the only way to prepare for judgment is to turn from sin and trust the Savior. The religious leaders did not obey God's call spoken through John (7:29-30; 20:1-8), and John called them "vipers" (Matt. 3:7-10). Jesus called them "children of the devil" (John 8:44-45; Matt. 23:33), for Satan is the serpent and has his "children" (Rev. 20:2; Matt. 13:36-43). John preceded Jesus because the preaching of judgment for sin must always come before the declaration of saving grace. First conviction, then conversion.

III. The Counselor (3:10-14)

John took time to counsel people personally and prepare them for baptism and their new life of faith. He admonished the people in general to be generous and share what they have (Acts 2:44-45; 4:32-37). He charged the tax collectors to be honest and the soldiers to be just. (Perhaps he knew that the soldiers and publicans worked together to extort money from the people.) Luke mentions tax collectors three other times (5:27; 15:1; 19:2). These soldiers were not likely Romans (see however Matt. 8:5-13), but were probably Jewish soldiers belonging to the temple guard or the court of Herod. It is interesting that John did not condemn the tax collectors' and soldiers' professions; he simply told the publicans and soldiers to do their jobs honestly and not to hurt people. They could remain in their vocations and serve God.

IV. The Witness (3:15-18, 21-22)

John did not come to talk about himself but to bear witness to the Son of God (John 1:19-34). It was his privilege to present the Messiah to the nation. Had they known the Scriptures, they would have been ready for this great event; but they were "in the dark," and so John had to "bear witness of the light."

The baptism of the Spirit takes place when the sinner trusts Christ and becomes a part of the body of Christ, the church (1 Cor. 12:13). The baptism of fire has to do with judgment, as vv. 9 and 17 make clear. John pictured Jesus as a harvester with a winnowing fork ("fan") in his hand, separating the wheat from the chaff. Harvesting is a familiar picture of judgment (Ps. 1:4; Jer. 15:7; Joel 3:12-13).

The Gk. word translated "preach" in v. 18 means "to preach the Good News." John was an evangelist who pointed sinners to the Savior. In v. 3, the word "preach" means "to herald a message." John was the herald who came before the King and proclaimed His coming to the people.

John baptized Jesus in order to present Him to the people (John 1:29-34) and not because Jesus was a repentant sinner. The Father and the Spirit both bore witness that Jesus of Nazareth is indeed the Son of God. Our Lord's baptism in water was a foreshadowing of His future baptism of suffering on the cross (12:50). It was through death, burial, and resurrection that He "fulfilled all righteousness" (Matt. 3:15).

Only Luke mentions that Jesus prayed during His baptism (v. 21), the first of many occasions of prayer mentioned in this Gospel (3:21; 5:16; 6:12; 9:18, 29; 11:1; 22:32, 41; 23:34, 46). If the perfect Son of Man had to pray in order to serve the Father, how much more do we His people need to pray!

V. The Martyr (3:19-20)

Luke does not give the full account of John's arrest and martyrdom, but Matthew and Mark do (Matt. 14:1-12; Mark 6:14-29). John could have compromised his message and spared his life, but he was a faithful witness who declared God's truth without fear or favor. His ministry was a brief one and may have appeared to be a failure, but he fulfilled his work (Acts 13:25) and was pleasing to the Lord (7:18-35).

Note on 3:23-38. The genealogy in Matthew 1:1-17 is that of Joseph, the foster father of Jesus, and traces his legal right to the throne of David. Luke gives us the genealogy of Mary, which proves Jesus' natural rights to the throne. Heli (Eli) was thus Mary's father. Verse 23 should read, "And Jesus . . . being (as was supposed, the son of Joseph) of Eli" (i.e., born of Mary, the daughter of Eli). Jesus was generally thought to be the son of Joseph (4:22; John 6:42, 45). The mother's name would not be put into the genealogy, so Mary is not named. Keeping with his focus on Jesus the Son of Man, Luke takes the genealogy all the way back to Adam (1 Cor. 15:45).

LUKE 4

One of the emphases in this chapter is our Lord's Spirit-led use of the Word. Our words may not always accomplish much, but His Word comes with authority and power.

I. The Word Conquers the Enemy (4:1-13)

Jesus was not tempted so that the Father could determine the Son's character and ability, for the Father had already approved the Son (3:22) and would do so again (9:35). Nor was He tempted to give Satan a chance to defeat Him, for Satan probably did not even want this confrontation, knowing that Jesus could overcome his every tactic. Jesus was tempted so that He could personally experience what we go through and so be prepared to assist us (Heb. 2:16-18; 4:14-16) and to show us how we can overcome the evil one by means of the Spirit of God (v. 1) and the Word of God (v. 4). The first Adam was tested in a beautiful garden and failed, but the Last Adam was victorious in a terrible wilderness.

The sequence of temptations reported by Luke is different from that in Matthew's Gospel, but Luke's account does not claim to be chronological. We do not know why Luke reversed the order of the last two temptations, and it is unprofitable to speculate.

In the first temptation, Satan wanted Jesus to use His divine powers to meet His own needs outside of the will of God. It was a question of putting immediate needs ahead of eternal purposes. In the next temptation, Satan asked for the worship that belongs only to God ("I will be like the Most High" — Isa. 14:14), offering Jesus all the world's kingdoms in return (Ps. 2:7-8). It was actually an opportunity for Jesus to escape the cross, but He said no. In the next temptation, Satan dared Jesus to test the Father's Word by jumping off the temple; and he backed up his dare with an "edited" quotation from Ps. 91:11-12.

Empowered by the Holy Spirit, Jesus used the "sword of the Spirit" (Eph. 6:17) to defeat the tempter, quoting from Deut. 8:3 and 6:13 and 16. Jesus did not use His divine powers to win the victory; He used the same spiritual weapons that any of us can use, if we will yield to Him (1 Cor. 10:13).

II. The Word Convicts the Sinner (4:14-30)

The events that occurred immediately after His temptation are recorded in John 1:19–4:45. Luke picks up the story at the start of His first tour of ministry in Galilee (4:14–9:50). Note the emphasis Luke gives in his book to the Holy Spirit (1:35, 41, 67; 2:25-27; 3:16, 22; 4:1, 14, 18; 10:21; 11:13; 12:10, 12). Luke tells about our Lord's first visit to Nazareth, but Matthew and Mark record only His second ministry there (Matt. 13:54-58; Mark 6:1-6). Since Nazareth was His hometown, you would think they would have been ready to receive Him.

It was customary in synagogue services to ask visiting rabbis to read the Scripture lesson and make whatever comments they felt were appropriate. By this time, Jesus had ministered about a year and was very popular; so it was natural that the synagogue leader ask Him to participate. The appointed lesson included Isa. 61:1-2, and Jesus used it as the text for His sermon in which He made three startling announcements.

First, He announced that the Scriptures were fulfilled in Him. He was anointed by the Spirit to minister to all kinds of needy people and bring them the salvation of the Lord. Second, He announced that the Year of Jubilee had begun. "The acceptable year of the Lord" refers to Lev. 25:8ff, the fiftieth year when everything in Israel was restored to its proper place. (Note that Jesus omitted part of Isa. 61:2, "the day of vengeance of our God," for that day is yet to come.) Finally, He announced that all of this was by the grace of God. He gave two examples from Jewish history to prove that God showed mercy to Gentiles (1 Kings 17:1-7; 2 Kings 5:1-15). The first two points were acceptable to the congregation, but not the third, for they wanted none of God's blessings to go to the Gentiles! Christ's words of grace were tolerable (v. 22), but not His words of judgment; and for His statement they tried to kill Him.

III. The Word Cures the Afflicted (4:31-44)

Jesus left Nazareth for Capernaum and there He set up His "headquarters." Each Sabbath Day, He taught in the synagogue, and His doctrine astonished the people (Matt. 7:28-29). To heal on the Sabbath was a violation of the rabbinical traditions, but Jesus went ahead and delivered this man anyway. Certainly He could have waited another day, but the miracle involved more than rescuing a possessed man. It also involved helping the people to learn the difference between man's traditions and God's truth. Jesus performed a number of Sabbath miracles, and this infuriated the religious leaders (4:38-39; 6:6-11; 13:10-17; 14:1-6; John 5; 9). Jesus came to bring them the true rest from God (Matt. 11:28-30), but the scribes and Pharisees preferred their own legalistic traditions.

Peter, Andrew, James, and John were partners in a fishing business in Capernaum (5:10). Peter was married (1 Cor. 9:5) and had a house in Capernaum with his brother Andrew (Mark 1:29). They had lived in Bethsaida (John 1:44). Jesus healed Peter's mother-in-law of a great fever, a "private miracle" that would not draw any attention from the authorities.

But the miracle He did in the synagogue brought a great crowd to Peter's door! People brought the sick and afflicted to Jesus, and He healed them. It was after sundown, so the Sabbath Day was over. Note that both in the synagogue and at Peter's house, the demons bore witness that Jesus is the Son of God, but Jesus did not encourage their testimony. In time, His words and His works would convince some people that He was indeed the Son of God and Israel's Messiah; but He did not want any testimony from the evil one. See Acts 16:16-18.

As important as it was to meet the physical needs of people, prayer (v. 42) and preaching (vv. 43-44) had higher priorities in our Lord's ministry; and so should they in ours.

LUKE 5

The four events described in this chapter illustrate our Lord's concern for individuals and His ministry to them.

I. Calling Laborers (5:1-11)

Peter, Andrew, James, and John had met Jesus a year before (John 1:35-42), had followed Him a short time, and then had returned to their fishing business. In v. 10 Jesus called His disciples to leave everything and follow Him permanently as His helpers. It is likely that there were seven fishermen in the disciple band (see John 21:2). Fishermen know how to work together, they do not give up easily, they have courage, and they labor diligently. These are ideal qualities for disciples of Jesus Christ. The fact that the men were planning to go out again after washing their nets is proof that they were not dismayed by a night of failure.

Peter was humbled, not by his night of failure but by his astounding success; this is a mark of real character. If success humbles you, then failure will build you up. If success puffs you up, then failure will destroy you. By faith, the men left all and followed Christ. They had been catching living fish and, when they caught them, the fish died. Now they would catch dead fish — sinners — and the fish would live!

II. Cleansing a Leper (5:12-15)

Lepers were not allowed to approach people (Lev. 13:45-46), but Jesus permitted this man to come to Him with his need. Our Lord is approachable, even by people who are rejected by others. Jesus not only spoke to the man, but He touched him, which meant that He was defiled by the disease. However, instead of the touch defiling Jesus, it delivered the leper from his disease! Those who wonder whether or not He is willing to save people should read 1 Tim. 2:4 and 2 Peter 3:9. Read Lev. 13 and 14 for the laws that governed the examination and ceremonial cleansing of the leper. Note that chapter 14 offers a wonderful picture of the atoning work of our Lord Jesus Christ.

III. Curing a Sinner (5:16-26)

Why was the crowd so large that it almost kept needy people from coming to Jesus? Many people were spectators who just came to watch; others wanted to hear the Word of God; and some were there to listen and criticize. The four men are to be commended for their faith and determination. They took the paralytic up the outside stairway to the roof, removed the thatching and tiles, and lowered him before Jesus. (The Gk. word translated "tiling" gives us our English word "ceramic.") It was easy to repair the roof so that no permanent damage was done. What a privilege to be a part of a miracle! It was worth all the effort!

Of course, it is much easier to say "your sins be forgiven" because nobody can prove that it did not happen. So, Jesus gave the scribes and Pharisees something visible and healed the man instantly. It is possible that the man's condition was the result of his sin (John 5:14). What healing is to the body, forgiveness is to the soul (Ps. 103:1-3). In claiming to forgive sins, Jesus was claiming to be God; His critics knew this and accused Him of blasphemy.

IV. Changing Men's Lives (5:27-39)

Luke introduces us to two tax collectors who trusted Christ — Levi (Matthew) (Matt. 9:9) and Zaccheus (Luke 19:1-10). It was bad enough when Gentiles collected taxes for Rome, but when Jews did it, the stigma was even greater. Levi not only followed Jesus, but he invited many of his "sinner friends" to meet Jesus. This is a good plan for new believers to follow: introduce your old friends to your new Friend before they drop you.

Once again, the scribes and Pharisees were on hand to criticize (vv. 21, 30). But Jesus defended Himself and His new friends by using three illustrations. First, He compared Himself to a physician who came to meet the needs of the sick. Jesus saw lost sinners as sick patients who needed healing, not as enemies who should be condemned. Second, He compared Himself to a joyful bridegroom who invited hungry and unhappy people to His feast. To the scribes and Pharisees, religion was a funeral; but to Jesus, it was a wedding feast!

His third illustration had to do with the old and the new. If you patch old garments with new cloth, the cloth will shrink when washed, and you will have a bigger tear than before. If you put new wine into old brittle wineskins, the fermenting liquid will produce gas, and the skins will burst. Jesus did not come to "patch" people's lives but to make them whole. He did not come to mix the old and the new but to bring new life to all who trust Him (2 Cor. 5:17). The tragedy is, people say "the old is better!" and do not want the new. The Book of Hebrews was written to explain how much better the new covenant faith is.

LUKE 6

I. Jesus the Ruler (6:1-5)

It was legal for people to pluck grain from a neighbor's field and eat it, but they could not use a sickle (Deut. 23:25). In allowing His disciples to do this on the Sabbath, Jesus once again violated the traditions of the elders. Just previously, He had healed a man on the Sabbath (John 5), and this angered the religious leaders even more. Our Lord's defense was simple: He was Lord of the Sabbath, and the King is not restricted by man's traditions. His example from the life of David bore this out (1 Sam. 21:1-9). Jesus was again claiming to be Son of David, the Lord, the Messiah. He wanted to give the people a new Sabbath of rest (Matt. 11:28-30), but they would not receive it.

II. Jesus the Healer (6:6-11)

The scribes and Pharisees attended the synagogue service, not to worship God, but to spy on Jesus. They knew that Jesus would be there, and perhaps they saw to it that the handicapped man was there. Jesus healed the man and defended Himself on the basis of the value of human life. Any Jew would rescue a farm animal on the Sabbath (Matt. 12:11-12), so why not rescue a man made in the image of God? When traditions become more important than people, the traditions must be examined and changed. As a result of this miracle, Jesus was hated even more; for miracles of themselves do not change the sinful human heart. The scribes and Pharisees even joined with the Herodians in their plot to destroy Jesus! (Mark 3:6)

III. Jesus the Master (6:12-16)

Once again, Luke mentions our Lord's retirement to pray (5:16). He had important decisions to make, and His enemies were after

Him; so it was necessary that He pray. This is a good example for us to follow in our own ministries (James 1:5).

Out of a crowd of many followers, Jesus selected twelve to be His apostles. An apostle is a person sent with a commission to perform a special task. These men lived with Jesus and learned from Him, for they were going to take His place after He returned to the Father. When the early church selected a man to replace Judas, they followed specific qualifications for not everybody could be an apostle (Acts 1:21-22; 1 Cor. 9:1).

Bartholomew is generally believed to be Nathanael (John 1:45-51), and Judas (not Iscariot) is another name for Thaddeus (Mark 3:18). In all the lists of the apostles' names, Peter is always first and Judas Iscariot is always last.

IV. Jesus the Preacher (6:17-49)

Jesus came down to "a level place" (NKJV) ("plain," KJV) on the side of the mountain, and there He preached the apostles' "ordination sermon." In his report of what we call "The Sermon on the Mount" (Matt. 5–7), Luke eliminated the "Jewish sections" that would not pertain to his audience of Gentiles. Jesus preached this sermon to the multitudes as well as to His apostles, and its message applies to us today. Nobody is saved by "keeping the Sermon on the Mount," because salvation comes only through faith in Jesus Christ.

The sermon deals with the disciples' relationships to possessions (vv. 20-26), people (vv. 27-45), and the Lord (vv. 46-49). In the section on people, Jesus tells us how to get along with our enemies (vv. 27-36) and our brothers (vv. 37-45). You can summarize the sermon in four words: being (vv. 20-26), loving (vv. 27-36), forgiving (vv. 37-45), and obeying (vv. 46-49).

A. Possessions (vv. 20-26).

The people who followed Jesus were, for the most part, poor people who lived from hand to mouth, a day at a time. They envied the rich and longed to be like them. The Bible does not teach that poverty is a blessing, for it tells us to take care of the poor and needy, but that poverty need not rob us of blessing. It has well been said that many people know the price of everything but the value of nothing. It is not a sin to be rich, but it is a sin to trust riches and think you are a special person in God's sight because of your wealth. Character is the important thing, not possessions.

B. People (vv. 27-45).

When you have values different from those of the people of the world, and when you stand up for what is right, you are bound to have enemies. If we retaliate, we are only living on their low level; but if we love them, do good to them, bless them, and pray for them, then we rise to a higher level and glorify the Lord. It takes little effort to love our friends and serve them, but it takes faith to love our enemies and do them good. The principles given in vv. 31 and 36 will encourage us to practice this difficult admonition. See also 1 Peter 2:13-25 and Rom. 12:17-21.

When it comes to our brothers and sisters (vv. 37-46), we must beware lest we treat them more severely than we treat ourselves. If you see a fault in your brother, before you talk to him, examine your own heart to see if perhaps you may be guilty as well. Are you a blind leader of the blind? Are you trying to "perform surgery" on your brother's eye when your own eye is damaged? It is not wrong to help a brother or sister (Gal. 6:1-5), but it is wrong if our attitude is judgmental and our lives are not right with the Lord. The great danger is hypocrisy (v. 42), which means pretending that we are more spiritual than we really are. In trying to help others, we must be careful to be honest with God and ourselves (1 John 1:5-10).

The illustrations of the tree (vv. 43-44) and treasury (v. 45) remind us of the importance of character. If the tree is not sound, the fruit will not be sound; if the heart is filled with evil, the mouth will speak evil. Build your character and you will be able to help others when they have spiritual needs.

C. The Lord (vv. 46-49).

Jesus is Lord, and He wants our works, not words (Matt. 7:24-27). To build "on the rock" means to obey what He says. To build "on the earth" means to profess obedience but not practice it. What we are building is tested today by the storms of life, but there will be a final and greater testing at the judgment seat of Christ (Rom. 14:10-13).

Matthew tells us that the listeners were amazed at Christ's teaching (Matt. 7:28-29). Yet many people today read the Sermon on the Mount and see it only as a beautiful piece of religious philosophy. How much we miss by being hearers and not doers!

LUKE 7

Our Lord's ministry as recorded in this chapter illustrates the Christian graces of faith, hope, and love (1 Cor. 13:13).

I. Faith (7:1-10)

A Roman centurion was in charge of one hundred soldiers. The four who are mentioned in the New Testament were men of character (Matt. 27:54; Acts 10 and 27:1, 3, 43). The fact that this particular centurion had built a synagogue for the Jews and had a loving concern for a servant speaks well of him. You also appreciate his humility in the way he asked Jesus for help and his faith in the power of Christ's word. Being a soldier, he realized that Jesus was under authority and therefore could also exercise authority. Diseases had to obey Jesus the way soldiers obeyed the centurion!

In Nazareth, Jesus marveled at unbelief (Mark 6:6); in Capernaum, He marveled at great faith (v. 9; see Matt. 15:28). It is appropriate that Jesus healed the boy at a distance, for He was ministering to Gentiles (Eph. 2:11-22). This Gentile soldier, who did not have all the spiritual privileges of the Jews, is a rebuke to our own small faith.

II. Hope (7:11-35)

Jesus encouraged two hopeless people: a lonely widow whose only son had died (vv. 11-18) and a discouraged prophet who felt his ministry had failed (vv. 19-35).

A. The widow (vv. 11-18).

Nain was about twenty-five miles from Capernaum, and Jesus traveled that long distance to bring comfort to a sorrowing widow. The boy had been dead probably a day, and it was evening when Jesus and His crowd met the widow and her crowd. The Prince of Life (Acts 3:15) is about to meet the last enemy, death (1 Cor. 15:26) and conquer it. The body was in an open coffin and was probably wrapped with spices in readiness for burial. Imagine the amazement of the mourners when the boy sat up and began to speak!

The Gospels record three miracles of resurrection: this young man who had been dead perhaps a day; a twelve-year-old girl who had just died (8:41-56); and an older man who had been in the tomb four days (John 11). The boy proved he was alive by sitting up and speaking, the girl by walking and eating, and Lazarus by shedding the graveclothes (Col. 3:1ff). In each instance, Jesus brought life by the power of His word (John 5:24).

B. The prophet (vv. 19-35).

John the Baptist had disciples serving him and bringing him reports of Jesus' ministry. John had announced the Messiah's ministry would be one of judgment (3:7-9, 16-17), but all the reports he heard spoke of a ministry of mercy. John should have remembered Isa. 29:18-19 and 35:5-6 and thanked God that the Messiah was fulfilling God's purposes, but John was walking by sight and not by faith. An outdoorsman confined in a prison by an evil king, John would find it very easy to get discouraged. We today get discouraged in much better circumstances!

Jesus praised John, although John's messengers were not there to hear Him and report His words to their master. John was not a wavering reed or a popular celebrity; he was the greatest of the prophets (Isa. 40:1-3; Mal. 3:1). However, the humblest believer today has a much higher position in Christ than John had as a prophet, for John belonged to the old dispensation of law. Believers today are seated with Christ in the heavenlies (Eph. 2:1-10), a privilege that was never given to John.

John thought that his ministry had failed, but Jesus pointed out that it was the Jewish leaders (vv. 29-30) and people (vv. 31-35) who had failed. The leaders rejected God's Word through John (20:1-8), and the people were childish instead of childlike. Nothing pleased them, neither the austerity of John nor the sociability of Jesus. When people are truly wise, they justify (prove right) that wisdom by demonstrating it in their lives (vv. 29-30).

III. Love (7:36-50)

We do not know why Simon the Pharisee invited Jesus to dine with him. Perhaps he wanted to get to know Jesus better, or perhaps he was hoping to get some new evidence with which to accuse Him. It certainly embarrassed Simon when a prostitute came into his house to anoint Jesus! This could have been a life-changing experience for Simon, but he was too blind to see the truths involved.

It is unfortunate that careless students confuse this woman with Mary Magdalene (8:2) and Mary of Bethany (Matt. 26:6-13), when the differences are obvious. According to the *Harmony of the Gospels,* just before this event, Jesus had spoken His great invitation to rest (Matt. 11:28-30), and it is likely that this sinful woman then and there responded and trusted Christ. She was transformed and came publicly to Jesus to give Him her love and worship. Having taken His yoke, she came to express her love.

Simon said to himself, "She is a sinner"; but he needed to say, "I am a sinner." In His parable, Jesus made it clear that all of us are in debt to God and are unable to pay because we are spiritually bankrupt. The two debts ($80 vs. $8) represent not the amount of sin, but the awareness of guilt. The woman knew she was guilty of sinning against God, but Simon had no conviction of sin. Yet he desperately needed to be forgiven! And he could have been forgiven if he had humbled himself and trusted Jesus.

Jesus tenderly pointed out Simon's sins of omission, for he had not treated Jesus with kindness and hospitality. The woman was guilty of sins of the flesh, but Simon was guilty of sins of the spirit: a critical attitude and a hard heart (2 Cor. 7:1). Verse 47 does not teach salvation by works, for v. 50 makes it clear that the woman was saved by her faith. Her works were the proof of her faith (James 2:14-26; Titus 3:4-7), and they were motivated by her love (Gal. 5:6).

Once again, His enemies charged Him with blasphemy because He forgave sins (5:21), but the woman knew she was forgiven because He told her so. How do we today know we are forgiven? We have the assurance of the Word of God (Isa. 55:6-7; Rom. 4:7-8; Heb. 8:12). Because the woman was justified by faith, she had "peace with God" (v. 50; Rom. 5:1). Jesus had offered her rest (Matt. 11:28-30), and she had received it by faith.

LUKE 8

Jesus continued touring Galilee with His disciples and the women who ministered to them. Jesus had cast seven demons out of Mary from Magdala (Mark 16:9). Joanna's husband worked for Herod Antipas; about Susanna, we know nothing. In his Gospel, Luke often mentions women, and it was not unusual in that day for Jewish women to share their wealth with the rabbis. However, it was unusual for women to travel with a rabbi; no doubt Jesus was criticized for this practice. (See Gal. 3:26-29.) One of the themes of this chapter is the Word of God and how we respond to it.

I. Hearing the Word (8:4-21)

A. *"Take heed that you hear!" (vv. 4-15)*

The word "hear" is used nine times in these verses, for it is by our hearing that we take the Word into our hearts where it can create faith (Rom. 10:17). The Word is like seed because it has life in it and can produce fruit when it is planted (received and understood). The human heart is like soil and must be prepared if the Word is to be planted and fruitful. It seems evident that three-fourths of the hearts did not produce fruit and therefore represent those who never were saved (3:8). It takes patience to cultivate the seed and produce a harvest (v. 15), and we must not give up (Gal. 6:9). It is important that we sow the seed in our own hearts as well as in the hearts of others.

B. *"Take heed how you hear!" (vv. 16-18)*

The image now is that of a lamp. We receive the Word so that we might share the truth with others; and the more we receive, the more we have to share. If we receive carelessly, we will have nothing to give. We will be like a lamp without oil. God shares His secrets with us, not for us to hide them, but so we can teach them to others.

C. *"Take heed why you hear!" (vv. 19-21)*

Do we hear the Word just to increase our knowledge and boast about it? (1 Cor. 8:1) Or do we hear God's Word because we want to obey it? Jesus was not being rude to His family. He used their appearance to teach a valuable lesson: if we desire spiritual intimacy with Jesus, we must listen to His Word, receive it, and obey it. Obedience not only enables us to learn more truth (John 7:17), but it brings us closer to the Lord in His spiritual family.

II. Believing the Word (8:22-25)

Jesus certainly knew that the storm was coming, yet He went to sleep in the ship. This fact alone should have encouraged the disciples not to be afraid. What was their problem? The same problem God's people face today: we know the Word of God, but we do not believe it when we face the tests of life. It is one thing to learn the truth and quite something else to live it. "Where is your faith?" is still the key question. Are we trusting God's promises, or are we trusting ourselves or our circumstances?

III. Rejecting the Word (8:26-40)

Jesus went through a terrible storm to visit two demon-possessed men in a graveyard in the Gentile territory of the Gerasenes. Mark and Luke mention only one man — the more vocal of the two — but Matthew tells us there were two of them (Matt. 8:28). The demons believe in God and tremble (James 2:19), but neither their "faith" nor their fear can save them.

Note the repetition of the word "besought." The demons begged Jesus not to send them to the pit but into the pigs (vv. 31-32). The citizens begged Jesus to leave their country (v. 37), and one of the former demoniacs begged Jesus to allow him to be one of His disciples (v. 38). Jesus answered the first two prayers but not the third one. He allowed the demons to enter the swine, and then He departed from that country and returned to Galilee. But He did not allow the healed man to go with Him, but rather sent him home to be a witness for the Lord. New converts may not be ready for full-time service for the Lord, but they can certainly tell others what He has done in their lives.

Critics of the Bible fault Jesus for destroying other men's property when He could have sent the demons elsewhere, but they miss the point of why He did it. It was not because He answers the prayers of demons but that He might demonstrate to the spectators what was really happening. When the herd of swine rushed down the escarpment into the water, there was no question that the demons had departed from the men and that Jesus had done it. By this dramatic act, Jesus made it clear that Satan will take a pig or a man; and if he gets a man, he will turn him into an animal! After all, our Lord is the Creator and Owner of all things; so can He not do what He pleases with His own?

The people rejected the Word and asked Jesus to leave them. What an opportunity they missed! They had seen a dramatic demonstration of the power of the Word of God, but they would not allow it to work in their lives. The people on the other shore were just the opposite: they welcomed Jesus, for they had been waiting for Him.

IV. Experiencing the Word (8:41-50)

An anonymous poor woman and a wealthy religious leader named Jairus both come to Jesus for help, she for herself and he for his daughter. The woman had been suffering for twelve years, while the girl had been well for twelve years and was now near death.

The ground is level at the feet of Jesus, and everybody is welcome to come and bring whatever needs they have.

Perhaps the woman's faith was a bit superstitious, but the Lord responded to it just the same. However, He would not permit her to steal away into the crowd and remain anonymous. Had she done that, she would never have glorified God by her testimony; and she would never have heard His special words of blessing (v. 48; and see 7:50). She had experienced the blessing of His power, but she also needed to experience the blessing of His Word. He called her "daughter," which suggests that she was now in the family. The phrase "made you whole" is a translation of the word that means "to be saved." (Healing is a symbol of salvation; see 5:20-26.) So, she had a healed body and a saved soul, and she went out in peace, all because of His word!

Jairus may have become frightened and discouraged as he waited for Jesus to minister to the woman, and then the bad news came that his daughter had died. It was then that Jairus experienced the power of the Word (v. 50); he trusted that Word as he and Jesus and the disciples made their way through that dense crowd to Jairus' home. What Jairus found there must have frightened him even more: people weeping and wailing (Matt. 9:23; Mark 5:38) and his daughter lying dead upon her bed.

Jesus is always master of every situation. He dismissed the mourners and told them to stop weeping. Why weep over a sleeping child? (When believers die, the body sleeps, but the spirit goes to be with the Lord—1 Thes. 4:13-18; Phil. 1:19-23. There is no evidence in Scripture that the spirit sleeps.) All He said was, "Little girl, I say to you, arise!" (v. 54, NASB) and her spirit returned to her body; she got out of bed and walked. She experienced the life-giving power of the Word of God! "For He spoke, and it was done; He commanded, and it stood fast" (Ps. 33:9). "He sent His word, and healed them" (Ps. 107:20). His Word still has power. Do we have the faith to release that power?

LUKE 9

Jesus is about to embark on His final "campaign" in Galilee before going to Jerusalem to die (v. 51). The background of this chapter is Matt. 9:35-38: His compassion for the multitudes and the desperate need for workers. How did Jesus respond to this challenge? He sent the apostles out to minister and prepared them in private for the ministry they would have after His return to glory. The Twelve still had a long way to go before they could assume places of leadership and service, but Jesus was patient with them, just as He is patient with us. Consider some of the lessons He sought to teach them.

I. Learning to Serve Him (9:1-17)

The first thing Jesus did was equip the Twelve for service. Power is the ability to do something; authority is the right to do it; and the apostles had both (Rom. 15:18-19; Heb. 2:1-4; 2 Cor. 12:12). They were sent only to the Jews (Matt. 10:5-6; Acts 3:26; Rom. 1:16), and they were to preach the Good News and heal the afflicted. This tour was not to be a vacation, so they were exhorted to "travel light" and live by faith. As they went out two by two to serve Him, they had to trust Jesus to enable them to do what He told them to do (Mark 16:20).

So effective was their ministry that even Herod Antipas took notice and began to make inquiries about Jesus. Still bothered by his conscience, Herod was sure that John the Baptist had returned to threaten him. According to John 10:41, John the Baptist did no miracles; so Herod was certainly a confused man. When Herod did finally meet Jesus, the Lord said nothing and did nothing (Luke 23:6-12).

Jesus and the apostles tried to get some rest after their demanding tour of ministry, but the crowds would not let Him go. What do you do with over 5,000 hungry people? The Twelve suggested that Jesus send them away (v. 12; see 18:15 and Matt. 15:23), Philip worried about the budget (John 6:5-7), and Andrew started with what they had and brought it to Jesus (John 6:8-9). Jesus taught the Twelve an important lesson for their future work: no situation is impossible if you take what you have, give it to God with thanksgiving, and share it with others.

II. Learning to Know Him (9:18-36)

Jesus now began to "retire" from public ministry so He could spend time alone with the Twelve and prepare them for what would happen to Him in Jerusalem. At each important milestone in His ministry, Jesus spent special times in prayer (v. 18). When the apostles ministered among the people, they heard what was being said about Jesus; but Jesus wanted the Twelve to have not the opinions of the crowd, but rather personal convictions of their own. He wanted their confession to be a spiritual experience from the Father (Matt. 16:16-17).

Now that they were clear in their confession of faith (all except Judas—John 6:67-71), the Twelve could learn more about Christ's coming suffering and death. Matthew tells us that Peter opposed the plan (Matt. 16:21-23), so Jesus had to explain to him and his associates the meaning of the cross. Peter was a saved man, but he knew little about discipleship, taking up a cross, and following Jesus. Salvation is God's gift to us because Jesus died for us on the cross. Discipleship is our gift to Him as we take up our cross, die to self, and follow the Lord in everything.

On the mount of transfiguration, the three chosen disciples learned that suffering leads to glory, a message Peter emphasizes in his first epistle (1:6-8, 11; 4:12–5:10). Moses represents the Law and Elijah the Prophets, both of whom find their fulfillment in Jesus Christ (Heb. 1:1-3). The word "decease" in v. 31 is the Gk. word *exodus* and refers to our Lord's total ministry in Jerusalem, His death, resurrection, and ascension. As Moses led the Jews out of the bondage of Egypt, so Jesus leads believing sinners out of their bondage to sin.

Peter wanted to make the event into a perpetual Feast of Tabernacles, but the Father interrupted his speech to remind Peter to "Hear Him!" This is the first of three interruptions in Peter's life: the Father interrupted him here, the Son in Matt. 17:24-27, and the Spirit in Acts 10:44-48. Peter learned from this experience to trust the unchanging Word of God (2 Peter 1:16-21) and to know that the glorious kingdom would come in spite of what sinful men may do (2 Peter 3).

III. Learning to Trust Him (9:37-43)

The nine apostles left behind were in trouble, for they could not heal a demon-possessed boy brought to them by a distraught father. Even more, some of the religious leaders were arguing with the apostles (Mark 9:14) and probably ridiculing them for their feeble efforts. Jesus had given these nine men the power and authority they needed (9:1-2), but something had happened. The explanation is given in Matt. 17:19-21. Apparently the nine apostles had stopped praying and fasting, and their faith had become weak. The powerful faith they had exercised on their tour (v. 10) was now too weak to claim the promises of victory Jesus had given them. We cannot live and serve on the basis of past victories. We must constantly be alert and disciplined, trusting the Lord to work.

IV. Learning to Love (9:44-56)

How strange that the Twelve should respond as they did to another announcement about the cross. Instead of being humbled, they argued over who was the greatest. Perhaps the failure of the nine to cast out the demon and the privilege of the three who went on the mountain with Jesus created rivalry among the men. How Peter, James, and John would have enjoyed telling the nine what they saw on the mountain, but Jesus had told them to be quiet (Matt. 17:9). The Twelve were walking in the flesh (Gal. 5:20) and thinking only of themselves. They had to learn to love one another if they were going to serve the Lord effectively.

They also had to learn to love others who were not a part of their special group (vv. 49-50). Jesus had not only His twelve apostles, but He also had seventy other men whom He could send out in service (10:1-2). John thought he was being spiritual by forbidding the anonymous man from serving, but Jesus lovingly rebuked him. For parallel situations, see Num. 11:24-30, John 3:26-30, and Phil. 1:12-18.

Finally, they had to learn to love their enemies (vv. 51-56). The Samaritans and Jews had been feuding for centuries, but Jesus would not participate in the fight (see John 4 and 8:48-49; Luke 10:25-37). We call John "the apostle of love," but Jesus called him and his brother "Sons of Thunder" (Mark 3:17). Perhaps their seeing Elijah on the mountain incited them to want to call down fire from heaven (2 Kings 1). But this is not the way to turn an enemy into a friend (Rom. 12:17-21; Matt. 5:10-12, 38-48).

V. Learning to Put Christ First (9:57-62)

These three men called Jesus "Lord" but did not do what He told them to do (6:46; Matt. 7:21-27). When he heard of possible hardships, the first man would not deny himself. The second man was concerned about the wrong funeral: he should have taken up his cross, died to self, and obeyed God's will. The third man had his eyes in the wrong direction and could not follow Christ. The conditions for discipleship are given in 9:23, and these three men failed to meet them. Their emphasis was "me first." No wonder the laborers are so few!

LUKE 10

I. The Greatest Privilege (10:1-24)

The seventy "ambassadors" had the privilege of serving the Lord and even of doing miracles, yet Jesus said that their greatest privilege was having their names written down in heaven (v. 20). Everything that they were and did grew out of that relationship with God; it was basic to everything and still is. "Apart from Me, you can do nothing" (John 15:5).

This commissioning of the seventy should be compared with the commissioning of the Twelve described in Matt. 10. The men went out in pairs to thirty-five different places where Jesus Himself expected to minister at a later time. They were "preparation men" as well as preachers of the Good News.

The images Jesus uses in this commission are vivid and arresting. These men were to be harvesters in a field that was ready but neglected (v. 2). They were also lambs among wolves and messengers of God's peace (vv. 3, 5-6). Above all else, these men were laborers (vv. 2, 7); they had a job to do. Their ministry in a city could bring blessing or judgment, depending on how the people responded. These seventy men were representing the Lord, and the way people treated them is the way they would treat the Lord Himself if He were there (v. 16).

Jesus knew something about cities rejecting Him (vv. 13-16). He had ministered in Chorazin, Bethsaida, and Capernaum, and had done wonderful things in each city; but they refused to receive Him. Chorazin was a small town in the hills, about two miles from Capernaum; and Bethsaida, the original home of three of the twelve apostles (John 1:44), was also near Capernaum and was condemned by Jesus on two occasions (Matt. 11:21-23; Luke 10:13-15). It is possible that Bethsaida ("fish town") was a special district in Capernaum where the fishermen lived and worked.

When the seventy returned, they were overjoyed with their experiences of victory; and Jesus saw in those victories the defeat of the devil (v. 18; John 12:31-32; Isa. 14:4-11; Gen. 3:15; Rom. 16:20). But even greater than these victories is the privilege of being enrolled in heaven (Phil. 4:3; Rev. 20:12-15). The verb "written" in the Gk. is in the perfect tense, which means that the believer's name stands written in heaven and always will be written in heaven.

If the seventy rejoiced in the privileges of service and salvation, Jesus rejoiced in the sovereignty of the Father and the privilege He had of submitting to Him. The entire Godhead was involved in this rejoicing: the Spirit (v. 21), the Son, and the Father. What a privilege it is to be one of His "babes" and learn His secrets! (1 Cor. 1:26-29)

II. The Greatest Responsibility (10:25-37)

Like some theologians and Bible students today, Jewish rabbis enjoyed debating the fine points of doctrine; and this lawyer (a student of the OT law) wanted to hear what Jesus had to say. We get the impression that the man was not seeking truth, but was only trying to involve Jesus in a debate that he hoped he would win. The lawyer proved to be evasive when it came to facing truth honestly and obeying it.

Our greatest responsibility is to obey the greatest of the commandments, which the man quoted accurately from Lev. 19:18 and Deut. 6:5. But we cannot rightly love God or our neighbor until we have God's love in our hearts (Rom. 5:5; 1 John 4:19). If we cannot keep the greatest of the commandments (Mark 12:28-34), how can we ever hope to please God? How important it is to see that salvation is by faith, not by keeping the law; but once a person has been saved, he or she can depend on the Spirit to help fill their hearts with love.

The Parable of the Good Samaritan was given to answer the evasive question of the lawyer. "Define your terms!" is an old trick of lawyers and debaters. Instead of getting involved in abstract terms, Jesus presented a concrete case; and the lawyer understood the point. We must not "spiritualize" this parable and turn it into an allegory of salvation. The point is simply that our neighbor is anybody who needs us, anybody whom we can help. The "hero" of the story is a Samaritan caring for a Jew; the priest and Levite— professional religious workers—are not heroes at all. The question we must answer is not "Who is my neighbor?" but "To whom can I be a neighbor?"

III. The Greatest Blessing (10:38-42)

The family at Bethany was especially dear to Jesus (John 11:1-5), and the Gospel record gives us three glimpses of Mary, Martha, and Lazarus (Luke 10:38-42; John 11; John 12:1-11). Each time you find Mary in the Gospels, she is in the same place: at the feet of Jesus. Most Jewish rabbis would not accept a woman for a student, but Jesus delighted in teaching Mary the Word. It was not wrong for Martha to prepare a meal, because people have to eat if they are to live; but it was wrong for her to be so preoccupied with work and her own "burdens" that she ignored her guest and was rude to her sister. She was "anxious and troubled" as she tried to serve the Lord, and yet she was missing the greatest and the most lasting blessing. Mary was occupied with Jesus; Martha was preoccupied with herself. What we do *with* Christ is far more important than what we do for Christ, *for* submission leads to obedience and service.

LUKE 11

I. Power in Prayer (11:1-13)

The fact that Jesus had to pray while He was ministering here on earth is proof enough that we need to pray. Jesus prayed at His baptism (3:21), before He chose the Twelve (6:12), at the Transfiguration (9:28), before He was arrested (22:40-44), on the cross (23:46), and at other times (5:16; 9:18). The Twelve soon learned the importance of prayer.

What we call "The Lord's Prayer" should probably be called "The Disciples' Prayer," because it contains things that did not pertain to the Lord Jesus. This is a "pattern prayer" that helps us organize our prayer burdens so that they comply with the will of God. Note that the pronouns referring to believers are all plural, for this is a "family prayer." We may pray in solitude (Matt. 6:6), but we do not pray alone, for we are a part of "the whole family" (Eph. 3:14-15). When we pray, we must put God's concerns first (v. 2) before we come with our requests (vv. 3-4).

True prayer is based on sonship and not friendship. This is not a parable teaching "persistence in prayer" (although that is an important factor) but the willingness of God to care for His own. If a weary, stubborn neighbor finally helps his friend, how much more will a loving Heavenly Father (who never sleeps) meet the needs of His own children! Yes, we should "keep on asking, seeking, and knocking," not to break down God's resistance but to reveal to Him our great concern that His will be done. It has well been said,

"The purpose of prayer is not to get man's will done in heaven but to get God's will done on earth."

Believers today need not pray for the gift of the Spirit, since the Spirit lives in each of God's children, but we should pray for the "good things" of the Spirit (Matt. 7:11) that we need for building character, guiding conduct, and empowering for service (Eph. 1:15-23 and 3:14-21).

II. Power over Satan (11:14-32)

Of themselves, miracles do not convict people of sin or give them faith for salvation (vv. 14-15). On seeing the miracle, some people marveled while others accused Jesus of being in league with the devil! "Beelzebub" means "lord of the flies" (2 Kings 1:1-3); "Beelzebul" means "lord of the house" and relates to vv. 18-26. Jesus showed how illogical it would be for Satan to fight against himself. Satan does have a kingdom (Eph. 2:1-3; 6:10ff), and Jesus has invaded it and conquered it (John 12:31-33; Col. 2:15; 1 John 3:8).

Verses 24-26 illustrate the danger of neutrality: the empty life is only an opportunity for Satan to do more damage. While the parable applies especially to the nation of Israel, cleansed of its idolatry, it also applies to people today who do not know the difference between reformation and regeneration.

The leaders had asked Jesus for a sign (v. 16; 1 Cor. 1:22), so He warned them that their seeking after a sign was an evidence of unbelief and a refusal to accept the evidence (vv. 29-32). The only sign He would give was the sign of Jonah, which is death, burial, and resurrection. If Gentiles like the Queen of Sheba and the people of Nineveh believed on the basis of the message God gave them, how much more should the Jews of that day repent, having seen all He did and heard His messages! Privilege always brings responsibility, and the nation was sinning against a flood of light. Lost people in so-called "civilized" societies will face a greater judgment than the so-called "heathen" in primitive societies.

III. Power from Purity (11:33-54)

The light of God shines in this world through the people of God who live for Him (Phil. 2:14-16; Matt. 5:14-16). We must have a single outlook on life and not be double-minded (Matt. 6:22-24; James 1:6-8). A "single eye" brings more and more light into the person, but a "divided eye" turns the light into darkness! The Pharisees were double-minded (16:13-15), but they thought they were "walking in the light." The outside was clean, but there was corruption in their hearts. In v. 41, Jesus urged the Pharisees to "dedicate to God what was within," and then everything else would be right.

Our Lord's six "woes" against the Pharisees and lawyers (students of the Mosaic law) were certainly spoken in anguish and not in anger (see Matt. 23). These religious men majored in trifles but ignored what was really important. They loved to be recognized and honored by men but forgot about the honor that comes only from God. They glorified the past but would not help those around them who were needy. Instead, the religious leaders only made the burdens heavier for the common people. Jesus saw this kind of religious hypocrite as the murderer of the truly righteous (2 Chron. 24:20-27), and He knew that soon they would crucify Him.

By rejecting Jesus Christ, the religious leaders took away the key that opened up the message of their own Scriptures (Luke 24:44-48). They did not enter into life themselves, and they stood in the way of others entering. It is bad enough to reject truth and be lost forever; but when you influence others to do the same thing, you are guilty of their blood.

LUKE 12

Jesus exhorted His disciples to have the right priorities in their lives.

I. Fearing God (12:1-12)

The religious leaders were trying to trap Jesus, the crowds were thronging Jesus, but He was neither afraid of the enemy nor impressed by the multitudes. He lived to please God alone. He saw that the Twelve were worried about the Pharisees, so He warned them to fear God alone and not fear men. If we fear God, we need not fear anyone or anything else (Ps. 112). When we start fearing people, then we are in danger of compromising in order to please them and protect ourselves, and this leads to hypocrisy ("playacting").

Jesus compared hypocrisy to yeast: it starts small, spreads, and eventually infects the whole. The Jews would recognize yeast as a picture of impurity (Ex. 12:15-20; see 1 Cor. 5:6-8; Gal. 5:9). But hypocrisy is destined to fail because eventually God will reveal all things (vv. 2-3), and God is the final judge.

The fear of man grieves the Father who cares for us (vv. 4-7), the Son who died for us (vv. 8-9), and the Holy Spirit who enables us to be strong in the Lord (vv. 10-12). In the power of the Spirit, we must confess Christ boldly and let men do what they will. God is in control (Acts 4:23-31).

The "blasphemy against the Holy Spirit" (v. 10) has special reference to the Jewish nation that was rejecting the evidence Jesus gave them of who He was and what they needed to do. When they refused the ministry of John the Baptist, they rejected God the Father who sent John; but there was still the witness of the Son. When they rejected Jesus, He prayed for them (Luke 23:34). They still had the witness of the Spirit (Acts 1:8). When they rejected the witness of the Spirit through the church (Acts 2–7), they sinned against the Holy Spirit (Acts 7:51), and there was no further witness left!

II. Trusting God (12:13-34)

This rich man was more concerned about getting money than hearing the Word of God (see 8:14). He wanted Jesus to solve his problems but not save him from his covetousness! Had Jesus made a just division of the property, this would not have solved the problem, for "the heart of every problem is the problem in the heart." The statement in v. 15 contradicts the philosophy of the world and is illustrated in the parable (vv. 16-21).

Money does not necessarily solve problems; it created new problems for this farmer. It is not a sin to be wealthy, but it is a sin to make wealth your god (Col. 3:5). Note the emphasis the farmer gave to himself ("I" and "my"). Wealth can be a window through which we see God (1 Tim. 6:17) or a mirror in which we see only ourselves. It can make us generous or selfish, depending on what is in our hearts.

The rich are prone to be covetous, and the poor are prone to worry. Both are sins. When we substitute *things* for *life*, we stop living by faith and trusting God. All of nature trusts God to meet their needs, and so should we. Worry only tears us down. The key to a worry-free life is a heart fixed wholly on God (v. 31; Matt. 6:33). This is the "undivided outlook" of 11:34-36. If we belong to God, then it is His obligation to care for us; so we need not worry.

III. Serving God (12:35-59)

Living for material possessions can blind us to the future and make us unprepared for the Lord's return. We can get so wrapped up in this world's goods that we neglect eternity. We must be servants who are faithfully waiting and watching for the Bridegroom (vv. 35-40) and working for the Master (vv. 41-48). He will come like a thief (v. 39; 1 Thes. 5:2; Rev. 16:15), so we must be ready.

If we decide that the Lord may not return today, then we start living for ourselves (v. 45); and this will mean judgment when we stand before the Lord (v. 46; 1 John 2:28). The phrases "cut him in two" (v. 46) and "beaten" (vv. 47-48) do not suggest that there will be physical discipline at the Judgment Seat of Christ, for we shall have glorified bodies. They are a vivid reminder that Jesus will deal with unfaithful servants and not give them their rewards. It is a serious thing to have a God-given responsibility.

If we think that serving Christ is demanding and difficult, think of what He experienced! (vv. 49-50) He felt the waves and billows of God's judgment in His baptism on the cross. Are we in the furnace of affliction? He felt that fire before we did. Are we experiencing "war" in the home because of our faith in Christ? He knew what that was like too (8:19-21; Micah 7:6; John 7:1-5).

We must take care that nothing keeps us from serving the Lord faithfully, neither the seeming delay of His coming (v. 45), nor persecution (vv. 51-53), nor the unbelieving attitude of the world (vv. 54-59). Our modern world understands science, can predict storms and comets, and can put men on the moon, but they cannot understand "the signs of the times." Like people in the days of Noah, they have a false security based on ignorance. A time of judgment was coming to Israel, but they would waste the opportunity for peace that God gave them (vv. 58-59; 19:41-44).

LUKE 13

As our Lord makes His way to Jerusalem (v. 22), He deals with some important questions.

I. Is There Justice in This World? (13:1-9)

Pontius Pilate, the Roman governor, was not known for his gentleness. He did not get along well with the Jews and did not hesitate to kill people who got in his way. This incident may have occurred when the Jews protested Pilate's taking money from their temple. The governor had in the temple crowd armed soldiers disguised as civilians, and they killed some unarmed Jews. Where was God when this happened? Why did God allow His faithful people to be killed without warning?

Jesus pointed out that these deaths in the temple were but one seeming tragedy in many that occur in our world. What about the fall of the tower of Siloam? Could not God have prevented this accident and spared the lives of eighteen people? According to Jesus, the real question is not "Why did others die?" but "Why am I still alive?" In vv. 3 and 5, Jesus made His answer very personal; and in the parable, He personalized it even more.

The Jewish nation was like that fruitless fig tree: it had the outward appearance of life, but it bore no fruit. John the Baptist had laid his axe to the root of the tree (3:9), and Jesus had ministered to the nation for three years; but there was still no fruit. God could have judged the nation immediately, but He gave them more time. In A.D. 70, He allowed the Roman legions to destroy Jerusalem and the temple.

But there is also an individual application: God expects us to bear fruit for His glory. Instead of asking, "Why did others die?" we should ask, "Is it worth it to God for me to be alive?"

II. Are We Concerned about Human Needs? (13:10-21)

Imagine the distress of the woman bound by Satan for eighteen years! Yet she still faithfully attended the synagogue and worshiped God. Like Abraham, she had faith to believe that God was able to do the impossible (v. 16; Rom. 4:19-25). Jesus healed her on the Sabbath to impress upon the people the true freedom that He alone can give. The Jewish religious leaders had so shackled the people with rules and regulations that they were bowed down with burdens, just as this woman was with her affliction. The ruler of the synagogue was a hypocrite: he would rescue one of his animals but would not help a human being made in God's image!

III. Is Our Salvation Personal or Theoretical? (13:22-30)

Once again, Jesus took an abstract question and brought it down to concrete reality. The question is not "Are there few who will be saved?" but "Will you be among the saved?" The word *strive* means "to agonize like an athlete." This does not imply that we are saved by our hard work, because we are saved by grace when we trust Jesus Christ. Rather, it warns us to avoid an easy, complacent, and theoretical attitude toward the eternal destiny of the soul. If we fail to take salvation seriously, we may find the door shut and somebody else taking our place at the feast! Those who think they are first (like the Pharisees) will find themselves last, while those who humbly think themselves last (the sinners) will find themselves first.

IV. Why Are Many People Lost? (13:31-35)

Since Jesus was in the territory ruled by Herod Antipas, the Pharisees thought they could frighten Him; but they were greatly mistaken. Herod's father, Herod the Great, had killed the little children in Bethlehem (Matt. 2:16-18), and Herod Antipas had slain John the Baptist (9:7-9), so this ruler was capable of doing the same thing to Jesus. The Pharisees wanted Jesus to go to Judea where they had authority to deal with Him, but He knew their plans and continued to follow His plan.

But Jesus was not afraid. He lived on a divine timetable and knew that He could not die until His hour had come (John 2:4; 7:30; 8:20; 13:1; 17:1). "The third day" refers to our Lord's resurrection from the dead when His earthly work of redemption would be completed. Note the "holy sarcasm" in our Lord's words in v. 33 and connect it with 11:47-51.

The nation was lost because it wasted its opportunities to be saved (vv. 34-35). During His years of public ministry, Jesus gave people many opportunities to believe the Gospel; but they preferred to go their own way. But God is long-suffering and gracious and will one day bring salvation to the nation, and they will welcome their Messiah (Zech. 12:10; 14:4ff; Matt. 24:30-31).

LUKE 14

I. Christ the Guest (14:1-14)

Sharing meals was an important part of Jewish life, and it became an important part of church life (Acts 2:46). In the East, eating together is a mark of friendship and a sign of commitment to one another. However, when Jesus was guest at a Sabbath meal, He saw some things that grieved His heart, and He spoke about them.

A. *Ignoring the needy (vv. 1-6).*

Was this handicapped man there as "bait" to catch Jesus? If so, what an awful way to treat him! Jesus healed the man and silenced His accusers. What a pity that people even today show more concern about protecting animals than they do helping human beings! Once again, Jesus deliberately violated their Sabbath traditions (4:31-39; 6:1-10; 13:10-17; and see John 5 and 9).

B. *Seeking for honor (vv. 7-11).*

The seats closest to the host were the best seats, and the guests looking for recognition tried to secure them. If where we sit makes us important, then we are not very important! It is what we are that really counts. Jesus probably had Prov. 25:6-7 in mind when He spoke these words. Verse 11 is a basic principle found in Scripture (18:14; Matt. 23:12; James 4:6, 10; 1 Peter 5:5; Prov. 3:34).

C. *Expecting to be repaid (vv. 12-14).*

The thrust of Christ's admonition to the host was, "Do not habitually invite only those who can invite you in return." R.G. LeTourneau used to say, "If we give only because it pays, it won't pay." Our motives must be pure if our service is to honor God and be a blessing to others (6:32-36). Fellowship that is based on selfish competition is not Christian fellowship at all.

II. Jesus the Host (14:15-24)

The Jews pictured their future kingdom as a great feast with the patriarchs as the honored guests (13:28-29; Isa. 25:6-9), and Jesus used this picture to illustrate the importance of accepting God's invitation to "salvation's supper." Salvation is a feast, not a funeral; everything we need has already been provided. All we must do is accept the invitation, come, and be filled!

When a host planned a feast, he told his guests the day of the feast, but not the hour. He had to know how many were coming so he could butcher enough meat and provide sufficient food. The servants would then go out near the hour of the feast and tell the guests to come. Remember, the guests in this story had already agreed to come; but then they backed out. Their action and excuses were a terrible breach of etiquette as well as an insult to the host.

The three people all had feeble excuses. In the East, real estate transactions are long and complicated; and how could he examine his property in the dark? Furthermore, anybody who buys ten oxen without first testing them is a fool. Finally, the third man's wife really had nothing to do with the event, for women were not usually invited to public feasts. It was only an excuse!

There were two responses by the host: he shut the door on the excuse-making guests, and he got others to take their places at the feast. God wants His house filled; and if those who are invited will not come, He will call others.

III. Jesus the Master (14:25-35)

It is important to note the contrast between vv. 23 and 25. When it comes to salvation, God wants everybody who will come; but when it comes to discipleship, He wants only those who will pay the price. Jesus was not impressed by the great crowds that followed Him because He knew their hearts. He was on His way to a cross outside Jerusalem, and the crowds were not ready for that. It is easy to be in the crowd but not so easy to carry the cross. After we "come in" and find salvation (v. 23), we must "come to" Him for our cross (v. 26), and then "come after" Him in obedience to His will (v. 27). Jesus is the Host at "salvation's supper," but He is the Master in our Christian walk of faith.

The builder (vv. 28-30) and the king (vv. 31-33) represent the Lord Jesus and not the believer. Jesus is building His church and needs to have the best materials. He is fighting a battle and must have the finest soldiers. Are we the kind of quality people that He can use for building and battling? If we are not faithful disciples, then He cannot use us to get the job done. Note the repetition of "cannot be my disciple" (vv. 26, 27, 33). There is no "cannot" for salvation's supper except "I cannot come" (v. 20), which really means, "I refuse to come." But when it comes to discipleship, God lays down qualifications and expects us to meet them. He is looking for those with "salty character" (Matt. 5:13) who will help Him influence this decayed world (vv. 34-35).

LUKE 15

The parables in this chapter were given in response to the criticism of the scribes and Pharisees that Jesus had received sinners and even ate with them. These "sinners" were Jews who were not obeying the Law or the traditions of the elders and were therefore "outcasts" in Israel. Jesus had already made it clear that He came to save sinners and not self-righteous people like the scribes and Pharisees (5:27-32; 14:21-24). Jesus saw what these "sinners" really were: lost sheep who needed a shepherd; lost coins that had value and needed to be put into circulation; lost sons who needed to be in fellowship with the Father.

I. Searching (15:1-10)

A shepherd is responsible for each of the sheep; and if one is lost or killed, he must make up for it himself. Sheep are lost because of their own stupidity; they wander away and fail to see the danger they are in. Jesus came to "seek and to save them that are lost" (19:10). Note the emphasis on rejoicing: the shepherd rejoices, the neighbors rejoice, and heaven rejoices.

The necklace of ten coins was a headband that signified that a woman was married. To lose one of the coins would be to ruin the necklace and embarrass the woman. Like that coin, sinners bear the imprint of the image of God and are valuable (20:24-25); but they are lost and "out of circulation." When found, sinners are once again useful and able to serve the Lord. Again, there is joy in the family because the lost has been found.

What does it mean to be lost? It means, like the sheep, to be away from safety and in a place of danger; or like the coin, to be useless and out of circulation. In the case of the younger son, it means to be out of fellowship with the Father and away from the joys of the family.

II. Waiting and Welcoming (15:11-24)

It is significant that the father did not go searching for his son, but waited at home for the boy to come back. When the boy did come back, the father ran to meet him. Like sheep gone astray, some sinners are lost through their own stupidity; and, like coins, some are lost by the carelessness of others. But the son was lost because of his own willfulness, and the father had to wait until that will was broken and submissive.

For the younger son to ask for an early inheritance was like asking his father to die! It must have broken the father's heart, but he gave the boy his share of the wealth! God likewise has shared

His wealth with a world of lost sinners, and they have wasted it (Acts 14:15-17; 17:24-28). It was not the badness of his life that brought the boy to his senses but the goodness of his father (v. 17; Rom. 2:4).

In the East, it is unusual for older men to run; but the Father had to run because of his compassion for the boy. Also, the son had disgraced his family and his village and could have been stoned to death (Deut. 21:18-21). If they threw any stones, they would have to hit the father! The best robe would be the father's expensive festal robe; the shoes indicated that the son was not a servant (in spite of his request); and the ring was the proof of sonship. Again, there is joy, for the lost has been found!

III. Pleading (15:25-32)

The elder brother is the forgotten person in this parable, and yet he is the key to the story. If the prodigal son symbolizes the "publicans and sinners," then the elder brother represents the scribes and Pharisees. There are sins of the spirit as well as sins of the flesh (2 Cor. 7:1). The religious leaders may not have been guilty of the gross things that the younger son did, but they were still sinners, guilty of a critical and unloving spirit, pride, and an unwillingness to forgive.

Because the younger son had received his inheritance, the estate belonged to the elder brother; but it was run by the father, who benefited from the profits. If the younger brother came back home, it would confuse the inheritance even more, so the elder brother did not want him back, nor was he looking for him.

Now we discover that the elder brother had a "hidden agenda" of his own, a longing to have a big party for his friends. He was angry with his brother for coming home and with his father for welcoming him and forgiving him. Like the scribes and Pharisees, he stayed outside the joy and fellowship of those who had been forgiven.

By staying outside the house, the elder brother humiliated his father and his brother. The father could have commanded him to come in, but he preferred to go out and plead with him. That is what Jesus did with the Jewish religious leaders, but they would not be persuaded. They thought they were saved because of their exemplary conduct, but they were out of fellowship with the Father and needed to repent and seek forgiveness.

LUKE 16

The parable of the two sons brought up the subject of wealth, and in this chapter Jesus pursued the subject further. The Jews thought that wealth was a sign of salvation and God's favor (Mark 10:17-27), but Jesus taught that wealth could lead to condemnation. In this chapter, we see three dangers to avoid.

I. Wasting Wealth (16:1-12)

Like the prodigal (wasteful) son, this steward wasted his master's goods, just as many people are doing today. All that we have comes from the Lord and must be used for the good of others and the glory of God. We are not owners; we are stewards of His possessions, and one day we must give an account of what we have done with what God has shared with us.

Jesus did not commend the steward for cheating his master, but for making good use of his opportunity. The people of this world are much better at seeing opportunities and profiting from them than are the children of God (Eph. 5:15-17). During this brief life, we have the opportunity to use wealth to make friends for God, friends who will meet us in heaven!

The key is faithfulness (vv. 10-12). The unrighteous mammon (money) is the least, but the eternal riches are "the most." If we use God's wealth as He wills, then He will give us true riches which are our own. Jesus did not see a "great gulf" fixed between the material and the spiritual, for one of the most spiritual things we can do is use material things to the glory of God in the winning of the lost.

II. Coveting Wealth (16:13-18)

The Pharisees were outwardly pious but inwardly filled with covetousness (Matt. 23:14; Titus 1:11). Believing as they did that wealth was a sign of God's blessing, they laughed at Jesus and what He taught. They were not unlike the "success preachers" today who equate happiness and holiness with prosperity. They were trying to serve two masters—the Lord and their money—and this is impossible to do. Either we serve money or we serve God; there can be no compromise (Matt. 6:24).

Material success and the power and prestige it brings are greatly admired by men, but God sees it as an abomination (Prov. 10:2-3).

It is not a sin to be wealthy, for godly men like David and Abraham were wealthy, nor is it a sin to enjoy one's wealth (1 Tim. 6:17); but it is a sin to have the world's attitude toward wealth and fail to use wealth to the glory of God.

The trouble with the Pharisees is that they were going along with the crowd and not "pressing into the kingdom" (v. 16). They were unwilling to pay the price to follow the Lord. In their desire to obey the letter of the Law, they were ignoring the inner meaning of the Law as taught by Jesus.

III. Worshiping Wealth (16:19-31)

Luke did not say that this narrative was a parable; perhaps it was an actual occurrence. The rich man used his wealth only to please himself and maintain his extravagant life-style. He did not use it to care for the poor and needy, not even the poor man begging at his very door. Lazarus in effect witnessed to the rich man (vv. 27-28); but in his false security, the rich man would not repent. To him, death seemed very far away.

When death came, it changed everything: the rich man was poor and tormented, and the poor man was rich and in paradise! Keep in mind that it was faith that made the difference. The rich man did not go to the place of punishment (Hades) because he was rich, just as the beggar did not go to paradise because he was poor. The beggar was a believer, and the rich man an unbeliever. Not only were their situations reversed, but they were also fixed and could not be changed.

How convicting it is to hear people in Hades calling for somebody to go to witness to their loved ones! People cannot be forced or frightened into trusting Christ: they must be persuaded (v. 31; 2 Cor. 5:11; Acts 18:4). If God's people could spend one second in hell, perhaps they would become bolder witnesses for the Lord. This is indeed a solemn account that both believers and unbelievers need to take to heart.

LUKE 17

I. The Unforgiving (17:1-6)

The word *offenses* means "occasions to stumble." The Gk. word gives us our English word "scandalize," and it originally referred to the stick that tripped a snare or a trap. These things must come because there is sin in the world, but they need not come from us. Before we cause somebody else to sin, we had better heed the Lord's stern warning in v. 2. By "these little ones," Jesus meant both new believers (such as the publicans and sinners in 15:1) as well as the little children (Matt. 18:1-7).

We must also take care not to sin against our brothers and sisters in Christ who are more mature in the faith. The church is a family of faith, and we minister to one another by admitting our sins, asking for forgiveness, and granting forgiveness to each other (Eph. 4:32; Matt. 5:43-48 and 18:21ff). It is not likely that a believer would commit the same sin seven times in one day, but we must be ready to forgive that often. Forgiveness should be a habit, not a battle.

You would expect the disciples to say, "Increase our love!" But forgiveness comes from faith in God's Word, the confidence that God will work out the best for everyone involved so long as we do what He wants us to do. Sometimes it is painful to forgive someone who has sinned against us, but we must obey God's Word by faith and believe Rom. 8:28. If our faith is like the seed, alive and growing, nothing will be impossible.

II. The Unprofitable (17:7-10)

Jesus knew how to balance one truth with another so that His disciples would not go to extremes. The miraculous faith of v. 6 must be balanced with faithful day-by-day "ordinary service" that may not be exciting. Here is a servant who plows, takes care of cattle, and even cooks! He does each job faithfully so that he might please his master. But when we do our jobs, we are still only "unprofitable servants." The word translated "unprofitable" means "without need," that is, nobody owes him anything. Even the rewards we get from the Lord are pure grace! He does not "owe" them to us because we have only done our duty.

III. The Ungrateful (17:11-19)

Jesus was still on His way to Jerusalem (9:51; 13:22, 33), and His journey took Him along the border of Samaria and Galilee where He met ten men who were lepers. These outcasts lived and traveled together because they were rejected by society. They recognized Jesus because immediately they begged Him for mercy. He commanded them to go see the priest (Lev. 13–14), and when they obeyed the command, they were all healed.

Only one of the ten men was grateful enough to come first to Jesus and thank Him for His merciful gift of healing. (See Ps. 107:8, 15, 21, and 31.) But the astounding thing is that this man was a Samaritan! Imagine a Samaritan giving thanks to a Jew! But because he did, this man received an even greater gift: he was saved from his sins. "Your faith has made you well" can be translated, "Your faith has saved you" (see 7:50, NKJV). Physical healing is a great blessing, but it ends at death; while the blessing of eternal life lasts forever.

IV. The Unprepared (17:20-37)

Just as many people today are excited about prophecy and future events, so the Jews in Jesus' day lived in expectation of the Messiah's coming. The Gk. word for "observation" means "to lie in wait, to spy." Jesus cautions us not to devote our time to spying on the future and trying to second-guess God. The Jews looked for the coming of their King, and there He was in their midst! We can be so wrapped up in the future that we miss the opportunities of the present.

The important thing is not to chart the future but to be ready for His coming at any time. This means paying no attention to the sensationalists and the people who claim to know all the "secrets" (v. 23). Jesus compared the last days to "the days of Noah" (vv. 26-27) and "the days of Lot" (vv. 28-33). Both men lived just before great judgments: the Flood (Gen. 6–8) and the destruction of Sodom (Gen. 19). Noah warned the world of his day that the flood was coming (2 Peter 2:5), and the angels warned Lot and his family that destruction was coming; but the warnings did no good. Only Noah and his family (eight people) were saved, and only Lot and his two unmarried daughters escaped from Sodom.

What will the world be like just before the final judgment and the coming of the Lord? It will be "business as usual" with little concern for the warnings God sends. People will eat and drink, attend weddings, and carry on their vocations; and then the judgment will catch them unprepared. In Noah's day, there was a great deal of violence (Gen. 6:11, 13); and in Lot's time, men were given to unnatural lusts (Gen. 19:4-11). We see both of these characteristics in our own day.

Verses 30-37 do not refer to the rapture (1 Thes. 4:13-18) but to the return of Christ to the earth to set up His righteous kingdom (Rev. 19:11ff; Matt. 24:15-20; Mark 13:14-18). When Christ comes suddenly for His church, there will certainly be no time to go back into a house to get something! (1 Cor. 15:51-52) The verb "taken" in vv. 34-36 does not mean "taken to heaven" but "taken away in judgment." Those left will enter into the kingdom.

Jesus saw human society at the end of the age to be like a rotten corpse that invites the eagles and vultures (v. 37); and this reminds us of Rev. 19:17-19, that last battle before Jesus establishes His kingdom. As believers in His church, we must obey v. 33 and seek to live wholly for Him (Matt. 10:39; John 12:25). That is the only way to be prepared for His coming.

LUKE 18

I. A Needy Woman Who Would Not Go Away (18:1-8)

When you live in a society that is rotting (17:37), the air is poisonous, and it is easy to faint! But prayer puts us in touch with the pure oxygen of heaven so that we can keep going. In this parable about prayer, Jesus is contrasting (not comparing) the selfish judge and the Heavenly Father. In that day, it was very difficult for poor widows to get justice because they lacked the means for bribing the officers who would get the judge to act. But this widow would not quit until the judge had given her what she was supposed to get.

Now, if a selfish judge finally meets the needs of a poor widow, how much more will the loving Heavenly Father meet the needs of His own children when they cry to Him? This parable is not urging us to "pester God" until He acts; it is saying that we do not need to "pester" Him because He is ready and willing to answer our prayers. (See 11:5-10 for a similar argument.) The widow had no lawyer, but we have a High Priest at the throne of God in heaven. She had no promises, but we have a Bible filled with promises we can claim. She was an outsider, but we are the children of God! What a privilege it is to pray!

II. A Sinful Man Who Went Away Justified (18:9-17)

Again we have a study in contrasts. The Pharisee talked to himself and about himself, but the publican prayed to God and was heard.

The Pharisee could see the sins of others but not his own sins (7:36-50), while the publican concentrated on his own needs and admitted them openly. The Pharisee was boasting; the publican was praying. The Pharisee went home a worse man than when he had come, but the publican went home forgiven.

Justified means "declared righteous." It is a legal term that means all the evidence has been destroyed, and there is no record that we have ever sinned. It also means that God no longer keeps a record of our sins (Ps. 32:1-4; Rom. 4). Instead, He puts to our account the righteousness of Christ (2 Cor. 5:21). All of this comes from the mercy of God (Luke 18:13) and not the merits of man. We are justified by faith (Rom. 5:1-5).

In contrast to the proud Pharisee are the little children that Jesus welcomed and blessed (vv. 15-17). His own disciples had some of the spirit of the proud Pharisee in the parable, and Jesus had to lovingly rebuke them. The publican, however, was childlike in his humility and faith and entered the kingdom of God.

III. The Young Man Who Went Away Sad (18:18-34)

When you combine the records in Matthew, Mark, and Luke, you learn that this man was rich, young, and a ruler, probably of a synagogue. It was unusual for a young man to have that position, so he must have been a most exemplary youth. However, he wanted salvation on his terms, not the Lord's; and Jesus could not accept him. Nobody is saved either by keeping the Law (Gal. 2:21 and 3:21-24; Rom. 3:20) or by becoming poor and generous. This was our Lord's way of making him face up to his sin of covetousness. It was true that outwardly the young man had obeyed the laws Jesus named in v. 20, but he forgot about "Thou shalt not covet" (Ex. 20:17; and see Col. 3:5 and Rom. 7:7-8). If we covet, we may end up breaking all the other commandments!

Our Lord's words about riches shocked the Twelve, for, like most Jews, they thought that riches were evidence of God's favor. It is not possessing riches that condemns the soul but trusting in riches. Abraham was a very wealthy man, but he was saved by faith in God's word, not faith in his money (Gen. 15:6). A desire to acquire and trust riches can hinder the growth of the Word of God in the heart (Matt. 13:22), cause us to forget God (Deut. 8:13-14), and lead to many kinds of temptations and sins (1 Tim. 6:9-10).

Verses 28-30 should be connected with Matt. 19:27–20:16. Was there a bit of boasting in Peter's statement and perhaps some pride? Jesus saw this dangerous attitude in Peter's heart ("What shall we get?" not "What can we give?") and gave the parable in Matt. 20:1-16 to warn him and the rest of the Twelve. He promised them blessings in this life and the life to come, but He also reminded them that He would soon die at Jerusalem (vv. 31-34). If their Lord had to suffer to enter into His glory, they would also have to suffer.

IV. The Man Who Went Away with Jesus (18:35-43)

Still on His way to Jerusalem, Jesus left the old city of Jerusalem, now in ruins, and approached the new city built by Herod the Great; and there He met two blind men (Matt. 20:30), one of whom, Bartimaeus, was the more vocal. Could Bartimaeus tell that the crowd walking with Jesus was different from the other bands of pilgrims that went by? Certainly the people who walk with Jesus ought to be so different that they can attract others.

Like the publican, the blind men cried out for mercy (vv. 13, 39) and kept it up in spite of the resistance of the crowd. Jesus always stops when a needy heart is calling to Him. The blind men could not find their way to the Master, but some of the people helped them; Jesus instantly healed them. Both of them followed Jesus and gave loud testimony of what He had done for them.

Read Mary's song of praise in Luke 1:46-55 and see how its various statements apply to persons you met in this chapter.

LUKE 19

I. Jesus Comes to Bring Salvation (19:1-10)

As chief among the publicans, Zaccheus ("righteous one") supervised the men who collected taxes and, of course, received his share of the money. No wonder he was rich! As Jesus and His followers made their way through Jericho to Jerusalem, Zaccheus "kept seeking" to see Jesus, but his small stature made this very difficult. In his eagerness, Zaccheus did two things unbecoming to a man of his position: he ran (in the East, men do not run), and he climbed a tree! But his boyish curiosity led to his conversion!

It was Jesus who wanted to see Zaccheus. Jesus stopped, looked up, and called Zaccheus to come down and receive Him as his guest. Zaccheus had been seeking, but now he was found! He received Jesus joyfully (John 1:11-13) and gave every evidence that he had experienced new life in his heart. Salvation had come to the house of Zaccheus (Rev. 3:20) because he had exercised the same kind of saving faith as Abraham (Rom. 4:12).

What a contrast between the attitude of our Lord toward Zaccheus and the attitude of the crowd (v. 7). Jesus came to seek and save the lost; they could only stand by and criticize (see 15:1-2). Verse 10 is a key verse in Luke's Gospel; for Luke describes the compassionate Son of Man, the Savior of the lost (1:47, 71; 2:11; 7:50; 9:56; 18:42). What happened to Zaccheus can happen to anybody who will trust the Lord Jesus Christ.

II. Jesus Comes to Bring Rewards (19:11-27)

Passover season brought a great deal of excitement to the Jewish people as they recalled the great victory of the Exodus and then pondered their plight as vassals of Rome. Perhaps the Messiah would come this year! This parable may have been based on history. Thirty years before, Archelaus, son of Herod the Great, went to Rome to ask Augustus Caesar for his kingdom; and some of the Jewish people sent a delegation to protest the appointment.

The Parable of the Pounds must not be confused with the Parable of the Talents (Matt. 25:14-30). The talents represent opportunities to use ability; and since we all have different abilities, we are given different opportunities. But the servants in this parable each received a pound (three months' wages), which represents the "deposit of the Gospel" that has been given to each believer (1 Tim. 1:11; 6:20; 2 Cor. 4:7). God wants us to multiply His message so that the whole world will hear (1 Thes. 1:8; 2 Thes. 3:1).

When Jesus returns, He will reward the faithful servants (vv. 15-19), deal with the unfaithful servants (vv. 20-26) and judge His enemies (v. 27). The unfaithful servant had no excuse; his fear paralyzed him when it should have mobilized him into service. At the Judgment Seat of Christ, the Lord will "balance the accounts" and give each of us exactly what we deserve. We must "occupy" (do business) until He comes.

III. Jesus Comes to Bring Peace (19:28-44)

The owners of the two animals were probably disciples of the Lord, and the plan was worked out secretly so the Jewish leaders could not interfere. When Jesus rode into Jerusalem, He fulfilled Zech. 9:9 and declared Himself to be the King of the Jews. But He also aroused the concern of the religious leaders so that they were forced to act (John 12:19). They wanted to arrest Him after Passover (Matt. 26:3-5), but God had ordained that His Son should die as the lamb of God on Passover (John 1:29).

There were three special groups in that Passover crowd: the native Judeans who were suspicious of Jesus, the Galileans who followed Him, and the visitors from outside Judea who did not know who Jesus was (Matt. 21:10-11). Within the crowd from Judea were people who saw Him raise Lazarus from the dead (John 12:17-18). The statement that "the crowd that cried 'Hosanna!' on Palm Sunday ended up crying 'Crucify Him!' on Good Friday" is not true. It was primarily the Jerusalem Jews, influenced by the priests, who asked for His blood (Matt. 27:20).

Jesus came to bring peace (2:14), but the people rejected Him and declared war (12:49-51). They wasted their opportunity! There is no peace on earth, but there is peace in heaven because of Christ's work on the cross (19:38); and there is peace with God for those who trust the Savior (7:50; 8:48; Rom. 5:1). As He thought of the terrible judgments that would come to His people, Jesus wept over the city.

IV. Jesus Comes to Bring Cleansing (19:45-48)

In God's scheme of things, righteousness and peace always go together (Ps. 85:10; Isa. 32:17; Heb. 7:1-2; James 3:17). The nation was wicked because its worship was corrupted. The holy temple had become a "religious market" where the high priest's family made money from foreign Jews who had to buy sacrifices and exchange currency. Jesus cited Isa. 56:7 and Jer. 7:11 to back up His cleansing of the temple. Like the Triumphal Entry, this public act aroused the hatred of the religious leaders so that they determined to act as soon as possible.

LUKE 20

The religious leaders wanted to arrest Jesus and condemn Him, but they did not know how to do it successfully during the Passover. The population of Jerusalem nearly tripled during the feast, and

Jesus was popular with the people. It was a volatile situation, and they had to find evidence great enough to convict Him. Judas eventually solved their problem; but meanwhile, the various religious and political parties in Jerusalem tried to get evidence against Him. This chapter tells us how Jesus dealt with these hypocritical religious leaders.

I. He Defended His Authority (20:1-18)

The chief priests, scribes, and elders were the first to attack, using His cleansing of the temple as their weapon. What authority did He have to do such a thing, and who gave Him this authority? When Jesus took them back three years to the ministry of John the Baptist, He was not evading the question; He was bringing them face-to-face with the basic issue of authority. Where did John get his authority? These religious leaders had rejected the authority of John's ministry, so why should they ask about the authority of Jesus' ministry? If they had accepted John, they would have accepted Jesus.

The parable (vv. 9-18) is based on Isa. 5:1-7 and Ps. 80, so the temple leaders knew what Jesus was talking about. For centuries, Israel had been guilty of abusing and even killing the messengers God sent to them; and they would treat the Son of God the same way. Jesus quoted Ps. 118:22 to show them how ignorant they were of the truth of God. They were the "religious experts" in the nation and did not even know when their own Messiah had come! (See Acts 4:11 and 1 Peter 2:7-8.) Verse 18 refers to Daniel 2:34-35 and 44.

II. He Destroyed Their Strategy (20:19-26)

His enemies kept watching Him, looking for an opportunity to catch Him in what He said; but He did not say anything that they could use as evidence to arrest Him. So they tried a new strategy and hoped to "bait Him" into saying something that was criminal. One of the most explosive questions of the day was whether or not Jews should pay the Roman poll tax. If Jesus said no, He would be in trouble with the Romans; but if He said yes, He would be in trouble with the Jews. It was a perfect trap!

But Jesus did not deal with it as a political question. He saw it as a spiritual issue. Just as the coin bore the image of Caesar, so man bears the image of God and has a responsibility to Him. But that also means he has a responsibility to Caesar (human government) because government was instituted by God (Rom. 13). It is not an either/or situation, but both/and. Even the Prophet Jeremiah counseled the people to cooperate with officials and seek to be peacemakers (Jer. 29:4-7; see 1 Peter 2:9-17 and 3:8-17). Our Lord's answer silenced His enemies.

III. He Demolished Their Theology (20:27-38)

The Sadducees thought they could trap Him with a theological question. They did not believe in the spirit world or in the resurrection of the dead (Acts 4:1-2; 5:17; 23:8), so they posed a hypothetical question based on the Jewish law of levirite marriage (Deut. 25:5-10). If a woman has seven husbands, which one will be her husband in the resurrection?

Jesus demolished their argument by pointing out that there is no need for marriage in the next life because there can be no death. If people cannot die, there is no need to get married and have children who will keep the population going! "Equal to the angels" (v. 36) does not mean that God's people become angels, for we are much higher than the angels in that we shall be like Christ (1 John 3:1-2). We shall be "equal to the angels" only in the matter of marriage, for angels do not marry and have families.

But Jesus took the argument a step further and showed the folly of their denial of spirits and the resurrection of the human body. He referred to Ex. 3, especially verses 6 and 15-16, to show that the patriarchs were then alive when God spoke to Moses. God did not say, "I was the God . . ." but "I am the God. . . ." A continuation of life after death implies a future resurrection; for God had made covenant promises to Abraham, Isaac, and Jacob that included future blessings. Would He give these blessings to disembodied spirits? Salvation is for the whole person, not just the spirit (1 Thes. 5:23); and this includes the body. While the doctrine of the resurrection of the body is not taught clearly in the OT Scriptures, the teaching is nevertheless there (Job 19:25-27; Ps. 16:9-10 and 17:15; Dan. 12:2). The full light on this doctrine came with the ministry of Christ (2 Tim. 1:10; John 11:25-26).

IV. He Declared His Deity (20:39-44)

Now it was time for Jesus to ask questions, and He focused on an accepted messianic psalm, Ps. 110. The scribes taught that Messiah was the Son of David, a title that was often ascribed to Jesus (Matt. 9:27; 15:22; 21:9). But in Ps. 110:1, David called the Messiah his Lord. How can Messiah be both the Lord of David and the son of David?

The answer, of course, is in the incarnation. Messiah is David's Lord because He is God, but He is David's son because He became man and was born into David's family. (See Rom. 1:3, Acts 2:32-36 and 13:22-23.) Jesus is both "the root and offspring of David" (Rev. 22:16). As the "root of David," He brought David into existence; but as the "offspring of David," David brought Him into the world (2 Sam. 7:13-14; Isa. 11:1).

V. He Denounced Their Hypocrisy (20:45-47)

Jesus moved from doctrine to practice and publicly exposed the hypocrisy of the religious leaders (see Matt. 23). In their garments, their desire for greetings and compliments, and their quest for prominent places, they proved themselves to be anything but servants. They used religion to rob the needy and keep the money for themselves. God is seeking servants, not celebrities; He sees the heart.

LUKE 21

Our Lord not only taught and healed in the temple, but He also watched the worshipers. He sees what we give and why we give, and He knows those who are giving God their best. He is interested in the proportion, not the portion—how much is left and not how much is given.

Jesus was not impressed with the beauty of the temple, for He knew that it was a "den of thieves" (19:46) that had been left desolate by God (Matt. 23:38). When He announced that the temple was destined to be destroyed, four of His disciples asked for details about this event. "Tell us, when will these things be?" (Mark 13:3-4, NKJV) This is Luke's version of the Olivet Discourse, found also in Matt. 24–25 and Mark 13.

I. Encouragements (21:8-9)

Since he was writing especially for Gentiles, Luke did not include all the prophetic details that relate particularly to the nation of

Israel. Jesus told His disciples that difficult times lay ahead of the church, but that they should heed His Word and not be led astray by deceivers. Neither should they be frightened by national, international, and natural calamities, or give up when persecution becomes intense. Times of tribulation can be times of testimony, and the Spirit would give them the wisdom and words that they needed. Because they know what will happen, they can be ready to meet it.

While our Lord was referring primarily to the ministry of the apostles in their day, as well as the ministry of believers during the tribulation period, these encouragements speak to all of God's people in every age. We must beware of deception and fear and trust the Spirit to empower us.

II. Admonitions (21:20-24)

In this paragraph, Jesus prepared His people for the fall of Jerusalem, which took place in A.D. 70. He admonished the people to get out of Jerusalem and Judea, and those who heeded His Word were spared. "The times of the Gentiles" refers to the period when the Gentiles would overrun Jerusalem and be in control. "The times of the Gentiles" began with the captivity of Jerusalem by the Babylonians in 606–586 B.C. (2 Chron. 36), and it will end when Jesus Christ returns to earth and delivers the city (Zech. 13–14).

III. Signs (21:25-33)

Jesus teaches what will happen in the last half of the Tribulation period, just before He appears in glory and returns to the earth. The last half of the Tribulation will be a very distressing time, with great judgments from heaven and great distresses on the earth (Rev. 13–19). Believers will find great encouragement from the signs that point to His coming, and they will look up expectantly as they await His return. We must not confuse this event with His coming for the church (1 Thes. 4:13-18), for that can occur at any moment. We are not looking for signs; we are looking for the Savior (Phil. 3:19-20).

However, since "coming events cast their shadows before," when we see these things "begin to come to pass" (paraphrase mine), we know that His coming will be soon. The budding of the fig tree has been interpreted as a symbol of the restoration of the nation of Israel. The phrase "and all the trees" (v. 29) may indicate the growth of nationalism among the nations of the world. In recent years, we have certainly seen a tremendous increase in nationalism.

"This generation" refers to the generation alive when all these things take place. God will preserve His people Israel and see them through their sufferings so that they can enter into their glorious kingdom.

IV. Dangers (21:34-38)

In view of the fact that the Lord Jesus could return at any moment, it behooves us as His people to be ready when He comes. We must beware of worldliness and the cares of this life. While we must not ignore our daily duties, we must be careful to live in the light of eternity. By reminding ourselves daily that Jesus may return before the day ends, we will walk carefully so that we will not be caught unprepared when He comes (1 John 2:28).

LUKE 22

I. Jesus Demonstrates His Love (22:1-20)

The enmity against Jesus that first revealed itself in the synagogue in Nazareth (4:28) and then infected the religious leaders (6:11; 11:15, 53-54; 19:47-48; 20:19) was now to reveal itself in the official condemnation of the Son of God. But how could they arrest such a popular rabbi during the Passover when the crowds might cause a riot? Judas solved their problem by turning traitor and promising to deliver Jesus to them without creating a scene.

While Judas was bargaining for money, Peter and John were making arrangements in the Upper Room for the celebration of the Passover (see Ex. 12). Judas was probably not informed beforehand lest he arrange to have the temple guard come there to arrest Jesus. It was unusual for a man to carry a pitcher of water since that was the job of the women; so it was not difficult for the disciples to find their man.

The traditional Passover feast began with a thanksgiving, which was followed by the first cup of wine. They then ate some bread dipped in the bitter herbs, sang Pss. 113–114 and drank the second cup. This was followed by the eating of the roasted lamb and the bread, the drinking of the third cup, and the singing of Pss. 115–118. The feast ended with the drinking of the fourth cup (v. 17).

It was then that Jesus gave new meaning to the bread and the wine and instituted the Lord's Supper (1 Cor. 11:23-26).

The Passover feast looked back to Israel's deliverance from Egypt, while the Lord's Supper looks back to Christ's death on the cross and ahead to His coming again ("til He come"—v. 18). Jesus saw a future fulfillment of the feast when His people would be gathered together in His glorious kingdom (vv. 16, 18, 29-30). Jesus is the Passover Lamb (John 1:29; 1 Peter 1:18-21) who died, not only for the sins of a nation but for the sins of the world. Both the Passover and the Lord's Supper were demonstrations of His love for a lost world.

II. Jesus Shares His Counsel (22:21-38)

A. About greatness (vv. 21-30).

When Jesus announced that His betrayer was at the table, the Twelve gave two responses: they each asked, "It is not I, is it?" (expecting a negative reply), and then they debated among themselves who was the greatest! Our Lord did not tell His disciples who the traitor was; in fact, in love, Jesus protected Judas to the very end. He washed Judas' feet, warned him, and gave him every opportunity to repent. We must never think that Judas was forced into betraying Jesus just because it was predicted in the Psalms (41:9; 55:12-14; 69:25; 109:8; and see Acts 1:15-20). It was Judas' own decision to sell Jesus for thirty pieces of silver; he alone bore the responsibility.

Why would the disciples be arguing over who was the greatest when Jesus had just washed their feet (John 13:1ff) and talked about His suffering and death? Perhaps it grew out of the order of seating at the table, for Judas was in the place of honor at our Lord's left and John was at His right. Or maybe the presence of an unknown traitor made them think they had to prove their loyalty to the Lord, and this could have led to their comparing one with another.

Whatever the reason, their attitude was that of the world, where competition and authority are important to success. In the kingdom of God, greatness is measured by how many you serve, not how many serve you. Jesus is the model for our ministry, and He was a servant (Phil. 2:1ff). The Lord assured them that the greatest glory was yet to come (vv. 29-30), so why settle for the transient glory of this world?

B. About Satan (vv. 31-34).

The "you" in v. 31 is plural; Satan wanted to have all the disciples to sift them. All of them would forsake Him and flee, and Peter would deny Him three times; yet Jesus prayed especially for Peter, that he would encourage the other disciples. "Converted" simply means "turned around" and refers to Peter's repentance and restoration to ministry (John 21). There is no doubt that Peter was a courageous man, but he would fail just the same because of his self-confidence. Had he heeded the Lord's warning, he would have spared himself a great deal of sorrow and shame.

C. About the future (vv. 35-38).

Verse 35 refers to their ministry described in Luke 9, a ministry that would not be repeated in exactly the same way now that Jesus was going to leave them and return to heaven. The disciples would face an entirely new set of circumstances and would need a new outlook. Jesus quoted Isa. 53:12 to show them that He would be treated like a criminal and that people would treat His followers the same way. What He said about the sword was only a metaphor for the dangers they faced, but the men took it literally. In fact, Peter used his sword in the garden (vv. 50-51).

III. Jesus Yields His Will (22:39-53)

The disciples were accustomed to praying with Jesus in the garden, and Judas knew the place well (John 18:2). Jesus could have taken the men to some other site, but He was not trying to avoid arrest. He was surrendered to the Father's will. As He faced the sufferings that lay ahead, especially being made a sacrifice for sin (2 Cor. 5:21), His holy soul was troubled to the depths. He did not pray in order to discover the Father's will or try to change it, but to be surrendered to it.

The three disciples with Him in the inner place of prayer (Mark 14:33) did not give Him the encouragement and strength He needed from His friends. Instead, they went to sleep—and Peter had boasted that he would die for Christ!

The healing of the slave's ear was our Lord's last miracle before the cross. Peter's rash action got him into trouble later (John 18:25-27). In healing Malchus, Jesus was practicing what He had preached to others (Matt. 5:38-48) and giving us an example of love and forgiveness. Peter would discover that "the sword of the

Spirit" is a much better weapon (Eph. 6:17; Heb. 4:12).

IV. Jesus Experiences His Sufferings (22:54-71)

A. In Peter's denial (vv. 54-62).

Those who criticize Peter for following "afar off" should remember that Jesus warned Peter not to follow at all (Matt. 26:31; John 18:8-9). Had Peter obeyed, he would not have walked into temptation. Peter lingered at the fire and sat down with the enemy, and ended up denying the Lord three times (Ps. 1:1). It grieved Jesus deeply to have Peter deny Him at the very time He was giving witness before His accusers. The Savior's loving look and the crowing of the cock (Mark 14:30) brought Peter to repentance.

B. In the soldiers' mockery (vv. 63-65).

Jesus had not been declared guilty, yet the soldiers mocked Him and beat Him. If a prisoner today were treated that way, the soldiers would be court-martialed. Jesus quietly took their brutality, and the heavens were silent (Matt. 26:52-53).

C. In the council's blindness (vv. 66-71).

Jesus was first taken to Annas, the former high priest (John 18:13), and then to Caiaphas, son-in-law to Annas, where the Jewish religious council (Sanhedrin) had assembled. The council was not allowed to pass judgment on such cases at night, so they met again early the next morning (Matt. 27:1). Having officially condemned Jesus, they led Him to Pilate (23:1-5), who sent Him to Herod Antipas (23:6-12), who in turn sent Him back to Pilate (23:13ff). The Jewish council was blind to their own Scriptures and deaf to the Word that Jesus had taught for three years.

By claiming to sit at God's right hand, Jesus was affirming that He was indeed the Son of God, the Messiah (Ps. 110:1; Dan. 7:13-14; see Acts 2:34 and 5:31).

LUKE 23

I. Jesus Presents No Defense (23:1-25)

The Jewish trial focused on the religious issue (blasphemy); but when the Jews sent Jesus to Pilate, it was the political issue they stressed ("He stirs up the people"). Pilate tried to send Jesus back to the Sanhedrin (John 18:31), but his ploy did not work. The chief priests and scribes insisted that the Roman governor ratify their decision. Pilate said he found no grounds for condemning Jesus, and this made the Jewish leaders even more vehement in their attempt to kill Jesus.

Always ready for another escape route, Pilate sent Jesus to Herod, since Jesus came from Herod's jurisdiction; but even this did not work. Herod had long wanted to meet Jesus (9:7-9), hoping to see Him do a miracle; but when the two finally met, Jesus did and said nothing. By killing John the Baptist, Herod had silenced the voice of God. Our Lord endured great humiliation at the hands of His enemies, but He bore it courageously (Isa. 53:7; 1 Peter 2:21-23).

Pilate tried a third escape when Jesus came back to him: he offered to beat Jesus and let Him go, since it was customary to release one prisoner at Passover season. Incited by the chief priests (v. 23; Mark 15:11), the crowd asked that Barabbas be released, and Pilate finally gave in. The job of a Roman governor was to see that justice was done, and yet Pilate gave in to the crowd after affirming three times that Jesus was innocent! Jesus "witnessed a good confession" before Pilate (1 Tim. 6:13), but Pilate would not accept the truth (John 18:33-39).

II. Jesus Asks No Sympathy (23:26-32)

It was required that the condemned criminal carry the cross to the place of execution. Jesus did so at the beginning of the journey (John 19:17) but could not continue, probably due to weakness from all He had suffered that night. Wanting to hasten the execution, the soldiers drafted Simon to carry the cross for Him (Matt. 5:41). It was an humiliating experience for this Jew from Cyrene who had come to Jerusalem for the feast (Acts 2:10), but it may have led to his conversion and the conversion of his family (Mark 15:21; Rom. 16:13). Simon Peter had offered to go to prison and death with Jesus (Luke 22:33), but it was another Simon who went with Jesus to Calvary.

Some of the people in Jerusalem who loved Jesus bewailed His plight, but He cautioned them not to weep for Him. Too often in our preaching and teaching, we so emphasize the physical aspects of our Lord's sufferings that we forget the spiritual agony that He endured on the cross in being separated from His Father. As Jesus looked to the future, He saw glory for Himself (Heb. 12:2) but judgment for the Jewish nation. Too much "religious devotion" is only sentimental emotion that is shallow and transient. Jesus wants us to share "the fellowship of His sufferings" (Phil. 3:10) and not try to duplicate the feelings of His sufferings.

III. Jesus Manifests No Resentment (23:33-49)

Crucifixion is perhaps the most humiliating and painful form of execution ever devised, yet Jesus offered no resistance and manifested no resentment. He even prayed for those responsible for His death (v. 34). His prayer did not automatically secure personal forgiveness for His enemies, but it did hold back the wrath of God for nearly forty years, thus giving the nation time to repent. Alas, they did not receive the Word and even committed another murder when they stoned Stephen (Acts 7).

In fulfillment of Isa. 53:12, He was crucified with two criminals, and He interceded for the transgressors. The mockery fulfilled Ps. 22:6-8, and the offer of the drink Ps. 69:21. The light and darkness remind us of Ps. 22:1-2, and the cry in v. 46 fulfills Ps. 31:5.

Luke is the only Gospel writer who records the conversation between Christ and the thief. How did the thief know Jesus had a kingdom? Probably from the official plaque hanging over His head (v. 38). How did he know that Jesus could save him? He heard the mockers cry, "He saved others!" (v. 35) Even the wrath of man can praise God. Our Lord in His compassion brought a thief out of sin and into salvation, and He did it in the nick of time. But we must never use this thief as an excuse for delay in deciding for Christ, for it is likely he was saved at his first opportunity. We have no evidence that he had ever met Jesus before.

The fact that Jesus dismissed His spirit is evidence that He was in full control of the situation (John 10:15, 17-18). The word translated "commend" in v. 46 means "to deposit, to commit for safekeeping." Paul used it in 1 Tim. 1:18 and 2 Tim. 2:2, and Peter in 1 Peter 4:19. This statement, quoted from Ps. 31:5, was used as a Jewish child's bedtime prayer.

IV. Jesus Suffers No Dishonor (23:50-56)

Our Lord's burial fulfilled Isa. 53:12. Condemned criminals lost the right to decent burial, but God had Joseph and Nicodemus (John

19:38-42) ready to care for Christ's body. It is important to the Gospel that we know for sure that Jesus actually died and was buried, for His resurrection depends on the reality of His death and burial (1 Cor. 15:1-11). Since all the members of the Jewish council condemned Jesus (Mark 14:64), and since Joseph had not consented with them, then he was probably not at that meeting to vote. Joseph lived twenty miles from Jerusalem, so he obviously did not prepare the tomb for himself. He was not likely to choose a site so near the place of public execution. He had the tomb and the spices all ready and was on hand the moment Jesus died. He and Nicodemus had searched the Scriptures (John 7:50-53) and learned when the Lamb of God would die, and they were ready. What a service they performed, and what a price they must have paid when the other council members found out what they did!

LUKE 24

I. Confusion (24:1-12)

The women who had lingered at the cross and seen the burial were the first at the tomb when the Sabbath was ended (23:55-56). They were worried about how to open the tomb (Mark 16:1-3), only to discover that the tomb was not only open but empty! The body of Jesus was not there! An angel had come and rolled the stone away (Matt. 28:2). On entering the tomb, they saw two angels (Mark mentions only one—see Mark 16:5) who told them that Jesus was alive and risen from the dead. Had they remembered His words, they would have saved themselves a great deal of sorrow (9:22; Matt. 17:9, 22-23; 20:17-19; John 2:19-22).

The first ambassadors of the resurrection message were the devoted women who were faithful to Jesus. They gave the message to the eleven apostles who did not believe it! Did the apostles think that the women were deceived or delirious? Peter and John ran to examine the evidence (v. 12; John 20:1-18), but this left them bewildered. What a difference it would have made had the believers only remembered and believed His promises!

II. Communion (24:13-32)

Cleopas and his companion were two disappointed men; for in the death of Jesus, all their hopes for Israel had been dashed (note

v. 21 and 1:68; 2:30-32, 38; 21:28, 31). Emmaus was about eight miles northwest of Jerusalem, and they were returning home to decide what to do next. As they walked, they conversed about the recent events and discussed what they might mean. They did the best they could with the limited knowledge they had, but they lacked the key that would unlock the prophetic Scriptures: the Messiah must suffer and die before He could enter into His glory. It was this key that Jesus provided as He walked and talked with them on the road.

These two men were "slow of heart to believe all that the prophets have spoken" (v. 25, paraphrase mine). They believed the promises about Messiah's glory, but they could not accept the prophecies about His suffering (1 Peter 1:8-12). Jesus opened their eyes and hearts to understand all the Scriptures, and this brought a warmth to their hearts (v. 32). They saw Messiah in the Word, but they did not realize He was walking with them! It was not until He blessed their simple meal that Jesus revealed Himself to them personally. What a revelation! It transformed them from discouraged pilgrims into enthusiastic witnesses!

III. Confirmation (24:33-45)

Excited about their good news, the two men rushed back to Jerusalem only to learn that Jesus had appeared to Peter (1 Cor. 15:5; Mark 16:7). We do not know when this meeting took place on that first Easter Day, but it brought Peter back into fellowship with his Lord. Later, Jesus restored Peter to his discipleship (John 21).

Then Jesus Himself appeared in the Upper Room, locked doors notwithstanding (John 20:19-25). Instead of welcoming Him and rejoicing, the believers were terrified, afraid, and troubled; so Jesus assured them that it was He and that He was alive. The wounds (not "scars") on His hands and feet (Ps. 22:16) and in His side (John 20:20) were identification enough. By eating some fish and honey He proved that He was not a phantom. His resurrection body had flesh and bones (v. 39) and yet could appear and vanish and even go through solid closed doors.

During that meeting, Jesus gave them His peace (v. 36), the assurance of His real presence, and a new understanding of the Scriptures (v. 45). During His years with them, He had taught them much from the Word; but now He gave them insight into what the OT said about Him and His redemptive ministry.

IV. Commission (24:46-53)

But the disciples were not to keep their knowledge of the Word to themselves. Starting at Jerusalem, they were to be both preachers (heralds of a message) and witnesses (sharers of an experience) of what the Lord had done for them and said to them (Acts 1:8). But how could this small group of men and women ever hope to reach a whole world with the message of redemption? Only through the power of the Holy Spirit. The early church did not possess the financial and technical resources that we have today, yet they got the job done.

Luke ended his Gospel at the point where his second book — The Acts of the Apostles — begins: the ascension of Christ and the waiting for the coming of the Holy Spirit. Had Jesus not gone back to heaven, the Spirit could not have come (John 16:7-15). Also, Luke's Gospel begins in the temple (1:8ff) and ends in the temple. It begins with Mary and Elizabeth rejoicing and ends with all the believers rejoicing. Before they became Spirit-empowered witnesses, the believers were joyful worshipers, a good example for us to follow.

JOHN

A Suggested Outline of John

Prologue (1:1-18)

I. Period of Consideration (1:19–6:71)

"Mine hour is not yet come." (2:4)

A. Christ and the disciples (1:19–2:12)
B. Christ and the Jews (2:13–3:36)
C. Christ and the Samaritans (4:1-54)
D. Christ and the Jewish leaders (5:1-47)
E. Christ and the multitudes (6:1-71)
Crisis #1: They would not walk with Him (6:66-67)

II. Period of Conflict (7:1–12:50)

(Note how the Jews oppose Christ: 7:1, 19, 23, 30, 32, 44; 8:6, 37, 48, 59; 9:22, 34; 10:20, 31-33, 39; 11:8, 16, 46-57; 12:10.)
"No man laid hands on Him, because His hour was not yet come." (7:30)

A. Conflict over Moses (7:1–8:11)
B. Conflict over Abraham (8:12-59)
C. Conflict over His Sonship (9:1–10:42)
D. Conflict over His power (11:1–12:11)
Crisis #2: They would not believe on Him (12:12-50)

III. Period of Climax (13:1–20:42)

"Jesus knew that His hour was come" (13:1)
"Father, the hour is come." (17:1)

A. Climax of preparation for the cross (13:1–17:26)
B. Climax of unbelief of the Jews (18:1–19:42)
Crisis #3: They crucified Him (19:13-22)
C. Climax of faith for the disciples (20:1-31)

Epilogue (21:1-25)

Introductory Notes to John

I. The Theme of the Gospel

A. Key verses: John 20:30-31.

John's theme is Jesus Christ, the divine Son of God. His book deals with the signs Christ gave during His ministry, signs that prove His deity. These signs were seen by dependable witnesses (His disciples and others) and therefore are trustworthy. John wants men to believe in Jesus Christ as Lord and receive new life through His name.

B. Comparison to the other Gospels.

The first three Gospels are called "The Synoptic Gospels" from a Greek word that means "to see together." Matthew, Mark, and Luke all view the life of Christ in a similar way, each with his own emphasis.

- Matthew pictures Christ as the King of the Jews.
- Mark shows Christ as the Servant, and writes for the Romans.
- Luke views Christ as the Son of Man, writing for the Greeks.
- John presents Christ as the Son of God, and writes for the whole world.

While the first three Gospels deal primarily with the events in Christ's life, John deals with the spiritual meanings of these events. He goes deeper and presents truths that are not emphasized in the other Gospels. For example, all four Gospels record the feeding of the 5,000, but only John gives the great sermon on the Bread of Life (John 6) that explains the meaning of the miracle. This is why John uses the word "sign" instead of "miracle," for a "sign" is a miracle that carries a message with it.

C. Key words.

Note as you read John's Gospel that these words are repeated: life, believe, light and darkness, truth, witness, world, glory, receive, Father, come, eternal and everlasting. These key words summarize the message of the Gospel.

II. Christ in John's Gospel

John emphasizes the Person of Christ as well as His work. He reports several sermons in which Christ talks about Himself and explains His mission. Note too the seven I AM statements of Christ:

- I AM the Bread of life — 6:35, 41, 48, 51
- I AM the Light of the world — 8:12; 9:5
- I AM the Door of the sheep — 10:7, 9
- I AM the Good Shepherd — 10:11, 14
- I AM the Resurrection and the Life — 11:25
- I AM the way, the truth, and the life — 14:6
- I AM the true Vine — 15:1, 5

These names, of course, speak of His deity; for God's name is I AM (see Ex. 3:14). Note these other occasions when Christ uses the I AM to speak of Himself: 4:26; 8:28, 58; 13:19; 18:5-6, 8. As you read this Gospel, you come to realize that Christ is the very Son of God!

III. The Signs in John's Gospel

Out of the many miracles that Christ performed, John selected seven to prove His deity. (The eighth in chapter 21 was for the disciples alone and forms a postlude to the Gospel.) These seven signs are given in a specific order (note 4:54, "This is again the second miracle") and forms a picture of salvation. The first three signs show how salvation comes to the sinner:

1. Water into wine (2:1-11) — salvation is by the Word
2. Healing the nobleman's son (4:46-54) — salvation is by faith
3. Healing the paralytic (5:1-9) — salvation is by grace

The last four signs show the results of salvation in the believer:

4. Feeding the 5,000 (6:1-14) — salvation brings satisfaction
5. Stilling the storm (6:16-21) — salvation brings peace
6. Healing the blind man (9:1-7) — salvation brings light
7. Raising of Lazarus (11:38-45) — salvation brings life

Of course, each miracle reveals the deity of Jesus Christ (see 5:20, 36). These signs also served as opportunities for Christ's discourses and interviews. Nicodemus came to Christ because of the signs He had performed (3:2); the healing of the paralytic (5:1-9) led to the discourse in 5:10-47; the feeding of the 5,000 was the basis for the sermon on the Bread of Life in chapter 6; the excommunicating of the healed blind man (9:34) led to the sermon on the Good Shepherd who never casts anyone out (chap. 10).

IV. Faith and Unbelief in John's Gospel

One major theme of John's Gospel is the conflict between faith and unbelief. John begins with rejection on the part of Israel (1:11), finally culminating in the crucifixion. Throughout the book, you see most of the Jews refusing to accept the evidence, growing harder and harder in their unbelief. On the other hand, you also see a small group of people willing to believe on Christ — the disciples, a nobleman and his family, the Samaritans, a paralytic, a blind man, etc. This same situation exists today: the world at large will not believe on Christ, but here and there you find people who see the evidence and accept Him as the Son of God.

You will note in the outline that the Jews begin their controversy with Christ after the miracle in chapter 5, since Christ healed the man on the Sabbath. In chapters 7 through 12, the conflict becomes more severe, and several times they try to arrest and stone Him. The climax comes in chapters 18–19 when they arrest and crucify Him.

There are three crisis events in John's Gospel (see outline): (1) 6:66-71, when the multitudes leave Him after wanting to make Him King; (2) 12:12-50, when the people refuse to believe on Him; and (3) 19:13-22, when they crucify Him. In the first crisis, they want to make Him King, yet they leave Him; in the second, they hail Him as King, yet reject Him; and in the third, they cry out, "We have no King but Caesar" (19:15).

He is the way, but they will not walk with Him; the truth, but they will not believe Him; the life, but they kill Him.

JOHN 1

The theme of John's Gospel is that Jesus is the Son of God (20:30-31), and in this first chapter he proves his claim. As you read this wonderful chapter, you cannot help but see that Christ is God's Son because of the names and titles He bears, the works He performs, and the witnesses who knew Him personally and declare who He is.

I. Christ's Names Prove He Is God's Son

A. He is the Word (1:1-3, 14).

Just as our words reveal our mind and heart, so Christ reveals the mind and heart of God to men. "He who has seen Me has seen the Father" (John 14:9, NKJV). A word is composed of letters; and Christ is the Alpha and Omega (first and last letters of the Gk. alphabet; Rev. 22:13) who spells out God's love to us. In Genesis 1, God created everything through His Word; and Col. 1:16 and 2 Peter 3:5 indicate that this Word was Christ. While God can be known in part through nature and history, He is known in full through His Son (Heb. 1:1-2). Christ as the Word brings grace and truth (1:14 and 17); but if men will not receive Him, this same Word will come in wrath and judgment (Rev. 19:13). The Bible is the written Word of God, and Christ is the living, incarnate Word of God.

B. He is the Light (1:4-13).

God's first creative act in Gen. 1 was producing light, for life comes from light. Jesus is the true light, that is, the original light from which all light has its source. In John's Gospel, you find a conflict between light (God, eternal life) and darkness (Satan, eternal death). This is indicated in 1:5 — "And the light shines [present tense] in the darkness, and the darkness has not been able to put it out or lay hold of it" (literal translation). Note 3:19-21, 8:12, and 12:46. Second Corinthians 4:3-6 pictures salvation as the entrance of light into the dark heart of the sinner (see also Gen. 1:1-3).

C. He is the Son of God (1:15-18, 30-34, 49).

It was this claim that aroused the Jews to persecute Christ (10:30-36). Note the seven persons in John's Gospel who called Christ the Son of God: John the Baptist (1:34); Nathanael (1:49); Peter

211

(6:69); the healed blind man (9:35-38); Martha (11:27); Thomas (20:28); and the Apostle John (20:30-31). The sinner who will not believe that Jesus is God's Son cannot be saved (8:24).

D. He is the Christ (1:19-28, 35-42).

"Christ" means the Messiah, the Anointed One. The Jews were expecting their Messiah to appear, and this is why they questioned John. Even the Samaritans were looking for Him (4:25, 42). Any Jew who said that Jesus was the Christ was thrown out of the synagogue (9:22).

E. He is the Lamb of God (1:29, 35-36).

John's announcement is the answer to Isaac's question, "Where is the lamb for the burnt offering?" (Gen. 22:7). The passover lamb in Ex. 12 and the sacrificial lamb in Isa. 53 point to Christ. There were many lambs slain in Old Testament history, but Christ is the Lamb of God, the unique one. The blood of lambs slain in the tabernacle or temple merely covered sin (Heb. 10:1-4), but Christ's blood takes away sin. The lambs offered in the Old Testament days were for Israel alone, but Christ died for the sins of the whole world.

F. He is the King of Israel (1:43-49).

Israel's people were tired of Roman rule and wanted a king. Because Christ fed them, they wanted to make Him King (6:15), but He left the crowd. He offered Himself as their King (recorded in 12:12-19) but the chief priests said, "We have no king but Caesar!" (19:15)

G. He is the Son of Man (1:50-51).

This title comes from Dan. 7:13-14, and every Jew knew it described God. (Note the Jews' question in John 12:34.) Christ alludes in 1:51 to "Jacob's ladder" in Gen. 28:10-17. Christ is "God's ladder" between earth and heaven, revealing God to men and taking men to God.

II. Christ's Works Prove He Is God's Son

A. He created the world (1:1-4).

He was in the beginning with God and was the divine Agent through whom the world was created.

B. He gives men salvation (1:9-13).

He came to His own world, and His own people (the Jews) received Him not. Salvation is a free gift that the sinner receives when he trusts Christ. "Believing" and "receiving" are the same thing. A new birth then takes place—not from human blood, or by the flesh, or by the will of men, but from God.

C. He reveals God (1:15-18).

Christ reveals God's grace and God's truth. Moses gave the Law that reveals sin and condemns; Christ reveals the truth that redeems. The Law prepared the way for Him.

D. He baptizes with the Spirit (1:33).

We see the Trinity in this chapter: the Father (1:14, 18); the Son (1:14, 18); and the Spirit (1:32-34). The descent of the Spirit identified Christ to John; and we cannot truly see Christ today unless the Spirit opens our eyes.

E. He has intimate knowledge of men (1:42, 47-48).

He knew Peter and Nathanael better than they knew themselves (see 2:23-25). Only God can see the hearts of people.

F. He forgives sin (1:29).
Nobody on earth can take away a person's sin!

G. He opens the way to heaven (1:50-51) and is the way to heaven.

Like Jacob in Gen. 28:10-17, sinners are away from home and in the night of sin. But Christ reveals the glory of heaven and opens it for us to enter in. Christ is God's "staircase to glory."

III. Witnesses Prove That Christ Is God's Son

John uses the word "witness" often in his Gospel (1:7-8, 15; 3:26, 28; 5:31-37; 8:18; 15:27; 18:23). The witnesses of the Bible can be trusted because they had a personal contact with Christ, and they gained nothing from men by witnessing for Christ. (In fact, they suffered for it.) There is no evidence that they lied; their witness would stand in court today. These witnesses are:

A. John the Baptist (1:7, 15, 29; see also 5:35).

B. John the Apostle (1:14, "we beheld His glory ... ")

C. The OT prophets (1:30, 45).

It is likely that Nathanael was reading in the Books of Moses when Philip found him.

D. The Holy Spirit (1:33-34).

E. Andrew (1:41).

He was a soul-winner, and he started at home.

F. Philip (1:45).

Philip backed up his testimony with the Word of God, a wise policy for all witnesses.

G. Nathanael (1:49).

John and Andrew were saved through a preacher, John the Baptist. Peter found Christ because of Andrew's personal work. Philip was called by Christ personally; and Nathanael found Christ through the Word and Philip's testimony. God uses different people and circumstances to bring people to His Son. He is a God of infinite variety.

JOHN 2

Some churches falsely teach that Christ performed miracles when He was a child, but John 2:11 clearly states that the turning of the water into wine was the beginning of His miracles. Keep in mind that John recorded these signs in order to prove that Jesus is God (John 20:30-31) so that people might believe in Him and be saved. We will make a threefold study of this first miracle to learn its dispensational lessons (a picture of Israel's failure), its doctrinal lessons (how the sinner is saved), and its practical lessons (how to serve Christ).

I. The Dispensational Lessons (2:1-12)

The failure of Israel.

Israel was ignorant of its own Messiah. "There stands One among you whom you do not know," said John the Baptist in 1:26. This wedding feast is a picture of the nation: the wine had run out, the people's supply was emptied, yet their Messiah stood there to help them. The six waterpots were used for ceremonial cleansing (see Mark 7:3ff), but the Jewish ceremonies could not help the spiritually bankrupt nation. It was without joy (wine is a symbol of joy in the Bible — see Ps. 104:15 and Jud. 9:13) and without hope. The people had external ceremonies, but they had nothing to satisfy them within.

Christ will one day bring joy again to Israel, when it receives Him as its King. Israel will be wedded again to its God (see Isa. 54 and Hosea 2), and the wine of its joy will run freely and Christ's glory will be revealed (John 2:11). Until that day comes, Christ must say to Israel, "What have I to do with thee?" (John 2:4) The nation has rejected Him, and it will not receive Him until that day when He returns in glory and power.

II. The Doctrinal Lessons

How the sinner is saved. If you refer to your introductory notes on John, you will see that the seven signs show how a sinner is saved and what the results are in his life. This first miracle teaches us that salvation is through the Word of God. Note the symbols here.

A. A thirsty crowd.

Isn't this a picture of the lost world today? They are tasting the world's pleasures but finding no personal satisfaction, and what fulfillment they have eventually runs out. The Bible invites thirsty sinners to come to Christ for salvation and satisfaction (John 4:13-14; 7:37; Isa. 55:1; Rev. 22:17).

B. Empty waterpots.

Representing the human heart, which is hard and empty. The Word of God compares the human being to a vessel (2 Cor. 4:7; 2 Tim. 2:20-21). The sinner's life may look lovely on the outside, but God sees it is empty and useless unless He is able to work a divine miracle.

C. Filled with water.

Water for washing is, in the Bible, an image of the Word of God. (See Eph. 5:26; John 15:3.) All that the servants had to do was fill the empty waterpots with water, which is like the servant of God filling the heart of the unbeliever with the Word. It is not our job to save souls, but it is our job to give people the Word and let Christ perform the miracle of salvation.

D. Water to wine.

When the sinner's heart has been filled with the Word, then Christ can perform the miracle and bring joy. In Acts 8:26-40, Philip filled the Ethiopian with the Word, and when the man believed, the miracle of salvation took place. The Ethiopian went his way rejoicing. Note John 1:17—"The law came through Moses"; in the Old Testament water was changed to blood (Ex. 7:19), which indicates judgment. But Christ turned water into wine, which speaks of grace and joy. Wine symbolizes the Holy Spirit (Eph. 5:18).

E. The third day.

This foreshadows the Resurrection, since Christ arose from the dead on the third day. It was the third day from "the day following" (1:43), which was the fourth of the days John wrote about in chapter 1 (Day #1—vv. 19-28; day #2—vv. 29-34; day #3—vv. 35-42; day #4—vv. 43-51). Perhaps John had Gen. 1 in mind when he wrote of this first week of "a new creation" (2 Cor. 5:17).

F. The beginning of miracles.

Salvation is the beginning of miracles, for after a person is saved, God performs one miracle after another for him; and the miracles we experience bring glory to Christ.

III. The Practical Lessons

A. How to serve Christ.

Mary's words should be heeded by all who would serve Christ: "Whatever He says to you, do it" (2:5). It must have seemed foolish for the servants to fill those waterpots, but God uses the foolish things to confound the mighty (1 Cor. 1:27). If we would see men saved, then we must obey Christ and give men the Word of God. It is not entertainment or recreation that saves souls, but the preaching and teaching of the Word. If we do our part, Christ will do the rest.

The servants knew where the wine came from, but the "important people" at the feast did not. When a person serves Christ, he or she learns His secrets. (See Amos 3:7.) We are Christ's servants and His friends (3:29; 15:15), and He tells us what He is doing. It is better to be a humble servant of Christ and share in His miracles than to sit at the head table at the greatest feast.

We should use every opportunity to serve Christ, "in season and out of season." Jesus brought glory to God at a wedding feast.

JOHN 3

This is perhaps the most important chapter in John's Gospel, for it deals with the subject of the new birth. Some religious groups have so confused this subject that many average church members, let alone religious leaders like Nicodemus, have no idea what it means to be born again.

I. The Necessity for the New Birth (3:1-51)

A. It is necessary to see (experience) the kingdom of God (v. 3).

Nicodemus was a moral, religious man, one of the chief teachers (rulers) of the Jews, yet he did not understand the truth about the new birth. Spiritual truths cannot be grasped by the carnal mind of sinful man (see 1 Cor. 2:10-14). Nicodemus came "by night," a symbol of the unsaved man; he is "in the dark" spiritually (see Eph. 4:18 and 2 Cor. 4:3-6). Being religious and moral does not make a man fit for heaven; he must be born again, that is, born from above.

Nicodemus confused the spiritual and the physical (see v. 4). He thought in terms of physical birth, while Christ was talking about a spiritual birth. All of us are born in sin. Our "first birth" makes us children of Adam, and this means we are children of wrath and of disobedience (Eph. 2:1-3). No amount of education, religion, or discipline can change the old nature; we must receive a new nature from God.

B. It is necessary to enter the kingdom of God (v. 5).

By "the kingdom of God" Jesus did not mean an earthly political kingdom. Paul described the kingdom of God in Rom. 14:17. When a sinner trusts Christ, he or she enters God's kingdom and family. Like most of his Jewish friends, Nicodemus thought that being born a Jew, and living according to the Law, would satisfy God (see Matt. 3:7-12; John 8:33-39). Ever since Adam's sin in Gen. 3, all men have been born outside paradise. Only by being born again can we enter the kingdom of God.

II. The Nature of the New Birth (3:6-13)

A. The new birth is a spiritual birth (vv. 6-7).

That which is born of the flesh (the old nature) is flesh, always will be flesh, and is under the wrath of God. That which is born of the Spirit (the new nature discussed in 2 Peter 1:4) is Spirit and is eternal. You cannot produce a spiritual birth with physical means. This is why "born of water" in v. 5 cannot mean literal water, for baptism would mean applying a physical substance (water) to the physical being. This action could never bring about a spiritual birth. (Read again John 1:11-13 and 6:63.) "Born of water" does not refer to water baptism, for in the Bible baptism speaks of death, not birth (Rom. 6:1ff). If baptism is essential for salvation, then nobody in the OT was ever saved, for there was no baptism under the Law. The great saints named in Heb. 11 were all saved by faith. Salvation is not of works (Eph. 2:8-10), and baptism is a human work. Christ came to save, yet He did not baptize (John 4:2). If baptism is necessary for eternal life, why did Paul rejoice because he had not baptized more people? (1 Cor. 1:13-17)

The new birth can only be produced by spiritual means. What are these means? The Spirit of God (John 3:6 and 6:63), and the Word of God (1 Peter 1:23; James 1:18). The "water" in v. 5 refers to physical birth (every baby is "born of water"), the thing Nicodemus mentioned in v. 4. A person is born again when the Spirit of God uses the Word of God to produce faith and impart the new nature when the person believes. The Spirit usually uses a believer to give the Word to another person (see 1 Cor. 4:15), but only the Spirit can impart life.

B. It is a mysterious birth (vv. 8-10).

No one can explain the wind, and no one can explain the working of the Spirit. Both the Spirit and the believer are like the wind. Nicodemus, instructed in the Law, should have known the truth of the renewing work of the Spirit. See Ezek. 37.

C. It is a real birth (vv. 11-13).

Many things are mysterious but still real. Jesus assures Nicodemus that the new birth is not a fantasy, it is a reality. If a person will but believe Christ's words and receive Him, he or she will discover how real and wonderful the new birth is.

III. The Basis for the New Birth (3:14-21)

A. Christ had to die (vv. 14-17).

Christ again refers Nicodemus to the OT, this time Num. 21, the account of the brazen serpent. The serpents were biting the Jews and killing them, and the strange solution to the problem was found when Moses made a serpent of brass! Looking to the serpent in faith brought healing. In like manner, Christ was made sin for us, for it was sin that was killing us. As we look to Christ by faith, we are saved. Brass symbolizes judgment, and Christ experienced our judgment when He was lifted up on the cross. Christ had to die before men could be born again; His death brings life. What a paradox!

B. Sinners have to believe (vv. 18-21).

Faith in Christ is the only means of salvation. God's command to Moses in Num. 21 was not that he kill the snakes, make a salve for the wounds, or try to protect the Jews from being bitten. It was that he lift up the brazen serpent and tell men to look by faith. Not to look meant condemnation; faith meant salvation. John here goes back to 1:4-13, the symbolism of light and life, darkness and death. Sinners not only live in darkness, but they love the darkness, and refuse to come to the light where their sins will be exposed and can be forgiven.

IV. The Confusion about the New Birth (3:22-36)

Verse 25 can be translated: "There arose a question between some of John's disciples and *a Jew* concerning ceremonial purification" (emphasis mine). Could this Jew have been Nicodemus, still searching after truth? Like many people today, Nicodemus was confused about baptism and religious ceremonies. Perhaps he thought "born of water" meant baptism or some Jewish purification rite. Note how John the Baptist pointed this Jew to Christ. If baptism were necessary for salvation, then this is the place for the Bible to say so; but nothing is said. Instead, the emphasis is on believing (v. 36).

It is evident that Nicodemus came "out of the dark" and finally became a born-again Christian. Here in John 3, we see Nicodemus in the darkness of confusion; in John 7:45-53, we see him in the dawn of conviction, willing to give Christ a fair hearing; and in John 19:38-42, we see Nicodemus in the daylight of confession, openly identifying himself with Christ.

JOHN 4

There are two sections in this chapter: (1) Christ's ministry to the Samaritan woman (4:1-42); and (2) Christ's miracle for the nobleman (4:43-54). In one sense, both experiences involved miracles; for the transformation of this sinful woman was as wonderful as the "long-distance" healing of the nobleman's son.

I. Christ's Ministry to the Samaritan Woman (4:1-43)

The Samaritans were "half-breeds," part Jew and part Gentile. As such, they were considered outcasts and were despised by the Jews. They had their own religious system in Samaria that competed with the claims of the Jews (see 4:20-24) and believed in the coming of the Messiah (4:25). Jesus "needed to go through Samaria" (v. 4) because God had planned for this sinful woman to meet Him and find in Him the water of life. In the interview recorded, we see the different stages by which this woman came to believe in Christ.

A. "You, being a Jew" (vv. 1-9, NKJV).

For a Jewish rabbi to ask a favor of any woman, especially a Samaritan, was surprising to her. She was aware of nothing more about Jesus than that He was a thirsty Jew. The sinner is blind to Christ and is more interested in the affairs of life (like getting water) than in the things of eternity.

B. "Are you greater than our father Jacob?" (vv. 10-15, NKJV)

In v. 10, Jesus tells her that she is ignorant of two things: the gift of God (salvation) and the identity of the Savior in her presence. Jesus speaks of living water—water of life—but she takes this to mean literal water. How typical of the sinner, confusing the physical and the spiritual! Nicodemus thought Christ spoke of physical birth (3:4), and even the disciples thought He spoke of literal food later on (4:31-34). Jesus points out to her that the things of the world do not satisfy, and men without Christ will always "thirst again." The parable in Luke 16:19-31 makes this so clear; the rich man who thirsted after physical pleasures in this life thirsted again when he found himself in Hades. Jesus promises that the water of life will spring up within the heart and keep us constantly refreshed and satisfied: and the woman, still confused, asked for that water. It was a shallow emotional response.

C. "You are a prophet!" (vv. 16-24, NKJV)

Having expressed interest in the living water (even though confused), the woman found herself confronted with her sins. Christ's command, "Go, call your husband!" (NKJV) was for the purpose of quickening her conscience and forcing her to face her own sin. No person can ever be saved who hides his sins. (See Prov. 28:13.) Note how the woman tried to change the topic of conversation! Like convicted sinners today, she began to argue about differences in religion! "Where should we worship?" "Which religion is right?" Jesus pointed out that the important thing is knowing the Father, and this can be done only through salvation, and salvation is of the Jews. He has now brought her face-to-face with her sins, her desire for satisfaction, and the emptiness of her own religious faith.

D. "This is indeed the Christ!" (vv. 25-42)

Her eyes are now opened to the Person of Christ, and on the authority of His Word, she trusts Him and is saved. She proves her faith by giving public testimony to the people in the town (and they certainly knew her character); and they too came to trust Him. Note the final testimony of these believers, "This is indeed the Savior of the world!" It is interesting to note the disciples' behavior in this chapter. They are more concerned about physical food than spiritual food. Christ was weary (v. 6) and thirsty, and certainly hungry; but He put spiritual matters above physical comfort. While the disciples were out buying food (a good thing), Christ was winning souls (a far better thing). The disciples, on coming to Samaria, had probably said, "We can never win anyone here. These people are hard-hearted and enemies of our people." But Christ told them to look on the fields that were white to harvest. He reminded them that all of God's people must work together in the harvest field, some to sow, others to reap. It is God who gives the increase (1 Cor. 3:5-9).

We might note the example Christ sets as a soul-winner. He did not allow personal prejudices or physical needs to hinder Him. He met this woman in a friendly way and did not force her into a decision. Wisely, He guided the conversation and allowed the Word to take effect in her heart. He dealt with her privately and lovingly presented the way of salvation. He captured her attention by speaking about something common and at hand — water — and used this as an illustration of eternal life. (Likewise, at the cool midnight hour, He spoke to Nicodemus about wind.) He did not avoid speaking of sin, but brought her face-to-face with her need.

II. Christ's Miracle for the Nobleman (4:43-54)

This is the second of the seven signs in John. These signs show the way a person is saved and the results that follow. (See the introductory notes to John.) The first two signs took place at Cana in Galilee. Turning the water into wine illustrates that salvation is through the Word. The healing of the son in this chapter shows that salvation is by faith.

The son lay dying in Capernaum, about seventeen miles away from Cana. The man wanted Christ to come with him, for he did not believe that He could cure the boy from a distance. (See Martha's similar reaction in John 11:21.) Jesus did not go with the man, but instead spoke the words: "Go your way; your son lives" (NKJV). He believed the Word!

It would have taken the man only three or four hours to get back home, yet v. 52 ("yesterday") indicates that he remained in Cana an entire day. The boy had been cured at 1:00 in the afternoon, and the next day the father arrived home. This proves he had real faith in Christ's word, for he did not rush home to see what happened. This is the way we are saved — by putting our faith in the Word of God. "Christ says it, I believe it, that settles it!" The nobleman apparently stayed in Cana, took care of some business, and then went home the next day. He had "joy and peace in believing" (Rom. 15:13) because his trust was in Christ's word alone. He was not surprised when his servants told him, "Your son lives!" He merely asked them when the cure took place and verified that it was the very hour that Christ spoke the word. The result: his whole family trusted Christ. "Faith comes by hearing, and hearing by the Word of God" (Rom. 10:17, NKJV).

Jesus in v. 48 gives the basic reason why people will not believe:

they want to see signs and experience wonders. Keep in mind that Satan is able to perform signs and wonders to deceive (2 Thes. 2:9-10). If your salvation is based on feelings, dreams, visions, voices, or any other fleshly evidence, then you are on dangerous ground. It is faith in the Word alone that gives us the assurance of eternal life. (See 1 John 5:9-13.)

JOHN 5

Like several other chapters in John, we have here a message based on a miracle (5:17-47).

I. The Miracle: Salvation Is by Grace (5:1-16)

This sign completes the three miracles that show how a person is saved. The first (water to wine) shows that salvation is through the Word of God. The second (healing the nobleman's son) shows that salvation is by faith. This third miracle demonstrates that salvation is by grace. This man was in a pitiable condition. Because of his past sin (see v. 14) he had been afflicted for thirty-eight years. He was surrounded by afflicted people, all of whom illustrate the sad condition of the unsaved; impotent (without power—Rom. 5:6), blind, halt (unable to walk correctly—Eph. 2:1-3), withered (paralysis), and waiting for something to happen (without hope—Eph. 2:12). If these people could get into the water when the angel came, they could be healed; but they lacked the power to get there! How like the sinner today: if he could keep God's perfect law, he could be saved; but he is unable to do so.

But see the grace of God at work. "Bethesda" (v. 2) means "house of grace," and this is what it became for this one man. What does "grace" mean? It means kindness to those who are undeserving. Jesus saw a multitude of sick people—but He chose only one man and healed him! This man was no more deserving than the others, but God chose him. This is a beautiful picture of salvation, and how it ought to humble us to know that we are chosen "in Him" and not because of our own merits but because of His grace (Eph. 1:4). What Christ says in 5:21 applies here: He quickens (gives life to) whom He will. We cannot explain the grace of God (Rom. 9:14-16), but if it were not for God's grace, nobody would ever be saved (Rom. 11:32-36).

Note several other points: There were five porches, and five in the Bible is the number of grace; and the pool was by the sheep gate, which speaks of sacrifice. The Lamb of God had to die before God's grace could be poured out on sinners. Christ healed him on the Sabbath, thus proving that Law had nothing to do with the cure. We are not saved by keeping the Law. He healed the man by Himself, for salvation is of Christ alone. The man complained, "I have no man" (v. 7), but had a dozen men been there to help him, they could not do what Jesus did. The lost sinner does not need help; he needs healing.

The man went to the temple, probably to worship (Acts 3:1-8), and publicly witnessed that Christ had healed him (v. 15). There is no evidence that this man trusted Christ for salvation.

When Jesus healed on the Sabbath, it was the beginning of the hatred and opposition from the religious leaders. This conflict grew worse and finally led to the crucifixion of Christ.

II. The Message: Christ Is Equal with the Father (5:17-47)

A. Christ's threefold equality with the Father (vv. 17-23).

Healing the man on the Sabbath was contrary to Jewish tradition, so the Jews persecuted Christ as a law-breaker. In the first part of His message, He showed them that He is equal to the Father in three ways:

(1) Equal in works (vv. 17-21). The Father's Sabbath rest was broken in Gen. 3 when Adam and Eve sinned. Since that time, God has been at work seeking and saving the lost. Christ states that the Father enables Him to do what He does and reveals His knowledge to Him personally. His works (miracles) come from the Father, including the miracle of raising the dead.

(2) Equal in judgment (v. 22). God has committed all judgment to the Son. This makes the Son equal with the Father, for only God can judge a man for his sins. See also v. 27.

(3) Equal in honor (v. 23). No mortal man would dare ask men to show him the honor that only God deserves. People who ignore Christ but who claim to worship God are deceived.

B. The threefold resurrection (vv. 24-29)

(1) The resurrection of dead sinners today (vv. 24-27). This is a spiritual resurrection (see Eph. 2:1-3) and takes place when sinners hear the

Word and believe. The man Christ healed was really a living dead man. When he heard the Word and believed, he was given new life in his body. Christ has life in Himself, for Christ is "the Life" (14:6) and therefore can give life to others.

(2) The Resurrection unto life (vv. 28-29a). This is the future resurrection of believers, described in 1 Thes. 4:13-18 and 1 Cor. 15:51-58. The Bible does not teach a "general resurrection" any more than it teaches a "general judgment." This "resurrection of life" is the same as "the first resurrection" in Rev. 20:4-6.

(3) The resurrection of damnation (v. 29b). This is described in Rev. 20:11-15 and takes place just before God makes the new heavens and earth. All who have rejected Christ will be judged, not to see if they get into heaven, but to see what their degree of punishment will be in hell. Hell is called "the second death," separation from God. No Christian will ever stand at the White Throne Judgment (John 5:24).

C. The threefold witness to Christ's deity (vv. 30-47)

(1) John the Baptist (vv. 30-35). The people listened to John and even rejoiced at his ministry, but rejected him and his message. Read 1:15-34 and 3:27-36 to see how John pointed people to Christ.

(2) Christ's works (v. 36). Even Nicodemus admitted that Christ's miracles proved that He came from God (3:2).

(3) The Father in the Word (vv. 37-47). The OT Scriptures are the Father's witness to His Son. The Jews searched the Scriptures, thinking that their studies would save them, but they read with eyes that were spiritually blind. Moses wrote of Christ and would accuse them at the judgment. They refused the Word (v. 38); they would not come to Him (v. 40); they had no love for God (v. 42); they would not receive Him (v. 43); they sought honor from men and not from God (v. 44); and they would not listen to His Word (v. 47). No wonder they could not believe and be saved!

JOHN 6

I. The Signs (6:1-21)

The first three signs illustrate how one is saved through the Word, by faith, and by grace. The fourth sign (feeding the 5,000) shows us that salvation satisfies the inner needs of the heart. Jesus is the Bread of Life. This miracle also reminds us that, while salvation is of the Lord and bestowed only by grace, God still uses human instruments to take the Gospel message to men. Jesus gave the bread and fish to His disciples, and they shared it with the people. "How shall they hear without a preacher?" asks Paul in Rom. 10:14. If, like the little lad in John 6:9, we will give Him our all, He will take it, break it, and use it to bless others. The last four signs in John's Gospel illustrate the results of salvation:

- *Feeding the 5,000 (6:1-14)* — Salvation brings satisfaction
- *Stilling the storm (6:15-21)* — Salvation brings peace
- *Healing the blind man (9:1-7)* — Salvation brings light
- *Raising Lazarus from the dead (11:34-46)* — Salvation brings life

Jesus would not be King to a group of people who were interested only in full stomachs (see v. 26). He dismissed the crowd and sent the disciples across the sea, knowing full well that the storm was coming. How like the church today: we are toiling against Satan's storms, but our Lord is praying for us on the mount and one day will come to bring peace. Note too that the ship miraculously arrived at its destination when Christ came on board. Salvation brings peace to the heart — peace with God (Rom. 5:1) and the peace of God (Phil. 4:4-7).

II. The Sermon (6:22-65)

In vv. 22-31 we have the setting for the sermon. The people, interested in food, have followed Christ over the sea to Capernaum, and they meet in the synagogue (v. 59). He revealed their shallow, carnal motives (vv. 26-27) and their ignorance of what it means to be saved by faith (vv. 28-29). Just as He graciously fed them the bread, and all they had to do was receive it, so He wanted to give them eternal life, but they instead thought they must work for it. The Jews threw out a challenge to Jesus in v. 30: "Show us a sign!" They reminded Him of the way Moses brought bread (manna) from heaven to feed the Jews (see Ex. 16); and Jesus used this as the basis for His sermon. There are three divisions to the sermon, each followed by a reaction from the crowd.

A. He reveals His Person: The Bread of Life (vv. 32-40).

This is a bold claim that He is the very Son of God! The Bread of God is a Person from heaven (v. 33), and He gives life, not just to the Jews (as Moses did) but to the whole world! The way to receive this Bread is to come and take it; and this Bread will give life not only today, but also life in the future at the resurrection. Note the reaction of the Jews (vv. 41-42) who denied His deity. Jesus said that God was His Father (v. 32), but they said Joseph was His father (v. 42). It is interesting to compare the manna to Jesus Christ:

(1) It came from heaven at night; Christ came from heaven when men were in darkness.

(2) It fell on the dew; Christ came, born of the Spirit of God.

(3) It was not defiled by the earth; Christ was sinless, separate from sinners.

(4) It was small, round, and white, suggesting His humility, eternality, and purity.

(5) It was sweet to the taste; Christ is sweet to those who trust Him.

(6) It had to be taken and eaten; Christ must be received and appropriated by faith (1:12-13).

(7) It came as a free gift; Christ is the free gift of God to the world.

(8) There was sufficient for all; Christ is sufficient for all.

(9) If you did not pick it up, you walked on it; if you do not receive Christ, you reject Him and walk on Him (see Heb. 10:26-31).

(10) It was wilderness food; Christ is our food in this pilgrim journey to heaven.

B. He reveals the process of salvation (vv. 43-52).

The lost sinner does not seek God (Rom. 3:11), so salvation must begin with God. How does God draw people to Christ? He uses the Word (v. 45). Read 2 Thes. 2:13-14 carefully for a clear description of what Christ means by "drawing men." To eat earthly bread sustains life for a time, but the person will ultimately die. To receive the spiritual Bread (Christ) gives one eternal life. Christ clearly states in v. 51 that He will give His flesh for the life of the world. The Jews revolted at this (v. 52) because eating human flesh was contrary to Jewish law. Like Nicodemus, they confused the physical with the spiritual.

C. He reveals the power of salvation (vv. 53-65).

What does Jesus mean by "eating" His flesh and "drinking" His blood? He is not speaking in literal terms. In v. 63 He clearly says, "The flesh profits nothing" (NKJV). What gives life? "It is the Spirit who gives life" (v. 63). "The words that I speak to you, they are Spirit, and they are life." In other words, a person eats Christ's flesh and drinks His blood—that is, partakes of Christ and receives Him—by receiving the Word as taught by the Spirit. Christ is not talking about the bread and cup of the Lord's Supper or any other religious rite. The Lord's Supper had not even been instituted, and when it was, Jesus clearly stated that it was a memorial. It did not impart life. To say that a man receives eternal life by eating bread and drinking wine is to deny the grace of God in salvation (Eph. 2:8-9).

Jesus is the Living Word (John 1:1-4), and He was "made flesh" for us (1:14). The Bible is the written Word. Whatever the Bible says about Jesus, it also says about itself. Both are holy (Luke 1:35 and 2 Tim. 3:15); both are Truth (John 14:6; 17:17); both are Light (John 8:12; Ps. 119:105); both give life (John 5:21; Ps. 119:93); both produce the new birth (1 John 5:18; 1 Peter 1:23); both are eternal (Rev. 4:10; 1 Peter 1:23); both are the power of God (1 Cor. 1:24; Rom. 1:16). The conclusion is obvious: when you receive the Word into your heart, you receive Jesus Christ. We "eat His flesh" by partaking of the Word of God. "I am the living Bread," said Jesus in v. 51; and in Matt. 4:4 He said, "Man shall not live by bread alone, but by every word that proceeds from the mouth of God." Peter grasped the meaning of the sermon, for in John 6:68 he said, "To whom shall we go? You have the words of eternal life."

The people were offended at the doctrine (v. 61) and would no longer walk with Christ. This is Crisis #1 in John's Gospel (see the suggested outline of John's Gospel).

III. The Sifting (6:66-71)

It is the Word of God, revealing the Person of Christ, that separates the true from the false. The crowd, desiring bread for the body, rejected the Bread of Life for the soul. Peter and ten of the disciples affirmed their faith in Christ. Their faith came by hearing the Word (Rom. 10:17). Judas, however, was a pretender and ultimately would betray Christ. (Note: the word "disciples" in v. 66 refers, not to the twelve apostles, but to the "followers" in the crowd.)

JOHN 7

We now move into the second section, The Period of Conflict. The Jewish leaders have seen Christ's signs and heard His sermons; now they begin to oppose Him. Check these verses to see their opposition: 7:1, 19, 23, 30, 32, 44; 8:6, 37, 48, 59; 9:22, 34; 10:20, 31-33, 39; 11:8, 16, 46-57; 12:10.

I. Before the Feast: Doubt (7:1-9)

The Feast of Tabernacles was held on the fifteenth day of the seventh month (Sept.-Oct.) and lasted for eight days. (See Lev. 23:34-44; Deut. 16:13-16; Num. 29:12-40.) It was a memorial of the time when Israel lived in booths during their wilderness wanderings. Exodus 23:16 indicates that it was also a harvest festival, one of the three feasts that all male Jews were required to attend annually (Deut. 16:16).

Christ's "brethren" here are His half brothers and half sisters, the children of Mary by Joseph. Jesus was Mary's "firstborn" (Luke 2:7), indicating that she had other children; see also Mark 3:31-35 and Matt. 13:55-56. These brethren are never called "cousins" of the Lord, as some who seek to defend Mary's perpetual virginity teach. Christ's brethren did not believe in Him at this time, although Acts 1:14 would indicate that after His resurrection they did receive Him. Psalm 69:8-9 predicted their unbelief and is another proof of the fact that Mary did bear other children.

Christ lived according to God's schedule for His life. Unsaved people can come and go as they wish, but the child of God must let the Lord lead. How sad that Christ's brethren left the Savior behind so that they might attend a religious feast!

II. In the Midst of the Feast: Debate (7:10-36)

The feeding of the 5,000 and the healing of the paralyzed man (5:1-9, see 7:23) had aroused the interest of the crowd. Because

Jesus healed the man on the Sabbath, the Jews said He was not from God. They called Him demon-possessed (v. 20) and even talked of killing Him; but God's time was not ready (v. 30). The Jews debated five different topics as they discussed Jesus at the feast:

A. His character (vv. 10-13).

Some called Him "good," others said He was a "deceiver." Why were they confused? Because they feared the Jewish leaders. "The fear of man brings a snare," warns Prov. 29:25 (NKJV). Christ's character was so spotless that when they finally did arrest Him, they had to get false witnesses to speak against Him. Pilate, Judas, and even a Roman soldier all pronounced Him faultless.

B. His doctrine (vv. 14-18).

The Jews were amazed at Christ's spiritual knowledge because He had never attended their schools or studied with a rabbi. Education is a blessing, but it is better to be taught by God than to borrow the ideas of men. Christ's doctrine comes from heaven; man's teaching comes from his darkened mind. Paul warns of what is falsely called "knowledge [science]" (1 Tim. 6:20, see also Col. 2:8ff). John 7:17 could be read, "if any man is willing to do My will...." A willingness to obey is the secret of learning God's truth. F.W. Robertson said, "Obedience is the organ of spiritual knowledge."

C. His works (vv. 19-24).

They pretended to defend the Law by accusing Him of working on the Sabbath; but He showed that their desire to kill Him was contrary to the very Law they revered. How inconsistent are people who oppose Christ and reject His Word! A man can be circumcised on the Sabbath, but he cannot be healed on the Sabbath! Like many today, they were shallow, judging by appearance, not truth.

D. His origin (vv. 25-31).

Verse 27 is not a contradiction of v. 42. The Jews knew where the Messiah would be born, but they also knew that His birth would be supernatural (Isa. 7:14). In other words, they would not know where He was from (see v. 28). The record states that Christ was born of the virgin Mary, but the Jews would not believe this. John 8:41 suggests that they accused Jesus of being born in sin; Mary's condition before she married Joseph would perhaps make people say this. In vv. 28-29, Christ affirms that He was sent from the Father and that if they knew the Father, they would know the Son.

E. His warning (vv. 32-36).

The "little while" that Christ spoke of lasted about six months. It is important that people seek the Lord "while He may be found" (Isa. 55:6). Many lost sinners who reject Christ today will seek Him tomorrow and He will be gone from them (Prov. 1:24-28). The Jews were ignorant of spiritual truth and thought He was talking about going to the Jews scattered among the nations. Because they were unwilling to obey the truth, they could not know the truth; they argued with Christ and lost their souls.

III. The Last Day of the Feast: Division (7:37-53)

The seventh day of the feast was a great day of celebration. (The eighth day was one of "solemn assembly" — Lev. 23:36; see Num. 29:35). Each morning of the feast, at the time of the sacrifice, the priests would draw water in a golden vessel from the Pool of Siloam and carry it to the temple to be poured out. This commemorated the wonderful supply of water God gave the Jews in the wilderness. This seventh day was known as "The Great Hosannah" and climaxed the feast. It takes little imagination to grasp what must have happened when Jesus cried out, "If any man thirst, let him come unto Me and drink!" (v. 37) as the priests poured out the water. Christ was the Rock out of which the waters flowed (Ex. 17:1-7; 1 Cor. 10:4). He was smitten on the cross that the Spirit of life might be given to save and satisfy thirsty sinners. In the Bible, water for cleansing symbolizes the Word of God (John 13:1-17; 15:3); water for drinking represents the Spirit of God (John 7:37-38).

Instead of heeding His gracious invitation to come, the people argued, and there was division among them. Some believed in Him, some rejected. (See Matt. 10:31-39 and Luke 12:51-52.) The soldiers could not arrest Him because His word gripped their hearts (v. 46). Because the Jewish leaders rejected Christ, they shut the door of salvation to others who followed their bad example (Matt. 23:13).

Nicodemus enters the picture again, and this time we see him defending Christ's legal privileges. In John 3, he was in the darkness of confusion; but here he is experiencing the dawn of conviction, willing to give Christ a fair chance. Because of this,

Nicodemus learned the truth, for a willingness to obey the Word is the secret of learning God's truth (v. 17). In John 19 we see Nicodemus in the daylight of confession, openly identifying himself with Christ. How did he come to make this decision? He studied the Word and asked for God to teach him. The rulers told him, "Search and look!" and that is just what he did. Anyone who will read and obey the Word of God will move out of darkness into God's marvelous light.

JOHN 8

This chapter shows Christ in conflict with the Jewish leaders and presents a series of important contrasts.

I. Light and Darkness (8:1-20)

The scribes and Pharisees brought this woman to Jesus in the court of the women, in the treasury section of the temple (v. 20). Their motive was to test Him (v. 6) and force Him into a dilemma. If He set the woman free, He violated Moses' law (Lev. 20:10; Deut. 22:22); if He had her stoned, He could not claim to be One who forgives sins. Arthur Pink suggests that Christ wrote on the ground with His finger twice to remind them of the two tablets of the Law, written with the finger of God (Ex. 31:18; 32:15-18; 34:1). The Jews sinned, and Moses broke the first stone tablets on the ground; but God forgave their sin, provided blood sacrifices, and gave them another set of tablets. Christ died for the sins of this woman and was able to forgive her.

The great I AM statement in v. 12 follows this incident. As the Light of the world, Christ claimed to be God, for God is light (1 John 1:5). Darkness speaks of death, ignorance, and sin; light speaks of life, knowledge, and holiness. The light reproves sin (John 3:20). The lost sinner lives in darkness (Eph. 2:1-3; 4:17-19; 5:8) and will spend eternity in darkness (Matt. 25:30) if he rejects Christ. The Jews, instead of submitting to Christ, argued with Him in the temple!

II. Heaven and Earth (8:21-30)

There are two births: from above, being born again by God's Spirit, and from this world, being born of the flesh. And there are two ways to die: the sinner dies in his sins, but the believer dies in the Lord (Rev. 14:13). Faith in Jesus Christ makes the difference.

Jesus told the Jews that He came from heaven; the Father sent Him (v. 26), taught Him (v. 28), and remained with Him (v. 29). The Father forsook His Son only when Christ was made sin for us on the cross. In v. 28, Christ spoke of being "lifted up," which means, of course, crucifixion. He had mentioned this to Nicodemus in 3:14-16, and He would mention it again in 12:32-34.

III. Freedom and Slavery (8:31-40)

The Jews who believed (v. 30) were admonished to prove their faith by their faithfulness. Faith in Christ makes one a child of God, but abiding in the Word and knowing the truth (and living it) makes one a true disciple of the kingdom. Christ is speaking about spiritual, not physical or political, bondage and liberty. The lost sinner is in bondage to lusts and sins (Titus 3:3), to Satan, and to the world (Eph. 2:1-3). By receiving the truth in Christ, slaves are set free!

Jesus' opponents, of course, appealed to their human advantages: "We are Abraham's children!" They said the same thing to John the Baptist (Matt. 3:8-9). Jesus made a distinction between Abraham's fleshly seed (v. 37) and Abraham's spiritual children (v. 39). Paul makes the same distinction in Rom. 2:28-29, 4:9-12, and 9:6, as well as in Gal. 4:22-29.

People reject Jesus because they confuse the physical and the spiritual. Jesus spoke to Nicodemus about a spiritual birth, but he asked about a physical birth (John 3:4). Christ offered the woman at the well eternal life (living water), but she talked about literal physical water (4:15). Salvation is a spiritual experience, and human birth has nothing to do with it.

IV. Children of God and Children of Satan (8:41-47)

The Bible speaks of four different kinds of "spiritual children." We are born by nature children of wrath (Eph. 2:3); when we reach the age of accountability and deliberately sin, we become children of disobedience (Eph. 2:2). When we put faith in Christ, we become the children of God (John 1:12). But the person who finally rejects the Savior and prefers self-righteousness (the devil's substitute) becomes a child of the devil. (See Matt. 13:24-30, 36-43, where the children of the devil are portrayed as counterfeit Christians.) Jesus pointed out the characteristics of the children of the devil:

A. They will not give place to the Word of God (v. 37).

B. They trust in the flesh—human birth, works (v. 39).

C. They hate Christ and seek to kill Him (vv. 40, 44).
Satan is a murderer and his children imitate him.

D. They do not love Christ or the things of Christ (v. 42).

E. They do not understand the Word—blinded by Satan (v. 43).

F. They are liars and love lies more than the truth (v. 44).

G. They will not hear the Word of God; they hate it (v. 47).

Remember, these "children of the devil" were not grossly immoral people; they were self-righteous religious people who rejected Christ. Many people today are deluded by Satan into an outward form of godliness that lacks the power of the Gospel, but these people think they are truly saved and going to heaven.

V. Honor and Dishonor (8:48-59)

God honors His Son, but self-righteous men dishonor Him. They dishonored Him verbally by calling Him a Samaritan and by accusing Him of having a devil. (Samaritans were the scum of the earth to the Jews.) Jesus told them that Abraham saw His day and rejoiced. How did Abraham see Christ's day? By faith (Heb. 11:8-16). He glimpsed at Christ's redemptive work when he offered Isaac on the altar (Gen. 22). God shared many secrets with His friend Abraham because of his faith and obedience (Gen. 18:16-22).

When the bright light of God's Word shines on hearts, men must either accept it and be saved, or reject it and be lost. See how these religious Jews hated Christ and sought to kill Him! This was proof indeed that they were children of Satan, the murderer. Jesus claimed to be Jehovah God when He said, "Before Abraham was, I AM" (see v. 58; also Ex. 3:14). In v. 24, He also said, "For if you do not believe that I am He, you will die in your sins" (NKJV). In v. 28, He said, "When you have lifted up [on the cross] the Son of Man, then you will know that I am" (NIV). Satan's lie is that Jesus Christ is not the Son of God (see 1 John 2:22; 4:1-3). It is impossible to honor God and at the same time dishonor His Son (5:23).

JOHN 9

This chapter presents the sixth of seven special miracles recorded in John's Gospel as witnesses to Christ's deity (20:30-31). The first three signs show how a person is saved: through the Word (water to wine), by faith (healing the nobleman's son), and by grace (healing the impotent man). The last four signs show the results of salvation: satisfaction (feeding the 5,000), peace (stilling the storm), light (healing the blind man), and life (raising Lazarus).

I. The Cure (9:1-7)

A. The man has the characteristics of the lost sinner.

(1) He was blind (Eph. 4:18; John 3:3; 2 Cor. 4:3-6). The unsaved, though intellectual like Nicodemus, can never see or understand spiritual things. See 1 Cor. 2:14-16.

(2) He was begging. The unsaved are poor in God's sight, though perhaps rich in the eyes of the world. They are begging for something to satisfy their deepest needs.

(3) He was helpless. He could not cure himself; others could not cure him.

B. The cure shows how Christ saves a sinner.

(1) He came to the man in grace. Christ could have passed him by, for it was the Sabbath and He was supposed to rest (v. 14). While the disciples argued about the cause of the blindness, Jesus did something for the man.

(2) He irritated the man. A speck of dirt irritates the eye; imagine how cakes of clay must have felt. But the dirt in his eyes encouraged him to go wash. It is just so with the preaching of the Word: it irritates sinners with conviction so that they want to do something about their sins. (See Acts 2:37.)

(3) He cured the man by His power. The man proved his faith in Christ by being obedient to the Word. "Religion" today wants to give men substitutes for salvation, but only Christ can deliver from the darkness of sin and hell.

(4) The cure glorified God. All true conversions are for God's glory alone. See Eph. 1:6, 12, 14; 2:8-10.

(5) The cure was noticed by others. His parents and neighbors saw a

change in his life. So it is when a person is born again—others see the difference it makes (2 Cor. 5:17).

II. The Controversy (9:8-34)

The religious leaders had let it be known that anyone who confessed Christ openly would be cast out of the synagogue (v. 22). This meant, of course, losing friends and family and all the benefits of the Jewish religion. It was this declaration that forced the blind man's parents and neighbors to "beat around the bush" when asked about his amazing cure. The son's simple confession in v. 11 exalted Christ, though at that time he did not fully know who "the man called Jesus" really was. The Pharisees attacked Christ by saying He was not of God (v. 16) and calling Him a sinner (v. 24). The son told what he knew (v. 25) and showed the Pharisees how foolish their thinking was (vv. 30-33). The simple-hearted believer knows more spiritual truth than unsaved educated theologians. (See Ps. 119:97-104.) The final result: they excommunicated the man from the synagogue.

It would have been easy for the son to hide his confession and thus avoid controversy, but he fearlessly stood his ground. He knew what a difference Christ had made in his life, and he could not deny it. Everyone who has met Christ and trusted Him should make it known openly.

III. His Confession (9:35-41)

The man did not realize it then, but the safest place for him was outside the Jewish religious fold. The Jews cast him out, but Christ took him in! Like Paul (see Phil. 3:1-10), this man "lost his religion" but found salvation and went to heaven.

Note carefully how this man grew in his knowledge of Christ:

(1) "A man called Jesus" (v. 11) was all he knew when Christ healed him.

(2) "A prophet" (v. 17) is what the man called Him when the Pharisees questioned him.

(3) "A man of God" (vv. 31-33) is what he concluded Jesus to be.

(4) "The Son of God" (vv. 35-38) was his final and complete confession of faith. (See 20:30-31.)

"The path of the righteous is like the first gleam of dawn, shining ever brighter till the full light of day," states Prov. 4:18

(NIV), and this man's growth in "light" proves it. A Christian is one who has light in his heart (2 Cor. 4:6) and who is a light in the world (Matt. 5:14). He walks in the light (1 John 1) and produces the fruit of light (Eph. 5:8-9). The man's "Lord, I believe!" was the turning point in his life.

The same light that leads one person can blind another (vv. 39-41). The Pharisees admitted that they could see, and therefore they were guilty because they rejected the evidence and would not receive Christ. The Gospel brings about different reactions from different kinds of hearts: the blind sinner receives the truth and sees; the self-righteous religious person rejects the truth and becomes even more blind spiritually. It is a dangerous thing to reject the light.

JOHN 10

The events in the first half of this chapter (vv. 1-21) took place right after the casting out of the man in 9:34, while teachings in the last half (vv. 22-42) took place two or three months later. The entire chapter is tied together by the symbolism of the shepherd and his sheep.

I. The Illustration (10:1-6)

These first six verses are a picture of the relationship between the shepherd and his sheep. Verse 6 calls this a "parable" but a better word is allegory. Christ is merely reminding the people of what shepherds and sheep act like. Later in the chapter He makes a more direct application.

The Middle Eastern sheepfold was very simple: a stone wall, perhaps ten feet high, surrounded it, and an opening served as the door. The shepherds in the village would drive their sheep into the fold at nightfall and leave the porter to stand guard. In the morning each shepherd would call his own sheep, which would recognize their shepherd's voice and come out of the fold. The porter (or one of the shepherds) would sleep at the opening of the fold and actually become "the door." Nothing could enter or leave the fold without passing over the shepherd.

Christ points out that the true shepherd comes through the door (v. 1), calls his sheep by name, which recognize him (v. 3), and leads the sheep, which follow (vv. 4-5). False shepherds and strangers, who are thieves and robbers, try to get into the fold some subtle way, but the sheep will not recognize or follow them.

II. The Explanation (10:7-21)

A. The door (vv. 7-10).

Jesus Christ is the door, and as such He leads the sheep "in and out." The blind man in chapter 9 was "cast out" (excommunicated) by the false shepherds because he trusted Jesus, but he was taken into the new fold by Christ. Theologian Arthur Pink points out that there are really three doors spoken of in this chapter, and we must distinguish them if we are to get the full meaning of this explanation:

(1) "The door into the sheepfold" (v. 1). The sheepfold here is not heaven but the nation of Israel (see Ps. 100). Christ came to Israel through the way appointed in Scripture; the porter (John the Baptist) opened the door for Him.

(2) "The door of the sheep" (v. 7). This is the door that leads people out of their present fold; in this case, Judaism. Christ opened the way for multitudes to leave the old religious system and find new life.

(3) The door of salvation (v. 9). The sheep using this door go in and out, which speaks of liberty; they have eternal life; they enjoy the pastures of God's Word. Satan, through his false teachers (thieves and robbers), wants to steal, kill, and destroy the sheep; but Christ gives abundant life and cares for the sheep.

B. The shepherd (vv. 11-15).

There is a contrast here between the Pharisees (hirelings) who had no concern for the sheep, and Jesus Christ, the Good Shepherd. The hirelings flee and protect themselves when the enemies come; but Christ willingly gives up His life for the sheep. (See Acts 20:29.) Christ as the Good Shepherd gives His life on the cross (Ps. 22); as the Great Shepherd, He cares for the sheep (Heb. 13:20 and Ps. 23); and as the Chief Shepherd He will come again in glory for His sheep (Ps. 24 and 1 Peter 5:4). In v. 18 He speaks of both His death and His resurrection.

C. The flock (vv. 16-21).

The "other sheep" are the Gentiles, who were not in the Jewish fold. Jesus must bring them, and He will do it through His voice, His Word. This we see happening in Acts 10 when Peter went to the Gentiles and preached the Word; they believed and were saved. Verse 16 can be read, "and there shall be one flock [the church] and one Shepherd [Christ]." The church is made up of Jews and Gentiles who trust Christ, and there is one body, one flock, one common spiritual life (see Eph. 2:11-22; 3:1-13; 4:1-5).

Christ is the Good Shepherd who dies for the sheep. (In the OT the sheep died for the shepherd!) He calls through His Word, and those who believe step through the Door, out of their religious fold, into the true flock of Christ, the church.

III. The Application (10:22-42)

Two or three months later the Jews were still arguing with Jesus about what He said! Christ pointed out to them that they were not "of His sheep" and therefore could not believe. He here gives a beautiful description of true Christians, His sheep:

(1) They hear His voice, which means they hear His Word and respond to it. The unsaved have little or no interest in the Bible; true sheep live in the Word.

(2) They know Christ and are known (vv. 14, 27), so that they will not follow a false shepherd. Church members who run from one religious system to another or one cult to another are proving they are not true sheep.

(3) They follow Christ, which speaks of obedience. No one has a right to claim to be one of Christ's sheep if he or she lives in willful, persistent, open disobedience, and refuses to do something about it. Just as there are false shepherds, so there are goats who try to pass for sheep. One day Christ will say to them, "I never knew you" (Matt. 7:23).

(4) They have eternal life and are secure. Verses 28 and 29 declare the wonderful security true believers have in Christ. We have *eternal* life, not just life "for as long as we don't sin." We are in Christ's care and the Father's hand, a double assurance of eternal preservation for His sheep. We are the Father's gift to the Son, and the Father will not take back a gift. Sheep are a beautiful illustration of

Christians. Sheep are clean animals, and Christians have been cleansed from their sin. Sheep flock together, and so do true believers. Sheep are harmless, and Christians should be blameless and harmless. Sheep are given to wandering—and so are we! Sheep need a shepherd for protection, guidance, and food; and we need Christ for spiritual protection, daily guidance, and spiritual food. Sheep are useful and productive; so are true Christians. Finally, sheep were used for sacrifices; and Christians are willing to yield themselves for Christ as "living sacrifices" (Rom. 12:1).

The Jews proved their unbelief by trying to kill Christ. He refuted them by quoting Ps. 82:6. If Jehovah called earthly judges "gods," then surely He could call Himself the Son of God! Careful never to put Himself in unnecessary danger, Christ left the scene; many came to Him and put their faith in Him. By faith, they stepped through the Door, out of the Jewish religious fold, and into the liberty and eternal life Christ alone can give.

JOHN 11

In this chapter is the seventh of the miracles John recorded. Here we see salvation pictured as resurrection from the dead, the giving of life to the dead. Use your concordance and see how much John has to say about life; he uses the word thirty-six times. Lazarus represents the salvation of the lost sinner in seven ways. Let's take a closer look at each of these.

I. He Was Dead (11:14)

The unsaved person is not just sick; he or she is spiritually dead (Eph. 2:1-3; Col. 2:13). When a person is physically dead, she does not respond to such things as food, temperature, or pain. When a person is spiritually dead, he does not respond to spiritual things. She has no interest in God, the Bible, Christians, or church until the Holy Spirit begins to work in her heart. God warned Adam that disobedience would bring death (Gen. 2:15-17)—physical death (the separation of the soul from the body) and spiritual death (the separation of the soul from God). Revelation 20:14 calls hell the second death, that is eternal death. What sinners dead to God's ways need is not education, medicine, morality, or religion; they need new life in Jesus Christ.

II. He Was Decayed (11:39)

There are three resurrections recorded in the Gospels, apart from that of our Lord Himself. Christ raised a twelve-year-old girl who had died (Luke 8:49-56), a young man who had been dead several hours (Luke 7:11-17), and an older man who had been in the tomb four days (John 11). They present a picture of three different kinds of sinners:

(1) The little girl. Children are sinners, but open corruption has not yet set in.

(2) The young man. Young people are sinners whose outward corruption begins to show.

(3) The older man. Adults are sinners whose definite outward corruption can be seen.

The point is that all three were dead. One person cannot be "more dead" than another. The only difference lay in the degree of decay. Is this not true of sinners today? The moral church member is not "decayed" like the person on skid row, but he is still dead.

III. He Was Raised and Given Life (11:41-44)

The sisters' Jewish friends could only sympathize and weep; it took Christ to give the man life. How did Christ give him life? By the power of His word. This is the way He raised all three dead people mentioned above (see John 5:24 and Eph. 2:1-10). Why did Christ raise Lazarus? Because He loved him (v. 5 and v. 36) and because it brought glory to God (v. 4). This is why He has saved us. We deserve to die and go to hell, but because of His great love, He rescued us. (Read again Eph. 1:3-14 and 2:1-10.)

Keep in mind that salvation is not a set of rules; it is life (John 3:14-21, 36; 5:24; 10:10; 1 John 5:10-13). This life is a Person— Jesus Christ. When dead sinners hear the voice of the Son of God (the Word) and believe, they are given eternal life (John 5:25). To reject that Word is to be dead forever.

IV. He Was Loosed (11:44)

Lazarus was bound hand and foot and so could not free himself. The believer is not to be bound by the graveclothes of the old life, but should walk in the freedom of the new life. Read carefully Col.

3:1-17 to learn how the Christian is to "put off" the graveclothes and "put on" the "grace clothes" of the new life. It is a poor testimony for a Christian to carry with him the things of the old life.

V. He Witnessed to Others (11:45)

In John 11:45 and 12:9-11 and 17, we see that Lazarus caused quite a stir in the area! People saw him and believed in Christ! In fact, he was a walking miracle, just as every Christian ought to be (Rom. 6:4). The great crowd that gathered on Palm Sunday came not only because of Jesus, but also because of Lazarus. In 12:11 we are told that Lazarus was causing people to trust Christ, but this kind of witness is the privilege and duty of every Christian.

VI. He Fellowshipped with Christ (12:1-2)

In looking ahead to 12:1-2 we see Lazarus sitting at the table with Christ, feasting with Him. This is the rightful place for the Christian who has been "raised . . . and made . . . to sit together in heavenly places in Christ Jesus" (Eph. 2:5-6). By spending time with Christ, Lazarus was showing his gratitude for Christ's mercy and love. He learned lessons from His Word and received new power to walk with Christ and to witness. The miracle of salvation gives us eternal life, but we must fellowship with Christ daily to be able to grow in the spiritual life.

It is interesting to note that the entire family at Bethany demonstrates what the Christian life is like. Mary is always found at Jesus' feet, listening to His Word (Luke 10:38-42; John 11:32; 12:3). Martha is a picture of service; she is found busily doing something for Christ. Lazarus speaks of testimony, a daily walk that leads others to Christ. These three practices must be in our Christian experience: worship (Mary), work (Martha), and walk (Lazarus).

VII. He Was Persecuted (12:10-11)

The Jews hated Lazarus because he convinced others of Christ's deity (12:10-11). Many of the chief priests were Sadducees who did not believe in the resurrection, and Lazarus was living proof that the Sadducees were wrong. Had the priests not been overruled by God, they would have put an extra cross on Calvary for Lazarus. ("Yes, and all that desire to live godly in Christ Jesus will suffer persecution"—2 Tim. 3:12 [NKJV].) Satan always fights a living miracle that testifies on God's behalf.

JOHN 12

I. Christ and His Friends (12:1-11)

While the Jewish leaders were plotting to slay Christ (11:53, 57), His friends were honoring Him at a feast in Bethany. Mark 14:3 indicates it was in the home of Simon, apparently a leper whom Jesus had healed. Martha served the meal, but this time she had none of the distraction and frustration she had experienced before. (See Luke 10:38-42.) She had learned the secret of letting Christ control her life. As mentioned previously, Martha represents working for Christ; Mary speaks of worship (in the Gospels, she is always found at Jesus' feet); and Lazarus speaks of our walk and witness.

The ointment Mary used would cost a year's wages for a common laborer. Mary had saved it to anoint Christ and show her love. How much better it is to show love to people before they die! She could have used this ointment on her own brother when he died, but she saved her best for Christ. Whenever a believer shows love to Christ, there is always a critic who will complain. Judas' heart was not right, so his lips spoke the wrong thing. See how Christ (our Advocate—1 John 2:1) defends Mary. "If God be for us, who can be against us?" (See also Zech. 3 where Satan accuses Joshua and the Lord defends him.)

Mary's example of devotion is one we should follow. She gave her best; she gave lavishly; she gave in spite of criticism; she gave lovingly. Christ honored her for her worship (see Mark 14:7) and defended her from Satan's attacks.

II. Jesus and the Gentiles (12:12-36)

At His birth, Gentiles came from the east; now at His death, Gentiles come once again. Why does John mention them at this point? Because the King has now been rejected by Israel. The Jews had said, "We want to see a sign!" (Matt. 12:38, NKJV); but the Gentiles said, "We want to see Jesus!" Philip had a Greek name, so the visitors wanting to see Jesus came to him; and he took the matter to Andrew, who also had a Greek name. (Note: whenever you find Andrew in John's Gospel, he is bringing somebody to Jesus: see 1:40-42, 6:8-9, and 12:22. What an example as a soul-winner!)

Christ mentions the Gentiles when He talks of being "lifted up" on the cross. In Matt. 10:5 and 15:24, Christ had taught His disciples to avoid the Gentiles; but now He says that the Gentiles also will be saved through the cross. Christ is the grain of wheat that must die before there can be fruit and the world given the opportunity to be saved.

Christ had to be lifted up so that "all peoples" (v. 32, NKJV) (Jews and Gentiles) could be drawn to Him. This does not mean all people without exception, but all people regardless of race. Christ again mentions "the hour" (vv. 23, 27). He first referred to it in 2:5; and again it is mentioned in 7:30, 13:1, and 17:1. It is the hour of His death, but He calls it the hour of His glory! Note that Christ invites "anyone" (v. 26). The ground is level at the foot of the cross; neither Jew nor Gentile has any special advantage. "All have sinned . . . there is none righteous" (Rom. 3:23, 10). God has condemned all to be under sin so that He might have mercy on all (Rom. 11:32).

III. Christ and the Jews (12:37-50)

The last words of Christ's public ministry (vv. 35-36) were a terrible warning against letting the opportunity for salvation pass by. Note the climax: "These things Jesus spoke and departed, and was hidden from them" (NKJV). In the verses that follow, the Apostle John explains why Christ hid Himself and why the Jews were condemned.

To begin with, they had rejected the evidence (v. 37). The light had been shining, but they refused to believe and follow the light. Note the terrible results of repeatedly rejecting Christ's Word (vv. 37-41):

(1) They would not believe (v. 37) though they had seen the evidence for His divine Sonship.

(2) They could not believe (v. 39) because their hearts became hard and their eyes blind.

(3) Therefore, God said, "They should not believe" (v. 39) because they had spurned His grace!

Isaiah 53:1 had foretold their unbelief, and Isa. 6:10 their hardness of heart. Note that John 12:40, which quotes Isa. 6:10, states that God blinds the eyes and hardens the hearts of those who persist in rejecting Christ! This verse is found seven times in the Bible, and each time it speaks of judgment: Isa. 6:10; Matt. 13:14; Mark 4:12; Luke 8:10; John 12:40; Acts 28:26; and Rom. 11:8. It is a repeated warning that reminds the unsaved not to take their spiritual opportunities lightly. "While you have light, believe in the light!" (v. 36) "Seek the Lord while He may be found" (Isa. 55:6, NIV).

We have noted before that John presents the conflict between light and darkness. Light symbolizes salvation, holiness, life; darkness stands for condemnation, sin, death. John speaks of four different kinds of darkness:

(1) Mental darkness (John 1:5-8, 26). The minds of sinners are blinded by Satan (2 Cor. 4:3-6), and they cannot see spiritual truths.

(2) Moral darkness (John 3:18-21). The unsaved love sin and hate the light.

(3) Judicial darkness (John 12:35-36). If men don't obey the light, God sends the darkness and Christ hides from them.

(4) Eternal darkness (John 12:46). To "abide" in darkness means to live in hell forever.

In vv. 42-50, John quotes Christ and shows why many people reject the light. Some reject Christ because of the fear of man (vv. 42-43). Rev. 21:8 lists the kind of people who will go to hell, and at the head of the list are the fearful. In v. 48 Christ states that rejecting the Word of God leads to condemnation. Salvation comes through the Word (John 5:24); and the very Bible that men reject today will be part of the evidence against them at the judgment.

This chapter closes John's record of Christ's public ministry. It is a solemn chapter. It reminds us again that we dare not trifle with spiritual opportunities. The light will not always be shining; Christ will some day hide Himself from those who have no concern for His salvation or His Word. Proverbs 1:20-33 is a good warning to heed.

JOHN 13

Contrast 1:11-12 and 12:36 with 13:1 and you will see that we have moved into a new section of John's Gospel. He came "unto His own [world] and His own [people] received Him not." Now He departs from His public ministry to the nation and gathers privately with "His own"—the disciples. Chapters 13 through 16 record Christ's "Upper Room" ministry to the disciples as He prepared them for His death and the work they would do after His ascension. Chapter 13 contains three important lessons for all Christians.

I. A Lesson on Humility (13:1-5)

Jesus' foot-washing was an example of humility and service (v. 15). In Middle Eastern countries, it was the slaves who washed the feet of guests; here Christ took the place of a slave. He makes this clear to His disciples in vv. 13-16: if their Lord and Teacher has washed their feet, then they should wash one another's feet and serve each other in humility. This must have been a striking rebuke to the Twelve, for just that evening they had been debating who was to be the greatest! (See Luke 22:24-27.)

Christ's actions in vv. 1-5 represent what He did when He left heaven to come to earth. He arose from His throne, laid aside the outward expression of His glory, became a servant, and humbled Himself to die on a cross. Philippians 2:5-11 outlines these steps beautifully. After He had completed the work of redemption, He put on His garments and sat down (v. 12), foreshadowing His resurrection, ascension to glory, and enthronement at the Father's right hand.

Peter must have recalled this lesson on humility years later when he wrote 1 Peter 5:5-6. Read these verses carefully. Too many Christians today are fighting for recognition and position and need to recall this lesson in humility. God resists the proud but gives grace to the humble.

II. A Lesson on Holiness (13:6-17)

Christ's words to Peter in v. 8 are important: "If I do not wash you, you have no part [communion] with Me" (NKJV). There is a difference between union and communion. Peter was in union with Christ as one of "His own" through faith, but sin can break our communion with the Lord. There is a difference between sonship and fellowship. Only as we allow Christ to cleanse us can we remain in fellowship with Him and enjoy His presence and power.

In v. 10, Christ makes an important distinction between washing and cleansing. The verse reads literally: "He that has been once-

and-for-all washed all over does not need to do anything more than cleanse his feet." In Eastern lands, people used public baths; as they walked in the dusty streets, their feet became dirty. On arriving home, they did not need another bath; they needed only to wash their feet. So it is with the believer. When we are saved, we are washed all over (1 Cor. 6:9-11; Titus 3:5-6); when we confess our daily sins to the Lord, we have our feet washed and our "walk" is cleansed (1 John 1:7-9).

When the Jewish priests were ordained, they were washed all over (Ex. 29:4), which pictures our once-for-all cleansing; but God also provided the laver (Ex. 30:17-21) for them to use in the daily washing of their hands and feet. Today, Christ is cleansing His church through the water of the Word (Eph. 5:25-26; John 15:3). As we daily read the Word, allow the Spirit to search our hearts (Heb. 4:12), and then confess our sins, we keep our feet clean and walk in the light. (See Ps. 119:9.) It is this daily cleansing that keeps the believer in communion with Christ. The lesson here has nothing to do with "getting" or "losing" one's salvation. It is strictly a matter of communion, fellowship with Christ. Many believers make the same mistake Peter made (v. 9); they want to be saved (washed) all over again when all they need is to have their feet washed.

III. A Lesson on Hypocrisy (13:18-38)

Judas was in the Upper Room, pretending to be Christ's own. In vv. 10-11, Christ made it very clear that He knew one of them was not saved. So successful was Judas' deception that even the other apostles did not realize he was a counterfeit.

Christ first quoted Ps. 41:9 (v. 18) to show that He would be betrayed. Christ had just washed Judas' feet; now Judas would lift up his heel against Christ! Yet Christ's death on the cross would defeat Satan, who was using Judas as his tool (vv. 2, 27). Satan first plants the thought in the heart, then enters into the person to control the life. Christ quoted this verse to the Twelve to keep them from stumbling in unbelief (v. 19). The Christian who knows the Word will not be easily discouraged by the defeats that occur along the way.

In v. 21, Christ openly told the disciples that one of their number would betray Him. Actually, this statement was a final warning to Judas. Christ had washed his feet, quoted the Word to him, and now openly warned him, thus giving Judas every opportunity to change his mind. John, leaning on Jesus' bosom, found out the secret and conveyed it to Peter, but apparently none of the men clearly understood the meaning of the Lord's words (v. 28). It is interesting to note that the Christian who is closest to Christ's heart is the one who discovers His secrets. When Judas accepted the sop, he finally yielded to Satan, who entered into him, making Judas a child of the devil. (See John 8:44.) Like the Holy Spirit, Satan works in and through human bodies and wills that are surrendered to him. "And it was night" (v. 30) — signifying the darkness of Judas' heart — and the fact that this was the hour for the power of darkness (Luke 22:53).

It is a dangerous thing to be a person like Judas. In Mark 14:21 Jesus said, "It were good for that man if he had never been born!" Judas pretended to be a Christian; he played with sin; he put off salvation; and any person who does these things may end up wishing he or she had never been born. There are some mysteries surrounding Judas, but one thing is clear: Judas made a deliberate choice when he betrayed Christ. In John 6:66-71, Christ warned Judas and called him "a devil." Peter thought Judas was saved, for he said, "We believe!" Jesus knew that Judas had never believed and therefore was not saved.

After Judas left the room, Jesus warned Peter about his own approaching testing and failures. Peter was anxious to discover another's sin (v. 24); now he had to face his own sin. "Judge not, that you be not judged" (Matt. 7:1, NKJV). Peter's boast showed his lack of understanding of his own heart. Self-confidence is dangerous in the Christian life. "You shall follow Me afterwards" (v. 36) probably refers to Peter's own death for Christ's sake (John 21:18-19; 2 Peter 1:14).

JOHN 14

Why were the disciples' hearts troubled? Christ had told them He was leaving them (13:33), that one of them was a traitor, and that Peter would fail Him (13:36-38). This undoubtedly disturbed them all, for they looked to Peter as their leader. Jesus Himself had revealed His own inward burden (13:21), although certainly His troubled spirit was in no way like their troubled hearts. In this chapter, Christ sought to comfort the Twelve and quiet their troubled hearts. He gave them five reasons why He had to leave them and go to the Father.

I. To Prepare a Place for Them (14:1-6)

Christ speaks of heaven as a real place, not merely as a state of mind. He pictured heaven as a loving home where the Father dwells. "Mansions" in the Gk. is actually "abiding places," speaking of the permanency of our heavenly home. Heaven is a prepared place for a prepared people. Christ "the Carpenter" (Mark 6:3) is building a heavenly home for all who have trusted Him. And He will return to receive His own to Himself. Paul later amplified this promise in 1 Thes. 4:13-18. "Absent from the body, present with the Lord." Had Christ remained on earth, He could not have prepared the heavenly home for His own.

How can sinners ever hope to get to heaven? Through Christ! Read Luke 15:11-24, the story of the Prodigal Son, in connection with John 14:6. Like the sinner, the boy was lost (15:24), ignorant (15:17—"came to himself"), and dead (15:24). But he came to the father! (15:20) He was lost, but Christ is the Way; he was ignorant, but Christ is the Truth; and he was dead (spiritually), but Christ is the Life! And he arrived at the Father's house when he repented and returned.

II. To Reveal the Father to Them (14:7-11)

Philip seemed to have trouble with his eyes: he wanted to see. Almost his first words in 1:46 are, "Come and see!" He saw the great crowd in John 6 and decided that Christ could not feed them (6:7). The Greeks who came to Philip said, "We would see Jesus" (12:21). Jesus made it clear that seeing Him is seeing the Father. "From now on you know Him," He promises in v. 7 (NKJV). It is by faith that we see the Father as we come to know Christ better.

III. To Grant Them the Privilege of Prayer (14:12-14)

While He was with the disciples, Christ supplied their needs (see 16:22-24); now that He was returning to heaven, He gives them the privilege of prayer. He promises to answer prayer that the Father might be glorified. To pray in "His name" means to pray for His glory, asking for whatever He Himself would desire. The "greater works" spoken of in v. 12 refer to the wonderful miracles and blessings the disciples experienced as recorded in the Book of Acts (see Mark 16:20; Heb. 2:4). The works He does through us today are "greater" in the sense that we are mere human vessels, while He was God incarnate ministering on earth.

IV. To Send the Holy Spirit (14:15-26)

Christ has much to say about the Spirit in these next chapters. Here He calls Him "the Comforter," literally, "The One standing alongside to help you." The word "another" means "another of the same kind," for the Spirit is God just as Christ is God. The Spirit living within the disciples would take the place of the Savior living beside the disciples. He is also called "the Spirit of Truth." The Spirit uses the Word to convict sinners and to direct saints, and God's Word is truth (17:17). The world cannot receive the Spirit because He comes in response to faith.

There is considerable discussion over what Christ means when He says, "I will come to you" (v. 18). Literally it reads, "I do [present tense] come to you." This statement probably includes several things: Christ's coming to the apostles after His resurrection; His coming to them in the Person of the Spirit; and His future coming to take them to heaven.

In vv. 21-26, Christ speaks of a deeper relationship the disciples will have with the Father and the Son through the Spirit. They thought they would be "orphans" (literal meaning of "comfortless" in v. 18), when actually Jesus' going to the Father made possible a deeper relationship between the saint and his Savior. This relationship involves obedience to the Word (v. 21) and a love for the Word (v. 24). It involves too the teaching ministry of the Holy Spirit (v. 26). The Christian who spends time learning the Word, then goes out to live the Word, will enjoy a close, satisfying communion with the Father and the Son. Love for Christ is not a shallow emotion to be talked about; it means loving and obeying His Word by the power of the Holy Spirit. In 14:1-3, Jesus talked about the saint going to heaven to abide with the Father and Son; but here He talks about the Father and Son coming to abide with the saint.

V. To Grant His Peace (14:27-31)

How the disciples needed peace! The peace that Christ gives is not that of the world, nor does He give it the way the world gives. The world's peace is shallow, unsatisfying, and temporary; while Christ's peace rests deep in the heart, is always satisfying, and will abide forever. The world offers peace through outward means; Christ gives peace that dwells in the heart. Psychologists talk about "peace of mind," but Christ, through His death, resurrection, and ascension, gives "peace with God" (Rom. 5:1). Philippians 4:4-9 outlines how the believer may have the peace of God.

"My Father is greater than I" (v. 28) refers to the days of His earthly life. As Son of God, He is equal with the Father; as Son of Man in a human body, He was obedient to the Father, who gave Christ His words and works (14:10, 24).

By dying on the cross and going back to heaven, Christ defeated Satan (v. 30), who is the author of confusion and unrest. Lest the disciples think that His death was a tragedy or a mistake, Christ assured them in v. 31 that the cross is proof of His love for the Father. He died because the Father commanded it, and Christ came to do the Father's will.

As you review this chapter, see how tenderly Christ seeks to comfort His perplexed disciples. These comforting words are for us today, so claim them by faith.

JOHN 15

John 14 closes with, "Arise, let us go hence!" which suggests that the next two chapters may have been spoken on the way to the Garden. It is probable that Christ and His disciples were passing some vineyards, or perhaps the temple with its golden vine decorations, when He gave the analogy of the vine and branches. This chapter divides into three sections: a parable (vv. 1-11), a commandment (vv. 12-17), and a warning (vv. 18-27).

I. A Parable (15:1-11)

It is important to remember that not everything in a parable must mean something. A parable teaches one main truth, and to try to make a parable "stand on all four legs" is often the first step toward misinterpretation. The main truth Christ is teaching in this parable is the importance of abiding in Him in order to bear fruit. The word "fruit" is used six times, and "abide" at least fifteen times (but it is not always translated "abide"). The main point of the teaching here is fellowship, not sonship.

251

To use v. 6 to teach that a Christian loses his salvation and is burned in hell if he fails to bear fruit is to twist the meaning of the parable. In the first place, such a teaching contradicts the plain teaching of other verses—John 6:27; 10:27-29; etc. Furthermore, note that the branch Christ speaks of in v. 6 withers after it is cast forth! If this branch pictures a backslidden Christian who loses his salvation, he should "wither" first, then fail to bear fruit, then be cast out. To abide in Christ does not mean to keep ourselves saved. It means to live in His Word and pray (v. 7), obey His commandments (v. 10), and keep our lives clean through His Word (vv. 3-4). The Christian who fails to abide in Christ becomes like a useless branch, like the salt that loses its taste and is good for nothing. First Corinthians 3:15 teaches that our works will be tested by fire. The Christian who fails to use the gifts and opportunities God gives him will lose them (Luke 8:18 and 2 John 8).

To be a branch in the Vine means we are united to Christ and share His life. As we abide in Him, His life flows through us and produces fruit. It is possible for the carnal Christian to produce "works," but only the spiritual Christian can bear lasting fruit. Note that the fruitful branches are "purged" (v. 2—same word as "clean" in v. 3) so that they will bear more fruit. God cleanses us through the Word, chastening us to make us more fruitful, which helps to explain why a dedicated Christian often has to go through suffering. As believers move from producing "fruit" to "more fruit" (v. 2) to "much fruit" (v. 8), they glorify the Father. The evidences of the "abiding life" are: a sense of the Savior's love (v. 9), obedience to His Word (v. 10), answered prayer (v. 7), and joy (v. 11).

II. A Commandment (15:12-17)

This is the "eleventh commandment," that we love one another. Certainly the Christian who abides in Christ ought to get along with other believers! Love for the brethren is a mark of a disciple. Now Jesus calls His disciples "friends." His own death on the cross proved His love for them; now they must prove their love for Him by loving His children. Friends love each other and help each other. The obedience that Christ asks from us is not that of the slave, but of the friend. Because we are His friends and abide in Him, we know His will and share His secrets. We are reminded that Abraham was God's friend, and God told him His plans for Sodom.

252

III. A Warning (15:18-27)

From the love of the brethren, Christ turns to the hatred of the world. Why does the world hate Christians? (1) Because it first hated Christ, and we belong to Him (1 John 3:13); (2) because we no longer belong to the world (1 John 4:5 and John 17:14); (3) because the world has rejected His Word (v. 20); (4) because the world does not know the Father (see 16:1-3); and (5) because the world's sin has been exposed by Christ.

Of course, by "the world" Jesus means the whole system of society that is opposed to Christ and the Father. It is made up of people and organizations, philosophies and purposes that are anti-Christian. "The world" has a prince in Satan (John 14:30), the archenemy of Christ. While Christians are in the world physically, they are not of the world spiritually. The old illustration of the ship and the water still applies: there is nothing wrong with the ship being in the water; but when the water gets into the ship, watch out!

Christians can become worldly, and they do so (like Lot) by degrees. First there is friendship with the world (James 4:4); then love for the world (1 John 2:15-17); and finally conformity to the world (Rom. 12:2). Anything in our lives that keeps us from enjoying God's love and doing God's will is worldly and should be put away. To live for the world is to deny the cross of Christ (Gal. 6:14). The world hates Christ; how can the Christian love the world?

In vv. 22-24, Christ lays down the basic principle that revelation brings responsibility. His words and His works revealed the will of God and the sinfulness of men. Mankind has no excuse. The fact that Jews and Gentiles alike joined together in hating and crucifying Christ is proof that all people are sinners and guilty before God.

To encourage the disciples, Christ quoted Ps. 69:4 (v. 25). It is the Word that strengthens and encourages us. He also promises them the ministry of the Holy Spirit. The Spirit's work is to testify of Christ and point to Him. He does this through the Word and through the good works the Christian performs in the Spirit's power (Matt. 5:16). The Spirit testifies to the Christian, who then witnesses to others (vv. 26-27). See Acts 1:8.

In summary, you will note that in the first section of this chapter (vv. 1-11) the Lord deals with the believer's relationship to Christ. In vv. 12-17, the focus is the believer's relationship to other Christians; while vv. 18-27 talk of the Christian's relationship to the world. Note too that our relationship to the Savior is presented first; for if we are abiding in Christ, we will love the brethren and get victory over the hatred of the world.

JOHN 16

The disciples could not understand why Christ had to leave them, so He showed them that His return to the Father made possible greater blessings because of the coming of the Spirit. The Christian life cannot be lived in the energy of the flesh. We need the Spirit of God if we are going to live lives that glorify Christ. Our Lord described how the Spirit works through the believer.

I. The Spirit Convicts the World (16:1-11)

The world is no friend to the Christian. Christ warned His own of coming persecution, lest when it came, they should stumble and fall. Paul, in his unconverted state, is a good picture of the kind of person talked about in v. 2. The reason Christ did not tell them this fact sooner was because He was with them to protect them. Now that He was going to leave them, He gave them this Word to encourage them. Of course, Christ had already spoken to them about persecution (Matt. 5:10-12), but had not explained the source (religious people) and the reason (the ignorance and hatred of the world).

He now explained the work the Spirit will do in the world through the church. The very fact that the Spirit is in the world is an indictment against the world. Actually, Christ should be in the world, reigning as King; but the world crucified Christ. Keep in mind that the Spirit does not come to the people of the lost world (14:17) but to the people of God. His Spirit is here, reminding mankind of its awful sin. There is a threefold conviction of the world by the Spirit:

A. Of sin (v. 9).

And this is the sin of unbelief. The Spirit does not convict the world of individual sins; the conscience must do this (see Acts 24:24-25). The Spirit's presence in the world is proof that the world does not believe on Christ; otherwise Christ would be here in the world. The sin that condemns the soul is unbelief, the rejection of Christ (see John 3:18-21).

B. Of righteousness (v. 10).

Note that this is not the same as unrighteousness, that is, the sins of lost souls. Christ is speaking of the Spirit's conviction of the world, not of individual unbelievers, although there is a personal application. The Spirit's presence in the world is proof of the righteousness of Christ, who is now returned to the Father. While on earth, Christ was accused of being a lawbreaker and a sinner, as well as a counterfeit. But the fact that the Spirit is present on earth is proof that the Father raised the Son and received Him back to heaven.

C. Of judgment (v. 11).

Do not confuse this with Acts 24:25, "judgment to come." Christ is speaking here of the past judgment at the cross, not a future judgment. He had spoken of judging Satan and the world (12:31-32; see also Col. 2:15). The presence of the Spirit in the world is evidence that Satan has been judged and defeated; otherwise Satan would be controlling this world.

You may apply these three judgments to the individual unbeliever. The Spirit uses witnessing Christians and the Word to convince the unbeliever of his sin of unbelief; of his need for righteousness; of the fact that, since he belongs to Satan (Eph. 2:1-3), he is on the losing side. There is no salvation without Spirit-led conviction, for the Spirit uses the Word to convict lost souls.

II. The Spirit Instructs the Christian (16:12-15)

The disciples must have felt their ignorance of the Word, so Christ assured them by explaining the teaching ministry of the Spirit. He had mentioned this in 14:26 and 15:26. "Not speak of Himself" (v. 13) does not mean that the Spirit never talks about or calls attention to Himself. He wrote the Bible, and there are hundreds of references to the Spirit in its pages! This phrase means that the Spirit will not teach whatever He pleases, but will get His leading from the Father and the Son. The Spirit teaches us truth from the Word, and in so doing, glorifies Christ. Guy King suggests three ways in which the Spirit glorifies Christ: (1) He wrote a Book about Him; (2) He makes a believer like Him; (3) He finds a bride for Him.

Any Christian who surrenders to Christ can be taught by the
Spirit. Read Ps. 119:97-104 to see how God can teach the humble
Christian. It is not age, experience, or education that counts so
much as a willingness to learn and live the Word.

III. The Spirit Encourages the Christian (16:16-22)

The disciples were greatly disturbed and discouraged because
Christ was going to leave them. Verse 16 seems to be a paradox:
"You will see Me, because I go to the Father" (NKJV). Christ
seemed to be saying, "Because I am going away, you will see Me
again!" There is a twofold meaning here. First, they would "see
Him again" after His resurrection from the dead; but they would
also "see Him" when the Spirit came to dwell with them. They
would exchange physical sight for spiritual insight. Today, believers
"see Jesus" (Heb. 2:9) through the Spirit's teaching of the Word of
God.

Christ compares the events of His suffering to the birth of a
child: travail is followed by joy. Isaiah 53:11 states, "He shall see of
the travail of His soul." The disciples did weep and lament, but
their sorrow was changed to joy. We today have sorrow and suffering; but when Christ returns, it will turn to joy. Christ gives the
kind of joy that the world cannot take away.

IV. The Spirit Helps the Christian Pray (16:23-33)

"In that day" refers probably to the day when the Spirit would
come and begin His ministry among them. While Christ was on
earth, the disciples were accustomed to taking their questions and
needs to Him personally. When Christ returned to heaven, He sent
the Spirit to assist them in their praying (Rom. 8:26-27), and instructed them to pray to the Father personally. Bible prayer is to
the Father, through the Son, in the Spirit. It will not be necessary
for Christ to beg the Father on our behalf (v. 26) because the
Father is willing to answer our requests (v. 27).

Prayer is a tremendous privilege! Consider these other words of
Christ about prayer: John 14:13-14; 15:7; 15:16. As the believer
allows the Spirit to teach him the Word, he grows in his prayer life,
for prayer and the Word go together. Jude 20 commands us to "pray
in the Holy Ghost." Too much praying today is in the flesh, asking
for things that are not in the will of God (see James 4:1-10). It is

wonderful to allow the Holy Spirit to burden us with prayer requests (Rom. 9:1-3). The Spirit knows the mind of the Father and can lead us to pray for those things God wants to give us. It has well been said that prayer is not overcoming God's reluctance; it is laying hold of His willingness.

The testimony of the disciples must have gladdened Christ's heart, but He warned them of their coming failure (v. 32). Even the Father would finally forsake Christ on the cross! What a blessing to hear the Lord say, "Be of good cheer!" (v. 33) He was about to be arrested and crucified, yet He gives peace and joy to His followers! He promises them His victory: "I have overcome the world" (John 16:33).

The Spirit has a special ministry in our lives. Are we allowing Him to have His way?

JOHN 17

Someone has aptly termed this chapter "The Holy of Holies of John's Gospel." We have the privilege of hearing the Son conversing with the Father. You could spend many weeks meditating on the truths in this chapter, but here we can only touch upon the highlights.

I. Christ Prays for Himself (17:1-5)

The great theme of these verses is that He has finished the work of salvation. Beginning at 2:4, John has often mentioned "the hour." Use your concordance and trace the pattern of these verses for yourself. "I have finished the work"—the work of salvation—and because of this, "I have glorified Thee on the earth" (v. 4). Christ always looked upon the cross as a means of glorifying God (12:23). Paul also saw glory in the cross (Gal. 6:14).

Christ prays that the Father will give Him again the glory He laid aside when He came to earth to die (Phil. 2:1-12). The only time that His glory was revealed on earth was on the Mount of Transfiguration (John 1:14; 2 Peter 1:16-18). Note the "gives" in in v. 2: (1) The Father has given the Son authority over all mankind; (2) the Son gives eternal life to (3) those the Father has given the Son. One of the precious truths in John 17 is that each believer is God's love gift to the Son! (John 6:37) This is a mystery we cannot explain, but we thank God for it! "The gifts and calling of God are without repentance" (Rom. 11:29). This means that our salvation is secure, for the Father will not take us from the Son!

"I have manifested Thy name" (v. 6) — this statement should be related to the "I AM" statements of Christ in John's Gospel. God's name is I AM (Ex. 3:13-14), and Christ reveals that God is to us whatever we need Him to be. To the hungry Christ says, "I am the Bread of Life." To the lost He says, "I am the Way." To the blind He says, "I am the Light of the World."

II. Christ Prays for His Disciples (17:6-19)

The key thought here is sanctification, that is, the disciples' relationship to the world. Jesus said, "I have given them Your word" (v. 14, NKJV), and in v. 17 He states that we are sanctified — set apart for God — through the Word. Sanctification does not mean sinless perfection, otherwise Christ could never say, "I sanctify Myself" (v. 19), for He had no sin. A sanctified Christian is someone who is daily growing in the Word and as a result is separated more and more from the world unto the Father.

Christ asked the Father to keep the disciples (v. 11). This request does not suggest the possibility that the disciples could lose their salvation. Note the full request: " . . . keep [them] through Your own name . . . that they may be one" (NKJV). Verse 15 asks that they be kept from the evil one. Christ was physically with the disciples and was able to keep them together, united in heart and purpose, separated from the world. Now that He was going back to heaven, He asked the Father to keep them.

Some use v. 12 as "proof" that a believer can lose his or her salvation, but a careful reading of the verse proves just the opposite! Jesus said, "None of them is lost but the son of perdition." This shows that Judas was never a part of the believing band of disciples. "But" is a word of contrast, showing that Judas was in a different class from the others. In v. 11 Jesus plainly stated that He kept all whom the Father gave Him; since Judas was lost, he could not have been among those who were given to the Son. Many people today who teach that Judas "lost his salvation" make the same mistake Peter made (6:66-71) in thinking that Judas had salvation, when he did not!

Christians are not of the world, but they are in the world to witness for Christ. We keep our lives clean through His Word.

Christ has actually sent us into the world to take His place (v. 18). What a responsibility we have!

III. He Prays for His Church (17:20-26)

The main theme here is glorification; "I have given them the glory that You gave Me" (v. 22, NIV). He does not say "I will give them" because in the plan of God, the believer has already been glorified (Rom. 8:30). This is another proof of the eternal security of the believer: we are already glorified as far as God is concerned. Christ prays that we might be with Him and see His glory. Colossians 3:4 states that we will share His glory; Rom. 8:18 promises we will show forth His glory!

Christ also prays for the unity of His church (v. 21). There is a vast difference between unity (oneness of heart and spirit) and uniformity (everybody exactly alike). Christ never prayed that all Christians would belong to one world church. Organizational mergers may bring about organizational uniformity, but they cannot guarantee unity. Unity comes from life within, not from pressure without. While true Christians belong to different denominations, they are all part of the true church, the body of Christ; it is this spiritual unity in love that convinces the world of the truth of the Gospel. It is possible for Christians to differ on minor matters and still love one another in Christ.

Every Christian who dies goes to heaven because Christ prayed that this might be so (v. 24), and the Father always answers His prayers (11:41-42).

In v. 26 Christ promises further revelations of the Father, which He gave to the apostles through the Spirit. He asks that we might enjoy the love of the Father in our daily experience (see 14:21-24).

We may summarize the major parts of this prayer as follows:

In vv. 1-5, Jesus emphasized salvation and the gift of eternal life (v. 2). In vv. 6-19, He dwelt on sanctification: "I have given them Your Word" (v. 14, NKJV). Verses 20-26 focus on glorification—"I have given them the glory" (v. 22, NIV). These gifts take care of the believer's past, present, and future.

Note also the wonderful assurances of the eternal security of the believer in this prayer: (1) Believers are the Father's gift to the Son (v. 2), and God will not take back His love gifts. (2) Christ finished His work. Because Christ did His work completely, believers cannot lose their salvation. (3) Christ was able to keep His own while on earth, and He is able to keep them today, for He is the same Savior. (4) Christ knows we will finally be in heaven because He has already given us His glory. (5) Christ prayed that we might be in heaven, and the Father always answers His Son's prayers (11:41-42).

JOHN 18

Jesus left the place of prayer for His meeting with His enemies. "The brook Kidron" reminds us of King David, who was exiled from his throne by the rebellion of his own friends and family and passed through that same body of water (see 2 Sam. 15).

I. The Arrest (18:1-14)

Jesus deliberately met Judas and his band, for He knew what was about to happen. (See 13:1-3 and 6:6. Jesus always knew what He would do, for He always knew the will of the Father.) It is interesting to note that the arrest took place in a garden. Christ, the Last Adam (1 Cor. 15:45), met the enemy in a garden and triumphed, while the first Adam met the enemy in a garden and failed. Adam hid himself, but Christ openly revealed Himself. As you meditate on these two garden scenes, see what other contrasts you can find.

Judas stood with the enemy. "And being let go, they went to their own company" (Acts 4:23). People will always go where their hearts are; Judas had Satan in his heart and so stood with Satan's crowd. Sad to say, Peter mixed with this same crowd! Note how Jesus stunned them when He used the divine name, "I AM!" (The word "he" in v. 6 is not in the original Gk. manuscripts.) The same name that saves believers (17:6) condemns the lost.

In v. 8, Jesus warned His disciples to go away, lest they fall into trouble. He had already told them they would scatter (16:32), but Peter preferred to remain and fight—and got into danger because of it. Peter's sin was not that he "followed afar off," but that he followed at all! He should have obeyed the Word and departed.

Verse 9 refers back to 17:12, where Christ spoke of the disciples' salvation. Here He is talking about their physical protection. Thus, Christ keeps us in two ways: He preserves our souls in salvation and keeps our bodies, sealing them by His Spirit, until the day of redemption (Eph. 1:13-14).

In using the sword, Peter was definitely disobeying Christ. Christ does not need our protection; the weapons we are to use to fight Satan are spiritual ones (2 Cor. 10:4-6; Eph. 6). Peter used the wrong weapon, had the wrong motive, acted under the wrong orders, and accomplished the wrong result! How gracious of Jesus to heal Malchus (Luke 22:51) and thus protect Peter from harm. Otherwise there might have been another cross on Calvary, and Peter would have been crucified before God's time had come (John 21:18-19).

II. The Denial (18:15-27)

The narrative focuses on Peter now, and we see his sad decline. In the Upper Room, Peter had boasted three times that he would remain true to Christ (Matt. 26:33, 35; John 13:37). In the Garden, he had gone to sleep three times (Mark 14:32-41) when he should have been praying. Then he denied the Lord three times, and in John 21 had to confess his love for Christ three times! In the Upper Room Peter fell into the snare of the devil (Luke 22:31-34); in the Garden he yielded to the weakness of the flesh; and now in the priest's courtyard, he would surrender to the pressures of the world. How important it is to watch and pray!

We do not know who the unnamed disciple was in v. 15. It may have been Nicodemus or Joseph of Arimathea; it is not likely that John (often called "that other disciple"—20:3) would have been on friendly terms with the high priest. See Acts 4:1-3. Whoever he was, this disciple led Peter into a sin by opening the door for him! Verse 18 says "it was cold," so Peter sat by the fire, but Luke 22:44 states that Christ had been sweating as He prayed that night! Peter was cold both physically and spiritually and had to warm himself at the enemy's fire. He had "walked in the counsel of the ungodly" and was now "standing in the way of sinners." He would soon "sit in the seat of the scornful" (see Ps. 1:1). While Christ was suffering, Peter was warming himself, not sharing Christ's sufferings at all.

III. The Rejection (18:28-40)

The fact that there were two men identified as high priests shows how corrupt the nation was at that time. Annas and Caiaphas were partners in the temple trade and hated Jesus for twice cleansing the temple.

Much has been written about the illegal aspects of Christ's trial. It was held at night; the prisoner was assumed to be guilty and treated that way; the court hired false witnesses; the judge permitted the prisoner to be mistreated while bound; the court allowed the accused no defense. After the secret night trial, the crafty religious leaders led Jesus to Pilate for the final death sentence. They would not enter a Gentile's hall, lest they "should be defiled," but they did not hesitate to condemn an innocent man to death!

In 18:33 through 19:15, we read the sad record of Pilate's cowardly indecision. At least seven times Pilate went from the hall to the Jews outside, trying to work out a compromise. Pilate crucified Christ because he was a coward, "willing to content the people" (Mark 15:15). How many sinners will be in hell because they feared people and sought to please them!

Christ explained to Pilate the spiritual nature of His kingdom but did not explain His statement "My kingdom is not of this world." Had the Jews received Him, He could have established His kingdom on earth. But they rejected Him, for His kingdom is of a spiritual nature, within people's hearts. One day when He returns, He will establish His kingdom on earth. How we long for that blessed day.

Pilate's question, "What is truth?" has been asked by philosophers for ages. In 14:6, Jesus says, "I am the truth." John 17:17 says, "Your Word is truth" (NKJV). First John 5:6 states that "the Spirit is truth." The Spirit and the Word point to Christ, the Truth.

The world makes the wrong choice when it comes to spiritual matters. The mob preferred a murderer to the Prince of Life! They chose the lawbreaker, not the Lawgiver! The Jews rejected their true Messiah, but they one day will accept Satan's false Messiah, the Antichrist (5:43).

Men reject Jesus for different reasons. Judas rejected Christ because he listened to the devil; Pilate listened to the world; Herod obeyed the flesh.

"You have a custom," said Pilate (18:39). How sad that Pilate knew the religious customs, but did not know Christ! People are like this even today, careful to observe religious holidays and customs, but ignorant of the Savior of the world. Rejection means eternal judgment, but faith means eternal life. Everyone must make a decision.

JOHN 19

I. Christ Mocked (19:1-22)

Pilate perhaps thought that scourging Jesus (which was illegal) would move the hearts of the Jews and that they would want to see Him released. But their hearts were hard (12:40), and they were determined to destroy Him. Pilate wrongly permitted the soldiers to ridicule Christ, presenting Him with a mock crown, robe, and scepter. Compare this scene with Rev. 19:1-21, when every knee will bow to Him.

The Jews accused Christ of breaking their law because He claimed to be God (see 10:33). Yet in His messages and miracles, Jesus had proved Himself to be God. But the hard-hearted sinners refused to consider the evidence; they were bent on destroying Him.

Why did Christ not answer Pilate's question in v. 9? For one thing, Pilate had not obeyed the truth he had already received; and God does not reveal more truth until we obey what He has already given. Pilate's boast in v. 10 was really his own sentence of condemnation! If he did have authority to release Christ and knew that Jesus was innocent (19:4), then Pilate should have set the prisoner free! Christ rebuked Pilate by reminding him that all authority comes from God (see Rom. 13:1ff and Prov. 8:15-16). Pilate was in the hands of God to fulfill a special purpose, but Pilate was still responsible for his decisions and guilty of sin. (See Luke 22:22.) "He that delivered Me to you" (v. 11) refers to Caiaphas, not Judas.

"We have no king but Caesar!" (v. 15) was their cry. In 6:15, the Jews wanted to make Christ king; and in 12:13 they hailed Him as king; and now they rejected Him. This is the third crisis in John's Gospel (see the suggested outline of John's Gospel for the listing of these crises).

Pilate had "the last word," for he wrote the title for the cross: "This is Jesus of Nazareth, the King of the Jews." It was customary for a Roman prisoner to wear the accusation on a placard around his neck, which then was hung above his head upon his cross. Christ's "crime" was that He made Himself king! The three languages of the title represented three great areas of human life: religion (Hebrew), philosophy and culture (Greek), and law (Latin). The title speaks of universal sin, for three great nations of the world participated in His death. Religion, philosophy, and law will not save lost sinners. The title also speaks of universal love—"God so loved the world." The title also announces salvation for a whole world, for Christ is the wisdom of God to the Greek, the power of God to the Jew, and the justice of God that fulfills His holy law (1 Cor. 1:18ff). The repentant thief read this title, trusted Christ, and was saved.

II. Christ Crucified (19:23-30)

John records but three of Christ's seven statements from the cross. He is careful to note the fulfillment of Scripture in the gambling for the seamless robe (Ps. 22:18), the giving of the vinegar (Ps. 69:21), and the piercing of His side without breaking any bones (Ps. 34:20 with Ex. 12:46; Zech. 12:10). Note, however, that v. 37 does not say Zech. 12:10 was fulfilled; rather, that Zech. 12:10 says He would be pierced. They will "look upon Him" at that future day when He returns in glory (Rev. 1:7). Every detail about the crucifixion was carefully worked out by the hand of God.

In giving John and Mary to each other, Christ was finally breaking the earthly ties of family. It was Christ who controlled the situation, not Mary. We admire Mary's devotion in coming to the cross (Luke 2:34-35). Her silence is proof that Jesus is God's Son, for one word from her could have saved Jesus. After all, who knows a son better than the mother who bore him?

"I thirst" spoke both of physical and spiritual agony, for Christ suffered the torment of hell for our sins. He thirsted that we might never thirst. "It is finished!" is one word in the Greek text— *tetelestai.* The word was a common one and was used by merchants to mean "The price is all paid!" Shepherds and priests used it when they found a perfect sheep, ready for sacrifice; and Christ died as the perfect lamb of God. Servants, when their work was completed, would use this word when reporting to their masters. Christ, the obedient Servant, had finished the work the Father gave Him to do. Christ willingly and deliberately gave up His life; He laid down His life for His friends.

III. Christ Buried (19:31-42)

The Jews were not interested in compassion or the awfulness of their crime; they only wanted to keep from violating their Sabbath laws! The fact that the soldiers did not break Christ's legs to hasten death was proof that He was already dead. The blood and water illustrate two aspects of salvation: blood to atone for the guilt of sin, and water to wash away the stain of sin. The blood speaks of justification and the water of sanctification. The two must always go together, for those who have trusted the blood of Christ to save them should live clean lives before a watching world.

From v. 35, we infer that John left Mary at his own house and came back to the cross. Staying with Christ was more important than caring for Mary. When we first find Mary in John's Gospel, she is attending a joyful wedding feast (2:1-11); her last mention is at Jesus' painful execution.

God had prepared Nicodemus and Joseph, two members of the Sanhedrin, to bury the body of Jesus. Otherwise, His body probably would have been thrown on the garbage heap outside Jerusalem. Isaiah 53:9 promised that His grave would be with the rich. This is the third and final mention of Nicodemus in John, and at last we see him coming out boldly into the sunlight of confession (see notes on John 3). Nicodemus and Joseph knew from studying the Scriptures when Christ would die, how He would die, and where He would die. They had the tomb all ready with the spices and were probably hiding in the tomb while Christ was on the cross. Joseph did not make this tomb for himself, for no rich man would want to be buried near the place where criminals were executed. He secured property close to Calvary that he might care for the body of Jesus quickly and easily.

We must not criticize Joseph for being a "hidden disciple," for we can see how God used him and Nicodemus to accomplish His purposes. Had their faith been known openly, they would have been prevented by the council from caring for the body of Jesus. When Joseph and Nicodemus touched the dead body of Christ, they defiled themselves for the Passover. But they did not care, for they had come to trust in the Lamb of God Himself!

The Lamb of God had given His life for the sins of the world. His work on earth was finished, and He rested on the Sabbath.

JOHN 20

This chapter records three post-resurrection appearances of Christ. Each appearance brought about a different result in the lives of those involved.

I. Mary Saw the Lord (20:1-18)

Christ had cast seven demons out of Mary Magdalene (Luke 8:2), and she dearly loved Him. In her confusion and disappointment, Mary jumped to conclusions and thought someone had stolen Christ's body. She ran to tell Peter and John, who in turn visited the tomb.

Why did John outrun Peter? (v. 4) There may have been a physical reason: perhaps John was younger than Peter. But there is also a spiritual lesson here: Peter had not yet reaffirmed his devotion to Christ, and therefore his "spiritual energy" was low. Isaiah 40:31 says that those who wait on the Lord "shall run and not be weary," but Peter had rushed ahead of the Lord and disobeyed Him. Peter's sin affected his feet (John 20:4), his eyes (John 21:7), his lips (He denied the Lord), even his body temperature (John 18:18; and see Luke 24:32).

What did the men see in the tomb? They saw the burial wrappings lying in the shape of the body, but the body was gone! The graveclothes lay like an empty cocoon. The napkin (for the face) was carefully folded, lying by itself. It was not the scene of a grave robbery, for no robbers could have gotten the body out of the graveclothes without tearing the cloth and disarranging things. Jesus had returned to life in power and glory and had passed through the graveclothes and the tomb itself! Verse 8 tells us that the men believed in His resurrection because of the evidence that they saw. Later they met Christ personally and also came to believe on the testimony of Scripture. There are, then, three types of proof that you can rest upon when it comes to spiritual matters: (1) the evidence God gives in His world, (2) the Word of God, and (3) personal experience. How can a man know that Christ is real? He can see the evidence in the lives of others; he can read the Word; and if he trusts Christ, he will experience it personally. Note that in v. 10 they go back home without proclaiming the message of the risen Christ. Mere intellectual evidence alone will not change people. We must meet Christ personally.

That is what happened to Mary: she lingered and met Christ. How many times it pays to wait! (See Prov. 8:17.) She saw two angels in the tomb (Luke 24:4 calls them "two men") but was too taken up with her grief to let them comfort her. The description of the angels in v. 12 reminds us of the mercy seat in the holy of holies (Ex. 25:17-19); the risen Christ is now our Mercy Seat in heaven. Mary turned from the angels, for she was seeking Christ; she would have rather had the body of Christ than the sight of angels! The person she then saw was really Christ, but her eyes were clouded so that she could not recognize Him. The one word "supposing" in v. 15 explains all her sorrow. Many Christians today are miserable because they "suppose" something that is not at all true. When Jesus spoke her name, she recognized Him. He calls His own by name (John 10:3-4), and they know His voice. See Isa. 43:1.

Verse 17 suggests that, early that Easter morning, Christ ascended to heaven to present His finished work to the Father. That secret ascension fulfilled the type of sacrifice discussed in Lev. 23:1-14, the waving of the "firstfruits sheaf" the next day after the Sabbath (see 1 Cor. 15:23). Mary's meeting with Christ made her a missionary!

II. The Disciples Saw the Lord (20:19-25)

Twice now "the first day of the week" has been mentioned (20:1, 19). This is Sunday, not Saturday (the Jewish Sabbath, the seventh day of the week). The Sabbath stands for rest after works and belongs to the dispensation of law. Sunday is the Lord's Day, the first day of the week, and speaks of life and rest before works. It reminds us of God's grace. Christ came through the locked doors in His glorified body and brought the fearful men peace. Note that twice He speaks of peace (vv. 19, 21). The first "peace" is peace with God, based on His sacrifice on the cross. That is why He showed them His hands and side. The second peace is the peace of God that comes from His presence with us (see Phil. 4). He commissioned them to take His place as the Father's ambassadors in the world. (See John 17:15-18.)

Our Lord's breathing upon them reminds us of Gen. 2:7, when God breathed life into Adam, and also of 2 Tim. 3:16, where "inspiration" means "God-breathed." This action was personal and individual, giving them the spiritual power and discernment they would need to fulfill His commission. The coming of the Spirit at Pentecost was corporate and empowered them for service and witnessing. The "remitting" power given in v. 23 does not apply to Christians today, except in the sense that we retain or remit sins as we give sinners the Gospel. There is no instance in the New Testament of any apostle forgiving sins. Peter (Acts 10:43) and

Paul (Acts 13:38) both spoke on the authority of Christ. There is no question that the disciples had special privileges, but these rights are not ours today.

III. Thomas Saw the Lord (20:26-31)

Thomas was not present at the first meeting. How many things we miss by being absent from the local assembly. Note Thomas' statement "Except I see . . . I will not believe!" (v. 25) He was called "Didymus" which means "twin." He has many twins today!

The next Lord's Day, when the disciples were together, Jesus appeared to them again and addressed Thomas. What forgiving love Jesus showed him! Thomas saw the Lord and forgot all about his demands for proof! His testimony thrills us: "My Lord and my God!" The sight of Christ's wounds won his heart. Christ states here that you and I today can have the same assurance and blessing, for we are among those who believe, yet have not seen Him.

As you review these three appearances of Christ, you can see the different results. With Mary, the issue was her love for Christ. She missed Him and wanted to take care of His body. With the disciples, the issue was their hope. All their hope was gone; they were locked in a room, huddling together in fear! With Thomas, the issue was faith: he would not believe unless he saw proof. Because Jesus Christ is alive today, our faith is secure. "And if Christ be not raised, your faith is vain" (1 Cor. 15:17). We have a living hope through His resurrection from the dead. First Corinthians 15:19 says, "If in this life only we have hope in Christ, we are of all men most miserable."

In vv. 30-31, John states the purpose of his Gospel: that sinners might believe and have eternal life through Christ. As you read this Gospel, you meet many people who did believe and received everlasting life: (1) Nathanael (1:50); (2) His disciples (2:11); (3) the Samaritans (4:39); (4) the nobleman (4:50); (5) the blind man (9:38); (6) Martha (11:27); (7) the Jews who saw Lazarus raised from the dead (12:11); and (8) Thomas (20:28). All of these gave the same witness, "I believe."

JOHN 21

The final chapter shows Christ as the Master of our service and the Friend of sinners. Were it not for this chapter, we would wonder what happened between Peter and the Lord and whether or not his disobedience was really dealt with.

I. A Night of Defeat (21:1-3)

Peter acted without orders in returning to his fishing. He had forsaken all to follow Christ (Luke 5:1-11), and now he was turning back to the old life. Everything about this scene speaks of defeat: (1) it is dark, indicating that they are not walking in the light; (2) they had no direct word from the Lord; (3) their efforts met with failure; (4) they did not recognize Christ when He did appear, showing that their spiritual vision was dim. Peter led the other six men astray when he made his hasty decision. How tragic is a bad influence! We need to keep in mind that God blesses us only when we abide in Christ and obey the Word. "Without Me you can do nothing" (15:5). Too many Christians enter into well-meaning but unscriptural activities, only to waste time, money, and energy for nothing. Let us beware of impatience. It is better to wait on the Lord for directions, and then let Him bless, than to involve ourselves in useless activities.

II. A Morning of Decision (21:4-17)

When Christ appears on the scene, then the light begins to shine. He instructs them from the shore, and they catch a great host of fish! A few minutes' labor with Christ in control will accomplish more than a whole night of carnal efforts! It is interesting to compare this miracle with the one at the beginning of Peter's career in Luke 5:

Luke 5	John 21
1. Followed a night of failure	1. Followed a night of failure
2. No exact number of fish given	2. 153 fish (v. 11)
3. The nets began to break	3. The net did not break
4. Christ instructed from the boat	4. Christ instructed from the shore

Some see in these scenes a picture of the church today (Luke 5) and of the church at the end of the age when Christ returns (John 21). Today we are casting out the Gospel net, but often the nets break, there is seeming failure, and we do not know how many souls are really won. But when Christ returns the exact number will be known, and none will be lost. Today there are many boats and fishermen at work, but when Christ returns, we will see the one church and all the redeemed in the one Gospel net.

There are actually several miracles in this chapter, besides the catch of fish. Peter is given miraculous strength to draw up a net that seven men were not able to draw together (v. 6 and v. 11).

The fact that the net did not break is amazing. The fire of coals and the cooked breakfast were certainly supplied miraculously. The entire scene was designed to awaken Peter's conscience and open his eyes. The catch of fish reminded him of his past decision to forsake all and follow Christ. The fire of coals would take him back to his denial (John 18:18). The location—the Sea of Galilee—reminded him of several past experiences with Christ: feeding the 5,000, walking on the water, catching the fish with the coin, stilling the storm, etc.

Because Peter had denied Christ three times publicly, he had to make it right publicly. Note that Christ fed Peter before He dealt with his sins. How like the Lord to bless us first, then deal with us! The issue was Peter's love for Christ. If a man really loves Christ, his life will be devoted and dedicated. Note that Christ gives Peter a new commission: he is now a shepherd (pastor) besides being a fisher of men. (See 1 Peter 5.) He is now to shepherd the lambs and sheep and feed them the Word of God. All Christians are expected to be fishers of men (soul-winners), but some have been called into the special ministry of shepherding the flock. What good is it to win the lost if there is no church where they might be fed and cared for?

III. A Day of Dedication (21:18-25)

There is a vast difference between sonship (being saved) and discipleship (following the Lord). Not all Christians are disciples. When Peter sinned, he did not lose his sonship, but he did fall away from his discipleship. For this reason Christ repeated His call, "Follow Me." Christ also confronts Peter with the cross (v. 18), indicating that Peter would one day be crucified himself. (See 2 Peter 1:12-14.) Before we can follow Christ, we must take up the cross. When you recall that earlier Peter tried to keep Christ from the cross, this commandment takes on new meaning (Matt. 16:21-28).

Peter now makes a tragic mistake: he again gets his eyes off the Lord and begins to look at others, in this case, John. If we are to follow Christ, we must keep our eyes on Him alone (Heb. 12:1-2). It is "none of our business" how Christ leads His other workers; our business is to follow Christ ourselves and obey Him. (See Rom. 14 for instructions on how we should relate to other Christians.)

John closes his Gospel by assuring us that the world itself could not contain all the books that could be written about Christ's life. The four Gospels are not "lives of Christ," but rather four different portraits of Jesus with a different emphasis. It would be impossible, says John, to record His life completely.

Had not Peter met Christ here in John 21, confessed his sin, and affirmed his love, we would not have read about Peter again in Acts 1. God was able to use Peter later because he made things right with the Lord. Christ blesses and uses those who obey and follow Him.

ACTS

A Suggested Outline of Acts

I. The Ministry of Peter: A Mission to Israel (1–12)

    A. Peter and the Jews (1–7)

        1. Preparation for Pentecost (1)

        2. Peter's first message (2)

        3. Peter's second message (3)

        4. The first persecution (4)

        5. The second persecution (5)

        6. Israel's final rejection: Stephen slain (6–7)

    B. Peter and the Samaritans (8)

    C. The Conversion of Paul (9)

    D. Peter and the Gentiles (10–11)

    E. Peter's arrest and deliverance (12)

II. The Ministry of Paul: Mission to Jews and Gentiles (13–28)

    A. Paul's first missionary journey (13–14)

    B. Paul defends the Gospel (15)

    C. Paul's second missionary journey (16:1–18:22)

    D. Paul's third missionary journey (18:23–21:17)

    E. Paul's arrest and journey to Rome (21:18–28:31)

Acts covers a time of transition as Israel moves off the scene and the Church comes to the fore. God's prophetic program as outlined in the OT gives way to a new program, the mystery of the Church. It was primarily through Paul that God revealed His new program (see Eph. 3).

Introductory Notes to Acts

I. Writer

Luke, the beloved physician, is the author of Acts. The "former treatise" (Acts 1:1) is the Gospel of Luke (see Luke 1:1-4). Luke was a doctor (Col. 4:14) who joined Paul's party at Troas (Acts 16:8-10; note the change from "they" to "we") and traveled with the missionary to Philippi. Apparently he stayed in Philippi and did not join Paul until Paul's return there on his third journey (Acts 20:6). It is generally believed that Luke was a Gentile.

II. Theme

It is vitally important that we understand the basic message of the Book of Acts, and to do this we must survey the book in a general way to grasp its message. In this book we see the kingdom message and the setting aside of Israel's status; we witness too the expansion of the church and the message of the grace of God. In chapters 1–7, we are definitely on Jewish ground. If we keep in mind that Acts is really a continuation of Luke and reflect on Luke 24:46ff, we will see why the disciples began in Jerusalem: Christ commanded them to stay there until the Spirit should come. Their ministry was to begin in Jerusalem, "to the Jew first" (Rom. 1:16). Even when we get to 8:1, we find the apostles courageously remaining in Jerusalem while others were fleeing. They were not disobeying the Lord but following the orders He gave them. Here are but a few of the many evidences in Acts 1–7 that the ministry of the apostles at that time was to the Jews and still was the message of the kingdom:

(1) The disciples expected the establishment of the kingdom (1:6), and Christ did not rebuke them for their request. He had promised that they would sit on twelve thrones (Matt. 19:28).

(2) It was necessary that they elect a twelfth apostle (1:22) to take Judas' place so that Christ's promise might be fulfilled. Paul was not supposed to be that new apostle, for his ministry was primarily to the Gentiles. Paul's ministry had to do with the one body, the church.

(3) Peter preached to the men of Judah, Jerusalem, and Israel in his message at Pentecost (2:14, 22). He did not address his words to Gentiles. It was primarily a Jewish message to a Jewish

congregation on a Jewish religious holiday.

(4) The prophecy of Joel (2:16ff) relates primarily to Israel, not the church.

(5) Peter portrayed the cross as an instrument of crime, not as God's gracious remedy for sin (2:22-23). Compare this with Paul's message in 2 Cor. 5.

(6) Peter's theme at Pentecost is the resurrection. Christ had promised to give Israel a sign—the sign of the prophet Jonah—which is death, burial, and resurrection (Matt. 12:38ff). This was the sign Peter preached. God was now giving Israel another chance to accept the Messiah and be saved.

(7) The apostles and first converts worshiped in the temple (2:46ff; 3:1ff) and maintained contact with the temple ministry until they were thrown out.

(8) Peter said that the days of blessing that were experienced in Acts had been prophesied by the OT prophets (3:21, 24). But the church was a mystery hidden by God and was not fully made known until Paul's ministry (read Eph. 3 carefully). The prophets spoke of the Jewish kingdom, not of the church. To confuse these two creates problems.

(9) Jerusalem was the center for blessing; everyone came there (5:16). It was definitely kingdom ground; see Isaiah 66:5ff.

(10) Peter clearly told the council that the message was one of repentance for Israel (5:31).

(11) In chapter 7, Stephen reviewed the history of Israel and showed how the nation had rejected the truth down through the years. It takes little effort to see that in the first seven chapters of Acts, we are concerned with the Jewish nation and that the message is meant primarily for the kingdom, not the church. It is important that we understand why.

There are three murders in Israel's history that mark out her rejection of God's will. John the Baptist came preaching the kingdom (Matt. 3:1ff), and the Jews allowed him to be slain. In this way they rejected the Father who had sent him. Then, Jesus came preaching the same message (Matt. 4:12-17), and they crucified Him. Thus, they rejected God the Son. On the cross, Jesus prayed for the Jews, "Father, forgive them for they know not what they do" (Luke 23:34). This prayer made possible a third offer of the kingdom through the apostles, recorded in the first seven chapters of Acts. What was the result? The religious leaders murdered Stephen! This was the sin of resisting the Holy Ghost (Acts 7:51), the "unpardonable sin" that Christ had spoken of in Matt. 12:31-32. The death of Stephen marks the close of God's offer of the kingdom to the Jews.

In chapters 8–12, we have a transition. In chap. 8, the Gospel goes from the Jews to the Samaritans. In chap. 9, Paul is saved in an unusual and miraculous manner, and God prepares His apostle for his ministry to the church. In chap. 10 the Gospel goes to the Gentiles, and Peter defends this new departure in chap. 11. In chap. 12, we see Peter for the last time as the leader among the believers. In chap. 13, it is Paul who takes the lead, here and through the rest of the book.

III. The Church in Acts

If the first seven chapters describe a message that is being offered to the Jews, then where does the church, the body of Christ, fit in? The answer: the church began at Pentecost but was not fully revealed by God until later, primarily through the writings of Paul. Christ had promised to build His church (Matt. 16:18); but almost in the same breath He gave Peter the "keys of the kingdom of heaven" (Matt. 16:19). Peter used these "keys" in opening the door of faith to the Jews at Pentecost (Acts 2), to the Samaritans (Acts 8), and to the Gentiles (Acts 10). In other words, there is a transition in these first seven chapters of Acts, with Israel and the kingdom moving off the scene, and the church and the Gospel of God's grace moving onto the scene.

Christ promised the apostles a baptism of the Spirit (Acts 1:5), and this took place at Pentecost (Acts 2, see 1 Cor. 12:13) and in the home of Cornelius (Acts 10:45, see Acts 11:15-17). These two events included both Jews and Gentiles, and thus the body of Christ was formed. The apostles did not know whether or not Israel would receive their kingdom offer (Acts 1:6-7), but Christ did know. Thus the church was about to take over God's purpose because of Israel's failure.

It is easy to see that as the action of the church begins to fill the pages of Acts, Israel becomes less and less significant in God's program on earth. In the final chapter (28:17ff) Paul pronounced God's judgment on the nation. As Romans 9–11 explains, God had set aside Israel so that "the fullness of the Gentiles" (Rom. 11:25) might be realized through the ministry of the church. This kingdom emphasis in the first seven chapters of Acts must be recognized; otherwise, one may apply certain practices to the church today that really do not pertain anymore. For example, some well-meaning Christians go "back to Pentecost" for their spiritual ideal; but in the light of the above analysis, Pentecost (a Jewish feast) involved signs for the Jews that do not necessarily have relevance to the church today. The "Christian communism" of Acts 4:31ff is not for us today. It was a temporary evidence of the gracious working of the Spirit, a picture of kingdom blessing to come. Of course, the spiritual principles given in these chapters apply to believers in all ages; but we must beware of mixing the kingdom truth of the Old Testament with church truth and thus confusing the message and the ministry.

IV. The Holy Spirit in Acts

This book could well be called "The Acts of the Holy Spirit." It is important to note the progress in the believers' experience as the book moves from Jewish ground to church ground.

Acts 2:38—Peter tells the Jews to repent, believe, and be baptized to receive the Spirit.

Acts 8:14-15—Peter prays for the Samaritans to receive the Spirit, lays hands on them, and they receive the gift of the Spirit.

Acts 10:44—The Holy Spirit comes on the Gentiles when they believe, and Peter can only stand by in amazement! Acts 10:44 is God's pattern for today: hear the Word, believe, receive the Spirit, and then be baptized as evidence of your faith.

V. Baptism in Acts

When Peter was offering the kingdom to the Jews, baptism was essential for their receiving the Holy Spirit (Acts 2:38). Baptism in the name of the rejected Messiah identified them with Him and separated them from the other Jews whom Peter termed "this perverse generation" (2:40). But the Samaritans' baptism did not grant them the Spirit (Acts 8:12-17). They had to call on Peter and John, two Jews, who prayed for the new believers and laid hands on them; and then they received the Spirit. This was Peter's second use of the "keys of the kingdom." But the pattern of baptism for this age is found in Acts 10:44-48—these believers were baptized after they had already received the gift of the Spirit.

ACTS 1

I. A New Book (1:1-2)

The "former treatise" referred to is the Gospel of Luke (see Luke. 1:1-4) in which Luke told the story of what Jesus began to do and teach while He was on earth. Acts picks up the account by telling what He continued to do and teach through the church on earth. The Gospel of Luke tells of Christ's ministry on earth in a physical body, while Acts tells of His ministry from heaven through His spiritual body, the church. For example, in 1:24 the believers ask the ascended Christ to show them which man to elect as apostle. In 2:47 it is the Lord who adds believers to the assembly. In 13:1-3, it is Christ through His Spirit who sends out the first missionaries; and in 14:27, Paul and Barnabas relate what God did through them.

Every Christian needs to move out of Luke's Gospel into Acts. Knowing about the birth, life, death, and resurrection of Christ is enough for salvation but not for Spirit-empowered service. We must identify ourselves with Him as our ascended Lord and allow Him to work through us in the world. The church is not simply an organization engaged in religious work; it is a divine organism, the body of Christ on earth, through which His life and power must operate. He died for the lost world; we must live to bring that world to Christ.

II. A New Experience (1:3-8)

Christ ministered to the apostles during the forty days He was on earth after His resurrection. Luke 24:36ff should be read in connection with these verses. In both places, Christ instructed the apostles to remain in Jerusalem and wait for the coming of the Spirit. They were to begin their ministry in Jerusalem.

This baptism of the Spirit had been announced by John the Baptist (Matt. 3:11; Mark 1:8; Luke 3:16; John 1:33). Note that Christ said nothing about a baptism with fire, for the fire baptism refers to judgment. The coming of the Spirit would unite all the believers into one body, to be known as the church (see 1 Cor. 12:13). The Spirit would also give the believers power to witness to the lost. Finally, the Spirit would enable the believers to speak in tongues and perform other miraculous deeds to awaken the Jews. (See 1 Cor. 1:22 — the Jews require a sign.) There are actually two occurrences of this Spirit baptism in Acts; in chapter 2, when He baptized the Jews; and in chapter 10 (see 11:16) when He came upon the Gentile believers. According to Eph. 2:11ff, the body of Christ is composed of Jews and Gentiles, all baptized into this spiritual body. It is wrong to pray for a baptism of the Spirit; we may ask God to fill us (Eph. 5:18) or empower us for special service (Acts 10:38), but we should not pray for His baptism.

Were the apostles correct in asking Christ about the kingdom (vv. 6-8)? Yes. In Matt. 22:1-10, Christ had promised to give the nation of Israel another opportunity to receive Him and the kingdom. In Matt. 19:28 Christ promised that the apostles would sit on twelve thrones (see Luke 22:28-30). In Matt. 12:31-45, Christ stated that Israel would have another opportunity to be saved even after sinning against the Son, and He promised to give them a sign to encourage them. It was the sign of Jonah: death, burial, and resurrection. The apostles knew that their ministry would begin with Israel (see the introductory notes); now they wanted to know what Israel would do. Would the nation accept or reject their message? Christ had not told them whether it would or would not. If He had told the apostles that Israel would spurn this good news, they could not have given their people an honest offer; their ministry would have been false. What He did tell them was that they would be witnesses, starting in Jerusalem, and eventually reaching across the world.

III. A New Assurance (1:9-11)

Do not confuse the promise of v. 11 with that of the rapture of the church as given through Paul in 1 Thes. 4. The angels here are promising that Christ will return to Mt. Olivet, visibly, and in glory. Luke 21:27 and Zech. 14:4 give the same promise. Had Israel accepted the apostles' message, Christ would have returned to Mt. Olivet (see Acts 3:19-21) and established His kingdom. The Jewish missionaries would have spread His Gospel to the ends of the earth, and Israel would have been the center of blessing for all mankind as promised in Isa. 35:1-6 and 65:19-23.

IV. A New Apostle (1:12-25)

Were the apostles correct in selecting this new man? Of course! There had to be twelve men to sit on the twelve promised thrones (Matt. 19:28; Luke 22:28-30) should Israel repent and receive the kingdom. Their decision was based on the Word of God (Ps. 109:8 and 69:25) and on continued prayer (vv. 14 and 24). The new choice, Matthias, was ratified by God since he, with the others, was filled with the Spirit on the Day of Pentecost.

Note that Peter took charge of the meeting. This is perhaps another use of his "binding and loosing" powers given by Christ in Matt. 16:19. Heaven directed them in their decision and ratified their decision after it was made.

Paul could not have been the twelfth apostle. For one thing, he did not meet the qualifications laid down in vv. 21-22; and furthermore, his special ministry had to do with the church, not the kingdom.

Everything was now in readiness for the coming of the Spirit. It was now a matter of time, and as the believers waited for the Day of Pentecost to arrive, they spent their hours in prayer and fellowship in the Upper Room.

ACTS 2

The Feast of Pentecost took place fifty days after the Feast of Firstfruits. (The word "Pentecost" means "fiftieth.") This feast is described in Lev. 23:15-21. Just as Passover is a picture of the death of Christ (1 Cor. 5:7), and Firstfruits a picture of the resurrection of Christ (1 Cor. 15:20-23), so Pentecost pictures the coming of the Holy Spirit (1 Cor. 12:13). The loaves of bread with leaven were presented that day, a picture of the church composed of Jews and Gentiles. (In 1 Cor. 10:17 the church is pictured as a loaf of bread.) The leaven in the bread speaks of sin yet in the church. There are two occurrences of the Spirit's baptism in Acts: upon the Jews in Acts 2, and upon the Gentiles in Acts 10. The two loaves presented at Pentecost foreshadow these events.

I. The Miracles (2:1-13)

The believers were waiting and praying as Christ had commanded (Luke 24:49), and at the proper time, the Spirit descended. When He did, He baptized them into one spiritual body in Christ (see Acts 1:4-5 with 1 Cor. 12:13), and He filled them with power for witnessing (2:4). The sound of rushing wind reminds us of John 3:8 and of Ezekiel's prophecy about the dry bones (Ezek. 37). The tongues of fire symbolize the divine power that would speak for God. Do not confuse these tongues of fire with the baptism of fire mentioned in Matt. 3:11. The baptism of fire mentioned there refers to the time of Israel's tribulation. Since every believer is baptized by the Spirit (1 Cor. 12:13), it is not proper to pray for a baptism of the Holy Spirit and of fire.

The believers spoke in tongues. They did not preach in tongues, but rather praised God in languages they did not naturally know (see 2:11). Apparently they were in the Upper Room when the Spirit descended (2:2), but must have moved out to the temple courts where a great crowd gathered. The purpose of the gift of tongues was to impress the Jews with the fact that a miracle was taking place. In 10:46, the Gentiles spoke with tongues as proof to the apostles that they had received the Spirit; and in 19:6 the Ephesian followers of John the Baptist spoke in tongues for the same reason.

II. The Message (2:14-41)

A. Introduction (vv. 14-21).

Peter first answered their charge that the men were drunk. No Jew would eat or drink anything before 9:00 a.m. on a Sabbath or feast day, and it was then the third hour, or 9:00 a.m. Note that throughout this sermon, Peter addresses Jews only (vv. 14, 22, 29, 36). Pentecost was a Jewish feast, and there were no Gentiles involved. In this sermon, Peter addressed the Jewish nation and proved to them that their Messiah had been raised from the dead. In vv. 16-21, Peter referred the men to Joel 2:28-32 (read that passage carefully). He did not say that this was a fulfillment of the prophecy, for Joel's words will not be fulfilled until the end of the Tribulation when Christ returns to earth. Peter does say that this is that same Spirit spoken of by Joel. Verses 17 and 18 took place at Pentecost, but vv. 19-21 did not, and will not until the end times. Between vv. 18 and 19 would unfold the entire church age.

B. The Explanation (vv. 22-36).

Peter now proved to the Jews that Jesus Christ was alive. He used five very convincing arguments:

(1) Christ's Person and life demand that He be raised from the dead (22-24). See John 10:17-18. He who raised others could not remain dead himself!

(2) Psalm 16:8-11 predicted the resurrection (vv. 25-31).

(3) The apostles themselves were witnesses and had seen the risen Christ (v. 32).

(4) The coming of the Spirit is proof Jesus is alive (v. 33).

(5) Psalm 110:1 promised His resurrection (vv. 33-35). Keep in mind that Peter was not preaching the Gospel of the cross as we preach it today. He was accusing Israel of a great crime (vv. 23) and warning them that they had rejected and crucified their own Messiah (v. 36). Peter was giving Israel one more opportunity to receive Christ. They had slain John the Baptist and Jesus, but God was now giving them another chance. The resurrection of Christ was the promised "sign of Jonah" that proved He was the Messiah (Matt. 12:38-40).

C. The application (vv. 37-40).

The men were convicted and asked Peter for counsel. Peter told them to repent, believe and be baptized; in that way they would be identifying themselves with Jesus as the Christ. This is the same message John the Baptist (Mark 1:4) and Jesus (Matt 4:17) preached. To make baptism essential for salvation and the receiving of the Spirit is to deny the experience of the Gentiles in Acts 10:44-48, which is God's pattern for today. (See the introductory notes on Acts.) The Jews in Acts 2 received the Spirit when they repented and were baptized; the Samaritans in Acts 8 received the Spirit by the laying on of the apostles' hands; but believers today receive the Spirit when they believe, as did the Gentiles in Acts 10. There is no salvation in the waters of baptism, for salvation is by faith in Jesus.

Peter stated that the promise of the Spirit was not only for the Jews present in Jerusalem, but also for the Jews scattered abroad (v. 39, see Dan. 9:7). This verse cannot refer to Gentiles because the Gentiles did not receive any promises (Eph. 2:11-12).

III. The Multitude (2:42-47)

Note that the believers remained in the temple and gave their witness and worship. The Spirit gave them unity of heart and mind and added believers to the assembly day by day. These verses are a beautiful description of what life will be like during the kingdom age. While the church (as we know it) was then in existence in the mind of God, the full revelation of it was not given until later by

Paul. Acts 2 is a message to the Jewish people, so do not read into these verses truths that were not revealed until later. The church today does not meet in the Jewish temple, nor is it required to practice communism. The kingdom offer was still open and would continue to be until the events of Acts 7, when the leaders of the nation resisted the Spirit one more time and killed Stephen.

ACTS 3

I. Power (3:1-11)

The fact that Peter and John still attended the temple and kept the Jewish customs is evidence that these first seven chapters of Acts are Jewish in emphasis. No Christian today who understands Galatians and Hebrews would participate in OT practices.

This cripple is a vivid illustration of the lost sinner in that: (1) he was born lame, and all are born sinners; (2) he could not walk, and no sinner can walk so as to please God; (3) he was outside the temple, and sinners are outside God's temple, the church; (4) he was begging, for sinners are beggars, searching for satisfaction.

Peter performed this miracle, not only to relieve the man's handicap and save his soul, but also to prove to the Jews that the Holy Spirit had come with promised blessings. Isaiah 35:6 promises the Jews that Israel would enjoy such miracles when their Messiah was received. The man's conduct after the miracle shows how every Christian ought to act: he entered the temple in fellowship with God's servants and praised God. His walk was new and different, and he did not run from persecution. His was such a testimony that the officers had no explanation for what had happened.

II. Preaching (3:12-26)

Peter used this healing as an opportunity to present Christ and offer forgiveness to the nation. Note that he addressed "Men of Israel" as he did in 2:14 and 22. He preached Christ to them and accused them of denying their own Messiah. Just a few weeks before, Peter himself had denied Christ three times. Yet because Peter confessed his sin and made things right with the Lord (John 21), he was able to forget his failure. (Read Rom. 8:32-34.)

Verse 17 is most important, for there Peter stated that Israel's ignorance caused them to commit this awful crime. Ignorance is no excuse, but it does affect the penalty handed out. This is why Jesus prayed, "Father, forgive them, for they know not what they do" (Luke 23:34). God was now giving Israel one more opportunity to receive their Messiah. Peter promised in vv. 19-20 that if the nation would repent and receive the Lord, He would blot out their sins (Isa. 43:25 and 44:22-23), send Christ to them, and give them "times of refreshing." These "times" were described in Jer. 23:5, Micah 4:3, and Isa. 11:2-9, 35:1-6, and 65:19-23. Peter was not describing individual salvation here so much as the blessing that would come to the nation if they would but repent and believe. Of course, national salvation depended on personal faith.

Heaven would receive and hold Christ until Israel would repent, and then the "times of restitution" would come. This refers to the kingdom Christ will set up when Israel turns to Him and believes. This event was spoken of by the prophets, Peter states in v. 21, which proves that he was not talking about events of the church. The "mystery" of the church was not revealed to the OT prophets. The prophets spoke of Israel's future kingdom, and that kingdom would have been set up had the rulers and the people believed Peter's message and repented.

What about the Gentiles? Peter answered this in v. 25. The Jews were children of Abraham and of God's covenant, and God would keep His promise to Abraham and bless the Gentiles through Israel. "And in your seed [Abraham's] shall all the families of the earth [Gentiles] be blessed" (see Gen. 12:3 and 22:18). God's program in the OT was to bless the Gentiles through restored Israel and Peter and the other Jewish apostles knew this. They realized that God promised to bless the Gentiles when Israel was established in its kingdom. This is why the apostles could not understand why Paul went to the Gentiles after Israel had been set aside. They did not realize then the "mystery program" that God then revealed through Paul, that through Israel's fall the Gentiles would be saved (see Romans 11:11-12). This program was a "mystery" hidden in OT days, but revealed through Paul (read Eph. 3). When the nation killed Stephen and committed that "unpardonable sin" against the Holy Spirit, God's prophetic program for the Jews came to a halt. From that day, Israel was set aside, and the church took center stage.

How did the nation respond to the invitation? Many of the common people believed and were saved, but the rulers had the apostles arrested. The Sadducees, of course, did not believe in the resurrection and rejected Peter's message that Christ had been raised from the dead. The Pharisees hated Jesus because He had condemned them (Matt. 23). The persecution that Christ promised the apostles in John 15:18–16:4 began to take place as we will see in the next chapter.

ACTS 4

I. The Arrest (4:1-4)

This is beginning of the persecution of the church. The Sadducees did not believe in the resurrection of the dead and were opposed to Peter's preaching. The priests, of course, did not want to be indicted for the crucifixion of Christ. Little did Israel's religious leaders realize that Peter's message was the one thing that could save their nation! Had they admitted their sin and received Christ, He would have bestowed the promises that the prophets had proclaimed centuries before.

II. The Trial (4:5-22)

The court assembled here, composed primarily of the high priest's family, had become corrupted over the years. This was an official meeting of the Sanhedrin, the highest Jewish council. Some of these very men had assisted in the "trial" of Christ not many weeks before. In fact, their question in v. 7 reminds us of Jesus' trial (read again Matt. 26:57ff). Jesus had promised the disciples that the world would treat them the same way it had treated Him (John 15:17ff). Note, too, that in Matt. 21:23-44 these same leaders had questioned Christ about His authority.

Peter's reply was directed by the Holy Spirit, in fulfillment of the promise in Luke 21:12-15 and Matt. 10:20. Believers today should never claim this promise as an excuse for neglecting to study or prepare for teaching or preaching. The Holy Spirit assists us in those emergency hours when preparation is impossible, if we have been faithful at other times. Peter boldly stated that Jesus Christ, the crucified and now living Lord, performed the miracle through His apostles. How those Jews must have trembled to come face-to-face with their awful crime! Yet it did no good, because their hearts had become calloused.

Verse 11 identifies Christ as the Stone and the Jewish leaders as the builders. This is a quotation from Psalm 118:22-23. Christ Himself used this passage in debating with these very leaders (Matt. 21:43). The Jews rejected Christ as the Chosen Stone on whom the kingdom would be established; that Rejected Stone became the Chief Cornerstone of the church (Eph. 2:20). Note that Peter stated clearly that Israel had rejected Christ. However, in v. 12, he invited them to believe on Christ and be saved. While this verse certainly applies to all sinners of every age, it had a special meaning for the nation in Peter's day. Had the leaders repented and received Christ, He would have saved the nation from the awful tragedy that came in just a few years when Rome destroyed the temple and the city.

In vv. 13-17 the "jury" recessed to consider the case. They were impressed with the boldness of the apostles. This is significant inasmuch as Peter had denied his Lord in fear just a few weeks before. The phrase "unlearned and ignorant" (v. 13) literally means "untaught and unlettered"; that is, the apostles had not been instructed in the official schools of the rabbis. Yet they knew so much more about the Scriptures than did the religious leaders. The leaders also realized that these men "had been with Jesus" (v. 13) in the Garden and during His last week in Jerusalem before His death. But they faced an even greater problem: how could they explain the healing of the beggar? They could not deny the miracle, so they decided to silence the messengers.

The apostles did not accept this verdict, for their loyalty to Christ meant more than any protection from the government. The judges finally had to let them go. The boldness of the disciples, the power of the Word, and the testimony of the healed beggar were too good a "case" and the judges had no answer.

III. The Victory (4:23-37)

True Christians always return "to their own company." (Read 1 John 2:19.) The assembly did not lament because persecution had begun; rather, the believers rejoiced and prayed! Note that in vv. 25-26 they referred to Psalm 2, which is a messianic Psalm, speaking about the day when Christ shall return to rule with power. Christians today ought to imitate the first Christians in their praying, for they tied their praying to the word of God (John 15:7).

They prayed for boldness, and God answered by filling them with the Spirit. This was not a "second Pentecost," for the Spirit came to fill with power and not to baptize the believers. The Holy Spirit also gave them a wonderful unity, so much so that they sold their goods and shared with those in need. This "Christian communism" was another proof of the presence of the Spirit, a sample of what will happen in the kingdom age when all nations have the Spirit and unselfishly love one another. This "communism" has no relation to Marxist communism. Please note that this sharing of goods was a temporary occurrence and is not required by the church of Christ today. While Christians today are to have the same spirit of love, they are not expected to sell their goods and form a separate community. In 11:27-30, the Christians at Antioch had to send relief to the Jerusalem believers. (See also Rom. 15:26; 1 Cor. 16:1-3; 2 Cor. 8:1-4 and 9:2.) When Israel rejected the message, this gracious working of the Spirit gradually disappeared. The pattern for NT church giving is found in 2 Cor. 8–9, 1 Tim. 5:8 and 2 Thes. 3:7-13.

"Boldness" seems to be a key thought in this chapter. See how the early believers received this boldness: they were filled with the Spirit (vv. 8 and 31), they prayed (v. 29), and they relied on the Word of God (vv. 25-28). You and I may have boldness in our walk and witness if we feed on the Word, pray, and surrender to the Spirit. We may have boldness on earth because Christ gives us boldness in heaven (Heb. 4:16 and 10:19).

ACTS 5

Satan is still attacking the believers, and as he does, he uses a dual plan: deception from within and persecution from without. Satan is a liar and a murderer, and we see him operating in both spheres in this chapter.

I. Opposition from Within (5:1-16)

Here we see Satan operating as the serpent, using believers within the assembly to hinder the work of the Lord.

A. The deception (vv. 1-2).

Ananias and Sapphira wanted to gain the reputation for being more spiritual than they actually were. When the others brought their donations (4:34-37), these two were jealous and wanted the same recognition. Please keep in mind that their sin was not stealing money from God, because Peter stated in v. 4 that it was in their own power to use the money as they wished. Their sin was hypocrisy, trying to appear more spiritual than they really were.

B. The discovery (vv. 3-4).

Peter was a man with Spirit-given discernment. Here we see him exercising the "binding and loosing" power given to him by Christ (Matt. 16:19). Sin is always discovered in one way or another. This couple had not mentioned anything openly, but the terrible sin was in their hearts. They had lied to the Spirit of God who was graciously working in the hearts of the believers, leading them to sell their belongings and share with others.

C. The deaths (vv. 5-11).

This was not a case of "church discipline" since God dealt with the sinners directly. The two deaths illustrate the kind of judgment Christ will exercise during the kingdom (see Jer. 23:5 and Rev. 19:15). Unlike local church discipline, where the pastor and the church investigate a matter, give opportunity for repentance and forgiveness, and seek to restore the erring ones, this was a definite case of divine judgment. It is interesting to compare this chapter to Joshua 7, where the covetous Achan tried to hide sin from God and was killed. Great fear fell on the church (v. 11) as people saw the hand of God at work.

D. The testimony (vv. 12-16).

The assembly was now unified and magnified, and it therefore multiplied. This will always happen when an assembly is purged of sin. Satan works inside the church and tries to divide it, disgrace it, and destroy it; but if we let the Spirit work, we will detect the devil's operation and avoid church problems. It is not the church that welcomes everybody that has the best testimony, for the people were afraid to join the church there in Jerusalem (v. 13). A local church must have standards and must let the Spirit lead. Note that Peter is the key man at this period of church history; even his shadow was thought to bring healing.

Satan still opposes the work of the church from within. Paul warned the elders that wolves would come in from the outside to attack the flock, but also that men would arise "from among yourselves" to harm the church (Acts 20:29-30, NKJV). The greatest danger the church faces today is not so much opposition from without, but sin from within. This is why it is important to seek God's guidance in receiving new members and in disciplining those who stray.

II. Opposition from Without (5:17-34)

The Jewish leaders (spurred on by the unbelieving Sadducees) were filled with jealousy ("indignation" in v. 17) at the success and popularity of the apostles. This time the entire apostolic band was probably put in prison, most likely in public prison and not a special ward. An angel of the Lord (this may have been Christ Himself) delivered them, and thus graciously God gave the nation another chance to hear the message of salvation. Note that the men went straight to the temple, for this is where they would find the people who needed their message. Imagine the surprise of the leaders when they discovered the prisoners gone! Keep in mind that deliverance is not always God's plan; He allowed Peter to be delivered but James to be slain (Acts 12) because each event worked out for His glory.

The leaders refused to pronounce the name of Jesus (v. 38)! "This man's blood" reminds us of what the nation had said in Matt. 27:25. The Jewish nation will not be cleansed until they see their Messiah and are purged from their sin (Zech. 12:9–13:1).

Peter and the apostles would not give in. Again they announced that God would save Israel if the leaders repented (v. 31). If the leaders turned from their sin, the people would follow their example (see John 7:48). The Word, like a sword (Heb. 4:12), cut the rulers to the heart, and they wanted to murder the apostles, just as they murdered Jesus!

Gamaliel then gave his advice to the council: stay neutral and find out whether God was in this movement or not. This appeared to be wise counsel, but actually it was not. No one can be neutral about Christ. To delay making a decision is to court disaster. God had given every evidence through signs and miracles that He was at work, and there was no reason to put off a decision. It is interesting to note that Gamaliel was a Pharisee, and not a part of the Sadducee group that led the arrest. He is also the great Jewish rabbi who taught the Apostle Paul (Acts 22:3). His pupil made a better decision than he did!

The apostles were beaten (see Deut. 25:2-3) and released, but they went away in joy, not defeat! They counted it a privilege to suffer for Christ (see Phil. 1:27-30). Note that the ministry of the church continued: (1) daily, (2) in public, and (3) in private homes, as the apostles taught and preached Jesus Christ. This must be the ministry of the church today.

ACTS 6

We meet now a second problem within the assembly. In chapter 5 it was deceit in the hearts of Ananias and Sapphira; here it is complaining in the ranks of the believers.

I. A Family Difficulty (6:1-7)

In one sense, the complaining was an evidence of blessing! The assembly had increased so rapidly that the apostles were not able to handle the daily distribution of food, and as a result some of the Grecian Jews had been neglected. It is encouraging to trace the growth of the church: 3,000 believed (2:41); then believers were added daily (2:47); then the church grew to 5,000 men (4:4); then this number multiplied (6:1); and then the number multiplied again greatly (6:7).

What was the secret of this amazing growth? Read 5:41-42 for the answer: the leaders were willing to pay any price to serve Christ, and the people lived their faith daily. Acts 5:42 is a good pattern for us to follow: (1) daily Christian service; (2) service in God's house; (3) service from house to house; (4) work from every member; (5) continuous service; (6) teaching and preaching the Word; (7) exalting Jesus Christ. Godly pastors and officers alone cannot make a church grow; every member must do his or her part.

The food problem was solved by putting first things first. The apostles knew that their primary ministry was prayer and the Word of God. If local churches would allow their pastors to obey Acts 6:4, we would see increase in spiritual power and in numbers. Prayer and the Word go together (John 15:7; Prov. 28:9). Samuel ministered in this way (see 1 Sam. 12:23); so did Christ (Mark 1:35-39) and Paul (Col. 1:9-10). In Acts 1, through prayer and the Word the apostles found God's will. Ephesians 6:17-18 states that prayer and the Word will overcome the devil. Second Cor. 9:9-15 indicates that the ministry of prayer and the Word will provide the financial resources a church needs. Prayer and the Word will build a church in every way (Acts 20:32-36).

These seven men are not actually called "deacons," although the word "ministration" in 6:1 is *diakonia* in the Gk., and this word is transliterated "deacon" elsewhere in the Bible. The word simply means "servant"; in 6:2 it is translated as "serve" and in 6:4 as "ministry." Note that the assembly did the choosing while the apostles did the actual appointing. The apostles also, led by the Spirit, laid down the requirements which the believers gladly accepted. This is a picture of unity and harmony between spiritual leaders and the members of the flock. It is possible that this early appointment grew into the office of deacon (1 Tim. 3:8ff). The deacons' main task was to take care of material needs and thus relieve the apostles for their spiritual ministry. Today, the deacon assists the pastor in counsel and service, helping him get as much work done as possible. Whenever deacons (or other church officers) shackle the pastor and make a sanctified "errand boy" out of him, and "boss him" around, God cannot bless.

Note that the men selected (v. 5) had Greek names! This shows the love of the early believers; in honor, they preferred one another (Rom. 12:10). Philip later became an evangelist (8:5, 26; 21:8). Every church officer ought to be an evangelist. See how God blessed the people when they faced their problem honestly and solved it (v. 7).

II. Faithful Deacon (6:8-15)

The name Stephen means "victor's crown," and certainly he earned a crown by being faithful unto death (Rev. 2:10). According to v. 3, Stephen had a good reputation among the believers, was Spirit-filled, and had practical wisdom. What a combination for any Christian! He had a two-fold witness: his words (v. 10) and his deeds (v. 8).

There were hundreds of synagogues in Jerusalem, many of them established by Jews from other lands. The synagogue of the Libertines was made up of Roman Jews who were descendants of Hebrew slaves who had been set free. ("Libertines" in v. 9 could be translated "freedmen.") It is interesting to note that Stephen testified in the place where there were Jews from Cilicia, for Paul was from that place (21:39) and might well have faced Stephen in debate there in the synagogue.

The enemy is always at work, and before long Stephen was arrested. They accused him of blaspheming Moses and the Law and charged him with saying that the temple would be destroyed; this may be a reference to Christ's words in John 2:19-21. The Jews treated Stephen the way they treated Christ: they hired false witnesses, made dubious accusations, and did not give him the benefit of a fair trial. (See Mark 14:58 and 64.) God gave witness to Stephen's faith by radiating His glory from his face (2 Cor. 3:18).

In the next chapter we will consider Stephen's great address, showing Israel's failure down through the centuries. Chapter seven will be the turning point in Acts, as Israel finally rejected Jesus Christ and persecuted the church. After this event the message went out of Jerusalem to the Gentiles.

ACTS 7

This chapter records the longest single speech in the Book of Acts as well as the turning point in Israel's spiritual history. It records the nation's third important murder (John the Baptist, Christ, and now Stephen) and their final rejection of the message of salvation. In his address, Stephen reviewed the history of Israel and pointed out that the nation always rejected God's chosen leaders when they first appeared, but received them the second time. Both Moses and Joseph were examples of this pattern (7:13 and 35). This is the very way Israel treated Christ: He was presented to the nation on earth by John the Baptist and the apostles, but it refused Him; but Israel will receive Christ when He appears the second time.

I. God's Covenant with Abraham (7:1-8)

The covenant with Abraham is recorded in Genesis 13:14-18, as well as in Genesis 15 and 17. It included the ownership by Abraham's seed of the land of promise, and the promise of a multiplied seed in the years to come. The seal of this covenant was circumcision. This covenant with Abraham was the foundation of the Jewish nation. God did not make this covenant with the Gentiles, nor does it apply to the church. To "spiritualize" these promises and apply them to the church is to misunderstand and twist Scripture. God promised the Jews a land and a kingdom; because of their disobedience, they lost possession of the land and failed to receive their kingdom

This covenant with Abraham still stands, however, and will be fulfilled when Christ returns to set up His kingdom on earth.

II. Israel's Rejection of Joseph (7:9-16)

Joseph bears a wonderful resemblance to Christ in many ways: (1) he was beloved of his father (Gen. 37:3; Matt. 3:17); (2) he was hated by his brethren (Gen. 37: 4-8; John 15:25); (3) he was envied by his brethren (Gen. 37:11; Mark 15:10); (4) he was sold for the price of a slave (Gen. 37:28; Matt. 26:15); (5) he was humbled as a servant (Gen. 39:1ff; Phil. 2:5ff); (6) he was falsely accused (Gen. 39:16-18; Matt. 26:59-60); (7) he was exalted to honor (Gen. 41:14ff; Phil. 2:9-10); (8) he was not recognized by his brethren the first time (Gen. 42:8; Acts 3:17); (9) he revealed himself to them the second time (Gen. 45:1ff; Acts 7:13; Zech. 12:10); (10) while rejected by his brethren, he took a Gentile bride (Gen. 41:45; Acts 15:6-18).

Stephen's argument here is that the Jews had treated Christ the way the patriarchs treated Joseph, but he did not bring this accusation out until the end. Just as Joseph suffered to save his people, so Christ suffered to save Israel and all humankind; yet the Jews did not receive Him.

III. Israel's Rejection of Moses (7:7-41)

Like Joseph, Moses was strikingly similar to Christ: (1) he was persecuted and almost slain when a child (Ex. 1:22 and 4:19; Matt. 2:13-20); (2) he refused the world that he might save his people (Heb. 11:24-26; Matt. 4:8-10; 2 Cor. 8:9); (3) he was rejected the first time he tried to help Israel (Ex. 2:11-14; Isa. 53:3); (4) he became a shepherd (Ex. 3:1; John. 10); (5) he took a Gentile bride during his rejection (Ex. 2:21); (6) he was received by his brethren the second time (Ex. 4:29-31; Acts 7:5); (7) he delivered the people from bondage through the blood of the lamb (Ex. 12; 1 Peter 2:24). Moses was a prophet (Deut. 18:15-19; Acts 3:22), a priest (Ps. 99:6), and a king (Deut. 33:4-5).

A comment may be needed on v. 38, where Israel is called "the church in the wilderness." This word *ekklesia* means "a called-out assembly" and does not suggest that Israel was the "church" in the OT. We do not find prophecies about the church in the OT. Israel (an earthly people) was not in the same relationship to God in the OT as believers (a heavenly people) were in the NT.

Though Israel had a godly leader and God Himself in their presence (v. 38), they still rebelled and rejected God's will! "In their hearts they turned back again to Egypt!" (v. 39) They turned to idolatry, and God gave them up. Had they not done the same thing while Christ was with them on earth? Moses performed miracles, met their needs in the wilderness, and gave them the Word of God; Christ also had performed mighty works, fed the people, and had given them God's Word—yet they turned away!

IV. Israel's Rejection of the Prophets (7:42-50)

In these verses Stephen refers to Amos 5:25-27 and Isa. 66:1-2. The Jews thought that because they had their temple, they were safe from harm, and God had to bless them. The prophets all warned them that the temple would not assure them of blessing if their hearts were not right. How can God, who fills all heaven and earth, be confined to a temple made with hands? Israel's religious life was a formality; they had the outward forms of religion but their hearts were not right with God. They rejected the voice of the prophets, even persecuting and killing them (see Matt. 23:29-39); and when The Prophet (Christ) appeared (v. 37), they rejected His Words and crucified Him!

V. Israel's Judgment Sealed (7:51-60)

Israel had committed two murders and was about to commit the third. In allowing John the Baptist to be slain, they rejected the Father who had sent John to prepare the way for Christ. When they crucified Christ, they rejected the Son. Now, in slaying Stephen, they were committing the final "unpardonable sin" (Matt. 12:31-32) of resisting the Holy Spirit. God would have forgiven the nation of its treatment of His Son, but He could not forgive the Jews once they resisted the Spirit who witnessed so mightily to His Son. God had given every evidence to the nation that Christ was their Messiah, but they preferred to harden their necks and hearts (7:51). How like sinners today!

Stephen used the Word, and this "sword of the spirit" (Eph. 6:17; Heb. 4:12) cut them in conviction to the heart. About to be slain, Stephen lifted his eyes to heaven and saw the glory of God. "Ichabod—the glory hath departed" (1 Sam. 4:19-22) could now be said of the nation of Israel; but Stephen saw that glory in Christ, where we see it today (2 Cor. 4:1ff). Verses like Ps. 110:1, Mark 16:19, and Heb. 1:3 and 10:12 indicate that Christ "sat down" because of His finished work; but v. 55 speaks of Him standing. Some have suggested that He stood to receive His martyr, Stephen, as he came to glory. Others think Christ stood as a witness, the usual posture of witnesses in the Jewish court, testifying to His servant's message and ministry. Another fact we want to note is that Stephen's death closed the offer of the King to the Jews and was the turning point in Acts, for now the church as the body of Christ begins to assume chief importance; and it is to the church that Christ has His ministry at the right hand of God. Perhaps Luke 22:69 should be kept in mind; the Jewish leaders would certainly recall Christ's testimony.

Stephen's prayer shows his own love for his people and reminds us of Christ's intercession on the cross. Perhaps Stephen thought, seeing Christ standing, that He was going to bring judgment on the nation for their repeated sin (see Ps. 7:6), and so he prayed for grace and a postponement of wrath. "He fell asleep" is a beautiful picture of what death means to a believer!

Israel's judgment was sealed; in the next chapters we will see the Gospel of grace (not the message of the kingdom) moving from the Jews to the Samaritans and the Gentiles.

ACTS 8

Chapters 1–7 have described the "Period of Testing," during which the kingdom was offered to Israel for the third time. Chapters 8–12 describe the "Period of Transition" during which the following changes take place:

(1) The center of activity moves from Jerusalem to Antioch.

(2) The message goes from the Jews to the Samaritans and then to Gentiles.

(3) Peter's activities assume less importance as Paul becomes leader.

(4) The communism of the "kingdom economy" is replaced by the activity of the church. The church had been in existence since Pentecost, but its meaning and place in God's program were now revealed through Paul's ministry of grace.

(5) The Gospel of the kingdom is replaced by the Gospel of the grace of God. If the Ethiopian eunuch was black (as some say he

was), then in chapters 8–10 you have three remarkable conversions paralleling the three sons of Noah in Gen. 10:18. The Ethiopian would have descended from Ham; Paul, a Jew, from Shem; and Cornelius, a Gentile, from Japheth. Thus we have a picture of the Gospel going to the whole of humankind.

I. Philip the Evangelist (8:1-25)

Satan again attacked as a lion, seeking to devour the believers. Paul was the chief leader in this great persecution and admitted it later several times (Acts 26:10-11; 22:4-5 and 18-20; 1 Tim. 1:13; 1 Cor. 15:9; Gal. 1:13). Note that Paul definitely stated that he persecuted the church of God, which proves that the church was in existence before Paul's conversion, though its place in God's plan had yet to be revealed. Some teach that God had to send persecution to force the apostles to leave Jerusalem and fulfill His commission, but this is entirely wrong. To begin with, the apostles did not leave the city, but courageously remained to give their message to the Jewish leaders and to witness to the lost. The apostles were hoping against hope that Israel would repent and be saved. They could have this ministry only in Jerusalem. Christ's commandment to them was to remain there; it was Paul who would take the Gospel "to the uttermost parts."

Persecution is an opportunity for service, and Philip is given here as an example of an evangelist (Eph. 4:11). Called to be a deacon (6:5), like Stephen before him, Philip discovered added spiritual gifts and became a mighty evangelist. He took the Gospel to Samaria, just as Christ had done in John 4; and thus for the first time in Acts we see the ministry of the Word moved from Jewish territory. Persecution only opened the door for soul-winning; what began as "great persecution" (v. 1) became "great joy" (v. 8).

What Satan could not accomplish through destruction he here sought to accomplish through deception; the lion becomes the serpent (John 8:44). Simon the sorcerer made a profession of faith in Christ and was even baptized; but subsequent events proved that his heart was never changed. His "faith" was like that described in John 2:23-25. That Simon was never saved is evident: (1) Peter said, "Your money perish with you" (v. 20); (2) he also said, "You have neither part nor lot [fellowship] in this word" (translated "matter" in v. 21); (3) v. 23 indicates Simon was in the bond of iniquity. Simon was a Satanic counterfeit, a "child of the devil." Wherever the true seed (Christians — see Matt. 13:36-40) is sown, Satan sows his counterfeits.

Peter made his first use of "the keys of the kingdom" at Pentecost, when he opened the door of faith to the Jews; he uses them for the second time here when he imparts the Spirit to the Samaritans. Until now, people had to be baptized to receive the Spirit; but now the gift was given through the laying on of hands (see Paul's case in 9:17). Those who teach that Peter's command in Acts 2:38 is God's demand today have a hard time explaining how these Samaritan believers received the Spirit several days after they were baptized. When we reach Acts 10 — concerning the Gentiles — we have God's order for today: hear the Word, believe, receive the Spirit, be baptized.

II. Philip the Personal Worker (8:26-40)

Any Christian would enjoy a revival such as that which God gave in Samaria, but not everyone would leave such a meeting to lead one soul to Christ! Philip obeyed the Lord and found an Ethiopian, undoubtedly a proselyte to the Jewish faith, a man who was a high officer in his land. We see in this event the factors necessary for effective personal work and soul-winning.

A. The man of God.

Philip was obedient to the Spirit, going where God led him. He knew Christ as his own Savior. God's method for winning others does not use organizational machinery, worldly attractions, or high-powered promotion. God uses people — dedicated men and women who will obey the Spirit. Philip was the kind of evangelist who was willing to leave the public meeting with its excitement to help a soul find peace in a private place where only God could see.

B. The Spirit of God.

The Holy Spirit is the Lord of the Harvest, and it's through Him that we have the power to witness (Acts 1:8). The Spirit opened the way for Philip to come to the man; He opened the Scriptures to the seeking sinner; and He opened the sinner's heart to the Savior. A man cannot be saved who does not understand what he is doing, and only the Spirit can teach the sinner the truths of the Gospel. When the Spirit brings a prepared servant and a contrite sinner together, there will be a harvest.

C. The Word of God.

"Faith comes by hearing, and hearing by the Word of God" says Rom. 10:17 (NKJV). Isaiah 53 was the chapter Philip used (vv. 32-33), that wonderful picture of the Lamb of God; from that chapter Philip preached Christ. He began where the man was and took him through the Scriptures, explaining who Jesus was and what He had done. There can be no real conversion apart from the Word of God. Consider these Scriptures: John 5:24; Eph. 1:12-14; 1 Thes. 2:1-6; 2 Thes. 3:1; 2 Tim. 4:1-5; Titus 1:3. The personal witness that finally bears fruit is the witness that plants the seed of the Word and exalts Jesus Christ.

The Ethiopian proved his faith by his baptism, in obedience to the Word of God. Philip was caught away for a ministry elsewhere; but the treasurer went on his way rejoicing! When Philip preached Christ in the city, there was great joy (v. 8), and when he presented Christ in the desert, he sent the new believer on his way rejoicing. Joy is one of the evidences of true conversion. See Luke 15:5-7, 9-10, 23-24, 32.

ACTS 9

The conversion of Paul is the great turning-point in God's dealings with Israel. His whole program for the evangelization of the world depended on this unusual man. If we are to rightly divide the Word of Truth, we must keep in mind that Peter and Paul in the Book of Acts represent two different ministries. Note these contrasts:

Peter	Paul
1. One of the twelve apostles	1. Called apart from the Twelve
2. Centered in Jerusalem	2. Centered in Antioch
3. Ministered mainly to Israel	3. Ministered to the Gentiles
4. Called on earth by Christ	4. Called by Christ from heaven
5. Saw Christ's glory on earth	5. Saw Christ's glory in heaven

Too many Christians confuse these two ministries and thus turn the local church into a hodgepodge of "kingdom truth" and "church truth." Paul is God's spokesman to the local church; even Peter admits this (2 Peter 3:15-16). To follow the practices of the local assembly in Acts 1–7, and thus ignore God's instructions to the church through Paul, is to disobey the Word. Even Peter did not fully understand God's new program revealed through Paul and had to be instructed further (see Gal. 2).

I. Paul and the Lord (9:1-9)

Paul's conversion was all of grace; God suddenly interrupted him on his murderous mission and by grace transformed him into a new person. Just as the church is one body composed of Jews and Gentiles, so Paul was one man with both Jewish and Gentile relationships. He was a Jew by birth, but a Gentile by citizenship. He was God's choice servant (v. 15) to announce the message of the church, this "mystery" that God had kept secret from ages past. Being associated with both Jews and Gentiles, trained in the OT Scriptures as well as the Greek philosophies and Roman laws, Paul was the ideal man to give this new message that there is no difference between Jew and Gentile in Christ.

His conversion experience can be summarized in these statements: (1) He saw a light; (2) He heard a voice; (3) He obeyed a call. Every sinner is in the dark until the light of the Gospel shines on him. Paul heard the voice of the Lord through the Word of God, although Paul heard Christ speak audibly. (The men with him heard sounds, but did not hear the words.) How Christ humbled Paul! He "fell" not only physically but in his heart as well; for unless we fall in humility we cannot be saved. Verse 4 is another proof that the body of Christ was in existence; otherwise how could Paul persecute Christ? When he laid hands on believers, he laid hands on the members of His body, and this affected the Head of the body, Christ.

III. Paul and Ananias (9:10-19)

Paul had seen in a vision that Ananias would visit him, for when God works, He works at both ends of the line. Ananias's fears were answered by God's promise that Paul would have a special ministry to the Gentiles, and how those words must have shocked this faithful Jewish believer! (See Acts 22:12-13.) Paul's ministry was primarily to the Gentiles; see Acts 13:46-47; 18:6; 22:21. The fact that Paul was already saved when Ananias arrived is seen in Ananias's greeting, "Brother Saul." Some misunderstand Paul's baptismal experience as recorded in Acts 22:16: "Arise, and be baptized, and wash away your sins" (NKJV). The tenses of the Gk.

verbs are important here: "Having arisen, be baptized and wash away your sins, having previously called upon His Name" (WUEST). When sinners call on God's name, they are saved (Acts 2:21; 9:14). Acts 10 illustrates this: sinners hear the Word, believe on Jesus Christ, receive the Spirit, and then are baptized.

III. Paul and the Jews (9:20-31)

Two evidences are given of Paul's conversion: he prayed (v. 11) and he preached (v. 20). Talking to God for men and to men for God are good proofs of conversion. Paul started where he was and preached what he knew, another good policy for new Christians to follow. His conversion was probably in the year A.D. 37. He spent time in Damascus preaching, then went to Arabia (Gal. 1:15-18), returning to Damascus "after many days" (Acts 9:23). This covered a period of probably three years, during which time Paul was being taught the truths of God's "mystery of the church." When back in Damascus, he was attacked by the Jews and had to leave through a window at night (2 Cor. 11:32-33; Acts 9:23-26.)

This takes us from A.D. 37 to A.D. 39, at which time he went to Jerusalem, where he met the apostles (Acts 9:26-29; 22:15-21; Gal. 1:17-20). The apostles were afraid of Paul, and it was Barnabas ("son of consolation," Acts 4:36) who introduced Paul to the group. The fact that Paul was a stranger (and even an enemy) to the apostles is important: it proves that he got his message of grace from Christ Himself and not from men. (See Gal. 1:15-18.) God took every precaution to keep separate the ministries of Paul and the twelve apostles. What a tragedy that people confuse them today. Paul stayed with Peter for fifteen days (Gal. 1:18), but he did not see any other apostle (Gal. 1:19). He did visit James, the Lord's brother (Gal. 1:19) who later took Peter's place as the spiritual leader in Jerusalem (Acts 15). Paul wanted to minister to the Jews in Jerusalem, but God commanded him to depart from the city (Acts 22:17-21). God's kingdom program at Jerusalem was now at a close, and Paul had a ministry to fulfill among the Gentiles.

Further persecution made it necessary for Paul to leave, so he returned to his home at Tarsus. Gal. 1:21 suggests that Paul preached in that region, and Acts 15:23 indicates that there were churches in that area. It is possible that during his stay of four or five years, Paul preached the Gospel of the grace of God and established Gentile churches. When the center of ministry moved from

Jerusalem to Antioch (a Gentile city), Barnabas went and sought for Paul and brought him back to minister with him (see Acts 11:19-30).

IV. Peter and the Saints (9:32-43)

Why does Luke discuss Peter at this point? The answer may have to do with the city he mentions: Joppa (vv. 36 and 43). This city reminds us at once of the prophet Jonah, who went down to Joppa to flee to Tarshish (Jonah 1:1-3). God called Jonah to carry His message to the Gentiles; and God was about to call Peter to do the same thing (Acts 10). Peter lived in Joppa with Simon, a tanner, suggesting that some of Peter's Jewish prejudices are now being set aside, for tanning was "unclean" as far as Jews were concerned. Peter was about to discover that nothing is unclean that God has sanctified.

ACTS 10

This chapter is one of the most important in the entire Book of Acts, for it records the opening of the door of faith to the Gentiles. Peter had used "the keys of the kingdom" to open the door of faith to the Jews (Acts 2) and the Samaritans (Acts 8:14ff), and now would complete his special ministry by opening the door to the Gentiles (see Acts 15:6-11). You should also read Acts 11:1-18 to get Peter's picture of this momentous event.

We noted in Acts 8 that, when God wants to do a work, He calls a man of God, empowers him with the Spirit of God, and enables him to preach the Word of God. This same program is seen in operation in this chapter.

I. Preparation by the Spirit of God (10:1-22)

A. The Spirit prepares Cornelius (vv. 1-8).

Caesarea was a Roman city, the Roman capital of Palestine. Cornelius was a God-fearing Gentile who did not know the truth of the Gospel. He was devout, honest, generous, and sincere; but he was not a saved man. It is possible to be very religious but still be lost! Were it not for the fact that God in His grace spoke to Cornelius, he would never have become a believer. We see here a fulfillment of Christ's promise in John 7:17, "If any man is willing to do His will, he shall know the truth." An angel spoke to him and told him to send for Peter. Why did not the angel give Cornelius the message himself? Because God has not given to angels the ministry of sharing the Gospel with sinners. What a privilege we have in telling the Gospel to lost souls, a privilege angels cannot have! Peter was thirty miles away at Joppa, but with soldier-like obedience, Cornelius called for two servants and a guard and sent them on this important mission. The Spirit was leading all of this activity (vv. 19-20).

B. The Spirit prepares Peter (vv. 9-22).

Whenever God is at work, He leads "at both ends of the line." He prepares us for what He is preparing for us. Peter saw all kinds of creatures, both clean and unclean (ceremonially speaking, cf. Lev. 11) and was commanded to kill and eat. His "Not so, Lord!" reminds us of Matt. 16:22, where he told Christ not to go to the cross. Anyone who says "Lord" cannot say "Not so!" If He is truly Lord, we must obey Him. While Peter thought about this vision, which occurred three times, the Spirit spoke to him directly and told him, "Arise and go!" Peter did not go to the Gentiles because he understood the vision, but because the Holy Spirit Himself told him to go (see 11:11-16). Later, he fully understood the meaning of the vision, that God had, through the cross, broken down all division between Jews and Gentiles.

II. Obedience of the Man of God (10:23-33)

Keep in mind that, up to this time, the Apostles had not preached to the Gentiles. Even the Samaritans (Acts 8) were "half-breed" Jews with reverence for the Mosaic law. Peter did not go to the Gentiles because he was obeying the Great Commission (although he was), but because the Spirit had distinctly commanded him to go. In fact, when he arrived at Cornelius' house, he asked, "For what reason have you sent for me?" (v. 29, NKJV) And when he preached, God had to interrupt him in order to accomplish His purpose (v. 44 and 11:15-16). Like the other apostles, Peter was still clinging to the Jewish outlook, and he knew that the Gentiles could not be reached until the Jews had accepted their Messiah and He had set up His kingdom. But now Peter was going to learn that God was introducing a new program—the church. Please do not assume that Peter understood all about this new program; in fact, Paul later had to rebuke Peter for his inconsistency (see Gal. 2). During this period of transition (Acts 8–12) we see Peter disappearing from the scene and with him the kingdom message to Israel.

III. The Preaching of the Word of God (10:34-48)

A prepared preacher and a prepared congregation make a wonderful team! Read Heb. 11:6 in connection with v. 35; Peter did not say that all who "do good" are saved. He began with the message of Christ to Israel, starting with the ministry of John the Baptist. He stated that Cornelius and his friends knew already the message about Christ's miracles, His death, and His resurrection and that these events were related especially to Israel. In v. 42 he said, "And He commanded us [Jewish witnesses] to preach unto the people" (meaning the Jews), which is what the apostles did up to that time. What Peter had said was simply that Christ came to save the nation of Israel, but now he realized that with God there is no difference between Jews and Gentiles. He spoke the key truth in v. 43 when he said, "whoever believes in Him will receive remission of sins" (NKJV).

At this point the Spirit interrupted Peter and wrought a miracle in the hearts of these Gentiles. They believed the Word! And when they believed, the Spirit was poured out upon them, the evidence being that they spoke with tongues. (See Gal. 3:2.) The Jews with Peter were astonished that God would save the Gentiles without first making them Jewish proselytes. Led by the Spirit, Peter commanded that they be baptized; and Peter and his friends stayed and ate with these new believers (11:3).

Review once again the relationship in Acts between the Spirit and baptism. In Acts 2, the Jews believed and had to be baptized to receive the Spirit. In Acts 8, the Samaritans believed and were baptized, but they received the Spirit by the laying on of the apostles' hands. But here in Acts 10 we are on true "church ground," for these Gentiles heard the Word, believed, received the Spirit, and then were baptized. The events of Acts 2:38 and 8:14-17 are not the pattern for the church today. Ephesians 1:13-14 should be read carefully. The Spirit's coming was actually a baptism, as Peter explained in Acts 11:15-16. Only two times is the word "baptism" used in Acts with reference to the Spirit: in Acts 2, when the Spirit came upon the believing Jews, and in Acts 10, when He came upon the believing Gentiles. This fulfills what Paul describes in 1 Cor. 12:13, "For by one Spirit are we all baptized into one body, whether we be Jews or Gentiles." This "one body" is the church (Eph. 2:11-22). In fact, in 11:15 Peter stated that the baptism in the home of Cornelius was identical to the one at Pentecost. Today, when sinners accept Christ, the Spirit comes into their bodies, and they are baptized into the body of Christ.

As we will see in Acts 11 and 15, the conversion of the Gentiles created a great problem for the Jewish believers, not because they were guilty of prejudice, but because they did not understand "the mystery" of the church (Eph. 3).

They thought that the Gentiles could be saved only through Israel's rise as a kingdom; but God revealed through Paul that through Israel's *fall* the Gentiles were saved (Rom. 11:11-25). The message of the kingdom given through the prophets (Acts 3:18-26) was replaced by the message of the grace of God, revealed in its fullness through Paul (Acts 13:38-43). Israel was set aside and will not be prominent in God's program on earth again until after the church has been raptured. (Read carefully Acts 15:13-18.) To mix kingdom truth and church truth is to confuse the Word of God and hinder the work of God.

The church's commission today is found in Matt. 28:19-20. We are to make disciples, which calls for evangelism; we are to baptize, which implies fellowship in a local assembly; and we are to teach the Word, which the Spirit uses to convict the lost. Let us be busy sowing the seed of the Word, watering it with our prayers and tears (Ps. 126:5-6; Acts 20:19) and patiently waiting for the harvest.

ACTS 11

In this chapter we learn of the relationship between believers in Jerusalem (a Jewish church) and the new Gentile disciples. Keep in mind that the Jerusalem church's problem is not prejudice but rather a misunderstanding of the purposes of God. The OT understanding of God's program was that of an earthly kingdom which would bless the Gentiles through the reign of Israel's Messiah. But the nation had rejected Christ and His kingdom; did this mean that the Gentiles could not be saved? Must they first become Jewish proselytes? Peter's experience at Caesarea (Acts 10) and Paul's revelation of "the mystery of the church" (Ephesians 3) helped to answer these questions. Both experiences proved that both Jew and Gentile stand condemned before God and can be saved only through faith in Jesus Christ.

I. The Jerusalem Church Accepts the Gentiles (11:1-18)

The faithful Jews contended with Peter because he had fellow-shiped and even eaten with Gentiles. As long as God's kingdom plan was still being offered to the Jews, Peter's actions were wrong. God's message was "to the Jew first" (Acts 1-7). Christ had commanded the disciples to start in Jerusalem (Luke 24:47; Acts 1:8), and when Jerusalem believed, the nation would receive the Messiah and the kingdom would be established (Acts 3:25-26). Peter did not go to Cornelius' house because he understood God's new program, but because he had been commanded personally by the Holy Spirit (11:12). These believing Jews who criticized Peter did so not because they hated the Gentiles, but because they wanted to be faithful to God's revealed will.

When Peter told them how the Spirit had guided him and sealed his ministry by coming upon the believing Gentiles, the Jewish Christians rejoiced and glorified God. Note that Peter proved what he did was God's will by appealing to: (1) his own personal experience (vv. 5-11), (2) the leading of the Spirit (v. 12), and (3) the Word of God (v. 16). Three essentials are always necessary if we are to do God's will: personal testimony, the leading of the Spirit in our hearts, and the clear teaching of the Word of God.

II. The Jerusalem Church Encourages the Gentiles (11:19-26)

Now the Gospel goes into new Gentile territory, Antioch, a key city in Syria. (Do not confuse this with Antioch in Pisidia, which is mentioned in Acts 13:14. Consult your Bible maps for these two cities.) The persecution described in 8:1ff had scattered Christians as far as Antioch, about 300 miles north of Jerusalem. True to their commission, they had preached to Jews only (this was before the events of Acts 10, of course); but some disciples began to preach to the Gentiles. The word "Grecians" in 11:20 is not the same as the word in 6:1, where it means "Hellenized Jews." Here, the word actually means "Greeks" — in other words, Gentiles. Many Gentiles came to know Christ as their Savior, and the Jerusalem church sent Barnabas to investigate the situation. But his mission was unlike that of Peter and John's in 8:14-17, for these believers had already received the Spirit and experienced the grace of God. In v. 23 we see for the first time the word "grace" is used in Acts with reference to salvation. (Acts 4:33 refers to the grace of God assisting believers.) Grace was to become Paul's great message in years to come. Note that these Gentiles were saved by grace (v. 23) through faith (v. 21). This is what Eph. 2:8-9 teaches.

Barnabas rejoiced at finding this Gentile assembly and exhorted them to continue in their faith. Then he did a strange thing: he left the church and went to find Paul. Why did he do this? Because Barnabas, filled with the Spirit, knew that God had given Paul a commission to preach the Gospel to the Gentiles (Acts 9:15, 27). Peter's importance was diminishing, as was God's kingdom program, and Barnabas knew that Paul was to be the next leader, preaching the message of God's grace. For an entire year, Paul and Barnabas taught the Gentiles the Word of God. From this church they went out on their first missionary journey. The church at Antioch assumed greater importance than the church at Jerusalem when Paul replaced Peter as God's special apostle who brought the revelation of the mystery of the church.

III. The Jerusalem Church Gets Aid from the Gentiles (11:27-30)

These "prophets" (v. 27) were Christians who ministered in the local assemblies and revealed the Word of God. That they came to Antioch from Jerusalem indicates that there was close fellowship between these two churches. "All the world" in v. 28 can mean either all the Roman world or possibly only the land (Judaea). The Gentile believers immediately sent material aid to the believers in Judaea as an expression of Christian love.

This famine is important, for if we read Acts 2:44-45 and 4:31-35, we see that a vital change has taken place in the Jerusalem church. In Acts 2–7, the church at Jerusalem had no needs at all; in 11:27-30 we read that these same people were in need of outside help. What had happened? The "kingdom program" with its special blessings had passed on. As long as the kingdom was being offered to the Jews, the Spirit conferred special blessings on the believers, and there was not one that lacked among them (4:34). But when the kingdom was finally rejected with the stoning of Stephen, these unusual blessings were withdrawn, leaving the Jewish believers in need. Several times in the Word we read of special aid sent to the "poor saints at Jerusalem" (Rom. 15:26; 1 Cor. 16:1ff.; 2 Cor. 8–9).

The pattern of giving in Acts 2:44-45 and 4:31-35 does not apply to the local church today, although the spirit manifested is certainly to be desired. Note that the believers in Antioch did not have "all things in common" but rather gave personal contributions according to their ability (11:29, see 2 Cor. 9:7). Paul instructs us to provide for our own (1 Tim. 5:8), warning that if we do not, we are worse than infidels. God's pattern for giving is that each believer give tithes and offerings to the Lord, starting with the local church. Barnabas and Saul (Paul) were chosen to take the offering to Jerusalem. They later returned to Antioch, bringing John Mark with them (12:25).

In chapter 12 we will see the close of Peter's special ministry, and chapter 13 ushers in the ministry of the Apostle Paul. These chapters close the period of transition when the message of the kingdom was replaced by the Gospel of the grace of God, Jerusalem was replaced by Antioch in Syria as the center of ministry, and Peter was replaced by Paul as the leader of God's work.

ACTS 12

Here we read one of the last instances of Peter's ministry among the early believers. In chapter 13 Paul assumes center stage and we do not meet Peter again until he gives his testimony (in support of Paul) in chapter 15. Here in chapter 12, we see several different powers at work.

I. The Power of Satan (12:1-4)

Herod Agrippa, the grandson of Herod the Great, was, like his forbears, a murderer. The Herods were Edomites, descendants of Esau. In one sense, we see Esau persecuting Jacob again, for "James" is simply another form of the name Jacob! This persecution is a picture of the time of tribulation the Jews will endure in the last days. Read again Matt. 20:20-23 where James and John were promised a baptism of suffering. James was the first of the apostles slain, and John, who lived a long life, endured great suffering (Rev. 1:9). Christ had promised the apostles that they would suffer persecution. So will all who seek to obey God's Word.

It is interesting to note that the apostles did not replace James as they had replaced Judas in chapter 1. Because the promised kingdom had been rejected, the apostles would not "sit on twelve thrones" in that kingdom (Matt. 19:28). This is another indication that a new plan had been revealed. There is a practical lesson here: when Satan wanted to hinder the work of the church, he went after Peter and James. He goes after the best Christians and seeks to hinder their work. Are we the kind of Christians that Satan wants to attack? It is significant that Peter was delivered while James was permitted to die. God has a unique purpose for each of His own.

II. The Power of Prayer (12:5-19)

The word "Easter" in v. 4 should read "Passover." This ceremony would last eight days, after which Herod promised to kill Peter to please the Jews. For safety's sake, he assigned four relays of four guards each to watch Peter. Two were at his side and two at the cell door. "But constant prayer was offered to God" (v. 5). How thrilling those words are to the believer! When Satan does his worst, Christians can turn to God in prayer and know that He will work.

How could Peter be so peaceful when he knew that he had only a short time to live? The prayer of the church certainly helped him, but Christ's promise in John 21:18-19 must have sustained him. Peter knew that he would not die until he was older, and that his death would not be by the sword (as with James, v. 2), but by crucifixion. Faith in the Word of God gave him peace. If we will but trust Christ's promises, we will have that same peace in the midst of tribulation.

The angel delivered Peter, but note that he did not do for the apostle what he could do for himself. The angel released him from the chains and led him out of the prison, but he told Peter to put on his own shoes, dress, and follow. When Peter was safely on the outside, the angel left him to make his own decision. We can expect God to do the impossible if we obey and do the possible.

We should never underestimate the power of a praying church. They prayed fervently (v. 5), definitely, and courageously. In spite of their unbelief when Peter did appear, God honored their prayers and drew glory to Himself. When Rhoda heard that knock at the door, she answered by faith; for all she knew, there may have been a company of Herod's soldiers outside, ready to arrest them!

The James mentioned in v. 17 is Christ's brother, who, it seems, became the chief elder of the Jerusalem assembly (see chapter 15). Do not confuse him with the son of Alphaeus or the James who was slain by Herod. See also Acts 21:18 and Gal. 1:19 and 2:9. Peter's departure remains a mystery: he went out "into another place," (v. 17) and what that place was, we do not know. He moved off the scene (although continuing his preaching, of course) to make room for Paul and his message of the church.

III. The Power of God's Wrath (12:20-23)

The relationship between the seaboard cities of Tyre and Sidon and Galilee stemmed from the days of Solomon (1 Kings 5:9ff). Herod, like the Antichrist who will appear one day, exalted himself and took the place of God. The people worshiped Herod and honored him strictly for their own gain, and one day the world will receive and worship the Antichrist so that they might be fed and protected. God smote him with a terrible death. Note that the angel who "smote" Peter in v. 7 brought salvation; but when he smote Herod, he brought condemnation. God hates pride and will not allow another to take His glory. Read Dan. 11:36 and 2 Thes. 2:3-8 to see how Herod typifies the coming man of sin, the Antichrist.

IV. The Power of God's Hand (12:24-25)

What a contrast! The great Herod was eaten with worms, "but the Word of God grew and multiplied." Whether Satan attacks as the murderer (as slaying James) or the liar (as in vv. 20-23), God's Word can overcome and bring victory. James was dead, but God's work went right on, for we see Paul and Barnabas, and their helper Mark, returning to Antioch after their ministry to the poor saints in Jerusalem (see 11:27-30). Mark had a godly home, for it was in his mother's house that the believers had met to pray (12:12). He was the cousin of Barnabas (Col. 4:10) and was later to be a cause of contention between Paul and Barnabas. He wrote the Gospel of Mark and eventually won Paul's approval (2 Tim. 4:11), although he had failed Paul in earlier years (13:13).

Let us never be frightened by the loud voices of Satan's world leaders. Their day is coming. The Word of God will never fail, and it is our responsibility to preach and teach that Word until Christ returns.

ACTS 13

We now begin the third and final section of Acts, "The Period of Triumph" (chaps. 13–28), during which the Gospel of the grace of God was preached to the Roman world and the local churches were established through the ministry of Paul and others. We witness, as it were, a new beginning of a new ministry from a new spiritual center—Antioch in Syria. We read of Paul's first missionary journey and his first sermon. We hear for the first time in Acts that wonderful word "justified" (13:39).

I. In Antioch: Called by the Spirit (13:1-3)

Keep in mind that the center of the church's operation had moved from Jerusalem and the Jews to Antioch and the Gentiles (Acts 11:19-30). Do not confuse Antioch in Syria, Paul's "home church," with Antioch in Pisidia (13:14-52). Note that as the servants of the Lord ministered in this local church, God called two of them (the first and last names on the list in v. 1—and soon the last would become first) to a world ministry. It is the servants who are faithful at home that God uses elsewhere.

"Prophets" (v. 1) means NT prophets (Eph. 4:11). These men spoke for God and were led directly by the Spirit. Now that we have the written Word of God, we do not have prophets in the church. Some suggest that Simeon was the man who carried Christ's cross (Mark 15:21) and also was the father of Alexander and Rufus. Manaen was "foster brother" to the Herod who killed John the Baptist. Not many people of nobility are called, but thank God, some do find Christ!

Verses 1-3 describe the NT program for sending out missionaries: (1) God calls those whom He chooses; (2) the church certifies this call; (3) the church and the Spirit send the missionaries ies forth, backing them with prayer and support. It is right that missionaries report to their churches (14:26-28). It is also not unbiblical for local churches to band together and organize agencies for sending out missionaries.

II. In Cyprus: Opposed by the Devil (13:4-12)

In the parable of the tares (Matt. 13:24-30 and 36-43) Christ promised that, wherever the true children of God were planted, Satan would plant counterfeits. This is what happened at the missionaries' first stop. Satan came in the person of an apostate Jew, a false prophet, a child of the devil (v. 10). In the power of the Spirit, Paul smote the deceiver with blindness. Isn't this like the nation of Israel, having rejected Christ, now smitten with blindness? See Rom. 11:25. Note that here "Saul" uses his better-known name "Paul," which means "little."

III. In Perga: Deserted by Mark (13:13)

Note that it is no longer "Barnabas and Saul" (v. 2) but "Paul and his company." We are not sure why Mark left the party, but Paul considered his act desertion (see 15:38). Was it because Paul had become prominent and Mark's cousin Barnabas was no longer leader? Was it because of the dangerous situations that lay ahead? Was the youth homesick? Whatever the reasons, his deed later caused the two missionaries to part company, although Paul later did forgive and receive Mark (2 Tim. 4:11). How wonderful it is that God gives us another chance! More than one servant of God has failed in his early ministry, only to be successful later.

IV. In Antioch of Pisidia: Received by the Gentiles — (13:14-52)

Why did Paul go to the Jewish synagogue when his special commission was to the Gentiles? For several reasons: (1) he knew he would get a hearing among the Jews in the synagogue, and this was the logical place to start; (2) he had a personal burden for his people (Rom. 9:1-3 and 10:1); (3) he wanted his nation to hear God's Word and so be without excuse.

In this sermon, he stated that Christ came "to the Jews first" (vv. 23-27 and v. 46), but he was careful to state that salvation is for "all that believe" (v. 39). In vv. 17-22 Paul showed how the OT was a preparation for Christ. In vv. 23-37 he outlined the life and death of Christ, proving His resurrection, and pointing out that Israel ("they that dwell at Jerusalem and their rulers," v. 27) rejected their Messiah. Verses 38-41 give the personal conclusion of the message showing that salvation was not through obedience to the law, but through faith in Christ. The warning in vv. 40-41 comes from Hab. 1:5. The "work" referred to here is God's program of saving the Gentiles. How unbelievable this must have been to the Jews! When the prophet Habakkuk spoke these words, the Gentile ruler Nebuchadnezzar was rising to power and would be invading nation after nation. Paul used these words to warn the Jews that, if they did not believe and receive the Gospel, they would perish like the unbelieving Israel of days past. He preached the Gospel of the grace of God (see v. 43), the message we are to proclaim today.

What were the results? Some Jews and Gentile proselytes immediately believed. It is obvious that these religious people, trained in the Scriptures, would be best prepared to receive the message. The next week the whole city was gathered together! This meant that the Gentile believers had spread the word among their friends, so that the majority of the congregation that Sabbath Day was Gentile. This provoked the Jews to jealousy and they hindered Paul's ministry, so he turned from them to a ministry among the Gentiles. He explained his action in v. 46; according to God's program outlined in the OT, it was necessary that the Word go to the Jews first; but now that they had (like their brethren in Jerusalem) proved themselves unworthy, the message would go to the Gentiles. Paul quoted Isa. 49:6, where God said that Christ (the "I" does not refer to Paul) was a Light to the Gentiles. See also Luke 2:29-32.

Do not "tone down" the phrase in v. 48 that indicates that certain people were "ordained to eternal life." The Gk. word actually means "enrolled," and has the idea of names written in a book. While salvation is by grace, through faith, there is also that mysterious working of God whereby we are "chosen in Christ" (Eph. 1:4). We do not know who God's elect are, so we offer the Gospel to all and have confidence that the Spirit will work.

Of course, where the seed is bearing fruit, Satan comes to oppose; and note that he can use "religious people" to do the work. True Christianity does not persecute anyone, but religious people have persecuted and murdered in the name of Christ. (For Paul's comment on persecution see 2 Tim. 3:11.) The opposition did not stop Paul and his associates; filled with joy and the Holy Spirit, they continued to minister the Word.

ACTS 14

This chapter records the completion of Paul's first missionary journey. You will want to refer to a map and trace it for yourself.

I. The Missionaries Suffer for Christ (14:1-20)

Wherever the Gospel is preached and some believe, you will find division and disturbance. See John 7:43, 9:16, and 10:19; also Luke 12:49-53. Even today, many Christians suffer at home because of loved ones who have rejected Christ. But the opposition did not stop Paul and Barnabas; instead, they stayed in the city and continued to preach. God honored their faith by granting signs and wonders. These miracles were proof that Paul was an apostle of God (2 Cor. 12:12) and would have an effect on the Jews (see 1 Cor. 1:22) and the Gentiles (Rom. 15:18-19). When the men discovered a plot to stone them, they left for Lystra and Derbe and there preached the Word. See Matt. 10:23.

At Lystra, Paul was enabled to perform a great miracle by healing a notable cripple. It is interesting to compare the ministries of Peter and Paul at this point: both healed a lame man (3:1-8; 14:8-12); both dealt with Satanic pretenders (8:18-24; 13:4-12); both were released from prison miraculously (12:5-10; 16:25-29); both raised the dead (9:40; 20:12); both performed special miracles (5:15-16; 28:8).

This miracle was accepted by the heathen citizens as proof that Paul and Barnabas were their gods come to earth; they named Barnabas "Jupiter" (or Zeus, the chief of the gods), and Paul they named "Mercury" (or Hermes, the messenger of the gods). The local priest of Jupiter was ready to offer sacrifices when the missionaries publicly stopped them. Paul took advantage of the situation to preach the Word to the crowd. Note that he did not use the OT Scriptures as he did in the synagogue service, but rather reasoned with these Gentiles on the basis of God's works in creation. Compare this sermon (given here in vv. 15-17 in brief) to Paul's message in Athens (17:16-34) and his statements in Romans 1:20ff. The works of God in nature leave the heathen "without excuse."

Paul's message was rejected, and the people stoned him and left him for dead. We wonder if Paul remembered the day he led the Jews in stoning Stephen. "Once I was stoned," he wrote later (2 Cor. 11:25); and in Gal. 6:17 he mentions the "brands" or marks he had on his body because of his suffering for Christ. Some students believe that Paul actually died and was raised from the dead miraculously, and they suggest that Paul's "third heaven" experience was at this time (2 Cor. 12:1-4). Years later, Paul reminded Timothy of these sufferings (2 Tim. 3:11). It is probable that

Timothy was converted to Christ at this point (see Acts 14:6 with 16:1).

II. The Missionaries Confirm the Churches (14:21-24)

Evangelism is not enough; there must be teaching and encouragement from the Word. This is why Paul established local churches wherever God led him. The local church is the one place the believer should be able to get a dependable diet of spiritual food, find Christian fellowship, and discover opportunities for service. We thank God for the many fine evangelistic organizations and programs that are winning souls today, but none of them can replace the local church.

Courageously, the missionaries returned to the very cities where their lives had been in danger. No wonder later on they had the reputation for being men who "hazarded their lives for the name of our Lord Jesus Christ" (Acts 15:26). Paul and Barnabas were not thinking of themselves but of those new Christians who needed spiritual help and guidance. They were at this point only 160 miles from Paul's home in Tarsus, and perhaps Paul would have loved to visit his home again; yet he set his own desires aside to serve the Lord. Also, on the trip back to Antioch, they bypassed Cyprus, which was the home of Barnabas.

Paul and Barnabas appointed elders in the churches. The Gk. word translated "appointed" has a double significance: it means "to designate" as well as "to elect by popular vote." Apparently the apostles selected the best candidates (see 1 Tim. 3 and Titus 1:5ff for the qualifications), and then the whole church voted as the Spirit guided them. This is the way church government ought to be. There is nothing in the Bible about a hierarchy of church leaders. If you will compare Titus 1:5 and 7, and Acts 20:17 and 28, you will see that the terms "bishop" and "elder" refer to the same office, the office of the pastor. Paul did not ordain the leaders until the return trip to the churches so as to give the men a chance to be tested. "Lay hands suddenly on no man," he warned (1 Tim. 5:22).

III. The Missionaries Report to the Home Church (14:25-28)

While boards and denominations can assist in the legal and technical aspects of sending out missionaries, the final responsibility lies with the local church. This is why Paul and Barnabas reported to the believers at Antioch, from whence they had been sent out in "the work" (see 13:2, 14:26, and 15:38). What a blessed meeting that must have been as these first missionaries reported what God had done! Remember that Acts records what Jesus "continued to do and teach" after He returned to heaven (Acts 1:2), so the work was really His.

As you review this first missionary journey, you can see the basic principles Paul followed as he sought to carry the Gospel to the world. The Spirit directed Paul in his work, and it is important that we follow these same principles today.

A. He worked in key cities.

For the most part, the places where Paul worked were important cities in the various provinces. Paul did not remain in some isolated corner; he attacked the great centers of population. This was where his strategic evangelism began. Then his converts reached out to the smaller towns in the area.

B. He established local churches.

His ministry was not a one-man affair, nor did it have a central headquarters for telling others what to do. He won souls to Christ and then organized them into local churches that had their own leaders. Of course, this meant teaching the people the Word and building them up in the faith. Today, we have many "support ministries" that are vital (schools, hospitals, radio and TV broadcasts, etc.), but all of them must assist in the winning of the lost and the building of the churches.

C. He taught the believers how to do the job.

Paul knew that missionaries must eventually make themselves dispensable. They must train new converts to carry on the ministry themselves. After all, 100 people in a local church can do 100 times the work any one missionary can do, and they know the language and culture of their own people. Ten years later, writing to the Romans (15:19 and 23), Paul was able to say that the entire area had been evangelized! How did he do it? He won converts, established churches, and trained Christians how to do the job. See 1 Thes. 1–2 for another example.

Our purpose is to evangelize, which simply means to give as many people as possible at least one opportunity to hear the Gospel. We know that not everyone will be saved, but we owe to everyone at least one chance to hear about Christ and the cross. Paul evangelized the Roman world without printing press, a radio station, television, airplanes, or any of the modern devices available to us. How much more we ought to be able to accomplish in this day of scientific wonders! "To whom much is given, much shall be required" (Luke 12:48).

ACTS 15

I. The Dissension at Antioch (15:1-2)

Whenever God's work is progressing, Satan begins to oppose it, and he usually works through lies. The reason many churches are ineffective today is because they believe "religious lies" instead of God's Word. Certain Pharisees from the Jerusalem church (v. 5 and 24) had gone to Antioch and told the Gentile Christians that their salvation was not valid unless they were circumcised and obeyed the law of Moses. Certainly Paul had not so preached (see 13:38-40)! Paul and Barnabas disputed with them, and it was decided to take the issue to the apostles and elders in Jerusalem. This was purely a voluntary decision and does not in any way indicate that a "denominational hierarchy" was intended to govern the affairs of the local church. Actually, Paul was expressly commanded by God to go to Jerusalem; see Gal. 2:1-2. "I went up by revelation" (v. 2) literally means, "I went up in obedience to, or guided by, a divine revelation." God wanted Paul to affirm once and for all the place of the Gentiles in His program.

It was easy for these Jewish believers to be confused about God's program. They knew the OT teaching that the Gentiles could be saved only through Israel. The only Gentiles that the Jerusalem church had seen saved were won by Peter, not Paul, and this had been a special act of God (Acts 11:18). News traveled slowly in those days, and they did not know all that God had done through Paul and Barnabas on their missionary journey. These men were sincere, but they were sincerely wrong. As Paul explains in Gal. 2:6ff, they preached a "gospel," but it was an incomplete gospel. They believed in the death and resurrection of Christ, but they had not yet progressed to see God's program for the Gentiles through the Apostle Paul.

II. The Deliberation at Jerusalem (15:3-21)

It appears that there were at least four different meetings involved in this strategic conference: (1) a public meeting during which the church welcomed Paul and his party (v. 4); (2) a private conference between Paul and the key leaders (Gal. 2:2); (3) a second public meeting at which time the strong Jewish party presented their case (Acts 15:5 and Gal. 2:3-5); and (4) the council proper which made the final decisions (Acts 15:6ff). Read Gal. 1–2 carefully as it gives Paul's report of the matter.

The debate continued and no progress was in sight until Peter arose and made his speech. It is interesting to note that his final act in Acts was to endorse Paul and his ministry, as did also Peter's last written words (2 Peter 3:15-16). Peter reviewed God's dealings with him relative to the Gentiles (Acts 10–11), emphasizing that God Himself had accepted the Gentiles by giving them the same Spirit He had given the Jews at Pentecost. They were saved by faith (v. 9) and grace (v. 11). Note what he says in v. 11: "We [Jews] shall be saved even as they!" It is not, "They should be saved the way we were," but the reverse. Not only was the law not applicable to the Gentiles, but it was no longer applicable to the Jews! "By grace, through faith" is the message, not "obey Moses and be circumcised."

Paul and his party were the next witnesses, and their reports of God's work among the Gentiles completely silenced the opposition. Then James took the floor and gave the final decision. This James is the Lord's brother who had become the leader of the Jerusalem church in Peter's place. His words in vv. 14-21 must be understood if the church is to carry on God's program in this age. What is God doing today? He is taking out from the Gentiles a people for His name. Jew and Gentile stand on the same ground as sinners before God, and the program of "to the Jew first" no longer applies.

But what about the promises to the Jews concerning the kingdom? James answered this in vv. 15-17, quoting from Amos 9:11-12. Note that James did not say that the calling out of the Gentiles is a fulfillment of Amos's prophecy, for the church is nowhere prophesied in the OT. James said that Amos's words agree with this new program: afterward, when the full number of Gentiles is saved, Christ will return and build again the house of David ("tabernacle" means "house" or "family," 2 Sam. 7:25-29) and establish the kingdom for Israel. Read Rom. 9:29-33 and 11:1-36 for Paul's explanation of this new program. Romans 11:25 is key: "hardening in part has happened to Israel, until the fullness of the Gentiles has come in" (NKJV). When the full number of Gentiles has been saved, then the church will be raptured, followed by a time of tribulation for seven years during which Israel shall be purged. Finally Christ shall return to earth to restore David's throne.

III. The Deputation to the Gentiles (15:22-35)

The council agreed with this decision and wrote letters concerning it to the Gentile churches, sending these letters with Paul and his associates. These admonitions were not official dogmas handed down by a superior body; they were wise suggestions that spiritual men had received as led by the Holy Spirit. Compare vv. 25 and 28. These prohibitions were not another "Law" but were rather admonitions that would help the Gentile Christians in their relationship with Jews, both saved and unsaved. Compare v. 29 with Gen. 9:1-5.

It was right that Paul and his associates should carry this report back to their home church. After all, had not God used them to open a door of faith to the Gentiles? Had they not risked their lives for the Gospel's sake? When they returned, they met with the entire church, and there was much rejoicing over the decision of the council.

The tragedy is that the decision of the Jerusalem Council is rarely heeded today. Far too many churches are still following the emphasis in the early part of Acts, seeking to "bring in the kingdom." Others try to "mix Peter and Paul" by making strange combinations of law and grace, of Israel and the church. It's time we began to listen to the chosen messenger to the Gentiles, God's special prophet to the church, the Apostle Paul. There is a curse pronounced on any who do not preach the Gospel of the grace of God (Gal. 1:6-9), and this does not apply only to "modernist" interpreters of the Gospel. It applies equally to churches where the Word of God is not rightly divided, and where kingdom truth is mixed with church truth.

IV. The Dispute Between Paul and Barnabas (15:36-41)

It is sad when Christians agree doctrinally (v. 12) but not personally. Since he was related to Mark, Barnabas did have an obligation to help the young man; but Paul felt that Mark was a failure. Perhaps both men were too severe, for later Paul accepted Mark (2 Tim. 4:11), and God used him to write the second Gospel. While Paul and Barnabas were ministering at Antioch, Peter had come up and debated Paul again about the Gentiles. Read Gal. 2:11-21, and note that even Barnabas was "carried away" by the Jews' hypocrisy. This may have been another reason why Paul chose Silas as he started on his second journey, for Silas had been a faithful servant (see 15:22 and 32). Differences between God's servants need not hold back God's work. "There are differences of administrations, but the same Lord" (1 Cor. 12:5).

ACTS 16

I. New Helpers (16:1-5)

You should read 15:36-41 to see how Barnabas and Paul severed their missionary partnership and took new associates. John Mark had failed, as far as Paul was concerned; but Barnabas, being a relative of Mark's, was willing to give the young man another chance. We regret differences between believers, but we are grateful that God can overrule even the mistakes of men for His own glory!

Silas had been a key man in the Jerusalem assembly (15:22) and was a prophet (15:32). He had shared with Paul in the ministry at Antioch, so they were not strangers to one another. Timothy, who took John Mark's place, was a youth who had been saved when Paul visited Lystra on his first missionary journey (14:6-22). Timothy witnessed Paul's sufferings in Lystra (2 Tim. 3:10-11) and had proved himself worthy of Christian service. Timothy was dear to Paul's heart; Paul called him "my son in the faith" (1 Tim. 1:2). If older, mature Christians do not "adopt" younger believers, who will fill in the ranks when God calls the "veterans" home? See 2 Tim. 2:1-2 for Paul's instruction on this matter. Timothy had been raised by a godly mother and grandmother (2 Tim. 1:5 and 3:15). The prophets of the church, with spiritual vision, predicted great things for this young man (1 Tim. 1:18 and 4:14). Philippians 2:19-23 states how faithfully Timothy served with Paul at Philippi.

Timothy's circumcision had nothing to do with salvation (Gal. 2:1-4). This was not an act of disobedience toward the council

(Acts 15:1ff). Rather, it was done to remove a stumbling block from the Jews to whom Paul and Timothy would be ministering (1 Cor. 9:20). Being the son of a Gentile father and Jewish mother, Timothy did not have to be circumcised; but being a child of God, he wanted to do nothing that would cause the Jews to stumble.

II. New Opportunities (16:6-12)

Check on your map the places mentioned in vv. 6-8. Paul and his group ministered the Word in these towns, but the Spirit did not permit them to go east into Bithynia. "Asia" in v. 6 does not mean the great continent we know today; rather, it was an area which we today call Asia Minor. However, had Paul gone east to Bithynia and continued in that direction, the Orient would have received the Gospel before Europe. Note that Peter ministered to these areas (1 Peter 1:1).

Paul was sensitive to the leading of the Spirit. Acts is truly the "Acts of the Holy Spirit," since He was at work in the lives of the apostles. God gave Paul a vision which instructed him to cross over the Aegean Sea into Macedonia. Some think that Luke (the author of Acts) was the man in the vision, because in v. 10 it says "we" rather than "they." At any rate, Doctor Luke joined them at Troas. See also 20:6-7.

III. New Christians (16:13-40)

Philippi was a Roman colony, named after Philip of Macedon, who had conquered that area in the fourth century B.C. Roman colonies were actually "little Romes," cities that followed Roman laws and customs; and the indication is that there were not many Jews in the area, for they did not have a synagogue. In his ministry here at Philippi Paul met three different kinds of sinners and saw them won to Christ:

A. A religious woman with an open heart (vv. 13-15).

Paul opened his European ministry by attending a ladies' prayer meeting! Lydia was a well-to-do merchant who had turned from pagan idolatry to worship the God of Israel. Not only did God open the doors for Paul to come to Europe, but He also opened Lydia's heart and she was saved. She shared the message with her household and they were also saved. The fact that Paul had these new

Gentile converts baptized is evidence that he was fulfilling the commission of Matt. 28:19-20. The word "household" implies that the members of the family (and the slaves) who understood the Word, believed and were saved, and then were baptized. There is no evidence that infants were baptized, here or anywhere else in the Book of Acts.

B. A slave girl with a possessed heart (vv. 16-18).

Paul and his company lived at Lydia's house and went to the prayer meetings with her. Satan is always at hand to oppose the work of the Lord, and in this case he used a slave girl. Note that her words appeared to be friendly to the apostles, as though she were promoting the work of the Lord. Satan came as an angel of light, using flattery (2 Cor. 11:13-15); but Christ never needs Satan's help in promoting the Gospel. This testimony was a hindrance, not a help; and Paul put a stop to it. In the next section we see how Satan the serpent became Satan the lion, throwing the apostles into jail.

C. A man with a hard heart (vv. 19-40).

It takes little imagination to see that this Roman jailer was a typical calloused official with no sympathy for man and no interest in Christ. Even though Paul and Silas had been humiliated and beaten, the jailer added to their sufferings by thrusting them into the inner prison and putting their feet in the stocks. Then he went about his business and finally went to sleep for the night.

But "At night His song is with me" (Ps. 42:8; cf. 77:6, NIV), and Paul and Silas praised God instead of complaining! What a testimony this meeting was! At midnight, God went to work and shook the prison so that all the prisoners were released. If a Roman jailer lost a prisoner, it meant his own life would be taken; so it is no wonder that the jailer, on awakening, tried to commit suicide. This is Satan the murderer at work again; for had Paul not called out and stopped him, that jailer would have died and gone to hell. As it was, Paul's love and God's grace reached the man's heart, and he was converted.

It is in this passage that so-called "household salvation" is refuted. Children cannot be saved simply because their parents are saved, nor are infants or unbelieving children to be baptized. The promise of salvation was to all of the jailer's household (v. 31); the preaching was heard by the household (v. 32); all the household was baptized (v. 33); but it was because all the household believed

(v. 34)! By no stretch of the imagination can we conceive of infants understanding the Word and believing! The jailer proved he had truly been converted by washing the apostles' wounds and feeding them in his own house. When a man opens his heart to Christ, his home should be opened as well.

Some Christians are puzzled by Paul's actions in vv. 35-40. Why did Paul humiliate the Roman officials by making them settle the case openly? Paul was simply making use of his Roman citizenship and legal rights to give proper respect to the Gospel and the new church he had just established. Had Paul quietly moved out of town, the citizens would have thought he had been guilty; and this would have hindered the work of the church. No, it is not wrong for Christians to use their legal rights, so long as it promotes the cause of Christ. This official apology and open settlement of the case (for Paul had been deprived of his legal rights) gave dignity to the Gospel and to the church. The church at Philippi was always a favorite with Paul, as you can see by reading his letter to the Philippians. The nucleus of that church was made up of a wealthy woman, a slave girl, and a Roman jailer! But such is the grace of God: Christ takes the weak things of the world and confounds the mighty.

ACTS 17

As we continue traveling with Paul on his second missionary journey, we see him in three different cities, and we see three different reactions to the Gospel.

I. Thessalonica: Opposing the Word (17:1-9)

Thessalonica was a busy city situated on the main highway to Rome. There were many Jews in the city, so Paul started (as was his policy) in the synagogue, reasoning with them for three weeks. He opened the Scriptures to them, which is the duty of all who teach or preach the Word. (See Luke 24:32.) Some Jews believed; a multitude of Greeks (Jewish proselytes) believed; and many of the leading women. But, as is always the case, Satan brought opposition from the unbelievers.

The Jews used "the rabble" from the marketplace to oppose Paul. The apostles had been staying with one Jason, so it was on his house that the mob centered its attack. If he is the same Jason mentioned in Rom. 16:21, then he was a kinsman to Paul, which would explain his hospitality and the reason for the attack. Note that their false accusation parallels the one made against Christ in Luke 23:2. If you read 1 and 2 Thessalonians (which Paul wrote from Corinth a little while later) you can see what a broad scope of doctrine Paul had given these people in just a few weeks. He told them of the coming kingdom of Christ, the rise of the man of sin, and many other important matters. We must never feel that new believers are too immature to receive the whole counsel of God. Paul's ministry must have been very effective, for the enemy accused him of turning the world upside down!

II. Berea: Receiving the Word (17:10-14)

That night, Paul, Silas, and Timothy (v. 14) set off for Berea, forty miles away. They left behind a local church that continued to witness for Christ. In fact, Paul congratulated them for getting the Gospel out so effectively (1 Thes. 1:6-10). This is the true NT pattern: win converts, teach them (1 Thes. 2), and challenge them to win others.

Berea was "on the byway" instead of the highway, but it was where God wanted the missionaries to go. How refreshing it must have been to meet Jews such as those in Berea! God knew that Paul and his company needed encouragement and refreshment, and they found both at Berea. We today should follow the example of the Bereans: (1) they received the Word; (2) they were of ready mind, prepared for the Word; (3) they searched the Scriptures and tested what the preacher said; (4) they studied the Word daily. Note the "therefore" in v. 12. When people have the attitude spoken of in v. 11, they cannot help but believe the Word! This is the attitude we should always have.

While the Thessalonian Christians were busy sending out the Gospel, Satan was busy stirring up trouble; and he sent some of his own "missionaries" to Berea. How Satan hates the simple preaching of the Word of God! Paul departed for Athens, leaving Silas and Timothy behind to strengthen the brethren. The two men did not come to minister with him at Athens as planned, but joined him later at Corinth (18:5). Paul's leaving at this time was not cowardice. Silas and Timothy could teach the church there while Paul carried the message on ahead.

III. Athens: Mocking the Word (17:15-34)

Paul came to Athens as a sightseer and became a soul-winner! This famous city was a center of religion and culture, but all Paul could see was sin and superstition; one ancient writer said it was easier to find a god than a man in Athens. Paul disputed with the Jews in the synagogue, but had little or no success. He then followed the pattern of the Greek teachers and took his message to the market (agora) where the men assembled to discuss philosophy or to transact business.

Two main philosophies controlled Athens at that time. The Stoics were materialistic and almost fatalistic in their thinking. Their system was built on pride and personal independence. Nature was their god, and they believed that all nature was gradually moving toward a great climax. We might say that they were pantheistic. The Epicureans desired pleasure, and their philosophy was grounded in experience, not reason. They were almost atheistic. Here we have two extremes in philosophy, and Paul confronted them both with the Gospel of Christ. The Athenians scorned him, calling him a "babbler," which means "a seedpicker." They thought he was preaching two new gods when he spoke of "Jesus and the resurrection." ("Resurrection" in Gk. is *anastasia,* and perhaps they took this for a proper name.) The Greeks led him to the Areopagus, their official court, also called Mars' Hill. There Paul preached a great sermon.

He began politely by saying, "I see that you are very religious" (not "too superstitious" as in KJV). He called attention to an altar dedicated "TO THE UNKNOWN GOD," and he used this object to preach to them the True God about whom they were ignorant. He presented in his sermon four great truths about God:

A. He is the Creator (vv. 24-25).

The Greeks believed different theories about creation, and even held to a form of evolution. Paul clearly stated that God created everything and did not live in temples made by men. God gives life to all; man can really give nothing to Him.

B. He is the Governor (vv. 26-29).

He appoints the boundaries of the nations. Through His government of the nations, He seeks to make men seek Him and find Him. Paul even quoted a Greek writer (v. 28) to show that God is the sustainer of life. This does not mean the Greek poet was inspired, but rather that his statement agreed with divine truth. Again Paul diplomatically pointed out that their temples and images were foolish and ignorant. We need this reminder today!

C. He is the Savior (v. 30).

Paul wipes away the great Greek culture by calling it "times of ignorance"! With all their wisdom and culture, the Greeks failed to find God (see 1 Cor. 1:18ff). God has commanded men everywhere to repent; and if they repent and believe, He will forgive.

D. He is the Judge (v. 31).

God has appointed a day of judgment, and the Judge will be His Son, Jesus Christ. God proved this by raising Him from the dead. If we trust Christ today, He will save us; if we reject Him, tomorrow He will judge us.

The reactions of the listeners were mixed: some mocked (this is often the attitude of pagan culture and philosophy); some delayed; but some believed!

This chapter presents three different attitudes toward the Gospel, and we find these same attitudes in the world today. Some people openly oppose the Word; some mock it or postpone making a decision; and some receive the Word and believe. Paul kept right on going as a faithful servant, and so must we, "for in due season we shall reap, if we faint not" (Gal. 6:9).

ACTS 18

From Athens, Paul made his way to Corinth, one of the greatest cities of that day. It was famous for several things: its bronze and pottery works; its great sporting events that were comparable to the Olympics; and its immorality and wickedness. From a cultured, refined city like Athens, Paul took the Gospel to the wicked city of Corinth, and by the grace of God established a church there!

I. Paul Finds New Friends (18:1-3)

It was customary for Jewish fathers to teach their sons a trade, even if the sons were going to be rabbis. Paul's trade was tentmaking, a skill which he used profitably to support his ministry at Corinth (see 1 Cor. 9:15). It was through his trade that he met a Christian couple with whom he lived and ministered while establishing the church in Corinth. How it must have rejoiced Paul's heart to fellowship with these saints! Paul had no home of his own, and his travels made it difficult to fellowship for long in any one place. Priscilla and Aquila later went with him to Ephesus where they instructed Apollos (vv. 18, 24-28). They had a Christian gathering in their house in Ephesus (1 Cor. 16:19), but later Paul greeted them in Rome (Rom. 16:3). They are good examples to us of Christians who open their hearts and homes to serve the Lord.

In vv. 24-28 we find Priscilla and Aquila explaining the Gospel of grace to the visiting speaker, Apollos. He knew only the baptism of John, which meant he had never learned of the baptism of the Spirit and the founding of the church. Instead of embarrassing him in public, Priscilla and Aquila took him home and taught him the Word. Apollos proves to us that it is possible to have eloquence, zeal, and sincerity, and still be wrong! God led Apollos to Corinth, and there God gave him a mighty ministry (see 1 Cor. 3:6; 16:12).

We might add one word about Paul's employment at Corinth. He himself recognized that his practice of earning his own bread was unique. The scriptural pattern is that "they which preach the Gospel should live from the Gospel" (1 Cor. 9:14, NKJV). In his pioneer missionary work, Paul deliberately paid his own way so that no one could accuse him of "preaching for money." Read 1 Cor. 9 for his clear explanation.

II. Paul Founds a New Church (18:4-17)

Paul began in the synagogue, but that witness lasted but a short time; then he turned to the Gentiles. (See 13:46.) At this same time, he moved out of the house of Priscilla and Aquila and moved in with a Gentile named Justus who was a Jewish proselyte and whose house was near the synagogue. Apparently Paul did not want to bring difficulties to his Jewish host and hostess, now that he had turned to the Gentiles. But v. 8 tells us that the chief ruler of the synagogue had believed, as did many of the Corinthians! Note the sequence in v. 8: hearing, believing, being baptized. This is the pattern today. In 1 Cor. 1:14-17, Paul informs us that he himself baptized some in Corinth (1 Cor. 1:11-17), which proves that water baptism is commanded for this age.

It is likely that Silas and Timothy (v. 5) did most of the baptizing, since Paul's special commission was to evangelize. God gave

Paul a special promise of success, and he continued for eighteen months in the city. A change in political leaders brought about new opposition, but Paul still tarried (v. 18) to preach and teach. Note that there is a new ruler of the synagogue, Sosthenes (v. 17, see also v. 8). It seems that Chrispus's salvation made it necessary for the Jews to elect a new ruler; but if the Sosthenes of v. 17 is the same one named in 1 Cor. 1:1, then he was also converted! Note that those who were baptized were believers (v. 8); this list excludes infants.

III. Paul Finishes His Second Journey (18:18-22)

The vow mentioned in v. 18 poses a problem, and perhaps we cannot answer all the questions it raises. Since it involved letting the hair grow, this may have been a Nazirite vow (Num. 6). The hair was cut at the close of the period of the vow, and this Paul did at Cenchrea, the seaport of Corinth. Whether Paul performed the sacrifices involved when he arrived at Jerusalem, we do not know, because the record is silent.

It is possible that this vow was taken after God had delivered Paul and his associates during the uprising described in vv. 12-17. The vow may have been made in thanksgiving to God, since such vows were purely voluntary. For the Jews, Paul became as a Jew (see 1 Cor. 9:19-23), not in compromise, but in courtesy. Certainly Paul knew that there were no merits in such vows, nor is he necessarily setting an example for us as believers today. The Apostle Paul clearly understood the meaning of God's grace and was not stepping back into legalism or ceremonial practices. Apparently, the completion of this vow in Jerusalem was uppermost in his mind, so much so that he did not tarry at Ephesus even though the Jews asked him to stay.

Paul returned to Antioch and reported to the church. He also saluted the brethren at Jerusalem. After some time (perhaps several months), Paul revisited the churches to establish them in the faith. If you will review Galatians, you will see why: the "Judaizing" teachers had invaded these young churches and were teaching the new converts that they had to obey the law of Moses. Paul was burdened for the churches and so made the trip again to teach them the Word and confirm them in the faith. Luke records this third journey in Acts 19:1–21:16. Most of the record deals with his great ministry for three years in Ephesus.

ACTS 19

This chapter tells of Paul's wonderful ministry in Ephesus and relates his contacts with three groups of people.

I. Paul and Twelve Ignorant Disciples (19:1-12)

It is likely that these twelve men were converts of Apollos before he came to a full understanding of the Gospel (18:24-28). All that this eloquent preacher knew then was the teaching of John the Baptist; and after Priscilla and Aquila instructed him, he apparently was not able to impart this new knowledge to his converts, since Ephesus was such a large city. When Paul met these twelve men, he detected something lacking in their spiritual lives.

Paul's question (v. 2) should read, "Did you receive the Holy Spirit when you believed?" To base a doctrine of "a second blessing" on this verse is wrong. The Spirit comes into our lives when we believe on Christ, not afterward (Eph. 1:13-14). The men replied, "We did not know that the Holy Spirit had been given." They knew there was a Holy Spirit, of course, because John the Baptist had promised a future baptism of the Spirit (Matt. 3:11). What they did not know is that this baptism had already taken place, on the Day of Pentecost (Acts 1:5 and 2:4) and in the home of the Gentile Cornelius (10:44-45 and 11:15-16).

Next, Paul asked about their baptism. Note that he assumes they had been baptized, another indication that water baptism is the expected and accepted thing for Christians. Why did Paul ask about their baptism when the real issue was the presence of the Spirit in their lives? In the Book of Acts, there is a definite relationship between water baptism and the Holy Spirit. Since Apollos had been their teacher, the only baptism they knew was John's baptism. But John's baptism was no longer valid. In other words, these twelve men were not saved: they had believed an outdated message ("Christ is coming") and had received an outdated baptism (the baptism of repentance). They were sincere, as was Apollos, but they were sincerely wrong.

Suppose they had answered Paul, "We were baptized on the Day of Pentecost after hearing Peter preach." Then they should have received the Spirit since in Acts 2:38 the Spirit was promised to all who repented and were baptized. If they had not received the Spirit, then it was evidence they had not truly believed. Or suppose they had replied, "We were baptized in Samaria" (Acts 8). Then they should have received the Spirit by the laying on of hands (8:17 and 9:17). Or suppose they had said, "We were in the house of Cornelius and heard Peter preach." Then they would have received the Spirit immediately upon believing (10:44-45) and would have been baptized in water. When they told Paul they had been baptized with John's baptism, he knew they were unsaved. They were believing a message that was no longer valid, since Christ had come, died, and gone back to heaven.

Of course, Luke does not record all that Paul told these men. But they believed the message of the Gospel (that Christ had already come and died) and were baptized with Christian baptism. They received the Spirit with the laying on of Paul's hands and gave evidence of it by speaking with tongues. This is the last time you find in Acts speaking with tongues as proof of the receiving of the Spirit. These twelve men became the nucleus of the church of Ephesus. The fact that God departed from the usual order and granted them the Spirit through the laying on of Paul's hands was proof that Paul was equal to the other apostles and therefore God's servant for establishing the church. This entire event points up several truths: (1) sinners must believe the right message before they can be saved; (2) baptism is important, but the kind of baptism described in Acts 2:38 is not intended for the church today; (3) a Christian can lead others only where he has been himself; (4) Paul was God's messenger and had equal standing with the other apostles.

II. Paul and Seven Jewish Pretenders (19:8-20)

Paul spent three years in Ephesus (20:31): three months in the synagogue, two years teaching in rented rooms at the school of Tyrannus, and about nine months in various places (19:8-10 and 22). All Asia heard the Word, for Paul taught the believers to pass the Word on to others. God attested to Paul's ministry with special miracles, an indication that such activities are not normal for ministry today. The use and sale of "prayer cloths and handkerchiefs" today is unscriptural. Seven Jewish men tried to imitate Paul's power (Satan is a great imitator), but their plan backfired and the demons left them naked and wounded. This event helped spread the Gospel, and many former sorcerers and magicians (dabblers in spiritualism and other Satanic practices) brought their books and burned them. Ephesus was a city noted for magical arts, and Satan was behind the whole program. It's wonderful to see the Gospel penetrate Satan's strongholds!

III. Paul and the Silversmiths (19:21-41)

Where Satan could not succeed in hindering the Gospel through the ignorant disciples or the Jewish pretenders, he almost succeeded with the businessmen and merchants of the city. Ephesus prided itself on being custodian of the image of the goddess Diana that was supposed to have fallen from heaven. Wherever you find superstition, you often find the exhibition and sale of such religious items. Remember the sale of sacrifices in the Jewish temple? True Gospel preaching always runs head-on into such superstitious money-making schemes, and Ephesus was no exception. The guild (or union) of silversmiths pretended that their concern was for the religion of the city, but their real worry was loss of business! The Gospel had so stirred the city that people were turning from idols to the true God, and this was hurting "religious" sales. During the Welsh Revival, it is reported that scores of taverns went out of business for lack of customers!

The silversmiths used religion to generate emotion among the people, and the result was a mob. The whole city was filled with confusion (v. 29) which proves the situation was born of the devil, for God is not the author of confusion (1 Cor. 14:33). The citizens rushed into the huge outdoor theater that seated at least 25,000 people. Wisely, Paul's friends prevented him from entering, for it is likely that the apostle would have been arrested by the authorities or even killed by the mob. The town clerk (city secretary) quieted the mob, warned them that they were in danger of breaking the law and sent them all home.

Satan was anxious to prevent the establishing of a strong church in Ephesus. This city had been one of his strongholds for years, with its superstition, idolatry, and magical practices. Demonic activity had prevailed in Ephesus, but now the Spirit of God was at work. What if Paul had not detected the shallowness of the profession of those twelve men and had tried to build a local church on their testimony? The work would have failed! What if those Jews had been able to counterfeit Paul's miracles? What if the mob had taken Paul and his associates and arrested or killed them? Would we have had the wonderful Epistle to the Ephesians? Satan did not want a church at Ephesus, yet God established one there; and a reading of the book of Ephesians proves that it was perhaps the most spiritual church Paul ever founded. That wonderful epistle outlines church truth in a clear way, and this is what Satan did not want.

Satan still hinders the work of the Lord in these three ways: false believers with an inadequate spiritual experience, counterfeits, and open opposition. But we may overcome the adversary if we trust God, depend on the power of the Spirit, and preach the Word of God.

Additional Notes on Acts 19:1-7

There are about several questions that should be answered in this difficult passage.

A. Were these twelve men saved?

Every indication is that they were not. The word "disciple" does not always mean "Christian" in the Bible. Paul assumed that they had believed some message (v. 2), but the basic issue was that they had not believed the right message. People of every age were saved by faith in God's revealed Word; but this Word was not always the clear Gospel of the grace of God that we preach today. Adam was saved by believing God's promise of a coming Seed. Noah was saved by believing God's Word about coming judgment. Abraham was saved by believing that God would make him a great nation. Nobody in this day of grace would be saved by believing these promises! Our salvation comes when we trust Christ and believe the Gospel. These twelve men had heard John the Baptist's message through Apollos some thirty years after John's ministry was ended. Calvary and the resurrection had intervened; John's message and baptism were no longer valid. John's ministry had been to point to Christ, and now that Christ had died and risen again, John's ministry was ended. "Simple faith" is all sinners need to be saved, but they must believe the right message.

B. Why were they ignorant of the Holy Spirit?

Certainly these men knew that there was a Holy Spirit since John himself had promised that the Spirit would be given. What they did not know was the Spirit had been given and had ushered in a new age of grace. These men had received their message from Apollos,

whose spiritual knowledge was meager. It is possible that Apollos
had been converted by trusting John's message before Calvary and
Pentecost, for we do not read in Acts 18:24-28 that he was baptized
again. None of the disciples of our Lord were baptized again after
Pentecost since their faith and baptism had taken place at the right
time. Apollos did not know that the Spirit had come, and thus he
was not able to give this knowledge to his converts.

C. Why did Paul baptize these men again?

The answer seems to be that baptism is a commandment for this
age, being a part of Christ's commission to the church in Matt.
28:19-20. Note that Paul assumed in his question of v. 3 that these
men had experienced some kind of baptism. If baptism were not
for this age, Paul would never have asked the question, and he
certainly would not have baptized these men. Wherever Paul went
with the Gospel of the grace of God, he obeyed Christ's instructions as given in Matt. 28: he evangelized, baptized believers, organized them into local assemblies, and taught them the Word. This
does not mean that Paul personally did the baptizing, for his special commission as an apostle was preaching the Gospel (1 Cor.
1:17). Few, if any, evangelists today do any baptizing; but this does
not mean baptism is not for this age. In fact, the NT indicates that
Paul baptized at least twenty people: Crispus, Gaius, the household of Stephanus (at least two people but probably more; 1 Cor.
1:14-16) the twelve disciples in Acts 19:1-7, Lydia and her household (a minimum of two people; Acts 16:15), and the jailer and his
household (a minimum of two people; Acts 16:30-33). The plain
facts prove that Paul did practice baptism and considered it important, having himself baptized more than twenty people. Paul was
God's special messenger to the church, and if baptism were not
intended for this age, he would have known it.

D. Why did these men not receive the Spirit when they believed?

The pattern in Acts is as follows. (1) Acts 1–7: the Jews received
the Spirit by believing and being baptized (see 2:38); (2) Acts 8–9:
the Samaritans and Paul received the Spirit by the laying on of
hands (see 8:17 and 9:17); (3) Acts 10: the Gentiles received the
Spirit when they believed on Christ (see 10:44-48). This is God's
pattern for today: hear the Word, believe, receive the baptism of
the Spirit, receive water baptism.

When we consider the whole situation at Ephesus, we can better understand why God departed from His normal program and imparted the Spirit to these twelve men through the laying on of Paul's hands. Ephesus was to become a great center of evangelism, reaching out into the surrounding provinces with the Gospel. The fact that Paul spent three years there indicates the importance of the city. It was a center of devil worship and Satanic activities, and Satan did all he could to prevent the establishing of a church. The Ephesian church was primarily a Gentile church. Paul was a Jew, and it was important that he establish his apostolic authority from the beginning. God gave Paul the privilege of imparting the Spirit to these men, thus proving his authority as God's messenger and his equality with Peter and John and the other apostles.

Keep in mind that whenever God advanced His program and established a new center, He put His seal of approval on the ministry with special miracles. When the Gospel moved from Jerusalem to Samaria, it was accompanied by attesting miracles, tongues, and the laying on of hands (Acts 8:5-17). Note that in Samaria, Satan tried to hinder the work through a magician. In Acts 9, when Paul was won to Christ, there was a light from heaven, a voice, and the laying on of hands. In Acts 10, when the Gospel came to the Gentiles, they spoke in tongues and magnified God. Now, the Gospel moves to the great city of Ephesus, a city controlled by Satan, and again God bore witness to His work and workers by giving "special miracles" (see 19:11). Satan resisted with counterfeit workers and miracles, but the Spirit proved them false.

The imparting of the Spirit by laying on of hands proved the apostles' authority. There are no apostles today, since none are living who saw the risen Christ (Acts 1:21-26; 1 Cor. 9:1). This means that laying on of hands is no longer in God's program, for if it were, He would provide the proper people to perform the act. God used Paul in this way to give him the credentials needed to found and lead the Ephesian church.

It is important to keep in mind the role Apollos played in this controversy. This able preacher went from Ephesus to Corinth (19:1) and became part of a church split involving him, Peter, and Paul (see 1 Cor. 1 and 3). Paul had founded the church at Corinth and laid the foundation, then Apollos came along to build on that foundation. Soon the church was divided three ways: one group followed Paul, the founder; another followed Apollos, the builder; and a third group wanted to follow "true apostolic leadership," so they chose Peter! These leaders did not cause or encourage these divisions, but they came just the same, and part of the cause was the church's refusal to accept Paul's apostolic commission (1 Cor. 9:1ff.). Now transfer this situation to Ephesus. Here are twelve men, converts of Apollos and the nucleus of the Ephesian church. Suppose God had granted them the Spirit when they believed (as in Acts 10)? They would always have looked to Apollos as their leader, and not Paul; the ministry in Ephesus would have been divided from the very first. It was Apollos who had taught them and baptized them, and they would have questioned the leadership of Paul.

No, God used Paul to give these men a fresh beginning; and from these twelve men he built a great church in Ephesus. Had He not worked in this way, we might not have had the magnificent Epistle to the Ephesians, with its glorious truths of the Head and the Body. Satan would have scored another victory!

John's baptism was a baptism of anticipation of the Spirit's coming; water baptism today symbolizes the realization of this Spirit baptism in our lives because of the finished work of Jesus Christ on the cross.

ACTS 20

I. Paul and the Local Church (20:1-12)

Soon after the riot described in chapter 19, Paul left Ephesus and made his way toward Macedonia, just as he had planned (19:21). At Troas, he expected to meet Titus and get a firsthand report of the situation in Corinth. He had sent Titus there to help correct some problems (2 Cor. 7:13-15 and 12:17-18). When Titus did not arrive, Paul continued to Macedonia, visiting the churches; there he met his fellow worker (2 Cor. 2:12-13). The report from Corinth encouraged him. He then spent three months in Greece, most of that time probably in Corinth. Here he wrote the Book Romans. The same Jewish opposition that had revealed itself in Corinth (Acts 18:12) before now appeared again (v. 3), so Paul left for Macedonia instead of heading for Syria. A number of Christians accompanied Paul, representatives of the churches that were contributing to the relief offering he was taking to Jerusalem. Luke joined the company at Philippi (note the "we" in v. 6), and they stayed at Troas seven days.

It is here that we see Paul in a local church setting. The believers were accustomed to meeting together on Sunday, the first day of the week. Paul may have tarried those seven days just to be with the church of Troas. He was burdened to get to Jerusalem, yet he put the Lord and the Lord's Day first. His is a good example for all to follow. It is probable that Luke describes in vv. 7-8 an evening assembly of believers, since it is not likely that Paul would preach all day. What a joy it would be to hear the great apostle to the Gentiles expound the Word of God! Yet there was one man who fell asleep, fell down, and was taken up for dead. The "many lights" of the torches (v. 8) would fill the air with smoke and make the temperature warm, ideal conditions for falling asleep. Luke the physician reported that the man was dead; Paul, with faith in God's power, announced that life was in him and raised him from the dead. Paul then talked (not preached, v. 11) a long time with the believers, possibly after the assembly was dismissed, and then sailed the next day.

Is there a spiritual meaning behind this miracle? Eutychus (which means "fortunate") had done nothing deserving of God's help; yet because of God's grace, he was restored to life. He had fallen (all have fallen in Adam), and he was dead (all are dead in sin); he was given life by grace alone.

II. Paul and the Local Pastors (20:13-38)

Paul decided to walk alone the twenty miles that separated Troas from Assos. Perhaps he was seeking the mind of the Lord regarding his visit to Jerusalem. While he loved the fellowship of other saints (v. 4), he knew he must get alone with God and seek His mind. The exercise was also good for his body. At Miletus he sent for the elders of the Ephesian church. Keep in mind that the NT teaches that churches should have a plurality of pastors, and this would be this would be especially true for a large church such as the one at Ephesus. These leaders are called elders and overseers (v. 28). Paul's address to the Ephesian pastors reveals the way he ministered to the local church. Note that there are three special addresses by Paul in Acts: (1) to the Jews in 13:16-41; (2) to the Gentiles in 17:22-34; and (3) to the church in Ephesus 20:17ff.

A. Paul's past ministry (vv. 18-21).

Paul did nothing in secret; all men knew his message and his methods. He served the Lord, not man. He was a humble leader, not a proud dictator (see Peter's admonition in 1 Peter 5). He knew what it was to water the seed of the Word with tears (vv. 19, 31). Paul preached the whole counsel of God publicly and from house to house. He preached to all the people and exalted Jesus Christ. This is the pattern for the pastor to follow today.

B. Paul's present burden (vv. 22-24).

Paul was bound in his spirit (not the Holy Spirit) to go to Jerusalem. There is serious doubt whether Paul was in the direct will of God in this matter. He admits in v. 23 that the Holy Spirit had told him in city after city (probably through local prophets in the churches) that he would suffer at Jerusalem. In 21:4 and 10-14 he was expressly warned not to go to Jerusalem. Years before, after his conversion, he was instructed by Christ that his witness would not be heard in Jerusalem (22:18ff); yet Paul's love for his people compelled him to ignore these warnings and press on to Jerusalem. If he was not in God's direct will, he was in God's permissive will. God overruled this burden of his and took him to Rome as a prisoner (see 23:11). Note how Paul described his ministry in v. 24: "To testify to the Gospel of the grace of God" (NKJV).

C. Paul's warning of future danger (vv. 25-35).

Paul was not concerned about himself; he was concerned about the church and its future. He warned the pastors to take heed, first to themselves. If they failed in their personal spiritual walk, the whole church would suffer. Later Paul repeated this warning to Timothy (1 Tim. 4:16). Then he warned them to shepherd the church. As overseers they were responsible for guiding the flock, feeding it, and protecting it from spiritual attacks. How precious the church is to Christ; He purchased it with His own blood. Paul warned of two dangers: (1) wolves attacking from outside the flock, v. 29; and (2) perverse teachers arising from within the flock, v. 30. Both have happened in the history of the church.

Paul gave himself as the example for the pastors to follow. He commended them to God (this is prayer) and to the Word (this is preaching and teaching), for "prayer and the Word" will build up a local church (see Acts 6:4). He warned them not to be covetous. Paul labored with his own hands, but he pointed out that this standard need not apply to the local pastor; see 1 Cor. 9. But the unselfish attitude he displayed certainly can be imitated by all of

God's servants. He reminded them of a beatitude of Christ's that
was never recorded in the Gospels: "It is more blessed to give than
to receive." Christian servants should seek to minister to others
rather than having others minister to them.

D. Paul's final blessing (vv. 36-38).

What a touching scene this is! Paul and his associates knelt down as
the great apostle prayed with them and for them. They wept because they knew they would see his face no more. When there is a
loving bond among God's servants and God's people, what blessings
God will send! Paul left them, heading for Jerusalem. He carried
with him the contributions for the Jews, and in his heart was a
burning desire to testify once more to his people. Paul the preacher
would, in Jerusalem, become "Paul, the prisoner of Jesus Christ."

ACTS 21

I. The Trip to Jerusalem (21:1-16)

Trace this voyage on your map. "Discovered" in v. 3 should read
"came in sight of." Paul and his company tarried in Tyre while the
ship's cargo was unloaded, and this gave them opportunity to fellowship with the believers there. Again the Spirit warned Paul of
trouble in Jerusalem. It seems that God did not want Paul to go
there, but He nevertheless stepped into Paul's plans for His own
glory. What a beautiful scene we have in v. 5 as the "church family" gathered on the shore for a time of prayer! How sad it is to see
children in church while parents are at home, or husbands worshiping while wives and children are elsewhere. Compare this verse to
20:36-38.

The company stayed one day in Ptolemais, then went to the
home of Philip in Caesarea. Philip had begun as a deacon (6:5),
became an evangelist (8:4ff), and now was settled in Caesarea with
his family, undoubtedly busy winning souls. His four unwed daughters
had the gift of prophecy (see Acts 2:17). God gives spiritual gifts to
women, and their ministries are important in the church, but women
must not take spiritual leadership over the men (see 1 Cor. 11:5 and
14:33-40; 1 Tim. 2:9-15). When God had a message to give to Paul,
he used the ministry of Agabus, and not that of any of Philip's daughters. This same prophet had foretold the famine (11:27-30).

In a dramatic way, Agabus warned Paul not to go to Jerusalem. But Paul was "bound in the spirit" (20:22) and willing to be bound and slain for Christ's sake. "I am ready!" was certainly Paul's watchword: ready to preach the Gospel anywhere (Rom. 1:15); ready to die for Christ at any time (Acts 21:13); ready to be offered and meet the Lord (2 Tim. 4:6).

"Carriages" in v. 15 should be translated "baggage."

II. The Bargain with the Jews (21:17-26)

It is easy to assume that everything the apostles did was right, though we realize they had passions like we do. While Paul's letters are certainly inspired of God and are to be trusted, his actions were not always in the will of God. We have already questioned his wisdom in going to Jerusalem (though his heart and motive were right); now it seems evident that after he got there, he made another mistake.

Paul met with James and the elders and reported God's blessing among the Gentiles. Paul gave God the glory—"what things God hath wrought" (v. 19). But James, as we have seen, was leader of the Jerusalem church and certainly interested in keeping the Jewish traditons in church life. Note in v. 20 that there were thousands of Jewish believers who were still practicing the Mosaic commandments. This would be easier to do in Jerusalem than anywhere else, since the temple with all its services was near at hand. We have here a confusion between law and grace, the kingdom and the church, a confusion we still have with us today. James and the elders thought Paul should prove to these zealous Jews that he was really not teaching against the Law of Moses.

It was a bad bargain, but Paul fell into it. He had already written the letters to the Romans and Galatians, which proved that no man could be saved or sanctified by keeping the law and showed that the Christian is free from the Law of Moses. Now he was denying all of this inspired truth with a "religious bargain" that was aimed at compromising with the Jews. Paul shared with the four men as they completed their vows and offered the sacrifices, the whole transaction taking seven days (v. 27). This was apparently a Nazirite vow since it involved shaving the head (Num. 11, and see Paul's own actions in Acts 18:18). Did the scheme work? No! It resulted in Paul being arrested! The very thing God had warned him about in city after city now took place.

Whether Paul was right or wrong is not for us to say with confidence. This we know: God used the whole episode to put Paul into the hands of the Romans and not the Jews, for he was safer with the Romans. God used the Romans to protect Paul and take him to Rome, where God had a special work for him to do.

III. The Arrest in the Temple (21:27-40)

Some of the foreign Jews, who knew Paul, had seen him in company with Trophimus, an Ephesian Gentile; and when they saw Paul in the temple, they assumed he had brought his Gentile friend with him into the forbidden area. It was a lie, but Satan is a liar and the father of lies. The very thing James was trying to prevent occurred just the same. Faith is simply trusting God without scheming, and the believer who walks by faith does not have to resort to plans and devices to influence or please others.

Paul would have been taken out of the city and stoned had not the captain of the temple guard rushed on the scene and rescued him. Then the oft-repeated prophecy was fulfilled: Paul was bound with two chains (v. 33; also v. 11). Note the confusion of the Jewish crowd, not unlike the confusion of the Gentile crowd in Ephesus (19:32). Satan is the author of confusion.

The guard thought Paul was a notorious Egyptian who had caused trouble earlier, but Paul once again used his Roman citizenship to protect himself. Government is instituted of God for our protection (Rom. 13), and it is right to use the law for the furtherance of the Gospel. Standing there on the steps, Paul signaled to the crowd; and when they heard him speaking in Hebrew, they quieted down.

While we do not want to be guilty of judging the great apostle, we must admit that it appears he made two mistakes: he went to Jerusalem when he was warned about what would happen, and he compromised with the church leaders by assisting the men in their temple sacrifices. One was a practical mistake, the other a doctrinal one. We understand, of course, that Paul's heart was so full of love and concern for his brethren in the flesh that he would have paid any price to give them the Gospel; but from the very beginning God had warned him not to witness in Jerusalem (22:17-21). Antioch and Ephesus were to be the great centers for the church, not Jerusalem.

The mixture of law and grace in churches has produced a false gospel of salvation by faith *and* works. It was Paul's Epistle to the Romans that changed Martin Luther and broke the shackles of superstition centuries ago, and Luther's exposition of Galatians which in turn brought liberty where there had been bondage. Through the centuries, faithful groups have been true to the Word of God and have laid down their lives for Christ. May we never mix law and grace; may we never compromise the truth of the Gospel.

ACTS 22

I. Paul's Defense (22:1-21)

This is the second of three accounts in Acts of Paul's conversion (see chaps. 9 and 26). By speaking in Hebrew, Paul helped to quiet and interest the Jews.

A. Paul's early conduct (vv. 1-5).

Paul was a Jew with valued Roman citizenship. In v. 28 he stated that he was "free born," which indicates that his father had been a Roman citizen as well. His early training at the feet of the great rabbi Gamaliel was the finest (see 5:34ff). Read Phil. 3 for another picture of Paul the Pharisee. No one could deny that the young Paul was zealous for the Law of Moses, even to the extent of persecuting Christians. What a paradox that Paul should say in v. 5 that his plan was to bring Christians "bound unto Jerusalem," when he himself stood there a prisoner!

B. Paul's amazing conversion (vv. 6-16).

When the heavenly light was at its brightest (noon), the satanic darkness in Paul's heart was at its deepest, for he was out to arrest all the Christians he could find. But God, in His grace, "arrested" Paul with a great light from heaven. The sinner is in darkness until God's light shines upon him (2 Cor. 4). Paul saw and heard the glorified Christ, trusted Him, and was saved. Note how Paul called Ananias "a devout man according to the law," a statement that would have impressed his antagonists. Some of the Jews in the city may have known Ananias, and this would have been in Paul's favor. Ananias declared that Paul had a special commission from God to be Christ's witness.

C. Paul's special commission (vv. 17-21).

Paul had a special meeting with the Lord while praying in the temple (see Acts 9:26). It is interesting to compare this experience with Peter's trance in Acts 10, when God prepared him to go to the Gentiles. Peter was hungry for physical food, while Paul had a "hunger" of heart to win his nation to Christ. But Christ clearly told Paul to get out of Jerusalem (v. 18). The apostle's pleading did not change the divine command: Paul had to go to the Gentiles. For one thing, the Jews would not receive Paul's testimony anyway, and they might arrest and stone him, thus ending his ministry too soon. The Jews listened intently to Paul's account until he spoke that hated word "Gentiles" (v. 21). Paul might have used another word, but then he would not have been faithfully quoting what the Lord said to him. See Eph. 3:1-13.

II. The Nation's Response (22:22-30)

Christ's prediction came true: the nation did not receive Paul's testimony. Instead, a riot broke out! The captain ordered Paul to be taken into the nearby castle where they could examine him under scourging. But Paul again used his rights as a Roman citizen to protect himself and his ministry. It was unlawful to treat a Roman citizen in this way (16:35-40), and Paul took advantage of these legal privileges. The chief captain had purchased his Roman citizenship and seemed proud of it, while Paul announced that he was "free born." This meant that his father was a recognized Roman citizen.

The captain released the bonds and kept Paul in ward until the Jewish council could meet the next day (an event covered in chap. 23).

At this point it is good to review the history of Israel in the Book of Acts. The people of the nation had already been involved in three murders: John the Baptist, Christ, and Stephen. They would have committed a fourth had not God delivered Paul through the intervention of the Roman guard. Paul's memory of the death of Stephen was still vivid (v. 20), and he wanted in some way to atone for his share in this national crime. But Israel was now set aside; Christ had forbidden Paul to witness in Jerusalem (v. 18) because its period of probation was over.

The remaining chapters of Acts describe Paul the prisoner, his trials before the Jews, and his appeal to Caesar. How these chapters would have read had Paul not gone to Jerusalem and been arrested, we do not know. But God overruled His servant's mistakes for His glory and the church's good. While a prisoner in Rome, Paul wrote letters to the Ephesians, Philippians, Colossians, and to Philemon, messages filled with church truth that is desperately needed today.

ACTS 23

I. Paul and the Council (23:1-11)

The next day the guard brought Paul to the official meeting of the Jewish council. This group had tried Peter and John (4:5ff), the twelve apostles (5:21ff) and Stephen (6:12ff). They had also tried Christ.

Paul felt at home in this meeting, having been an active Pharisee himself. He immediately spoke in his own defense, stating that his public life had been blameless and his conscience clear. This infuriated the high priest, Ananias, who ordered one of the men near Paul to hit him on the mouth. Christ suffered similar treatment (John 18:22). There is division of opinion concerning Paul's reply in v. 3. Some say he was acting in carnal haste by condemning the high priest; others feel Paul was justified in his words since smiting him was illegal, and the high priest was a wicked man. History tells us that Ananias was one of the worst high priests the nation ever had. He stole money from the other priests, used every political trick to enlarge his power, and finally was assassinated. "Whited wall" (v. 3) may refer to Ezek. 13:10ff, where the hypocritical rulers of the land are compared to walls painted over with whitewash but unable to stand up.

Did Paul know who the high priest was? Some students feel that the apostle's eye trouble (Gal. 4:13-15) may have hindered him from recognizing the high priest. This was not a formal meeting of the council, since the Roman captain had summoned the Jews together; thus the high priest may not have been wearing his usual garb or been seated in his usual place. Another possibility is that Paul refused to recognize him as high priest. He quoted Ex. 22:28 perhaps in irony and meant by this that the priest was not really the ruler of the nation.

Paul then used a "political" tactic, seeking to divide the council and set the strict Pharisees against the liberal Sadducees. It is difficult to believe that the great Apostle to the Gentiles, the minister of the grace of God, would shout, "I am a Pharisee!" He would later call his Pharisaical life "garbage" (Phil. 3:1-11). He stated that the real issue was the hope of the resurrection, knowing that the Sadducees did not believe that doctrine. He hoped, no doubt, to be able to prove the resurrection of Christ; but the argument that ensued put him in danger of his life and the captain had to rescue him again. It looked hopeless, but that night the Lord graciously stood by Paul and encouraged him. He knew he would go to Rome!

II. Paul and the Conspirators (23:12-22)

Jerusalem was certainly far from God when more than forty men could conspire in the name of religion to slay a godly Jew! Even the chief priests and elders were a part of the crime! But God was in control and was going to take His messenger to Rome in spite of the opposition of men and Satan. Whether or not Paul's coming to Jerusalem was in God's revealed will, the Lord still graciously diverted and encouraged His servant. What an encouragement this incident is to us as we make ministry decisions!

We know nothing about Paul's sister or his nephew. We are not even sure they were believers. But God used them to foil the conspiracy and get Paul away from dangerous Jerusalem. We must certainly admire the honesty and integrity of that Roman captain. He could have scorned the boy's message or listened to the lies of the Jews; but instead, he did his job faithfully. Often God's servants are helped and protected by unbelievers who are honest and faithful. Paul had now been delivered into the hands of the Gentiles, as was His Lord in Jerusalem years before.

III. Paul and the Captain (23:23-35)

The captain's name was Claudius Lysias. In his letter to Felix, he told how he rescued Paul from the Jews because the apostle was a Roman citizen. He further stated that the issue was one of Jewish law and not Roman law, and he did not feel that Paul was worthy of arrest or death. But that Paul might be kept safe, Claudius sent him to Felix for trial.

What a procession that was! Those forty Jews must have been terribly hungry before they broke their vow! But Paul was carried safely to Caesarea, where he would face his Jewish accusers before Felix the governor.

We can see now why God used Paul as his great missionary to the Gentiles. His Roman citizenship gave him the protection of the Roman laws and army for one thing, and it also gave him opportunities to witness to the Gentiles. How wonderful it is that God prepares His servants beforehand, even seeing to their birthplace and citizenship!

It is interesting to note that on several crisis occasions, the Lord appeared to Paul to sustain him. During the Jewish attacks at Corinth, Christ assured Paul that He was with him and would give him many converts (18:9-11). Aboard ship, going to Rome, when the storm broke loose, Christ assured Paul that He would not forsake him (27:21-25). We wonder if Paul leaned heavily on Ps. 23:4, "Yea, though I walk through the valley of the shadow of death, I will fear no evil; for Thou art with me."

ACTS 24

I. A False Accusation (24:1-9)

Paul next had a hearing before Felix the governor. Felix was the husband of Drusilla (v. 24), his third wife. She was the youngest daughter of Herod Agrippa I and was not yet twenty years old.

It was customary for the accusers to present oratorical arguments and try to flatter the judge. Tertullus was such an orator-lawyer whose flattering words about Felix sound hollow and false. The "five days" in v. 1 refer to the period since Paul's arrest. The summary of Paul's activities would look like this: Day 1—arrived in Jerusalem, 21:17; Day 2—visited James, 21:18; Day 3—visited the temple, 21:26; Days 4, 5, and 6—in the temple with the vow upon him; Day 7—arrested in the temple, 21:27; Day 8—before the Council, 22:30–23:10; Day 9—the Jews' plot and Paul's trip to Caesarea, 23:12-31; Day 10—presented to Felix, 23:32-35; Days 11 and 12—waiting at Caesarea; Day 13—the hearing before Felix. You will note that there are five days (8 through 12) between Paul's arrest and the trial.

There were three accusations by the Jews against Paul: (1) a personal accusation: "we have found this man a pestilent fellow"; (2) a political accusation: "a mover of sedition"; and (3) a religious accusation: "a ringleader of the sect of the Nazarenes." Compare the trial of Christ and the accusations they made against Him (Luke 23:22). Of course, they had no proof for any of these matters! They considered Paul "a plague" (v. 5) while generations of Christians have looked to him as God's great apostle to the Gentiles. Unbelievers today do not realize that their "pesky Christian friends" are really their best friends. The rich man in Luke 16:19-31 begged from hell that Abraham should send Lazarus to visit his brothers and witness to them!

The political argument was also false. Paul never sought to change men's politics, but he did preach the lordship of Christ. This conflicted with Caesar's demand that people worship him as a god. "We have no king but Caesar!" is what the Jews cried to Pilate (John 19:8-15). These men considered the Christian faith a sect, a group of people alien to the true Jewish faith. Thousands of Jews had believed in Christ but still participated in temple worship, so they were looked upon as a sect within Israel and not as a new religion. The term "Nazarene" was one of contempt; "Can there any good thing come out of Nazareth?" asked Nathanael (John 1:46).

Tertullus even lied about the courageous soldier Lysias! Note how he "softened" the story of the temple riot (v. 6) but exaggerated what Lysias did (v. 7)! Men who oppose the truth will stop at nothing to distort the truth or promote a lie. God had used Lysias to rescue Paul, and the Jews hated him for this. Men pretend to obey the law, but these children of the devil (John 8:44) were murderers and liars!

II. A Faithful Answer (24:10-21)

Christians have the right to use the law (established by God) to protect themselves and the Gospel. Note that Paul did not depend on flattery; see 1 Thes. 2:1-6. He waited until the governor had given him permission to speak, then he quietly and honestly gave his story.

Felix had been governor about six or seven years, which was enough to be considered "many years" (v. 10) according to the records of those days! Paul answered their accusations with facts. Just twelve days before (recall the timetable given earlier) he had come to Jerusalem to worship. There was no way that he could have organized a revolt in such a short time! The accusers had no witnesses to prove that he had caused trouble or even raised his voice in the temple! Then the apostle began to use the court for a pulpit, giving witness of his faith in Christ. "I will confess to heresy, as they call it!" But he went on to state that this "heresy" was actually the fulfillment of the Jewish faith. Paul believed the Law and the Prophets, that is, the entire OT Scripture. He believed (as did the Pharisees) that there would be a resurrection of the dead. He tried daily to have a conscience void of offense to man or God.

Was Paul anti-Jewish? How could he be, when he was now bringing a gift of love to his nation to help them in their time of trial! The "many years" of v. 17 would have been three or four years. Paul visited Jerusalem on five different occasions: these events are found in Acts 9:26 (A.D. 39); Acts 11:27-30 (A.D. 45); Acts 15 (A.D. 50); Acts 18:22 (A.D. 53); and Acts 21:17 (A.D. 58). It had been five years since his last visit to Jerusalem. The accusers could not prove with witnesses that he had caused any trouble; in fact, they were the ones who started the riot in the temple (21:27ff).

III. A Foolish Attitude (24:22-27)

Felix had an understanding of "that Way" (the Christian faith) but refused to make any decision. He postponed the decision with the excuse that the Roman captain would have to appear first. The governor was kind to Paul by allowing him liberty and access to his friends.

Felix held another trial, this time with his teenage wife Drusilla present. As young as she was, she had already lived in sin, not unlike the Herod family from which she came. She probably enjoyed all the pomp and parade of being a governor's wife — until Paul began to preach the Word! Paul stood before them and spoke, not for himself, but for their own salvation! He had a three-fold argument telling them why they should accept Christ: (1) righteousness — they had to do something about past sin; (2) temperance (self-control) — they had to overcome today's temptations; (3) judgment to come — they had to be prepared for tomorrow's judgment.

The message was so powerful that Felix trembled! But the governor had a foolish attitude, even though God had spoken to his heart: he put off deciding for Christ and used Paul as a "political pawn" with the hopes of getting money from him. Paul had admitted that he carried alms for the Jews (v. 17), and perhaps Felix thought the Apostle would bribe his way to freedom. Seeking to please the Jews, Felix left Paul in jail two more years, before he was succeeded by Porcius Festus.

We cannot help but admire Paul as he faced false charges from wicked men. What an example he is for us today. Paul faced facts honestly and demanded that the truth be presented. His concern was for the souls of men, not for the safety of his own life. God had promised that Paul would witness before Gentiles and kings (9:15), and this experience was a fulfillment of that promise.

Many sinners today are like Tertullus, who flatter and refuse to face the truth. Others are like Felix, who hear the truth and understand it, and are even convicted, but who refuse to obey. Still others are like Drusilla; she heard the Word and saw her husband deeply moved, yet the record says nothing about her own decision. Undoubtedly her youthful sins had already hardened her heart. Historians tell us that she died twenty-one years later in the eruption of Mt. Vesuvius.

ACTS 25

I. Paul Appeals to Caesar (25:1-12).

It is now two years since the events of chapter 24. Luke did not record Paul's activities at Caesarea since his purpose is to explain how Paul finally got from Jerusalem to Rome. Festus, the new governor, was a more honorable man who was unwilling to give Paul a false trial (see v. 16). In a state visit to Jerusalem, Festus found "a multitude of Jews" (v. 24) who insisted that he do something with Paul. Even the high priest and the chief rulers lied about Paul, asking Festus to bring the prisoner to Jerusalem for trial. They wanted to attempt again to kill Paul along the way (see 23:12ff). God guided Festus to refuse the Jews' suggestion, and in this way He protected His servant. Man proposes, but God disposes. We must admire this pagan governor for his honesty and fairness.

After a ten day visit to the Jews, Festus returned to Caesarea and held another trial for Paul. Again, the Jews came with their complaints which they could not prove. How patiently Paul waited for God to fulfill His promise to take him to Rome! Like Joseph in the

Egyptian prison, Paul was tested and tried as he waited for the Word to be fulfilled (Ps. 105:17-20).

The politician in Festus now came to the fore as he asked Paul if he wanted to go to Jerusalem for trial. Like Felix, he wanted to please the Jews and make a good impression as the new governor (24:27). But Paul clung to Christ's promise that he would go to Rome. Years before, Christ had told him not to stay in Jerusalem (22:17-18). God had sovereignly overruled Paul's decisions, and Paul was careful now to stay away from Jerusalem. Again, in this way God protected him and took His servant to Rome for his final years of ministry. Every Roman citizen had the right to appeal to Caesar and have his trial in Rome, and this right Paul now used.

II. Paul Perplexes Festus (25:13-22)

The new governor now had a real problem on his hands. Paul was a notable prisoner and his trial involved the Jewish leaders and their whole nation. If Festus did the honest thing and released Paul, he would incur the anger of the Jews, and as a new governor, he desperately needed their goodwill. It seemed that his problem was solved with the coming of Agrippa and Bernice, two seasoned rulers and politicians. Agrippa was the son of the Agrippa of Acts 12, and Bernice was the older sister of Drusilla, Felix's wife. The Herodian dynasty had intermarried and lived in sin for years.

Festus did not give Paul's case to Agrippa right away, but waited for the proper time. He explained the situation to his guest as though the problem were too much for him and called for experienced help. This approach undoubtedly appealed to Agrippa's pride. Festus called the whole case "a matter of superstition" (v. 19)! The unsaved have no understanding of spiritual matters and see little difference between one religion and another. Festus also recognized the fact that Jesus was involved in the case: Paul said He was alive, but the Jews said He was dead.

Then Festus gave the real reason for wanting Agrippa to hear Paul: the governor had to send Paul to Caesar, but he had no real accusation against him! See v. 27.

III. Paul Faces Royalty (25:23-27)

With great pomp and ceremony the royal party assembled in the judgment room on the next day. The world has nothing within to satisfy, so it must have "the lust of the eyes and the pride of life" (1 John 2:15-17) to make it happy. The Christian needs none of these things. In fact, believers feel ill at ease in the presence of such pomp and pride.

Note how Festus introduced Paul: "You see this man!" (v. 24, NKJV) Yet Paul was the noblest of all the people present at that meeting! He was the apostle of Jesus Christ, an ambassador in bonds, a king and a priest of Jesus Christ! Christians need never feel that the world has more than they do; Christ has made us rich and given us a heavenly calling and a hope of glory!

Paul's trial was similar to Christ's in that all the people involved admitted that he was not worthy of death and should have been released. Captain Lysias admitted that he had no case against Paul (23:29); Festus here admitted that Paul had done nothing worthy of death (25:25); and even Agrippa agreed with this verdict (26:31). "How can I send a prisoner to Caesar if I have no crimes to accuse him of committing?" asked Festus, and then Agrippa gave Paul permission to speak.

ACTS 26

I. Paul's Personal Explanation (26:1-23)

Paul's hands were bound (v. 29) so when he stretched them forth, it must have been a sermon in itself. Here was the great apostle, bound because of his faithfulness to Christ. In Phil. 1:13 he said his bonds were "in Christ" and were a blessing rather than a burden. Note the polite manner in which Paul addressed the king. Though Paul could not respect the man, he did respect his office. See Rom. 13 and 1 Peter 2:13-17. Agrippa was an "expert" in matters relating to the Jews, so Paul felt he would have a fair, intelligent hearing. Paul's personal defense and explanation can be summarized with several key phrases:

A. "I lived a Pharisee" (vv. 4-11).

See 22:3ff, 9:1ff, and Phil. 3 for additional information about Paul's early life. So famous was Paul as a young rabbi that he could say that "all the Jews at Jerusalem" knew his life! Yet in Phil. 3, Paul said that he considered all this position and prestige but garbage compared to knowing Christ and living for Him. In vv. 6-8 he mentioned again the matter of resurrection. (See 23:6-10.) God had promised the nation a kingdom and glory. In Acts 13:27-37, Paul explained that the promises made to David were fulfilled through the resurrection of Christ from the dead. Had Israel (in Acts 1–7) received Christ, they would have received their kingdom. But the Jews were sure that Christ was dead (25:19); Paul stated that Christ's resurrection is what gives hope to Israel. Paul went on to describe his days as a persecutor and murderer, taking the account up to the day of his conversion.

B. "I saw a light" (vv. 12-13).

Nobody else has ever experienced the amazing kind of conversion that Paul did. While engaged in his murderous plans, Paul saw the glory of God shining from the heavens. Certainly he had been in spiritual darkness up till then (see 2 Cor. 4:1-6), but now the Son of God had been revealed to him. See 1 Tim. 1:12ff.

C. "I heard a voice" (vv. 14-18).

The Word of God is what convicts and converts the soul. All his life, Paul had heard the "voices of the prophets; but that day he heard the voice of the Son of God." See John 5:21-25, where this miracle of spiritual resurrection is described. Note that Paul was persecuting Christ and not simply His people. As members of His body, the believers were sharing in His sufferings and He in theirs. "It is hard for you to kick against the goads," (v. 14, NKJV) said Christ, referring to the stick farmers used to prod their cattle. Jesus was comparing Paul to a stubborn animal that would not obey! What "goads" was God using to bring Paul to Christ? The death of Stephen was certainly one, for Paul never forgot it (22:17-20). The godly conduct of the saints he persecuted must have touched Paul's heart. Surely the OT Scriptures spoke to his heart with new conviction. God used different means to bring Paul to repentance, just as He does with sinners today.

Paul called Jesus "Lord," and then the Savior revealed His name. See Rom. 10:9-10. Read Christ's commission to Paul carefully, noting his special ministry to the Gentiles; and compare the other records in Acts of Paul's conversion. Verse 18 is a beautiful description of salvation!

D. "I was not disobedient" (vv. 19-21).

Paul saw the light and opened his heart to Christ, and then immediately began to testify to others. Obeying God meant incurring the wrath of men, but Paul was faithful.

E. "I continue unto this day" (vv. 22-23).

These five phrases certainly summarize the life of Paul, and the life of any sinner who has trusted Christ and seeks to serve Him. Paul was faithful to continue. Faithfulness to Christ is an evidence of true salvation.

II. Paul's Passionate Exhortation (26:24-32)

Paul got to the word "Gentiles" and Festus interrupted him, just as the Jews had done in the temple (22:21). Festus accused Paul of being out of his mind, just as the friends and relatives of Christ had done to Him (Mark 3:20-21 and 31-35). Festus attributed Paul's "madness" to his great scholarship, which shows that Paul was a brilliant man and a great student. God never discredits learning unless it discredits His Word.

The apostle "cornered" Agrippa and ignored Festus. Paul knew that Agrippa was expert in these matters, that he read and believed the prophets, and that he was acquainted with the events concerning Christ. The more light a person has, the more responsible he or she is to make a right decision. Note that it is possible to have faith short of salvation. Agrippa believed the prophets, but this faith did not save him.

Agrippa's response has been variously interpreted. Some say that he was under real conviction and was about to be saved. Our touching invitation song "Almost Persuaded" is based on this idea. But the literal meaning of v. 28 is, "With but a little will you persuade me to be a Christian?" There is no evidence of conviction here, and Agrippa is using the word "Christian" as a term of contempt. "It will take more than this to make a Jew like me into one of those hated Christians!" is the idea behind his response.

But Paul used this remark as the basis for a passionate appeal in v. 29, pleading with the royal assembly to trust in Jesus Christ. Sad to say, there are two kinds of people—"almost Christians" and "altogether Christians." Agrippa was an "almost Christian"—he understood the Word, heard the truth, but refused to do anything about it. His intellect was instructed, his emotions touched, but his will was unyielding.

This exchange closed the trial. The king and his party left the

351

room with Festus and held a private meeting, at which all agreed that Paul was innocent. Agrippa's words in v. 32 are a criticism of Paul's request for a Roman trial. He is looking at the situation through the eyes of an unbeliever, not realizing that the burden of Paul's heart was to go to Rome. This trial was God's means of getting him there. The Jews would have killed Paul, but the Romans helped Paul fulfill God's will.

ACTS 27

Be sure to consult your maps as you read this account of Paul's voyage and shipwreck. In 2 Cor. 11:25, written some three years before, Paul mentioned he had been in three shipwrecks; so the one described in this chapter would be his fourth. Paul was willing to take any risk to carry the Gospel to the lost world. Are we?

I. The Voyage to Fair Havens (27:1-8)

Paul was accompanied by Luke (note the "we" sections) and Aristarchus (see 19:29 and 20:4; also Phile. 24 and Col. 4:10). How comforting it must have been to Paul to have these men at his side! The centurion, Julius, was kind to Paul, for "when a man's ways please the Lord, He makes even his enemies to be at peace with him" (Prov. 16:7, NKJV). The centurions in the Bible are usually presented as kind, intelligent men. Julius permitted Paul a visit to the church gathering at Sidon, which refreshed the apostle physically and spiritually. At Myra, they changed ships.

From the very beginning, the voyage was not encouraging. "The winds were contrary" and they "sailed slowly many days" (v. 7). The ship finally arrived at Fair Havens.

II. Paul's Warning of Danger (27:9-14)

It was now October; "the fast" referred to in v. 9 was the Day of Atonement. Sailing was dangerous for several months after the fall season began, and there was some debate whether or not the ship should continue to Rome. Directed by God, Paul warned them that the voyage would be disastrous, but the centurion would not listen. There were at least five factors that contributed to this wrong decision by the centurion:

A. *Impatience.*

Much time was spent (v. 9). Whenever we get impatient, we usually rush ahead and disobey the will of God. We should not be like the horse that rushes ahead, or the mule that lags behind (Ps. 32:9), but like the obedient sheep that follows the shepherd.

B. *Expert Advice.*

The centurion listened to the pilot (master) and the owner of the ship, and not to God's messenger. The centurion had faith—but his faith was in the wrong people! God's wisdom is far above the wisdom of men. The person who knows the Word of God knows more than the "experts" (Ps. 119:97-104). While knowledge is important, we also need wisdom (James 1:5).

C. *Discomfort.*

"The haven was not commodious to winter in" (v. 12). The centurion could not see staying three months in an uncomfortable place.

D. *Majority rule.*

He took a vote (v. 12), and Paul was out-voted! In the Bible, the majority is usually wrong; yet today the common excuse is "Everybody's doing it!"

E. *Favorable circumstances.*

"The south wind blew softly" (v. 13) The very wind they needed came along and seemed to prove how wrong Paul was. We must beware of "great opportunities" and "ideal circumstances" that seem to contradict the Word of God.

Each of the above factors can work in the lives of Christians today. We must be careful to obey God's Word by faith, even when circumstances seem to prove us wrong.

III. The Storm (27:15-26)

The balmy south wind soon turned into a terrible storm, as is usually the case when we disobey the Word of God. "Euroclydon" is part Greek and part Latin, a word that means "east wind and north wind." Note that Luke uses "we" in this section, indicating that all the crew and prisoners were busy trying to save the ship. First, they pulled in the little boat that was behind the ship (v. 16). Then, they put cables around the ship to help hold it together (v. 17). The next move was to pull down part of the sail, leaving enough to steady the ship (v. 17b). The next day they began to lighten the ship by throwing out some of the cargo (v. 18); and by the third day (v. 19) even the "furniture" (which is what the Gk. word means) or gear was thrown out. All of this was necessary because people did not believe the Word of God!

By comparing v. 27 with v. 19, we learn that the "many days" of v. 20 amounted to eleven days. There was no light and no hope! What a picture of lost souls today, driven in the storm of disobedience and sin, without God, without hope! (See Ps. 107:23-31.) Paul then stood up and took command, reminding the men that their plight was the result of not listening to God's warning. But Paul had more than a rebuke for them; he also had a message of hope from God (23:11). God had promised Paul that he would minister in Rome, and Paul believed God's Word. It is faith in the Word of God that gives us hope and assurance in the storms of life. God had also told Paul that the ship would be wrecked upon a certain island, but that all the passengers and crew would be saved.

IV. The Shipwreck (27:27-44)

Three days later, at midnight, Paul's words came true. The sailors heard breakers and knew they were getting near land. They took several soundings and learned that the water was indeed getting shallower and that land was near. Now a new fear arose: would the boat be dashed on the rocks and everybody killed? As a safety measure, four anchors were put out, only to be taken in (literally, "cast off") later on (v. 40). Some of the sailors tried to escape on the small boat that had been taken in before (v. 16), but Paul detected the plot and stopped them. Note that Paul said in v. 31 "you cannot be saved" and not "we" as though he were thinking only of himself and his friends.

For the first time in two weeks, light began to appear, and Paul encouraged the men to take some food. The effects of the storm, the necessity for constant watch, the lack of food from lightening the ship, and perhaps the desire to fast to please their gods had kept the passengers from eating. Without shame, Paul gave thanks before 275 people (v. 37) and set the example himself by eating.

As day broke, they saw a creek on an island, cast off (cut off) the four anchors, and, hoisting the sail, headed for this haven. The front of the ship stuck in the mud, while the stern was beaten by the waves. Satan was again at work as the soldiers planned to kill all the prisoners (including Paul), but the centurion believed Paul this time and told all on board to make for land the best way they could. The last statement (v. 44) vindicates the truth of God's promise in vv. 22 and 34: "They escaped all safe to land." They were on the island of Malta.

God spared 276 people because of one man—the Apostle Paul! How precious His saints are to Him! God was willing to spare Sodom and Gomorrah for ten righteous people (Gen. 18), and He did not send His wrath until Lot and his family had safely escaped. God holds back His judgment on this wicked world because the church is still in the world; but when we are taken away, His judgments will fall (2 Thes. 2). Satan tried to prevent Paul from getting to Rome, but God's Word prevailed. "There has not failed one word of His good promise" (1 Kings 8:56, NKJV).

ACTS 28

I. The Ministry at Malta (28:1-10)

To the Greeks, "barbarians" were any people who did not speak Greek. For three months (v. 11) the party stayed in Malta, and the natives treated them kindly. We can imagine how cold and wet the prisoners were when they arrived on shore! Though Paul was now the leader and savior of the group, he still helped gather fuel for the fire. (See 20:34-35.) Satan, the serpent, attacked him but God protected him. (See Mark 16:18.) The reaction of the natives was exactly opposite to that of the people at Lystra (14:11-19). Beware of trusting the opinions of the crowd!

The leading man on the island was Publius, who allowed Paul and his companions to lodge with him three days. Paul healed the man's father and then cured many of the natives who were diseased. God allowed Paul to perform these miracles to win the confidence of the people who, in turn, assisted Paul and his party when they left for Rome three months later (v. 10). It appears that the gift of miracles and healing gradually disappeared during Paul's ministry. God gave Paul "special miracles" at Ephesus (Acts 19) to witness to the Gentiles; and here at Malta, God gave Paul the power to heal. Yet, when Paul wrote from Rome two years later, he reported that Epaphroditus had been ill and had almost died (Phil.

2:25-30); and in 2 Tim. 4:20, he stated that he had to leave Trophimus sick at Miletus.

II. The Trip to Rome (28:11-16)

The party remained at Malta during November, December, and January; then, taking a grain ship that had wintered on the island, they headed for Rome. "Castor and Pollux" were "patron saints" of navigation, and their images were often carved on ships. We have another "south wind" in 28:13—quite different from the "south wind" of 27:13! At Puteoli, Paul fellowshiped with the believers for a week, probably while the ship was delayed with business.

When the word got to Rome that Paul had arrived (Puteoli was the principal port of Rome), the believers arranged to meet him. Since Paul remained at Puteoli a week, there was ample time to carry messages between the churches. How wonderful it is to be a part of the fellowship of the Gospel and find "brothers and sisters" in Christ wherever we go! "Appii forum" is literally "the Market of Appius" and refers to a town about forty miles from Rome on the famous Appian Way. Here Paul met one deputation of believers; then, ten miles further, he met another group at Three Taverns. (This Latin word translated "tavern" does not mean what the English word commonly means today. A Roman "tavern" was any kind of shop.) Seeing these believers, to whom he had written his Roman epistle some three years before, brought Paul courage.

"And when we came to Rome" (v. 16). How simply Luke described Paul's arrival at the city he had longed to see for years. There is no description here of the beauty of the city, for Paul was not there as a sightseer, but as an ambassador. See Rom. 1:11-13.

III. The Introduction to the Roman Jews (28:17-22)

As in other cities, Paul wanted to begin with his own nation and seek to win them to Christ. See Rom. 9:1-2 and 10:1 for his burden. He began by stating his innocence and then told them the real reason for his calling them together. "The hope of Israel" in v. 20 refers to the resurrection of Christ, and verses 5:31, 23:6, 24:14-15, and 26:6-8 have similar themes. See also 13:27-37 and the notes on 26:6. The resurrection proved that Christ was the Messiah, and all of Israel's blessings rested in Him. Note, however, that Paul did not offer the kingdom to Israel, but rather preached the kingdom of God, which means the Gospel of the grace of God (see v. 31).

The Roman Jewish leaders had not heard any accusations against Paul, but they had heard about "the sect" of Christians which had been spoken against. Three sects are mentioned in Acts: the Sadducees (5:17), the Pharisees (15:5), and the Christians (24:5 and 28:22). The Jews appointed a time to meet Paul and discuss the Word.

IV. The Jews Reject the Gospel (28:23-31)

Paul was not in a prison, but rather in his own rented house, chained to a Roman soldier, but with liberty to have visitors. When the Jewish leaders arrived, Paul explained the OT Scriptures and presented to them Jesus as the Christ. Compare v. 23 with Luke 24:13-35, where Christ used Moses and the Prophets to open the hearts and minds of those two dejected men. There is a contrast in results, however: the Emmaus disciples believed the Word and became missionaries, while the Roman Jews for the most part rejected the Word and would not believe. The phrase "from morning to evening" (v. 23) aptly describes the history of Israel — from the light of God's revelation into the darkness of unbelief (2 Cor. 4).

Please keep in mind that Paul is not making an offer of the kingdom to these men. He had written the Epistle to the Romans three years before, explaining in chapters 9–11 that Israel had been set aside. The church would now take up God's program for the age to come.

For the fifth time in Israel's history, the prophecy of Isaiah 6 was fulfilled. Over 700 years before, God had told Isaiah that Israel would reject His Word and refuse His message. When Christ was accused of being in league with Satan (Matt. 12), our Lord quoted this same prophecy as He gave the Parables of the Kingdom (Matt. 13:14-15). At the close of His ministry, Jesus spoke of this prophecy again (John 12:37-41). Paul quoted it in Rom. 11:8; and now he used it for the last time. God had been speaking to His people for over 700 years — what patience! Verse 28 does not mean that for the first time Paul went to the Gentiles. It simply means that, now that Israel in Rome had been given an opportunity and had refused, Paul would turn to the Gentiles. Paul's hands were free of their blood; he had given them the opportunity to be saved. This had been Paul's pattern from the very beginning (Acts 13:44-49).

Paul was a prisoner for two years, freely preaching and teaching the Word. It was during this time that he wrote the letters to the Ephesians, Philippians, Colossians, and to Philemon. People often imagine Paul chained to a dungeon wall, when actually he enjoyed a great deal of liberty. His first period at Rome lasted from A.D. 61–63; then he was released for about three years, during which time he wrote his first letter to Timothy and another to Titus. He probably visited Philippi, Colosse, and several other Asian churches at this time. He may also have made his intended trip to Spain (Rom. 15:24, 28). He was imprisoned again in A.D. 66, and this time his situation was not so easy. As we read 2 Timothy, written at that time, we see the loneliness and suffering he endured. He was martyred in late A.D. 66 or early 67, having finished his course and kept the faith.

ROMANS

A Suggested Outline of Romans

Introduction (1:1-17)

A. Salutation (1:1-7)

B. Explanation (1:8-17)

I. Sin (1:18–3:20 — Righteousness Needed)

A. The Gentiles under sin (1:18-32)

B. The Jews under sin (2:1–3:8)

C. The whole world under sin (3:9-20)

II. Salvation (3:21–5:21 — Righteousness Imputed)

A. Justification explained (3:21-31)

B. Justification expressed: the example of Abraham (4:1-25)

C. Justification experienced (5:1-21)

III. Sanctification (6–8 — Righteousness Imparted)

A. Our new position in Christ (6)

B. Our new problem in the flesh (7)

C. Our new power in the Spirit (8)

IV. Sovereignty (9–11 — Righteousness Rejected)

A. Israel's past election (9)

B. Israel's present rejection (10)

C. Israel's future redemption (11)

V. Service (12:1–15:13 — Righteousness Practiced)

A. Consecration to God (12)

B. Subjection to authority (13)

C. Consideration for the weak (14:1–15:13)

VI. Conclusion (15:14–16:27)

A. Paul's faithfulness in the ministry (15:14-21)

B. Paul's future in the ministry (15:22-33)

C. Paul's friends in the ministry (16:1-23)

D. Final benediction (16:24-27)

Introductory Notes to Romans

I. Importance

While all Scripture is inspired of God and profitable, there are some parts of the Bible that contain more doctrinal truth than others. Certainly what Paul has to say in Romans is of more practical value to us than some of the lists in Numbers. St. Augustine was converted through reading Romans. Martin Luther launched the Reformation on Rom. 1:17: "The just shall live by faith." John Wesley, founder of Methodism, was converted while listening to someone read from Luther's commentary on Romans. If there is one book that every Christian should understand, it is this epistle. Why?

(1) It presents doctrinal truth—justification, sanctification, adoption, judgment, and identification with Christ.

(2) It presents dispensational truth in chapters 9–11, showing the relationship between Israel and the church in the eternal plan of God.

(3) It presents practical truth, teaching the secret of Christian victory over the flesh, the duties Christians have toward each other, and their relationship to government.

Romans is a great exposition of the faith. It is the complete and most logical presentation of Christian truth in the entire NT. While some topics (such as the priesthood of Christ and the return of the Lord) are not dealt with in detail, they are mentioned and related to the other great doctrines of the faith.

If a Bible student wishes to master any one book of the Bible, let it be Romans! An understanding of this book is a key to unlocking the entire Word of God.

II. Background

Romans was written by Paul during his three-month visit in Corinth (Acts 20:1-3). In Rom. 16:23 he indicates that he was with Gaius and Erastus, both of whom are associated with Corinth (1 Cor. 1:14; 2 Tim. 4:20). The letter was probably carried by Phoebe (16:1), who lived at Cenchrea, the seaport that served Corinth (Acts 18:18). Paul's friends Aquila and Priscilla were originally from Rome (Acts 18:2), and from the greeting to them in Rom. 16:3, we discover that they are back in Rome.

How did there come to be groups of believers at Rome? Note

that Paul does not address his letter to "the church at Rome" but rather "to all that be at Rome" (1:7). When you read chapter 16, you cannot help but note different groups of believers, which suggests that there was not one local assembly (16:5, 10-11, 14-15). One tradition, without historical or scriptural foundation, is that the ministry at Rome was founded by Peter. It is claimed that Peter lived in Rome for twenty-five years, but this fact cannot be proved. If Peter had started the work at Rome, then certainly there would have been an organized church rather than scattered bodies of believers. Paul greets many friends in chapter 16, but not Peter; yet in his other letters, he always sent greetings to spiritual leaders. Certainly somewhere in his prison epistles (Ephesians, Philippians, Colossians, Philemon, 2 Timothy) Paul would have mentioned Peter if that great apostle were ministering anywhere in Rome. The most telling argument against Peter as the founder of the work in Rome is Romans 15:20, where Paul states that he did not build on another man's foundation. Paul was anxious to visit Rome to minister to the saints there (1:13; 15:22-24, 28, 29; Acts 19:21; 23:11); but he would not have made these plans if another apostle had already started the work there.

How, then, did the Gospel get to Rome? Acts 2:10 indicates that there were people at Pentecost from Rome. Priscilla and Aquila were Roman Jews who knew the Gospel. Note that the names in chapter 16 are all Gentile, indicating that Gentile Christians from other cities had gravitated to Rome and carried the Gospel with them. These people were probably converts of Paul from other churches. Rome was the great center of the world in that day, and it was not unlikely that thousands of pilgrims made their way over Roman highways to the imperial city. Romans 1:13-15, 11:13 and 15:14-16 all indicate that the majority of the believers who received the letter were Gentiles. Naturally there was also a Jewish element in this Christian community as well as many Gentiles who had been Jewish proselytes.

III. Reason for Writing

Paul was about to close his work in Asia (15:19) and go to Jerusalem with his love gift from the churches of Asia (15:25-26). His heart's burden had always been to preach at Rome, and this long letter was his way of preparing the Christians for his coming. While at Corinth (Acts 20:1-3) he also wrote his letter to the Galatians, seeking to answer the Judaizers who were confusing the churches of Galatia. Paul may have wanted to warn and teach the Christians at Rome lest these Judaizers arrive there before him and upset his plans. Note that in Rom. 3:8 he mentions false accusations certain men had made about him. Paul's reasons, then, for the letter may be summarized as follows:

(1) To prepare the Christians for this planned visit, and to explain why he had not visited them sooner (1:8-15; 15:23-29).

(2) To instruct them in the basic doctrines of the Christian faith lest false teachers upset them.

(3) To explain the relationship between Israel and the church, lest the Judaizers lead them astray with their doctrines.

(4) To teach the Christians their duties to one another and to the state.

(5) To answer any slander about Paul (3:8).

IV. Position in the Bible

Romans is the first of three letters in the NT based on one verse of Scripture—Hab. 2:4, "The just shall live by his faith." This verse is found in Rom. 1:17 (the theme of Romans is *the just*), Gal. 3:11 (the theme of Galatians is how the just *shall live*), and Heb. 10:38 (the theme of Hebrews is living *by faith*).

Romans is the first epistle in the NT. You will note that the order of the NT letters follows 2 Tim. 3:16, "All Scripture is given by inspiration of God and is profitable for . . .":

Doctrine—Romans (the great doctrinal book)
Reproof—1 and 2 Corinthians (where Paul reproves sin)
Correction—Galatians (where Paul corrects false teaching)
Instruction in righteousness—Ephesians and Paul's remaining letters (where Paul teaches holy living based on Christian doctrine)

V. Theme

Paul's basic theme is the righteousness of God. The word "righteous" in one form or another is used over forty times in these chapters. In chapters 1–3 he presents the need for righteousness; in 3–8, God's provision of righteousness in Christ; in 9–11, how Israel rejected God's righteousness; and in 12–16, how righteousness must be lived in daily practice.

ROMANS 1

I. Salutation (1:1-7)

All thirteen of Paul's letters begin with the apostle's name. It was customary in those days to open a letter with the writer's name and personal greeting, rather than place them at the end, as we do today. Paul identifies himself as a servant and an apostle, and gives all the glory to God by saying that he was called by God's grace (v. 5) and separated unto this wonderful ministry (see Acts 13:1-3).

He immediately states that his ministry is that of the Gospel, which he calls "the Gospel of God" (v. 1), the "Gospel of His Son" (v. 9), and the "Gospel of Christ" (v. 16). He states that this "Good News" is not something new that he invented, but that the OT promised the coming of Christ and His death and resurrection. (See 1 Cor. 15:1-4, where "the Scriptures" obviously means the OT writings, since the NT was then being written.) By relating the Gospel to the OT, Paul appealed to the Jewish believers reading his letter.

The Gospel concerns Christ: according to the flesh, a Jew (v. 3), but according to God's power through the resurrection, proved to be the very Son of God (v. 4). This proves the humanity and deity of the God-Man who alone can be our Mediator. What is the purpose of this Gospel that cost Christ His life? Verse 5 tells us: to bring all nations into obedience to the faith. When a person truly trusts Christ, he or she will obey Him.

In vv. 6-7, Paul describes his readers, the saints in Rome. They are also "called" by Christ, not to be apostles, but to be saints. Note that a saint is a living believer in Jesus Christ. Only God can make a sinner into a saint! They are also "beloved of God," even though they live in the wicked city of Rome! How wonderful it is that God calls us "beloved" just as He did His Son (Matt. 3:17). Jesus states that the Father loves us just as the Father loves Him (John 17:23)!

In this brief salutation, then, Paul identifies: (1) the writer, himself; (2) the recipients, the saints at Rome (and not unbelievers); (3) the theme, Christ and the Gospel of salvation.

II. Explanation (1:8-17)

Paul now gives a two-fold explanation of (1) why he is writing, (vv. 8-15); and (2) what he is writing about (vv. 16-17).

For a long time, Paul had desired to visit the saints in Rome. Their testimony had spread throughout the Roman Empire (v. 8, and see 1 Thes. 1:5-10), and Paul was anxious to visit them for three reasons: (1) that he might help establish them in the faith, v. 11; (2) that they might be a blessing to him, v. 12; and (3) that he might "have some fruit" among them, that is, win other Gentiles to the Lord, v. 13. Keep in mind that Paul was the chosen messenger of God to the Gentiles, and he certainly would have a burden for the saints (and sinners) in the capital of the empire! He explains that he had been hindered ("let," v. 13, in KJV) from visiting them sooner, not by Satan (see 1 Thes. 2:18), but by his many opportunities to minister elsewhere (Rom. 15:19-23). Now that the work was ended in those areas, he could visit Rome. Note the motivating forces in Paul's life (vv. 14-16): "I am debtor . . . I am ready . . . I am not ashamed." We would do well to emulate the apostle's example in our lives.

In vv. 16-17 we have the theme of the letter: the Gospel of Christ reveals the righteousness of God, a righteousness based on faith and not works, and available to all, not just the Jews. Paul explains in Romans how God can be both "just and justifier," that is, how He can make sinners righteous and still uphold His own holy law. He quotes Hab. 2:4 (see introductory notes), "The just shall live by faith."

III. Condemnation (1:18-32)

We now begin the first section of the letter, which discusses sin (1:18 — 3:20 — see outline). In these closing verses of chapter 1, Paul explains how the Gentiles got into the awful darkness that engulfs them and how God's wrath was revealed against them. Note the steps downward in Gentile history:

A. They knew God (vv. 18-20).

God had given them a twofold revelation of Himself "in them" (conscience) and "unto them" (creation), v. 19. Man did not begin with ignorance and gradually work his way up to intelligence; he began with a blazing revelation of the power and wisdom of God and turned his back on it. God had revealed Himself from the very time of creation, so that people who have never heard the Gospel are still without excuse. (How God judges such people will be taken up in chap. 2.)

B. They glorified Him not as God (vv. 21-23).

Vain thinking and foolish reasoning turned men from the truth to lies. We see indifference leading to ingratitude, resulting in ignorance. People today bow before the Greek and Roman philosophers and honor their words above the Word of God; but Paul calls all of these philosophies "empty imaginations" and "times of ignorance" (Acts 17:30)! The next step was idolatry, honoring the creature (including man) rather than the Creator.

C. They changed the truth of God (vv. 24-25).

This word "changed" should really read "exchanged." People replaced God's truth with Satan's lie! What is Satan's lie? Worshiping the creature and not the Creator; worshiping man instead of God; worshiping things instead of Christ. Satan tempted Christ to do this (Matt. 4:8-11). Note that in Rom. 1:18, the Gentiles "held down the truth," and now they "exchange the truth" for a lie! The truth believed and obeyed sets us free (John 8:31-32); the truth rejected and disobeyed makes us slaves.

D. They rejected the knowledge of God (vv. 26-32). These people had begun with a clear knowledge of God (vv. 19, 21) and His judgment against sin (v. 32); but now they reached the lowest level of their downward fall: they did not even want to have knowledge of God! "The fool has said in his heart, 'There is no God' " (Ps. 14:1, NKJV).

It is sad to see the tragic results of this decline. Evolutionists want us to believe that humans have "evolved" from primitive, ignorant, beast-like forms into the marvelous creature they are today. Paul says just the opposite: man began the highest of God's creatures, but he made himself into a beast! Note the three judgments of God:

- God gave them up to uncleanness and idolatry, vv. 24-25.
- God gave them over to vile passions, vv. 26-27.
- God gave them over to a reprobate mind, vv. 28ff.

God gave them up! This is the revelation of the wrath of God (v. 18). The sins listed here are too vile to define or discuss, yet they are practiced today around the world with the approval of society. People know that sin will be judged, yet they take pleasure in it anyway. Were it not for the Gospel of Christ, we would be in this slavery to sin ourselves. "Thanks be unto God for His unspeakable gift" (2 Cor. 9:15).

ROMANS 2

From 2:1 to 3:8, Paul turns the searchlight on his own people, the Jews, and shows that they are equally condemned as sinners before God. In 1:20 he states that the Gentiles are without excuse, and in 2:1 he states that the Jews are without excuse. This news comes as a thunderbolt to the privileged Jews! Surely God would deal with them, they thought, differently from the Gentiles! No, states Paul; the Jews are under the condemnation and wrath of God because God's principles of judgment are fair. In this chapter he points out three divine principles of judgment that prove the Jew is equally condemned with the Gentile.

I. Judgment is According to God's Truth (2:1-5)

As the Jew read Paul's indictment of the "heathen" in the first chapter, he must have smiled and said, "Serves them right!" Their attitude would have been that of the Pharisee in Luke 18:9-14 — "I thank Thee that I am not as other men!" But Paul turns the Jew's judgment of the Gentile right back upon him: "You do the same things the Gentiles do, so you are just as guilty!" God's judgment of men is not according to hearsay, gossip, our own good opinions, or man's evaluations; it is "according to truth" (v. 2). Someone has said, "We hate our own faults, especially when we see them in others." How easy it is for people today, as in Paul's day, to condemn others, yet have the very same sins in their own lives.

But the Jew may have argued back: "Surely God wouldn't judge us with the same truth He applies to the Gentiles! Why, see how good God has been to Israel!" But they were ignorant of the purpose God had in mind when He poured out His goodness on Israel and waited so patiently for His people to obey: His goodness was supposed to lead them to repentance. Instead, they hardened their hearts and thus stored up more wrath for that day when Christ will judge the lost (Rev. 20). Have you not heard lost sinners today say, "Oh, I'm sure God isn't going to send me to hell. Why, He's done so many good things for me." Little do they realize that God's goodness is the preparation for His grace; and instead of bowing in humble gratitude, they harden their hearts and commit more sin, thinking that God loves them too much to condemn them.

These same two "excuses" that the Jews used in Paul's day are still heard today: (1) "I am better than others, so I don't need Christ"; (2) "God has been good to me and will certainly never condemn me." But God's final judgment will not be according to men's opinions and evaluations; it will be according to truth.

II. Judgment Is According to a Person's Deeds (2:6-16)

The Jews thought they held the highest "status" among God's people, not realizing that it is one thing to be a hearer of the Law, and quite another to be a doer (v. 13). Keep in mind that these verses do not tell us how to be saved. They describe how God judges mankind according to the deeds performed in the course of life. Verses 7-8 are not talking about a person's occasional actions, but the total purpose and drift of his life, the "life-choice" as William Newell describes it. People do not get eternal life by patiently seeking it; but if they are seeking for life, they will find it in Christ.

"Every man" (v. 6), "every soul" (v. 9), "every man" (v. 10) — these phrases show that God is no respecter of persons but judges all mankind on the basis of the lives they have lived. One might ask, "But is God just in judging men this way? After all, the Jews have had the Law and the Gentiles did not." Yes, God is just, as vv. 12-15 explain. God will judge people according to the light they have received. But never think that the Gentiles (who were unaware of Moses) lived apart from law; for the moral law of God was written on their hearts (see 1:19). Dan Crawford, veteran missionary to Africa, came out of the jungles and said, "The heathen are sinning against a flood of light." "It is most evident from Scripture," writes Dr. Roy Laurin, "that men will be judged according to the knowledge of God which they possess and never according to any higher standard they do not possess." The Jews hear the Law but refuse to do it, and will be thus judged more severely. The same will happen to sinners who hear God's Word today but will not heed it.

III. Judgment Is According to the Gospel of Christ (2:17-29)

Twice now Paul has mentioned a "day of judgment" (vv. 5 and 16). Now he states that this judgment will be of the heart, when God will reveal all secrets. Christ will be the Judge, and the issue will be, "What did you do with the Gospel of Christ?"

The Jews boasted of their racial and religious privileges. Because

367

God had given them His Word, they knew His will and had a finer sense of values. They looked upon the Gentiles as blind, in the dark, fools, and babes (vv. 19-20). The Jews considered themselves to be God's exclusive favorites; but what they failed to see was that these very privileges obligated them to live holy lives. They disobeyed themselves the very law they preached to the Gentiles. The result was that even the "wicked Gentiles" blasphemed God's name because of the sins of the Jews! Paul is referring perhaps to Isa. 52:5, Ezek. 36:21-22, or Nathan's words to David in 2 Sam. 12:14.

If any people had "religion," it was the Jews; yet their religion was a matter of outward ceremony and not inward reality. They boasted of their rite of circumcision, a ceremony that identified them with the living God; yet what good is a physical rite if there is no obedience to God's Word? Paul even goes so far as to say that the uncircumcised Gentile who obeyed God's Word was better off than the circumcised Jew who disobeyed it (v. 27), and that the circumcised Jew who disobeyed God was looked upon as uncircumcised! For a true Jew is one who has faith inwardly, whose heart has been changed, and not one who merely follows outward ceremonies in the flesh. Verse 27 boldly states that the Gentiles who by nature, though uncircumcised, fulfill the Law are going to judge the Jews who transgress God's standards!

The Gospel of Christ demands an inward change: "You must be born again" (John 3:7). It is not obedience to a religious system that will allow one to pass the test when Christ judges the secrets of men's hearts. It is the Gospel of Christ that is God's power unto salvation, both to Jew and Gentile (Rom. 1:16). If a person has never believed the Gospel and received Christ, then he or she stands condemned. The Jews, with all their religion and legalism, were (and are) just as much under sin as the Gentiles—and more so, because to them were given greater privileges and opportunities to know the truth.

How many people are going to hell because they think God is going to judge them according to their own good opinion of themselves, their status, or their religion? God does not judge according to these principles, but according to truth, according to our deeds, and according to the Gospel of Christ. Thus, in chapter 1 Paul proves that the Gentiles are without excuse, and here in chapter 2, that the Jews are without excuse. In chapter 3, he will prove that the whole world is under sin and condemnation, desperately needing the grace of God.

ROMANS 3

This chapter forms the bridge between Section 1 "Sin" and Section 2 "Salvation." In the first section (vv. 1-20), Paul deals with condemnation and concludes that the whole world—Jew and Gentile alike—is under sin. In the last section (vv. 21-31), he introduces the theme of justification by faith, which will be his theme in the next two chapters.

In fact, chapter 3 is really the seedbed for the rest of the book. In vv. 1-4, he deals with Israel's unbelief, and this is his subject in chapters 9–11. In v. 8, he mentions the question of living in sin, and this matter is discussed in chapters 6–8. (Note that 3:8 is closely related to 6:1.) Verse 21 brings up the topic of justification by faith, his theme for chapters 4–5. Finally, in v. 31, he mentions establishing and obeying the law, the theme presented in chapters 12–16 (note 13:8-14).

I. The Bad News: Condemnation Under Sin (3:1-20)

Paul asks and answers four important questions in this section:

A. Is there any advantage in being a Jew if Jews are condemned? (vv. 1-2)

The answer is "Yes," because the Jews were given the oracles of God, His revealed will in His Word. Had Israel believed the Word and obeyed it, the nation would have received Christ and been saved. Then, through them, God would have spread the blessing to the whole world. We today are certainly privileged to have the Word of God. May we never take it for granted.

B. Has Israel's unbelief canceled God's Word? (vv. 3-4)

Of course not. The unbelief of people could never cancel the faithfulness of God ("faith" in v. 3). God is true though every man is a liar! Here Paul quotes Ps. 51:4, where King David openly admitted his sin and God's righteousness in judging him. Even in admitting his sins, David declared the righteousness of God and the truth of His Word.

C. Then, why not sin and glorify God the more? (vv. 5-8)

"After all, if God is honored in judging my sin, then I am really doing Him a favor by sinning! Instead of judging me, He should let me sin that He might be glorified all the more! He certainly is not righteous to judge me!" Paul quickly disposes of this argument for sin by pointing out in v. 6 that such a position would mean God could never judge the world, and even Abraham recognized God as the "Judge of the world" (Gen. 18:25). Paul does not explain how God judges sin and gets glory from it; he merely states that all truth and justice would collapse if God did what such people claimed. Paul's Jewish enemies had lied about him and said that he taught this very doctrine: "Let us do evil that good may come" (v. 8). See also 6:1 and 15. This statement is so contrary to all reason and Scripture that Paul dismissed it by saying that "the people who say this deserve condemnation themselves!" (v. 8).

D. Then is the Jew better than the Gentile? (vv. 9-18)

No, nor is the Gentile any better or worse than the Jew: for both are sinners and stand under the awful condemnation of God. "There is no difference" is the great message of Romans—no difference in sin (3:22-23) or in salvation (10:12-13). God has regarded both Jew and Gentile as under sin that He might, in grace, have mercy upon all (11:32).

Paul now proves that the whole world is guilty by describing the total sinfulness of mankind. In vv. 10-12, he comments on its sinful character and refers to Ps. 14:1-3. In vv. 13-18, he reminds us of its conduct, quoting from Ps. 5:9, 140:3, 10:7, and 36:1, and also Isa. 59:7-8. Please read these verses and their settings carefully. His final verdict is given in vv. 19-20: the whole world is guilty before God! The Law that the Jews thought would save them merely condemns them; for the Law gives the knowledge of sin.

II. The Good News: Justification by Faith (3:21-31)

A. Apart from the Law.

Verse 21 can be paraphrased, "But now, in this age of grace, a righteousness—a new kind of righteousness—has been revealed, but not one that depends on the Law." People today want righteousness by the Law and by works, but Paul has already proved that the Law condemns and can never save. This grace-righteousness was, however, seen in the OT. Abraham, for example, was declared righteous because of his faith (Gen. 15:6). Habakkuk 2:4 says, "The just shall live by faith." Read Rom. 9:30-33 and see why Israel missed this righteousness by faith.

B. Available through Christ (vv. 22-26).

Note how often Paul uses the word "faith." Verse 23 can be read, "For all have sinned [once-for-all in Adam] and are constantly coming short of the glory of God." Then Paul introduces several important terms:

Justified — declared righteous in God's sight through the merits of Christ, secure in our position in Christ before the throne of God. Justification is God's righteousness imputed, put to our account. Sanctification is righteousness imparted, or lived out in our daily lives.

Redemption — deliverance from sin and its penalties, by the payment of a price. This price was Christ's blood on the cross.

Propitiation — Christ's sacrifice satisfied God's holy law, thus making it possible for God to forgive sinners and remain just Himself. God's justice has been satisfied; He may now look with kindness and grace upon a lost world.

"Justified freely by His grace" (v. 24)! What a thrilling statement! Not by works, good intentions, gifts, or prayers, but freely by His grace alone. It is in this letter that Paul explains how God can be both "just and justifier" (v. 26), and the answer is the cross. When Jesus died, He bore our sins in His own body (1 Peter 2:24) and thus paid the price God's law demanded. But He arose again! Thus He is alive and able to save all who will believe!

Verse 25 teaches that in the ages before the full revelation of the Gospel of Christ, God appeared to be unjust in "passing over" the sins of mankind and forgiving such people as Noah, Abraham, and Enoch. True, He did send wrath in some cases; but generations of sinners seemed to escape the judgment of God. How was God able to do this? Because He knew that at the cross, He would give a full display of His wrath against sin, and yet through Christ's death provide a redemption for sins that had merely been "covered" by the blood of bulls and goats (Heb. 9–10).

C. Accepted by faith (vv. 27-31).

"Hear the conclusion of the whole matter!" The Jew has nothing to boast of, because all sinners are justified by faith and not by the works of the Law. If justification is by the Law, then He is a God of the Jews only, because only Israel had the Law. But God is also the God of the Gentiles. Therefore, both Jews and Gentiles are saved the same way — by faith. And this simple means of salvation does not cancel the Law, for the Law demanded death for sin, and Christ died for our sins. Thus, the Gospel establishes the Law. God's Law reveals my need of grace, and God's grace enables me to obey the Law.

ROMANS 4

By all means seek to master this chapter! It explains how God justifies (declares righteous) ungodly people through the death and resurrection of Jesus Christ. "Salvation" is a broad term and includes all that God does for the believer in Christ; "justification" is a legal term describing our perfect standing before God in the righteousness of Christ. In this chapter, Paul uses the example of Abraham to illustrate three great facts about justification by faith.

I. Justification Is by Faith, Not Works (4:1-8)

Every Jew revered "Father Abraham," and from Gen. 15:6 knew that Abraham had been justified before God. Abraham's acceptance by God was so certain that they referred to heaven as "Abraham's bosom." Knowing this, Paul points to Abraham and asks, "How was Abraham, our father in the flesh, justified?" Was it by works? No, for then he could have gloried in his accomplishment, and we have no record of such action in the OT. What does the Scripture say? "Abraham believed God!" (See Gen. 15:1-6.) The gift of righteousness came, not by works, but by faith in God's revealed Word.

Note that in his argument, Paul used the words "reckon," "impute," and "count" (vv. 3-6, 8-11, 22-24). These words all mean the same thing: to put to a person's account. Justification means righteousness imputed (put to our account) and gives us a right standing before God. Sanctification means righteousness imparted (made a part of our life) and gives us a right standing before men, so they believe we are Christians. Both are a part of salvation, as James 2:14-26 argues. What good is it to say that I have faith in God if my life does not reveal faithfulness to God?

Salvation is either a reward for works or a gift through grace; it cannot be both. Verse 5 states that God justifies the ungodly (not the righteous) through faith and not works. The Jews thought that

God justified religious people on the basis of their works; yet Paul has proved that "Father Abraham" was saved simply on the basis of faith. Then Paul refers to David and quotes Ps. 32:1-2, proving that Israel's great king taught justification by faith, apart from works. God does not impute sin to our account, because that was charged to Christ's account (2 Cor. 5:21, and see Phile. 18). Rather, He imputes Christ's righteousness to our account purely on the basis of grace! What a wonderful salvation we have!

II. Justification Is by Grace, Not Law (4:9-17)

Now the important question arises: "If salvation is by faith, then what about the Law? What about the covenant God made with Abraham?" Paul answers this question by pointing out that Abraham's faith and salvation took place fourteen years before he was circumcised! Circumcision was the seal of the covenant, the rite that made a Jewish child a part of the system of law. Yet Abraham, the "Father" of the Jews, was in effect a Gentile (that is, uncircumcised) when he was saved! Circumcision was merely an outward sign of a spiritual relationship, as baptism is today. No physical ceremony can produce spiritual changes; yet the Jews of Paul's day (like many "religious" people today) trusted in the ceremonies—the outward signs—and ignored the saving faith that was required of them. Abraham is actually the "father" of all believers, all who belong to the "household of faith" (see Gal. 3:7, 29). As Paul pointed out in Rom. 2:27-29, not all "Jews" are truly the "Israel of God."

In vv. 13-17, Paul contrasts law and grace, just as in vv. 1-8 he contrasted faith and works. The key word here is "promise" (vv. 13, 14, 16). God's promise to Abraham that he would be "the heir of the world" (v. 13—indicating the glorious kingdom ruled over by the Promised Seed, Christ) was not given in connection with the Law or circumcision, but by God's grace alone. Read Gen. 15 again and note Abraham was "at the end of himself" when God stepped in and gave him His gracious promise. All Abraham had to do was believe God! The Law was never given to save anyone; the Law only brings wrath and reveals sin. The Law completely cancels grace, just as works will cancel faith; the two cannot exist side by side (vv. 14-15). How could Abraham be saved by the Law when the Law had not yet been given? Paul concludes in v. 16 that justification comes by grace, through faith; and thus all people—

Jews and Gentiles—can be saved! Abraham is not only the father of the Jews, but he is "the father of us all," all who follow in his steps of faith. (Read Gal. 3.)

III. Justification Is by Resurrection Power, Not Human Effort (4:18-25)

The first section (vv. 1-8) contrasted faith and works; the second (vv. 9-17) contrasted law and grace; and now the third (vv. 18-25) contrasts life and death. Note that Paul in v. 17 identifies God as "He who quickens the dead." Abraham and Sarah were "dead," their bodies being well past the age of child-bearing (see Heb. 11:11-12). How could two people, one ninety years old and the other one hundred, ever hope to have a son? But when the flesh is dead, then the resurrection power of the Spirit can go to work!

We ought to marvel at the faith of Abraham. All he had was the promise of God that he would be the father of many nations; yet he believed this promise, gave the glory to God, and received the blessing. What a perfect illustration of the miracle of salvation. As long as people depend on the flesh and feel they still have enough strength to please God, they will never be justified. But when we come to the end of ourselves, admit we are dead, and cease to strive in our own efforts, then God is able to "raise us from the dead" and give us new life and a perfect standing before Him. It was Abraham's simple faith in God's Word that justified him, and that is how sinners are justified today.

But perhaps Abraham was somebody of importance. No, says v. 24; God wrote that statement in His Word for our sakes, not Abraham's. We are saved the same way he was saved: by faith. Note how important this word "believe" is in Romans: it appears in 1:16; 3:22, 26; 4:3, 24; 5:1; 10:4, 9-10; etc. When a sinner believes the promise of God in the Word, then the same resurrection power enters his life, and he becomes a Christian, a child of God, as was Abraham. We must confess that we are dead and believe that Christ is alive and will save us.

Verse 25 explains the basis for justification: the death and resurrection of Christ. Paul will go into detail on this subject in chapter 5. The verse reads, "[Jesus our Lord] was delivered because of our offenses, and was raised again on account of our justification." The fact that He died proves we were sinners; the fact that God raised Him from the dead proves we have been justified by His blood.

This is evidence again that justification is a matter of resurrection power and not feeble human effort.

ROMANS 5

This chapter is an explanation of the last word in chapter 4, justification. A clear understanding of Paul's argument is essential if we are to grasp the meaning of justification by faith.

I. The Blessings of Justification (5:1-11)

Keep in mind that justification is God's declaration that the believing sinner is righteous in Christ. It is righteousness imputed, put to our account. Sanctification is righteousness imparted, worked out in and through our lives by the Spirit. Justification is our standing before God; sanctification is our state here on earth before others. Justification never changes; sanctification does. Note the blessings we have in justification:

A. We have peace (v. 1).

There was a time when we were enemies (v. 10); but now in Christ we have peace with God. Peace with God means that our problem with sin has been settled by the blood of Christ. God is our Father, not our Judge.

B. We have access to God (v. 2a).

Before our salvation, we stood "in Adam" and were condemned; but now in Christ, we have a perfect standing before God and can enter into His presence (Heb. 10:19-25).

C. We have hope (v. 2b).

Literally, "We boast in the hope of the glory of God." Read Eph. 2:11-12 and note that the unsaved person is "without hope." We cannot boast in good works that bring salvation (Eph. 2:8-9), but we can boast in the wonderful salvation God has given us in Christ.

D. We have daily confidence (vv. 3-4).

"We boast [glory] in testings also." The true Christian not only has a hope for the future, but he has confidence in the present trials of life. The "formula" looks like this: testing plus Christ equals patience; patience plus Christ equals character [experience]; experience plus Christ equals hope. Note that we do not glory over trials, or about trials, but in trials. Compare Matt. 13:21; 1 Thes. 1:4-6; and James 1:3ff.

E. We experience the love of God (vv. 5-11)

The Spirit within sheds God's love to us and through us. God revealed His love at the cross when Christ died for those who were "without strength," who were "ungodly," "sinners," and "enemies," thus proving His great love. Paul's argument is this: if God did all that for us while we were His enemies, how much more will He do for us now that we are His children! We are saved by Christ's death (v. 9), but we are also saved by His life (v. 10) as "the power of His resurrection" (Phil. 3:10) operates in our lives. We have received "reconciliation" (atonement, v. 11), and now the love of God is experienced in our lives.

II. The Basis of Justification (5:12-21)

This is a complex section, so read it over several times and use a modern translation, too. Paul is explaining here how it is that all men are sinners, and how it is that one Man's death could give an ungodly sinner a right standing before God.

Please note, first of all, the repetition of the word "one" (vv. 12, 15-19—eleven times). Note also the use of the word "reign" in vv. 14, 17, and 21. The key thought here is that when God looks upon the human race, He sees but two men—Adam and Christ. Every human being is either "in Adam" and lost, or "in Christ" and saved; there is no middle ground. Verse 14 states that Adam is a type (figure) of Christ; he is the "First Adam," and Christ is the "Last Adam" (1 Cor. 15:45).

We may contrast the two Adams as follows: (1) The first Adam was made from the earth, but the Last Adam (Christ) came from heaven (1 Cor. 15:47). (2) The first Adam was the king of the old creation (Gen. 1:26-27), while the Last Adam is King-Priest over the new creation (2 Cor. 5:17). (3) The first Adam was tested in a perfect garden and disobeyed God, while the Last Adam was tested in a terrible wilderness and obeyed God; and in the Garden of Gethsemane, He surrendered His will to God. (4) The disobedience of the first Adam brought sin, condemnation, and death upon the human race, but the obedience of the Last Adam brought righteousness, salvation, and life to all who will believe. (5) Through the first Adam, death and sin reign in this world (vv. 14, 17, 21); but through the Last Adam, grace reigns (v. 21) and believers can "reign in life" (v. 17).

The OT is "the book of the generations of Adam" (Gen. 5:1-2) and ends with the word "curse." (Mal. 4:6). The NT is "the book of the generation of Jesus Christ" (Matt. 1:1) and ends with "no more curse" (Rev. 22:3). The paradise of Genesis that Adam lost is restored in Revelation through the cross of Christ.

What Paul is teaching here is the unity of the human race in Adam (see Acts 17:26). When he says in v. 12 that "all have sinned" he means that all of us sinned in Adam when he sinned. We are identified with him as the "head" of the human race, and his sin is our sin, his death is our death. Paul's argument in vv. 12-14 goes like this: We all know that a man dies if he disobeys God's law. But there was no law from Adam to Moses, yet men died! We know that Adam died because he disobeyed a divine law; but the generations from Adam to Moses did not have such a law to disobey. Then death must be from another cause, and that cause is Adam's sin. Because we are born "in Adam," we inherit his sin and condemnation. But in His grace, God has given a "Last Adam," a new "Head" who has by His life and death undone all that Adam did in his sin. Paul now presents several contrasts between salvation and sin:

vv. 15-16 — The offense vs. the free gift: Adam's offense brought condemnation and death, while the free gift of God's grace brings justification and life.

v. 17 — Death vs. life: Death reigned as king because of Adam, but now believers reign in life (right now, not only in the future) through Christ, and have abundant life!

v. 18 — Condemnation vs. justification: Adam's sin plunged the human race into condemnation; Christ's death brings right standing with God. Adam hid from God; in Christ we have free access to God!

v. 19 — Disobedience vs. obedience: Adam disobeyed God and made us all sinners; Christ obeyed God and, through faith in Him, we are made righteous.

v. 20 — Law vs. grace: God did not give the Law to save mankind, but rather to reveal sin. But God's superabounding grace met the demands of the Law when Christ died, and then supplied what the Law could not supply — salvation from sin.

The whole transaction is summarized in v. 20; in the new creation (2 Cor. 5:17, being "in Christ") sin no longer reigns, grace does! Death does not reign, life does! And we reign in life! "Christ . . . has made us kings and priests to God" (Rev. 1:5-6, NKJV).

Now, the important question is this: Am I "in Adam" or "in Christ"? If I am "in Adam," then sin and death reign over my life and I am under condemnation. If I am "in Christ," then grace reigns and I can reign in life through Christ, and sin no longer has me in its slavery (the theme of chapter 6). In 5:6-11, Paul teaches substitution—Christ died for us on the cross. But in 5:12-21, he goes further and teaches identification—believers are in Christ and can live in victory over sin.

Hallelujah, what a Savior!

Introductory Notes to Romans 6–8

The church today desperately needs to emphasize practical holiness in the life of the believer. Every Christian (if he is truly born again) lives as described in Rom. 5; but so few progress into the Christians described in chapters 6 through 8! It is essential that we understand the meaning of this section on sanctification. Not only should we understand it, but live it.

Definition

To sanctify means simply "to set apart." It says nothing essentially about the nature of a thing, only its position with reference to God. The tabernacle and its furnishings were sanctified, set apart for God's exclusive use. The wood, cloth, metal, and other materials were not of themselves "holy," but they were set apart to God. In John 17:19 Jesus says that He sanctified Himself. Certainly the holy Son of God had no need to be made "more holy" than He was! What He means is simply that He set Himself apart to serve God and, through His act of salvation, was able to set believers apart to the glory of God.

Sanctification in Scripture is three-fold: (1) positional—the Christian is taken out of the world and seated with Christ (John 17:16); (2) practical—the believer has day-by-day victory over sin and grows in holiness and in likeness to Christ; (3) perfect—"We shall be like Him for we shall see Him as He is" (1 John 3:1-2).

Unless we keep the message of Rom. 6 separated from that of

Rom. 7, we will confuse Paul's message and lose a great blessing. This chart explains the difference between the message of Rom. 6 and the message of Rom. 7.

Romans 6	Romans 7
1. Shall we continue in sin that grace may bound?	1. How can we do anything but sin when our very nature is so sinful?
2. Bondage to the body of sin.	2. Bondage to the Law.
3. We are dead to sin.	3. We are dead to the Law.
4. Analogy of a servant and master.	4. Analogy of a wife and husband.
5. The problem of avoiding evil when we have sinful natures.	5. The problem of doing good when we have sinful natures.
6. Problem solved by knowing we have died to sin, reckoning ourselves dead to the Law, and yielding to the Spirit.	6. Problem solved by knowing we have died to the Law, admitting we cannot please God of ourselves, and yielding to the indwelling Spirit.

Romans 7 presents a deeper problem than that of chapter 6. Every Christian realizes the problem of chapter 6—that his sinful nature drags him down and tries to enslave him. But not many Christians have entered into the experiences of chapter 7, the humbling realization that we are incapable in ourselves of even doing *anything* good! Many Christians live under the Law: they have a set of rules and regulations that they obey religiously in the energy of the flesh, and they call this "dedicated Christian living." How far from the real thing! Only when the Holy Spirit directs our lives from within and we obey out of a heart of love is there God-honoring Christian living.

The flesh enjoys being "religious," trying to obey laws, rules, and codes. The most deceitful thing about the flesh is that it can appear so sanctified, so spiritual, when in reality the flesh is at war with God. Romans 6, then, deals with the flesh as it generates evil; chapter 7 deals with the flesh that through law tries to generate "good."

Romans 5 is important to this discussion, too, even though in our outline we have placed this chapter under the heading "Salvation." Note the contrasts:

Romans 5	Romans 6 and 7
1. Christ died for us	1. We died with Christ
2. Substitution	2. Identification
3. Christ died for sins	3. Christ died unto sin
4. He paid sin's penalty	4. He broke sin's power
5. Justification	5. Sanctification
6. Righteousness imputed	6. Righteousness imparted

The Flesh: This phrase does not mean the body as such, but rather the nature of man apart from God's influence and power. Other terms used for the flesh are: the old man, the body of sin, and the self. It is difficult for refined people (even Christians) to admit that in us is no good thing. Everything the Bible says about the flesh is negative, and until believers admit that they cannot control the flesh, change the flesh, cleanse the flesh, or conquer the flesh, they will never enter into the life and liberty of Rom. 6–8. Paul the "preeminent Pharisee" (see Phil. 3) had to admit in Romans 7 that even his flesh was not subject to God's laws! Perhaps he did not commit gross outward acts of sin, but he certainly cherished inward attitudes that were contrary to God's will. The law of God is holy and good, but even a holy law can never control sinful flesh.

This truth comes as a shock even to well-taught believers: the Christian life is not lived in the energy of the flesh, attempting to "do good works" for God. No believer on earth can ever do anything in the flesh that can please God. We must admit that "the flesh profits nothing" (John 6:63, NKJV) and surrender to the Spirit before we can hear God say of our lives, "I am well pleased." What a tragedy to live under the bondage of laws, resolutions, and rules, when we have been called into glorious liberty through the Spirit!

Our Responsibility: Christian living is not a passive thing, in which we merely "die" and let God do everything for us. The three key words of chapter 6 are know, reckon and yield. We must *know* our spiritual position and privileges in Christ, and this means spending time with the Word of God. We must *reckon* that what God says about us in the Bible is true in our lives, and this means showing a faith that is born of the Spirit. Finally, we must *yield* all to the Spirit, not just occasionally, but all day long. This is "walking in the Spirit."

The old nature is strong to do evil, and yet "the flesh is weak" (Matt. 26:41) when it comes to doing anything spiritual. We must feed the new nature on the milk, meat, bread, and honey of the Word of God, and we must reckon ourselves to be dead to sin. Why feed a corpse? Yet many Christians feed the old nature on the husks of the world while the new nature starves for the manna from God and for fellowship with God in prayer. God has already done His part; our responsibilities are clear: know, reckon, yield.

ROMANS 6

We move now into the third section of Romans — "Sanctification" (chaps. 6–8). These three chapters belong together and should not be studied independently, so it would be wise for you to read all three chapters carefully. Note that chapter 6 deals with the believer being dead to sin; chapter 7, with the believer being dead to the Law; and chapter 8, with the believer alive in Spirit-given victory. All three chapters are an explanation of the little phrase in 5:17 — "reign in life." Chapter 6 tells us how sin no longer reigns over us (6:12); chapter 7 explains how the Law no longer reigns over us (7:1); and chapter 8 explains how the indwelling Spirit gives us life and liberty (8:2-4).

The believer faces two problems: (1) How can I achieve victory over the old nature (the flesh, the body of sin)? and (2) how can I live so as to please God? Chapter 6 answers the first question: we get victory over the old nature by realizing that we have been crucified with Christ. But the second question is more complex; for how can I please God when everything I do — even the "good things" — is tainted by the old nature? Sin is not simply an outward action; it also involves inward attitudes and dispositions. Chapter 7 answers this problem (along with chapter 8) by showing that the Christian is dead to the Law and that the Spirit fulfills the righteousness of the Law in us (8:4).

The secret of victory over the flesh is found in our obeying those three instructions: Know, reckon, and yield.

I. Know (6:1-10)

Notice how often Paul uses the word "know" in this chapter (vv. 3, 6, 9, 16). Satan wants to keep us in the dark when it comes to the spiritual truths we should know, and this is why many Christians are living beneath their privileged station. "If God's grace abounds where sin is (5:20)," a person might say, "then the Christian ought to live in sin to know more of God's grace!" Paul shows, however, that this is impossible because the true Christian is dead to sin. This is the wonderful truth of our identification with Christ. Not only did Christ die for us, but we died with Him. When the Spirit baptized us into the body of Christ, then we were buried with Him and raised to newness of life.

Verses 3-4 do not refer to water baptism but the operation of the Spirit in putting us "into Christ" as members of His body. (This operation is illustrated by water baptism.) When Christ died, we died with Him; when He was raised, we were raised to newness of life with Him. This is our new position in Christ. Christ not only died for sin, but He also died unto sin (6:10). That is, He broke the power of sin and put out of commission (destroyed) the old nature (6:6). The old nature is still there, this we know; but it has been robbed of its power by the cross of Christ, for we died with Christ to all that belongs to the old life.

Sin and the old nature are hard masters. The unsaved person is a slave of sin (Eph. 2:1-3), but even many Christians still serve sin even though their slavery to sin has been broken by Christ. People read Rom. 5, discover that Christ died for their sins, and receive Him into their hearts; but they fail to take up the words of Rom. 6 and discover the glorious liberty they have in Christ. Read 6:1-10 again and see for yourself that the believer is dead to sin (v. 2); the old nature has been crucified (v. 6); the believer is freed from sin (v. 7). The old nature can no longer reign as king over the Christian who knows the truth, reckons on it, and yields to the Lord.

II. Reckon (6:1)

It is not enough merely to know our new position in Christ; we must, by faith, reckon it to be true in our own individual lives. Reckoning is simply that step of faith that says, "What God says about me in the Bible is now true in my life. I am crucified with Christ." Reckoning is faith in action, resting on the Word of God in spite of circumstances or feelings. God does not tell us to crucify ourselves, but rather to believe that we have been crucified and that "the old man" has been put to death. Crucifixion is one death you cannot inflict on yourself; you must be crucified by another. Reckoning is that step of faith that believes God's Word and acts upon it.

III. Yield (6:12-23)

If believers truly reckon themselves dead to sin, then they will prove their faith by yielding themselves to God. This is step three in the process of getting victory over the old nature, the flesh. Notice that stern "Let not!" in v. 12. This yielding is an act of our own wills, a step of obedience to the Lord. It is not enough to know this wonderful doctrine, or even reckon on it; we must take this final step of yielding the members of our bodies to Christ.

In vv. 16-23, Paul gives the example of master and servant. No man can serve two masters. Before we were saved, we yielded ourselves to sin, and were the servants of sin. Consequently we received the "wages" of sin—death (v. 23). But now that we have received Christ as Savior, we have been made free from sin; that is, our new position in Christ gives us a new Master as well as a new nature. We are now the servants of righteousness instead of the servants of sin! As we yield the members of the body to Christ as his "tools" or "weapons" ("instruments," v. 13), then He comes to control our lives, and we bear fruit unto holiness (v. 22).

The Christian who deliberately yields himself to sin will commit sin and reap sorrow. Why should sin be our master when we have died to sin? Why must we be obedient to a master that has already been defeated by Christ? Christians who deliberately sin are people who have yielded themselves to the old nature instead of to the Holy Spirit. They are living beneath their exalted position in Christ. They are living like slaves when they could be reigning like kings.

It is important that we keep these three steps in order. We cannot yield to God and get victory over the flesh unless we first reckon ourselves to be dead unto sin and alive in Christ. But we cannot reckon ourselves dead unless we know our position in Christ. Satan does not want us to live up to our high position in Jesus Christ, so he tries to confuse us about our victory in the Son of God. It is not enough to know that Christ died for us; we must also know that we died in Christ. It is not enough to know that we have new natures within; we must also know that the old nature was dealt with on the cross. Know—reckon—yield: these three steps lead to daily victory over the flesh. These three steps lead to the throne where Christ is exalted on high, and where (with Him) we "reign in life," servants of righteousness and not slaves of sin. We enjoy life and true freedom in Him.

Keep in mind that these three steps should represent a daily attitude of life. They are not "emergency measures" that are to be used when we face some special temptation. Believers who spend time with the Word of God daily will know their position in Christ. They will have the faith to reckon themselves dead to sin and will be able to yield themselves to the indwelling Spirit, obtaining victory. The answer to the problem of sin is not simply determination, discipline, reformation, legislation, or any other human endeavor. Victory comes through crucifixion and resurrection.

ROMANS 7

This chapter is a greatly misunderstood, but nevertheless important one. Many students cannot understand why Paul deals with victory in chapter 6 and then discusses defeat in chapter 7! They feel that he should move immediately from the victory of chapter 6 to the great blessings of chapter 8, but the inspired writer knew better. Chapter 7 deals with a vital issue in Christian living: the believer's relationship to God's law. Romans 6 explains that believers are dead to sin because they are identified with Christ in His death and resurrection. It answers the question, "Shall we continue in sin?" (6:1). But note that Paul asks a second question in 6:15: "Shall we continue in sin because we are not under the Law?" He answers this question in chapter 7 and explains that believers are dead to the Law just as they are dead to sin (7:4).

What does Paul mean in 6:14 when he says we are not "under law but under grace"? To be "under law" means that we must do something for God; to be "under grace" means that God does something for us. Too many Christians are burdened with religious rules and regulations and good resolutions, not realizing that it is impossible to find holiness through their own efforts. How tragic it is to see Christians living "under law," striving in their own efforts to please God, when the new position they have in Christ and the new power in the Spirit (8:3-4) make it possible for them to enjoy victory and blessing by grace. Paul explains this in chapter 7 by giving us a series of "duets."

I. Two Husbands (7:1-6)

The marriage relationship illustrates our relation to the Law. (Keep in mind that when Paul speaks of "the Law" he means not only the law of Moses but any kind of legislation that the believer uses to try to curb sin or attain holiness.) The two husbands are the Law and the Lord Jesus Christ.

When a woman is married to a man, she is bound to that man until he dies. Then she is free to marry again. Before we met Christ, we were bound by the Law and condemned by it. The Law, however, did not "die" when we were saved; instead, we died in Christ. We are no longer "married" to a system of regulations; we are "married" to Jesus Christ, and the Law has no control over us. Read v. 4 again and again and absorb its wonderful message. Our old "husband" has no control over us: we are in a wonderful new relationship through and in Christ. When we were lost, the Law triggered the "arousings of sin" in our old nature, and this produced death (v. 5). But now we are delivered from the Law and can serve Christ in newness of the Spirit, not in the oldness of the letter (v. 6).

Verse 6 does not suggest that Christians have no obligation to obey God. Actually, our obligations are now greater since we know Christ and belong to God's family. The demands now are far more severe than under the Mosaic law. For example, the Sermon on the Mount goes beyond outward actions to deal with inward attitudes. The law of Moses found murderers guilty, but Jesus said that hatred is equivalent to murder. But Rom. 7:6 teaches that our motivation for obeying is different: we do not mechanically obey a set of rules, but we lovingly, from the heart, obey the Spirit of God who fulfills the righteousness of the Law in us (8:4). A beginning pianist can play a number "letter perfect" and still not capture the inner spirit of the song the way an accomplished musician can. Our obedience to God is not that of a slave fearing a master, but that of a bride lovingly pleasing her bridegroom.

II. Two Discoveries (7:7-14)

Then why did God give the Law if it does not produce holiness? What purposes did God have in mind? Well, Paul made two discoveries that answer this question: (1) the Law itself is spiritual, but (2) the believer is carnal, sold under sin. What a humiliating discovery it was to that proud Pharisee that his very nature was unspiritual and unable to obey the law of God! The Law reveals sin (v. 7), for when we read the Law, the very things it condemns appear in our lives. The Law energizes sin (v. 8), and sin agitates in our nature. The Law slays the sinner and deceives him (vv. 9-11), making him realize that he is too weak to meet God's standard. Finally, the Law reveals the sinfulness of sin (v. 13), not just our outward actions, but especially our sinful attitudes. The reason the believer cannot make himself holy by means of law is not because God's law is not holy and good, but because our nature is so sinful that it cannot be changed or controlled by law. It is a wonderful day in the life of the Christian when he or she discovers that "the old nature knows no law and the new nature needs no law."

III. Two Principles (7:15-25)

After his defeating experience with the Law, Paul concluded that there are two principles (or "laws") that operate in the life of the believer: (1) the law of sin and death, and (2) the law of the Spirit of life in Christ (see 8:2). He is dealing, then, with the presence of two natures in the child of God. Salvation does not mean that God changes the old nature, cleanses it, or reforms it. The believer's old nature is just as wicked and opposed to the Spirit today as the day he was saved! Salvation means that God gives the believer a new nature and crucifies the old one. The Christian still has the ability to sin, but he now has an appetite for holiness. The dynamic for sin is still there, but not the desire.

The law of sin and death is simply the operation of the old nature, so that when the believer wants to do good, evil is present. Even the "good things" we do are tainted with evil! (See v. 21.) It is here that you see the difference between the victory of chapter 6 and that of chapter 7: in chapter 6, the believer gains victory over the evil things of the flesh, that is, he ceases to do evil deliberately; but in chapter 7 he triumphs over the "good things" the flesh would do in obedience to law. But God will not accept the flesh, for in our flesh there is no good thing. "The flesh profits nothing!" (John 6:63, NKJV). Yet how many Christians set up laws for their lives and seek to discipline the flesh into obedience, when God plainly says, "The carnal mind [old nature] is not subject to the law of God, neither indeed can be" (8:7).

The law of sin and death is counteracted by the law of the Spirit of life in Christ Jesus. It is not by submitting to outward laws that we grow in holiness and serve God acceptably, but by surrendering to the indwelling Spirit of God. This law (or principle) is elaborated in chapter 8, especially in the first seventeen verses. We cannot fulfill the righteousness of the Law by our own strength; the Spirit fulfills it in us by His power (8:3-4).

What is the practical application of all this? Simply this: In our new position before God, as dead to the Law, we are not expected to obey God in our own strength. God has not enslaved us under a "Christian Law" that we must obey in order to be holy. Rather, He has given us His Holy Spirit who enables us to fulfill the demands of God's holiness. Christians may have the victory of chapter 6 and no longer be enslaved to the body of flesh, but there is more to the Christian life. Shouldn't we produce fruit for God? Certainly! But the minute we start doing works in our own strength, we discover that we are failures; and, sad to say, many well-meaning Christians stop right there and become spiritual casualties. Rather, we should accept the truths of Rom. 7—that we are indeed failures in ourselves, that the Law is good but we are carnal, and then allow the Spirit to work out God's will in our life. May God enable us to reckon ourselves dead to sin (chap. 6), and dead to the Law (chap. 7) that we might, through the Spirit, enjoy the blessed liberty of God's children and glorify God in holy living.

ROMANS 8

This chapter is the climax of the section on "Sanctification" (chaps. 6–8) and supplies the answers to the questions raised about the Law and the flesh. The Holy Spirit dominates the entire chapter, for it is through the indwelling Spirit that we overcome the flesh and live a fruitful Christian life. The chapter can be summarized in three phrases: no condemnation, no obligation, and no separation.

I. No Condemnation: The Spirit and the Law (8:1-4)

These verses actually form the conclusion to the argument in chapter 7. Keep in mind that Paul is not dealing with salvation in chapter 7 but with the problem of how the believer can ever do anything good when he has such a sinful nature. How can a holy God ever accept anything we do when we have "no good thing" dwelling in us? It would seem that He would have to condemn every thought and deed! But there is "no condemnation" since the indwelling Holy Spirit fulfills the righteousness of the Law in us.

The Law cannot condemn us because we are dead to the Law. God cannot condemn us, for the Holy Spirit enables the believer to "walk in the Spirit" and thereby meet God's holy demands.

It is a glorious day in the life of the Christian when he or she realizes that God's children are not under the Law, that God does not expect them to do "good works" in the power of the old nature. When the Christian understands that "there is no condemnation," then he realizes that the indwelling Spirit pleases God and helps the believer to please Him. What a glorious salvation we have! "Stand fast therefore in the liberty by which Christ has made us free, and do not be entangled again with a yoke of bondage!" warns Paul in Gal. 5:1 (NKJV).

II. No Obligation: The Spirit and the Flesh (8:5-17)

The believer can have two "dispositions" (minds): he can lean toward the things of the flesh and be a carnal Christian ("carnal" means "of the flesh") who is at enmity with God; or he can incline toward the things of the Spirit, be a spiritual Christian, and enjoy life and peace. The carnal mind cannot please God; only the Spirit working in and through us can please God.

The Christian has no obligation to the flesh: "Therefore, brethren, we are debtors, not to the flesh, to live after the flesh" (v. 12). Our obligation is to the Holy Spirit. It was the Spirit who convicted us and showed us our need of the Savior. It was the Spirit who imparted saving faith, who implanted the new nature within us, and who daily witnesses within that we are God's children. What a great debt we owe to the Spirit! Christ loved us so much, He died for us; the Spirit loves us so much, He lives in us. Daily He endures our carnality and selfishness; daily He is grieved by our sin; yet He loves us and remains in us as the seal of God and the "down payment" ("earnest," 2 Cor. 1:22) of the blessings waiting for us in eternity. If a person does not have the Spirit dwelling within, that person is not a child of God.

The Holy Spirit is called "the Spirit of adoption" (v. 15). To live in the flesh or under law (and to put yourself under law is to move toward living in the flesh) leads to bondage; but the Spirit leads us into a glorious life of liberty in Christ. Liberty to the believer never means freedom to do as he or she pleases, for that is the worst kind of slavery! Rather, Christian liberty in the Spirit is freedom from law and the flesh so that we can please God and become what He wants us to become. "Adoption" in the NT does not mean what it typically means today, the taking of a child into a family to be a legal member of the family. The literal meaning of the Gk. word is "son-placing" — the taking of a minor (whether in the family or outside) and making him or her the rightful heir. Every believer is a child of God by birth and an heir of God through adoption. In fact, we are joint-heirs with Christ, so that He cannot receive His inheritance in glory until we are there to share it with Him. Thank God, the believer has no obligation to the flesh, to feed it, pamper it, obey it. Instead, we must "put to death" (mortify) the deeds of the flesh by the power of the Spirit (v. 13, see Col. 3:9ff) and allow the Spirit to direct our daily lives.

III. No Separation: The Spirit and Suffering (8:18-39)

Though believers endure suffering now, they will enjoy glory when Christ returns. In fact, the whole creation ("creature" in vv. 19-21) is groaning under the bondage of sin, thanks to Adam's disobedience. When Christ finally imprisons Satan, He will deliver the entire creation from this bondage, and all nature will enjoy with us "the glorious liberty of the children of God" (v. 21). What a thrilling salvation we have: free from the penalty of sin because Christ died for us (chap. 5); free from the power of sin because we died with Christ to the flesh (chap. 6) and to the Law (chap. 7); and someday we shall be free from the very presence of sin when nature is delivered from bondage.

We have the Spirit of adoption, but we are "waiting for the adoption, that is, the redemption of the body" (v. 23). The soul has been redeemed, but not the body. We wait in hope, however, because the indwelling Spirit is given as "the firstfruits" of the deliverance God has for us in the future. Even if we die, the Spirit who has sealed us unto the day of redemption (Eph. 1:13-14) will raise our body to life (v. 11).

Note the three "groans" in vv. 22-26: (1) all creation groans, v. 22; (2) the believer groans awaiting Christ's coming, v. 23; and (3) the indwelling Spirit groans as He intercedes for us, v. 26. Note John 11 where Jesus "groaned within Himself" as He visited the grave of Lazarus. How the heart of God is burdened because of the bondage of creation. What a price Christ paid to deliver us.

Paul points out that while we endure this suffering in hope we have the privilege of praying in the Spirit. Perhaps too much of our praying is of the flesh—long, beautiful, "pious" prayers that glorify man and nauseate God (Isa. 1:11-18). Paul indicates that the most spiritual prayer could be a wordless groan that comes from the heart! "Sighs too deep for words" is the way one translation renders v. 26. The Spirit makes intercession for us, the Father searches our hearts and knows what the Spirit desires, and this He grants to us. The Spirit always prays in the will of God. What is the will of God? That believers might be conformed to the image of Christ (v. 29). We can claim the promise of v. 28 because of the purpose of v. 29. Note that all the verbs in v. 30 are past tense: the believer has been called, justified, and glorified. Why faint under the sufferings of this world when we have already been glorified? We simply wait for the revelation of this glory at the return of Christ.

Paul closes by asking five questions (vv. 32-35) and answering them clearly. There is no need to fret over what God will do, for God is for us and not against us. The proof is that He gave His very best on the cross. Surely He will freely give us anything else we need. Can anyone indict us for sin? No! We have been justified, and that standing before God never changes. Can anyone condemn us? No! Christ died for us and lives now as our Advocate (lawyer) at God's right hand. Can anything separate us from God's love? No! Not even the devil himself ("principalities and powers"—v. 38).

No condemnation—no obligation—no separation! "Yet, in all these things we are more than conquerors through Him who loved us" (NKJV).

ROMANS 9

The next three chapters deal with Israel's spiritual history: past (chap. 9), present (chap. 10), and future (chap. 11). Paul's purpose is to explain how God could set aside His chosen people and save the Gentiles, and how He will restore the nation at some future date.

I. Israel's Election Described (9:1-13)

A. The blessings of the election (vv. 1-5).

We cannot help but admire Paul's burden for Israel. His words remind us of Moses in Ex. 32:31-32. Do we have that kind of a burden for lost souls? Christ loved us so much He became a curse for us.

(1) The adoption — chosen by God because of His love (see Isa. 43:20-21).

(2) The glory — the presence of God in the tabernacle (Ex. 24:16-17).

(3) The covenants — through Abraham, Moses and David, God gave unchanging covenants to His people Israel.

(4) The giving of the Law — God never so dealt with the Gentiles. Israel heard God's voice and received His laws to govern their lives.

(5) The service of God — the priestly service in the tabernacle was a privilege from the Lord.

(6) The promises — many OT promises have been fulfilled, and many are yet to be fulfilled for the Jews.

(7) The fathers — Abraham, Isaac, Jacob, and the twelve sons of Jacob formed the foundation for the nation.

(8) The Messiah — Christ was a Jew, of the tribe of Judah, born according to the Law. Note in v. 5 that Paul calls Christ "God blessed forever."

No other nation had these wonderful blessings; yet Israel took them for granted and ultimately rejected the righteousness of God. The Christian today also belongs to God's elect and has similar blessings to enjoy: adoption (Eph. 1:5); glory (Eph. 1:6-7); the new covenant in Christ's blood (Heb. 9–10); the law written on the heart (2 Cor. 3; Heb. 10:16-17); priestly service through Christ (1 Peter 1:4); and we have Abraham as the father of the believing (Gal. 3:7) — all because we have Christ.

B. The basis of the election (vv. 6-13).

In election, God exercises His sovereign will to accomplish His perfect plan. Keep in mind that the election discussed in Rom. 9–11 is national and not individual. To apply all the truths of these chapters to the salvation or security of the individual believer is to miss their message completely. In fact, Paul carefully points out that he is discussing the Jews and Gentiles as peoples, not individual sinners.

(1) Abraham — He was chosen as the father of the Hebrew nation, but Paul states that not all Israelites are true sons of Israel. (See also 2:25-29.) Abraham had many children (Gen. 25:1-6), but only one chosen son, Isaac, who was the child of promise by faith.

(2) Isaac — He was the child of promise by faith (see Gal. 4:21-31), while Ishmael was a child of the flesh through works. The true

"seed of Abraham" are the believers, and not just all who have Jewish blood in their veins.

(3) Jacob—God bypassed Esau, the firstborn, and chose Jacob, and this choice was made even before the children were born. Why? To show that God's purpose in electing His nation would be fulfilled. Esau made the choice to rebel against God, but God's purpose does not depend on man's decisions. We cannot explain the relationship between man's choice and God's purpose, but we know that both are true and are taught in the Word.

II. Israel's Election Defended (9:14-33)

The doctrine of Israel's national election raises several crucial theological questions:

A. Is God unrighteous? (vv. 14-18)?

Of course not! For election has nothing to do with justice, but rather free grace. "God is unjust if He chooses one and leaves another!" ignorant people often say. But the purpose of God goes beyond justice; for if God did only what was just, He would have to condemn all of us! Paul uses Moses (Ex. 33:19) and Pharaoh (Ex. 9:16) as proof that God can do what He wishes in dispensing His grace and mercy. Nobody deserves God's mercy, and nobody can condemn God for His choice of Israel or His bypassing of other nations.

B. Why does God find fault if none can resist His will? (vv. 19-29)

Paul replies with a parable about the potter, possibly borrowed from Jer. 18:1-6. God is the Potter, and the nations of the world (and their leaders) are the vessels. Some are vessels of wrath that God patiently endures until their time of destruction (Gen. 15:16). Others are vessels of mercy that reveal His glory. Paul then quotes Hosea 2:23 and 1:10 to show that God promised to call a "people" from among the Gentiles, a people to be called "children of the living God." This is the church (see 1 Peter 2:9-10). He also quotes Isa. 10:22-23, showing that a remnant of Jews would also be saved (see Isa. 1:9). In other words, God's purpose in election makes it possible for both Jews and Gentiles to be saved by grace. Neither Jew nor Gentile could be saved any way other than by the grace of God.

C. What shall we say about the Gentiles? (vv. 30-33)

Here is the paradox of history: the Jews tried to be righteous and were rejected; the Gentiles, who did not have the privileges the Jews had, were received! The reason is because the Jews tried to attain righteousness by works, while the Gentiles received righteousness by faith through the grace of God. The Jews stumbled over a crucified Messiah (see Isa. 8:14; 28:16; Matt. 21:42; 1 Cor. 1:23; and 1 Peter 2:6-8). They wanted a Messiah who would lead the nation to political freedom and glory; they could not believe in a crucified Christ.

Paul's purpose in this chapter is to explain Israel's position in the plan of God. Israel was an elect nation, given privileges that no other nation had; yet it failed miserably to follow God's program of blessing for the world. The entire chapter exalts the sovereign grace of God without minimizing the responsibility of men and women for making right decisions. God's Word will prevail regardless of human disobedience; but disobedient sinners will miss the blessing. No human mind can fathom or explain the wisdom of God (see 11:33-36), but this we know: without the sovereign grace of God, there would be no salvation.

ROMANS 10

In this chapter, Paul explains why Israel is in its present spiritual condition nationally.

I. The Reason for the Rejection (10:1-13)

The key word in this chapter is "righteousness." The Jews wanted righteousness, but tried to obtain it in the wrong way. Like the Pharisees described in Matt. 23:15, the Jews expended energy in securing a right standing with God, but their deeds were done in ignorance. "Religious people" today are no different; they think that God will accept them for their good works.

The Bible speaks of two kinds of righteousness: "works righteousness," which comes from obeying law; and "faith righteousness," which is the gift of God to those who trust His Son. The Jews would not submit to faith righteousness; their racial and religious pride turned them from simple faith to blind religion. They rejected Christ and clung to the Law, not realizing that Christ was the very one for whom the Law had been preparing the way, and that He Himself had ended on the cross the reign of the Law. The Mosaic law is no longer God's basis for dealing with mankind; He deals with us at the cross, where Christ died for the world. Righteousness by the Law is described in Lev. 18:5; faith righteousness is described in Deut. 30:12-14.

The Deuteronomy passage is used to show that the Word of God is readily available to the sinner, and that Christ is near him and ready to save. Verses 6-8 are a good illustration of Paul's use of OT passages that convey NT truth. In Deut. 30:11-14, Moses warned the people against disobedience to the Word of God. Lest they argue that the Law was far from them (applying especially to the time when Israel would be scattered among the nations, Deut. 30:1-5), Moses reminded them that they did not have to go to heaven, or across the sea, to find God's Word: it was on their lips and in their hearts. Paul applied this to Christ, the Word (John 1:1), and pointed out that Israel need not bring Christ down from heaven, or up from the underworld, because the Word of salvation is near to them so that they can believe and be saved. Salvation comes when sinners confess that "Jesus is Lord [Almighty God]" and believe in their hearts that Christ is alive from the dead. What is believed in the heart is confessed openly with the mouth. Some of the Jews in Jesus' day would not openly confess Him (John 12:42-43). When the sinner receives Christ by faith and confesses Him openly, thus proving his faith, he receives the gift of righteousness.

In v. 11, Paul again quotes Isa. 28:16 (see Rom. 9:33): "Whoever believes on Him will not be put to shame (NKJV)." The Jews disliked that word "whoever" since they thought they were the only "chosen people." But in v. 13 Paul cites Joel 2:32 to prove that whoever calls upon Christ is saved—and not the Jew only!

II. The Remedy for the Rejection (10:14-17)

The sequence here is as follows: (1) messengers are sent; (2) they declare the Word; (3) sinners hear the Word; (4) sinners believe the Word; (5) they call upon Christ; (6) they are saved! The argument here is simply that sinners cannot be saved apart from the Word of God, for "faith comes by hearing, and hearing by the word of God" (v. 17, NKJV). In v. 15, Paul refers to Isa. 52:7, a verse that will have its complete fulfillment in the day when Israel is established in its kingdom. Think of the joy Israel will have when the news comes that its Messiah is reigning! Paul applies this passage to the taking of the Gospel of peace (peace with God and peace between Jew and Gentile, Eph. 2:13-17) to lost Israel today. We often use Rom. 10:14-15 as the basis for our sending missionaries to Gentile nations, and certainly this application is valid; but the basic meaning here is that of taking the Gospel to Israel today. We take the Gospel to the Jew, not because of Rom. 1:16 ("to the Jew first"), but because of Rom. 10:14-15. If we share Paul's burden for the people of Israel, we will want to share the Gospel with them. The witness who bears the Gospel to the lost (whether Gentile or Jew) certainly has "beautiful feet" in the eyes of God.

What is Israel's attitude today? That of Isa. 53:1 — "Who has believed?" (NKJV) Just as Israel turned away in unbelief in Christ's day (John 12:37-38) and during the time of witness of the apostles in Acts 1–7, so the nation today is settled in unbelief. Paul quotes Ps. 19:4 in v. 18 to show that the Word of God, even through nature, has reached around the world; Israel is without excuse.

III. The Result of the Rejection (10:18-21)

The result of Israel's rejection is that God has turned to the Gentiles and is now taking out of them a people for His name (see Acts 15). But even this should be no surprise to the Jews, for in Deut. 32:21, God promised to use other nations to provoke the Jews to jealousy, and in Isa. 65:1-2, He announced that Israel would be disobedient, but that the Gentiles would find Him and His salvation.

Keep in mind that the OT did promise the salvation of the Gentiles; but nowhere did it teach that Jews and Gentiles would be part of the same plan or that believers from both races would be one in Christ. The OT program provided that the Gentiles would be saved through Israel's rise, that is, its establishment as a kingdom. But Israel fell! What then would God do with the Gentiles? Paul points out in Rom. 9–11 that through Israel's fall, mercy was extended to the Gentiles (see 11:11). God has committed all people, Jews and Gentiles, to unbelief; in this way He can have mercy upon all through the grace made possible at Calvary (11:32).

Verse 21 certainly states God's attitude toward Israel, even today. Though the nation is set aside in blindness and unbelief (2 Cor. 3:15–4:6; Rom. 11:25), God yearns after the unsaved Jew just as He does the lost Gentile. No doubt many Jews who are hearing the Word today will trust Christ after the church has been caught up and the Tribulation period begins. Instead of criticizing the Jews for their spiritual blindness, we ought to thank God that they gave us the Bible and Savior, and that even through their fall, salvation was made available to Gentiles!

Before we leave this chapter, note several practical points:

(1) Salvation is not difficult: "Whosoever shall call upon the name of the Lord shall be saved!" (v. 11).

(2) It is important that the Word of God be presented to lost sinners. It is the Word that convicts, that gives faith, that leads to Christ.

(3) There are only two "religions" in the world: works-righteousness and faith-righteousness. Nobody can fulfill the first, but everybody can respond to the second.

ROMANS 11

This chapter discusses Israel's future and answers the question, "Has God permanently cast aside His people, or is there a future for Israel?" Paul says the answer is "Yes!", and presents several proofs.

I. The Personal Proof (11:1)

"I am an Israelite!" states Paul, "and my salvation is proof that God is not through with Israel." In 1 Tim. 1:16 Paul states that his conversion (told three times in Acts) was to be a pattern for other Jewish believers. Certainly it is not a pattern for the conversion of a Gentile today, for no lost sinner sees the glorified Christ, hears Him speak, and is blinded for three days! But Paul's experience is a picture of the way Israel's people will be converted at the coming of Christ in glory. Like Paul, they will be in rebellion and unbelief. They will see Him whom they pierced (Zech. 12:10 and Rev. 1:7) and will repent and be saved. In 1 Cor. 15:8, Paul says he was "born out of due time"; that is, as a Jew, he saw Christ and was saved long before his people would have that same experience.

II. The Historical Proof (11:2-10)

Paul reached back into 1 Kings to show that God has always had a faithful remnant even in the times of greatest unbelief. In fact, as we read OT history, we cannot help but be impressed with the fact that it was always the remnant that God used and blessed. See Isa. 1:9, for example. It is a basic teaching of the Word that the majority falls from the faith and cannot be reformed, so God must take the remnant and begin over again. Verse 5 states that God has a remnant according to grace, that is, in the body, which is the church. Though not many, there are Jews in the body, although, of course, all national distinctions are removed in Christ. But if God is saving Jews during this age of the church when Israel is blind, how much more will He do in that coming age when Israel moves back on the scene again? God has never forsaken His people; this is the testimony of history.

We need to remind ourselves that during this church age, God is not dealing with the nation of Israel as such. According to Eph. 2:14-17 and Gal. 3:28, we are all one in Christ. No Jewish group can claim to be God's elect remnant. In vv. 8-10, Paul shows that this "blinding" of Israel as a nation was prophesied in Isa. 29:10 and Deut. 29:4. (Compare Matt. 13:14-15 and Isa. 6:9-10.) In vv. 9-10 he refers to Ps. 69:22, where God promises to turn Israel's blessings into curses because it had refused His Word.

III. The Dispensational Proof (11:11-24)

Paul in these verses is discussing Jews and Gentiles, not individual sinners or saints. In this section he proves that God has a dispensational purpose behind the fall of Israel; namely, the salvation of the Gentiles. Through Israel's fall, God was able to commit all people to disobedience and thus have mercy upon all! Gentiles do not have to become Jews before they can become Christians.

Paul argues that if the fall of the Jews has brought such blessing to the world, then how much greater will the blessing be when Israel is again restored! The restoration of Israel will bring resurrection to the world (v. 15). In other words, Paul was certain that there was a future for Israel as a nation. The teaching that the church today is God's Israel, and that the OT kingdom promises are now fulfilled in the church in a "spiritual way" is not scriptural. Paul looked forward to the day when Israel would be received into fullness of blessing as a nation.

The parable of the olive tree must be examined carefully. Paul is not talking about salvation of individual Christians, but the position of Jews and Gentiles as peoples in the program of God. Israel is the olive tree that failed to bear fruit for God. God then broke off some of the branches and grafted into the tree the Gentiles, "a wild olive tree." This was done "contrary to nature" (v. 24), for it is the practice to graft the good branch into the poorer stock; but God grafted the weak Gentiles into the good stock of Israel's religious privileges! This act shows the goodness and the severity of God: His goodness in saving the Gentiles, His severity in cutting off rebellious Israel. But the Gentiles dare not boast because they now have Israel's place of spiritual privilege, for God can cut them off too! And He will do just that at the end of this age, when the Gentile nations join together in a world coalition that refuses the Word of God and the Son of God. Then He will call out the true church, judge the Gentile nations, purge Israel, and set up His promised kingdom for Israel.

Again, remember that the theme of chapter 11 is national and not personal. God will never "break off" true believers from their salvation, for there is no separation between Christ and His people (Rom. 8:35-39). The church today is primarily made up of Gentiles, and we Gentiles benefit from the spiritual heritage of Israel (the rich sap of the olive tree). In a spiritual sense, we are children of Abraham, who is the "father" of all who believe (Gal. 3:26-29).

IV. The Scriptural Proof (11:25-36)

Paul has used the OT often in these three chapters, but in this section, he turns to Isa. 59:20-21, Isa. 27:9, and Ps. 14:7 to show that the OT promised a coming Deliverer who would cleanse and restore Israel. He states the "mystery" of Israel's blindness, a mystery being a truth hidden in past ages but now revealed in its fullness in the NT. "The fullness of the Gentiles" (v. 25) refers to the number of Gentiles that will be saved during this church age. When the body of Christ is completed, He will catch it away in the air; then will begin the seven-year Tribulation here on earth, "the time of Jacob's trouble" (Jer. 30:7). At the end of that period, the Deliverer will come, and the believing remnant will enter into its kingdom. "All Israel" does not mean every last Jew; rather, it means that the nation of Israel at that day will all be saved; it will be a redeemed, regenerated nation. God's promised covenant is quoted (Jer. 31:31-34) in v. 27. This "new covenant" will apply to Israel when it trusts Christ as its Redeemer and turns from its sins. Though the Jews may seem like enemies of God's will today, they are still beloved in God's sight because of the covenants He made with their fathers. Men may change, but God cannot change or revoke His promises (v. 29).

In the final paragraph (vv. 30-32), Paul explains that the Gentiles at one time rejected God (Rom. 1:18ff), yet now were being saved by faith; so today the Jews are in unbelief, but shall one day receive mercy. God had committed both Jews and Gentiles to unbelief and sin, that He might be able to save both through grace (v. 32).

After reviewing God's gracious and wise plan for both Jews and Gentiles, is it any wonder Paul broke out in a hymn of praise to the Lord (vv. 33-36)!

ROMANS 12

This chapter begins the final section of Romans — "Service" (12–16). Paul tells us how to put our learning into practice; and in this chapter, the apostle gives us four pictures of the Christian and reminds us of our spiritual duties.

I. A Sacrifice on the Altar (12:1-2)

True Christian service and living must begin with personal dedication to the Lord. The Christian who fails in life is the one who has first failed at the altar, refusing to surrender completely to Christ. King Saul failed at the altar (1 Sam. 13:8ff and 15:10ff), and it cost him his kingdom.

The motive for dedication is love; Paul does not say, "I command you" but "I beseech you, because of what God has already done for you." We do not serve Christ in order to receive His mercies, because we already have them (3:21–8:39). We serve Him out of love and appreciation.

True dedication is the presenting of body, mind, and will to God day by day. It is daily yielding the body to Him, having the mind renewed by the Word, and surrendering the will through prayer and obedience. Every Christian is either a conformer, living for and like the world, or a transformer, daily becoming more like Christ. (The Gk. word for "transform" is the same as the one for "transfigure" in Matt. 17:2.) Second Corinthians 3:18 tells us that we are transformed (transfigured) as we allow the Spirit to reveal Christ through the Word of God. It is only when the believer is thus dedicated to God that he can know God's will for his life. God does not have three wills (good, acceptable, and perfect) for believers in the way that there are three choices for merchandise in the mail order catalogs ("good, better, best"). Rather, we grow in our appreciation of God's will. Some Christians obey God because they know that obedience is good for them, and they fear chastening. Others obey because they find God's will acceptable. But the deepest devotion is in those who love God's will and find it perfect.

As priests, we are to present "spiritual sacrifices" to God (1 Peter 2:5), and the first sacrifice He wants each day is our body, mind, and will in total surrender to Him.

II. A Member of the Body (12:3-8)

In 1 Cor. 12 we find the same truth spoken of in these verses, that the believer is baptized by the Spirit into the body and is given a gift (or gifts) to use for the benefit of the whole church. There is a "universal body" made up of all believers in Christ from Pentecost to the rapture; but there is also the local body, through which each believer ministers to the Lord. Most of the 112 references in the NT to the church refer to a local congregation of believers.

Service in the local body begins with personal dedication (vv. 1-2) and then an honest evaluation of the spiritual gifts the believer possesses (v. 3). Paul does not tell us not to think of ourselves at all, but that we should not think of ourselves more highly than our spiritual gifts warrant. If a man is called to pastor, God will reveal it as he uses his gifts in the assembly. Our gifts differ, but they all come from the Spirit and are to be used for the glory of Christ. Just as we are saved "by grace, through faith" (Eph. 2:8-9), so we are to exercise our spiritual gifts "according to the measure of faith" (v. 3) and "according to the grace given" (v. 6).

Paul lists seven ministries: (1) *prophecy*, which is defined in 1 Cor. 14:3; (2) *ministry*, which is literally "deaconing" (serving) and may refer to that office; (3) *teaching*, according to 2 Tim. 2:1-2, an important responsibility; (4) *exhorting*, which means encouraging people to serve the Lord and be faithful to Him; (5) *giving*, which should be done in singleness of heart out of pure motives (see Acts 5); (6) *ruling*, pertaining to the government of the local church (1 Tim. 3:4 and 12); (7) *showing mercy*, sharing with those in need.

Eph. 4:7-12 describes the gifted people which Christ has given to the church; Rom. 12 and 1 Cor. 12 both describe the gifts which the Spirit has given believers in the local body. It is a dangerous thing to try to serve the Lord when no gift has been given; and it is also tragic to refuse to use a gift for His glory (2 Tim. 1:6). The twelve men in Acts 19:1-7 were ignorant of the Spirit and His gifts; the seven men of Acts 19:13-16 tried to counterfeit gifts they did not possess.

III. A Member of the Family (12:9-13)

Each believer has his or her own spiritual service to perform, but vv. 9-13 tell us how every Christian should behave in the family of God. Love should be honest and without hypocrisy (see 1 John 3:18). We should hate evil and cling to the good (see Ps. 97:10). Love should lead to kindness and humility, faithfulness in business, fervency in spiritual things ("fervent" here means "boiling, aglow with power"). Note how the characteristics mentioned in this section parallel the fruit of the Spirit that Paul describes in Gal. 5:22-23.

Christians in the local church should care for each other and share with each other. Note how the prayer of v. 12 is followed by the care of v. 13. "Given to hospitality" is literally in the Gk. "pursuing hospitality" — going after people! First Peter 4:9 tells us to stop complaining when we open our homes to others. Unspiritual hospitality is pictured in Prov. 23:6-8. See also Luke 14:12-14; 1 Tim. 3:2 and 5:10; Heb. 13:2; 3 John 5-8.

IV. A Soldier in the Battle (12:14-21)

Christians have their battles as well as their blessings, and Paul instructs us how to handle those who oppose the Word. We are to bless them (Matt. 5:10-12) and not curse. Of course, no believer should get into trouble because of wrong living (1 Peter 2:11-25). We should have sympathy (v. 15) and humility (v. 16), for selfishness and pride generate ill will. Christians are never to "pay back" their opponents; rather, we should wait for God to "repay" (v. 19), either in this life or in the future judgment.

"Provide things honest in the sight of all men" (v. 17) suggests that the Christian lives in a "glass house" and must be aware of the scrutiny of others. "I'm going to live my own life!" is a sinful attitude for a believer, in the light of Rom. 14:7-8. People are watching us, and as much as possible, we should live peaceably with all people. Of course, we cannot compromise with sin or have a "peace at any price" attitude. The attitude and spirit of Matt. 5:38-48 will help us be "peacemakers" (Matt. 5:9).

In vv. 19-21, Paul refers to Prov. 25:21-22 and Deut. 32:35. (See also Heb.10:30.) The principle stated here is that the believer has turned himself over to the Lord (12:1-2), and therefore the Lord must take care of him and help fight his battles. We need spiritual wisdom (James 1:5) when it comes to dealing with the enemies of the cross, lest we be a bad testimony on the one hand, or cheapen the Gospel on the other. Paul used the Roman law on three occasions to protect himself and the testimony of the Gospel (see Acts 16:35-40; 22:24-29; 25:10-12), yet he was willing to become all things to all men that he might win some to Christ. If we practice Rom. 12:1-2 daily, we can be sure He will direct us in obeying the rest of the chapter.

ROMANS 13

Christians have been called out of this world (John 15:18 and 17:14), but they still have responsibilities to the state. The best citizen ought to be the Christian citizen. Though the church is not to get involved in party politics, individual believers certainly should use their God-given privileges as citizens to see to it that the best leaders are elected and the best laws are enacted and enforced justly. When we think of godly leaders like Joseph, Daniel, and Esther, who were able to exercise spiritual ministries in pagan governments, we can see what the Spirit can do through the dedicated believer. In this chapter, Paul gives us four motives for obeying human government.

I. For Wrath's Sake (13:1-4)

The "higher powers" (v. 1) are the rulers of government, even though they may not be Christians. We thank God that the Gospel can reach a government official, such as Erastus, the city treasurer (Rom. 16:23), and some of Nero's officials (Phil. 4:22). But we must recognize the fact that even an unsaved government official is a minister of God. Even if we cannot respect the person, we must respect the God-ordained office.

Rulers are a terror to bad people, not to good people; so people who live consistent Christian lives need not fear. (Of course, where the government is openly opposed to Christ, Acts 5:29 is the principle to follow.) Keep in mind that God ordained human government, including capital punishment, after the flood (see Gen. 8:20–9:7). The church is not to bear the sword; the government does that. God has established only three institutions on earth: the home (Gen. 2), the church (Acts 2), and human government (Gen. 9). Their functions are not to overlap; when they do, there is confusion and trouble.

II. For Conscience's Sake (13:5-7)

Fear is perhaps the lowest motive for Christian obedience; a Spirit-directed conscience lifts us to a higher level. The Christian should experience the Spirit witnessing to his or her conscience (Rom. 9:1); and, if we disobey the Lord, we know it when the Spirit convicts our consciences. Some people have an evil conscience that is unreliable. The obedient Christian should have a good conscience (1 Tim. 1:5). To disobey constantly and refuse the witness of the Spirit in the conscience leads to a defiled conscience (Titus 1:15), a seared (or calloused) conscience (1 Tim. 4:2), and finally a rejected conscience (1 Tim. 1:19).

Paul admonishes us to pay taxes (tribute), pay customs (on material things), and show proper honor to all officials. See 1 Peter 2:17ff.

III. For Love's Sake (13:8-10)

Now Paul enlarges the circle to include not only government officials, but our neighbors as well. Keep in mind that the NT definition of a neighbor has nothing to do with street addresses or geography. In Luke 10:29, the lawyer asked, "Who is my neighbor?" In the parable of the Good Samaritan (Luke 10:30-36), Jesus changed the question to, "Which of these three was neighbor to him?" The issue is not "who is my neighbor?" but "to whom can I be a neighbor for the glory of Christ?" It is not a matter of law, but love—and this is what Paul deals with here.

While the believer lives under the law of the land, he also lives under a much higher law as a citizen of heaven: the law of love. In fact, love is the fulfillment of the law, because love from the heart enables us to obey what the law demands. A husband does not labor all day because the law tells him to support his family, but because he loves them. Where there is love there will be no murder, dishonesty, stealing, or other kinds of selfishness.

Note that Paul says nothing about the Sabbath; the Sabbath Law was actually part of the Jewish ceremonial code and never applied to the Gentiles or to the church. Nine of the Ten Commandments are repeated in the epistles for Christians to obey, but the commandment about the Sabbath is not repeated.

It is often difficult for us to love those who reject the Gospel and ridicule our Christian testimony, but this love can come from the Spirit (Rom. 5:5) and reach out to them. "Love never fails" (1 Cor. 13:8). More people are won through love than through arguments. The Christian who is walking in love is the best citizen and the best witness.

IV. For the Savior's Sake (13:11-14)

We reach the pinnacle of motives in these verses: from fear to conscience to love to devotion to Christ. "Our salvation" is nearer in the sense that Christ's coming for the church is nearer today than ever before. By "salvation" Paul means the total blessing that we will have when Christ comes — including new bodies and a new home.

Christians belong to the light, not the dark. They should be awake and alert, behaving as those who have seen the light of the Gospel (2 Cor. 4). Moreover, no believer wants to be found in sin when Christ returns! "The day is at hand!" (See Heb. 10:25ff.)

Paul lists a number of sins here, sins that ought never to be named among the saints. Note that drinking and immorality often go together and result in strife and division. How many homes have been broken up over drink! Verse 14 gives us the dual responsibility of the believer: positively, to "put on Christ" — that is, make Christ Lord of your daily life; negatively, to "make no provision for the flesh" — that is, deliberately avoid that which tempts you to sin. It is wrong for Christians to "plan for sin." Vance Havner said that when David left the battlefield and returned to Jerusalem, "he was making arrangements to sin." In the light of the soon-coming Christ, it is our responsibility to live sober, spiritual, clean lives.

The last days will be days of lawlessness (see 2 Tim. 3 and 1 John 3:4). It will be increasingly difficult for dedicated Christians to maintain their testimony. Governments will become more opposed to the Bible and to Christ, until at last the Man of Sin welds the world into one great satanic system to oppose the truth. Read 2 Tim. 3:12–4:5 to see what God expects from us in these last days.

ROMANS 14

Romans 14:1–15:7 deals with the problem of questionable things in the Christian life and what to do when sincere Christians disagree about personal practices. Paul recognizes that in each local church there are mature believers ("We that are strong," 15:1) as well as immature ("him that is weak in faith," 14:1), and that these two groups may disagree on how the Christian is to live. The Jewish Christians might want to cling to special holy days and OT dietary laws, while the Gentile believers might turn their Christian liberty into license and offend their Jewish brothers and sisters. Many Christians have the false notion that extreme legalism (observing days and diets) shows strong faith, but Paul states that just the opposite is true! It is the Christian that is mature in the faith who recognizes the truths found in Col. 2:18-23.

In the church today we have differences on how to regard such things as worldly amusements, and Paul tells us how to face and solve these differences. He does not give a list of rules; rather, he lays down six basic principles that can be applied by all Christians of all stages of growth. We can state these principles in the form of questions and test our own lives.

I. Am I Fully Convinced? (14:1-5)

Christians are not to act from mere emotion, but from settled inward convictions that are the result of diligent prayer and study of the Word. There would be no serious disagreements if every Christian acted from conviction. Someone has said that opinions are what we hold, while convictions are what hold us. The stronger Christian is not to despise the weaker one for his or her immaturity; neither is the weaker believer to judge his or her more mature brothers and sisters for their liberty. God has received both in Jesus Christ and we should receive each other. Our lives are to be directed by Him, not by people's ideas or judgments. Mature Christians know why they behave as they do, and these convictions control their lives.

II. Am I Doing This Unto the Lord? (14:6-9)

"I'm living my own life!" is a statement no Christian ought to make, for we belong to the Lord, whether we live or die. He is the Lord, and we must live to please Him. So often the Christian who has questionable practices in his or her life cannot honestly say that these practices are done as "unto the Lord"; for in reality, they are practiced for selfish pleasure and not to honor the Lord. Christians who observe special days as unto the Lord will be accepted by the Lord, and we should not judge them. It is between them and their Lord.

III. Will It Stand the Test at the Judgment Seat? (14:10-12)

We have no right to judge our brethren, for we will all have our works tested at the judgment seat of Christ—not the White Throne Judgment of Rev. 20:11-15, but the testing of the Christian's works after the church is called home (2 Cor. 5:10; 1 Cor. 3:10ff). We do not have to give an account of our brother's life, so we have no right to condemn him today. Certainly all of us want to live lives that will stand the fiery test before Christ, lives that will win rewards for His glory.

IV. Am I Causing Others to Stumble? (14:13-21)

There is one thing we should judge: we should judge ourselves to see whether we are abusing our Christian liberty and making others stumble. Certainly nothing is unclean of itself, but some practices and habits are considered unclean by others. Therefore, if we deliberately do something that makes our brothers stumble, we're not living according to the rule of love.

It is a serious thing to cause another person to stumble and fall into sin. Note Christ's words in Mark 9:33-50, where "offend" means "cause to stumble." The believer who holds on to his questionable practice and causes another Christian to fall in his walk with God is blind to the price Jesus paid on the cross. Our good should not cause evil talk. After all, the Christian life is not a matter of eating or drinking (or any other practice), but one of righteousness and peace and joy, all of which come from the Spirit. Our aim should be not to please ourselves, but to build up (edify) other Christians in love. 1 Corinthians 10:23 states that all things are lawful for the believer (for we do not live under law), but not everything builds us up or helps to build up others. See also 1 Cor. 8. "Destroy" in Rom. 14:15 and 20 means "tear down." How selfish for a Christian to tear down another believer's spiritual life because of his own selfish living. His practices may be lawful, but they do not come under the law of love.

V. Am I Doing This by Faith? (14:22-23)

The Gk. word for "faith" in v. 22 means almost the same as "conviction," for our convictions are born of faith in God's Word. These two verses lay down the principle that the Christian life is between the believer and his Lord, and that the believer must always be sure he is right with the Lord. If there are doubts about some of his practices, he cannot have joy and peace. "Damned" in v. 23 has nothing to do with eternal punishment; it should read "condemned." That is, the Christian who engages in practices with a doubtful mind is condemning himself and those practices by his very attitude. Whatever we do that is not of faith is sin, for the Christian lives by faith. "Faith comes by . . . the Word of God," says Rom. 10:17 (NKJV); so anything I do that I cannot back up by the Word of God is sin, because I cannot do it by faith.

"If it's doubtful, it's dirty!" is a good policy to follow. No one would drink milk or water that possibly was contaminated; nor would we accept food that might possibly be poisoned. Yet many Christians carelessly engage in practices that even the world questions. They never face the fact that whatever is doubtful is not of faith, and therefore is sin.

VI. Am I Pleasing Myself or Others? (15:1-7)

These verses fit best in chapter 14's outline. The strong ought to bear the weaknesses of the immature Christians, and while doing this, seek to build them up in the faith. We should follow Christ's example and seek to please others, not ourselves (Ps. 69:9). Does this OT verse apply to the NT Christian? Of course it does, for the OT was given for our learning, that we might receive patience (endurance), comfort, and hope from the promises of God. We ought to be like-minded, and we will be if all believers seek to help others grow in the Lord. Paul's final conclusion in v. 7 is: receive one another, for Christ has received you. This will bring glory to God.

Local churches have the right to establish standards, but not beyond what the Word teaches. We must lovingly allow for differences among Christians and not use these differences as opportunities for division.

ROMANS 15

This chapter concerns the Jews and the Gentiles in the church, and reveals three different ministries that we must recognize and understand:

I. Christ's Ministry to Jew and Gentile (15:8-13)

The Bible student who fails to recognize Christ's dual ministry, first to the Jew and then to the Gentile, will never rightly divide the Word of truth. When Christ was born, His coming was announced to the Jewish nation and related to the OT promises. As v. 8 states clearly, Christ was first a minister to the Jews for the purpose of confirming the OT covenants and promises. See Luke 1:30-33, 46-55, and 67-80. These Spirit-filled Jews knew that Christ had come to deliver them from the Gentiles and establish the promised kingdom.

But what happened? The people of Israel rejected their King on three occasions: (1) they allowed Herod to murder the King's messenger, John the Baptist; (2) they asked for Christ to be murdered; (3) they themselves murdered Stephen. In the Gospels and Acts, the Gospel is delivered "to the Jew first." Had Israel received Christ, the kingdom would have been set up, and the blessings would have flowed out to the Gentiles through a converted Israel. Paul has already shown in Rom. 9–11 that it is through Israel's fall (not her rise to glory) that the Gospel of God's grace has now gone to the Gentiles. There is a pattern of progress in vv. 9-11; the Gentiles hear the Word (Ps. 18:49); the Gentiles rejoice with the Jews (Deut. 32:43); all the Gentiles praise God on their own (Ps. 117:1); and the Gentiles trust Christ and enjoy His reign (Isa. 11:10). These verses almost summarize the spiritual history of Israel: v. 9 (see Acts 10–14), when the Jews witnessed to the Gentiles; v. 10 (see Acts 15–28), when Jews and Gentiles shared in the church's witness; v. 11 (Acts 28), when Israel was finally set aside and the Gentiles given the prominent place in God's program (as described in Paul's letters to the Ephesians and Colossians); and

v. 12, the future kingdom, shared by the Gentiles.

The theme of the Gentile praise is Christ. Speaking of that future day when the King reigns, v. 12 says, "In Him shall the Gentiles trust" (or hope). Paul then picks up the theme of "hope" in the prayer of v. 13. We do not have to wait to have joy, peace, and hope; the Spirit can give us those blessings now.

II. Paul's Ministry to Jew and Gentile (15:14-22)

Paul is anxious to emphasize that he is the apostle to the Gentiles. Failure to see the special place of Paul's ministry in the program of God will bring confusion to one's Bible study. In v. 16, Paul pictures himself as a NT priest, offering up the Gentiles to God as his sacrifice of praise. Every time we win a soul to Christ, it is offering another sacrifice to His glory.

His special ministry involved a special message (the Gospel of the grace of God, v. 16), special miracles (vv. 18-19), and a special method (v. 20, going where Christ had not been preached). Paul was a pioneer; he did not mix law and grace, faith and works, or Israel and the church, the way some teachers do today. We know that the Jews require a sign (1 Cor. 1:22), but God also gave miracles for the Gentiles (at Ephesus for instance — see Acts 19:11-12). We should not think, then, that because there are miracles recorded after Acts 7 (Israel's final rejection) that God is still dealing with the nation of Israel.

Paul had been hindered from going to Rome, not by Satan, but by the demands of ministry in so many places where the Gospel had not been preached. Now that he had covered all the ground possible, he was ready for his visit to Rome. The fact that Paul was willing to preach in Rome indicates that no other apostle had been there (Peter, for example); for his policy was to go to areas untouched by the Gospel.

III. The Gentile Churches' Ministry to the Jews (15:23-33)

Paul desired to go to Spain; whether or not he ever got there, the Bible does not say. Tradition says he did. At any rate, at the time he wrote this letter he was engaged in taking a relief offering to the poverty-stricken Jews in Palestine, an offering contributed by the Gentile churches he had founded. For details, see 1 Cor. 16 and 2 Cor. 8–9.

Paul gives several reasons for this offering:

(1) *Spiritual obligation, v. 27.* Since the Gentiles had received all their spiritual blessings through the Jews, the Gentiles were to pay them back in some measure with material things. Christians today need to bear in mind that the Gentiles are debtors to the Jews.

(2) *Personal love, v. 29.* Paul had a great burden for the Jews, and by bringing the offering, he would express this love to them.

(3) *Christian unity, v. 31.* Some of the Jewish believers (remember Acts 15) were not happy about the entrance of Gentiles into the fold. This offering was to help to heal the breach that some caused by saying that Gentiles had to become Jews before they could become Christians.

This passage raises the question of the responsibility Gentile Christians have to Jews today. Certainly the program of "to the Jew first" (1:16) was valid during the period of the Gospels and Acts 1–7 but no longer applies today. Our obligation to the Jews stems from the Great Commission, the grace of God, who chose us and grafted us into the olive tree (Rom. 11:20ff), and the plain logic of Rom. 10:11-17. As far as condemnation is concerned, there is no difference between Jew and Gentile. As far as salvation is concerned, there is also no difference. But Israel is still God's chosen nation, though set aside and blinded temporarily; Israel is beloved for the fathers' sakes (Rom. 11:28). No Christian should be guilty of anti-Jewish feelings or practices. Rather, we should seek to witness to them and win them to Christ. As a nation, Israel has been blinded; but individual Jews can find Christ as the Spirit opens their eyes.

Note that in v. 31 Paul anticipated trouble with the unbelieving Jews, and that trouble came! Review Acts 21:15ff and note how the unsaved Jews treated Paul.

This chapter emphasizes once again the importance of distinguishing between the Jew, Gentile, and church (1 Cor. 10:32). In fact, Paul's last words to the Romans (16:25-27) deal with that great mystery of the church, which Paul was to reveal through his message. May we never fail as stewards of His mysteries!

ROMANS 16

This chapter may appear to be a boring one, but it is filled with surprises. As we read this list of names, we cannot help but be impressed with the fact that Paul loved people and was interested in them. No doubt many of these people were his converts who had found their way to Rome; Paul had never visited Rome and certainly had to have met these saints in other cities. Like his Master, Paul knew the sheep by name and had a personal concern for each one.

I. Some Saints to Greet (16:1-16)

It seems that the believers in Rome did not meet in one general assembly but were members of various household flocks. Note vv. 5, 10, 11, and 15. There was no "church at Rome" in the organized sense (compare Phil. 1:1). Rome was a large city, and it is possible that some of the assemblies were composed mainly of Jewish believers.

Phoebe was evidently a deaconess on her way to Rome, and hence the bearer of the epistle. "Receive her and assist her" (v. 2) are good admonitions for Christians today. Some scholars suggest that she was going to Rome for assistance with a legal problem, and thus Paul was asking the saints to aid her with this special problem.

We meet Priscilla and Aquila again! What dear friends they were to Paul! Review Acts 18:2-28, 1 Cor. 16:19, and 2 Tim. 4:19. The incident where these two saints risked their lives for Paul is not recorded in the NT, but how indebted the church is to them for saving him! They had left Rome because of persecution, had met Paul in Corinth, and now were building a church in their house back in Rome. How wonderful are the ways of the Lord and the workings of His providence!

Nine women are mentioned in this chapter: Phoebe, v. 1; Priscilla, v. 3; Mary, v. 6; Tryphena, v. 12; Tryphosa, v. 12; Persis, v. 12; the mother of Rufus, v. 13; Julia, v. 15; and the sister of Nereus, v. 15. Some critics have accused Paul of being against women, but no man ever did more to emancipate women from heathen bondage and dignify them in the manner God intended from the beginning. Paul teaches that women have a special and important place in the ministry of the local church.

In several verses, Paul mentions his "kinsmen" (vv. 7, 11, 21). This does not necessarily mean blood relative, but more likely fellow Jews, possibly of the tribe of Benjamin.

Verse 7 mentions two men who were saved before Paul was, and were also noted by the apostles. They were not apostles themselves, but were held in repute among the apostles.

Rufus is an interesting man (v. 13). Mark 15:21 states that the Simon who carried the cross was the father of Alexander and Rufus, as though these two men were well-known among the churches at the time Mark wrote his Gospel. It is possible that Simon was actually the father of the Rufus of v. 13, and that he also won his mother to the Lord. If he and his family stayed in Jerusalem, it is possible that they had Paul in their home, and that Paul "adopted" Rufus's mother as his own.

II. Some Sinners to Avoid (16:17-20)

This warning sounds foreign in a chapter filled with greetings, but Paul knew the dangers in the churches and wanted to warn the saints. Certainly we as individual Christians are to love and forgive one another; but sins against the church body must be dealt with according to scriptural discipline. Christians who cause trouble because of their selfish desires (usually pride — they want to tell everybody else what to do) are not to be received into the local fellowship. "Mark them — avoid them!" The word "mark" means "watch them; keep your eyes on them." It is right for the church to keep an eye on "church tramps" who run from one church to another, causing trouble and division. These people are smooth talkers and know how to fool the simple, but the discerning saint will see through their disguises. Conquer Satan — don't let him conquer you!

III. Some Servants to Honor (16:21-24)

What a grand list of veterans! In these verses we find Timothy, Paul's son in the faith and a servant of the Lord (Phil. 2:19-22), and Lucius, who was associated with Paul in the early days at Antioch (Acts 13:1). (It is not likely that this person is Luke.) Jason traveled with Paul from Thessalonica (Acts 17:5-9); Sosipater was a Berean (Acts 20:4). Paul loved these companions and could not have ministered without them. Not everyone can be a Paul, but all of us can help others to serve Christ more effectively.

Tertius was the amanuensis (secretary) to whom Paul dictated the letter, as the Spirit directed him. It is probable that he was a Roman, known by the believers to whom the letter was sent.

Gaius may be the same person mentioned in Acts 19:29; or

perhaps Gaius of Derbe (Acts 20:4). He is surely the Gaius of 1 Cor. 1:14, one of the men whom Paul baptized during his ministry at Corinth. Paul was at Corinth when he wrote to the Romans, so this would mean he was staying at the home of Gaius. See how many people the Lord uses to give us His Word: an inspired apostle, a faithful secretary, a friendly Christian host, and a sacrificing woman!

Erastus was the city treasurer, thus showing that the Gospel had reached into the official families of the city. (See Phil. 4:22.) He may be the same man mentioned in 2 Tim. 4:20. "And Quartus, a brother!" No saint is too insignificant for Paul to mention! Read 1 Thes. 5:12-13 and see how this thought applies there.

Paul always signed his letters personally with his "grace signature" (2 Thes. 3:17-18), and he does so here in v. 24. It is likely that he went on to add personally this great doxology that emphasizes the mystery of the church. The prophets mentioned in v. 27 are the NT prophets through whom God revealed the truths of the church and the Gospel of grace. See Acts 13:1, 15:32, 21:10; 1 Cor. 12:28-29, 14:29-32; Eph. 2:20, 3:5, 4:11.

Thus the letter to the Romans is completed. If we understand it and apply it, v. 27 will be true: "To God only wise, be glory through Jesus Christ forever!"

1 CORINTHIANS

A Suggested Outline of 1 Corinthians

Greeting (1:1-3)

I. Reproof: The Report of Sin (1:4–6:20)

    A. Divisions in the church (1:4–4:21)
        1. Not living up to their standing (1:4-16)
        2. Not understanding the Gospel (1:17–2:16)
        3. Not understanding ministry (3:1–4:21)
    B. Discipline in the church (5)
    C. Disputes in the courts (6:1-8)
    D. Defilement in the world (6:9-20)

II. Instruction: Reply to Questions (7–16)

    A. Concerning marriage (7)
    B. Concerning idols (8–10)
        1. The example of Christ (8)
        2. The example of Paul (9)
        3. The example of Israel (10)
    C. Concerning church ordinances (11)
    D. Concerning spiritual gifts (12–14)
        1. Origin and purpose of gifts (12)
        2. Using gifts in love (13)
        3. Principles of spiritual worship (14)
    E. Concerning the resurrection (15)
        1. Proofs of the resurrection (15:1-34)
        2. Process of the resurrection (15:35-49)
        3. Program for the resurrection (15:50-58)
    F. Concerning the offering (16:1-12)

Farewell (16:13-24)

Introductory Notes to 1 Corinthians

I. The City

Without question, Corinth was the most important city of Greece. It was the capital of the Roman province of Achaia and was ideally located on the empire's most important travel route from east to west. Fourth in size among the great cities of the Roman Empire, Corinth was noted for commerce, culture, and corruption. Everyone knew what "a Corinthian girl" was, and "a Corinthian feast" was the depth of luxury and license. Corinth was the headquarters for the worship of Venus and for some of the mystery cults from Egypt and Asia.

II. The Church

Paul visited Corinth on his second missionary journey, after he had met with seeming failure in cultured Athens (Acts 18:1-17). He made friends with two Jewish tent-makers, Aquila and Priscilla, and stayed in Corinth for a year and a half. He reasoned with Jews in the synagogue week after week, and Silas and Timothy joined him after they had completed their ministry in Berea. The ruler of the synagogue was converted and baptized by Paul (Acts 18:8, see also 1 Cor. 1:14-16). Christ gave Paul special encouragement to stay in Corinth (Acts 18:9); after a year and a half, he departed for Ephesus. He left behind a church richly gifted in spiritual things (1 Cor. 1:4-7), but sorely tempted by the worldly wisdom and the wickedness of the city itself.

III. The Correspondence

Paul remained at Ephesus for three years (Acts 19:1ff). It is likely that he made a second visit to Corinth (see 2 Cor. 13:1) to correct some of the problems there. Once back in Ephesus, he wrote them a strong letter about fornication (see 1 Cor. 5:9), but this letter has been lost to us. The church at Corinth then wrote a letter to Paul, possibly sending it with Stephanas, Fortunatus, and Achaicus, who were members of the church (1 Cor. 16:17). This letter asked several important questions about both doctrine and practice, and Paul answers these questions (as well as rebuking them for their sins) in 1 Corinthians. (Note 1 Cor. 7:1, 8:1, 11:17.) He also sent Timothy on ahead to help the leaders unify and purify the church (Acts 19:22; 1 Cor. 4:17 and 16:10-11). It is likely that the three Corinthian Christians mentioned in 1 Cor. 16:17 carried 1 Corinthians back with them.

Timothy returned to Paul with news that the church had received his letter but that some things were still not right. Paul then dispatched Titus to Corinth to see that the believers obeyed his apostolic orders (2 Cor. 7:13-15). Titus then met Paul (2 Cor. 7:6-17) with the good news that the offender (1 Cor. 5) had been disciplined and that the church had obeyed Paul's instructions. It was then that Paul wrote, along with Timothy (2 Cor. 1:1), to commend the church and to encourage them to go on and finish the good work. Titus took this letter to Corinth and waited there to assist the church in raising its share of the collection for the poor saints in Jerusalem (2 Cor. 12:17-18 and 8:6). Paul made one final visit to Corinth (Acts 20:1-4).

Paul had two basic purposes for writing 1 Corinthians: (1) to reprove the Corinthian Christians for the flagrant sins that were being permitted in the church (1–6); and (2) to answer their questions about Christian life and doctrine. He had received reports of sin from the household of Chloe (1:11) and from Stephanas, Fortunatus, and Achaicus (16:17). His own visit to the city from Ephesus gave him firsthand information about the divisions and disputes in the church. No letter in the NT deals so forcibly with local church problems, and perhaps no NT letter is more neglected today.

1 CORINTHIANS 1

I. Commendation: Their Standing in Christ (1:1-9)

In a most tactful way, Paul opened his letter by reminding the believers of the wonderful blessings they had in Christ. He does this before he reproves them for their sin, for they were living beneath their privileges as Christians. They were not walking in a manner worthy of their calling in Christ (Eph. 4:1ff). He lists some of their spiritual blessings that they were ignoring and thus depriving themselves of spiritual power.

A. Called of God (v. 2).

This means they were sanctified (set apart) and members of that elect group, the church! They were not living like saints, but they were saints!

B. Grace of God (vv. 3-4).

Grace means that God gives us what we don't deserve; mercy means He doesn't give us what we do deserve. This grace came through Christ by faith.

C. Gifts from God (vv. 5 and 7).

Paul discusses spiritual gifts in chapters 12–14, but it is evident that the Corinthians were wonderfully blessed with spiritual gifts, especially the gifts dealing with utterance (see 14:26). They were enriched with knowledge, too. Yet with all their gifts and knowledge, they lacked love (13:1-3) and could not get along with each other. Spiritual gifts do not take the place of spiritual graces.

D. Testimony for God (v. 6).

Everything Paul said that Christ could do for them came to pass in their lives. God's Word came true in their lives.

E. Hope from God (vv. 7-9).

They were waiting for Christ to return but were not living in the light of His coming (1 John 2:28). Though the Corinthians were sinful on earth, God would be able to present them as blameless in heaven. We should not use this passage as an excuse for sin; rather it should be seen as an encouragement that God is faithful even though we may fail Him.

II. Accusation: Their Sinful State as Christians (1:10-16)

Now that he has tactfully commended them, Paul launches into his discussion of their sins, dealing first with the matter of church divisions. The sad news of their "splits" had come to him from the household of Chloe, and also from the friends who visited him (16:17-18). Why is it that bad news of church troubles spreads so rapidly, while the good news of the Gospel never seems to spread quickly at all? There were divisions and contentions in the church (3:3, 11:18, 12:25), even at the Lord's Table (11:20-34)! Paul begs them to be "perfectly joined together" (v. 10), which in the Gk. is a medical term that refers to the setting of a bone that was broken or out of joint. Whenever Christians cannot get along, the body of Christ suffers.

Paul explains why they were divided: they had their eyes on men instead of on Christ. They were trusting in the wisdom of men (2:5); they were glorying in the works of men (3:21); and they were comparing one servant with another and boasting about men (4:6). In chapter 3, Paul proves that this infatuation with men was a mark of carnal living, evidence that these "spiritual Corinthians" were actually babes in Christ.

There were four factions in the church. One group followed Paul, and they may have been predominantly Gentiles, because he was the apostle to the Gentiles. Another group followed Apollos, the learned orator (Acts 18:24-28), probably because they enjoyed his wonderful speaking. The third group, probably Jews, leaned toward Peter, the apostle to the Jews (Gal. 2:7), and the fourth group tried to prove it was more spiritual than the rest by following "Christ alone" and rejecting human leaders. Paul explains that Christ is not divided; we are all part of the one body (12:12-31). Christ, not human leaders, died for us; and we are baptized in the name of Christ, not the names of human leaders! Paul goes on to say that he is happy he did not baptize more believers in Corinth than he did, lest the division be even worse. Paul's associates in the ministry did the baptizing, since Paul's special commission was to evangelize. This fact does not minimize baptism in any way. Imagine how difficult it would be for an evangelist today to take time to examine candidates and baptize them. (The word "sent" in 1:17 is the Gk. word that means "sent with a special commission.") Acts 18:8 informs us that many of the Corinthians believed and were baptized, so Paul did practice water baptism.

III. Explanation: The Reason for the Divisions (1:17-31)

The Corinthian believers were divided and not living up to their standing in Christ because: (1) they were mixing the Gospel with the wisdom of the world, and (2) they were glorying in men and were confused about the meaning of the Gospel ministry. In chapters 1–2, Paul deals with the wisdom of the world in contrast to the wisdom of God, and in these verses he gives seven proofs to show that the Gospel is sufficient for all people.

A. Paul's commission (v. 17).

He was sent to preach the Gospel alone, not the Gospel plus man's philosophies. How we must guard against mixing anything with the Gospel!

B. Personal experience (v. 18).

The Corinthian church had experienced the Gospel's power personally.

C. Scripture (vv. 19-20).

Paul quotes from Isa. 19:12, 29:14, and 33:18 to prove that God does not need the world's wisdom; in fact, He will destroy it!

D. Human history (vv. 20-21).

With all its "wisdom," the world was not able to find God or salvation. When we trace human history, we discover a record of man gaining more and more knowledge, but less and less real wisdom, especially about spiritual matters. Review Rom. 1:18-32 to see how the world turned from God. God's plan was so simple and unique that it seemed to be foolishness to the world! God saves those who believe what He says about His Son.

E. Paul's ministry (vv. 22-25).

Paul had preached to Jews and Gentiles across the Roman world. He knew that the Jews looked for miraculous signs and the Greeks looked for philosophical wisdom. But God bypassed both ways to make salvation available through a crucified Christ. This message about a crucified Christ was a stumbling block to the Jews, whose idea of the Messiah was far different; it was foolishness to the Greeks because it seemed contrary to their philosophical systems. But Paul saw that this "foolish Gospel" was God's power and wisdom to those Jews and Greeks who were called. Christ is our wisdom and power; He is all we need.

F. Their own calling (vv. 26-29).

"If God needs man's wisdom and glory," says Paul, "then why did He ever call you?" There were not many mighty people in the church at Corinth, not many nobles or worldly-wise people. But God still saved them! In fact, God deliberately hides His truth from "the wise and prudent" and reveals Himself to the humble. Reflect on the history of the Bible and recall how God called the "nobodies" of history, making great leaders out of them—Abraham, Moses, Gideon, David, etc.

G. Christ's sufficiency (vv. 30-31).

Every saint is "in Christ Jesus" (v. 30), and Christ is to every saint all that he or she ever needs. When it comes to spiritual things, we don't need man's wisdom or power because we have Christ. He is our redemption, our righteousness, our wisdom, our all. To add anything to Christ or His cross is to diminish Him and His work and rob them of their power.

Whenever Christians take their eyes off Christ and start depending on, trusting in, and glorifying man, then they cause divisions. Such divisions rob the church of its power.

1 CORINTHIANS 2

This chapter continues Paul's discussion of the Gospel and the wisdom of men. There were Christians at Corinth who admired the philosophies of men (perhaps the oratory of Apollos encouraged this), and they thought that the church would be better off to use man's wisdom and philosophy to win converts rather than the simple and despised message of the cross.

I. The Two Messages Paul Preached (2:1-8)

A. The Gospel.

When Paul came to Corinth, it was from a seeming defeat at Athens (Acts 17:32-34) where he addressed the Greek philosophers but won few converts. This experience, plus his conviction that only the plain Gospel is the power of God, led Paul to minister in

Corinth in fear and trembling. He did not use the enticing (persuasive) words of the orator or philosopher; he simply preached in the power of the Spirit. He was anxious that the believers put their faith in God and not in people. It is sad when pastors or evangelists make converts to themselves and fail to teach people how to walk with Christ alone. How sad when Christians have to lean on other believers and never learn to walk on their own. In chapter 3 Paul calls these Christians "babes in Christ" (3:1-4).

B. The mystery.

But Paul did not stop with a mere declaration of the Gospel, as important as that is. He also taught a deep wisdom of God to those who were more mature in the faith. Sad to say, there were few of these in Corinth! These people had their eyes on human leaders, were comparing men, and were failing to grow in the Word. It is necessary in the local church for the pastor and teachers to declare the Gospel to the lost, but it is also important that they teach God's wisdom to those who are maturing in the faith. It is impossible to build a strong church on the preaching of the Gospel alone; there must be the teaching of the plan and "mystery" of God. (A mystery is a truth hidden in the ages past revealed by the Spirit to those who belong to God's family. It is a "family secret" known only to the initiated, not the outsiders.) Of course, the mystery that Paul taught at Corinth was the program of God for the present age as outlined in Ephesians 2–3: that Jew and Gentile are "one in Christ" through faith, and make up the one body which is the church. This mystery, or hidden wisdom of God, could never be known by the "rulers of this world," because it is understood only through the prompting of the Spirit. Many professed Christians do not really understand God's purpose for this age! This is why our churches are still cluttered with OT "antiques" that do not belong to this age.

In chapters 1 and 2, Paul has contrasted the wisdom of this world with the wisdom of God:

Wisdom of this world	Wisdom of God
1. A wisdom of words (1:17; 2:4)	1. A wisdom of power, not words alone (2:4-5)
2. Man's words (2:4)	2. The Spirit's words (2:13)
3. The spirit of the world (2:12)	3. The Spirit of God (2:12)

4. Foolishness to God (1:20)
5. The philosopher (1:20)
6. Ignorance (1:21)
7. Leads to condemnation (1:18)

4. Foolishness to men (2:14)
5. The preacher (1:31; 2:4)
6. Knowledge of God (2:12)
7. Leads to glory (1:18; 2:7)

II. The Two Spirits in the World Today (2:9-13)

A. *The spirit of this world (2:12).*

Satan is certainly the energizing spirit in the world today (Eph. 2:1-3). He has given lost men a "wisdom" that inflates their egos and blinds their minds; he has led them away from the simple truths of the Word of God. The great centers of learning today do not want the Bible; they reject the deity of Christ and the need for salvation through the cross. This ignorance led men to crucify Christ—and men (even "learned" men) have been crucifying Him ever since.

B. *The Spirit of God.*

We must never forget that the Holy Spirit is the One who teaches us the things of God. In v. 9, Paul refers to Isa. 64:4 and states that God has prepared wonderful things for His children here and now.

God has prepared these blessings for us today! How does God reveal these blessings to us? Through His Spirit (v. 10). Just as a man's spirit within him understands what outsiders never know, so the Spirit of God understands the heart and mind of God and reveals these truths to us through the Word. God wants His children to be "in the know" and not in the dark. This is why He has given us the Word of God and the Spirit to teach us.

Note that the Spirit teaches us in words (v. 13). Here we have the verbal inspiration of the Bible—the very words given by the Spirit. "Comparing spiritual things with spiritual" (v. 13) may also be translated, "combining spiritual things with spiritual words" or "explaining spiritual things to spiritual people." In either case, the truth is clearly given that the Bible is the Word of God, given by the Spirit of God. We either trust God's Word, taught by God's Spirit, or the words of men.

III. The Two Kinds of People in the World Today (2:14-16)

A. *The natural man.*

This man is the unsaved man, the man who belongs to the world and is happy in it. He cannot receive the things of the Spirit (the Word) because he does not have spiritual discernment; he does not have the Spirit dwelling within his mind and body. In fact the things of the Spirit are foolishness to him! In 1:23, Paul states that the Greeks thought the Gospel was foolishness. The Greeks were great philosophers, but their philosophy could not explain a God who died on a cross, or, for that matter, a God who even cares about people. Their gods were not interested in the problems of mortals, and the Greek attitude toward the human body was such that they could not conceive of God coming in human flesh.

B. The spiritual man.

This man is the believer who is controlled by the Spirit. (In the next chapter, Paul will deal with the Christian controlled by the flesh — the carnal man.) The spiritual man is a man of discernment and is able to judge and evaluate things with God's insights. This is true wisdom. The people of the world have a great deal of knowledge, but they lack spiritual wisdom. We could paraphrase v. 15 like this: "The spiritual person understands the things of the Spirit and has wisdom, but the people of the world cannot understand the spiritual person." We are a puzzle to the unbeliever!

The spiritual person has the mind of Christ (see Phil. 2). This means that the Spirit, through the Word, helps the believer think as Jesus thinks. It is an amazing thing to say that human beings possess the very mind of God! Down through the years, spiritual Christians have predicted things that the people of the world said could never happen, but these events came to pass. The spiritually minded saint understands more about the affairs of this world from his Bible than the leaders of the world understand from their human perspective.

In these two chapters, Paul has been emphasizing the message of the Gospel and the warning that we must not mix it with human wisdom or human philosophy. In the next two chapters, he will deal with the ministry of the Gospel and show that we must take our eyes off of people and keep them on Christ alone.

1 CORINTHIANS 3

In chapters 3 and 4, Paul deals with the ministry of the Gospel and tells us what a minister of the Gospel is and does, and how the church should look upon him and his work. It is sad that we have such extremes today: some churches "deify" their ministers and make gods out of them, while other fellowships "defy" their ministers and refuse to respect them. In these two chapters, Paul gives six pictures of Christ's servants, three in chapter 3 and three in chapter 4.

I. A Servant to Others (3:1-5)

The word "minister" here is the same word from which we get our word "deacon," and it means "a servant." For eighteen months Paul was Christ's servant in Corinth, feeding people the Word, disciplining them, encouraging them, and helping them win others.

If there were problems in the church, it was not Paul's fault; it was their fault for being such immature Christians. They were babes in Christ and could not receive the solid meat of the Word, the deeper truths of the Scriptures (Heb. 5:11-14) about the heavenly ministry of Christ as High Priest. He had to feed them with milk like a nurse! Just like little children they argued and divided into cliques, following human leaders. Read James 3:13–4:17 to see why there are wars and divisions in the church.

A true pastor must be a servant. He must have a servant's mind (Phil. 2) and be willing to put Christ first, others second, and self last. This is not always easy to do! We must pray for our spiritual leaders, that God will give them grace and strength to be servants to others.

II. A Sower of Gospel Seed (3:6-9)

Paul now changes the image from that of a family to that of a field; he portrays the minister as a farmer working in the field. The seed is the Word of God (note the Parable of the Sower in Matt. 13:1ff), and the hearts of the people are the different kinds of soil. The local church is a "spiritual garden" where the pastor acts as the gardener (note v. 9—"You are God's husbandry [God's garden]").

On any farm, many different workers are needed. One prepares the soil; another plants the seed; a third pulls the weeds; and a fourth reaps the harvest. But all of them share in the harvest, and each receives wages. "How foolish of you to compare one worker with another!" says Paul. "We are all working together. I planted the seed by founding the church at Corinth; Apollos came along and watered the seed by his preaching and ministering; but only

God can give the harvest. Apollos and I deserve no glory! We are nothing, but God is everything!" The church was divided over human leaders, but Paul says in v. 8 that the workers are one, united in purpose and heart; therefore the church should also be one. How tragic when Christians compare pastors, evangelists, and Bible teachers in the way the people of the world compare athletes or movie stars! "Laborers together" must always be our motto and motive. We must take care that the soil of our own hearts is not hard and cold and unable to receive the seed of the Word.

III. A Builder of God's Temple (3:10-23)

This section is one of the most misunderstood passages in all the Bible. The Roman Catholics use it to "prove" their doctrine of purgatory, that fire will purify people in the next life and make them fit for heaven; the modernists use it to "prove" salvation by good works; and many evangelical Christians interpret this section as applying to the judgment of individual Christians rather than the building of the local church. While this passage teaches that there will be a judgment of believers' works at the judgment seat of Christ, the basic application is to workers and pastors of the local churches. The local church is compared to a building, or a temple, and the pastor is a builder whose responsibility is to keep the materials in the temple at their very best. Paul was the builder God used to lay the foundation at Corinth, and that foundation was Christ as preached in the Gospel. Along came Apollos, who built upon that foundation, and other pastors followed him. "Each one should be careful how he builds" (v. 10, NIV) is Paul's warning. He then describes three kinds of Christian workers:

A. The wise builder (v. 14).

The first worker uses lasting materials (gold, silver, jewels) and not the cheap, shabby things of the world (wood, hay, stubble). This builder seeks to honor Christ, aiming for quality that will glorify Christ, not quantity that will win the praise of men. Wise builders use the Word, they pray and depend on the Spirit; as a result, their work is lasting. When the fire tries their work in glory, it will stand!

B. The worldly builder (v. 15).

The second builder uses materials that cannot stand the test. This is the Christian worker who is in a hurry to build a crowd, but does not take time to build a church. The materials come from the world—wood, hay, stubble. These workers do not test people's professions by the Word to see if they are truly born again; they merely take them into the church and rejoice in bigger statistics. When this ministry is tested in eternity, it will burn up. The worker will be saved, but there will be no reward. Like Lot, the worker will be saved, as by fire.

C. The destroyer (v. 17).

Finally, the destroyer does not build the church but tears it down. The word "defile" in v. 17 really means "destroy." It takes no talent or intelligence to tear something down; even a child (and the Corinthians were like babies) can destroy something. Sad to say, there are Christian workers whose selfish ministries destroy local churches instead of building them up. God has a severe judgment awaiting them.

Keep in mind that Paul is saying all this to teach the Corinthian Christians to love and respect their pastors and to pray for them because they had this tremendous task of building the local church for God's glory. The Christian who is a "preacher follower" is helping to build with wood, hay, and stubble. The church member who loves the Word, obeys the pastor's teaching of the Word, and seeks to keep the local church at its best spiritually is helping the pastor build with gold, silver, and precious stones. The judgment seat of Christ will reveal that many great churches were not great at all.

In 2:5, Paul warned the Corinthians not to trust in men; now he warns them not to glory in men (vv. 18-23). Immature Christians love to bask in the light of "great men." Paul refers to Job 5:13 and Ps. 94:11 in vv. 19 and 20. Why must we glory in people when, in Christ, we have all things? If Paul or Apollos was a blessing to them, they should glorify God and not the men. All that we have comes from God, whether it be gifted men and women, the blessings of life, or things yet to come. And, if these blessings come from God, we should give the glory to God and not to men.

It is important that new Christians realize their relationship to the local church and the pastor. As members of the family (vv. 1-5), we receive the food and grow (see Eph. 4:1-16).

As "plots" in God's garden (vv. 6-9), we receive the seed of the Word and bear fruit. As living stones in the temple (vv. 10-15, and see 1 Peter 2:4-8), we help the temple grow and be strong for the glory of God. The lives that we live help to determine whether the church is being built with gold, silver, and precious stones, or wood, hay, and stubble. The Christian is not to glorify his pastor, but is to respect him and obey him as he obeys the Lord (see Heb. 13:17).

1 CORINTHIANS 4

Paul continues in his discussion of the ministry by giving three more pictures of the pastor:

I. The Steward of God's Wealth (4:1-7).

A steward owned nothing; he was a slave who managed his master's wealth. Read Gen. 24 for a picture of the oriental steward who handled Abraham's wealth and did his bidding. Note also Luke 12:35ff; 15:1-8; 16:12-27, and Matt. 25:14-30. The pastor is a servant who is a steward. The word "minister" in v. 1 is literally "the slave who rows on the lowest level of a boat." What humility Paul had!

A steward's responsibility is to be faithful to the Master, and the pastor's responsibility is to be faithful to teach the things of the Lord, especially those truths that relate to the mystery of the church. He will be judged by his own master according to his faithfulness. How tragic it is when Christians judge different workers and compare one with another. In vv. 3-5, Paul presents three kinds of judgment: (1) the judgment of people, which he does not fear; (2) self-judgment, and he says he "knows nothing against himself" (not "by" himself); and (3) the judgment of God, which is the only true judgment. The Corinthians were evaluating different servants of God, comparing one with another, and thinking themselves to be very spiritual. Paul told them they were carnal and that their judgment meant nothing to a spiritual servant of God. A true servant of God is a steward of God's wealth, and his only concern is pleasing God, not men. At the judgment seat of Christ, God will reveal the secrets and give out the rewards, and every man will have his own reward (3:8) and his own glory from God (4:5). To live for the praise of men is to be false to our stewardship.

In vv. 6-7, Paul summarizes the whole matter: they were not to go beyond the Word of God and treat men other than as Scripture allows. They were to love and honor their spiritual leaders, and obey them as they teach the Word; but to compare one leader with another, or to give glory to one over another, was contrary to God's Word and had to be avoided. After all, it is God who makes one believer differ from another; every gift a believer has comes from God! Who dares to boast over a gift?

II. A Spectacle to the World (4:18-13)

The world and its wisdom are contrary to Christ and His ministers. Paul uses some "loving sarcasm" here when he says: "You Corinthians brag about one another and compare one man with another, as though you were kings on a throne! How wonderful it must be to reign as kings and look down on others! I wish I could reign with you. But, no, I must be a hated apostle, a spectacle to the world, a fool for Christ's sake."

The verbal picture he painted was a familiar one to the people of Paul's day. Whenever a victorious general came home from a war, he was given a glorious parade through the city streets. As a way of boasting, he would display the captured nobles and generals. At the very end of the parade came the soldiers who were to be thrown to the wild beasts in the arena. Paul compared himself and the other apostles to these captured soldiers, "appointed to death for Christ's sake," (vv. 9 and 10) while the Corinthian Christians were boasting at the front of the parade!

What a spectacle a true servant of God must be to the world! Paul could have been a great Jewish rabbi, with authority and esteem; yet he gave it up for Christ's sake (Phil. 3) to have hunger, nakedness, peril, and death! The world cannot understand this attitude and calls such a person a fool. How convicted these Corinthians should have been when they compared their carnal living to the sacrifices Paul and the other apostles were making. Paul was a fool; they were wise. Paul was weak; but they were strong. Paul was hated by the world, but they were courting the world's wisdom. Paul went so far as to call himself the "the scum of the earth—the world's garbage" (v. 13).

This attitude of heart must be shared by Christ's servants today as well. How easy it is to settle down and live like the world, accepting the world's standards and courting the world's honors, when we ought to beware "when all men speak well of us" (see Luke 6:26).

III. A Spiritual Father (4:14-21)

Jesus warns us that we should call no man on earth "father" (Matt. 23:9), but it is still true that those who lead souls to Christ are, in a sense, "fathering" them. (See 1 Thes. 2:11.) Paul had been their spiritual father in that he gave them the Gospel and helped to lead them to Christ. A sinner is born into God's family through the Spirit of God (John 3:6) and the Word of God (1 Peter 1:23), but God uses human instruments to bring sinners the Gospel. It had been Paul's "spiritual travail" (Gal. 4:19) that had made possible a church in Corinth.

The men who followed Paul may have been their instructors, but the Corinthians had only one spiritual father; they should have showed him more respect and listened to his word. Paul had warned them about sin, but they had failed to listen. Now he sent Timothy to help them settle their church problems; if that did not help, Paul intended to come himself. Their own attitude would determine whether he would come with a father's rod of correction, or with a word of commendation and approval. History tells us that they did not listen to Timothy, so it was necessary for Titus to go to Corinth.

Several times in this chapter you find the phrase "puffed up," referring to the Corinthians' attitude of superiority and carnal pride (vv. 6, 18, and see 5:2). What made them "puffed up"? Was it not the leaven of sin in their church (5:6)? As the yeast of sin grew, it inflated them into a false spirituality; therefore, Paul found it necessary to warn them. This "puffed up" attitude often reveals itself in much talking. "Paul will never come here!" they were saying (vv. 18-19). "He writes stern letters and tries to scare us, but he will never come back!" "Be careful!" warned the apostle. "Talk is cheap! When I do come, I want to see how much power these Christians have, and not how much they talk. A carnal Christian is often a bragging Christian, but there is no demonstration of God's Spirit in his or her life (see 2:4).

Certainly it grieved Paul's heart to have to write this way to his spiritual children, but he had to be faithful. Just as parents must warn and chasten their children, so "spiritual fathers" must warn and discipline the children of God in love. This is not an enjoyable experience, but it is a necessary one.

These two chapters illustrate the proper attitude of the church toward its spiritual leaders. Such Christians should thank God for them, pray for them, love them, honor them, and obey the Word which they teach and follow themselves. There must never be in a church a worldly attitude of exalting men and ministries. The pastor ministers the Word, sows the seed, builds the temple, dispenses the mysteries of God, suffers shame before the world, and lovingly fathers the church family. These are great responsibilities, and only the sufficiency of God enables anyone to fulfill them.

1 CORINTHIANS 5

Paul now deals with the second problem that had been reported to him: immorality in the church and the refusal of the leaders to deal with the offender. How sad that such awful sin should be "commonly reported" and thus ruin the testimony of the church! Paul gave three reasons why the church had to exercise loving but firm discipline and deal with the offending member.

I. For the Good of the Offender (5:1-5)

Discipline in the church is not like a policeman arresting a culprit; rather, it is like a father chastening his son. The first motive is to help the sinner, to show Christian love in seeking to bring him to repentance. For us to allow church members to live in open sin hurts them as well as Christ and the church. This particular member apparently was living with his stepmother (see Lev. 18:8) in an immoral relationship. The woman was apparently not a part of the church family, otherwise Paul would have had the church deal with her as well.

What a terrible thing for a Christian to live in sin with an unsaved person while the church does nothing about it!

The church was "puffed up" and boasting about its "liberal attitude." Paul told them that they should be mourning, and the Gk. word he used means "to mourn over the dead." (Later on he compares their sin to leaven, and leaven always "puffs up" whatever it infects.) Their "broad-minded attitude" toward sin was only hurting the offender and the church, not to speak of the sorrow it was causing Paul and the Lord Himself. Paul judges the man and instructs the church to dismiss him from the fellowship. "But doesn't Jesus tell us not to judge?" some may ask, referring to Matt. 7. Yes, He does; but this does not mean we should close our

431

eyes to sin that is known by sinners and saints alike! We cannot judge another believer's motives (which is what Matt. 7 refers to), but we can and must judge the actions of God's people.

The discipline was to be handled by the church collectively, and not by the leaders alone (v. 4). The matter was known publicly, so it had to be dealt with publicly. If the man refused to repent, he was to be dismissed from fellowship. To "deliver a man to Satan" (v. 5) does not mean to send him to hell, for no church can do that. Rather, it means to cut him off from church fellowship so that he must live in the world, which is controlled by Satan (John 12:31 and Col. 1:13). The purpose of such discipline is not to lose a member, but rather to bring the sinner to the place of repentance that he might be saved from loss of reward on the day of judgment.

Church discipline is a forgotten ministry in many churches these days. Yet, if we really love one another, and if the pastor really loves his flock, he will see to it that wandering ones are warned and disciplined for their own good.

II. For the Good of the Church (5:6-8)

How foolish for a church to say it is "open-minded" and willing to accept any and all members, no matter how they live! Would you open the door of your home to all who want to enter? Then why should we allow any and all who want to enter to come into the fellowship of the church? It is harder to join many worldly organizations than it is to unite with the average local church! "Your glorying is not good," warns Paul. "Don't you realize that one member living in open sin can defile the entire church?" (see v. 6).

Paul used the Passover supper to illustrate his point; see Ex. 12:15ff. Leaven to the Jews was always a symbol of sin and corruption; so, before Passover, they always scoured their houses to remove all traces of leaven. Christians must have the same attitude; we dare not allow the yeast of sin to grow quietly in the church and produce trouble and shame. Christ died for us, not to make us like the world, but to make us like God. "Be holy for I am holy" (1 Peter 1:16). This does not mean that church leaders are to be "spiritual detectives" who pry into the lives of the members. But it does mean that each church member must see to it that the leaven of sin is not growing in his or her life. And, if sin becomes known, the leaders must take steps to protect the spiritual welfare of the church.

There are several kinds of Christians that we are warned about in the Bible, believers who should not be permitted fellowship in the local church: (1) the member who will not settle personal differences, Matt. 18:15-17; (2) the member who has a reputation for being a flagrant sinner, 1 Cor. 5:9-11; (3) those who hold false doctrine, 1 Tim. 1:18-20 and 2 Tim. 2:17-18; (4) those who cause divisions, Titus 3:10-11; (5) Christians who refuse to work for a living, 2 Thes. 3:6-12. Those who are suddenly overtaken by sin we should lovingly seek to restore; see Gal. 6:1.

III. For the Good of the World (5:9-13)

The church cannot change the world if the church is like the world. Read these verses carefully and note that Paul makes a distinction between sin in the lives of Christians and sin in the life of unbelievers. Sin in the lives of believers is worse! Paul had commanded them in a previous letter not to fellowship with Christians and church members who had sinful reputations as fornicators, coveters, or idolaters. He did not tell them to stay away from all sinners of this kind, otherwise they would have to leave the world! We expect the unsaved man to live in sin, but even the world expects the Christian to be different. One reason the church today has so little influence in the world is because the world has too much influence in the church.

Faithful Christians are not even to eat with church members who have ruined their testimony by open sin and have never made things right with the church and the Lord. This is a part of the discipline outlined in v. 5. If a faithful church member fellowships in a friendly way with a Christian living in sin, that member is condoning his sin and disobeying the Word of God.

It shocks some Christians when they realize that God expects us to exercise spiritual judgment in the church. We are not to judge the outsiders; God will do that. But we are to expel from church fellowship any Christian who will not confess sin and make things right. This is not to be done hastily; all parties involved must be permitted to state their case. There must be prayer and the ministry of the Word. There must be sincere Christian love. The very act of church discipline is a testimony to the world and a warning to the church, and especially to new believers, that God expects His children to be different from the world. To condone sin is to deny the very cross of Christ!

1 CORINTHIANS 6

This chapter deals with the two remaining problems that had been reported to Paul.

I. Disputes in the Courts (6:1-8)

It was probably the Gentiles (Greeks) in the church who were the guilty parties in this case, for the Greeks were very much wrapped up in courts and law. Each Greek city had its courts and councils, and it was not uncommon for a son to sue his own father! Of course, the basic problem was carnality (3:1-4); when Christians are immature and not growing, they cannot get along with one another. They lack the spiritual discernment to settle and solve personal problems. How tragic it is when a local church is torn asunder by lawsuits among the members! We are living in an era when lawsuits are the "going thing" and a quick way to try to make money. It seems that the purpose of the court is not justice but income.

Paul is not condemning courts of law (see Rom. 13), for the government is instituted by God for our good. But matters between believers must not be exposed before unbelievers, and certainly an unsaved judge lacks the spiritual understanding to deal with spiritual matters (2:14-16). By dragging one another to court, the church members at Corinth were ruining the testimony of the church and disgracing the name of the Lord.

How should Christians settle personal differences? They must first have the right spiritual values. How trivial these personal disputes become when compared to the great eternal matters we will decide in glory! The church is going to judge the world and the angels! This realization makes worldly disputes rather insignificant. Too many Christians have warped values; the things of this world (especially money) are more important to them than the glory and praise of God.

Matters between Christians should be settled quietly according to the principles of Matt. 18:15-17 and 1 Cor. 6:5. If the two parties cannot reach an agreement, then they should invite some spiritual believers to meet with them and help decide. If the matter becomes known to the church (or outside the church), the members should appoint a group to examine the matter and give spiritual counsel.

Far better that a Christian should lose money than lose his spiritual stature and bring shame to Christ's name! We can find this same attitude in Matt. 5:38-42. Of course, the Christians in Corinth were so carnal that they lacked spiritual vision and wisdom, and thus their church was split into warring factions. "You are brethren!" Paul cried. "Show love for one another!"

There is some question concerning the meaning of Paul's statement about "the least esteemed" (v. 4). Some take it that Paul is using "loving sarcasm" as though to say, "You don't even have a wise, mature Christian in your church who can handle these matters!" Or, he may have been saying, "Far better to lay these disputes before some humble believer in your church than to spread them before an unsaved judge."

II. Defilement in the World (6:9-20)

While we cannot excuse the Corinthians for their terrible sins, we can certainly understand why they fell into them; no city presented more opportunities for immorality and vice than did Corinth. The very religion of the city (the worship of Aphrodite) was nothing but prostitution in the name of religion! These believers had been rescued from lives of horrible sin but were tempted to go back. Paul knew that some of the believers were looking for excuses to sin, so he clearly refuted every argument that they might bring up.

A. "If we are saved, then we can sin and still go to heaven!" (vv. 9-11)

Certainly people who are truly born again will go to heaven in spite of their many failings; but the new birth brings a new nature, and a new nature means a new appetite. The Christian still has the ability to sin, but not the desire. Any teaching that makes it easy to sin is not Bible doctrine. "Be not deceived!" Paul listed the awful sins that once had ruled their lives, then reminded them of what Jesus had done for them. "Such were some of you! But you are washed . . . sanctified . . . justified!" The Christian is a new creation (2 Cor. 5:17) and proves it by breaking with the old life. We do not inherit the kingdom of God by refraining from sin, but we prove that we are going to heaven by the godly lives that we live.

B. "Don't Christians have liberty? Aren't we free from the Law?" (vv. 12-14)

Certainly we are free from rules and regulations, but we are not free to sin. Christian liberty is never license. Christian liberty does not mean I am free to do what I please, but that I have been freed to do what pleases Christ. Furthermore, "liberty to sin" is really the worst kind of slavery! We must not be brought under the power of sin (Rom. 6). "But," you say, "if God gave us these physical appetites, certainly He wants us to use them." That's right: use them, but not abuse them. Your body is the Lord's; and if you live in sin, that sin will destroy you and God will someday judge you.

C. "Can I not use my body as I please?" (vv. 15-20)

Of course not! To begin with, it is no longer your body; it belongs to Christ. He purchased you with His own blood. Back in Paul's day, a slave could set himself free by saving his money and depositing it with the priest at the local heathen temple. When he had enough money to purchase his freedom, he would take his master to the temple and the priest would give the master the money and declare that the slave now belonged to that particular god. Christ paid the price to set us free from sin, and we must use our bodies to please Him.

Furthermore, when we sin against the body, we sin against Christ and the Holy Spirit who has made the body His temple. Gen. 2:24 states that two persons joined physically become "one flesh." How can a Christian join his body—which is a member of Christ's body—in such horrible sin? How can he defile the temple of the Spirit?

Christians are to glorify God with their bodies. This means the way we care for the body, the way we dress the body, the places we take the body, the deeds we do in the body. It is dangerous for Christians to use their bodies for sin. Remember what happened to Samson and David!

In these latter days, we see a shameless increase of sexual sins. We dare not close our eyes to it. (See 2 Tim. 3:1-7, and note that v. 5 states that these sinners will be professing Christians, and not people of the world!) The attitude of the world is, "Everybody's doing it, so why be different?" It is sad when Christians think they can violate God's moral code and get away with it. Sexual sins are sins against Christ (who purchased our bodies), against the Spirit (who indwells our bodies), and against ourselves (v. 18). Single people in particular need to read and ponder Prov. 5:1-23, 6:20-35, and 7:1-27. These are plain chapters, but they warn against sexual license.

Married Christians need to read and ponder 1 Thes. 4:1-8, where God warns Christians in the church against breaking their wedding vows.

This closes the first section of the letter dealing with the sins in the church. Keep in mind that all of these problems—division, immorality, disputes, and defilement with the world—come from one common source: the believers in Corinth were spiritual babes and were not growing in the Lord. They had their eyes on men, not on Christ; they were feeding on milk, and not the meat of the Word; they were unwilling to admit sin and deal with it. Most serious church problems begin as personal problems and sins in the lives of church members.

1 CORINTHIANS 7

This chapter deals with problems of marriage and the home. Beginning with this chapter, Paul is answering the questions the Corinthians asked in the letter they wrote him (see 7:1; 8:1; 12:1; 16:1). Some modern liberal critics accuse Paul of being cruel to women in his teaching, but nothing could be farther from the truth! Paul's ministry of the Gospel did more to raise the position of women than people realize. Wherever Christianity has gone, it has improved the lot of workers, women, and children. Paul himself must have been married, otherwise he could not have been a member of the Jewish Sanhedrin. (He may have been a widower.)

As you read this chapter, keep in mind: (1) that Corinth was noted for its immorality and lack of standards for the home; (2) that Paul was dealing with local problems that we may not face in the same way today; (3) that it was a time of persecution for the Christians (v. 26). In this chapter, Paul discusses the problems of three groups of believers.

I. The Unmarried Christians (7:1-9)

Note v. 8, "I say therefore to the unmarried and widows." Paul is giving counsel to those without mates, and he begins by saying that believers should not think themselves unspiritual because they are single, or that they are especially spiritual because they are married. One version translates v. 1, "It is perfectly proper, honorable, morally befitting for a man to live in strict celibacy" (WUEST). The

Roman Catholic church teaches that celibacy is a more devoted form of life than marriage, but Paul teaches otherwise. Celibacy is honorable, but so is marriage (see Heb. 13:4). In v. 7 he says that God gives different gifts to people when it comes to the marriage relationship, and this idea resembles our Lord's teachings in Matt. 19:10-12. Keep in mind that the Greeks looked down on the body and were prone to separate "body" and "soul" in a manner not taught in the Bible. Paul states that God had given him the ability to live without marriage, and he would that they had the same self-control. But he does not say that celibacy is more spiritual than marriage.

There are, however, reasons for marriage, and the main one is to avoid sexual sin. "It is better to marry than to burn with lust" says v. 9. In v. 2, Paul unmistakably teaches monogamy: every man is to have his own wife, every woman her own husband. Husband and wife must be considerate of one another when it comes to the privileges of marriage. Lack of consideration can give Satan an opportunity to tempt one of the partners, and the result might be tragic. "Incontinency" (the deliberate refusal of the marriage bed) is not necessarily a mark of spirituality. It can be a cause of conflict and sin. If a Christian cannot control oneself, then he or she ought to marry. Of course, Paul is not suggesting that the only—or main—reason for marriage is physical; for a marriage built on physical bonds will fall apart in only a short time. Paul treats marriage in this chapter as a privilege, a blessing from God that can enrich the lives of both partners.

II. Christians Married to Unsaved Partners (7:10-24)

Christians are to marry other Christians (note v. 39—"married . . . in the Lord"—and see 2 Cor. 6:14-18). But some of the Corinthians were saved after they had married. What should they do? Should they leave their unsaved mates? Should they refuse the marriage bed? What if the unsaved mate wants to end the marriage? Paul's counsel is clear: stay where you are and use every opportunity to try to win the lost mate. If the unsaved mate is willing to live with you, remain in the home and be a good witness. The Christian might win the unsaved mate. The children from such a marriage are not "unclean" (illegitimate), as would be the case if an OT Jew married a Gentile; their children would not be accepted into the covenant. (Verse 14 does not mean that children born in a

Christian home are saved; only that the Christian mate "sets apart" for God's blessing the unsaved in the home. God blesses the lost because of the saved.) However, if an unsaved mate refuses to continue in the home, then the believer can do nothing but let the mate depart. "God has called us to peace." Does the abandoned wife or husband have the right to remarry? Verses 10-11 would indicate that the ideal is to work toward reconciliation, but v. 15 seems to teach that abandonment does break the marriage relationship and thus gives the faithful partner right to divorce and remarry. Christ taught that unfaithfulness breaks the marriage bond and is grounds for the innocent party to remarry. Keep in mind that Paul is not commanding separation; he is permitting it in certain cases. Ideally the Christian is to patiently bear the burdens and seek to win the lost mate. (See 1 Peter 3 for further counsel.)

The fact that a person becomes a Christian does not change his or her status in society. In vv. 17-24, Paul tells the Corinthians not to try to "undo" their situation, but to abide in their calling and allow Christ to make the changes in His way and His time.

III. Parents of Marriageable Girls (7:25-40)

"No commandment of the Lord" in v. 25 simply means that Christ gave no teaching on this subject as He did about divorce (as noted in v. 10, where Paul refers to His teaching). Keep in mind that in those days, the parents arranged marriages for their children; it is different today. Paul presents several facts for these parents to consider.

A. It is a time to distress (vv. 25-31).

Marriage is a serious matter, and Christians were facing difficult times. These testings were not to cause the married to divorce or the unmarried to be frightened out of marriage (v. 27); but due consideration had to be given to the situation at hand. Living a dedicated Christian life means sometimes forsaking even the good things of the world.

B. Marriage brings responsibilities (vv. 32-35).

One reason why Paul remained unmarried was so that he might devote himself completely to the service of Christ. His calling was such that he did not want to force a wife and family to suffer because of the Lord's demands on him. While this is not the normal standard for Christian servants, we must admire men like Paul, David Brainerd, Robert Murray McCheyne, and others who gave their all to Christ in this sacrificial way. If these parents wanted their daughters to serve God, then they had to face the fact that marriage involves many cares and demands.

C. Each case is individual (vv. 36-38).

It is next to impossible to lay down rules that fit each case when it comes to marriage. Paul warns them that they must be convinced in their own hearts, and not merely follow the crowd or try to appear superspiritual.

D. Do not be in a hurry, for marriage is for life (vv. 39-40).

The marriage cannot be broken because of some whim or fancy. Too many people (including some Christians) have the idea, "If our marriage doesn't work out, we can always get a divorce." Not so, says Paul! When you marry, be sure it is "in the Lord"—that is, be sure you marry a Christian and that your mate is the one God has chosen for you. How tragic to see young lives ruined by hasty marriages.

1 CORINTHIANS 8

Chapters 8 through 10 deal with the church's questions about meat offered to idols. This was a serious problem to them, especially since the church was composed of both Jews and Gentiles, and the Jewish believers were anxious to avoid any contact with heathen idolatry. The situation was this: most of the meat in Corinth was slaughtered at the temples. The priest kept part of the meat, but the rest was used for private feasts or sold in the markets. In fact, sacrificial meat was sold at a cheaper price, making it that much more attractive to these poor Christians. If a friend or neighbor invited a Christian to a feast, it was likely that the meat had been dedicated to an idol. Should the Christian participate in the feast? Would some demonic power be present in the meat and injure the believer? Would eating such meat defile the Christian?

We don't face this same problem today, but the basic situation is still with us: does a Christian, because he is set free from the Law, have the right to live any way he pleases? There are many practices that we know from Scripture are definitely wrong, but there are also many borderline problems about which even dedicated Christians disagree. In these three chapters, Paul outlines the basic principles that should govern our lives when it comes to questionable things. Here in chapter 8, he uses the example of Christ and states that we must be controlled by love so as not to cause others to stumble (see Matt. 17:24-27). In chapter 9, Paul uses himself as an example, pointing out that it is not necessary for Christians to use their rights in order to be happy; for Paul laid aside even legitimate rights in order to serve Christ. Finally, in chapter 10, he uses the example of Israel to warn believers about presumptuous sins, particularly those connected with idolatry and immorality.

Here in chapter 8, Paul gives four admonitions for us to follow in discerning right and wrong in the area of questionable things.

I. Consider Your Own Attitude (8:1-3)

Too often strong Christians who know the Bible are prone to be "puffed up" when they deal with weaker Christians. Paul admits here, as well as in Rom. 14, that some believers are strong in the faith and mature, while others are weak and have legalistic views of the Christian life. "Knowledge puffs up, but love builds up!" (v. 1). In fact, the man who thinks he knows everything is admitting that he knows nothing! Paul is not encouraging us to be "ignorant brethren," but rather is warning us that a proud attitude is not Christ-like. Knowledge must be balanced with love, love for God and for our brethren. We must not judge one another or reject one another (Rom. 14:4-12).

II. Consider Your Brother's Knowledge (8:4-8)

The Christian life cannot be lived in its fullness if a man is ignorant of the Word. We must always take into consideration that some Christians do not understand the blessings of liberty we have in Christ. They live in religious bondage and try to regulate their lives with rules and rituals (see Col. 2:16-23). Paul clearly states that idols are not real, and that meat offered to idols could never hurt anybody's body or spirit (v. 8). There is one God and Savior, and we worship and obey only the Lord. But some Christians do not have this knowledge. They do not realize that no food is sinful of itself (note Rom. 14:14), and that meat and drink can never make anybody a better Christian. How patient Christ was with His ignorant disciples! And how patient we must be with one another!

As a Christian grows in grace and knowledge, through reading and obeying the Word, he understands the truth, and the truth sets him free (John 8:32). He sees knowledge as a tool with which to build, not a weapon with which to fight.

III. Consider Your Brother's Conscience (8:9-11)

Conscience is that inner judge that condemns us when we do wrong and commends us when we do right. It "bears witness" to us (Rom. 2:15 and 9:1). The Christian's conscience has been purged (Heb. 9:14 and 10:22) and is termed a "good conscience" (1 Tim. 1:5, 19). Repeated sin not judged and confessed will make it a defiled conscience (Titus 1:15) and eventually a seared conscience (1 Tim. 4:2) that no longer convicts. We must strive to have a conscience void of offense (Acts 24:16).

The new Christian, or the untaught Christian, will have a weak conscience (1 Cor. 8:7, 10, 12). If he sees another Christian eating meat that had been dedicated to a heathen god, this experience might offend him and perhaps lead him into sin. Because his spiritual senses are not fully developed, he will go to the other extreme and perhaps disgrace the name of Christ (see Heb. 5:11-14). A mature Christian, with a strong conscience, will not be affected by the heathen around him; but the believer with a weak conscience will be confused and, if he follows his brother's example, might get into trouble.

Paul takes up this same principle in 10:25-33, so we might look ahead at these verses. "Don't go around being a spiritual detective!" he states. "If invited to a feast, and if you are disposed to go, then go right ahead; but don't ask a lot of questions. However, if the host tells you that the meat was sacrificed to an idol, do not eat it! Why? So that you can be a testimony to the weaker Christian who might be offended and lead into sin." Paul then anticipates an argument. "But, you ask, why should we have our liberty limited by somebody else's immaturity? If we bless the food and eat for God's glory, isn't that enough?" No! Believers are to follow a different rule. We Christians must do everything possible not to offend the Jews, Gentiles, or other Christians.

It boils down to this: whatever a Christian does, even if it does not hurt him, must never hurt anyone else. While we may think that this principle limits us, it really does not, for it allows us to be a greater blessing to others and to win the lost to Christ (10:33).

IV. Consider Christ (8:12-13)

Our Lord, in the days of His flesh here on earth, was careful never to cause others to stumble. The incident in Matt. 17:24-27 illustrates this. "Lest we should cause them to stumble" is a wonderful principle to follow, for it means putting Christian love into daily living. Christ died for the weaker Christian, therefore we dare not cause them to sin. To sin against another Christian is to sin against Christ! It would be better to go without meat than to make others fall, says Paul.

We can think of dozens of applications of this principle in modern life. Take the world of amusements, for example. One person might be able to attend a theater and not suffer from it spiritually; but if this act leads a weaker Christian astray, then the stronger Christian has sinned. A mature Christian might be able to read a popular novel and not be affected; but if his selection causes another to stumble, he has sinned. Yes, we have liberty as Christians; but we are not at liberty to become stumbling blocks to others. What a tragedy if a believer were to backslide, or a lost sinner reject Christ, because a Christian selfishly asserted "his rights" and set the wrong example. "Let no man think only of his own good, but let him think of the good of others," Paul states in 10:24—that is a wonderful principle to follow!

1 CORINTHIANS 9

In the previous chapter, Paul pointed to the example of Christ and laid down the principle that we should do nothing that would offend another Christian, especially weaker Christians. In this chapter, he points to himself as an example of one who had privileges, but, for the Gospel's sake, did not use them. Keep in mind that he is still dealing with the problem of meat offered to idols. "Certainly we have privileges as Christians," he states, "but we must never use our privileges in such a way that we will hinder the Gospel."

I. Paul's Claims to Privileges (9:1-14)

While in Corinth, Paul worked with his own hands and took no support from the church. He willingly laid aside even the privilege of marriage. Paul could have claimed the privilege of financial support from the church, and proved this by citing five arguments.

A. *Other apostles and workers (vv. 1-6).*

Paul states his apostleship in no uncertain terms. He had seen the Lord (Acts 1:21-22) and was called to his apostleship by the risen, glorified Christ. His work and ministry in Corinth proved his apostleship. The other apostles, including Peter, received support from the churches and took their wives with them from place to place as they ministered. If other servants had these privileges, then so did Paul!

B. *Human custom (v. 7).*

No soldier supports himself, but receives supplies and wages from his government. The farmer who toils in the vineyard is privileged to eat the fruit. The shepherd expects to get milk and meat from the flock. Is it unreasonable to expect a local church, then, to support the pastor? Verse 11 lays down a basic principle: if others bless us with spiritual things, we should show our appreciation by sharing material ("carnal") things (see Gal. 6:6-8). It is interesting to note that we have here three more pictures of a pastor: he is a soldier to protect the church and battle Satan; he is a farmer who tends the spiritual field or vineyard and looks for fruit; and he is a shepherd who leads and feeds the sheep. Pray for your pastor; a pastor's work is never easy.

C. *The Old Testament law (vv. 8-11).*

Paul refers to Deut. 25:4. The OT practice was to have the oxen walk on the sheaves and thus separate the grain from the chaff. Here, and in 1 Tim. 5:18, Paul uses this law to illustrate the principle given in v. 11. If oxen benefit from their physical work, should not God's servants benefit from their spiritual work? The plowman and the harvester both work in hope, expecting to share in the harvest.

D. *The Old Testament priests (vv. 12-14).*

The Law allowed the priests to share generously in the sacrifices from the altar. He took the hides from the burnt offerings, all the flesh (minus the fat) from the sin offering and the trespass offering, most of the meal offering, the breast and right shoulder of the peace offering, plus various firstfruits, tithes, and special offerings. If they served faithfully, the people shared generously.

E. *Christ's command (v. 14).*

Read Matt. 10:10 and Luke 10:7. While Paul personally did not use these privileges, he does not say that they are wrong. "The laborer is worthy of his hire." It is right for Christians to support those who serve them in the Lord.

II. Paul's Sacrifice of Privileges (9:15-27)

Though he had all these privileges, Paul did not use them (vv. 12, 15) and he gives several reasons to explain why.

A. He wanted to make the Gospel free (vv. 15-18).

He gloried in a free Gospel of free grace! As one writer puts it, "Paul's pay was to get no pay!" He preached the Gospel willingly and rejoiced at the privilege. How tragic it is when Christians look upon their responsibilities as burdens instead of blessings.

"But even if I did not preach willingly," says Paul, "I would still have to preach, because God has committed a stewardship (dispensation) to me." There is a practical principle here: we should do nothing that would reflect on the grace of God and the free offer of salvation. We wonder what sinners must think when they attend "Gospel meetings" where a leader spends thirty minutes taking offerings or scolding the crowd for not giving more!

B. He wanted to work independently (v. 19a).

More than one Christian worker has soft-pedaled the message because of money. Some pastors dare not offend members who are "heavy givers." Others are afraid of losing their denominational support or insurance. Paul wanted no master but Christ.

C. He wanted to win as many as possible (vv. 19b-23).

Though Paul enjoyed liberty as a worker, he willingly made himself the servant of all men that he might win them to Christ. This does not mean that Paul followed the worldly slogan, "When in Rome, do as the Romans do." That would be compromise rooted in fear. Paul's attitude was based on love, not fear. He was not lowering his standards; rather, he was laying aside his personal privileges. It was not hypocrisy, but sympathy: he tried to understand those who needed Christ and enter into their experiences. He was a Jew, so he used this as a key to open the Jewish heart. He was a Roman citizen, so he used this as a key to open the door to the Gentiles. He sympathized with the weak and encouraged them. "All things to all men" (v. 22) simply means the wonderful ability of accommodating ourselves to others, understanding them, and seeking to lead them into the knowledge of Christ. Paul was no tactless "bull in a china shop" who used the same approach on all he met. Rather, he used tact to get contact; he willingly sacrificed his own privileges to win the lost.

D. He wanted to gain a lasting reward (vv. 24-27).

What good are daily privileges if we lose our eternal reward? Every Christian needs to govern his or her life "with eternity's values in view." For Paul to set aside his personal privileges meant discipline and hard work, and he describes this discipline in vv. 24-27. His illustration from the Greek games was familiar to his readers, for the famous Isthmian Games (similar to the Olympics) were held near Corinth. The contestants had to discipline themselves and lay aside even good things in order to win a prize. If athletes can give up their rights in order to win a fading olive-leaf crown, certainly Christians can lay aside privileges to win an eternal crown! Only one athlete could win each event at the Isthmian Games, but all Christians are given the opportunity to win Christ's approval.

Paul's fear of becoming a castaway had nothing to do with his salvation. He is not talking about salvation but Christian service. We are not saved by running the race and winning; we run the race because we are saved (Phil. 3:12-16 and Heb. 12:1-3). The word "castaway" means "disapproved, disqualified"; it is translated "not well pleased" in 10:5. Paul compares himself to the herald who called the athletes into the arena, yet who himself did not pass the tests to be a contestant! Paul was not afraid of losing his salvation but of losing his reward for faithful, sacrificial service.

1 CORINTHIANS 10

This chapter closes the section dealing with meat offered to idols. Paul has cited the example of Christ (chap. 8), his own example (chap. 9), and now points to Israel's past history. He probably had in mind the overconfident members of the church at Corinth, believers who thought they had such wisdom and knowledge that they did not have to beware of temptation or sin. He warns them in v. 12 and uses a bit of "holy sarcasm" as he calls them "wise men" in v. 15. While the believer has liberty to eat and drink, he must beware of at least three dangers.

I. The Danger of Falling into Sin (10:1-13)

Paul uses Israel to illustrate the temptations and sins of God's people. While Israel in the OT is different from the church in the NT (note v. 32), there are several parallels between the two.

A. Israel had spiritual advantages (vv. 1-4).

Paul compares its passing through the sea and under the cloud to the believer's experience of baptism. Just as Christian baptism identifies the believer with Christ, so Israel's "baptism" identified the people with Moses. Israel was delivered from Egypt by the blood of the lamb just as Christians are delivered from the world and sin by the cross. God opened the sea to let the Israelites through, thus separating them from their slavery in Egypt; in like manner, the resurrection of Christ has separated the Christian from the world and the bondage of the flesh. The Jews ate manna, and Christians feed on Christ, the Bread of Life, as they partake of the Word. Israel drank water supernaturally provided, and Christians drink the living water (John 4:10-14) of salvation and the refreshing water of the Spirit (John 7:37-39). Some are puzzled by "that spiritual rock that followed them" (v. 4), as though a literal rock rolled along in the wilderness with the Jews. Two explanations are possible: (1) Paul states that a spiritual rock followed them, and certainly Christ did travel with His people and met their needs; (2) the word "them" is not in the original text, so that Paul may be saying, "They drank of that spiritual rock that followed [after the manna was given]." First the bread, then the water followed.

B. Israel fell because of sin (vv. 5-10).

God was "not well pleased" with them (v. 5), which is the same Gk. word as "castaway" in 9:27. They were disapproved; they lost their lives because of sin. They lusted (Num. 11:34); they worshiped idols (Ex. 32:1-14); they committed fornication (Num. 25:1-9); they tempted God by deliberately trying His patience (Num. 21:4-9); they complained (Num. 16:41-50). What a list of sins! Yet, God had to judge their sins even though they had been wonderfully delivered from Egypt. Spiritual privileges never give us license to sin. Rather, they lay upon us the greater responsibility to obey God and glorify Him. (Note on v. 8: Paul gives 23,000 slain, while Num. 25:9 says 24,000. However, Paul is recounting how many died in one day, while Moses records the total number of deaths, for obviously some died later.)

C. Israel is a warning to us today (vv. 11-13).

The people of God, whether in the OT or the NT, must never presume to sin. In v. 12, Paul warns the overconfident, and then encourages the fearful in v. 13.

II. The Danger of Fellowshiping with Demons (10:14-22)

Paul uses the Lord's Supper to illustrate his point that while idols are not real (8:4-6), Satan can use idols to lead people astray. This is not superstition, for Deut. 32:17 and 21 clearly teach that demons can be worshiped through idols. Just as the believer has fellowship (communion) with Christ in partaking of the cup and loaf, and just as OT priests had fellowship with God as they feasted on the sacrifices from the altar, so an idolater has fellowship with demons in his idolatrous feast. Paul is actually describing "Satan's communion service" here! Just as Satan has a counterfeit church and gospel, so he has a counterfeit communion service. Anthropologists may study and admire heathen worship and idols, but God says the whole system is of the devil and is actually demon worship. Wherever there are idols, there will be demons.

Of course, Paul is not saying that the eating of the bread and drinking of the cup actually and literally make a person a partaker of Christ. He is not talking about union but communion, fellowship with Christ. It is inconsistent for a Christian to share the Lord's Table one day and sit at a table of demons the next day.

Christians must take care not to get involved in the devil's religion. Not everything that passes for Christianity is scriptural. We may think we are sharing half-heartedly in a religious ceremony, when actually we are opening ourselves up to Satanic attack. The recent rise of Satanism ought to be a warning to the church.

III. The Danger of Failing a Fellow Christian (10:23-33)

As he closes his discussion, Paul now repeats the principle laid down in chapter 8: do nothing that would weaken your brother's conscience or cause him to stumble. Yes, Christians are free and all things are lawful; but not everything builds up (edifies). We dare not use privileges to tear down the work of the Lord. He closes with several very practical guidelines:

A. Live to please others (vv. 23-24).

This is a summary of his teaching in chapter 9.

B. Don't be overly "fussy" (vv. 25-27).

The Christian who goes around asking questions about foods will be a poor testimony to the lost and of no help to the saved. Buy your meat in the meat market ("shambles") without asking questions. All food comes from God and is good for us, and Satan cannot hurt us with meat (8:8). When invited to a feast in an unsaved friend's house, ask no questions. However, if another Christian there tells you the meat came from a heathen altar, and if that Christian is bothered by it, do not eat the meat. It is better to go hungry than to cause that weaker brother to stumble.

C. Live for God's glory, even if it means sacrifice (vv. 29-31).

Paul anticipates an argument in vv. 29-30. "Why should my strong conscience be judged by a brother's weak conscience? And what damage can there be in meat for which I have given thanks?" The answer is: regardless of what we do, be it eating or drinking, we must do it for God's glory and not just to please ourselves. Humanly speaking, it may seem wrong for a strong Christian to bow to a weaker brother, but this is what glorifies God. Making that weaker brother stumble into sin would disgrace the church and the name of Christ.

D. Live to win souls (vv. 32-33).

There are only three groups of people in the world: the Jews, the Gentiles, and the church. God expects the church to seek to win Jews and Gentiles to the Lord. If a Christian lives to win souls, these questions about conduct will take care of themselves. It is the idle Christian, the carnal Christian, who frets over how far he can get involved with the world. When believers live to build the church and win the lost, they put first things first and glorify the name of Christ.

1 CORINTHIANS 11

In chapters 11–14, Paul deals with the disorder in the public assembly at Corinth. As you read these chapters, certain problems become evident: their meetings were disorderly and unscriptural; women were taking the lead over the men; various members were competing for leadership and opportunity to speak; in general, there was confusion and a poor testimony before the lost. Chapter 11 concerns disorder at the Lord's Supper in particular, while chapters 12–14 discuss public worship in the assembly and the principles that should govern our services.

I. The Causes of Disorder at the Lord's Supper (11:1-22)

A. Lack of subordination by the women (vv. 1-16).

Paul is often accused of being critical of women and placing them in an inferior position, but this is not true. He realized that God is a God of order, and that when anything is out of order, there is confusion and loss of power. Paul nowhere teaches that women are inferior to men in the eyes of God, but rather that God has laid down the principle of headship (not dictatorship) that makes Christ the Head of man and man the head of woman. At Corinth, this important principle was being violated. Women were competing with men for public leadership in the church. Furthermore, in the observing of the Lord's Supper, women were not keeping their proper place and were coming with their heads uncovered; it is this matter that Paul now discusses.

Keep in mind that Corinth was an immoral city, with temple "priestesses" who were prostitutes. One mark of a sinful woman was her short hair; such a woman often walked about the city without the usual veil for a covering. In some Eastern countries even today, women do not appear in public unveiled. This is a sign of disrespect to their husbands and would be interpreted as an invitation to sin. In fact, even among the Jews, a shorn head was a mark of immorality (see Num. 5:11-31, especially v. 18). So, Paul warns the women of the church not to lose their testimonies by worshiping in public without a veiled head. That veil (or covering) was a mark of subordination to the Lord and to their husbands and a recognition of the principle of headship.

Orthodox Jewish men even today wear a prayer cap in their synagogue worship, but this is a practice Paul forbids in the local church. Christ is the Head of man; so, if a man wears a hat in worship, he dishonors his Head. If a woman does not wear a covering, she dishonors her husband, because "woman [was created] for the man" (v. 9). Of course, the mere wearing (or not wearing) of a piece of cloth never changes the heart. Paul assumes that these Christian women obeyed the principle of headship from their hearts and were simply not complying outwardly.

Paul gave several reasons why women must keep their proper place in the church: (1) it shows honor to their husbands; (2) it honors Christ, the Head of the church; (3) it agrees with the plan of creation itself, for God created woman for man; (4) the angels watch our worship and know what we do, v. 10; (5) nature itself gives the woman long hair and the man short hair, thus teaching subordination; (6) this is the practice in all the churches, v. 16. How does this matter of "wearing hats" and "wearing short hair" apply to us today? While we do not have all of the same circumstances that Paul had to deal with in Corinth, we must admit that a woman or a man out of place is always a hindrance to the work of God. There ought to be modesty in the local church, both in dress and action. We dare not conform to the world, lest we lose our testimony.

B. Divisions in the church (vv. 17-19).

When there are divisions and factions (heresies) in the church, even though they seem hidden, they will show up in the public meetings. The Lord's Supper speaks of the unity of believers; divisions in the church would negate this wonderful message.

C. Selfish motives (vv. 20-22).

The early church often held a "love feast," a fellowship meal, in conjunction with the Lord's Supper. But at Corinth, the rich came with their bounties while the poor sat on the side with a crust of bread. "Eat at home!" Paul commands them. "Your gluttony and drunkenness are a disgrace to the Lord!" (v. 22). If believers do not love one another, they can never partake of the Lord's Supper and be blessed.

II. The Consequences of This Disorder (11:23-30)

A. They were judged instead of blessed (vv. 23-29).

Apparently Christ had given Paul instructions about the Lord's Supper personally, for the apostle was not in the Upper Room when the ordinance was instituted. Paul's words speak of the broken body and shed blood of Christ for His church which are a constant reminder of His love and His coming again. We look back to the cross and forward to the coming. But the Supper had ceased to be a blessing to the church at Corinth, for the way they abused it was a cause of judgment. Their meetings were "for the worse, not the better" (v. 17)! This is the way spiritual matters always work: if our hearts are not right, whatever should be a blessing becomes a curse.

B. They were chastened (v. 30).

God allowed sickness and even death to come to the Corinthian church because it was partaking of the Lord's Supper in an unworthy manner. Paul never tells us we must be "worthy" to eat at the Lord's Table; for if that were the case, no one would be able to partake. Though we are not worthy, we can partake in a worthy manner by understanding what the Supper means: having a heart free from sin; being filled with love for Christ and His people; being willing to obey His Word. Christians often think they can "get away" with carelessness in church, but this is impossible. If our hearts are not right, God has to chasten us to bring us to the place of blessing.

III. The Correction of This Disorder (11:31-34)

A. Self-judgment (vv. 31-32).

If we face our sins honestly, judge them, and confess them, then God will not chasten us. "Let a man examine himself" is Paul's command in v. 28. At the Lord's Supper, we take three "looks": we look within and confess our sins; we look back and remember Calvary; and we look ahead and eagerly anticipate His return. The principle is clear: if we do not judge our sins, God will have to judge us.

B. Mutual love (v. 33).

"Don't think only of yourself!" Paul wrote; "think of others." This is Christian love: putting others ahead of ourselves. How few Christians obey this principle when it comes to worship. We come to church asking, "Will I get anything out of the service today?" when we should be asking, "What can I say or do that will give somebody else a blessing?"

C. Spiritual discernment (v. 34).

While there is nothing wrong with church fellowship meals, the place to eat is at home. It takes spiritual discernment to keep the church doing what it is supposed to do and not get sidetracked on detours. The ministry of the local church is not to entertain or feed the saints; it is one of building one another spiritually that all might be able to go out to win others. It may be put down as a basic principle that the local church is not to do what God ordained the home or the state to do. The church is not meant to raise children, yet people blame the church and Sunday School when their children go wrong!

If we follow these principles, then our assemblies will come together for blessing and not for judgment ("condemnation" in vv. 29, 32, 34).

1 CORINTHIANS 12

This chapter opens the discussion on spiritual gifts (chaps. 12–14), and in this day when churches and denominations are emphasizing the work of the Spirit, we need to know what God has to say on this subject. However, we must study these chapters in the light of the problems in the Corinthian church—division, immorality, stunted spiritual growth, and confusion in the assembly. Here in chapter 12, Paul explains the work of the Holy Spirit in the body of Christ as He bestows spiritual gifts upon the members. Chapter 13 emphasizes that Christian graces, flowing from love, are more important than spectacular gifts; in chapter 14 he lays down the principles that should govern worship in the community of the church.

I. We Belong to Each Other (12:1-20)

Division was a major problem in the church at Corinth (1:10-16; 6:1-8; 11:18-22). Each group followed its chosen human leader, exercised its gifts selfishly, and cared little for the health or ministry of the whole body. The Christians at Corinth had received an abundance of spiritual gifts (1:4-7), but they were lacking in spiritual graces—the kind of Christian character that the Holy Spirit longed to form in them. Keep in mind that Christian gifts are not necessarily a mark of Christian character or spiritual maturity. These Corinthian believers were carnal, yet they exercised wonderful and miraculous gifts.

A. We share the same confession (vv. 1-3).

A citizen of the Roman Empire was required once a year to put a pinch of incense on the altar and say, "Caesar is Lord!" This was anathema to believers. No true Christian could call anyone but Christ "Lord," so this was a definite test of whether or not a person was saved. It is only by the Spirit that we can confess Christ as Lord (Rom. 10:9-10).

B. We serve the same God (vv. 4-6).

The church, like the human body, has diversity in unity. Our human members all differ, yet they work together for the health of the body. In the spiritual body of the church, we possess gifts from the Holy Spirit (v. 4), partake in service to the same Lord Jesus Christ (v. 5), and share in the workings (operations) of the same Father (v. 6).

C. We seek to build the same body (vv. 7-13).

Paul now lists the spiritual gifts and shows that they are given for the benefit of the whole church, and not for the private enjoyment of the individual Christians. We must distinguish between: (1) the spiritual Gift, which is the Spirit Himself, received at salvation (Eph. 1:13-14); (2) spiritual gifts, which are ministries to the church through the Spirit, and not just natural abilities or talents; (3) spiritual offices, which are positions of trust in the local church, as discussed in 1 Peter 4:10; 1 Cor. 12:28; Rom. 12:4; (4) spiritual graces, which are the fruit of the Spirit (Gal. 5:22-23; 1 Cor. 13:4-7) in Christian conduct. Paul makes it very clear that each Christian has the Gift (12:3) and at least one spiritual gift (12:7). Not all Christians have spiritual offices, but all Christians should manifest the graces of the Spirit, which are far more important than miraculous gifts.

It is clear from 1 Cor. 13:8 that some of the gifts granted to the early church were never meant to be permanent. When the church was in its infancy (13:11), before the completion of the NT Scriptures, these gifts were needed; but they are not needed today. God can grant them if He pleases, for He is sovereign in all things; but these "sign gifts" are not necessary for the ministry of the church.

D. We share the same baptism (vv. 14-20).

The baptism of the Spirit refers to the placing of members into the body at the moment of their conversion. The Jews were first baptized into the body at Pentecost (Acts 1:5 and 2:1ff); the Gentiles were first baptized into the body at the household of Cornelius the centurion (Acts 10:44 and 11:15-16); and ever since, whenever a sinner trusts Christ, he or she is made a part of that same body by the operation of the Holy Spirit. The Spirit places each believer in the body as He sees fit, but each part of the body has an important ministry to perform. "Many members in one body" is the program for this present age.

II. We Need Each Other (12:21-25)

Those believers who possessed spectacular gifts looked down upon the others and thought them unimportant. Yet here Paul teaches that every member of the body is essential to the life, health, and growth of the church. (Read Eph. 4 to see how God uses gifted people to help build the saints who in turn build the body.) No Christian can say to his less-gifted brother, "I don't need you!" In fact, those parts of our body that seem the least important can do the most good — or cause the most trouble if not functioning properly! Doctors used to list several organs or members of the human body that (they said) were not important. That list is much shorter today!

III. We Affect Each Other (12:26-31)

There should be no division (schism) in the body (v. 25), since we all share the same life through the Spirit. But it is not enough simply to avoid division; we must also care for each other and seek to build the church and strengthen the body. In the human body, the weakness or pain of one member affects the other members. This is also true in the spiritual body: if one believer suffers, we all suffer; if one member grows in strength, we all receive help. This fact lays upon each Christian the responsibility for being the strongest member possible. Ephesians 4:16 indicates that every part of the body makes some kind of contribution toward the growth of the church.

It is essential that we keep in mind God's method for strengthening the body. He has chosen spiritual leaders, given them spiritual gifts, and placed them in the body as He chooses. There were, in the early days of the church, apostles, and prophets. There are no apostles today, since it was necessary to have seen the risen Christ to qualify for apostleship (1 Cor. 9:1; Acts 1:21-22). The apostles were special ambassadors who took the Gospel to the lost, established churches, and delivered God's messages. Prophets were preachers who spoke as directed by the Spirit. They did not expound the Bible as such, but conveyed God's will immediately to the church, and not mediately through the written Word, since the NT was not yet written. First Cor. 13:8-13 teaches that the spectacular gifts that the early church possessed in its "childhood" stage were not meant to be permanent. They were the heaven-sent credentials that told the people that God was at work in their midst (Heb. 2:3-4).

Note that tongues stand last on the list. Apparently the believers at Corinth were given to abusing the gift of tongues, so much so that there was confusion in their public services (14:23ff). In fact, the "tongues members" looked down upon the other believers who did not have this particular gift. So Paul closed by reminding them that we do not all possess the same gifts (vv. 29-30). "Do all speak with tongues?" No. Never let anyone convince you that the gift of tongues is necessarily a mark of special spiritual power or character. This gift was possessed by Christians whom Paul called "carnal— babes in Christ" (1 Cor. 3:1).

It is important that we realize our relationship to one another in the church. Yes, there are many denominations today, but all true Christians, indwelt by the Spirit, are members of His body. There can be unity even where there is not uniformity. Christ never prayed for uniformity in His church, but for the same spiritual unity that exists between Him and His Father (John 17:20-23). We should likewise pray for spiritual unity and do all we can to guard it and extend it (Eph. 4:1ff).

1 CORINTHIANS 13

It is tragic when the world takes a chapter like this (as it does) and divorces it from its true Christian meaning. The unsaved man can no more experience this kind of love than can a marble statue! It takes the indwelling of the Spirit of God in the life, and the empowering of that Spirit, for anyone to display this kind of character in daily life.

Keep in mind that Paul is still dealing with the question of spiritual gifts. Here he is emphasizing the fact that gifts without graces are nothing. The fruit of the Spirit (Gal. 5:22-23) is more important in the Christian life than the miraculous gifts of the

Spirit. Whenever the church strives for miraculous experiences rather than Christian holiness and character, there will be division, confusion, and carnality.

I. Love Is Essential (13:1-3)

The word "charity" means "love" in action. It is not simply an emotion; it is the heart reaching out to others. "Charity" today makes us think of giving away old clothes or making gifts to "charitable institutions." These activities can be Christian love in action, but Paul is demanding much more. The word he uses for love is *agape*, which is love that sacrifices for the good of others.

Notice how he takes up some of the spiritual gifts of 12:8-10 and shows their emptiness apart from love. Tongues apart from love become mere noise, like the clanging of a cymbal. Prophecy without love makes the prophet nothing. This application can also be made to knowledge (spiritual insight given immediately by the Spirit) and faith. Paul is not minimizing these gifts; he is simply saying that they will have no good effect on the individual or on the church unless there is love in the life of the Christian in the exercise of his or her gifts. We might go so far as to sacrifice our body, but apart from love, this act would amount to nothing. Love is the measure of all things.

It is evident that the Corinthians were using their spiritual gifts and offices with an attitude of competition and not of love. The church was divided, and the situation was getting worse because the very spiritual gifts that were supposed to build the church were doing more harm than good! Preaching without love is just so much noise. Praying without love becomes an empty speech. Giving without love is just a ceremony. Is it any wonder that Christ asked Peter, "Do you love me?" (John 21:17)

II. Love Is Effectual (13:4-7)

Gifts have no spiritual effect on the life of the church if there is no love, for it is love that the Spirit uses to build the church. "Knowledge puffs up, but love builds up," says 1 Cor. 8:1. Note the qualities of love:

A. Love is patient and kind (v. 4).

Love rises above petty things and is generous in the way it treats others. It is easy to "love" when people are lovable; how difficult it is to love when they injure or attack us in one way or another. Think of Christ's patience with Peter after the times Peter sinned against Him, and you have some idea of what this means. Love not only patiently bears with wrongs, but it positively acts in deeds of kindness.

B. Love never simmers with jealousy (v. 4).

Envy is a terrible sin; Cain envied his brother and killed him! How do we react when other Christians receive blessings or benefits that we lack? Do we allow the sparks of envy to burn and then come to a full flame?

C. Love is not boastful or proud (v. 4).

"Puffed up" refers to the inward feeling; "vaunteth" refers to the outward displays of self-importance.

D. Love is not rude or self-seeking (v. 5).

There is a graciousness about the person who acts from Christian love, a charm that the world cannot give. True love seeks only the good of others; it is unselfish. Can you see this love displayed in Christ's life?

E. Love is not provoked, nor does it harbor evil thoughts (v. 5).

The word "easily" does not belong here. Christian love shows no irritation, as the flesh too often does. Love does not keep account books of the evil things people do, or the hurts received from them. In fact, love is never glad when others get involved in evil, but love is always glad when others are walking in the truth.

F. Love gives victory (v. 7).

Through Christ's love in us, we can bear up under anything, have faith, and continue in hope. "It gives us power to endure in anything" v. 7, (wms). Love always leads to victory!

In these verses, Paul gently rebuked the sins of the Corinthians. They did not have patience with each other in the assembly (14:29-32); they envied the spiritual gifts others possessed (14:1); they were proud and critical (12:21-26); they did not have modesty or grace in their behavior (12:2-16); they sought to uphold their own rights (chaps. 8–10) even if it hurt others; they were easily provoked, and even sued one another (6:1-8); and they rejoiced at sin when they should have judged it (5:1-13). We can also see in these verses a picture of Christ who alone perfectly manifests the love of God to us. We can substitute the word "Christ" for "charity" in this chapter.

III. Love Is Eternal (13:8-13)

The Corinthians were spiritual babies, and, like babies, they were striving for the temporary and neglecting the permanent. They wanted passing spiritual gifts instead of lasting Christian character. Love will never "fail" (cease to have force or authority). These other gifts will pass away; prophetic utterances would be replaced by the written Word of God; tongues would no longer be needed; gifts of special knowledge would be put aside for the teaching ministry of the Spirit from the Word. But love, and the graces it produces, will last forever.

Paul explains that these special gifts were necessary during the infancy period of the church. Special manifestations of the Spirit were the credentials of the apostles (Rom. 15:18-19). God did not always use miracles to attest His truth, but often He did. In Thessalonica, for example, the Spirit revealed Himself in the mighty preaching of the Word, and not in miracles (1 Thes. 1:5-6). In v. 11, Paul uses a simple example from childhood. We do not condemn a child because he talks like a child, but we do condemn an adult for using baby talk. "It is time," says the apostle, "for you babies to grow up and start talking like adults! Tongues and other special manifestations belong to spiritual childhood. Grow up!" Paul in 14:20 again tells them to quit acting like children.

There will always be room for growth in the church, and while we are growing, we will know and see imperfectly. Corinth was famous for its metal mirrors, so Paul used that as an illustration. One saw only a dim reflection of the real person in those mirrors, just as we see only a dim reflection of God today. But when Christ comes, we shall know Him as we are known by Him! And we shall be like Him!

The church grows closer to perfection through love: believers loving Christ and one another; holding the truth in love; practicing the truth because they love Him. "Building the body up in love" is the way Eph. 4:16 puts it, and this is a ministry all of us share.

Faith, hope, love — these abide forever; and love is the greatest, for "God is love" (1 John 3:18).

1 CORINTHIANS 14

The first thing we want to do is go through this chapter and cross out the word "unknown." Paul is not discussing "unknown" tongues; those words were added by well-meaning but confused translators. Wherever you find "tongues" in the Bible, it refers to known languages (note Acts 2:4, 6, 8, 11). The Jews at Pentecost heard the believers extolling God's mighty works in their own dialects, so no interpreter was needed. In 1 Cor. 14:10 and 21, Paul definitely states that he is discussing known languages, not a strange "heavenly language" or unknown tongues.

I. The Inferiority of Tongues (14:1-25).

Some want us to believe that the gift of tongues is a mark of superior spirituality, and that Christians cannot truly be spiritual as long as they neglect this gift. Paul teaches exactly the opposite! He gives three reasons why tongues are an inferior gift.

A. Tongues do not edify (build up) the church (vv. 1-19).

We must keep in mind that spiritual gifts have as their purpose the building up of the church of Jesus Christ (12:7) and not the personal enjoyment of the believer. Gifts are for employment, not enjoyment. In this section, Paul contrasts tongues and prophecy. Prophecy, you will recall, was the giving forth of the truth of God under the immediate leading of the Holy Spirit. It is not identical to preaching, because the preacher interprets the written Word as instructed by the Spirit; he does not speak the very Word of God. Note the contrasts:

Prophecy	Tongues
1. Speaks to men for their good, v. 3	1. Speaks to God for the speaker's own good, v. 2
2. Can be understood, vv. 2, 5	2. Not understood unless there is an interpreter
3. Edifies the church, vv. 3–4	3. Edifies the speaker, v. 4
4. The greater gift, vv. 5, 19	4. The lesser gift, v. 5 (note 12:10)

Paul makes it clear that tongues, apart from utterances that are interpreted, are of no value to the church. For that matter, they bring no personal blessing to the speaker himself unless he understands what is being said (vv. 14-15). Those who say that Christians should practice this gift in private ignore what Paul says here. In the first place, how can we edify the church if we use our spiritual gifts in private and not to serve others? And, second, if we do not understand what is being said, how can we profit from it ourselves? It is possible for the flesh and the devil to imitate spiritual gifts and lead a believer into a religion of shallow emotionalism instead of one of solid understanding and faith. This is not to deny the place of sincere emotions in the Christian life, for the fruits of the Spirit certainly involve the emotions (Gal. 5:22-23); these emotions, however, must be instructed by the mind and controlled by the will, or they will be destructive.

B. Tongues do not edify the believer (vv. 20-21).

Some suggest that the gift of tongues is a mark of spiritual maturity and of a deeper Christian life; but Paul says just the opposite. The Christians at Corinth were "babes in Christ" and "carnal" (3:1-4). They boasted of their "spirituality" (8:1-2; 10:12), yet had to be warned by Paul and taught in the most elementary manner. In 13:8-13, Paul explains that their passion for emotional spiritual gifts was a mark of infancy and not maturity. Mature believers have the Spirit and the Word and seek no emotional "crutches" to prop them up. Dr. M. R. DeHaan has an interesting view of 14:22 that backs up this teaching. He says that "them that believe" (v. 22) refers to spiritual Christians who live by faith in God's Word, while "them that believe not" refers to immature believers without strong faith. God has to give emotional signs to immature Christians to bolster their faith, but the mature believer builds his life on the Word.

C. Tongues do not win the lost (vv. 22-25).

In Acts 2, God gave the apostles the gift of tongues that they might share the Word with the Jews at Pentecost. It was a sign to the Jews that God was at work, fulfilling Isa. 28:11-12. We find incidents involving tongues four times in Acts, and each time they give evidence to Jews present that God is working: (1) Acts 2; tongues are evidence to the unbelieving Jews at Pentecost; (2) Acts 8; evidence to the believing Jews that the Spirit had come upon the Samaritans; (3) Acts 10; evidence that the Spirit had come upon the Gentiles; (4) Acts 19; evidence that the twelve Ephesian men had received the Spirit. But tongues would never reach the unbeliever for the Lord, especially the confusion of tongues that existed at Corinth. It was another Babel! Far better that the unbelieving visitor should hear a message from the Word, something he can understand, and then make his decision for Christ, than hear a confusion of messages he cannot grasp.

II. The Importance of Order (14:26-40)

A. Tongues (vv. 26-28).

Tongues are not to be allowed without interpretation. Only three are to speak, and then in order.

B. Prophecy (vv. 29-33).

Two or three prophets are to speak, and the others are to test their messages to see if they come from God. (Note the gift of "discerning of spirits" in 12:10, and see 1 Thes. 5:20-21). Speakers are to edify the church and maintain proper order. If a speaker gets "carried away," it is proof that the Spirit is not speaking; for when the Spirit is at work, there is self-control.

C. Women in the church (vv. 34-35).

Relate these verses to 11:5ff and 1 Tim. 2:12. It seems that the women were abusing their gifts and using them out of place. Paul does not say that women have no spiritual gifts, or that they should be slaves to the men. He teaches that both men and women, if acting out of place in the church, tear down the church instead of building it up. Paul also lays a responsibility upon the men; they were to teach their wives spiritual truths, but to do so at home. Sad to say, in many families it is the wife who has to teach the husband!

D. Obedience to the Word (vv. 36-40).

"If any of you are spiritual," says Paul, "you will prove it by obeying the Word of God!" The Spirit of God never works apart from or contrary to the Word of God, and nowhere is this principle needed more than in the area of spiritual gifts. We cannot be guided by somebody's subjective emotional experience, but we can be guided by the unchanging objective Word of God.

Note the basic principles for spiritual worship that Paul gives to the church:

(1) The teaching and preaching of the Word takes precedence over everything else.

(2) The church must be built up.

(3) There must be nothing that would hurt the testimony before unbelievers.

(4) There must always be self-control.

(5) Everything must be done "decently and in order," following the Word of God.

(6) Women are not to exercise authority over men.

(7) There must be understanding before there can be blessing. It is evident from Scripture that there was an informality about the meetings of the early church. We must avoid formality on one hand and fanaticism on the other. It is a fine line to toe. A planned service is not an unspiritual service, for the same Spirit can lead in the planning beforehand just as He can lead in the service itself. But even in a planned service, we must make room for the Spirit to lead, lest we grieve Him.

Additional Notes on First Corinthians 12–14

We want to examine the claims of some charismatics with reference to manifestation of tongues and of the Spirit to see if they meet the test, "What say the Scriptures?" Some claim:

A. "There is a baptism of the Spirit after salvation."

Some teach that it is necessary to "tarry for the power" in prayer and fasting, basing this on Acts 1 and Luke 24:49. But 1 Cor. 12:13 teaches that all believers have been baptized by the Spirit into the body of Christ. This was true even of the carnal Corinthians! There are "fillings" of the Spirit after conversion, and we are commanded to be filled with the Spirit (Eph. 5:18); but we are never commanded in Scripture to be baptized with the Spirit. There is one baptism that takes place at conversion, but many fillings of the Spirit as we daily yield to God.

B. "The evidence of this baptism is speaking in tongues."

If this is true, then most of the Corinthians had never experienced the baptism, because not all of them spoke in tongues (12:10 and 30). Yet 12:13 says they were all baptized by the Spirit. Therefore, if the charismatics are correct, all of the Corinthian believers should have spoken in tongues; but they did not. John the Baptist was filled with the Spirit before birth, yet never spoke in tongues. Great saints down through the ages have never spoken in tongues.

C. "The gift of tongues is a mark of spirituality."

Not at Corinth! This was the most carnal church Paul ever had to deal with. They were babes in Christ (1 Cor. 3:1-4). Instead of being a mark of deeper spiritual life, tongues are a relatively inferior gift that has little value to the individual Christian or the church collectively. It is possible to have spiritual gifts and not have spiritual graces, and 1 Cor. 13 clearly teaches this. The important issue is not how many gifts I have, but is my life like Christ's and am I attracting people to Him?

D. "Tongues are for the church today."

There is every evidence that several of the gifts were temporary. Prophecy, tongues, and knowledge (the imparting of immediate spiritual truth by the Spirit) seemed to have passed away with the completion of the writing of the NT. First Cor. 13:8-13 indicates that these gifts would pass away and no longer be needed. They belonged to the "childhood" of the church. Today the church's life and ministry are founded on the Word of God. Read Acts 20:17-38 for a picture of the ideal NT ministry; here you will find nothing about tongues.

E. "A believer can benefit from tongues privately."

But spiritual gifts are given for the profit of the whole church (12:7), not just one saint. There is no suggestion in these chapters that any gift is granted for the private enjoyment of the believer. In fact, in 14:13-15 Paul clearly states that the private use of the gift of tongues is not right. If there is interpretation, allowing the believer to know what is being said, then there can be spiritual benefit; but without understanding, there is no blessing. The private use of tongues is contrary to the letter and spirit of 1 Cor. 12–14.

F. "The gift of tongues ties believers together."

There is a new kind of ecumenicity among Christians in the charismatic movement that says, "You don't have to deny your basic beliefs to be a part of our fellowship." But did the so-called "baptism of the Spirit" unify the believers at Corinth? The church was divided four ways (1 Cor. 1:10-13)! Yet all of the believers there had experienced the baptism of the Spirit (12:13)! There was discord, division, and dispute in the church; yet there was also the gift of tongues. It has been our experience that the emphasis on "tongues" and "Spirit baptism" divides the church instead of unifying it. The "tongues Christians" think themselves superior to the others, and then trouble starts.

G. "It makes no difference what terms you use as long as you have the experience."

This is a subtle lie of Satan. The very words of Scripture are given by the Spirit, and we must obey them (1 Cor. 2:9-16). It is wrong to confuse the baptism of the Spirit with the filling of the Spirit, for God has definitely separated them. We must base Christian experience on the Bible, and not interpret the Bible by experience. If we understand Bible words and truths, we will understand how to live the Christian life. Notice how many times Paul uses the word "ignorant" in writing to the Corinthians. "Be not children in understanding!" he admonished them in 14:20. It is possible for Satan and his demonic powers to counterfeit "spiritual experiences" for shallow Christians. But Satan cannot work where Christians understand the Word of God.

1 CORINTHIANS 15

The Greeks did not believe in the resurrection of the dead. When Paul preached the resurrection at Athens, some of the people actually laughed at this doctrine (Acts 17:32). Their philosophers taught that the body was the prison of the soul, and the sooner the soul was set free in death, the better off a person would be. The Greeks looked upon the human body as a source of weakness and wickedness, and they could not conceive of a body that continued to exist after death. It was this kind of thinking that Paul had to deal with when he wrote this chapter.

I. The Proofs of the Believer's Resurrection (15:1-34)

A. Historical proof (vv. 1-11).

The Corinthians did not doubt the resurrection of Christ, so Paul began there in his argument for the resurrection of the human body. The resurrection of Christ is an historic fact proved by the message of the Gospel, the testimony of witnesses and the conversion of Paul himself. If there were no resurrection, there would be no salvation, for a dead Savior can save nobody! "Now," argues Paul, "I know that you Corinthians believe in the resurrection of Christ, otherwise your faith is empty (vain). Christ was a man, and now He has a resurrection body. If He has a glorified body in heaven, why should we believers not have one also?" This is another aspect of the believer's union with Christ: because He has been glorified, we shall also be glorified one day.

B. Personal proof (vv. 12-19).

Paul points to the Corinthians' own personal experience. He had preached the Gospel to them, they had believed, and their lives had been transformed (6:9-11). But if the dead rise not, then Christ is dead, and that Gospel was a lie! Their faith was vain, and they were still in their sins! The Christian faith is good only if a person lives; there is no hope after death.

C. Doctrinal proof (vv. 20-28).

Here Paul deals with the Bible doctrine of "the two Adams." (He uses this argument also in Rom. 5.) It was through the first Adam's sin that death came into the world; but through the Last Adam (Christ), death has been conquered. Christ is the firstfruits; that is, He is the first of a great harvest that is yet to come. Christ is God's "Last Adam," and He will reverse the wrong that the first Adam brought into this world. When Christ comes, the dead in Christ will be raised (v. 23 and 1 Thes. 4:13-18). Jesus will finally put all things under His feet, including death. In other words, to deny the resurrection of the dead is to deny the future kingdom of Christ. If believers are "dead and gone," then God's promise for the future is null and void.

D. Practical proof (vv. 29-34).

Paul mentions several practices in daily life that prove the resurrection of the body. For one thing, the Corinthians were "baptizing for the dead." There is some disagreement over what this means. Were they baptizing living people on behalf of saints who had died before being baptized (which is not likely), or were they baptizing new converts to take the place of those who had died (which is likely)? In any event, the church at Corinth was still practicing baptism, and baptism is a symbol of death, burial, and resurrection. (New Testament scholars generally agree that the early church baptized by immersion.) The ordinance has no meaning if there is no resurrection of the dead. In vv. 30-32, Paul cites the many dangers in his ministry, and says in effect, "Surely it is foolish for me to risk my life daily if there is no resurrection!" In v. 32 he argues, "If there is no resurrection, then we ought to eat, drink, and be merry! Enjoy life while we can!" It is easy to see that these practical points make sense. "Shame on you!" he concludes in v. 34. "You ought to have this knowledge!"

II. The Process of the Believer's Resurrection (15:35-49)

"How are the dead raised?" is the key question here. Paul uses illustrations from nature to show that there is no life apart from death. The seed that is planted dies and bears fruit, and the fruit, while identified with the original seed, is different from it. The resurrection body, like the bodies in the heavens, will have its own kind of glory. It is not the same body that was planted (v. 37), but there is continuity between the buried body and the resurrection body. The physical body laid in the grave is liable to corruption; it is humble, a body of humiliation; it is weak; it is suited to a natural environment. The resurrection body will not decay; it will have power and glory; it will be suited to a spiritual environment. It will bear the image of the heavenly.

The resurrection body of Christ illustrates what Paul is teaching here. The believers recognized Him, so there was continuity between His crucified body and His glorified body. But He was also able to change His appearance. He passed through locked doors, yet He also ate fish and honey (Luke 24:41-43) and invited the disciples to feel Him. It was the same body, yet it was also a different body. The resurrection body retains the personal identity and individuality of the believer, but it will be suited to a new way of life.

III. The Program of the Believer's Resurrection (15:50-58)

Here Paul deals with the second coming of Christ and what it means to both the living and the dead. "We shall not all die (sleep)," because some saints will be alive when Christ returns; "but we shall all be changed." This mystery concerns the rapture of the church. When Christ returns, the dead shall be raised first, the living caught up with them, and all will be changed to be like Christ. And all of this will happen in the twinkling of an eye.

Paul closes with a note of victory. There can be no sting in death
when a person is a Christian, for Christ has taken out that sting.
There can be no victory in the grave, for Christ will one day empty
the graves and bring forth His own in resurrection power. How
hopeless the Greeks were when they thought about death! Inscrip-
tions on tombs in ancient Greece and Rome indicate that death
was their greatest enemy, that they saw no hope beyond the grave.
In Christ we have life and hope!

Verse 58 is often quoted out of its context. Christians can be
steadfast and immovable, because they know that if their worst
enemy (death) has been overcome, they need fear no other enemy.
They can abound in Christian service, for that work will count for
eternity. Their labor is not in vain.

Several times in this chapter Paul uses the phrase "in vain." It
means "empty, without content." Because the tomb is empty, our
faith is not empty! But if the tomb is not empty, then everything
else is in vain: our preaching is empty (v. 14), our faith is empty
(v. 14), and our works are empty (v. 58). The resurrection of Jesus
Christ is God's answer to Solomon's lament in Ecc. 1:2: "Vanity of
vanities, all is vanity!" Thanks be to God for the victory we have in
the resurrection of Christ!

1 CORINTHIANS 16

In this final chapter Paul gives instructions concerning the offering
for the poor saints in Jerusalem, and also exhortations to the believers in Corinth concerning their church life.

I. How to Take the Offering (16:1-4)

A local church gets its financial instructions from the Word ("as I
have given order") and not from the world. How sad it is when
churches reject the biblical method of financing and adopt worldly
methods. All the churches in Paul's day followed the same biblical
pattern; there were to be no exceptions. While these instructions
deal with a "missionary relief offering," the principles apply to
Christian giving in general; see 2 Cor. 8–9.

A. Giving was church-centered.

Otherwise, why would Paul mention "the first day of the week"?

The churches gathered on the Lord's Day, and this was when they brought their offerings to the Lord. Paul did not encourage the members to send their offerings to him personally. He wanted the church to give an expression of its love for the needy Jewish believers in Judea. Note in Phil. 4:15-16 that Paul was grateful for churches that shared with him. A church member owes it to the Lord and to his church to bring his or her tithes and offerings to the church. This does not mean that it is wrong to give personal support to workers (2 Tim. 1:16-18), but giving to persons must not take the place of our faithfulness to the church.

B. Giving was regular.

Paul encouraged them to bring the money weekly, if possible. Some people are paid weekly, others by the month. Paul is saying, "Don't let your tithes and offerings accumulate at home." Systematic, regular giving makes for spiritual growth.

C. Giving was for everyone.

Giving was not just for the rich, but rich and poor alike. In fact, in 2 Cor. 8–9, Paul tells us that the poor saints in Macedonia gave liberally out of their poverty. Here is the biblical model for giving. The church member who is able to give but does not give faithfully is a thief: he is robbing God (Mal. 3:7-12); he is robbing other Christians, for they pay the bills while he gets the blessings; moreover, he is robbing himself of blessings.

D. Giving was proportionate: "as he may prosper" (v. 2).

The tithe was the minimum standard for giving in the OT, and there is no reason why this standard should not apply to the NT Christian as well. Tithing was practiced long before the Law was given (Gen. 14:20; 28:22), so it cannot be argued that tithing is a legalistic practice.

E. Giving was carefully handled.

Paul was always careful about the handling of money. He wanted church-appointed representatives to assist him, lest anyone accuse him of stealing money for himself. It is right for a church to have a financial system that includes receipts and records. The church's financial status should always be the best possible as a testimony to the lost, and it will be, if the members are faithful to give and if the funds are carefully, prayerfully dispersed.

II. How to Help the Servants (16:5-12)

Paul outlined his future plans, trusting that the church would want to share in his ministry. He was then at Ephesus where there were both battles and blessings; Paul, in faith, looks at the blessings, not the battles!

Paul dearly loved young Timothy but knew his timidity and fears. Paul encouraged the saints to receive and assist Timothy because the youth was doing God's work. We should never despise a worker because he is not another Apostle Paul!

Apollos followed Paul at Corinth (Acts 18:24-28), and he and Paul had good fellowship. It is wonderful when successive pastors have good relationship one with another. Both Paul and Apollos were implicated in the church divisions (1:12), but they were careful to show themselves one in the work.

It is important that churches receive the Lord's servants and treat them right. It is wrong to compare one person with another; this behavior is carnal. The teaching of Scripture is clear on this point. If these servants do the work of the Lord, we should assist them as much as possible.

III. How to Strengthen the Church (16:13-24)

Paul's commands in v. 13 sound like military orders, suggesting that the church is an army and ought to act like one. "Act like adults!" he exhorts them, and how we need that exhortation today. Too often the church does not have the discipline and maturity of an army. The Corinthians were acting like babies; it was time they grew up and acted like adults.

We must love and appreciate faithful laborers in the church. Paul mentions several workers in vv. 15-19, including his beloved Priscilla and Aquila. Paul could never have done his work were it not for the assistance of many Christians, and he was glad to acknowledge his indebtedness to them.

Paul closes with his own signature (vv. 21-24). He undoubtedly dictated the letter to a secretary, then took the pen and affixed his own name. This proved that the letter was authentic and not a forgery. "Grace" was always the key word whenever he signed his name.

The words *anathema* and *maranatha* are not translated here; they are Aramaic words that mean, "accursed" and "our Lord come!" What a peculiar combination of words! "If any man does not love our Savior, let him be accursed! The Lord is coming!"

Paul does not end on a note of judgment, however; he closes with, "My love to you all!" which even included the followers of Cephas and Apollos! Even the people who were causing confusion in the assemblies! Even the man who needed to be disciplined! What an example Paul gives us here: he loved them in Christ even though he did not love their sins.

2 CORINTHIANS

A Suggested Outline of 2 Corinthians

I. Paul's Explanation of His Ministry (1–5)

    A. Suffering, but not defeated (1)

    B. Sorrowing, but not despairing (2)

    C. Spiritual, not carnal (3)

    D. Sincere, not deceitful (4)

    E. Serious, not careless (5)

II. Paul's Exhortation to the Church (6–9)

    A. Paul's ministry examined (6:1-13)

    B. Paul encourages separation from sin (6:14–7:1)

    C. Paul requests reconciliation in the Lord (7:2-16)

    D. Paul asks for co-operation in the offering (8–9)

III. Paul's Vindication of His Apostleship (10–13)

    A. Paul defends his manner (10)

    B. Paul explains his motives (11)

    C. Paul asserts his merit (12)

    D. Paul tells of his mission (13)

Note the many references in this letter to Paul's sufferings (1:3-11; 4:8-11; 6:4, 8-10; 7:5; 11:23-28; 12:7-10), and also to encouragement (1:3-6; 2:7; 7:4, 6-7, 13).

Introductory Notes to 2 Corinthians

I. Background

Review the introduction to 1 Corinthians for the background of the founding of the Corinthian church.

Paul wrote 1 Corinthians from Ephesus, where he had been ministering for three years. He sent this letter to the church by Timothy (1 Cor. 4:17), but problems in the church only grew worse. Perhaps it was young Timothy's timidity that made the believers at Corinth disobey Paul's words. At any rate, Paul then sent Titus to Corinth to make sure the church obeyed the apostolic orders Paul had given them (2 Cor. 7:13-15).

Meanwhile, the riot discussed in Acts 19:23-41 forced Paul to leave Ephesus. Paul had promised the Corinthians that he would visit them (1 Cor. 16:3-7), but circumstances were such that he was delayed along the way. He had hoped to meet Titus at Troas (2 Cor. 2:12-13), but this plan failed. As you read 2 Cor. 1–2, you feel the burden and heartache of Paul, suffering both physically and emotionally. While at Troas, Paul did some preaching, then made his way to Macedonia. He and Titus finally met, probably at Philippi (2 Cor. 7:5-6), and Titus gave Paul the good news that the majority at Corinth were behind him and would obey his word. It was this joy that prompted him to write this second letter to the Corinthians.

II. Purposes

Paul had several purposes in mind when he wrote this letter:

(1) To commend the church for disciplining the offender (1 Cor. 5), and to encourage them to forgive and receive him (2 Cor. 2:6-11).

(2) To explain why he had apparently "changed his plans" and not visited them as he had promised (1 Cor. 16:3-7, 2 Cor. 1:15-22).

(3) To answer those in the church who were questioning his apostolic authority (2 Cor. 10–12).

(4) To answer those who accused him of wrong motives (2 Cor. 4:1-2).

(5) To encourage the church to share in the offering for the Jerusalem saints (2 Cor. 8–9).

(6) To prepare them for his planned visit (2 Cor. 13).

This letter is in direct contrast to the tone of 1 Corinthians, for it is intensely personal and filled with the deep emotions of the dedicated apostle. If 1 Corinthians "takes the roof off" the church at Corinth and lets us look in, then 2 Corinthians "opens the heart" of Paul and lets us see his love and concern for the work of the Lord. In the first letter, Paul is the instructor, answering questions and setting matters right; in this second letter he is the loving pastor, the minister of Christ, pouring out his life that his spiritual children might be perfected in the faith.

No letter in the NT reveals the true character of the Christian ministry as does this one. No letter says so much about Christian giving, suffering, or spiritual triumph.

2 CORINTHIANS 1

Few chapters in the NT reveal the heart of Paul as does this one. Here we see the great apostle admitting his fears and failings as he tells of the sufferings he had endured. The problem of pain has always perplexed thinking people. "Why must the righteous suffer?" is a question that is found in Scripture from Job to Revelation. In this chapter, as Paul recounts his personal experiences, he gives us three reasons why God permits His people to suffer.

I. That We Might Comfort Others (1:1-7)

The word "comfort" is used ten times in vv. 1-7 ("consolation" in 5, 6, and 7) and literally means "to call to one's side." It is the same word Jesus used in John 14:16 for the Spirit, the Comforter (Paraclete). What a joy it is to know that God stands at our side to help whenever we go through troubles (Isa. 41:10, 13; 43:2-3). Each member of the Trinity is a comforter: the Father (2 Cor. 1:3), and the Son and Spirit (John 14:16). God is the God of all comfort, just as He is the God of all grace (1 Peter 5:10). There is comfort and grace for every situation!

But this comfort that we receive from God is not simply for our personal relief; it is shared with us that we might be able to help others. Paul went through tribulation (1:4 and 8; 2:4; 4:17; 6:4; 7:4; 8:2) that he might be able to minister to others. God prepares us for what He is preparing for us. We cannot lead others where we have not been ourselves. Paul looked upon his trials as "the sufferings of Christ" (1:5 and 4:10-11); as he states in Phil. 3:10, he was experiencing the "fellowship of His sufferings." This does not mean that we share in the sufferings of Christ to atone for our sin, since that was a ministry He alone could perform. Rather, it suggests that we suffer for His sake and for His glory, and that He suffers with us (see Acts 9:4).

The mathematics of God's mercy is wonderful! As the trials abound, the comfort of God abounds as well! Where sin abounds, so does grace (Rom. 5:20)! Paul used this word "abound" often in 2 Corinthians, so check your concordance for these references. In v. 6 Paul teaches the wonderful truth that a Christian's affliction brings a double blessing: first, to the individual believer ("effectual" means that it works in the believer; see 1 Thes. 2:13; Phil. 2:12-13), and then to others. We as Christians ought to be willing to endure trials, since we know they bring spiritual good to us personally, and blessings to others as we share God's comfort with them. The Gk. word for "partakers" in v. 7 can also mean "fellowship" or "partners." We ought to be willing "partners" with Christ in suffering since this "partnership" leads to comfort and edification.

II. That We Might Have Confidence in God Alone (1:8-11)

It takes a great soul to admit failure. Paul bares his heart here and shares with the believers the troubles he endured in Asia. He wrote this not to win their sympathy, but to teach them the lesson he learned: trust God alone. We are not sure just what trouble Paul is referring to; probably it involved the riot in Ephesus (cf. Acts 19:23-41 and 1 Cor. 15:32) as well as the sad news of the troubles in the Corinthian church. In 7:5 he indicates that there were troubles without and within; so perhaps it was both physical weakness and danger as well as spiritual concern for the infant church at Corinth. Whatever these troubles were, they were sufficient to crush Paul and cause him to pass sentence on his life! He despaired even of life itself! (How comforting to know that even the great saints of God are still made of clay!) But Paul learned the lesson God had for him: he would not trust himself, but God alone. Note the three tenses of the believer's deliverance in v. 10, and compare Titus 2:11-15. However, Paul is quick to acknowledge the helpful prayer of his friends (v. 11). He states that his deliverance in answer to prayer will cause many to praise God and give Him the glory He deserves.

We have come a long way in our Christian lives when we learn to put faith in God alone and not in self, circumstances, or men. Abraham took Lot with him, and Lot left for Sodom. Moses insisted on Aaron's help, and Aaron led the people into sin. David's choice advisers deserted him. Even the disciples forsook Christ and fled! The believer who fears the Lord and lives to please Him enjoys peace and confidence even in the midst of trouble. What a lesson to learn!

III. That We Might Claim the Promises of God (1:12-24)

The connection between this passage about Paul's plans and the general topic of suffering is easy to see; but by understanding the background, we can follow Paul's thinking. Paul had promised to visit Corinth, first when he made his way to Macedonia, and then a second time as he headed to Jerusalem with the special offering. This is the "double blessing" mentioned in v. 15 ("second benefit"). But circumstances forced him to change his plans, and his enemies at Corinth accused him of being fickle and undependable. "You cannot trust Paul's letters!" they said. "All the same he claims these letters are God's message to us!"

Paul answered these charges by showing that he was sincere in promising them two visits, and that his motives were pure and godly. He assured them that his letters were honest and trustworthy, as they will discover when Christ returns to judge (vv. 12-14). It was Paul's confidence in their love and understanding (vv. 15-16) that led him to change his plans. One paraphrase puts it: "It was because I was so sure of your understanding and trust that I planned to stop and see you on my way to Macedonia" (TLB). Where there are love and confidence, there should never be doubt or questions about motives. Paul was not like the men of the world who say "Yes" when they mean "No." It is here that Paul teaches us a lasting lesson: the Word of God is trustworthy, and all the promises of God find their "Yes" in Jesus Christ. One way to translate v. 20 is, "All the promises of God find their yes in Christ, and through Him we say amen." In other words, the promises of God are true in Christ—He fulfills them, and He gives us the faith to claim them.

How grateful we ought to be for the unchanging Word of God! Often it takes trouble and trial in our lives before we claim and trust the promises of God. We make plans, but God overrules them. We make promises and are not always able to keep them. But in Christ, all the promises of God's Word find their fulfillment, and in Him we have the power to claim these promises for ourselves and our situation.

In the closing verses (vv. 21-24), Paul reminds the believers that his Christian life came from God. He was established in Christ by the Spirit, anointed and sealed, and had been given the earnest (down payment) of the Spirit. How could he be insincere when the Spirit was working in his life? The sealing of the Spirit refers to the work of the Spirit in marking us for eternal salvation. Once we have trusted Christ, we are sealed and secure in Him (Eph. 1:13-14; 4:30). The "earnest" refers to the blessings of the Spirit in our lives today which are but a "down payment" of the eternal blessings we will enjoy in glory (see Rom. 8:9, 14, 23; Eph. 1:14).

Finally, Paul states that he was glad God changed the planned trip, because it would have been necessary for him to rebuke them at that time had he visited them. Instead of sailing from Ephesus to Corinth, he had traveled to Troas and Philippi, and thus had given the church more time to straighten things out. A visit at that time would have been painful; but, now that matters had been attended to (2:6-11), he could visit them in joy and not in grief.

2 CORINTHIANS 2

In this chapter, Paul continues his explanation of the changed plans (1:15ff) and shows his love and concern for the church and its spiritual needs.

I. Paul's Tears over the Church (2:1-4)

In 11:23-28, Paul lists the many trials he had endured for Christ's sake, and he names as the greatest burden "the care of all the churches" (v. 28). A true shepherd, Paul had these infant churches on his heart and on his shoulders, like the High Priest of Israel (Ex. 28:12-21). Tears are an important part of a spiritual ministry. Jesus wept; Paul ministered with tears (Acts 20:19 and 31); and Ps. 126:5-6 states that there will be no harvest apart from tears.

Paul did not want to visit the church as a stern father, but as a loving friend. The church should have brought joy to his heart, not sorrow. If he had made them sorry, how could they in turn make him glad? He wanted to give them time to make matters right in the church; then he would visit them and their fellowship would be joyful. When he wrote to them, he wrote with a pen dipped in tears. He even wept over that letter. (v. 4). (He may be referring to 1 Corinthians, or to an even sterner letter that we do not have.)

In chapter 1, Paul's theme was abundant comfort; here it is abundant love. "Love never fails" (1 Cor. 13:8). Where there is love, there is always the burden to see others enjoy the very best. How many times pastors weep over wayward Christians. Yet God honored Paul's tears and worked in the church so that sin was put away.

II. Paul's Testimony to the Offender (2:5-11)

This section takes us back to 1 Cor. 5, where Paul had admonished the church to discipline the man who was living in open sin. Here

Paul states that the offender did not cause Paul alone trouble and sorrow: he had brought trouble to the whole church! He had instructed them to call the church together and dismiss this man from the fellowship. This act of discipline would then bring him to a place of sorrow and repentance. Well, they had done this, but then they went to the opposite extreme! The man had evidenced sorrow for sin, but the church was not willing to receive him back after his confession!

"Forgive him and take him back," says the apostle. "If you don't, Satan will overburden him with too much sorrow." How often Christians confess their sins and yet fail to believe that God will forgive and forget. There is an abnormal sorrow that is not really true repentance; it is remorse, the sorrow of the world. Peter showed repentance; his was a godly sorrow that led him back to Christ. Judas showed remorse; his was a hopeless sorrow, a sorrow of the world, that led him away from Christ into suicide. Satan wants us to believe that we cannot be forgiven (see Zech. 3:1-5); yet read Rom. 8:31-39. If Satan can accuse us of sin and discourage us with our past failures, he will rob us of our joy and usefulness to Christ.

If God forgives a person of sin, we must forgive the person, too (Eph. 4:32).

III. Paul's Triumph in Christ (2:12-17)

Paul picks up his account of the trip from Ephesus to Philippi. What had started out as trouble ended up as triumph! How often this happens in the Christian life. The women came to the tomb that Easter morning burdened with disappointment, only to find that a great victory had been won. Paul came to Troas and could not find Titus, but he did find a "tremendous opportunity" to preach the Gospel (Rom. 8:28). In every place of trial there is always an open door of opportunity. Joseph turned trials into triumph in Egypt; Daniel did in Babylon; Paul did at Troas.

But service is no substitute for peace, and Paul longed to see Titus and get word about the church at Corinth. He left Troas and made his way to Macedonia (probably Philippi), bypassing Corinth completely. At Philippi he met Titus and received the good news that the offender had been disciplined, the majority of the church was behind Paul, and things were looking better. This so rejoiced Paul that he broke into a song of praise.

The picture in vv. 14-17 was familiar to every Roman but is not to twentieth-century Christians. Whenever a victorious general returned home from battle, Rome gave him a public parade, not unlike our modern ticker-tape parades. This parade was filled with pomp and glory, and a great deal of incense was burned in honor of the hero. In the parade soldiers and officers would enjoy glory and praise, but slaves and captives also present would end up in the arena to die fighting the wild beasts. As the victors smelled the incense, they inhaled an aroma of life and joy; but to the captives, the incense was a reminder of their coming death.

In the "Christian parade" Paul describes, Jesus Christ is the Victor. Through His death on the cross, He has conquered every foe. We Christians ride in that procession with Him, sharing His victory (1 Cor. 15:57). The Christian, however, is the incense (sweet savor of Christ) in this procession as the Spirit spreads the knowledge of Christ in and through our lives. This savor, or perfume, means life to other believers, but to the unbeliever headed for eternal condemnation, it means death. Joseph was a savor of death to the baker, but a savor of life to the butler (Gen. 40).

Paul's description is a beautiful and challenging picture. What a tremendous responsibility it is to introduce people to life, or to have them reject Christ and go off to death! Being a Christian is a serious responsibility, for our lives are leading people either to heaven or hell. No wonder Paul exclaims, "Who is sufficient for these things?" (v. 16). How can a Christian possess all he needs to be the best Christian possible, the best witness, the best soldier? Paul answers the question in 3:5—"Our sufficiency is of God." Paul uses this word "sufficient" several times in this letter. Christ is sufficient for our spiritual needs (3:4-6), our material needs (9:8), and our physical needs (12:7-10).

In v. 17, Paul returns to the accusation that his word could not be trusted. Unfortunately, there are, even today, religious leaders who "make merchandise" of (v. 17—corrupt) the Word of God, who are insincere and deceptive. The word "corrupt" has the idea of "peddling" the Gospel, using the ministry only as a means of making a living rather than building the church of Jesus Christ. A form of this Gk. word was used to describe an innkeeper or peddler, and carries the idea of doing any kind of business just to make a profit. Paul's ministry was not a business; it was a burden. He was not serving men; he was serving Christ. He was sincere in method, message, and motive. He realized that God's eye was upon him and that Christ's glory was at stake.

In these two chapters we have seen that Paul's ministry was full of suffering and sorrow, yet he experienced triumph and joy in Christ. Let us remember that "our sufficiency is of God" (v. 5).

2 CORINTHIANS 3

This chapter is a key one, for it shows the relationship between the OT message of Law and the NT ministry of the Gospel of God's grace. It seems that the Jewish faction at Corinth was saying that Paul was not a true apostle because he did not have letters of commendation from the church at Jerusalem. Apparently some teachers had arrived at Corinth with such letters, and this lack of credentials seemed to discredit Paul. The apostle used this accusation as an opportunity to contrast the Gospel of grace with the Law of Moses.

I. Written on Hearts, Not Stones (3:1-3)

"I don't need letters of recommendation!" says Paul. "You Christians at Corinth are my letters, written on hearts, not on stones!" "By their fruits you will know them" (Matt. 7:20, NKJV). A person's life and ministry may be seen in his or her work. Paul pictures himself as God's secretary, writing the Word into the lives of God's people. What an amazing truth: every Christian is an epistle of Christ being read by all men!

> You are writing a Gospel, a chapter each day,
> By the deeds that you do and the words that you say.
> Men read what you write, whether faithful or true.
> Just what is the Gospel according to you?

Moses wrote God's Law on stones, but in this age, God writes His Word on our hearts (Heb. 10:16-17). The Law was an external matter; grace dwells internally, in the heart. But Paul did not write even with ink, for that would fade; he wrote permanently with the Spirit of God. The Law, written on stone, held in a man's hand, could never change his life. But the Spirit of God can use the Word to change lives and make them like Jesus. The NT ministry, then, is a spiritual ministry, as the Spirit writes the Word on men's hearts.

II. Bringing Life, Not Death (3:4-6)

When Paul says, "The letter kills," he is not talking about the "letter" of God's Word as opposed to its "spirit." Often we hear confused people say, "It is wrong to follow the letter of the Bible; we must follow the spirit of it." Keep in mind that by "the letter," Paul means the OT law. In this chapter, He uses different phrases when referring to the OT law: the letter (v. 6); ministry of death (v. 7); ministry of condemnation (v. 9).

The Law was never given to impart life; it was definitely a ministry of death. Paul was a minister of the New Covenant, not the Old Covenant of works and death. No man was ever saved through the Law! Yet there were teachers at Corinth telling the people to obey the Law and reject Paul's Gospel of grace. Trace the word "life" in John's Gospel, for example, and you will see that the NT ministry is one of life through the Holy Spirit.

III. Lasting Glory, Not Fading Glory (3:7-13)

Certainly there was glory to the OT ministry. Glory filled the temple; the glory of God hovered over the people in the wilderness. The temple and its ceremonies, and the very giving of the Law to Moses, all had glory attached to them. But it was a fading glory, not a lasting glory. Paul cites the experience of Moses from Ex. 34:29-35. Moses had been in God's presence, and His glory was reflected on his face. But Moses knew that this glory would fade, so he wore a veil over his face whenever talking to the people, lest they see the glory fade and lose confidence in his ministry. (It is commonly taught, but in error, that Moses wore the veil to avoid frightening the people. Note v. 13, "And not as Moses did, who put a veil over his face so no one could see the glory fade away" (TLB). God never meant for the glory of the Old Covenant to remain; it was to fade away before the abounding glory of the Gospel. If the ministry of condemnation (the Law) was glorious, then the ministry of righteousness (the Gospel) is even more glorious! Paul needs no veil; he has nothing to hide. The glory of the Gospel is there!

IV. Unveiled, Not Veiled (3:14-16)

Paul makes a spiritual application of Moses' veil. He states that there is still a veil over the hearts of the Jews when they read the OT, and this veil keeps them from seeing Christ. The OT will always be a locked book to the heart that knows not Christ. Jesus removed that veil when He rent the veil of the temple and fulfilled the OT types and prophecies. Yet Israel does not recognize that the ministry of the Law is temporary; it is holding on to a ministry that was never meant to last, a ministry with fading glory. There is a two-fold blindness upon Israel: a blindness that affects persons, in that they cannot recognize Christ as revealed in the OT, and a judicial blindness whereby God has blinded Israel as a nation (Rom.11:25). Satan blinds the minds of all sinners, hiding from them the glorious Gospel of Christ (2 Cor. 4:4).

But when the heart turns to Christ, that veil is taken away. Moses removed his veil when he went up to the mount to see God, and any Jew who turns honestly to the Lord will have his spiritual veil removed and will see Christ and receive Him as Savior. The NT ministry is one that points to Christ in the Word of God, in both the OT and the NT. We have nothing to hide, nothing to veil; the glory will last forever and will grow continually brighter.

V. Liberty, Not Bondage (3:17-18)

Verse 17 is grossly misused and quoted to excuse all kinds of unspiritual practices. "The Lord is that Spirit"; when sinners turn to Christ, it is through the ministry of the Spirit. And the Spirit gives liberty from spiritual bondage. The Old Covenant was a covenant of works and bondage (Acts 15:10). But the New Covenant is a ministry of glorious liberty in Christ (Gal. 5:1ff). This liberty is not license; it is freedom from fear, sin, the world, and legalistic religious practices. Every Christian is like Moses: with an unveiled face, we can come into the presence of God and enjoy His glory — yes, receive that glory and become more like Christ!

In v. 18, Paul illustrates the meaning of sanctification and growing in grace. He compares the Word of God to a mirror ("glass" — James 1:23-25). When the people of God look into the Word of God and see the glory of God, the Spirit of God transforms them to be like the Son of God (Rom. 8:29). "Changed" in this verse is the same as the Gk. word for "transformed" in Rom. 12:2 and "transfigured" in Matt. 17:2, and explains how we have our minds renewed in Christ. The Christian is not in bondage and fear; we can go into the very presence of God and enjoy His glory and grace. We do not have to wait for Christ to return to become like Him; we can daily grow "from glory to glory" (v. 18).

Truly our position in Christ is a glorious one! The ministry of grace is far superior to Judaism or any other religion, even though the NT Christian has none of the ceremonies or visible trappings that belonged to the Law. Ours is a glorious ministry, and its glory will never fade.

2 CORINTHIANS 4

Some at Corinth were accusing Paul of being insincere in his ministry. "Paul is in it for what he can get out of it!" was their accusation. In this chapter, Paul gives the evidence that proves his ministry is sincere.

I. His Determination (4:1)

Why would Paul keep on preaching, with all the dangers and toils involved, if he were not sincere? A man with lesser motives, or a less spiritual view of the ministry, would have given up long ago. Paul looked upon his ministry as a stewardship: God gave it to him, and God also gave him strength to continue and not faint. The Gospel was too glorious for Paul to give up! It was too great a privilege for him to be a minister of the Gospel to risk falling by the wayside.

II. His Honesty (4:2-4)

There are some things Paul refused to do. He refused to use underhanded, deceitful practices to gain followers. False teachers were doing these very things. "We do not try to trick people into believing," is the way TLB puts it. Paul would not walk in craftiness or use the Word deceitfully, that is, "adulterating the Word of God." We handle the Bible deceitfully by mixing philosophy and error with God's truth in order to win human approval. Not so with Paul. His ministry was honest. He used the Word in an open, sincere way and encouraged people to search the Scriptures for themselves (see Acts 17:11).

If the Gospel is hidden, it should never be the fault of the teacher. Satan blinds the minds of sinners because he does not want them to see Christ's glory. Multitudes who today refuse to look upon His face in salvation will some day try to hide from His face (Rev. 6:15-17). The sinner's mind is blinded and ignorant

(Eph. 4:17-19), and only the light of the Word can bring the knowledge of salvation. But we must never twist or corrupt the Word of God to attempt to win converts. We must handle the Word with a good conscience toward men and God.

III. His Humility (4:5-7)

If Paul wanted to get a following for himself and make money, then he should have preached himself, not Christ. Yet he would not preach himself; he sought only to honor Christ. Read again 1 Cor. 3:1-9 to see how Paul presents himself as a servant of God and a slave for Jesus' sake. No, there can be no light if we exalt men; God alone can cause the light to shine out of the darkness.

Here Paul refers us back to Gen. 1:1-5 where God brought light at creation and from this brought life and blessing. The lost sinner's heart is like that original earth: formless and empty and dark. The Spirit broods over the heart. The Word comes and brings light — the light of the glorious Gospel. The sinner then becomes a new creation, and starts to bring forth fruit for the glory of God.

"Yes, I have a treasure," Paul admits, "but it is in an earthen vessel. I don't want to be seen; I'm just the vessel. The most important thing is that Christ is seen and that Christ gets the glory." It is too bad when Christian workers make the vessel more important than the treasure of the Gospel.

IV. His Suffering (4:8-10)

If Paul were out for personal gain, as they said, then why did he suffer so much? The man who compromises the Word of God will not suffer; men will welcome him and honor him. But people were abusing Paul, rejecting him, and making life difficult for him. They were treating him the way men treated Christ.

Paul's willingness to suffer for Christ is one of the greatest proofs of his sincerity as a servant of God. Read these verses in a modern translation to get the vigor of their message.

V. His Unselfishness (4:11-15)

Paul was willing to face suffering and death for Jesus' sake and for the sake of the churches. The experiences that brought death to him meant life for the believers as he suffered to bring the Word to them. The false teachers knew nothing of suffering or sacrifice. All through this letter, Paul points to his scars as the credentials of his ministry. In Gal. 6:17 he said, "I bear in my body the marks [brands] of the Lord Jesus!"

"All things are for your sakes!" What an unselfish spirit! Paul was willing to go anywhere, willing to endure anything, if it brought glory to God and good to the churches. He had the Spirit of faith; he knew that his sufferings would mean blessings.

VI. His Faith (4:16-19)

These verses bring wonderful assurance to the believer in times of suffering. Though the outward man is perishing day by day, the inward man, the spiritual man, is being renewed day by day (see 3:18). Paul is here weighing his sufferings on God's scales. He discovers that his sufferings are light when compared to the weight of glory God has stored up for him. His days and years of trial are nothing compared to the eternity of bliss that awaits him. How important it is for us to live "with eternity's values in view." Life takes on new meaning when we see things through God's eyes.

Verse 18 is a paradox to the unbeliever, but a precious truth to the Christian. We live by faith, not by sight. It is faith that enables the Christian to see things that cannot be seen (Heb. 11:1-3); this faith comes from the Word of God (Rom. 10:17). The things that the world lives and dies for are temporal, passing; the things of the Lord last forever. The world thinks we are crazy because we dare to believe God's Word and live according to His will. We pass up the "things" that men covet because our hearts are set on higher values.

It is important that we have a sincere Christian life and ministry. Our motives must be pure. Our methods must be scriptural. We must be true to the Word of God. Paul had this kind of a ministry, and so should we.

2 CORINTHIANS 5

In this chapter, Paul is still discussing his ministry, answering the accusations of his enemies. He points out that his ministry is serious, not careless; that he works from honest motives and not fleshly desires. Paul explains four motives that control his life and his ministry.

I. His Confidence of Heaven (5:1-8)

In the previous chapter, Paul mentioned his determination to serve Christ in spite of suffering and even death. He lived by faith, not by sight. But this faith was not blind trust; it was a certain confidence in the Word of God. When you know where you are going, no storm can frighten you or enemy defeat you. The outward man might be perishing (4:16), but what difference did that make? Paul knew that glory lay on the other side.

The "building" Paul is talking about here is not the home Christ is preparing for believers (John 14:1ff); it is the glorified body that will be ours when Christ returns (Phil. 3:21; 1 Cor. 15:50ff.). Our earthly house is but a tent (tabernacle) that will one day be taken down (dissolved). But God has a glorified body for us! However, our desire as Christians is not to have this earthly body taken down in death, but to have it "clothed upon" and transformed when Jesus comes. How do we know we have this glorious future? We have the earnest of the Spirit (v. 5), that "eternal down payment" that assures us the rest of the promised blessing will be ours. We are today "at home in the body but absent from the Lord." Our yearning is to be "at home with the Lord" and living in glorified bodies that will never change. See Phil. 1:19-24.

II. His Concern to Please Christ (5:9-13)

But Paul is not selfish; his Christian service is motivated by more than a hope for the future. He seeks to please Christ and be acceptable to Him right now. Paul wanted to be found "well-pleasing" to Christ (v. 9). He had a healthy fear of the Lord ("terror" in v. 11), for he knew that all believers will one day be judged at Christ's Judgment Seat (see 1 Cor. 3:10-15; Rom. 14:7-13). Knowing that his works would some day be revealed and tested, Paul wanted to live the kind of life that pleased and honored Christ.

The Gk. word for "appear" in v. 10 means more than "stand" or "show up." It carries the idea of being revealed; "for we shall all be shown as we are" is the meaning. There will be no pretending at that judgment; our character and works will be revealed as they are, and the suitable rewards will be given. But the true servant of God is careful even today to have an open life, manifest both to God and men (v. 11). How important it is that we let God do the judging, for He sees the heart. The Corinthians were "glorying in appearance" (v. 12) as they boasted about various preachers and criticized Paul. Keep in mind that "results" are not the only test of a worker's life and service. The motives of the heart are very important.

III. His Constraint of Love (5:14-17)

Paul had been accused of being mad (see Acts 26:24) since he went to such extremes to win men to Christ. But the controlling power of his life was the love of Christ. This does not mean Paul's love for Christ, although certainly that was there. It means rather the love Christ had for Paul. The apostle was so overwhelmed by Jesus' love for him that to serve and honor Christ became the controlling motive of his life. He describes in vv. 14-17 this love that led Christ to the cross to die for sinners. Why did He die? That we might live *through* Him (1 John 4:9); that we might live *with* Him (1 Thes. 5:10); and that we might live *for* Him (2 Cor. 5:15). There can be no selfishness in the heart of the Christian who understands the love of Christ.

One of the problems at Corinth was that believers were judging after the flesh (1 Cor. 4:1-7). They were comparing Paul with other teachers and using carnal judgment instead of spiritual discernment. They were forgetting that the Christian life is a new creation with new values and motives. To judge Christ after the flesh is wrong; that is, to look upon Him (as the world does) as only a great teacher or example. Paul, as an unconverted Jewish rabbi, probably did look upon Christ after the flesh. But when he saw the glorified Christ, Paul changed his point of view. We must have a spiritual evaluation based on the Word of God. Other teachers said Paul was beside himself; they were judging after the flesh and proving that they lacked that love of Christ as the controlling force of their lives.

IV. His Commission from God (5:18-21)

We have seen three motives that controlled Paul's life and ministry: his confidence of heaven, his concern to please Christ, and his constraint of love. There was a fourth motive: Paul's commission from God. Paul was an an ambassador for Christ! His message was one of peace: God had paid the price for sin; God was not at war with sinners; sinners could now believe and be saved. What a tremendous message! Consider some facts about ambassadors.

(1) Ambassadors are chosen, and Christ had chosen Paul to be

His representative. Paul did not represent himself (see 4:5) but Christ. His message was the Gospel Christ had committed to his trust (1 Thes. 2:4). His aim was to please Christ and be faithful to the task given to him.

(2) Ambassadors are protected. An ambassador must be a citizen of the nation that he represents, and Paul (as is every Christian) was a citizen of heaven (see Phil. 3:20 where "conversation" is equated with "citizenship.") The nation supplies their ambassadors' every need and stands ready to protect them. Likewise Christ supplied Paul's every need and stood with him in every crisis.

(3) Ambassadors are held accountable. Ambassadors represent their countries and say what they are instructed to say. They know that they must one day give an account of their work.

(4) Ambassadors are called home before war is declared. God has not yet declared war on this wicked world, but one day He will. There is a coming day of wrath (1 Thes. 1:10) that will judge the wicked, but Christians will be called home before that day comes (1 Thes. 5:1-10). The church, God's ambassadors, will not go through the Tribulation.

The message of the church today is one of reconciliation: God in Christ on the cross has reconciled the world to himself and is willing to save all who will trust His Son. Ours is not a message of social reform (although the Gospel reforms lives, Titus 2:11-15); ours is a message of spiritual regeneration. We represent Christ as we invite the lost to receive Him. What a privilege—what a responsibility!

All believers are ambassadors, whether we accept the commission or not. "As the Father has sent me, also I send you," said Christ (John 20:21, NKJV). Let us make sure that our message, methods, and motives are right, so that our work might be lasting and might stand the test of fire when we stand before Him.

2 CORINTHIANS 6

Chapters 6–9 are composed of a series of loving exhortations to the Christians at Corinth. In 6:1-13, Paul exhorts them to examine his life and ministry and to enlarge their hearts to make room for him. Second Corinthians 6:14–7:1 (the chapter division here is unfortunate) is a call to separation, while in 7:2-16 is a plea for reconciliation. Chapters 8–9 deal with the offering Paul was taking for the poor saints of Judea, and he appeals for the Corinthians' cooperation. We note, then, two appeals here in chapter 6.

I. An Appeal for Examination (6:1-13)

Paul has been defending his life and ministry in the first five chapters. His enemies at Corinth had accused him of wrong methods and motives, and he successfully answered them. His final statement in chapter 5 deals with his ministry of reconciliation, so it is just one step forward for him to appeal to the Corinthians to be reconciled to him and to receive God's grace. He not only beseeches the sinners in 5:20, but he beseeches the saints in 6:1. How tragic it is when churches and Christians receive God's grace in vain. The Corinthians were babes in Christ, immature saints, because they failed to grow in grace and knowledge. They had the greatest pastor available — Paul — and yet they failed to benefit from his ministry!

Paul had been careful to do nothing that would make others stumble or would in any way discredit the ministry. In vv. 3-10, Paul gives several arguments to prove that his ministry was blameless.

A. The battles he waged (vv. 3-5).

"Patience" here means "endurance." It is not a picture of the Christian in a rocking chair, doing nothing, but rather of the soldier in battle, pressing on to victory in spite of opposition. The battles Paul fought in obedience to Christ were proof of his sincere, unselfish ministry. This distress came, not because he was disobedient and needed chastening, but because he was obedient and a threat to Satan. Stripes refer to the beatings Paul endured; tumults, the mobs he faced; "labors" reminds us of his toil day and night to support himself and his companions; "watchings" describes his sleepless nights of prayer and ministry of the Word; "fastings" indicates that he often went without food. No counterfeit minister would have endured so much!

B. The weapons he used (vv. 6-7).

Paul's character and conduct were always Christ-like. He had clean hands and a clean conscience, and his love for the saints was honest, not "put on." He used the Word of God and prayer as weapons to defeat Satan. Dishonest ministers would have used carnal methods to promote their work.

491

C. The reputation he gained (vv. 8-10).

We have here a series of paradoxes, or seemingly contradictory statements. Certainly the Christian servant is looked upon differently by the saints and the sinners. The sinners see him in one light, the saints in another, just as men look at Jesus with differing opinions. What a thrilling description is v. 10 of the Christian who is sold out to Christ!

Paul closed this appeal by reminding them of his love. His heart was wide open with love, but their hearts had been narrowed (straitened). He appealed to them as his children to receive him.

II. An Appeal for Separation (6:13–7:1)

The problems in the Corinthian church were spiritual: the members were living like worldly people and not like Christians. There was compromise with sin. Paul presents two major arguments for separation from the world.

A. The argument from principle (vv. 13-16).

It is a basic principle of life that opposites cannot fellowship together. The "unequal yoke" takes us back to Moses' admonition in Lev. 19:19. These Corinthians were yoking themselves with unbelievers in marriage, business life, and other ways, and were losing their testimonies for Christ. After all, if Christians live like the world, how can they witness to the world?

Note the series of contrasts here: righteousness/unrighteousness; light/darkness; Christ/Belial (an OT name for Satan); believer/unbeliever (infidel); temple of God/idols. The attitude of too many Christians today is that the church should court and please the world in order to try to win it. Nothing could be further from the truth! There must be separation from sin. This does not mean isolation, retreating from the world; it does mean keeping ourselves from the defilement of the world. It is fine for the ship to be in the water, but when water gets into the ship, look out! Paul cites Lev. 26:11-12 to show that God lives and walks in the believer, so that his relationship to the world affects his fellowship with God.

B. The argument from promise (vv. 17-18).

God promises to bless those who keep themselves pure. Worldliness is subtle; it creeps in gradually. This downhill progression begins in friendship with the world (James 4:4); then love for the world (1 John 2:15-17); then conformity to the world (Rom. 12:1-2). But God promises to bless those who will separate themselves unto Him (Isa. 52:11). The compromising Christian loses the enjoyment of God's love and a deeper fellowship in the Spirit.

Chapter 7 begins with the verse that should end chapter 6. This verse summarizes in a compact way what Paul has to say about personal holiness.

(1) Two motives for separation from the world: love for God ("dearly beloved") and the fear of God. Both conditions must operate in our lives. Just as the loving wife keeps herself pure because she loves her husband, so the Christian keeps his life clean because he loves Christ. But also necessary is that healthy fear of God, lest He should have to discipline us to teach us obedience.

(2) Two responsibilities: we must cleanse ourselves (this is negative) and perfect holiness (this is positive). It is good to ask God to cleanse us (Ps. 51:2, 7), and His promise in 1 John 1:9 affords full cleansing. But we must also cleanse ourselves by putting out of our lives all that displeases Him. "Wash yourselves, make yourselves clean!" says Isa. 1:16, (NKJV). We should not expect God to remove things that we ourselves must deal with. "If your hand makes you sin, cut it off!" (cf. Matt. 6:30) Then we can grow in holiness through the Spirit.

(3) Two kinds of sin: filthiness of the flesh and of the spirit. There are sins of action as well as of attitude. The prodigal son was guilty of sins of the flesh, but his elder brother committed sins of the spirit. See Ps. 51:17.

Separation is the negative; perfecting holiness is the positive. How sad it is to see churches and Christians who are separated from sin, but who have never grown in personal holiness and developed the fruits of the Spirit. The Pharisees were separated from sin, but there was an absence of love and true obedience.

2 CORINTHIANS 7

In 1:12-13, Paul began to tell the Corinthians of his experience with Titus in Macedonia, and in this chapter he completes the account. Just as the word "comfort" appeared often in chapters 1–2, so it reappears here (vv. 4-7, 13). The appeal in this chapter is for the Corinthians to be reconciled to Paul. They had been critical and disobedient, but now it was time to receive him and fellowship with him again, particularly in light of his coming visit. In the early part of his letter, Paul told of the trials he went through when he left Ephesus, waited for Titus, and worried about the situation at Corinth. Now he explains how God comforted him and gave him joy. Three comforts are mentioned.

I. The Comfort of the Arrival of Titus (7:1-6)

"Receive us" literally means "Make room for us in your hearts" (note 6:11-12). Paul again reminds them of his clean life and honest ministry; he hastens to assure them that his writing in this way was not to condemn them. How could he condemn those who were in his heart and such a vital part of his life? It is assuring to us today to see that Paul knew the meaning of distress and disappointment (v. 5). Where was Titus? What was the situation like in Corinth? Would the church last at Ephesus? All these questions and many more crowded into Paul's mind as he traveled to Macedonia.

But the arrival of Titus was a source of great comfort to Paul. He admits he was "cast down" (downcast—v. 6), but that the arrival of his friend brought him great relief. This is the way Christians ought to help one another. We ought to bear one another's burdens (Gal. 6:2); encourage one another (Heb. 10:25); minister to one another (1 Peter 4:10-11). Christ sent the disciples out two by two, knowing that "it is not good for a man to be alone" (cf. Gen 2:18) even in Christian service. Lonely Christians are often defeated Christians. Ecclesiastes 4:9-12 states that "two are better than one." What a privilege and responsibility it is for Christians to encourage one another! When Elijah thought he was the only one faithful to God, he began to backslide. Jonah ministered alone and developed a bitter spirit.

II. The Comfort of the Corinthians' Obedience (7:7-12)

"As cold waters to a thirsty soul, so is good news from a far country" (Prov. 25:25). It was a comfort to see Titus again (see Acts 28:15), but an even greater comfort to hear the good news that Paul's stern letter had brought results. Verse 7 lists the results: they had an earnest desire to see Paul again; they had mourned over their sin; they had rekindled their love for Paul; they had repented and dealt with the offender (v. 8). Read 1 Cor. 5 for Paul's commands for disciplining the fornicator in the church. In

v. 11, Paul indicated several of their other reactions: they were full of care, or concern, to obey Paul; they sought to clear themselves with men and God; they showed indignation at the sin, instead of being puffed up (see 1 Cor. 5:2); they feared lest God would deal with them; and they sought to obey God with strong determination. "Revenge" in v. 11 does not carry with it any idea of personal vindictiveness. It indicates that the offender was punished adequately.

Paul teaches here the important doctrine of repentance. He states that there is a vast difference between repentance and regret. Repentance is from God and is a sorrow that draws people closer to God and brings them to a place of confessing and forsaking sin. Regret is from the world; its drives people away from God and into the hand of Satan. For example, Peter showed repentance and was forgiven; Judas showed regret and took his own life. Godly sorrow is good; it leads to life. But the sorrow of the world leads to death. Some people commit suicide because they know nothing of true repentance and the gracious forgiveness that God shares with those who call upon Him in faith.

In v. 12, Paul indicates that he had written that stern letter (about which even he had been temporarily sorry, v. 8) to prove his love for them. It was not simply to correct the offender, or to protect the one against whom this man had sinned, but to prove Paul's care and concern for them. Spiritual workers who shun correction and avoid facing facts do not sincerely love their people or their Lord. Paul was anxious that the believers there suffer no loss spiritually (damage, v. 9); his sharp rebuke was from a heart of love, for their good and God's glory.

III. The Comfort of Their Reception of Titus (7:13-16)

Titus was overjoyed when he met Paul, and this joy was due to the warm reception he had received at Corinth. The church had not been so gracious to Timothy (1 Cor. 4:17), otherwise Titus would never have been sent. Note 1 Cor. 16:10-11.

Paul had boasted to Titus about the Corinthian church, and now his "godly boasting" had proved true. How thrilled Paul was at the love the Corinthians had shown to his co-worker. To receive Titus so warmly, Paul believed, was the same as receiving him. Paul knew that his next visit to Corinth would be an enjoyable one.

The Corinthians had received Titus with "fear and trembling."

This is because they had received God's Word from Paul and were willing to obey it. God wants us to tremble at His Word (Isa. 66:2). Oddly enough, Paul's first ministry at Corinth was one performed in fear and trembling (1 Cor. 2:3). They respected Titus as God's servant and received his leadership as from the Lord (see 1 Thes. 2:13 and 5:12-15). "Obey them that have the [spiritual] rule over you," is the command of Heb. 13:17. The way we treat God's faithful servants is the way we treat Christ, for His servants represent Him (2 Cor. 5:20; John 13:20).

It is interesting to read through the Bible and note that God's servants rejoice when God's people are obedient and are burdened when God's people disobey. Moses often felt like giving up because the people were rebellious. Jeremiah wept bitterly over the hardness of Israel. Jesus Himself wept because the Jews were ignorant of the day of their visitation. Paul's ministry was one of tears (Acts 20:19, 31). God's servants are human; they have the treasure "in earthen vessels" (2 Cor. 4:7) and know the disappointments and discouragements that life can bring. How important it is for us to "remember them which have the rule over you" (Heb. 13:7), "obey them that have the rule over you" (Heb. 13:17), and "salute [i.e., greet in love] all them that have the rule over you" (Heb. 13:24).

Having now replied to his critics and defended his ministry, and having been assured of the love of the church, Paul moves to a plea for the missionary offering for the poor saints of Judea. It is dangerous to take offerings from Christians who are not right spiritually. We do them harm, and we do the cause of Christ harm. Paul dealt first with the Corinthians' spiritual needs, and then he reminded them of their promise to help in the missionary relief collection.

2 CORINTHIANS 8

Chapters 8 and 9 deal with the missionary offering Paul was receiving for the believers in Judea (1 Cor. 16:1-3 and Romans 15:25-28). In the early days of the church (Acts 2–10), these Jewish believers had given up everything and had "all things common" (Acts 4:32-37). It was a foretaste of the kingdom God promised to Israel. But when Israel was set aside and the church brought onto the scene, this "Christian communism" died away, leaving these saints in great need. It was to them Paul was taking this offering. While these chapters focus primarily on a special missionary relief offering, they help us grasp some of the principles and promises of Christian giving.

I. Gifts Should Be Brought to the Church (8:1)

In chapter 8 are the same directions Paul gave in 1 Cor. 16:2, but they had not yet been obeyed. On the first day of the week (the Lord's Day), the believers (the Lord's people) were to bring their offerings (the Lord's tithes and offerings) to the church meeting (the Lord's house). The believer's first responsibility is to his own local church. Furthermore, since this offering was to be a witness to the Jews from the Gentile churches, it was important that each congregation be represented.

Spiritual giving is biblical giving. If Christians do not bring tithes and offerings to the local church, then their hearts are not in the ministry of the local church (Matt. 6:21). Individual giving other than to the local church is certainly allowed, for Paul received help from many individuals (2 Tim. 1:16-18, and see the many names in Romans 16); but our first obligation is to the church where we fellowship and serve.

II. Gifts Should Come from the Heart (8:2-9)

Christian giving does not depend on material circumstances so much as spiritual convictions. The believers in Macedonia (v. 1) were poor and going through suffering; yet because they loved Christ, they wanted to share in the offering. They did not say, "We must keep this for ourselves!" They were willing to give that others might be helped. They looked upon their giving as a grace (note vv. 1, 6, 7, 9, 19, and 9:8). Christian giving flows from the heart, the spontaneous expression of love to Christ for His full and free salvation.

The Corinthians were enriched with many spiritual blessings (v. 7), and Paul urged them to have also the grace of giving. For us to profess to be spiritual, and yet not give faithfully to the Lord, is to deny what we profess. Faith, preaching, witnessing, studying the Bible—none of these is a substitute for the grace of giving.

Paul uses not only the example of the Macedonian churches, but also the example of Christ Himself. How rich He was—and how poor He became! Read Phil. 2 for the details. To give is to be Christ-like, for His whole life was spent in giving.

III. Gifts Should Be Measured Proportionately (8:10-15)

A year before, the Corinthian church had suggested the offering and announced its willingness to share in it. Titus had assisted in the beginning of the project (v. 6), and now Paul was exhorting them to finish what they had started. How easy it is to make promises and then fail to keep them! If they had fulfilled their other financial obligations in the same manner, they might have been thrown in jail!

Paul then laid down in v. 12 the principle of proportionate giving, as he did in 1 Cor. 16:2 ("as he may prosper, NKJV"). Tithing is the only fair way to give. Tithing robs no man; it is fair to rich and poor alike. It permits all men to give and receive God's blessing. It is not the *portion* but the *proportion* that God seeks. This is the only way there could be any "equality" (v. 14) in the project. Paul cites Ex. 16:18 to show that just as God blessed the Jews as they obeyed Him, so He will bless Christians who obey His Word concerning giving. God does not send more blessings on the person who gives 10 percent of $500 than He does on the person who gives 10 percent of $100, if this is what they have to give. The person who opposes tithing is opposing the only fair way of giving.

IV. Gifts Should Be Handled Honestly (8:16-24)

Paul was anxious that nobody accuse him of misusing these missionary funds, so he had the churches appoint three messengers to handle the money. They were Titus (vv. 16-17), another brother (vv. 18-19), and a third associate (v. 22). This is a good business practice. It is sad to see churches and Christian organizations handle funds in an unbusinesslike manner. All money should be receipted and recorded. Funds should be counted by more than one person. Many a Christian worker has lost his power and testimony because of a misuse of funds or because of carelessness in handling the Lord's money.

Verses 20-21 are the key: there should be no opportunity for accusation, either from God or men. It isn't enough for the Christian worker to say "God knows my heart." We must remember that others are watching us, and we dare not give the enemy any opportunity to accuse us of dishonesty.

No Christian or local church should send money to works that are not financially sound. The fact that "there is a need" is not reason enough for giving; there must be proof that the money is handled honestly and spent wisely. We are not obligated to pay a debt we never incurred.

2 CORINTHIANS 9

Having discussed in chapter 8 the principles of Christian giving, Paul now shares the promises that we can claim if we are faithful in our giving to God. These two chapters present giving as a Christian grace, a blessing, not as a legal obligation that burdens people. If giving is difficult for a Christian, then there is something wrong with his heart! Note the three-fold promise that Paul gives:

I. Giving Will Bring Blessing to Others (9:1-5)

In 8:1-5, Paul used the churches of Macedonia as examples to encourage the Corinthians, and now he uses the Corinthians as an encouragement to the churches of Macedonia! Christians ought to be an encouragement to one another. Paul had been "boasting" to others of the generosity of the church at Corinth (8:24), and now he wants to make sure that the Corinthians do not embarrass him. He knew they had readiness of mind and were willing and anxious to share in the missionary offering, but he wanted to remind them just the same.

"Your enthusiasm has stirred most of them to action" (v. 2, NIV) What a testimony! Unfortunately, some Christians provoke people in the wrong way. Hebrews 10:24 urges us to provoke one another to good works, and this is what the Corinthians were doing. A year before, they had urged Paul to take up this missionary offering and had pledged their support. The apostle had used their zeal as an encouragement to the other churches, and now he reminds them of their promise. He seems to be saying, "If you fail to do your share, you will discourage other Christians and hurt the whole offering."

Paul called this offering "a bounty," that is, a blessing. He wanted them to look upon it as an opportunity to be a blessing and get a blessing, and not as a yoke on their necks. How often people misunderstand the true blessing of giving! Giving is a blessing to others, both to those who receive (v. 12—it supplied their want) and to those who share. When a Christian is faithful in giving, he or she is being a blessing to others and encouraging other Christians to be obedient to the Word.

II. Giving Will Bring Blessing to Ourselves (9:6-11)

Paul uses an agricultural principle here to illustrate his point. The farmer that sows bountifully will reap bountifully. See Prov. 11:24; Luke 6:38; and Gal. 6:7-8. "Bountifully" here is the same word as "bounty" in v. 5. To sow bountifully means to "sow with blessing" and to reap bountifully means to "reap with blessing." God will be no man's debtor; He is faithful to bless when we are faithful to obey.

Verse 7 is often misapplied. Paul is not talking here about how much we give so much as how we give. He told them how much to give in 8:12-15; it was to be in proportion to what they had. But for a believer to give grudgingly, or out of a sense of obligation, is to miss the blessing of giving. Giving must be from the heart, and God loves a cheerful ("hilarious" in the Gk.) giver. Some Christians take this verse to mean that it matters not how much we give, so long as we give cheerfully what we have purposed in our hearts. Absolutely not! A cheerful heart is not a substitute for an obedient heart. Our hearts should be both faithful and cheerful, because we give the right gift with the right motive.

Note the "alls" in v. 8—all grace; always; all sufficiency; all things; every good work. Nothing is left out! This is God's promise to those who obey Him. This word "sufficiency" is found again in 3:5 and 12:9. God is faithful to supply what we need spiritually (2:6), materially (9:8), and physically (12:9). But God meets our needs, not simply for our own enjoyment, but that we might be able to serve Him and help others. We are to abound "to every good work" (v. 8). Paul exhorts Christians to go to work that they might be able to help others (Eph. 4:28). Here he refers to Ps. 112:9 and Isa. 55:10 to prove that God blesses the person who is faithful in giving. God supplies seed so that sowers might make bread for food and also have more seed for sowing.

Humanly speaking, the person who gives should be the person who loses; but such is not the case. "It is more blessed to give than to receive" (Acts 20:35). "Give and it shall be given unto you" (Luke 6:38). This does not mean that we should bargain with God or look at our giving as a means of purchasing God's blessing. No! Rather, we should look upon giving as an opportunity to show our love for God and our trust in His Word. Christian industrialist R. G. LeTourneau used to say, "If you give because it pays, it won't pay!"

III. Giving Will Bring Glory to God (9:12-15)

How many times Paul reminds the Corinthians of their spiritual riches in Christ (see 1 Cor. 1:5 and 4:8; 2 Cor. 8:9 and 9:11). God enriches us, we enrich others, and God receives the thanksgiving and glory! Paul points out that the distributing of this offering would not only bring help to the saints, but it would bring glory to God.

Verse 13 gives two reasons why the Jews receiving this offering would glorify God: (1) because the givers showed obedience to God's Word and (2) because this liberal offering helped them and all men. The recipients in turn would pray for the churches and love them the more.

There was, of course, a very practical thought behind this offering. Paul was anxious to bind the Gentile churches he had founded to the hearts of the Jewish Christians in Judea. This offering would prove that Paul was not an enemy of the Jews, and that there was a unity in the church regardless of racial, national, or ethnic distinctions.

Paul closes the chapter with a word of praise. He has been writing about giving, and his heart has been so filled with God's goodness to him that he shouts, "Thanks be unto God for His unspeakable gift!" This gift is, of course, the gift of His Son, Jesus Christ, and His gift of eternal life.

One cannot read these two chapters without gaining a new attitude toward giving. In the Christian life, there is no such thing as "material" and "spiritual." All that we have comes from God, and all that we have must be used for spiritual ends. Paul teaches that giving is not a burden but a blessing. He shows us that true Christian giving enriches the life and opens the fountains of God's blessings. Giving is a grace (8:1, 6-7, 9, 19; 9:8 and 14), and the Christian who understands something of grace will understand how to give.

2 CORINTHIANS 10

This last section of 2 Corinthians (chaps. 10–13) presents Paul's vindication of his apostleship. In these chapters he answers the accusations of his enemies at Corinth. As we read his reply, we can discover the lies they were telling about Paul: that he was not a true apostle since he lacked credentials from the Jerusalem church; that his motives were insincere; that his physical presence was so weak that he deserved no respect; that his letters were bold but he would never back them up in person; and that his promises could not be depended upon.

Keep in mind that Paul was not defending himself in these chapters; he was defending his apostolic office and, therefore, the message he preached. These lies were being furthered by the false teachers who had visited Corinth and won over part of the church to their false doctrine, which was a mixture of Judaism and the Gospel. Paul was not merely answering critics; he was answering Satan himself (11:13-15). When Paul speaks of "boasting," it is with a touch of sarcasm. "Your favorite teachers like to boast," he said, "so I will try to win your love by doing some boasting of my own!" Of course, Paul's boasting was in the Lord and not in himself. Here in chapter 10, Paul gives several answers to the accusation that his presence was weak while his letters were powerful.

I. I Follow Christ's Example (10:1)

The Corinthians loved to glory in men (1 Cor. 3:21 and 4:6-7) and were "swept off their feet" by the Judaizing preachers from Palestine. Even though they were preaching a false doctrine (11:4) and taking advantage of the Christians (11:18-20), they were welcomed by the church and honored above Paul, who had founded the church and risked his life for it. "Paul is so weak!" these teachers said, as they lorded it over the church. "Follow us, because we display real power!"

"If I am weak," Paul replied, "it is not weakness — it is the meekness of Christ" (see v. 1). Christ never "lorded it over" people; His power was exercised in meekness and humility. Meekness is not weakness; meekness is power under control, the ability to be angry at sin, yet willing to suffer abuse for the sake of Christ. Let's not make the mistake of judging after the outward appearance (10:7) and thinking that some "powerhouse preacher" is necessarily displaying the power of God.

II. I Use Spiritual Weapons (10:2-6)

Simply because Paul did not use carnal methods and exert the power of a "strong personality," the believers thought he was a weakling! His weapons were spiritual, not fleshly. Like all of us, Paul "walked in the flesh" (that is, had all the weaknesses of the body), but he did not war after the flesh by depending on fleshly wisdom, human abilities, or physical prowess. Moses had to learn that God's weapons are spiritual (Acts 7:20-36) and Paul taught this principle in Eph. 6:10ff. The Word of God and prayer are the only effective weapons in this battle against Satan (Acts 6:4).

There was disobedience in Corinth because Christians were believing lies instead of the truth of God's Word. Paul warned them that he would smash their arguments and false doctrines and bring their hearts and minds to the place of obedience. Church problems are not solved simply by changing the constitution, revising the church program, or reorganizing a board, but by confronting people and problems with the Word of God.

III. I Don't Judge by Appearance (10:7-11)

The person who judges by appearance always lives to give a good appearance. Paul lived to please God and never tried to be a man-pleaser. He was confident of his calling and credentials from the Lord, and that was all that mattered. Certainly he could have pulled rank and invoked his apostolic authority, but he preferred to use that authority to build up the church, not to tear it down. Of course, often it is necessary to tear down before we can make room for real building (Jer. 1:10).

How foolish of these Christians to discredit Paul because he lacked the physical stamina of Peter or the oratorical power of an Apollos! Carnal Christians are "preacher judges" and like to compare one servant of God with another. Paul warns them that his presence at his next visit would be just as powerful as his letters!

IV. I Let God Do the Commending (10:12-18)

These false teachers were members of a "mutual admiration society," comparing themselves with one another; consequently they thought very highly of themselves. (See what Jesus says about this in Matt. 5:43-48. Also see Gal. 6:3-4.) But, says Paul, where were these "great teachers" when I risked my life to start the church in Corinth? Anybody can come along after the hard work is done, criticize the founder, and take all the glory! Paul had stretched himself out to reach the people in Corinth with the Gospel, and he was hoping to get their assistance in taking the Gospel "to the regions beyond." The Judaizers had come along and were boasting in a work that they had never accomplished. Paul's policy was to take the Gospel where nobody else had ever gone (see Rom. 15:20), while the Judaizers' policy was to invade another man's territory and take over the work he had done.

Paul was wise enough to leave the matter of commendations to the Lord alone. He refers to Jer. 9:24 in v. 17 (a thought he also quoted in 1 Cor. 1:31). After all, it is the Lord who gives the grace that we might serve Him, and He alone knows our hearts and motives. The apostle was willing to wait for God's "Well done!" and we should be also.

As you review this chapter, you will note several important lessons all of us should learn for being effective workers in the service of Christ.

(1) Don't be influenced by physical matters. The greatest servants of God are not always the most handsome or the strongest, humanly speaking. How easily some Christians are awed by a "Hollywood-style" Christian worker who sweeps them off their feet with imposing looks or hypnotic oratory. This does not mean, of course, that we should deliberately strive for a careless appearance or practice a mock humility. God has made each of us differently, and we must use all that He gives us for His glory.

(2) The most lasting work is done when we use spiritual weapons and tools. It is one thing to build a crowd, and something else to build a church. Theatrical programs, Madison Avenue promotional schemes, man-honoring displays that depend on the efforts of the flesh—all of these may grab popular attention, but they will never receive the approval of God. We build through prayer and the Word of God, and this takes time, dedication, and sacrifice.

(3) Don't judge before the time (1 Cor. 4:5). Let God do the commending. Live for His approval, and your life and ministry will be blessed. You may seem to be a failure in your eyes and the eyes of others, but God may see you and your work as a great success for His glory.

2 CORINTHIANS 11

This chapter presents what Paul calls his "boasting." Keep in mind that there is "holy irony" in this chapter as Paul turns his enemies' accusations on themselves. "Since your new teachers love to boast," Paul says, "then I will use their approved method and do some boasting, too!" He admits that he is not following Christ's example in this action (11:17), but he knows his "boasting" will glorify Christ because all that he has endured has been for Christ's glory. Paul boasts over three matters.

I. His Jealousy over the Church (11:1-6)

There is a difference between jealousy and envy. Envy is of the flesh and is selfish; jealousy is based on love and seeks the welfare of others. It is right for a husband to be jealous over his wife or for a pastor to be jealous over his church. Paul compares the local church to a bride, just as in Eph. 5:22-33 he compared the church universal to Christ's bride. Both examples are valid. Just as Israel in the OT is compared to the wife of Jehovah ("wife" because already married to Him at Sinai), so the church is called the bride of Christ ("bride" because not yet wedded to Him). Paul's desire was to keep the church pure, free from false doctrine and worldly living. In the OT, going after false gods is compared to adultery; in the NT, worldliness is called adultery (James 4:1-4).

How can a local church be seduced from Christ? By following Satan's false teachers (vv. 3, 13-15). Just as Satan deceived Eve's mind in Gen. 3, so false teachers deceive the minds of believers and lead them away from the truth. "Simplicity" (v. 3) means single-hearted devotion. We cannot serve God and mammon. How important it is for the church to stay true to the Word of God! Religious leaders today try to give us another Jesus, and not the Christ Paul preached; or another Spirit, and not the Holy Spirit of God; or another Gospel, and not the Gospel of God's grace (see Gal. 1). The only defense against spiritual adultery is faithfulness to the Word of God. How jealous we should be over the church for which Christ died!

II. His Generosity to the Church (11:7-21)

"Paul cannot be a true apostle," said his enemies, "otherwise he would accept money for his services. The fact that he refused to accept support from the church in Corinth is proof he knows he is not an honest man." How tragic when a good man's generosity is judged and his motives questioned! Paul uses a bit of irony here when he suggests that he committed a sin by refusing the Corinthians' material support (v. 7)! He had supported himself that the ministry might not be accused (1 Cor. 9 deals with this), and still his enemies found fault!

He assures them that it was because he loved them that he refused their support. He allowed the church at Philippi to send him support, but he did not take support from the people at Corinth, though his apostolic calling would have permitted it. He wanted to "cut off" any opportunity his enemies would have for accusing him (v. 12).

For the first time, Paul openly accuses these teachers of being servants of the devil. Satan's most effective weapon is imitation (see Matt. 13:24-30, 36-43). Yet the Christians should have known that these teachers were from Satan, since their lives and ministries manifested nothing of the spirit of Christ. Verse 20 is a description of a carnal ministry: it is one that brings people into bondage, not liberty; it devours them selfishly; its leaders exalt themselves and not Christ; it smites the saints instead of helping to heal their wounds. How unlike Paul's ministry! What is there about the flesh that enjoys bondage, honors, and human schemes, instead of the simple love and grace of Christ?

III. His Sufferings for the Church (11:22-33)

Paul's chief credentials of apostolic ministry were the wounds on his body that he received in serving Christ (see Gal. 6:17). Keep in mind that Paul wrote these things before the events in Acts 20ff transpired, and that most of the items on this list are not even mentioned in Acts! And the great apostle would never have mentioned them at all were it not for the fact that he was defending the Gospel. It is an arresting fact that Paul claims that his suffering, not the praise of men, was the best proof he had for asserting his apostleship. When selecting a spiritual leader, look for the scars.

These sufferings need little comment; they speak for themselves. Suffice to say that Paul went anywhere, endured anything, that he might take the Gospel to lost souls. Why is it that we do so much less today, when we have tools at our disposal that make the task much easier and faster?

It seems that Paul's heaviest burden was "the care of all the churches." Spiritual battles are always more costly than physical ones. Praying for the new Christians, feeding the lambs and the sheep, and warding off Satan's attacks are demanding tasks.

Notice that Paul did not boast of things that attested to his strengths, but rather his weaknesses! While the Judaizers were boasting of their converts, Paul was counting up the number of times he had been put in jail, beaten, or left in the sea! "I will glory in my infirmities while they boast about their powers!" he says, leading up, of course, to his account of the thorn in his flesh in chapter 12.

He closes with an especially interesting item: his escape from Damascus (Acts 9:23-25). How humiliating it must have been for this great rabbi to be lowered over a wall in a basket! Would the Judaizers have stooped this low? No! They would have compromised their message and walked out of the city gate! Paul faced suffering from the very first days of his ministry until the very last days. "Yea, and all who desire to live godly in Christ Jesus will suffer persecution" (2 Tim. 3:12, NKJV).

These attitudes Paul had toward the church ought to be in the heart of every pastor and church member today. We must be jealous over our churches and beware lest some satanic lie begin to lure the church away from true devotion to Christ. How easy it is for churches (and Christians) to rob Christ of the love He deserves. "You have left your first love!" Christ warned the church at Ephesus (Rev. 2:4). Unless Christians exercise a holy jealousy over the church, it will drift away into sin.

Likewise, we must have an unselfish and generous attitude toward the church. We should not have the attitude "How much can I get?" but rather "How much can I give?" We should be willing to sacrifice so that the church might grow for the glory of God.

2 CORINTHIANS 12

While we often extract parts of this chapter for devotional blessings, we must keep in mind Paul's purpose in answering his critics and proving his apostolic calling. In the previous chapter, he had decided to recount those things that showed his infirmities, that Christ might receive the glory. We find in this chapter four proofs of Paul's apostleship.

I. His Revelations from Christ (12:1-6)

The "man" Paul is talking about here is, of course, himself. Imagine being able to keep a thrilling experience like this secret for fourteen years! (Imagine, too, bearing suffering silently for fourteen years!) Certainly Paul was given divine revelations that no other man saw or heard. He was God's chosen instrument to reveal to the world the greatness of God's grace (note carefully Acts 26:16). The "third heaven" (v. 2) is paradise, the very heaven of the presence of God. What Paul heard from God, we do not know. Paul himself said nothing about this experience lest any Christian start honoring him more than he deserved. What humility!

God would not have given these revelations to Paul if he were not his chosen servant. As Paul argues in Gal. 1:11ff, the truths he taught came directly from God; Paul did not receive them second-hand from another apostle.

II. The Thorn in His Flesh (12:7-10)

We do not know what this thorn was, but the best suggestion is an eye ailment. Paul was supernaturally blinded when converted (Acts 9:9), and it is possible that some weakness remained even in later years. Galatians 4:15 and 6:11 ("with what large letters") suggest eye trouble. This would have been a trial to Paul both physically and emotionally, and could honestly be called a thorn (stake) in the flesh. (Sometimes prisoners were impaled on stakes and left to die a horrible death.) Whatever the thorn was, it was a burden to him, and it brought pain. He asked to have it removed.

The presence of this thorn was proof of his heavenly experience related in vv. 1-7; for God gave him the thorn (what a gift!) to keep him from getting proud. The enemies at Corinth had been accusing Paul of being weak (see 10:1 and 10; 11:6 and 29), and now he admits that he was weak, but that his weakness was a gift from God. The very weakness they accused him of was actually an argument for his apostolic authority!

There are several very practical lessons to be learned from Paul's experience with the thorn:

(1) Spiritual blessings are more important than physical ones. Paul thought he could be a better Christian if he were relieved of his weakness, but just the opposite was true. "Faith healers" who preach that sickness is a sin have a hard time with this chapter.

(2) Unanswered prayer does not always mean the need is not met. Sometimes we get a greater blessing when God does not answer our prayers! God always answers the need even though it seems He is not answering the prayer.

(3) Weakness is strength if Christ is in it. Read 1 Cor. 1:26-31 for proof; remember Gideon's pitchers, David's sling, and Moses' rod.

(4) There is grace to meet every need. Grace enabled Paul to accept his weakness, glory in it, and take pleasure in it! Paul knew that his weakness would bring glory to Christ, and that is all that mattered. See 2 Cor. 4:7.

III. His Apostolic Signs (12:11-18)

Paul is not exalting himself when he claims to be second to none of the apostles; he is simply defending his office. Note that Paul lists several "signs" that proved his apostleship, starting with patience! We expect him to mention miracles and wonders, but not patience! Yet it was Paul's steadfast endurance under trial that gave evidence that he was divinely called and commissioned (see chap. 4).

He mentions too his attitude toward money. It can be stated as an accepted fact that the servant's attitude toward material things indicates his spiritual life and outlook (Luke 16:1-15). A true servant of Christ cannot have a love of money. Paul reminds them that he and Titus proved their sincere love for the church in the way they supported themselves and generously helped the Corinthians.

Miracles and signs alone are no proof that a man is sent from God, for Satan himself has miraculous credentials (see 2 Thes. 2). When a servant's life and motives are pure, then we can trust any miracles that God may give; but when his or her life is not right, those miracles cannot be from the Lord.

IV. His Courage in Dealing with Sin (12:19-21)

"When I come to you, you will see how weak I am!" writes Paul. "I would rather you start cleaning up the church now," he advises. "If you wait for me to do it, you'll see how humble I can be in the hands of the Lord!"

When the hireling sees the wolf coming, he runs away (John 10:13), but the true shepherd stays and protects the sheep. Paul was not about to run away. He even went so far as to name the sins that were rampant in the church. Though they had taken care of the offender mentioned in 1 Cor. 5, there were other sins now that needed attention. "A little leaven" had indeed leavened the whole lump (1 Cor. 5:6).

There are two types of sin mentioned here: the social sins

(v. 20) and the sexual sins (v. 21). There were both prodigal sons and their elder brothers in the church, and both needed to repent. What began as factions in 1 Cor. 1:10 had now grown into debates, strifes, and tumults! Satan was in command, for God is not the author of confusion. False teaching leads to false living.

This chapter might well serve as a test for Christian servants. While none of us receives special divine revelations today, we all must be in communion with God and receive our messages from Him only. We all must have grace to endure suffering. There dare not be any love of money or any fear of man that would hinder us from dealing with sin. May God help us to be the kind of servants that God can commend and bless!

2 CORINTHIANS 13

Paul has reached the end of his letter, and he closes with several admonitions to the church.

I. Be Ready for My Visit (13:1-4)

In 12:14 he had mentioned his third visit, and now he repeats his admonition. He refers to the OT law that two or three witnesses are needed to settle the truth of a matter (Deut. 19:15), as though his third visit were God's final opportunity for the church to make matters right. He had told them before, and was now reminding them, that this visit would mean unsparing judgment to those who were guilty of sin. His boldness in dealing with sin would be proof enough that he was not a weakling! (See 10:10 and 11:6.)

His statement in v. 4 is interesting. In His death, Christ seemed to reveal weakness; but His resurrection revealed the power of God. In his previous visit, Paul showed seeming weakness as he served; this next visit would be different. There are times when we show His power in us by our seeming weakness; there are other times when we must be severe through the power of God. Paul's thorn in the flesh experience is an example of being "weak in Him" yet living by the power of God.

Had the Corinthians obeyed the Word of God, they would have spared themselves and Paul a great deal of agony. It is when Christians ignore or oppose the Word of God that they bring trouble upon themselves, others, and the church. How many pastors have gone through Gethsemane because of Christians who refuse to listen to God's Word!

II. Be Sure You Are Saved (13:5-7)

The Corinthians were spending a great deal of time examining Paul; now it was time they examined themselves. Socrates said, "The unexamined life is not worth living." A true Christian experience will bear examination. "Are you even in the faith?" asked Paul. "Are you truly saved?" Every believer must prove his or her faith; no one can tell others whether or not they are born again.

A true Christian has Christ in him. The word "reprobate" means "counterfeit." The word literally means "not passing the test." His enemies had charged Paul with being a counterfeit (a false apostle), a charge that he denied in v. 6. He begged the Corinthians to turn away from evil living and speaking, not simply that they might thereby prove that Paul was a true apostle, but for their own good. If they repented, he would not have to prove his apostleship by coming to discipline them. He was willing to set aside this privilege for their sakes. Paul would have rather lost his reputation to see them helped spiritually than to have them continue in sin and force him to exercise his apostolic authority. Peter warns pastors that they should not exercise lordship over the church (1 Peter 5:1ff), and Paul is here manifesting that same humble spirit. The warning of discipline is never for the purpose of exalting the pastor, but always for leading the offender to the place of repentance.

In this day of satanic counterfeits, it is important that professing Christians know that they are saved. Remember the warnings in Matt. 7:15-29 and the startling truths of 2 Cor. 11:13-15.

III. Be Obedient to God's Word (13:8-10)

In v. 8, Paul is not suggesting that there is no way to oppose the truth. Satan certainly opposes the truth with his lies, and people are more prone to believe his lies than they are to believe God's truth! Paul is saying that the repentance of the Corinthians would be "that which is honest" (v. 7) and according to the Word of God. Since they would be obeying the truth, Paul could do nothing against them in terms of judging sin or disciplining the offenders. He himself did not want anything other than the truth in the church at Corinth.

In fact, Paul goes on to say that he would be glad to make this next visit another demonstration of his weakness (1 Cor. 2:1-5) if it meant that they would be living in the power of God. His aim was their perfection—their spiritual maturity in Christ. They were babes in Christ, carnal and worldly, and needed to mature. "I want to build you up, not tear you down," he assured them. "This is why I am writing such a stern letter. I want you to start heeding God's Word and making matters right in the church. If you do, I'll not have to speak with sharpness when I come."

IV. Be Mature in Your Faith (13:11-14)

Notice the love that flows from these final words. He calls all of the Corinthian Christians brethren, and makes no distinction between those who attacked him and those who supported him. "Farewell" (v. 11) means "rejoice." Paul has written with tears (2:1-5), yet he found it in his heart to "rejoice evermore" and "in everything give thanks."

"Be perfect" is another admonition to grow up in the faith (see v. 9). If they were mature Christians, then the blessing Paul closes with in these verses would be their portion. There would be comfort, unity, peace, and fellowship with one another and with God.

The "holy kiss" (v. 12) was an oriental custom among believers; a modern version might read (as J.B. Phillips puts it), "Shake hands all around" (PH).

Paul closes with one of the greatest of the Bible benedictions, the benediction of the Trinity (v. 14). The "grace of our Lord Jesus Christ" takes us back to Bethlehem, where He became poor for us (2 Cor. 8:9); "the love of God" takes us to Calvary, where God the Father gave His Son; and "the communion of the Holy Spirit" takes us to Pentecost, where the Spirit baptized all believers into the body of Christ. How fitting this benediction was for this divided, unspiritual church! Many churches need this benediction today.

GALATIANS

A Suggested Outline of Galatians

I. Personal: Grace and the Gospel (1–2)

   A. Grace declared in Paul's message (1:1-10)

   B. Grace demonstrated in Paul's life (1:11-24)

   C. Grace defended in Paul's ministry (2:1-21)

      1. Before the church leaders collectively (2:1-10)

      2. Before Peter personally (2:11-21)

II. Doctrinal: Grace and the Law (3–4)

   A. Personal argument from experience (3:1-5)

   B. Scriptural argument—Abraham's faith (3:6-14)

   C. Logical argument (3:15-29)

   D. Dispensational argument (4:1-11)

   E. Sentimental argument (4:12-18)

   F. Allegorical argument (4:19-31)

III. Practical: Grace and the Christian Life (5–6)

   A. Liberty, not bondage (5:1-5)

   B. The Spirit, not the flesh (5:16-26)

   C. Others, not self (6:1-10)

   D. God's glory, not man's approval (6:11-18)

Introductory Notes to Galatians

I. Background

Ancient Gaul was peopled by warlike tribes which migrated across Europe into Asia Minor several centuries before the Christian era. They founded a nation called "Galatia" which means "the country of the Gauls." About a quarter of a century before Christ was born, the Romans made Galatia a part of one of their larger provinces, and called the entire area "Galatia." In other words, when you spoke about "Galatia" back in Paul's day, you had to specify whether you meant the smaller nation of Galatia, or the larger Roman province. The problem was somewhat like the one we face when someone says, "I'm going to New York." Is he going to the state of New York or to New York City?

This problem presents itself as we study the Epistle to the Galatians. Did Paul write this powerful letter to churches in the country of Galatia, or to churches in the Roman province of Galatia? Check a map of the apostolic world in the back of your Bible and you will see what is involved. Most Bible students today believe that Paul wrote to the churches of the province, ones he founded on his first journey (see Acts 13:1–14:28). In other words, he was writing to Christians in Iconium, Lystra, and Derbe. If this is true, it means that Galatians was the first of Paul's epistles, proving that the Gospel of the grace of God was just as clearly presented by Paul at the start of his ministry as at the close.

II. Theme

It will benefit you to review the introductory material to Acts and the notes on Acts 15. You will recall that the message of the kingdom was presented by Peter and the rest of the Twelve in the first chapters of Acts, offering Christ to the Jews. Their answer was to stone Stephen (Acts 7). It was then that the message was taken to the Samaritans (Acts 8) and to the Gentiles (Acts 10–11). Between these two events, Paul was saved (Acts 9). God especially revealed to Paul that He was doing a new thing and that the prophecy message of the kingdom had been replaced (temporarily) by the mystery of the church. However, the masses of believers (some of whom continued to be faithful to the Jewish religion) did not realize that this wonderful new program of grace, for both Jew and Gentile, had come onto the scene.

The issue was debated finally at Jerusalem (Acts 15). The believers concluded (led by the Spirit) that: (1) God's program for today was to take out of the Gentiles a people for His name; (2) Paul was His apostle to the Gentiles, with a special ministry to the body, the church; (3) the kingdom program would be resumed after the body was completed. However, there were Jews who would not receive the simple message of grace and who tried to mix it with the Law, blending improperly the kingdom message and the church message. We call these people "Judaizers," since their aim was to entice Gentile believers into the Jewish system. They taught that a person was saved by faith *and* by keeping the Law, and that the believer was sanctified and enabled to live a holy life in the same manner. These teachers had visited the Gentile churches in Galatia and were upsetting the people (Gal. 1:6-9; 3:1; 4:8-11; 5:7-9; 5:12; 6:12-13). They wanted the believers to follow the Jewish laws and customs of religious holidays, circumcision, etc. This was the "other Gospel" that Paul condemned in Gal. 1:6-9. The only Gospel that God approves and blesses is the Gospel of the grace of God, justification by faith in Christ Jesus alone. We are not saved by making promises to God but by believing His promises.

III. Its Value Today

Galatians is God's strongest word against legalism. The flesh loves to do things religious—celebrate holy days, practice rituals, attempt to do good works for God. Many religious systems today mix law and grace and present a garbled, confused way of salvation that is actually a way of bondage (Gal. 2:4; 4:9; 5:1). Keeping the Sabbath, dietary laws, an earthly priesthood, holy days, obeying rules—all of these are swept away in Galatians and replaced by the glorious liberty the believer has through faith in Christ!

GALATIANS 1

The first two chapters are personal, and the key word in them is "Gospel," found ten times in these forty-five verses. Paul's aim was to show that his message and ministry came directly from Christ and not from men. Paul did not preach a secondhand message that he learned from Peter or any of the apostles. Rather, God took every measure necessary to keep Paul's ministry separate from that of the Twelve, lest anyone think Paul's ministry was given to him by the apostles.

I. Paul's Announcement of His Gospel (1:1-5)

The Judaizers who "bewitched" the Galatians (3:1) were telling them that Paul's apostleship and message were not trustworthy because he lacked official endorsement from Jerusalem. "We have our credentials from Peter!" they would say, as though the approval of men is proof that a preacher is sent of God. Paul begins his letter by affirming that his message and ministry came directly from Jesus Christ. (Note Paul's use of "not neither" in vv. 1, 12, and 17.) He immediately spells out the Gospel that he preached.

Paul's Gospel was centered in Christ—His death, burial, and resurrection—and not in Moses or the Law. It was a Gospel of grace that brought peace. It was a Gospel of liberty: "that He might deliver us" (v. 4). The Judaizers were bringing the churches into bondage through the Law (see 2:4; 3:13; 4:9). Christ's death has delivered us from this present evil age and has given us a new standing in liberty (5:1ff). No wonder Paul adds, "To whom be glory for ever and ever!" (v. 5)

May we never be confused as to the content and intent of the Gospel. The Gospel is not "follow Christ and imitate His life" but "receive Christ by faith and allow Him to set you free." There is no place in the Gospel for a salvation that is attained by keeping the Law.

II. Paul's Astonishment at Their Removal (1:6-10)

Two things astonished Paul: (1) that so soon after experiencing the blessing of salvation (3:1-5) they were turning away to another message; (2) that they would remove from him (Paul) who had suffered to bring Christ to them. The Gk. word for "removed" (v. 6) is a present participle—literally "removing." They were then in the process of turning from simple grace to a mixture of law and grace. In 5:4 Paul says, "You are fallen from [out of] grace" (NKJV). This did not imply they had lost their salvation, but rather that they had moved themselves out of the sphere of grace into the sphere of the Law. Grace means I depend on God to meet my needs; through the Law I try to handle matters by myself, in my own strength.

The apostle speaks forcefully in condemning any other gospel, regardless of who the preacher might be—even an angel! Keep in mind that there are many "gospels" (messages of good news), but only one Gospel of the grace of God as Paul preached it. Abraham believed "the gospel" (3:8), the "good news" that through his seed all the nations would be blessed. In every age, men have been saved by believing whatever promise God revealed to them. Noah believed God's Word about a flood and the ark; Abraham believed God's Word about his promised seed; today we believe God's Word about His Son's death and resurrection. Since the advent of Paul and the revelation of justification by faith, there is no other Gospel. The "Gospel of the kingdom" that was emphasized from Matt. 3 to Acts 7 is not our message today.

III. Paul's Argument for His Ministry (1:11-24)

In these verses, Paul seeks to show how he was completely independent of the Twelve and the assembly in Jerusalem.

A. He received his Gospel personally from Christ (vv. 11-14).

Paul saw the risen Christ (Acts 9) and received his commission and message directly from Him. This experience qualified him to be an apostle. Paul was never meant to be the twelfth apostle to replace Judas (Acts 1:16-26). For one thing, Paul could not have met the qualifications; also God deliberately kept Paul separated from the Twelve so no one could accuse Paul of borrowing his message. Nobody could accuse Paul of inventing his message, because he had been a persecutor of the church, not a friend. His life was radically changed after he met Christ on the Damascus road. The only way to explain such a remarkable transformation is to accept the fact that Paul met Christ.

B. He received his Gospel apart from the apostles (vv. 15-17).

Again let it be said that God never meant for Paul to belong to the

Twelve. Their ministry was primarily to the Jews and was related to the kingdom; Paul's ministry was to the Gentiles and was related to the mystery of the church, the one body. The Twelve received their call from Christ on earth because their message presented the hope of Israel's earthly kingdom. Paul received his call from heaven, because his message presented the "heavenly calling" of the church in Christ. There were twelve apostles, associated with the twelve tribes. Paul was one man (and a Jew with Gentile citizenship) representing the one body in Christ.

Paul did not confer with men after he received his calling. Had he met immediately with the Twelve, people could have said that he borrowed his message and received his authority from them. Instead, God sent Paul to Arabia for a time of meditation and investigation. Someone has said, "Paul went to Arabia with the Law and the prophets and came out with Romans and Galatians!" Like Moses and Elijah before him, Paul went to the desert to wrestle with God's program and plan for his life. Then he went back to Damascus where he had first witnessed for Christ.

C. He received acknowledgement for his Gospel from the churches (vv. 18-24).

The believers there were actually afraid of Paul; and were it not for Barnabas, Paul would never have been accepted. This fact in itself proved that Paul had never leaned on the Jerusalem church for approval. After this visit, he went to Syria (Antioch). His ministry there is recorded in Acts 11:22-30; but he was personally unknown to the believers in Judea. However, the churches there heard the wonderful news of Paul's conversion and glorified God.

How tragic it is today that men reject Paul's revelation of the Gospel and try to mix law and grace. They try to "fit" Paul into the early chapters of Acts where the kingdom program is still emphasized. They are robbing Paul to pay Peter! We need to get back to the simple message of grace, the Gospel of Jesus Christ alone. To mix church and kingdom, law and grace, Peter and Paul is to create confusion and "twist" (pervert—1:7) the Gospel of Jesus Christ.

GALATIANS 2

In the first chapter, Paul proved that his Gospel and apostleship came directly from Christ, independent of the Twelve. His readers would naturally ask, "Then what was Paul's relationship to the Twelve and the Jerusalem church?" He answers that question in this chapter.

I. His Gospel Was Approved By the Apostles (2:1-10)

Fourteen years after Paul's visit to Jerusalem (Acts 9:26-29), he was back in the "holy city" to attend a council on the problem of law and grace (Acts 15). Paul went to this conference "by revelation"; that is, Christ personally directed him to go, just as He had personally given him the Gospel years before (1:11-12). Paul had been ministering among the Gentiles; he and Barnabas had seen many Gentiles saved and many local churches established; now the fate of the Gentile ministry was being discussed by the church leaders. Read Acts 15 again for the account of this important conference.

Some have suggested that there were four different meetings involved: (1) a public meeting, at which Paul recounted what God had done among the Gentiles, Acts 15:4; (2) Paul's private meeting with the leaders, Gal. 2:2; (3) the public debate of Acts 15:5 and Gal. 2:3-5; and (4) the council session at which the matter was finally settled, Acts 15:6ff.

Paul met with the leaders privately, but not because he was afraid his message was wrong. He knew his message was the right one because it had come from Jesus. Rather, he met with them privately to keep out the "spies" (2:4) and to avoid any open disagreements that would only add fuel to the fire.

Titus was with Paul, and, being a Gentile, was uncircumcised. According to the Judaizers, Titus was not even saved (Acts 15:1)! But the church leaders did not compel Titus to be circumcised; so, Paul concludes, this proves that circumcision has nothing to do with salvation. There were false brethren there, people who wanted to rob the believers of the glorious liberty they have in Christ. This party must have argued for Titus' circumcision, but Paul "beat them down." The group was divided: some were for legalism; some were for liberty; some were for a compromise between the two. The church today is still divided, with some teaching salvation by ritual; others insisting on mixing law and grace. The minority hold to Paul's Gospel of the grace of God.

The conclusion of the matter was that the church leaders agreed that Paul's message and ministry were of God, and that he should minister to the Gentiles while Peter and the Twelve ministered to the Jews. In v. 8, Paul is careful to point out that the same Spirit who worked in Paul worked in Peter as well. Both had the same message and the same Spirit but were responsible for different spheres of ministry. The council added nothing to Paul's message (v. 6), and endorsed it as well. Paul had preserved the "truth of the Gospel" (2:5) from the lies of the enemy.

II. His Gospel Was Defended before Peter (2:11-21)

Paul was right in ignoring the "spiritual positions" of the people mentioned in v. 6. Even the best leaders can make mistakes, and Paul cites Barnabas and Peter as examples. After the Jerusalem conference, Peter had visited the Gentile church at Antioch where Paul and Barnabas were still ministering (Acts 15:35). In Acts 10, God had clearly revealed to Peter that no foods or peoples were unclean; but the apostle fell back into legalism just the same. When he first came to Antioch, Peter mingled with the Gentiles and ate with them; but after some visitors came from Jerusalem, he withdrew himself and put up the old Jewish barriers again. Even Barnabas fell into the trap (v. 13), amazing his missionary companion, Paul. The reason was fear (v. 12); for "the fear of man brings a snare" (Prov. 29:25, NKJV).

Peter and Barnabas were not walking uprightly. What we believe determines how we behave. Because Peter and Barnabas were confused about spiritual truth, they were unable to walk a straight line. The "truth of the Gospel" is not only something for us to defend (v. 5), but it is also something for us to practice (v. 14). In vv. 14-21 we have a summary of the rebuke Paul gave to Peter. Certainly Paul said more than this, but the following digest summarizes the matter very well:

"You are a Jew," said Paul to Peter, "but you used to live like the Gentiles, with no barriers between you and other Christians. Now you want the Gentiles to live like Jews, doing what you did not even do yourself!"

The "we" in vv. 15-17 refers, of course, to the Jews. "We Jews have had special privileges and may not be guilty of Gentile sins; but we are saved the same way they are!" We would expect Paul to say, "They must be saved the way we are," but he reverses the order. Salvation did not mean that Gentiles had to become like Jews, but that the Jews had to go to the level of the condemned

Gentiles! "We are justified—given a right standing before God—by faith in Jesus Christ,"argues Paul. "The works of the law will never justify a man. Was any Jew ever saved by keeping the law? Of course not!"

In vv. 17-18, Paul showed Peter the folly of going back to the Law. "You say you have been saved by faith in Christ. Well, if you go back to the Law, you are confessing that you are still a sinner needing to be saved and that Christ did not save you. In fact, you are saying that your faith in Christ made you a sinner again, and that makes Christ the minister of sin!" To turn back to the Law denies the work of Christ on the cross. "You preached the Word to the Gentiles yourself," Paul went on, referring to Acts 10, "but now you have changed your mind. You preached salvation by faith; now you preach salvation by law. You are building up the very things you once tore down, which makes you a sinner, because you tore down something that God wanted to keep standing." In other words, Paul showed Peter the inconsistency of his actions and his beliefs.

"The Law is not a way of life, Peter; it is a way of death. The Law kills us (v. 19) that the Gospel might raise us up again. A Christian is not someone who is trying to obey an outward law. A Christian is one who has the living Christ within. By faith, I am united to Christ forever. When He died, I died; when He arose, I arose with Him. He lives out His life through me as I walk by faith—this is the Christian life! It is not a set of rules and regulations. To go back to the Law is to frustrate (make empty) the grace of God! If the Law is God's way of salvation, then Christ died in vain!"

Neither Galatians nor Acts records Peter's response, but we know that Paul's rebuke accomplished its purpose. In fact, one of the last admonitions Peter wrote was that believers should read Paul's letters to find God's truth about this present age (2 Peter 3:16-18).

GALATIANS 3

Chapters 3–4 are doctrinal, for in them Paul explains the relationship between law and grace. Three words that are repeated frequently are faith (fourteen times), law (nineteen times) and promise (eleven times). Paul presents six arguments, three in each chapter, seeking to prove that salvation is by grace, through faith, apart from the works of the Law.

I. The Personal Argument (3:1-5)

Paul began with the Galatians' own personal experience with Christ, for this is one of the best evidences of how God works. Paul had preached Christ crucified, not obedience to the Law; this message they believed, and it changed their lives. They had received the Spirit (the evidence of salvation, Rom. 8:9) by the hearing of faith, and by believing the Word of God (Eph. 1:13-14), not by obeying some law. Certainly the Gospel Paul preached, the Gospel that changed his life and their lives, was the true message. For them to go back to the Law after all the Spirit had done for them was to act like fools!

They had willingly suffered for their faith. Through the gifts of the Spirit, the ministers in the Galatians' church were doing wonderful works, works that could never be done through the Law. Everything in their personal experience pointed to one fact: salvation is by grace, not by law.

Christians today need the truth of v. 3, for many feel that the same Spirit who saved them is not able to keep them or help them live for Christ. They have the idea that salvation is by grace through faith, but that living the Christian life depends on their own strength. How wrong this is! Romans 7 teaches clearly that believers cannot do anything of themselves to please God; Rom. 8 teaches that the Spirit continues the work of grace and fulfills the demands of the Law in us.

II. The Scriptural Argument (3:6-14)

By "scriptural" we are not suggesting that Paul's other arguments were not true to the Word, but rather that in this section he appeals strongly to the OT. In fact, you will want to check each of these references and contexts carefully.

A. Verses 6-7 quote Gen. 15:6.

The Judaizers pointed to Abraham, the "father of the Jews," as their example, and Paul does the same thing. How was Abraham saved? By faith! And all who trust Christ are children of Abraham, the father of the believing. See Rom. 4:1-8 for an amplification of this argument.

B. Verses 8-9 quote Gen. 12:3.

God promised to bless the heathen (Gentiles) through Abraham, which means that Jews and Gentiles are saved the very same way. The "gospel" that Abraham believed was certainly not the full Gospel of the grace of God that we preach today; even the apostles did not fully understand the meaning of Christ's death until it was explained to them. The gospel Abraham believed was the good news that God would bless Abraham and make him a mighty nation. Abraham believed this promise and this faith was accounted for righteousness.

C. Verse 10 quotes Deut. 27:26.

"You want to be saved by the works of the law? But the law does not save—it curses!"

D. Verse 11 quotes Hab. 2:4.

We have met this verse before: "The just shall live by faith" (Rom. 1:17; Heb. 10:38). This little verse from Habakkuk is so rich that God wrote three NT commentaries on it!

E. Verse 12 quotes Lev. 18:5.

There is a vast difference between "doing" and "believing"! Nobody was ever saved by doing the Law, because nobody can ever fully obey the Law.

F. Verses 13-14 quote Deut. 21:23.

The law puts us under a curse, but Christ died to remove that curse. He died on a tree (the cross—1 Peter 2:24) and fulfilled the word given in Deuteronomy. Because He has taken our curse upon Himself, we are free to live in Christ. The blessing God promised Abraham is now available to the Gentiles by faith.

Read again these six quotations and see how they prove conclusively that even the OT law itself taught that salvation is by grace, through faith.

III. The Logical Argument (3:15-29)

Of course, all of Paul's arguments are logical. But the particular arguments here depend especially on reasoning, as Paul compares the Law to a human contract. "When two people make a contract, it is illegal for a third party to step in and change it or cancel it.

Now, God made a contract (covenant) with Abraham four hundred years before the Law was given. The law of Moses could never cancel God's original promise to Abraham. God gave that promise to Abraham's seed as well, and v. 16 indicates that this Seed is Christ. The Mosaic law was not a new way of salvation that canceled God's promises to Abraham; this would not be logical. Promise and faith go together, but not promise and law.

"But why then did God even give the Law?" his objectors would argue. Paul gave three answers:

A. The Law was temporary and only for Israel (vv. 19-20).

Rom. 2:14 and Acts 15:24 make it clear that God never gave the Law to the Gentiles. The moral law was already written in the Gentiles' hearts (Rom. 2:15). But the ceremonial law (including the Sabbath laws) was never given to the Gentiles. The law was "added" and was not a replacement for the Abrahamic promises. Once the Seed (Christ) came, the Law was superseded. "But the Law was given with such glory!" the Judaizers would reply. "How can you say it was only temporary?" Paul is ready with an answer: the Law was given by angelic mediators, but God spoke personally to Abraham. God is one—and the fulfillment of His promise to Abraham depended on Him alone.

B. The Law convicted us of sin but never saved us from sin (vv. 21-22).

If there were a law that saved sinners, then God would have spared His Son and used that law instead of the cross. The Law is not contrary to God's promises; by revealing sin, the law forces the sinner to trust God's promises. Law shows us our need of grace; grace enables us to please God through faith. The Law places all under sin, which means that all can be saved by grace. If God permitted even one sinner to be saved by law, then no man could be saved by grace. All must be saved the same way.

C. The Law prepared the way for Christ (vv. 23-29).

"Before the faith we now know came, the law shut men up, revealing their need for a Savior." As L.E. Maxwell has put it, "We were crowded to Christ!" The Law was God's "schoolmaster" (tutor) for the Jews in their national infancy. The Greek and Roman tutor used to guard and teach the minor children until they reached legal adulthood, after which the children were on their own. The Law kept the Jews "in line," so to speak, until Christ came and the full revelation of the Gospel was given to Jews and Gentiles.

GALATIANS 4

Paul continues with three more arguments to prove that salvation is by grace and not by law.

I. The Dispensational Argument (4:1-11)

Anyone who reads the Word carefully must admit that at different times, God deals in different ways with different people. When we speak of "dispensational truth," we mean the truth of the Word as related to God's program of the ages for Jews, Gentiles, and the church (1 Cor. 10:32). In this section, Paul explains that the period of Law was a dispensation, a special way in which God dealt with Israel for a special purpose. God never gave the Mosaic law to the Gentiles. To impose Jewish regulations on Gentiles (or even on Jews today) is totally unscriptural.

The Jews were heirs, for God had made wonderful promises to them through Abraham, but it took many centuries before they received these promises. Paul is continuing his comparison between the situation of the Jews and the tutelage of the Roman or Greek child. The child, Paul reasons, might be heir to a fortune, but so long as he or she has not reached the legal age of inheritance, the child is no different from the slave. Even so, the Jews were in their "spiritual childhood" under the law. The rules and rituals of the Law were the "religious ABCs" they had to learn before they could graduate into their full inheritance. This legalism was bondage to the Mosaic system ("elements of the world" — see Col. 2:8, 20). But this dispensation of law ran its course, having prepared the way for Christ. Christ was born at the right time, in the right manner (of a woman — a virgin birth), and for the right purpose — to set us free. Christ was made under the Law, obeyed the Law, and fulfilled the Law in His life and death. His death on the cross set the Jews free from their legalistic bondage and opened the way for the fulfillment of the promises to Abraham.

Had Israel received its Messiah when Peter presented Him at Pentecost (and again throughout Acts 2–7), the nation would have entered into its adulthood. The blessing would have flowed out to the Gentiles through Israel, and the Abrahamic promises would have been fulfilled. The nation collectively rejected Christ, but God in His grace opened the blessings up to Jews and Gentiles alike on an individual basis. The Gentiles were not saved through Israel's rise, but through Israel's fall (read Rom. 11:1-12). Now, individual Jews have received their adoption — their "son-placing," as mature, grown-up children in God's family. They are no longer little children under the guidance of tutors; believers are sons, not servants, enjoying the full inheritance in Christ.

Paul now applies his argument: "Why do you want to go back into bondage, into a second childhood? Leave the ABCs and enjoy the full inheritance that you have in Christ!"

II. The Sentimental Argument (4:12-18)

"Brethren, I beseech you!" This is the appeal of a loving spiritual servant, a concerned father addressing his spiritual children. "I became as one of you when I first preached to you," writes Paul; "now become as I am and be true to Christ." He reminds them that it was through some physical affliction that he first came to them, and that they had then treated him like an angel. Now they treated him like an enemy because he was telling them the truth. "Your false teachers make a big show of their love for you ("zealously affect you" — v. 17), but their motives are not pure. They want to use you to show off their spiritual conquests!" (See 6:12-14.)

III. The Allegorical Argument (4:19-31)

An allegory is an event or story that has a hidden meaning. Paul uses the story of Abraham's two sons (Gen. 16 and 21) to show that the new covenant of grace has superseded the old covenant of law. We may illustrate the contrasts in this way:

The Old Covenant of Law	The New Covenant of Grace
1. Symbolized by Hagar the slave-girl	1. Symbolized by Sarah, the free woman
2. Ishmael, a son born after the flesh	2. Isaac, a son born miraculously by God's promise
3. Represents Jerusalem in Paul's day, still in spiritual (and political) bondage	3. Represents the heavenly Jerusalem which is free and glorious

We Christians are children of promise, like Isaac (v. 23), and therefore children of liberty (v. 31). God had promised Abraham a son long before Ishmael was born. Ishmael "was added" (like the Law, 3:19) and was a son of the flesh, a slave's son. The old covenant of law was never God's final plan for Israel. It was added, like Ishmael, and brought bondage and sorrow. God's commandment to Abraham was to cast out Ishmael and Hagar! Law and grace, faith and works, promise and commandment, can never live in the same household. The Judaizers in Galatia wanted to invite Hagar and Ishmael back into the family again!

Paul refers to Isa. 54:1 and applies this verse to the church. Just as Sarah was barren and had to wait for many years for her son, so the Jews had to wait many years before God's promises to Abraham were fulfilled. Isaiah described the joy of Jerusalem after the return from exile. Paul sees a deeper meaning: joy in the church in spite of its persecution and suffering.

The danger Paul saw in Galatia is with us today. The flesh loves and craves "religious excitement" and feels gratified when it can keep some religious law. While there is nothing wrong with church traditions that are tied to Scripture and magnify Christ, we must beware of inviting Hagar and Ishmael back into the family. There can be no mixture of law and grace. May God help us to hold fast to His simple grace.

GALATIANS 5

We now move into the final section of the letter in which Paul makes the practical application of Christian liberty to the lives of believers in a series of four contrasts.

I. Liberty, Not Bondage (5:1-15)

"Your doctrine of grace and liberty is dangerous!" Paul's enemies argued. "Why, if Christians are free from the Law, they will live wicked lives! We need the Law to control them!" So people have argued down through the centuries, little realizing that grace, not law, is the greatest teacher and "controller" in the world (Titus 2:11-12).

Paul admonishes us to stand fast in our Christian liberty. If we step back into legalism, we risk entanglement and bondage. How well the Jews of Paul's day knew what legal bondage meant (Acts 15:10). Circumcision was the seal of the old covenant, so Paul warns the Galatians that to turn back to the old covenant is to rob themselves of the blessings Christ had purchased for them. Christ cannot profit the sinner who rejects grace and trusts law; Christ cannot profit the saint who seeks to live by law instead of grace. "Circumcision" in vv. 2-3 stands for the entire Mosaic system. People who put themselves under the Law become debtors to the whole system.

"Fallen from grace" (v. 4) does not mean "fallen from salvation." Paul is not writing to people who have "lost their salvation" because such a thing is not possible. He is writing to saints who have moved out of the sphere of grace into the burdensome sphere of law. Watchman Nee says, "Law means I must do something for God; grace means that God does something for me." How wonderful it is for the Christian to enjoy the liberty of grace! This means moving out of the bondage described in Romans 7 into the glorious liberty of Romans 8! Paul describes the true Christian walk in vv. 5-6: our power is in the Spirit; we receive this power by faith; this faith produces love and works in our lives. In other words, the doctrine of Christian liberty does not encourage a wicked life; instead, it binds us closer to Christ, and Christ lives out His life through the believer (2:20).

How did such false teaching get into the Galatians' lives? Just the way yeast (leaven) gets into good meal. Leaven is always compared to that which is evil (cf. Matt. 13:33; 1 Cor. 5:1-7). The false doctrine was planted as a little bit of leaven in the church, but then it grew and infected the whole body. The Galatians had run well up to that point; now they were being hindered in their Christian walk.

Paul then points to himself and reminds them of how he had suffered to preach the Gospel. His enemies were probably lying about him and saying that he actually did preach circumcision (that is, obedience to the OT law). But, Paul argues, that if he was preaching legalism, the Jews would never have persecuted me! "The offense of the cross" (v. 11) means the stumbling block of the cross to the Jews (1 Cor. 1:23-25), who could not accept a crucified Savior. Using circumcision as an example, Paul says, "I wish they were cut off who trouble you!"

Paul closes this section with the reminder that liberty is not license. "By love serve one another," he says. We fulfill the law when we live in love (Rom. 13:8-10). The Christian who says, "I have liberty to sin!" understands nothing of the cross or of God's grace.

II. The Spirit, Not the Flesh (5:16-26)

Paul's first admonition was "Stand fast!" Now he says, "Walk in the Spirit!" Our standing in Christ determines our walk in Christ. The words "flesh" and "Spirit" are each found ten times in chapters 5–6. Those who live according to law depend on the energy of the flesh; those who live by grace depend on the power of the Spirit. To "walk in the Spirit" means to have our daily lives under His control, and this means under the direction of the Word of God. To be "led of the Spirit" means to be delivered from a life of bondage to legalism. The elder brother in the parable of the prodigal son (Luke 15) lived in bondage and had no joy in his walk or service. How many Christians are like him!

"The flesh" refers to the fallen nature still with the believer. The body itself is not sinful; appetites are not necessarily sinful, but the tendencies of the old nature are downward. In Romans 6, Paul tells us that the old man has been crucified and that we can overcome the flesh by reckoning ourselves dead to sin and by yielding ourselves to God. Here in Galatians, Paul spells out the conflict between the believer's two natures. Immediately after conversion, new Christians enjoy several days or weeks of wonderful victory; then temptation and defeat come, and they become discouraged. Somebody should have told them that the old nature would rise up again! The last phrase in v. 17 does not teach that the believer cannot get victory. The phrase should be translated, "so that you may not do what you would." That is, mere determination on the part of the Christian will never control the flesh or produce the fruit of the Spirit. Paul amplifies this theme in Rom. 7, where he shows that the believer's determined attempts to please God in his own strength are destined to fail.

What a contrast between works and fruit! Fruit is the result of a living union; a machine may produce works, but it can never produce fruit. Even the Law produces works, but God calls them dead works (Heb. 6:1). The Law could never produce the gracious fruit described here. Read this list of "flesh works" in a modern version to get the full import of their meaning. What a terrible catalog of sins! How many of them are found even among Christians!

Christian character comes from within, by the power of the Spirit. The Spirit seeks to transform us into Christ's likeness (2 Cor. 3:18; Rom. 8:29 and 12:1-2). We could meditate for hours on the nine-fold fruit of the Spirit! Note especially that love heads the list. Paul clearly states that no law could ever produce this kind of character. When will people learn that making resolutions will never sanctify them!

"If we live in the Spirit" (this is salvation, being made alive by the Spirit), "let us also walk in the Spirit" (this is sanctification, allowing the Spirit to command and control our lives). Compare Eph. 5:18-24 with Col. 3:15-19 and you will see that to be filled with the Spirit is to be controlled by the Word of God, for the results are identical. "Walking in the Spirit" is not some emotional experience, detached from everyday life. It is the daily experience of the believer who feeds on the Word, prays, and obeys what the Bible says.

In closing, note that Paul uses three pleas as he beseeches these Christians to live lives of holiness by the grace of God: God the Father has called them (v. 13); God the Son has died for them (v. 24); and God the Holy Spirit indwells them (vv. 16-23). Each Person of the Trinity is assisting us in our battle against the flesh.

GALATIANS 6

In this final chapter, Paul presents two more contrasts in the Christian life. Keep in mind that he is describing the spiritual life of the believer who lives under grace and not under law. It is a life of liberty, not bondage (5:1-15), and one that is lived in the Spirit, not in the flesh (5:16-26).

I. Others, Not Self (6:1-10)

There is a law that the believer obeys; it is the law of love in Christ. "A new commandment I give to you, that you love one another as I have loved you" (John 13:34, NKJV). The Spirit of God is the Spirit of love, for God is love. If we are walking in the Spirit, we will not use our liberty in Christ for selfish purposes; we will allow the Spirit to work through us to help others. "Others" is the great Gospel word! Jesus lived for others, and we must follow His example. Being free from the Law does not mean we are independent of one another, for we are members of the same family, and we minister to each other.

A. Spiritual help (vv. 1-5).

Suppose a believer is suddenly caught by the enemy and falls into sin. (Or it may be that the word "overtaken" suggests being caught in sin and found out by other believers.) Should our attitude be one of judgment and condemnation? No! If we are spiritual (walking in the Spirit, led by the Spirit, bearing fruit through the Spirit), we will seek to restore the fallen one. This Gk. word for "restore" is a medical term used for the setting of a broken bone. Christians are members of Christ's body, and a Christian in sin weakens the body. Of course, if the person does not submit to restoration, then the measures of discipline outlined in Matt. 18 and 1 Cor. 5 must be considered.

We are to bear each other's burdens, but we must also bear our own burdens. See Paul's words to the Galatians in Gal. 6:1-5. There are some burdens that we can share with others, but there are also some that we alone can carry. To avoid my own responsibilities while seeking to help another is to sin. There must be the spirit of meekness as we seek to help others, not thinking we are better than they. Let God do the judging and the rewarding; He never makes a mistake.

B. Material help (vv. 6-10).

The believer who listens to the Word should share material blessings with those who teach; this is the lesson of vv. 6-8. We often apply these verses to reaping what we sow in terms of sin, and certainly this principle is true. But the basic lesson here is that of giving; "communicate" in v. 6 simply means "to share." This principle is stated in Rom. 15:27; where we receive spiritual blessings, we have the privilege and obligation of sharing material blessings. "Sowing to the flesh" means living for the flesh, investing time and money on things that will not last; "sowing to the Spirit" means spending time and money on things eternal. How many Christians use their time and money (and money is merely time minted so we can spend it again) on things fleshly—and they wonder why they never grow in grace or reap spiritual fruits! Certainly it takes faith and patience to sow to the Spirit, but God promises the harvest in due season. It takes time to grow a spiritual harvest. We must be faithful sowers in our activities.

II. God's Glory, Not Man's Approval (6:11-18)

To the very end of the letter, Paul has grace in mind. The Christian who depends on grace, through the Spirit, will always bring glory to God; the legalist who "practices religion" will earn the approval of men. How the world honors "religious people" and hates the dedicated Christian!

Paul usually used a secretary when he wrote, dictating the letter, and then adding his personal "grace signature" to the end (1 Cor. 16:21-24; Col. 4:18; 2 Thes. 3:17-18). But apparently he wrote Galatians personally, and, because of his poor eyesight (note Gal. 4:15) had to write in large letters. "How large a letter" does not mean the number of words, because the letter is relatively brief; it means the size of the individual letters. Paul did not permit his physical handicap to hinder him from obeying God and warning his Christian friends of the evils of legalism.

"These Judaizers want to use you for their glory," Paul asserts (v. 12). "They are not ministering to you for your good, but for their own praise. They want to avoid the persecution that comes to those who preach the cross. But they do not even obey the law themselves!" What a stinging rebuke! These Judaizers, like the Pharisees of Christ's day, would cross land and sea to make a convert (Matt. 23:15), not to help the convert, but to add more glory to their own names. But Paul was not of this type: he gloried in the cross and willingly took all of the shame and persecution that was attached to it. Paul could glory in the cross because he knew the Person of the cross, the purpose of the cross, and the power of the cross.

Again, Paul mentions his own crucifixion (6:14, see 2:20). Salvation means Christ died for me — substitution; sanctification means I died with Christ — identification. "These false teachers belong to the world and are living for the world," states the apostle. "The world has no attraction for me: I have been crucified to the world, and the world has been crucified to me." Today, the cross is often a polished piece of jewelry; back in Paul's day, the cross was a shameful instrument of pain and death. "Religion" has made the cross a symbol; the Spirit makes the cross a reality in the life of the Christian who lives by grace.

The Christian belongs to a "new creation" (2 Cor. 5:17), the "true Israel of God" (v. 16). This does not mean that the NT church has taken the place of OT Israel, for in Christ there are no racial distinctions (3:28). Rather, Paul is saying that these Judaizers are not a part of the true Israel, the real people of God. Gentiles who receive Christ as Savior are not children of Abraham genetically, but spiritually (3:7). The church today is the true Israel of God, because God's ancient people have been set aside temporarily in unbelief and are termed "not my people" (Hosea. 1:9-10; 2:23; Rom. 9:25-26). One day Israel will become God's people and inherit their national promises.

The "rule" we are to walk by is that of grace and the new creation in Christ. How many well-meaning but ignorant Christians are walking by a different rule, trying to "bring in the kingdom" or reform the world.

With one sweep of the pen, Paul brushes away these legalistic troublemakers. "Your false teachers are marked with circumcision," he writes, "but I have on my body the marks [brands] of Jesus Christ." This does not mean Paul had five wounds on his body similar to Christ's wounds; it means rather that he had scars on his body to prove that he bore reproach for the cross of Christ. In Paul's day, men branded soldiers, slaves, and people who dedicated themselves to a god. Paul was Christ's soldier, slave, and devoted follower.

What a wonderful benediction: "The grace of our Lord Jesus Christ be with your spirit!" (v. 18)

EPHESIANS

A Suggested Outline of Ephesians

I. Doctrine: The Believer's Blessings in Christ (1–3)

    A. Our possessions in Christ (1:1-14)
        1. From the Father (1:1-6)
        2. From the Son (1:7-12)
        3. From the Spirit (1:13-14)
    B. Prayer for enlightenment (1:15-23)
    C. Our position in Christ (2)
        1. Raised and seated on the throne (2:1-10)
        2. Reconciled and set into the temple (2:11-22)
    D. Prayer for enablement (3)

II. Duty: The Believer's Behavior in Christ (4–6)

    A. Walk in unity (4:1-16)
    B. Walk in purity (4:17-32)
    C. Walk in love (5:1-6)
    D. Walk in the light (5:7-14)
    E. Walk carefully (5:15-17)
    F. Walk in harmony (5:18–6:9)
        1. Husbands and wives (5:18-33)
        2. Parents and children (6:1-4)
        3. Masters and servants (6:5-9)
    G. Walk in victory (6:10-24)

Ephesians balances doctrine and duty. First Paul reminds us of what God has done for us; then he tells us what we must do for Him in response to His mercies. Christian living is based on Christian learning. The believer who does not know his wealth in Christ will never be able to walk for Christ. Our conduct depends on our calling. Too many Christians live in chapters 1–3 and study the doctrines but fail to move into chapters 4–6 and practice the duties.

Introductory Notes to Ephesians

I. The City

Ephesus was one the great cities of Asia Minor: a Roman capital, a center for the worship of Diana, and a wealthy commercial center, located on an ample harbor that invited world trade. The temple of Diana was one of the seven wonders of the ancient world, and the worship of this goddess was jealously guarded (see Acts 19:23ff). Ephesus was the chief city of that area, so it is no wonder Paul stayed there for three years (Acts 20:31) and that from the city the Gospel spread out to "all Asia" (Acts 19:10).

II. The Church

Paul paid a brief visit to Ephesus on his second journey, leaving his associates Priscilla and Aquila there (Acts 18:18-28). He returned to Ephesus on his third journey and remained there for three years (Acts 20:31). He began his ministry in the Jewish synagogue; when his countrymen rejected his message, he moved into the school of a teacher named Tyrannus (Acts 19:9) and preached and taught for about two years. His ministry had a tremendous effect on the city: those who practiced witchcraft turned to Christ and burned their books of magical incantations; many people were won to the worship of the true God; and the profits of the silversmiths (who sold shrines of Diana) were greatly undermined. Paul's clear teaching and preaching of the Word of God so aroused the enemy that a riot resulted, and Paul was forced to leave the city. Later (Acts 20) he met the Ephesian elders while he was traveling back to Jerusalem.

III. The Letter

Paul was a Roman prisoner when he wrote this letter (Eph. 3:1; 4:1). How he became a prisoner is recorded in Acts 21:15ff. While in Jerusalem, Paul went to the temple and was arrested on false charges. His "trial" was indecisive, but he was imprisoned for two years at Caesarea (Acts 21:27–26:32). When Paul appealed for a trial before the emperor, he was then sent to Rome (Acts 27–28). While a prisoner in his own house, Paul was free to receive visitors, and it was at this time that he wrote Ephesians. The letter was carried by Tychicus (6:21), who probably also helped to deliver the letter to Colosse, along with Onesimus (Col. 4:7-9).

While the letter was directed to the church at Ephesus, there is reason to believe that it was circulated among the many churches of Asia Minor. You will note that the letter deals with church truth in general, not the kind of local problems you would find in the two Corinthian letters or 1 Thessalonians. In every sense, Ephesians is Paul's greatest word on the church, teaching us what the church is in the mind of God, and what it ought to be in practice before the eyes of men. Paul's theme is Christ and the church, the eternal plan of God to gather together all things in Christ Jesus. The letter begins in eternity past and carries us to eternity future! We see the believer seated in the heavenlies, but also walking with Christ on earth and fighting against Satan. While Ephesians does not tell us all God wants us to know about the church, there is no part of the Bible that soars any higher in church doctrine or practical Christian living. It is interesting to compare the description of Paul's Ephesus ministry in Acts 20 with the doctrines taught in the Ephesian epistle.

IV. The Church in Ephesians

In the prison letters (Ephesians, Philippians, Colossians), Paul deals with the church collectively as the body of Christ, the bride, and the temple. In the pastoral epistles (such as Timothy and Titus), he deals with the church serving Christ as a local body. Both emphases are necessary for a balanced ministry. Certainly God sees the whole body with Christ as the Head; but as far as the ministry is concerned, He works through the local assemblies in different places. The "church universal" (body of Christ) into which the believer is baptized by the Spirit is a valid concept; but the "universal church" concept is not a substitute for the action of the local church. The "universal church" never sent out a missionary, built a hospital, observed the Lord's Supper, or helped a needy family. It is the local church that receives the greater emphasis in the NT, but the ministry of the local church will be stronger if the members realize their position in the body of Christ.

EPHESIANS 1

The key thought in this chapter is the wealth of blessings we have as Christians, spiritual blessings that are ours because we are in Christ (1:3). Paul informs us that each Person of the Godhead has blessed us (vv. 1-14), and then he prays that we might understand these blessings and the power they can be in our lives (vv. 15-23).

I. Blessings from the Father (1:1-6)

A. He has chosen us (vv. 3-4).

This is the wonderful doctrine of election, a doctrine that we cannot fully explain but one we can fully enjoy. Do not try to explain away the mystery of grace. God did not choose us in ourselves; He chose us in Christ, by grace. Note 1 Cor. 1:26-29; 2 Thes. 2:13-14; and John 6:37.

B. He has adopted us (v. 5).

"Election" refers to persons; predestination to purposes for those persons. God elects us to be saints (set-apart ones), then predestines that certain purposes in our lives shall come to pass (see Rom. 8:28ff). "Adoption" in the NT refers to the official act of a father who bestows the status of full adulthood on a son of minor status. It is not the taking in of an outsider; it is the placing of a family member into the privileges and blessings of adulthood. This means that even the youngest Christian has everything that Christ has and is rich in grace.

C. He has accepted us (v. 6).

In ourselves, we are not acceptable to God, but in Christ, we are "made accepted." Read the Epistle to Philemon for a beautiful illustration of this truth. Paul wrote, "Receive your slave Onesimus as you would receive me" (Phile. 17). Though we have sinned, Christ says to the Father, "Receive this saint as you would receive Me." Trace that wonderful phrase "in Christ" throughout Paul's letters—you will be thrilled!

II. Blessings from the Son (1:7-12)

A. He has redeemed us (v. 7a).

By giving His life on the cross, Christ purchased us from the slavery of sin. We have a present redemption in that He has delivered us from the penalty and power of sin; we shall have a future redemption (v. 14) when Christ delivers us from the presence of sin at His return.

B. He has forgiven us (v. 7b).

The word "forgive" literally means "to send away." Sin is a terrible burden that is sent away when a sinner turns to Christ. Christ carried the burden on the cross (1 Peter 2:24). It is pictured by the scapegoat on the Day of Atonement, taken into the wilderness (Lev. 16:20-22).

C. He has revealed God's will to us (vv. 8-10).

A "mystery" is a divine truth known only by God's people through revelation. In Christ we are a part of God's eternal purpose to gather together "all things in Christ" (v. 10). This present world is falling apart with war, strife, and sin. But one day God will usher in a new creation, with all things united in Christ.

D. He has made us an inheritance (vv. 11-12).

God has not only given us an inheritance in Christ (1 Peter 1:3-4), but He has made us an inheritance for Christ. The church is His body, temple, and bride; we shall some day share His glory.

III. Blessings from the Spirit (1:13-14)

A. He has sealed us (v. 13).

This important verse outlines the way of salvation. The sinner hears the Word of Truth, trusts in Christ, receives the Holy Spirit, and is sealed forever. "After that ye believed" ought to be "when ye believed," for the Spirit enters the heart the instant the sinner trusts Christ. This sealing means God owns us and will keep us. Nobody can break God's seal!

B. He has given us an earnest (v. 14).

"Earnest money" in business means money given as a down payment for a purchased possession. Christ has purchased our future for us, but we have not yet entered into all the blessings. God has given us His Spirit as the "down payment" to assure us that we will experience total redemption and receive God's promised blessings in glory.

Please note that at the end of each of these three sections, Paul tells why the Father, the Son, and the Spirit have given us these blessings: "To the praise of His glory" (vv. 6, 12, 14b). Salvation is by God's grace and for God's glory! God does not have to save anybody; when He does save the sinner, He does so for His own glory.

IV. Prayer for Understanding (1:15-23)

There are two prayers in Ephesians: (1) "that you might know," 1:15-23; and (2) "that you might be," 3:13-21. The first is for enlightenment, the second for enablement. Paul prays first that we might know what Christ has done for us; then he prays that we might live up to these wonderful blessings and put them to work in our daily lives. Notice Paul's requests:

A. *That God may give you spiritual understanding (vv. 17-18a).*

Spiritual truths must be spiritually discerned (1 Cor. 2:9-16), and this understanding can come only from the Spirit. He wrote the Word; He alone can teach us what it says.

B. *That you might know the hope of His calling (v. 18b).*

Because God chose us in Christ before the foundation of the world, we have a blessed hope for all eternity that depends not on our goodness but on His grace. Review vv. 4-6, where this calling is summarized for us. The Christian who does not know his high calling (Phil. 3:14), holy calling (2 Tim. 1:9), and heavenly calling (Heb. 3:1) will never be able to walk worthy of that calling (Eph. 4:1, where "vocation" is "calling").

C. *That you might know the riches of His inheritance (v. 18c).*

We not only have an inheritance in Christ, but we are an inheritance to Christ (see v. 11). The word "riches" appears often in Ephesians, suggesting that there is nothing lacking, nothing more that we need. Christians mature in the Lord when they learn how much they mean to Christ and then start living to bring joy to His heart.

D. *That you might know His power (vv. 19-23).*

The very power that raised Jesus from the dead is available for our daily lives! Christ has already won the victory over sin, death, the world, and Satan. God's people do not fight for victory but from victory! We are seated with Him in the heavenlies, where there are power, peace, and victory.

Of course, all these blessings are only for those who meet the conditions set forth in vv. 1-2. Note that Paul writes to living saints (not dead ones), people who have put faith in Christ. These saints (set-apart ones) have experienced God's grace and now enjoy God's peace. Nowhere does the Bible teach that the church makes people saints; only God can make a sinner a saint. And the sinner must become a saint while he is still alive, for after death is the judgment (Heb. 9:27).

EPHESIANS 2

Chapter 1 emphasized our possessions in Christ; chapter 2 emphasizes our position in Christ. Your position determines your possessions and authority. Regardless of where the President of the United States may be physically, his position as the man who sits behind the desk in the White House gives him power and authority. So with the Christian. Regardless of where we might be physically (Paul was a prisoner when he wrote this letter), we have power and authority in the spiritual realm because of our position in Christ.

I. We Are Raised and Seated on the Throne (2:1-10)

A. *What we were (vv. 1-3).*

What a picture of the lost sinner! To begin with, sinners are dead spiritually; that is, the inner man is dead to spiritual things and cannot respond to them. The Gospels describe the resurrections of three people that Jesus raised from the dead: (1) a twelve-year-old girl, Luke 8:49-55; (2) a young man, Luke 7:12-15; and (3) an older man, John 11. Each of them was dead; the only difference was their state of decomposition. Lazarus had been buried for four days and had begun to smell! All sinners are dead, regardless of age; the only difference between the unsaved church member and the vagrant on skid row is the state of decay. Sinners are not only dead, they are enslaved by the world and live for its pleasures and fashions. Tell them that this world is under the condemnation of God and is passing away, and they will laugh at you. They are also enslaved by

Satan, who is at work in the lives of unsaved people. This does not mean that he necessarily makes them drunkards or murderers; his usual tactic is to give people false security through self-righteousness. Jesus called the Pharisees "children of the devil" (John 8:44), yet they were religious, upstanding citizens.

We are born by nature children of wrath; when we reject Christ knowingly after reaching an age of accountability, we become children of disobedience by choice. When we trust Jesus Christ, we become children of God.

B. What God did (vv. 4-9).

"But God!" These words are among the greatest in the Bible. God could have allowed us to go on in sin and live eternally with the devil in hell, but instead He chose to save us. He gave us life (quickened us), raised us from the grave of sin, and took us out of the graveyard! More than that, He made us members of Christ! We have been quickened together, raised together, and we sit together in the heavenlies. God did this because He is rich in mercy and great in love. Mercy means that God does not give me what I do deserve; grace means that He gives me what I don't deserve.

C. What we are now (v. 10).

We are His workmanship, His new creation (2 Cor. 5:17). Read Phil. 2:12-13 and dare to believe that God works in you! What does the future hold? We do not know, but we do know who holds the future. The same loving Father that chose me, called me, and saved me has also marked out a wonderful plan for my life! "Oh, to grace how great a debtor, daily I'm constrained to be!"

II. We Are Reconciled and Set into the Temple (2:11-22)

In the first half of this chapter, Paul has been telling us what God has done for sinners in general; now he discusses Jews and Gentiles in particular. God had made no messianic covenants with the Gentiles, but God had promised the Jews a kingdom. What is the status of Jews and Gentiles in God's program today?

A. What the Gentiles were (vv. 11-12).

God makes a distinction between Jews and Gentiles racially (1 Cor. 10:32), but not individually (Rom. 10:11-13). The Gentiles were without Christ; that is, they had no promise of a Messiah. They were not a part of the nation of Israel; in fact, the OT laws put a great gulf between Jews and Gentiles. Instead of being "the people of God," the Gentiles were aliens. They were strangers, without hope and without the true God in the world. Contrast this sad plight with the privileged position of Israel described in Rom. 9:4-5. Verse 13 sums up the Gentiles' condition in two words: "far off." While the problem of sinners in general (vv. 1-10) was spiritual death, the problem of the Gentiles in particular was spiritual distance from God and His blessings. Note in the Gospels that whenever Christ helped a Gentile, He did it at a distance (Matt. 8:5-13; 15:22-28).

B. What God did (vv. 13-17).

"But now" in v. 13 parallels "But God" in v. 4. When Christ died on the cross, He broke down every barrier that stood between Jews and Gentiles. In the Jewish temple, there was a wall that separated the "Court of the Gentiles" from the rest of the structure; and on this wall was a sign giving warning that any Gentile who passed beyond it would be killed. Jesus Christ tore down that wall! He tore down the physical wall, for in Christ all are made one (v. 15, and see Gal. 3:28-29). He tore down the spiritual wall and brought the "far off" Gentiles near (v. 13). He tore down the legal wall, for He fulfilled the Law in Himself and ended the reign of the Mosaic law that separated Jews and Gentiles (vv. 14-15). Christ not only made peace between sinners and God (Rom. 5:1), but He also made peace between Jews and Gentiles. He took sinful Jews and sinful Gentiles and through His cross made a "new man" — the church.

Keep in mind that the mystery of the church was revealed through Paul (as we shall see in chapter 3), and that it took some time for the Jewish Christians to understand God's new program. For centuries, God had kept Jews and Gentiles separated, and the Jews had taught that the only way a Gentile could be brought near to God was by becoming a Jew. Now the truth was revealed that the cross of Christ condemns both Jews and Gentiles as sinners, but also reconciles to God in one body those that believe on Jesus.

C. What the Gentiles and Jews are now (vv. 18-22).

Both have access to the Father in the Spirit. Under the Jewish economy, only the high priest could go into the presence of God, and that only once a year. But in the new creation, every believer has the privilege of coming into the holy of holies (Heb. 10:19-25). Both Jews and Gentiles now belong to the household of God, and the Jew can no longer claim greater privileges. It is through faith in His blood that Jews and Gentiles are justified.

Paul closes by picturing the church as a temple. This would be a fitting image not only for the Jews, who revered their holy temple at Jerusalem, but also for the Ephesians, who had the great temple of Diana in their city (Acts 19:21-41). Each believer is a living stone set into the temple (1 Peter 2:4-8). The apostles and prophets (NT prophets, 4:11) are not the foundation; they laid the foundation since they were the first to proclaim the message. Christ is the foundation of the local church (1 Cor. 3:11) and the chief cornerstone of the whole building. The church today is a living, growing temple; when it is completed, Christ will return and take the temple to glory. God dwelt in the Jewish tabernacle (Ex. 40:34), in Solomon's temple (2 Chron. 7:1), in the temple of Christ's body (John 1:14 and 2:18-22), and today in the individual believer (1 Cor. 6:19-20) and the church (Eph. 2:21-22). What a privilege to be the very habitation of God through the Spirit!

EPHESIANS 3

This chapter closes the first half of Ephesians in which Paul has described our wealth in Christ. Paul is about to move into the practical section (our walk with Christ), but first he pauses to pray. He begins his prayer in v. 1, but does not continue until he gets to v. 13! The intervening verses form a long parenthesis, but they are important, because they explain Paul's special ministry to the church body and to the Gentiles.

I. Paul's Explanation of His Ministry (3:1-12)

The first thing we note is that Paul calls himself a prisoner and that he connects his imprisonment to the Gentiles! Go back to Acts 22 for the explanation. Paul had been arrested in Jerusalem and was making his defense to his people. They listened to him until he got to the word "Gentiles" (Acts 22:21), and then a riot broke loose! The relationship of Gentiles to Jews was even a problem among the early Jewish believers, as Acts 10 and 15 reveal.

Paul explains that God had given him a special revelation and a special stewardship (dispensation). He terms this revelation "the mystery of Christ." (It would be well for you to review the introductory notes to Acts, as well as the notes for Romans 9–11.) In the OT, God revealed through prophecy His program for the people of Israel: that He would establish them in their kingdom when they received their Messiah, and then through Israel He would convert the Gentiles. God offered them the kingdom through the ministry of John the Baptist (Matt. 3:2), whom the Jews permitted to be slain; through Christ's ministry (Matt.4:12-17), whom the Jews asked to be slain; and through the apostles and Stephen (Acts 2–7), whom the Jews themselves actually killed (Acts 7:54-60). Three offers of the kingdom were made to Israel, but the nation rejected each of them. They had rejected the Father, who had sent John; the Son; and the Spirit, who was energizing the witnessing apostles. With the death of Stephen, the offers of kingdom ceased temporarily; the message went out to the Samaritans and the Gentiles (Acts 8 and 10); in the meantime Paul was saved miraculously in Acts 9.

Paul's ministry was to the Gentiles, and his message was that of grace, Paul's special task was to share the truth of the one body, the mystery of the church. Note Rom. 16:25-26; Col. 1:26-27 and 4:3-4; as well as Eph. 6:19. Here in v. 6, he states the mystery clearly: that believing Gentiles and Jews are one body in Christ. This mystery had not been made known before this time; but now God had revealed it to His apostles and NT prophets by the Spirit. To say that the twelve apostles from the beginning understood the mystery of the church is to deny Paul's inspired words here. Even Peter had to have a vision from heaven in Acts 10 before he would go to the Gentiles. The truth of the one body was given to Paul and its significance dawned gradually upon the early church.

"Unsearchable riches" in v. 8 is literally "untraceable riches." You cannot detect the mystery of the one body in the OT Scriptures; it was a mystery hidden in Christ. In vv. 9-10 we see a dual ministry: Paul was to make known the dispensation ("fellowship," same word as v. 2) of the mystery to people in general; the church was to reveal the wisdom of God to angelic beings ("principalities and powers," see 6:12). Angels are learning about God's grace through the church! (See 1 Peter 1:10-12.) Satan knows the Scriptures; by keeping His program for the church hidden, God prevented Satan from hindering the plan. Satan took Christ to the cross, and by so doing sealed his own doom! It is tragic today when we see pastors and churches wandering about aimlessly in their ministries because they do not understand God's purpose for the church in this age. If they would move out of the message of Acts 1–6 and into that of Ephesians and Colossians, they would not be wasting time, talent, and money "building the kingdom" but instead would be building the church.

II. Paul's Intercession for the Saints (3:13-21)

You will recall that the two prayers in Ephesians (here and in 1:15-23) complement each other. The first is a prayer for enlightenment; the second is for enablement. Paul wants the Ephesians to learn all they have in Christ and then live what they have learned. He prays for God's family in heaven and earth, for that is where His family is; none are "under the earth" (see Phil. 2:10). This means there is no purgatory where people are being prepared for heaven. He prays that the inner person might know spiritual strength. How carelessly some Christians treat the inner person! The Holy Spirit empowers us from within through the Word of God and prayer. In vv. 20-21, Paul points out that as we pray, God's Spirit goes to work in us; and 1 Thes. 2:13 (along with Col. 3:16) teaches that God empowers us through His Word. The early saints gave themselves to "prayer and the Word of God" (Acts 6:4), and God worked mightily in them and through them.

He wants Christ to "feel at home" (dwell, v. 17) in their hearts. Of course, Christ does dwell in the heart of every true believer, but not every heart is a comfortable home for Him. Christ loved to go to Bethany because his friends there loved Him, fed on His Word, and served Him. When Christ came to earth to talk to Abraham (Gen. 18), He sent two angels ahead to visit Lot (Gen. 19) because He did not feel at home in the house of a worldly believer. Does He feel at home in our hearts?

Christ feels at home in our hearts when He finds faith and love. "Rooted" (v. 17) suggests a steady position, a habit of faith and love, like a tree rooted in the soil. Too many Christians want the fruits of the Spirit without being rooted in spiritual things.

"Comprehend" in v. 18 should be "apprehend—lay hold of." Paul has already prayed that they might understand; now he prays that they might lay their hands on these wonderful blessings and grasp them for themselves. By faith we lay hold of God's promises. Paul especially wants them to lay hold of God's immeasurable love, a love that fills all things. Far too many Christians think of God as an angry Judge or a stern Master instead of a loving Father.

"Filled with all the fullness of God" (v. 19): this is God's ultimate purpose for our lives. Read carefully John 1:16 and Col. 2:9-10. "You are complete in Him" states Col. 2:10, NKJV. Why live like paupers when God has given us His fullness? An empty life is disappointing and dangerous; if the Spirit of God does not fill us, then the spirit of disobedience (2:2) goes to work and we fall into sin.

Verses 20-21 declare a thrilling benediction, closing this first section of the letter. God works in us! God works through us! God is glorified in us! What a wonderful salvation we have! This power works in us as we open our hearts to Christ, cultivate this abiding fellowship, pray, and submit to the Word. There is no reason for us believers to be "down in the dumps" when we are seated with Christ (2:6) and filled with God's fullness.

As we close this first section, it would be helpful to note Paul's "spiritual postures," for they give us the secret of God's blessing. Paul is seated with Christ (2:6), built upon Christ (2:20), and is bowing his knees to the Father (3:14). This is what makes it possible for him to walk (4:1), grow up (4:15), and stand against Satan (6:14ff). Our spiritual position in Christ makes possible our victorious walk on earth.

EPHESIANS 4

We now begin the second half of the letter, which emphasizes the Christian's walk (4:1, 17; 5:2, 8, 15). The Christian life is compared to a walk because it starts with one step of faith, involves progress, and demands balance and strength. If we do not learn to walk, we will never be able to run (Heb. 12:1-2) or stand in the battle (Eph. 6:11ff).

I. Walk In Unity (4:1-16)

We have been called to one body; therefore, as we seek to walk in unity, we are walking worthy of the calling (vocation) we have from God. Paul has described this high calling in chapters 1–3; now he pleads with us to live up to these blessings. We do not live for Christ to get something; we live for Christ because He has already done so much for us! Note that Paul does not tell us to manufacture unity, but to maintain the unity already existing in the body. This is not organizational uniformity, a "super church"; this is organic, living union and unity. Note John 17:20-23.

The grounds for this unity are listed in vv. 4-6. You will note that the central item in this list is "one Lord." The fact that there is "one body" does not minimize the importance of the local bodies of believers. You will notice that Paul is dealing here with spiritual truths relating to the whole program of God. When we read his other epistles (such as Corinthians and the letters to Timothy and Titus) we see the practical outworking of these truths. The major emphasis in the NT is on the local assembly; but the administration of the local assembly must be based on what Paul teaches about the "one body."

The gifts for unity in the church are given in vv. 7-11. When Christ ascended, He gave gifts to His people through the coming of the Holy Spirit. He also gave these gifted people to the local assemblies. While vv. 1-6 deal with the one body and its unity, vv. 7-11 deal with the many local bodies and the diversities of gifts.

The goal of the church is described in vv. 12-16. The pastor-teacher is to nourish the saints with the Word of God and equip them for service; the saints, in turn, perform the work of the ministry. As each saint grows and wins others, the entire body grows in Christ. Verse 12 should read: "For the maturing of the saints unto the work of the ministry, unto the building up of the body of Christ." Each saint shares in the growth of the church. Unfortunately, there are some Christians who are still babies (v. 14, and see 1 Cor. 3:1ff), who are unstable and easily led astray. Satan and his ministers (see 2 Cor. 11:14-15) are waiting to tear down the church with their lies. The church is edified (built up) through the Word of God (Acts 20:32 and 1 Cor. 14:4). Churches are not built up and strengthened through man-made programs, entertainment, recreation, or "drives." The church is a body and must have spiritual food; this food is the Word of God. When the body is completed, Christ will return and take His body (of which He is the Head, 1:22-23) home to glory.

II. Walk In Purity (4:17-32)

The first part of this chapter described the believer's relationship to the church; now Paul deals with the believer's relationship to the world. Certainly we are "in Christ" and a part of the body; but we are also in the world, where there is temptation and defilement. We cannot depart from the world because we have a responsibility to witness to it; but we must walk in purity and not allow the world to defile us.

Paul starts with the negative: do not walk the way the unsaved heathen walk. He explains the reasons for their godless walk: (1) their minds are darkened because they believe lies and have not received the truth; (2) they are spiritually dead; (3) they have surrendered themselves to do all kinds of sin. Compare this description with 2:1-3 and 2 Cor. 4. We might summarize their plight by saying they were walking in the wrong way because they did not know the truth and had never received the life. Only the Christ of John 14:6 could meet their spiritual needs.

The Christian life must be radically different from the old life. Paul expected the Ephesians to experience changes, and he gave three admonitions: "put off" (vv. 22-23), "put on" (v. 24), and "put away" (vv. 25ff). Romans 6 teaches us that the old self has been crucified and buried, and that, as we reckon this to be true, we "put off" the old man. God has done His part; it remains for us to believe what He has said and "change clothes." The instruction Jesus gave concerning Lazarus applies to each believer: "Loose him—take off the grave clothes—and let him go!" But it is not enough simply to die to the old life; there must also be resurrection and the manifestation of the new life. We put off the "grave clothes" of the old life and put on the "grace clothes" of the new life. We are a part of God's new creation (v. 24 and 2:10) and therefore we walk in newness of life (Rom. 6:4).

We must "put away" (once-for-all) certain sins, and he names these in 25ff. Note how Paul ties each commandment to a spiritual truth: we are members of each other (v. 25); we are sealed until the day of redemption (v. 30); God has forgiven us (v. 32). Doctrine and duty are twin blessings in the Bible, both the Christian's wealth and his walk in Christ.

If we belong to the truth, how can we indulge in lies? Satan is the father of lies (John 8:44); his spirits tell lies (1 John 2:21, 27); one day the whole world will believe "The Lie" (2 Thes. 2:9-11).

There is an anger that is not sinful (Mark 3:5). If we are angry at persons, then sin will come along; if we are angry at sin and sinful principles, we can maintain a holy walk. How easy it is for Christians to call their tempers "righteous indignation"! The wrath of man never brings about the righteousness of God (James 1:20).

Giving place to the devil (v. 27) involves both lying and anger; for Satan is a liar and a murderer. Do we realize that lies and hypocrisy and anger give Satan a foothold in our lives? Cain's lies and anger led to murder (Gen. 4).

Verse 25 ties in with 1 Thes. 4:11 and 2 Thes. 3:6-12. The unsaved thief used to rob to please himself; now that he is saved, he should work to be able to give to others. This is the wonderful change grace makes in the heart of a person.

Our lips should speak that which builds up (Col. 4:6; Ps. 141:3). Corruption from the lips only means that there is corruption in the heart. The Spirit has sealed us (1:13-14); we should not grieve Him by allowing these sins of action and attitude to be in our lives. In Scripture, the Spirit is pictured as a dove (John 1:32), and a dove is a clean bird that loves peace. Anger and clamor should be done away with by means of forgiveness and Christian love.

EPHESIANS 5

Paul continues his description of the Christian's walk.

I. Walk in Love (5:1-6)

"Followers" (v. 1) means "imitators, mimics"; as God's children, we should imitate our Father. God is love, and we should walk in love. The example of Christ's love should inspire us. See John 15:9 and 12 and 1 John 3:16-18. Here Paul pictures Christ as the sweet-savor offering, bringing joy to the heart of God as He gives Himself for sinners.

Of course, the right kind of love implies that we hate certain things (Rom. 12:9). There are some sins that should not even be named among saints. In v. 4, Paul is not objecting to humor, but to unsuitable and unclean jesting. Certainly no Christian should use his or her lips to spread questionable stories. We should never have to say, "Take this with a grain of salt" because our speech should always be seasoned with salt (Col. 4:6). False teachers may say that you can be a Christian and live in habitual, deliberate sin; but Paul calls these teachings "empty [vain] words." Compare vv. 5-6 with Gal. 5:21ff and 1 Cor. 6:9-10. We were "children of disobedience" (2:1-3); now we are children of God, and we ought to walk in love.

II. Walk in the Light (5:7-14)

The word translated "partakers" (v. 7) implies having in common; it is often translated "fellowship" or "partnership." Christians are partakers of: (1) the divine nature, 2 Peter 1:4; (2) God's promises, Eph. 3:6; (3) Christ's sufferings, 1 Peter 4:13; (4) holiness, Heb. 12:10; (5) the heavenly calling, Heb. 3:1 and (6) God's glory, 1 Peter 5:1. Since we have this wonderful partnership with God, how could we ever become partners with that which belongs to sin and darkness? "What communion has light with darkness?" asks 2 Cor. 6:14 (NKJV). We are children of light and ought to walk in the light. Darkness produces sin and lies; the fruit of the light (a better translation of v. 9) is goodness, righteousness, and truth. The light cannot compromise with the darkness; it can only expose it. Note John 3:19-21 and 1 John 1:5-10.

III. Walk Carefully (5:15-17)

The word "circumspectly" (v. 15) carries the idea of looking around carefully so as not to stumble. It means walking intelligently and not in ignorance. How foolish to stumble along through life and never seek to know the will of the Lord! Instead of walking "accurately" (which is equivalent to "circumspectly"), they miss the mark, miss the road, and end up suffering on some detour. God wants us to be wise and understand His will for our lives. As we obey His will, we "buy up the opportunities" (redeem the time, v. 16) and do not waste time, energy, money, and talent in that which is apart from His will. Lost opportunities may never be regained; they are gone forever.

IV. Walk in Harmony (5:18–6:9)

This section concludes in chapter 6 and deals with harmony between husbands and wives, parents and children, and workers and masters.

The secret of harmony in the home and on the job is the fullness of the Spirit. The unity of the church and the harmony of the home both depend on the Spirit (4:3; 5:18). It is power from within, not pressure from without, that holds the church and the home together. Note the evidences of a Spirit-filled life: joy (v. 19), gratitude (v. 20), obedience (v. 21ff). Compare Col. 3:15-17 and you will see that when Christians are filled with the Word of God they will have the same characteristics. In other words, to be filled with the Spirit of God means to be controlled by the Word of God. The marks of a Spirit-filled Christian are not unusual emotional experiences, miracles, and tongues, but rather Christian character.

The principle of headship is what helps bring harmony to the home. "As unto Christ" is the motive. Wives are to submit to their husbands as unto Christ; husbands are to love their wives as Christ loves the church; and children are to obey as unto the Lord. Family members who are right with the Lord will be right with each other.

The church is pictured as the bride of Christ. It is interesting to compare the church to the first bride in the Bible, Eve (Gen. 2:18-25). She was taken from Adam's side, and Christ's side was pierced for us on the cross. She was formed when Adam was asleep, and Christ experienced the sleep of death to create the church. Eve shared Adam's nature, and the church partakes of Christ's nature (vv. 30-31). Eve was the object of her mate's love and care, and Christ loves the church and cares for it. Adam was willing to become a sinner because of his love for his wife (1 Tim. 2:11-15), and Christ willingly was made sin because of His love for the church. Eve was formed and brought to Adam before sin entered the human family; the church was in the mind and heart of God before the foundation of the world. Note Rom. 7:4 and 2 Cor. 11:2 for the application of this truth of marriage to the individual believer and the local church.

What is Christ's present ministry to the church? He is sanctifying and cleansing the church through the Word of God, and He does this by the work of the Spirit in His chosen servants (4:11-16). The water in v. 26 is not baptism. For one thing, Paul is talking about a continuous process, and no Christian is baptized continuously. Water for washing is a symbol of the Word of God (John 15:3 and 13:1-12). When Christ takes His church to glory, it will then be perfect, spotless, and without blemish. See John 17:22-24.

The Word is not only water that cleanses the church, but it is also food that nourishes the church (v. 29). It is the spiritual food for the new nature of the believer.

In 6:1-9, Paul applies the same truth to children and to servants. Children are to obey their parents for several reasons: (1) it is right; (2) it is commanded; (3) it brings blessings. The father who honors the Lord will have little trouble winning the love and respect of his children or the sincere love of his wife. Paul also warns fathers in

v. 4 to refrain from provoking their children with undue demands. The Golden Rule applies to the home, and children must be treated like people and not things. Fathers are to discipline children (nurture) and counsel them (admonition) in the Lord.

Servants must remember that they serve Christ first of all. To be double-minded and try to serve two masters will lead to trouble (Matt. 6:24); singleness of heart means the heart is fixed on pleasing Christ, and not on worldly gain. "Eyeservice" means working when the master is watching and loafing when he is gone; but if we serve Christ on the job, we are aware that He is always watching us!

EPHESIANS 6

This final section (6:10-24) tells us how to walk in victory. It is a sad thing when believers do not know the provisions God has made for victory over Satan. Christ has completely overcome Satan and his hosts (Col. 2:13-15 and Eph. 1:19-23), and His victory is ours by faith.

I. The Enemy We Fight (6:10-12)

Satan is a strong enemy, so Paul exhorts us to be strong. Paul knows that the flesh is weak (Mark 14:38) and that we can overcome only in Christ's power. Note that before Paul tells us to stand in v. 11, he commands us in v. 10 to be strong. How do we receive this strength to stand? By realizing that we are seated with Christ in the heavenlies far above all of Satan's principalities and powers (1:19-23), and that the very power of God is available to us through the indwelling Spirit (3:14-21). We must sit before we can walk, and we must walk before we can stand. We must understand our spiritual position before we can have spiritual power.

Many Bible students believe that Satan was the anointed cherub whom God placed in charge of the newly created earth (Ezek. 28:11-19). Through pride, he fell (Isa. 14:9ff) and took with him a host of angelic beings who now make up his army of principalities and powers. Satan has access to heaven (Job 1–3), but one day will be cast from heaven (Rev. 12:9ff). He is the deceiver (2 Cor. 11:3) and the destroyer (Rev. 9:11, where Abaddon means "destroyer"), for he goes about as a serpent and a lion (1 Peter 5:8-9). We

Christians need to realize that we do not fight against flesh and blood but against the "spirit who now works in the sons of disobedience" (Eph. 2:2, NKJV). Just as the Spirit of God works in believers to make them holy, so the spirit of disobedience (Satan and his demons) works in the lives of unbelievers. How foolish to fight flesh and blood when the real enemy is merely using that flesh and blood to obstruct the Lord's work. This is the mistake Peter made in the Garden of Gethsemane when he tried to overcome the devil with the sword (see Matt. 26:51). Moses made the same mistake when he killed the Egyptian (Acts 7:23-29). The only way to fight spiritual enemies is with spiritual weapons — the Word of God and prayer.

We must beware of the wiles of the devil (Eph. 6:11) which means his strategy, devices (2 Cor. 2:11) and snares (1 Tim. 3:7). He is the ruler of darkness and uses darkness (ignorance and lies) to further his cause (2 Cor. 4:1ff; Luke 22:53).

II. The Equipment We Wear (6:13-17)

It is important that the Christian not "give place to the devil" (4:27), that is, leave any area unprotected so that Satan can get a foothold. The armor Paul describes is for protection; the sword (God's Word) is for actual battle. Each part of the spiritual armor tells us what believers must have if they are to be protected against Satan:

Truth — Satan is a liar, but the Christian who knows the truth will not be deceived.

Righteousness — This means the consistent daily walk of the Christian. Satan is the accuser (Rev. 12:10), but the believer who walks in the light will give Satan no opportunity to attack. We stand in the imputed righteousness of Christ, and we walk in the imparted righteousness of the Holy Spirit.

Peace — Satan is a divider and a destroyer. When the believer walks in the way of peace, the Gospel way, then Satan cannot reach him. The Christian's feet should be clean (John 13), beautiful (Rom. 10:15), and shod with the Gospel. Christians who are ready to witness for Christ have an easier time defeating the evil one.

Faith — Satan is the source of unbelief and doubt. "Has God indeed said?" is his favorite question (Gen. 3:1). Faith is what overcomes every foe (1 John 5:4). As believers use the shield of faith, the fiery darts of unbelief and doubt are kept away.

Salvation—This verse (17) probably refers to our ultimate salvation when Christ returns (see 1 Thes. 5:8). The believer whose mind is fixed on Christ's imminent coming will not fall into Satan's traps. The blessed hope must be like a helmet to protect the mind. Satan would love to have us believe that Christ is not coming back, or that He may not come back today. Read Matt. 24:45-51 to see what happens to the person who takes off the helmet of salvation.

These pieces of armor are for the believer's protection; the sword of the Spirit and prayer are weapons for attacking Satan's strongholds and defeating him. The Christian must fight spiritual enemies with spiritual weapons (2 Cor. 10:4), and the Word of God is the only sword we need. God's sword has life and power (Heb. 4:12) and never grows dull. Christians conquer as they understand God's Word, memorize it, and obey it.

III. The Energy We Use (6:18-24)

Armor and weapons are not sufficient to win a battle; there must be energy to do the job. Our energy comes from prayer. We use the sword of the Spirit, and we pray in the Spirit: the Holy Spirit empowers us to win the battle. Read again Eph. 3:14-21 and dare to believe it. The Word of God and prayer are the two resources God has given the church to overcome the enemy and gain territory for God's glory. Note Acts 20:32 and Acts 6:4; also 1 Sam. 12:23.

Christian soldiers must pray with their eyes open. "Watch and pray" is God's secret for overcoming the world (Mark 13:33), the flesh (Mark 14:38), and the devil (Eph. 6:18). We should also "watch and pray" for opportunities to serve Christ (Col. 4:2-3).

We should not only pray for ourselves, but we should also pray for our fellow soldiers (6:19ff). Paul was never too proud to ask for prayer. He wanted to have the power to be able to share the mystery (see 3:1-12), the very message that had brought him to jail. "Ambassador in bonds" is a peculiar title, yet that is exactly what Paul was. Chained to a different Roman soldier every six hours, Paul had a wonderful opportunity to witness for Christ.

Paul closes this magnificent epistle with several personal items, knowing that his friends would want to know his condition. Certainly they could pray for him more intelligently if they knew his needs. But Paul wants to give them comfort, too (v. 22). Paul was a true saint, drawing upon God's supply for his every need.

PHILIPPIANS

A Suggested Outline of Philippians

I. The Single Mind (1)

    A. The fellowship of the Gospel (1:1-11)
    B. The furtherance of the Gospel (1:12-26)
    C. The faith of the Gospel (1:27-30)

II. The Submissive Mind (2)

    A. Example of Christ (2:1-11)
    B. Example of Paul (2:12-18)
    C. Example of Timothy (2:19-24)
    D. Example of Epaphroditus (2:25-30)

III. The Spiritual Mind (3)

    A. The Christian's past: salvation (3:1-11)
    B. The Christian's present: sanctification (3:12-16)
    C. The Christian's future: glorification (3:17-21)

IV. The Secure Mind (4)

    A. God's presence: "at hand" (4:1-5)
    B. God's peace (4:6-9)
    C. God's power (4:10-13)
    D. God's provision (4:14-23)

Introductory Notes to Philippians

I. The City

Philippi was a Roman colony, governed by Roman laws and subject to Roman rule. It was a little Rome in the midst of a Greek culture, just as the church is a "colony of heaven" here on earth (Phil. 3:20, where "conversation" means "citizenship"). The original city, named after King Philip, who had won it from the Thracians, was noted for its gold as well as its farming. Its soil was very fertile. Check your map to see its location in Macedonia.

II. The Church

The first church founded in Europe was planted by Paul in Philippi (see Acts 16) on his second missionary journey. After Paul moved on to Thessalonica, the Philippian believers sent him support (Phil. 4:15, and see 2 Cor. 11:9). Five years later, while on his third journey, Paul visited Philippi on the way to Corinth, and then on the return trip (Acts 20:1-6). There was a deep love between Paul and the people at Philippi. Certainly their church gave the apostle little trouble! No wonder he enjoyed fellowshipping with them!

III. The Letter

The church had heard of Paul's house arrest in Rome and wanted to send him aid. They sent one of their men (perhaps an elder) named Epaphroditus to carry their offering to the needy apostle in Rome. The journey from Philippi to Rome usually took about a month. Epaphroditus remained with Paul in Rome and ministered to him and with him, so much so, in fact, that he became ill (Phil. 2:25-30). Apparently when Paul wrote his acknowledgment to the church, he mentioned his friend's illness. The church then became concerned about him as well as Paul. It is also possible that Epaphroditus stayed with Paul a few months too long and was criticized by the church for his tardiness. At any rate, when Epaphroditus regained his strength, Paul sent him back home with the letter that we know as the Epistle to the Philippians. Paul had several purposes in mind when he wrote the letter: (1) to explain his circumstances to friends who were concerned about him; (2) to explain Epaphroditus' situation and defend him to his critics; (3)

to thank the Philippians again for their generous support; (4) to encourage them in the Christian life; (5) to encourage the unity of the church.

IV. The Emphasis

One of the key themes in Philippians is joy. "Joy" is mentioned in one way or another nineteen times in these four brief chapters. Another emphasis is the mind. As we read Philippians, note how many times Paul talks about remembering and thinking. We can summarize the theme of the book as "the Christlike mind that brings Christian joy." In each chapter, Paul describes the kind of mind Christians must have if they are to enjoy Christ's peace and joy. Certainly our thoughts have a great influence on our lives, and wrong thinking leads to wrong living. We should notice in our suggested outline that there are four minds described: the single mind, the submissive mind, the spiritual mind, and the secure mind.

Of course, we should not conclude that this is the only lesson to be gained from this wonderful letter. Paul teaches us much about Christ in this epistle: Christ is our life (chap. 1), our example (chap. 2), our goal (chap. 3), and our strength (chap. 4). The word "sin" is nowhere mentioned in Philippians, and the only suggestion of sorrow is in 3:18, where Paul weeps over the professed Christians who are worldly minded and thereby dishonor Christ.

PHILIPPIANS 1

Certainly Paul's circumstances were anything but joyful! He had been arrested illegally, taken to Rome, and was now awaiting trial. There was division among the Christians there (1:14-17), and some were trying to make matters worse for the apostle. How was he able to have such joy in the midst of uncomfortable circumstances? He had the "single mind"—his concern was not for Paul, but for Christ and the Gospel. Five times in this chapter he mentions the Gospel (vv. 5, 7, 12, 17, 27), and Christ is mentioned seventeen times! Paul looked upon these circumstances as sent by God (v. 13) for the purpose of exalting Christ (v. 20). If Paul had been double-minded, he would have complained because life was so uncomfortable. The single mind is concerned with three priorities.

I. The Fellowship of the Gospel (1:1-11)

To be "in Christ" and a part of the Christian fellowship is a source of joy when things become difficult. Here is Paul, a prisoner in Rome, yet rejoicing because of the fellowship of the Gospel. Three phrases summarize his joyful attitude.

A. "I have you in my mind" (vv. 1-6).

Paul was not thinking about himself; he was thinking instead about the dear saints (set-apart ones) in far-off Philippi. Every memory was a blessing to him—including the suffering he experienced in that Philippian jail (Acts 16). As he prayed for them, he rejoiced over their salvation and growth. He knew that what Christ had begun in their lives would be completed, for Christ is the Alpha and Omega, the Author and Finisher of our faith (Rev. 1:8; Heb. 12:1-2).

B. "I have you in my heart" (vv. 7-8).

The Philippian church was composed of a mixed group of people, but they were bound together by love. Among them were wealthy Lydia, the jailer, the slave girl (all found in Acts 16), plus other believers, mostly Gentiles. They had shared in the Gospel ministry with Paul; their hearts were united in their love for Christ and each other. How different they were from the Corinthian church! (2 Cor. 12:20-21)

C. "I have you in my prayers" (vv. 9-11).

Paul always took time to pray for people; his prayer here is that they might live full lives. An empty Christian is a tragedy! He prayed that they might be full of love and discernment; that they might be faithful in their daily walk; and that they might be fruitful in Christian service. This was a prayer for Christian maturity.

II. The Furtherance of the Gospel (1:12-26)

Notice how Paul describes all the suffering he had been through; he calls these trying events "the things that have happened unto me" (1:12). Most of us would have gone into great detail about shipwreck and chains, but not Paul. His desire was to honor Christ and promote the Gospel.

A. He put Christ first (vv. 12-21).

Were there chains on his wrists? These were his "bonds in Christ." Were his enemies causing trouble by their selfish preaching? "So what? They are preaching Christ!" Were his friends worried about him and praying for him? "Fine! This will exalt Christ!" Was there a possibility that he might die? "Then Christ will be magnified by life or by death!" This is the single mind—putting Christ and the Gospel ahead of everything else.

When we take Christ into every circumstance, we will have joy. Paul was not the prisoner of Rome; he was the "prisoner of Jesus Christ" (Eph. 3:1; 4:1). The soldiers chained to his wrist were not guards; they were souls for whom Christ died. Paul had a "captive audience," and from 1:13 and 4:22, we conclude that he won some of them to Christ. The single-minded Christian does not allow circumstances to overcome him; he or she turns those circumstances into opportunities to magnify Christ and win souls.

B. He put others second (vv. 22-26).

Selfishness always breeds unhappiness. Paul had joy because he loved others. He prayed for others, encouraged others, and sought to bring joy to others. Paul's "heaven on earth" was helping others! While he longed to be with Christ, he eagerly yearned to remain and help these believers grow in Christ.

C. He put himself last.

His body was not his own; his future was not his own; his reputation was not his own. In contrast, when we put ourselves first, it always brings misery.

561

Whenever difficulties affect our lives, we should always be sure that we have the single mind that says, "Lord, whatever comes, I want Christ to be glorified." This is the secret of Christian joy.

III. The Faith of the Gospel (1:27-30)

There are battles to fight in the Christian life, and Paul warns here about the enemies that would attack us. New Christians go through these three stages: (1) they become sons or daughters in the family (the fellowship of the Gospel); (2) they become servants (the furtherance of the Gospel); and then (3) they become soldiers (the faith of the Gospel). Satan is out to defeat the church, and Christians need to have the single mind to face him and "fight the good fight of faith." Paul gives several encouragements here to help the Christian defend the faith of the Gospel.

A. "You are not standing alone" (v. 27).

How wonderful it is to know that others are standing right with us as we fight the battles of life. There is no substitute for the unity and harmony of the Christian church. Satan is the great divider and destroyer; Christ is the uniter and builder.

B. "You are on the winning side" (v. 28).

"Don't let the enemy frighten you!" Paul counsels. "He knows he's losing and you're winning!" The unity and faith of the believers is an "evident token" (clear omen or sign) to the enemy that he is going to lose.

C. "It is a privilege to suffer for Christ" (vv. 29-30).

It is wonderful to believe on Christ and receive the free gift of salvation, but there is another gift: the gift of suffering for Jesus' sake. Philippians 3:10 points out that our suffering is in fellowship with Him; see also Acts 5:41. What a privilege to follow in the train of such saints as Paul as we suffer for Jesus' sake!

But, whatever happens, a Christian should always act like a Christian. "Let your behavior be such that it can be identified with the Gospel," Paul warns in 1:27. Someone once asked Gandhi, "What is the greatest hindrance to Christian missions in India?" Gandhi replied, "Christians." Such criticism may also apply to Christians in other lands besides India. Even in the midst of battle, we must behave like Christians.

In the midst of trouble, Paul showed quiet confidence. He was confident that the Philippians would continue in their Christian walk (v. 6); he was rejoicing that his trials had given the believers in Rome new confidence (v. 14); and he was confident that he would come through these trials and be restored to his friends again (v. 25). This is the blessing of the single mind—that joyful confidence in God, knowing that He is in control of circumstances.

PHILIPPIANS 2

Circumstances may cause us to lose our joy, but *people* can also bring trials that rob us of joy. How many times we lose our peace and joy because of what people say or do. The best remedy for these trials is the submissive mind, the humble mind that seeks only to honor Christ. Pride is the cause of much unrest and contention (read James 4), but humility brings peace and joy. Paul gives four examples for us to follow so that we may achieve the submissive mind.

I. The Example of Christ (2:1-11)

There is the suggestion in this passage of disunity in the Philippian church (see also 4:1-3). Paul appeals to them on the basis of their Christian experience to have unity of mind and heart and to put others ahead of themselves. What motives are there for unity in the church? Christ is the greatest incentive; if we are in Christ, we ought to be able to live with one another! Other incentives include love, the fellowship of the Spirit, the deep-seated desires we have in Christ, and the joy we can bring to others. Paul saw strife and selfish ambition among the Roman believers (1:14-17), and he warns that it must not be present at Philippi. "Lowliness of mind"—this is the submissive mind that thinks not of itself but of Christ and others. "Humility is not thinking meanly of ourselves; it is just not thinking of ourselves at all." Paul points to the attitude of Christ before His incarnation. Was He selfishly trying to hold on to His privileges as God? No! He willingly laid aside His glory and "put on" the form of a servant. He did not cease to be God, but He did lay aside His glory and the independent use of His attributes as God. His life as the God-Man on earth was completely subjected to the Father. "I do always those things that please

Him" (John 8:29). Jesus humbled Himself to become flesh, and then to become sin as He willingly went to the cross.

But Christ's experience proves that exaltation always follows humiliation. "Humble yourselves therefore under the mighty hand of God, that He may exalt you in due time," promises 1 Peter 5:6. The person who exalts himself will be humbled (Luke 14:11). Remember what happened to Pharaoh, King Saul, Nebuchadnezzar, Haman, and Herod? We do not worship a "babe in a manger" or a "sacrifice on a cross"; we worship an exalted Lord seated on the throne of the universe. Christ's life, death, and resurrection proved eternally that the way to be exalted is to be humbled before God. There is no joy or peace in pride and self-seeking. When we have the submissive mind that Christ had, then we will have the joy and peace that He alone can give.

II. The Example of Paul (2:12-18)

Wherever there is the submissive mind, there will be sacrifice and service. This was true of Christ (vv. 7-8), Paul (v. 17), Timothy (vv. 21-22), and Epaphroditus (v. 30). The single mind leads to the submissive mind: as we seek to live for Christ, we live for others. How true this was in Paul's life! The secret? Christians allow God to work in them. The flesh cannot "work up" humility or dedication; this must come from within by the power of the Spirit. God works in us before He works through us, and He uses the Word (1 Thes. 2:13), the Spirit (Eph. 3:16, 20-21), and prayer.

Paul gives us several pictures of Christians who have the submissive mind. He portrays them as obedient children of God, seeking to honor the Father; as stars shining in a dark world; and as athletes who hold out their batons to the next runner. In vv. 17-18, Paul describes himself as a drink-offering being poured out on the altar. Where there is the submissive mind, the humble mind, there must be sacrifice and service.

III. The Example of Timothy (2:19-24)

Paul called Timothy his "son in the faith" because he had won this lad to Christ. (See Acts 16:1-5; 2 Tim. 1:1-6; 1 Cor. 4:15-17.) Like Paul, Timothy lived for others, not for self. Too many Christians live in the way discussed in Phil. 2:21 instead of that in Phil. 1:21! Timothy was Paul's helper and representative and had proved himself faithful to the Lord. Though a young man, he knew how to serve Christ and was willing to sacrifice for Him.

Paul did not call Timothy into service right away; he let him stay at home and grow for five or six years. Timothy had a good testimony of service at home when Paul added him to his missionary staff (Acts 16:2; 1 Tim. 3:6-7). It is dangerous to give new Christians important tasks right away.

IV. The Example of Epaphroditus (2:25-30)

A. He was a balanced Christian (v. 25).

He was a brother, which means he knew the fellowship of the Gospel; a companion in labor, which tied him to the furtherance of the Gospel; and a fellow soldier, which means he knew how to battle for the faith of the Gospel. How easy it is for Christians to get out of balance! Some Christians think only of the fellowship, the brotherhood, and have no time to win souls or fight the enemy. Others are so wrapped up in service that they forget fellowship. This was the mistake Martha made (Luke 10:38-42). Still others are always fighting, so much so that they neglect fellowship and service. We need to be balanced Christians.

B. He was a burdened Christian (vv. 26-27).

He had the submissive mind and thought of others, not self. Though he was sick, and almost died, his burden was for Paul and the church back at Philippi. We need more Christians who are burdened not only for foreign missions, but also for their own local churches.

C. He was a blessed Christian (vv. 28-30).

What a blessing Epaphroditus was to Paul! How he must have encouraged Paul in those difficult days as they prayed and labored together. He was also a blessing to his own church. He made it possible for the Philippians to share in Paul's important ministry. Moreover, Epaphroditus is a blessing to us today! Here we are, centuries later, studying his character and benefiting from his life and ministry!

Faithful servants of Christ ought to be honored in the right way. "Receive him in the Lord" is Paul's admonition. See 1 Thes. 5:12-13. "Hold such in reputation" (v. 29) in no way contradicts 2:7, "made Himself of no reputation." The phrase in 2:7 literally means that Christ emptied Himself. Paul told the church to show proper honor to their leader because he "gambled his life" (v. 30, "not regarding his life") for their service to Paul.

How different it is for us to exercise the submissive mind, the mind of Christ! Walking by sight as we do, we think that to humble ourselves means to lose; yet the Word teaches that the only way up is down. Christ had the submissive mind, and God highly exalted Him. Paul, Timothy, and Epaphroditus had the submissive mind, and they were honored for their sacrifice and service. The best way to get the victory over people and pride is through the submissive mind, the mind of Christ. And we receive this mind only as we allow the Spirit and the Word to work in our lives (vv. 12-13).

PHILIPPIANS 3

Too many Christians get wrapped up in "things" and lose the joy and peace they ought to have in Christ. They "mind earthly things" (3:19) and lack that spiritual mind of the dedicated believer. Notice how many times the word "things" is used in this chapter. Here Paul describes the spiritual mind—the mind that thinks God's thoughts and is directed toward God's goals. Read Rom. 8:1-17 for more about the spiritual mind. In this chapter, Paul describes his past, present, and future, a full biography of the Christian life.

I. Salvation: The Christian's Past (3:1-11)

Paul was religious before he was saved, but his religion could not save him. He had to lose his religion in order to find eternal life! He begins this chapter by warning the believers against religion apart from Christ. The Jews called the Gentiles "dogs," but here Paul uses the term "dogs" to describe the Jewish teachers who emphasized circumcision and keeping the Law. (We met those teachers in Acts 15 and Galatians.) In fact, he does not even call the rite "circumcision"; he calls it "concision," which means "a cutting, a mutilation of the flesh." True worship is in the Spirit (John 4:20-24) and not in the flesh; it honors Jesus Christ, not religious leaders; it depends on God's grace, not on fleshly strength. How much of what passes for the Christian faith in this world is really only fleshly religion.

Paul had the best possible reputation as a Jewish rabbi. In birth and training, he far surpassed all of his friends (see Gal. 1:11-24). He was sincere too; his Jewish religion meant life and death to him. So sincere was he that he even persecuted those who differed with him. If any man could get to heaven on the basis of character and religion, it was Paul—and yet he was a lost sinner apart from Jesus Christ! When he met Christ, he considered all of his earthly and fleshly attainments mere rubbish! "I counted" (v. 7) is the way he puts it. He measured carefully, took stock of himself, and decided that all of his religion and worldly honors were not worth it. He wanted Christ!

What did Paul obtain through faith in Christ? Righteousness, for one thing (v. 9). Paul had plenty of legal righteousness (v. 6), but he lacked that true righteousness that God demands and that He alone can give. It is one thing to be religious enough to get into the synagogue, and quite another to be righteous enough to get into heaven. Paul also obtained a personal knowledge of Christ. Salvation is not knowing about Christ; it is knowing Him (John 17:3). Paul also experienced resurrection power (see Eph. 3:14ff) in his life. Added to these blessings was the privilege of suffering for Christ (Phil. 1:29). Finally, through Christ he was given a new promise: the "out-resurrection from the dead" (v. 11). The Jews believed in the resurrection, that is, a general resurrection at the end of the age; but Christ introduced a resurrection of the just out from among the dead. This is called the first resurrection (1 Thes. 4:13-18; Rev. 20:5). When Paul says "If by any means . . ." he is not suggesting uncertainty but humility. To think that he, a murderer, should share in that glorious resurrection!

II. Sanctification: The Christian's Present (3:12-16)

In the previous section, Paul is a "spiritual accountant" figuring his gains and losses. In this section he is a runner, pressing toward the prize. The figure of a runner is a favorite with Paul (see 1 Cor. 9:25-27; 1 Thes. 2:19-20; Heb. 12:1-3; 2 Tim. 2:5). Of course, Paul is not suggesting that we run to get to heaven! The Olympic runners in ancient Greece had to be citizens of the nation they represented. They also had to be free men, not slaves. The unsaved sinner is a slave, but the Christian is a citizen of heaven (3:20) and has been set free by Christ. Each Christian is given a special place on the "track" for his or her own service, and each one has a goal established by Christ. Our task in life is to "lay hold of that for which Christ laid hold of us" (v. 13). Paul is not talking about salvation but sanctification—growth and progress in Christian life and service.

How do we reach the goal God has set for us? For one thing, we must be honest with ourselves and admit where we are: as Paul declared. "Not that I have already attained" (v. 12). Then, we must keep our eyes of faith on Christ and forget the past—past sins and failures, and also past successes. We must press on in His power. The Christian life is not a game; it is a race that demands the very best that is in us: "This one thing I do" (v. 13). Too many Christians live divided lives. One part enjoys the things of the world and the other part tries to live for the Lord. They get ambitious for "things" and start minding earthly ambitions. Our calling is a "high calling" and a "heavenly calling"; and if we live for this world, we lose the prize that goes with our high calling.

III. Glorification: The Christian's Future (3:17-21)

Nothing will keep our minds spiritual more than looking for the coming of Christ. "Watch out for the worldly crowd!" Paul warns his readers. He expresses here great sorrow in a letter filled otherwise with joy. Paul is weeping over the professed Christians whose lives were bearing the fruit of worldly-mindedness. He describes them: (1) they mind earthly things, which means they think only of this world and what it has to offer; (2) they live for the flesh, for their god is their stomach; and (3) their end is destruction! These people are the enemies of the Cross of Christ. The Cross defeated the world and the flesh; the Cross speaks of sacrifice and suffering, yet these people live for the world and seek only to please themselves. What an awful thing, to be an enemy of the Cross, yet a professed Christian!

Our citizenship ("conversation") is in heaven (v. 20). When people become members of God's family, their names are written down in heaven (Luke 10:20). They become citizens of heaven. This means that they live for the glory of heaven and not for the praise of this earth. Citizens should honor their own countries, and surely the Christian will honor heaven! The people in Philippi were governed not by Macedonian laws, but by Roman laws; likewise, the church lives by heaven's laws. Philippi was a colony of Rome in Macedonia, and Christians make up a colony of heaven on earth. Many times the laws of heaven conflict with the laws of earth, but our responsibility is to obey God, not men.

What a blessed future the citizen of heaven has! Paul proclaims, "We shall be like Him!" This humble body ("vile" means "body of humiliation") will be changed to be like His glorious body. Read 1 Thes. 4:13-18 to see what a happy event the return of Christ will be for the saint. Of course, this will be a day of resurrection and reunion, but it will also be a day of reckoning and reward. May we be found faithful to Him and not ashamed at His coming (1 John 2:28–3:3).

PHILIPPIANS 4

Worry, worry, worry! How many Christians lose their joy and peace because of worry! In this chapter, Paul tells us that the secure mind—the mind that is guarded by the peace of God—frees us from worry. Of course, the believer who does not have the single mind (chap. 1), the submissive mind (chap. 2), and the spiritual mind (chap. 3) can never have the secure mind. We must first live what Paul describes in the previous three chapters before we can claim the promises and provisions of this final chapter.

What is worry? Our English word "worry" comes from an Anglo-Saxon word that means "to strangle"; worry certainly does strangle people physically, emotionally, and spiritually. The Bible term "be careful" or "be anxious" means literally "to be torn apart." Worry comes when the thoughts in our mind and feelings in our heart pull in different directions and "tear us apart." The mind thinks about problems, and these feelings weigh down the heart, creating a vicious circle that wrecks our emotional state. Our minds tell us we should not fret, but we often cannot control the anxiety in our hearts! We have to break this circle of worry before we can enjoy peace.

What causes worry? Wrong thinking and attitudes toward people, circumstances, or things. Notice here in chapter 4 that Paul has no worry about people (vv. 1-5), circumstances (vv. 10-13), or the material things of life (vv. 14-19). Of course, Paul had the single mind of chapter 1 and gained victory over circumstances; he had the submissive mind of chapter 2 and overcame troublesome people; and he had the spiritual mind of chapter 3 and triumphed over physical circumstances. So it was natural for him to have the secure mind of chapter 4. His mind and heart were at peace and could not be disturbed by people, circumstances, or things. In this chapter, Paul gives us God's four-fold remedy for worry.

I. God's Presence (4:1-5)

"The Lord is at hand" does not mean "His coming is soon," but that He is near to help us right now. Euodia and Syntyche (v. 2) were two women in the Philippian church at odds with each other, and Paul encouraged them to make things right. Remember this: worry often comes when we do not make things right with people. We must face differences honestly and do what God wants us to do (see Matt. 18:15-17).

"Moderation" in v. 5 means "sweet reasonableness." It is wonderful when Christians can have convictions and yet be easy to get along with! If we keep in mind that the Lord is with us in every circumstance, then it is easy to obey Him and get along with other people. If we would but rejoice in Him and get our eyes on Him instead of on people, we would have His joy and peace. Note the admonitions Paul gives: stand fast in the Lord; be of one mind in the Lord; rejoice in the Lord; the Lord is near at hand! This is "practicing the presence of Christ," seeing Him in every situation of life, and letting Him work out His perfect will.

II. God's Peace (4:6-9)

"Peace with God" is the result of faith in Christ (Rom. 5:1); "the peace of God" and the presence of "the God of peace" will come when the believer practices right thinking, right praying, and right living. Worry is tension between the mind and heart. The peace of God will guard (garrison) our hearts and minds if we but meet the conditions He gives.

A. Right praying (vv. 6-7).

Not just praying, but *right* praying. The Bible nowhere says that any kind of praying will bring peace to our hearts. What is right praying? It begins with adoration, for this is what the word "prayer" means in v. 6. This is love, enjoying the presence of God, honoring Him in worship. Rushing into His presence and begging for peace of mind will never get results. We must bow before Him in worship and let Him search our hearts and minds. Next comes supplication, which means the earnest, sincere desire of the heart. True prayer comes from the heart, not the lips. What a joy it is to present our requests to Him! Finally, there is appreciation or thanksgiving (see Eph. 5:20 and Col. 3:15-17). It takes faith to thank Him for uncomfortable circumstances or for requests not yet granted. How God loves to hear His children thank Him! Read Dan. 6:10 and you will see that this is the way Daniel prayed. No wonder he had such peace in that lions' den!

B. Right thinking (v. 8).

Peace involves the mind (see Isa. 26:3 and Rom. 8:6). Thoughts are powerful; "as he thinketh, so he is" (Prov. 23:7). Wrong thoughts will lead to unrest and discouragement, but spiritual thinking will lead to peace. Paul tells us in this verse what to think about; if you compare these virtues to Ps. 19:7-9, you will see that the Word of God meets all of these requirements. Meditation on the Word of God will always bring peace (Ps. 119:165).

C. Right living (v. 9).

If there is something in my life I dare not pray about, then I will never have peace. Right living always brings peace; see Isa. 32:17 and 48:18, 22. It is not enough to use the Bible as a basis for praying and claiming its promises; we must also use it as a basis for our living, obeying its precepts. Read carefully James 4:1-11 and note that wrong praying (4:3), wrong living (4:4), and wrong thinking (4:8) produce war instead of peace!

III. God's Power (4:10-13)

Paul was never the victim of circumstances; he had learned by experience the secret of peace: "I can do all things through Christ who energizes me!" The J.B. Phillips translation says, "I am ready for anything through the strength of the One who lives in me" (v. 13, PH). Turn back to Phil. 2:12-13 and you will see that God cannot work through us until first He works in us; He works in us through His Word (1 Thes. 2:13), through prayer by the Spirit (Eph. 2:14ff), and sometimes through suffering (1 Peter 5:10). If we depend on our own power, we will fail; but if we depend on His strength, we can do all things through Him. This explains why Paul could rejoice even in prison: he had learned the secret of the secure mind through the power of God.

IV. God's Provision (4:14-23)

How easy it is to worry about "things"! Jesus warns us in the Sermon on the Mount (Matt. 6:19-34) that we must not worry about things, but we do it just the same. Paul had peace in his heart concerning his personal needs, for God had promised to supply all of them! Paul thanks the Philippians for their gifts and assures them that the spiritual meaning of their gifts is far more important to him than the gifts themselves. What a blessing it is to know that our gifts are looked upon as spiritual sacrifices to the Lord that rejoice His heart! Paul believed in the providence of God, that God was in control of events and that He was able to meet every need (Rom. 8:28). When the child of God is in the will of God, all of the universe works for him; but when the child of God is out of the will of God, everything works against him. This is the providence of God.

COLOSSIANS

A Suggested Outline of Colossians

I. Doctrine: Christ's Preeminence Declared (1)

   A. In the Gospel message (1:1-12)
   B. In the cross (1:13-14)
   C. In creation (1:15-17)
   D. In the church (1:18-23)
   E. In Paul's ministry (1:24-29)

II. Danger: Christ's Preeminence Defended (2)

   A. Beware of empty philosophies (2:1-10)
   B. Beware of religious legalism (2:11-17)
   C. Beware of man-made discipline and asceticism (2:18-23)

III. Duty: Christ's Preeminence Displayed (3–4)

   A. In personal purity (3:1-11)
   B. In Christian fellowship (3:12-17)
   C. In the home (3:18-21)
   D. In daily work (3:22–4:1)
   E. In Christian witness (4:2-6)
   F. In Christian service (4:7-18)

Colossians emphasizes Christ, the Head of the body, while Ephesians emphasizes the church as the body of Christ. These two letters complement each other; in fact, you can find many parallels between them. In emphasizing Christ's headship of the church, Paul shows that our Lord is all-sufficient for our every need.

Introductory Notes to the Colossians

I. The City

Colosse was one of a trio of cities (Hierapolis and Laodicea being the other two) located about 125 miles southeast of Ephesus. This was a rich area both in mineral wealth and merchandising, with a large population, both Jewish and Gentile. These three cities were almost within view of each other.

II. The Church

Paul had never visited Colosse (see 2:1). During his three years of ministry in Ephesus, "all Asia" heard the Gospel (Acts 19:10, 26). One of Paul's converts in Ephesus was a man named Epaphras, whose home was in Colosse. Epaphras had taken the message of the Gospel back home, and through his ministry the church was founded (1:4-7; 4:12-13). This fellowship may have met in the home of Philemon, for he lived at Colosse (Col. 4:9 and Philemon).

III. The Crisis

Paul was now a prisoner in Rome. Epaphras had come to visit him and to report that a new teaching was invading the church and causing trouble. This heresy today is generally called "gnosticism," from the Gk. word *gnosis* which means "to know." The Gnostics were "in the know" — that is, they professed to have a superior knowledge of spiritual things. Their doctrine was a strange blending of some Christian truth, Jewish legalism, Greek philosophy, and Eastern mysticism.

For one thing, these heretics taught that all matter was evil, including the body; and therefore God could not come in contact with matter. How, then, was the world created? By a series of "emanations" from God, they claimed. And, since Christ had a human body, He was only one of these "emanations" and not truly the Son of God. The Gnostics proposed a complex series of "emanations" (including angels) between man and God and thus denied the preeminence of Christ.

Their system was supposed to give the believer a special "full knowledge" not possessed by others. The Gnostics loved to use the word "fullness," and so you find Paul using it many times in this letter. Their doctrine called for legalistic practices (2:16) and strict discipline of the flesh (asceticism, 2:18-23). "Touch not, taste not, handle not!" was one of their rules. They taught that certain days were holy and certain foods sinful. The Gnostic system had a semblance of spirituality but was of no real spiritual value (see Col. 2:21-23).

IV. The Correspondence

It is likely that Paul sent Onesimus and Epaphras, along with Tychicus, back to Colosse with the letters to the Colossian Christians, to the Ephesians (Eph. 6:21-22), and to his friend Philemon. Some students think that the letter to the Laodiceans (Col. 4:16) is our Ephesians.

Colossians emphasizes the preeminence of Christ. As you read it, note the repetition of the words "all" and "fullness" or "filled" (see 1:9-11, 16-20, 28; 2:2-3, 9-10, 13, 19; 3:8, 11, 14, 16-17, 20, 22; 4:9, 12). Paul's theme is that "Christ is all and in all" (3:11) and that we are "made full in Him" (2:10). Since believers are made full in Christ, Christ is all they need! Legalism, man-made philosophies, strict diets, compulsory observance of holy days, discipline of the flesh—all of these must go when Christ is given His place of preeminence. Colossians is a letter pleading for spiritual maturity (note the prayer in 1:9-12). Religious practices done in the flesh may appear to be spiritual, but they are of no value in the inner life of the person. How easy it is even for evangelical Christians to substitute man-made rules for true spirituality.

COLOSSIANS 1

Many people today, like the false teachers at Colosse, will give
Jesus Christ a place of eminence, but they will not give Him His
rightful place of preeminence. He is not a "great man among great
men"; He is God's Son, preeminent in all things! In this first
chapter, the apostle declares Christ's preeminence in several areas
of life.

I. Preeminent in the Gospel Message (1:1-12)

The false teachers had a message, but their message had no power
to it. They taught about angels, "emanations" from God, legalistic
rules, and bodily disciplines, but their message had no power to
transform lives. In these verses Paul reviews the effect the Gospel
of Christ had on the Colossians. He had not visited this church
personally but had heard from Epaphras the good news of their
salvation (vv. 4, 7).

A. *How they were saved.*

Epaphras apparently had heard the Gospel of Christ from Paul at
Ephesus and had taken this life-changing message back to Colosse
(v. 7). Witnessing ought to begin at home (Mark 5:19). Epaphras
gave them "the word of the truth of the Gospel" (v. 5) in contrast
to the lies of the false teachers. Faith comes by hearing; these
people heard the Word, believed, and were saved.

B. *The evidences of their salvation.*

These believers demonstrated faith, hope, and love (vv. 4-5, 8).
Only Jesus Christ can give faith, change a selfish heart into a heart
of love, and then give a blessed hope for the future. The Word
brought forth fruit in their lives (v. 6); fruit is the evidence of true
salvation (Matt. 13:23).

C. *Paul's prayer for their growth (vv. 9-12).*

Since salvation is a personal experience with Jesus Christ, and not
merely the acceptance of a set of doctrines, a believer can experience daily growth and development. The heretics taught a mystical
"fullness" that their followers would gain; but here Paul states that
every believer in Christ can be filled. We have been "made full in
Him" (2:9-10); now he prays that they might experience this full-

ness in their daily lives. Note the requests he makes: (1) that they might know His will; (2) that they would walk so as to please God; (3) that they would work to bear fruit; (4) that they would understand the Word better; and (5) that they would know His glorious power. These are things the heretics falsely promised their followers, but these blessings can be found only in Christ. He is preeminent!

II. Preeminent in the Cross (1:13-14)

It is His cross that causes Jesus Christ to stand out head and shoulders above any other person in history. Religious leaders have died, but only Christ, God's Son, died on the cross for the sins of the world. The picture in these verses is that of a great general setting a nation free from bondage and moving the people into a new land of blessing. What angel ever died to redeem sinners (set them free)? What religious rules ever produced forgiveness? It is the cross that lifts Jesus Christ high above all.

III. Preeminent in Creation (1:15-17)

The Gnostic teachers claimed that God made the worlds through a series of "emanations" from Himself and that Christ was one of these emanations. Paul asserts that Christ is not an emanation from God, but God Himself! "Image" means "the exact reproduction." Christ is not one of God's creatures, but the highest (firstborn) of all creation. The term "firstborn" does not refer to time (as though Christ were the first thing God created) but to position. All things were created by Him (see John 1) and for Him; He holds all things together! ("Consist" means "to hold together.")

IV. Preeminent in the Church (1:18-23)

The church is His body, and He is the Head. The church is the new creation, and He is "the Beginning," that is, the Originator of the new creation. His resurrection gives Him title to the throne of preeminence, for He is "firstborn" from the dead, that is, first to rise from the dead, never to die again. Note the repetition of the word "all" in this chapter, showing the universal rule of Jesus Christ over everything that exists.

The details of the meaning of "the body" are given in Eph. 2:11ff; this passage describes how Christ made peace between Jews and Gentiles and reconciled both in one body, the church. But His cross not only reconciled Jews and Gentiles; it made possible the reconciliation of "all things"—the entire universe! Paul applies this to the believers personally (vv. 21-23), reminding them that Christ has completely changed their lives and reconciled them to God. The false teachers might spin spider webs of doctrine about angels and "emanations," but Christ still has preeminence as the Head of the church! He is "the firstborn" of creation (v. 15) and of the dead (v. 18), signifying His priority and sovereignty.

V. Preeminent in Paul's Ministry (1:24-29)

How foolish it would have been for Paul to suffer for a Christ who was only an "emanation"! Why risk death to tell people that Jesus Christ is not preeminent! Paul's first words when he saw the glorified Savior were, "Who are You, Lord?" The lordship of Christ— His preeminence over all things—was the heartbeat of Paul's life and ministry. He looked upon his personal sufferings as suffering for Christ's sake. In v. 24, Paul is not saying that he suffered as Jesus did or that his suffering was a part of Christ's suffering on the cross. Rather, he is saying that as Christ suffered for others, so he suffers for others, and his suffering is on behalf of the body, the church. The word for "suffering" here is never the one used for the sufferings of Christ on the cross. It speaks rather of His sufferings during His earthly ministry, sufferings that God's people experience as they seek to live for Christ in a hostile world.

Paul next described "the mystery"—that truth about Christ and the church that had been hidden in times past but was now revealed (see Eph. 3). Actually, Paul speaks of a three-fold mystery: (1) the mystery of the church, vv. 24-26; (2) of the indwelling Christ, v. 27, and (3) of the Person of Christ, the fullness of God, 2:2-3.

Paul had a balanced ministry: he preached, taught, and warned; he sought to take the truth to all people, not just a few; and his goal was to present each believer mature (perfect) in Christ. Christian perfection is not sinlessness, but maturity—growing up unto Christ in all things (Eph. 4:15). The whole theme of Colossians is "Christ is all you need." We are made full in Him, and that is all that is needed! How tragic when Christians substitute man-made rules, disciplines, and rituals for the fullness we have in Christ!

But Paul did not run his ministry by his own power: God worked in him, and then he worked for God. See Phil. 1:12-13 and Eph. 3:20-21.

COLOSSIANS 2

In this chapter, Paul gets to the heart of the problem and denounces the false teachers. He asserts clearly the sufficiency of Christ for every need. He sounds three warnings, and these warnings are needed just as much today as in his day.

I. Beware of Empty Philosophies (2:1-10)

So burdened was Paul, he was in spiritual conflict, wrestling in prayer against Satan who was seeking to lead these believers astray. Paul knew how to overcome Satan—prayer and the Word of God (Eph. 6:17-18). He longed to see the saints united in Christ, enjoying the riches of blessing in Him. The false teachers had their fascinating philosophies, but in Christ we have "all the treasures of wisdom and knowledge" (v. 3). Any man-made philosophy that has no place for Christ is unworthy of our consideration. We are rich in Him; why lower ourselves to follow man-made doctrines? Let religious teachers come along with their "hidden doctrines"; we have all wisdom hidden in Christ, and we are "hid with Christ in God" (3:3).

Man's philosophies are attractive. They give a show of wisdom and intelligence, and too often young Christians are "beguiled" by these "enticing words" (v. 4). How tragic it is when young people go off to secular schools and fall prey to man-made philosophies that deny Jesus Christ and the Bible. "Beware lest any man take you captive" (spoil you—v. 8), warns the apostle. How is the believer to overcome these philosophies?

A. Walk in Christ (v. 6).

As you were saved by faith, so walk by faith. As you were saved by the Word, so walk according to the Word. As you were saved through the work of the Spirit, so walk in the Spirit. The Christian life continues as it began, by faith in God.

B. Grow up in Christ (v. 7).

Have roots that dig down into the richness of the Word. Have foundations that are strong, laid upon Jesus Christ. How important it is to be taught the Word of God! Believers fall prey to religious philosophies unless they are rooted in Christ, grounded in the Word, and built up in Bible truth.

C. Make Christ the test (v. 8).

Test every high-sounding religious system by asking, "Does it give Christ the place of preeminence?" Almost every religious system today gives Christ an eminent place, but only true Bible Christianity gives Him the preeminent place.

D. Draw on His fullness (vv. 9-10).

Realize that there is no substitute for Christ and that in Him we have all that we need. When believers drift into worldly living, or are taken prey by man-made systems, it is usually because they feel they lack something that Jesus Christ cannot supply. "You are made full in Him!" What a wonderful position we have in Christ!

II. Beware of Religious Legalism (2:11-17)

These false teachers had mixed oriental mysticism with Greek philosophy and Jewish legalism—what a mixture! But the flesh loves to be religious, so long as that religion does not have a cross to crucify the flesh. The Colossian believers were involved in Jewish legalism—rituals, diets, holidays, and so on. "You are going out of the sunlight into the shadows!" Paul cries (v. 17). "You are forsaking the reality (Christ's body) for the symbol!" Like the child who admires his father's photo while he ignores his father's presence, so these Christians had turned from the fullness of Christ to the ABCs ("elements"—2:8, 20) of the world.

All that we need has been accomplished by Christ on the cross. The circumcision of v. 11 is not His physical circumcision as a child (Luke 2:21), but rather His death on the cross. Just as Christ's water baptism was a symbol of His baptism of suffering on the cross (Luke 12:50), so His circumcision as an infant prefigured His "putting off the body" when He took our sins on Calvary. "Your spiritual circumcision in Christ is far more wonderful than physical rituals!" Paul states. "Why replace Christ with Moses? Why have a physical cutting instead of a spiritual operation on your heart? Circumcision removes a fragment of the flesh from the body, but our identification with Christ puts off the whole fleshly nature."

All of this is made possible through our union with Christ, when the Spirit baptized us into His body. We died with Him, and we are risen with Him. The Old Covenant laws are now set aside; Satan has been completely defeated (v. 15); therefore enjoy the liberty you have in Christ. "Let no man judge you!" Paul urges (v. 16).

III. Beware of Man-made Disciplines (2:18-23)

How the flesh loves legalism: fasting, regulations about food, bodily disciplines. Special religious observances with their regulations make many people "feel spiritual." "Let no man sit as an umpire in your life" (beguile you, v. 18). Beware of affected humility, a counterfeit that tries to imitate genuine spiritual humility. There is nothing wrong with exercising discipline in the Spirit of God, to the glory of God; but when it is done in the flesh and for our own praise, then it becomes sin. While we believe wholeheartedly that believers should not abuse their liberty and become stumbling blocks (1 Cor. 8:9-10), we do not for one minute believe that the giving up of certain habits or pleasures automatically makes a believer spiritual.

Our relationship to Christ is a living union — He is the Head, we are members of the body. A body functions through nourishment, not legislation. Who can say to his stomach, "Start digesting! Stop hurting!" How foolish! Yet people think the Christian life personally, and the church collectively, can be made spiritual by carnal regulations and disciplines. We believe in standards ("Love not the world"), but we reject the idea that outward obedience to standards necessarily produces inward spirituality. We are dead to the elements of the world; we are alive in Christ, and Christ is all we need. Obeying man-made religious regulations (vv. 21-23) might impress some people as spiritual, but Paul states clearly that these practices cannot control or overcome the flesh. Yes, these regulations appeal to us and might seem to help us develop piety and superior spirituality, but they are useless as far as God is concerned.

This, then, is the main theme of Colossians: all the believer needs is Jesus Christ. Man-made systems and regulations seem very spiritual, but they are merely worldly principles (rudiments, v. 20). This is "kindergarten" living; we must graduate into a higher level of Christianity. Man-made disciplines (asceticism) are attractive, but it is impossible for the flesh to control itself, better itself, or perfect itself. "Having begun in the Spirit, are you now being made perfect by the flesh?" asks Gal. 3:3 (NKJV).

Our union with Christ is a living union. This life cannot be controlled by man's laws, but only by the principles that God has put into the body. Only another life can control life, and we have His life within us.

COLOSSIANS 3

It is not enough for Christ to be preeminent in the Gospel, the cross, creation, and the church; He must also be preeminent in our lives. Paul states very specifically how we should "practice the preeminence of Christ."

I. In Personal Purity (3:1-11)

"Since you are risen with Christ, set your mind (affection) on things above!" (v. 1) In other words, let your earthly practice be worthy of your heavenly position. Once you were dead *in* sin (Eph. 2:1-3), but now you are dead *to* sin. Christ is in you, the hope of glory (1:27), and someday soon that glory will be revealed (v. 4). In brief, Paul says, "Live up to what Christ has done for you!" This simple principle of Christian living is more powerful than all the rules and regulations men can devise. "You are made full in Him" (2:10); now live out that fullness in daily life.

Oriental, Greek, and Roman religions said little or nothing about personal holiness. A person could bring sacrifices, say prayers, and go away from the altar to commit terrible sins, and nobody would think he or she was inconsistent. Not so with Christianity! The new life within demands a new life without. Since we have died with Christ, we should put to death ("mortify," v. 5) impure behavior (see Rom. 6). "Don't live the way you used to live," Paul cautions, "the way the unsaved crowd lives. Christ is your life, and you died with Him. Now, let His life show through you day by day."

In vv. 8-11, Paul compares the new life to a change of clothes: "Put off the old sins as you would take off a filthy garment, and put on the new life of holiness." But notice that we are able to do this because in Christ we have already put off the old man (v. 9); that is, in Christ the body of flesh (the sinful nature) has been put off through His true circumcision on the cross (2:11). Physical circumcision to the OT Jew meant entering into a covenant relationship with God. Our spiritual circumcision in Christ means the old nature has been put off, and we may now walk in newness of life.

II. In Christian Fellowship (3:12-17)

In Christ there are no barriers (v. 11); we are one in Him, and He is All. If Christ is preeminent in our lives, then we will be able to get along with others for His glory. If there are differences, the peace of God will be "umpire" (rule) in our hearts as we feed on the Word and worship Christ. Christian fellowship in the local church cannot be legislated by a constitution, although constitutions are useful; true fellowship must come from within, from the hearts of the believers. If a believer is out of fellowship with another believer, it is because one or both of them have gotten out of fellowship with God. "Do all in the name of Christ!" Paul admonishes (v. 17). Read James 4 and you will see that wars and fightings come when Christians do things for their selfish reasons and not for God's glory. Compare 3:15-18 with Eph. 5:18-22, and you will see that being filled with the Word produces the same blessings as being filled with the Spirit. To be filled with the Spirit means to be controlled by the Word.

III. In the Home (3:18-21)

The first place our Christian faith should go to work is in the home. "Let them learn first to show piety at home," commands 1 Tim. 5:4. If the wife is drawing her spiritual nourishment from Christ, the Head (2:19), then she will be submissive and obedient for Christ's sake. Read Eph. 5:22ff and 1 Peter 3 for additional information on this theme.

Of course, the husband too will show love and tenderness toward his wife and family. The headship of the husband in the home is a reflection of the headship of Christ in the church, according to Eph. 5:23ff.

Children are to obey their parents for Christ's sake, to please the Lord. It is sad when children who are professing Christians rebel against their parents and thereby sin against Christ and the church. Christian sons and daughters need to live up to their high position in Christ as members of His body.

What blessings would come to our homes if each member of the family said, "I will live each day to please Christ and make Him preeminent in all things." There would be less selfishness and more love; less impatience and more tenderness; less wasting of money on foolish things and more living for the things that matter most.

IV. In Daily Work (3:22-4:16)

Slaves were attached to households in Paul's day, but we can apply these same truths to Christian employers and employees today.

Paul reminds servants that they have masters according to the flesh as well as a heavenly Master, Christ. The Christian employee is to work to honor and please Christ. "Eyeservice" (v. 22) means working when the employer is watching. But the heavenly Master is always watching! We are not to be men-pleasers, but Christ-pleasers.

"Singleness of heart" implies a heart fixed on one goal—to honor Christ. What a blessing it is to know that Christian employees are actually ministers of Christ as they operate their machines, use their tools, drive their trucks, or work at whatever vocation they might have.

Work must come from the heart: "Do it heartily as unto the Lord!" Half-hearted work is a poor testimony. The half-hearted, unfaithful worker will be judged when Christ returns, so it behooves all of us to do our best for Jesus' sake.

Employers too must manage their affairs as Christians. It is not right for the Christian employer to shortchange his Christian workers because they are all in Christ. He should give them that which is just and equal. In these days of union contracts, government regulations, and competitive economic conditions, it is a challenge for the Christian employer to put Christ first in business, but God promises to honor the believer who will do so. If the employer works to put Christ first and gives Him preeminence, then he will be able to face his Master with a clean heart.

Too many Christians rejoice at the great doctrines of chapters 1–2 but ignore the duties of chapters 3–4. The believer who lives a shallow, disobedient life does not really believe in the all-sufficiency of Christ. Once the Christian depends on the Head—his risen, glorified Savior—for nutrition, guidance, and wisdom, he will discover mature Christian living in its fullness.

COLOSSIANS 4

Paul continues his application of the preeminence of Christ in our lives.

I. In Christian Witness (4:2-6)

Paul was a prisoner in Rome, but this did not stop him from bearing witness for Christ. He tells believers how to be effective witnesses for Christ.

A. Watch and pray.

"Watch" carries the idea of being alert, praying with your eyes open. This truth first appears in Neh. 4:9, when the enemy threatened the Jews as they tried to rebuild the walls of Jerusalem. "We made our prayer . . . and set a watch," was Nehemiah's solution; and it worked! Prayer is never a substitute for our own alertness. Christ teaches us that to watch and pray is the way to victory over temptation (Mark 14:38). We should watch and pray for opportunities to witness and serve. Certainly Paul had his eyes open as he prayed for that Philippian jailer; when the apostle saw the man reaching for his sword, he cried out and stopped him (Acts 16:27-28). If each believer would pray for the lost, and watch for God's open doors of opportunity for witness, we would win more people to the Savior.

B. Walk in wisdom.

"Them that are without" refers, of course, to the lost who do not belong to the Christian family. What a sad thing to be "without" — without Christ, without hope, without peace, without forgiveness! It is important that we Christians live wisely when among the lost, for unsaved people look at our lives and try to find things to criticize. First Thessalonians 4:12 admonishes us to walk honestly toward them that are without. What a terrible testimony it is for a Christian to be dishonest with an unbeliever! Far better for believers to suffer loss than to ruin their testimony and bring reproach on the name of Christ. We wonder what unsaved people think of Christ and the Gospel when the Christians they do business with fail to pay their bills or keep their promises.

C. Have godly speech.

The salt of holiness must always flavor our speech. Old Testament Jews used salt in their sacrifices, symbolizing purity and the preservation of that which is good. The Greeks called salt *charitas* — grace — because it gave flavor to things. Our speech must not be corrupt (Eph. 4:29); salt (God's grace) holds back corruption. A thoughtless word of criticism, a questionable remark, an angry word — any of these could tear down in a minute whatever Christian testimony others have tried to build up.

"Redeeming the time" (v. 5) means "buying up the opportunity." As Christians, we must be alert to seize every opportunity to witness for Christ and win others.

II. In Christian Service (4:7-18)

While we honor Paul as the great apostle, we must never forget the many dedicated Christians who assisted Paul in his ministry. No pastor, evangelist, or missionary can do the Lord's work alone. "We are laborers together with God" (1 Cor. 3:9).

Tychicus (vv. 7-8) had been with Paul for several years. He accompanied Paul from Ephesus (Acts 20:4) as he returned to Jerusalem and possibly was a citizen of Ephesus. He had labored there with Paul for those three years. Tychicus was to carry the letters to the Colossians and the Ephesians (Eph. 6:21-22). This man had a long and dangerous journey ahead of him. How thankful we are that he was faithful to deliver the Word, otherwise we could not study it today! See also 2 Tim. 4:12.

Onesimus (v. 9) was the runaway slave of Philemon, whom Paul had won to Christ. The apostle was now sending Onesimus back home to Colosse. (Read the letter to Philemon.) He and Tychicus traveled together, with Onesimus carrying the precious letter to his master, Philemon.

Aristarchus (v. 10) is seen during the Ephesian riot (Acts 19:29), where he was singled out as a leading Christian. He also accompanied Paul (Acts 20:4) and was with him during that terrible storm en route to Rome (Acts 27:2). What a faithful Christian he was, to "stick by" Paul through thick and thin!

Marcus (v. 10) is John Mark, cousin to Barnabas. Mark had "fallen out" with Paul years before (Acts 13:13 and 15:36-41). It is possible that the Colossians knew about Mark's failure, but Paul wanted them to receive this young man and show him love. When he wrote his last letter, Paul admitted that Mark was "profitable" in the ministry (2 Tim. 4:11). We need to forgive the failures of others and give believers the opportunity to "make good" in the Lord's work.

Jesus-Justus (v. 11) was a Jewish believer. His Hebrew name was Joshua, which is translated "Jesus" in the Greek. His other name signifies one who obeys the Law (Justus). He worked with Paul and comforted (encouraged) him. What a help he was to the apostle during those days in prison!

Epaphras (vv. 12-13) was a Gentile and probably the founder-pastor of the church at Colosse. This godly man believed in the ministry of the Word of God and prayer (1:7 and 4:12). What a prayer warrior he was! He did not simply "say prayers"; "he labored [agonized] in prayer." It is the same word that is used for the struggles of athletes in contests. If Christians prayed as hard as they played, they would see more of God's blessings. Epaphras prayed that the Colossians might stand "mature and full" in God's will (see 1:28-29). He wanted them to live up to their "fullness" in Christ. Yet his prayers were not for the Colossians only; he was zealous for the saints in the neighboring cities as well. What Christian love!

Luke (v. 14) was the Gentile physician who joined Paul at Troas (Acts 16:10) and later wrote the books of Luke and Acts. Luke and Demas are linked again in 2 Tim. 4:10-11, "Only Luke is with me . . . Demas has forsaken me" (NKJV). You can summarize the life of Demas in three verses: "Demas, my fellow laborer" (Phile. 24); "Demas . . . " (Col. 4:14); "Demas has forsaken me" (2 Tim. 4:10, NKJV). Since Colossians and Philemon were written during the same time, Demas' backsliding must have been rapid. What a tragedy!

In his closing instructions, Paul sends a greeting to some of the saints and tells the Colossians and Laodiceans to share their respective letters with each other. It may be that the epistle to the Laodiceans is our Ephesians. "All Scripture is profitable" (2 Tim. 3:16), so we must not neglect any of God's Word. He closes by warning Archippus not to faint but to fulfill his ministry in the Lord. Perhaps he was the son of Philemon, since he is mentioned in that letter too (Phile. 2).

Paul's usual salutation of grace closes the letter, marking it as authentic.

1 THESSALONIANS

A Suggested Outline of 1 Thessalonians

I. Personal: "We give thanks remembering..." (1–3)

  A. How the church was born (1)
    1. An elect group (1:1-5)
    2. An exemplary group (1:6-7)
    3. An enthusiastic group (1:8)
    4. An expectant group (1:9-10)
  B. How the church was nurtured (2)
    1. A faithful steward (2:1-6)
    2. A gentle mother (2:7-8)
    3. A concerned father (2:9-16)
    4. A loving brother (2:14-20)
  C. How the church was established (3)
    1. Through the Word (3:1-5)
    2. Through prayer (3:6-13)

II. Practical: "We beseech you..." (4–5)

  A. Walk in holiness (4:1-8)
  B. Walk in love (4:9-10)
  C. Walk in honesty (4:11-12)
  D. Walk in hope (4:13-18)
  E. Walk in light (5:1-11)
  F. Walk in gratitude (5:12-13)
  G. Walk in obedience (5:14-28)

Each chapter of this epistle ends with a reference to the second coming of Christ. Paul relates His coming to: salvation (1:9-10); service (2:19-20); stability (3:13); sorrow (4:18); and sanctification (5:23).

Introductory Notes to the Thessalonian Epistles

I. The City

You can find the modern city of Soloniki on your map, and when you do, you have found the site of the ancient city Thessalonica. It had originally been named Therma, from the hot springs in the area; but 300 years before Christ, Cassander, king of Macedon, renamed it in honor of the sister of Alexander the Great. It was a free city, with its own government, and it also was the capital city of Macedonia. Thessalonica stood on the important Egnatian Way, Rome's greatest highway.

II. The Church

The record is found in Acts 17:1-15. Paul, Silas, and Timothy left Philippi and traveled thirty-three miles to Amphipolis, then twenty-eight miles farther to Apollonia. It is interesting to note that no ministry was carried on in either of those cities. Their next trip was some forty miles to Thessalonica, where Paul ministered in the synagogue for perhaps three weeks and saw a number of people converted. In the city was a large group of Gentile proselytes ("devout Greeks," Acts 17:4) in the synagogue, and they responded enthusiastically, along with some of the Jews. This kind of success enraged the orthodox Jews, and they engineered a mob scene to embarrass the Christians and hinder Paul's ministry. The believers thought it best for Paul and his party to leave, which they did, going first to Berea. Paul left his associates at Berea and went alone to Athens. When Timothy joined Paul at Athens, the apostle promptly sent him back to Thessalonica to encourage the new church (1 Thes. 3:1-3). The men finally met together at Corinth (Acts 18:5). Timothy reported on the state of the infant church in Thessalonica. It was from Corinth, about the year A.D. 50, that Paul wrote 1 Thessalonians. Second Thessalonians was written just a few months later.

III. The Correspondence

The first letter had several purposes behind it: (1) to encourage and confirm the new believers in the things of Christ; (2) to answer false charges made against Paul and his ministry, 2:1-12; (3) to explain that the Christian dead would participate in the second coming of Christ; (4) to warn the Christians against pagan immorality, 4:4ff; (5) to remind the church members to honor and follow their spiritual leaders, 5:12-13; and (6) to warn believers who had given up their jobs and were idle because they thought Christ would soon return, 2:9.

Second Thessalonians was written a few months later. The persecutions against the church were getting worse (2 Thes. 1:4-5) and the people needed encouragement. The "idlers" in the church had not gone back to work (2 Thes. 3:6-12). To make matters worse, the people were confused about the Day of the Lord (the Tribulation), thinking that they were already in it! It is possible that the church had received a counterfeit epistle, claiming to be from Paul (2:1-3) and teaching that the Day of the Lord had already begun. (Note that the phrase "day of Christ" in 2 Thes. 2:2 should be "Day of the Lord," referring to the tribulation period on earth that follows the rapture of the church.) Paul wrote 2 Thessalonians to: (1) encourage the church to persevere in spite of testing; (2) explain the events leading up to the Day of the Lord; (3) warn the busybodies to get back to work. Note that in 2 Thes. 3:17-18, Paul gives his personal "trademark" so that the people could easily detect any forged letters in the future.

Keep in mind that 1 Thessalonians deals with *the rapture*, Christ's return in the air for the church, while 2 Thessalonians deals with *the revelation*, Christ's return with the church to the earth, to defeat His enemies and establish His kingdom. "The Day of the Lord" referred to in 2 Thessalonians is that period of tribulation that comes to the earth after the church has been raptured. First Thessalonians 1:10 and 5:9 teach clearly that the church will not go through the Tribulation.

1 THESSALONIANS 1

It is a wonderful thing when a pastor can think of his church and say, "We give thanks always for all of you!" Paul loved the church at Thesssalonica; these people were on his heart, and he was concerned for their spiritual welfare. In this chapter, Paul tells us what kind of a church he left in that wicked city. When we see the characteristics of this church, we should examine our own lives and ask, "Am I helping to make my church a model church in the Lord?"

I. They Were an Elect People (1:1-56)

The word "church" in the Gk. is *ekklesia*, which means "a called-out group." The church is not a social club; it is a spiritual organism, an organization composed of people whom God has "called out of darkness into His marvelous light" (1 Peter 2:9). This calling is purely of grace (Eph. 1:3ff). Though we are in the world physically, we are not of the world spiritually (John 15:19). These saints lived in Thessalonica but dwelled in Christ. Paul explains the miracle of this calling in 2 Thes. 2:13-14. God sent Paul and Silas to Thessalonica with the Word of God. The people heard the Word, believed, and were saved. After receiving Christ, they discovered that they had been chosen in Him by God through grace! Read also 1 Peter 1:1-4.

The mystery of God's election and man's decision will never be fully explained this side of heaven. Just keep in mind that the Bible teaches both. "How do you reconcile these two truths?" a man once asked Spurgeon. The preacher replied, "I never try to reconcile friends." These twin truths of election and decision are not contradictory; they are complementary. As far as God the Father is concerned, we were saved when He chose us in Christ before the foundation of the world (Eph. 1:4); as far as the Spirit is concerned, we were saved when we responded to His call and received Christ; as far as the Son is concerned, we were saved when He died for us on the cross.

How did Paul know these people were saved? Because of the evidences in their lives:

A. Work of faith.

When people honestly trust Christ, that faith will be shown by works. Works will not save, but faith that does not lead to works is not saving faith. True Christian faith results in a changed life. See James 2:14-26.

B. Labor of love.

Unsaved people live for themselves (Eph. 2:1-2), but the true believer is willing to toil because of love. He has a new motive for living; he loves Christ and loves others. See Heb. 10:24-25; also Rom. 8:35-39.

C. Patience of hope.

The lost are without hope. Believers have endurance in life's trials because they know Christ is coming again. Believers need not give up in times of trial because they know the Savior is coming to deliver them (1 Peter 1:1-9; 4:12-16).

It has been pointed out that vv. 9-10 parallel these three evidences of salvation: the work of faith (they turned to God from idols); the labor of love (they served the living God); the patience of hope (they waited for Christ to return). Faith, hope, and love are evidences of true salvation (Col. 1:4-5; Rom. 5:1-4).

II. They Were an Exemplary People (1:6-7)

It is wonderful when "hearers" become "followers"! These people heard the Word, welcomed it, believed it, and suffered for receiving it into their lives. The Word imparts faith (Rom. 10:17) and brings joy (Acts 8:8, 39; Jer. 15:16). Having believed, these new Christians followed Paul, associated themselves with a local fellowship, and became examples to all around them. They were not only followers of Paul, but also of the churches (2:14); for in the NT, Christians were expected to be a vital part of the local fellowship. Their testimony reached throughout the whole area and helped lead others to Christ.

III. They Were an Enthusiastic People (1:8)

These people had been saved just a few months. They did not have the instruction most saints today have, yet they were enthusiastic in their witness for Christ. They witnessed by their walk ("examples" in v. 7) and by their talk (v. 8). The verb "sounded out" has the idea of blowing a trumpet. While these saints were waiting for the trumpet to blow to call them home (4:16), they were "trumpeting the Gospel" loud and clear to all their lost friends.

Too often we are like the Pharisees, blowing our own trumpets, instead of trumpeting for Christ and the Gospel (Matt. 6:1-4).

IV. They Were an Expectant People (1:9-10)

The second coming of Christ is a basic theme in this book. Each chapter relates Christ's return to a basic Christian truth (see the suggested outline). In this chapter we see that Christ's coming is the blessed hope of the saved. While the lost are blindly worshiping and serving their idols, the saved are serving the living God and rejoicing in the living hope that Christ will come again.

How are Christians supposed to wait for Christ's return? By being busy when He comes (see Matt. 24:44-51). In 5:1-11, Paul warns the saints to be awake and alert, and not to sleep and be drunken, like the people of the world. The blessed hope of Christ's return must be more than a doctrine in our creed: it must be a dynamic in our lives.

How do we know Christ is coming again? God proved Christ is His Son by raising Him from the dead. Read carefully Acts 17:22-34 for Paul's argument. Christ could not come again if He were dead and His body decomposing in a Jewish tomb. We cannot separate the living hope and the living Christ (1 Peter 1:1-5).

Paul had instructed these people concerning the return of Christ and the time of tribulation that God has promised would come on a Christ-rejecting world. But he is careful to point out that the church will not share in that tribulation. The verb "deliver" in v. 10 is present tense — "who delivers us"; or it could be recast as a title — "Jesus, the Deliverer." The church will not go through the Tribulation. Read 1:10 and 5:1-9, as well as 2 Thes. 1 and 2. The next event on God's calendar is the return of Christ in the air, at which time the church will be caught up to meet Him. Then will follow seven years of tribulation on earth. When the cup of iniquity on earth starts overflowing, Christ and the church will return to defeat Satan and His hosts and usher in the 1,000-year reign of Christ (see Rev. 19:11–20:5).

1 THESSALONIANS 2

Chapter 1 describes the ideal church; chapter 2 provides a picture of the ideal pastor or Christian servant. Paul has told us how the

Gospel came to Thessalonica; now he tells us how he ministered to the young believers. This is an outline of Paul's "Follow-up Program," and it explains why most of his converts stayed true to the Lord and why his churches grew. He gives us four pictures of the ideal Christian worker.

I. The Faithful Steward (2:1-6)

What a tremendous privilege to be "put in trust with the Gospel"! (2:4) We often speak of the stewardship of material things, but we need also to remember that every believer is a steward of the Gospel and the Word of God. God gave the message to Paul (1 Tim. 1:11); Paul in turn committed it to Timothy (1 Tim. 6:20), and Timothy was expected to commit it to faithful people in the churches who would then commit it to others (2 Tim. 2:2). The main responsibility of a steward is to be faithful (1 Cor. 4:1-2); and it is on the basis of this faithfulness that we will be tested and rewarded when Christ comes.

In order to be faithful to his or her stewardship, a believer must be willing to suffer. Paul and Silas had been treated shamefully in Philippi (Acts 16:19-24), and they could have made all kinds of excuses for taking a vacation. But they knew that God had entrusted them with the Gospel and that they had to carry the message to other cities. Instead of being fearful, they were bold to proclaim the Good News.

The faithful steward must live to please God, not men (v. 4). It is tempting to compromise the message in order to win friends, but God cannot bless a steward whose message and ministry are not according to His divine pattern. In v. 3, Paul states that his message was not of deceit or error; that is, it was the true Word of God. His motive was pure, and not one of uncleanness; and his method was honest, not guileful (or "baiting the hook" as for catching fish). Verse 5 states that Paul did not resort to flattering people for personal gain. Paul always honored faithful workers and gave praise where it was due; but he did not stoop to flattery to win converts or influence followers. (See Gal. 6:10ff; John 8:29; Acts 4:18-21.)

II. The Gentle Mother (2:7-8)

It seems odd that the man Paul should compare himself to a "nursing mother" in v. 7. (Consider also 1 Cor. 4:14-15 where he states that as a spiritual parent he had "begotten" the Corinthian saints through the Gospel.) In 2:9-13, Paul uses the image of a father, but the main thought here is that of loving care. New Christians need love, food, and tender care, just as a mother would give to her own children. Newborn babes need the milk of the Word (1 Peter 2:2) and then must "graduate" to the meat (1 Cor. 3:1-4; Heb. 5:11-14), the bread (Matt. 4:4, and see Ex. 16, the manna), and the honey (Ps. 119:103).

How a mother feeds her child is almost as important as what she feeds it. How important it is that we who are older Christians feed the younger believers lovingly and patiently.

III. The Concerned Father (2:9-16)

Note the "fatherly" ministry of Paul: he labored (v. 9a), he preached (v. 9b), behaved himself (v. 10), exhorted (v. 11), and suffered (v. 14). A father must watch over his family and make sacrifices for their welfare. Children are great imitators, and it is important that "spiritual fathers and mothers" live lives that are exemplary.

Paul could have claimed his rights as an apostle and required the church to support him (2:6); but instead, he sacrificially labored with his own hands in order to minister to the church. Fathers do not make little children pay for the care that they receive. Paul was also careful to live a life that was holy (to God), just (to man), and blameless (to self).

One of the duties of fathers is to exhort and educate their children, and this Paul did in Thessalonica. He provided individual and personal teaching ("each one of you") as well as the public ministry to the church. Spiritual leaders dare not depend on their public ministry alone; their spiritual children need personal encouragement and counsel as well. Paul's three-fold ministry as a father was to: (1) "exhort" or entreat; (2) "comfort" or encourage; and (3) "charge" or witness, testify. Paul not only taught them the Word, but he encouraged them from his own experiences in the Lord.

The apostle rejoiced over the way his spiritual children received the Word of God. He knew that the Spirit of God would work in their lives if they received the Word and believed it. If we will tie together Phil. 2:12-13, Eph. 3:20-21, and 1 Thes. 2:13, we will see that God works in us through His Word, His Spirit, and prayer.

Finally, Paul warned his spiritual family of the enemies who would persecute them. If Christians become followers of the Lord

(1:6) and of the churches (2:14), then they can expect to be persecuted by Satan and his followers.

IV. The Loving Brother (2:17-20)

How Paul loved to call these saints "brethren"! He used the word twenty-one times in his two Thessalonian epistles. (Of course, this also included the sisters.) He saw himself as one of them, a part of the family. In v. 17 he says that he was "orphaned" from them for a short time, like a child away from home. He loved them, prayed for them, and greatly desired to see them again. After all, the test of our spiritual life is not what we do when we are in church with "the family," but how we behave away from church. Paul was not the kind of church member who "took a vacation" from the house of God.

As mentioned before, each chapter of this epistle ends with a reference to the return of Christ. In chapter 1, Christ's return is related to salvation; here in chapter 2, it is related to service. Why was Paul able to minister faithfully and lovingly to these saints? Because he saw them in the light of Christ's coming. He was looking forward to the glorious day when he would rejoice over them in the presence of Christ! Jesus endured the cross "for the joy that was set before Him" (Heb. 12:2); this "joy" is surely the joy of presenting the church to His Father (Jude 24). Paul endured all kinds of suffering for this same joy. Do we rejoice as we contemplate seeing Jesus one day?

1 THESSALONIANS 3

The key word in this chapter is "establish" (vv. 2-3, 8, 13). New Christians go through times of testing and affliction (vv. 3, 5); and unless they are established in the Lord, they will be upset by the devil. Paul was not satisfied just to have these people saved (chap. 1) and nurtured (chap. 2); he wanted to see them established in the faith (chap. 3), able to walk (chap. 4). After all, little children must learn to stand before they can learn to walk. What means did Paul use to establish these believers in the faith?

I. He Sent Them a Man (3:1-2)

What an asset young Timothy was to Paul! Every Paul must have his Timothy—the younger person who works with the older. Paul knew how to select and train Christian leaders, and Timothy was one of his finest. This young man had proved himself for several years in his own local church (Acts 16:1-3) before Paul enlisted him to be a helper. Young Timothy (probably a teenager) did not start his ministry by teaching or preaching; he was Paul's "minister" to help him in the tasks of daily travel and living. Actually, Timothy replaced John Mark, who had turned back when the going got tough. Paul's estimate of Timothy is found in Phil. 2:19-24 and throughout his two epistles to Timothy.

God uses gifted believers to strengthen the church (Eph. 4, and see Acts 14:21-23, and 15:32, 41). Paul was willing to be left at Athens alone in order that Timothy might return to Thessalonica to encourage the believers and establish them in the faith. If church members would "adopt" new Christians, encourage them, teach them, and fellowship with them, there would be fewer spiritual casualties. The mature saints in the church must help younger Christians to grow in Christ.

II. He Wrote Them a Letter (3:3-4)

The believer is built up by the Word of God (2 Thes. 2:15-17; Rom. 16:25-27; and 2 Peter 1:12). Note how Paul reminds them of the Word he had already taught them. He had warned them that afflictions were coming, but they seemingly had forgotten what he had taught them. There is no substitute for the Word of God. The Christian who is ignorant of the Bible is prey to every wind of doctrine and never will be established in the Lord (Eph. 4:11-16). Timothy reminded them of the Word Paul had taught them, and this encouraged and established them.

Read Acts 17:1-4 for a description of how Paul ministered the Word at Thessalonica. He reasoned, which suggests debate or discussion; he opened the Word, which implies explaining its meaning (Luke 24:32, 45); he alleged certain truths, which means he gave evidence for them or laid them out in an orderly way for all to see; and he preached, which means the proclaiming of the Gospel. The pastor and Christian worker must be sure to have a balanced ministry of the Word. It is not enough merely to preach and declare the Word; there must be teaching, proving, explaining. The word "allege" (Acts 17:3) can mean "the setting of a table"; thus the spiritual worker must "set the food on the table" so that every saint, young or old, may reach it and partake of it.

III. He Prayed for Them (3:5-10)

The two-fold ministry of the Word of God and prayer is what establishes a church. If there is all teaching and preaching and no prayer, then the people will have light but no power. If there is all prayer but no teaching of the Word, you may have a group of enthusiasts who have more heat than light! The pastor, Sunday School teacher, missionary, or Christian worker who talks to God about his people, and then talks to his people about God, will have a balanced and established ministry. Christ's ministry consisted of both the Word and prayer (Luke 22:31-32). Samuel ministered in this way (1 Sam. 12:23, and do not forget the last clause); so did Peter and the apostles (Acts 6:4) and Paul himself (Acts 20:32).

Paul's concern was not so much their safety or happiness, but their faith. The word "faith" is used five times in this chapter. Satan is the enemy of our faith, for if he can get us to doubt God and His Word, he will rob us of the enjoyment of every blessing we have in Christ. Paul wanted them to have mature (perfected) faith (v. 10). Faith is not a deposit that sits within the heart and never changes; it is like the grain of mustard seed that looks small, but contains life and is able to grow. Paul wanted to see these people abounding in love, established in hope, and growing in faith—faith, hope, and love!

There is no substitute for a consistent prayer life. Christians are commanded to pray for one another and for the lost. When there is a combined ministry of prayer and the Word, Satan is defeated and the church is established.

IV. He Reminded Them of Christ's Return (3:11-13)

As we have noted before, the theme of both epistles to the Thessalonians is the second coming of Christ. No truth establishes the believer faster or better than this one. In the midst of testing and tribulation, these believers could assure and encourage themselves with the promise of His coming. When temptations came their way, as they did daily in those heathen cities, they could keep themselves clean by remembering that Christ might come that very day. If weary of laboring and witnessing, they could take on new strength and courage by looking for His return. No truth in the Bible has a greater effect on the believer's heart, mind, and will than the truth of the second coming of Christ.

Read Luke 12:42-48 to see what happens to the servant who

forgets the coming of Christ. This man did not say anything openly; he merely said in his heart, "My Lord has delayed His coming!" He did not love Christ's appearing. Is it any wonder this servant backslid and could not get along with other workers?

Paul was anxious that their hearts be established blameless; note also 5:23. Christians are supposed to be blameless and harmless (Phil. 2:15). This does not mean they are sinless, for perfection is not possible until Christ returns. The little child, copying his name on the blackboard, does not perform faultlessly, because he is only a child; but if he does the best he can, he is blameless. If we live up to the light God has given us and seek to grow in Him, we can live lives that are blameless in God's sight. The daily expectancy of Christ's return will help the believer keep his or her life clean (1 John 2:28–3:3).

1 THESSALONIANS 4

We move now into the second half of the letter dealing with the practical instructions for these new believers in Christ. The key word is "walk" (4:1, 12), and Paul beseeches them to obey the Word (4:1, 10, 12, 14). The Christian's behavior is compared to a walk for several reasons: (1) it demands life, for the dead sinner cannot walk; (2) it requires growth, for a little baby cannot walk; (3) it requires liberty, for someone who is bound cannot walk; (4) it demands light, for no one wants to walk in the dark; (5) it cannot be hidden, but is witnessed by all; and (6) it suggests progress toward a goal. Paul describes the kind of walk the believer should have.

I. Walk in Holiness (4:1-8)

Here Paul deals with marriage and the home. The marriage vows in heathen cities said nothing about purity, so there was great danger of immorality in the lives of these new Christians. While love and purity certainly prevailed in many heathen homes, the general atmosphere of these city-states (before the Gospel came) was one of lust and selfishness. The Christian has the responsibility of building a Christian home that will glorify God, so Paul begins here.

Immorality is basically selfishness and robbery. Thus Paul exhorts them to live to please God and not themselves. He had set the example (2:4), and now he expected them to follow. He had commanded them, from the Lord, to live in holiness and purity by the power of God. God's will for their lives was that they be sanctified. The word *sanctified* simply means "set apart for a purpose." You can rent the Jefferson Hotel in Washington, D.C. but you cannot rent the White House. The latter has been sanctified, set apart for a special purpose. The believer has been set apart for God; he or she is a saint, a set-apart one. We have the daily responsibility of devoting ourselves more and more to God so that in body, soul, spirit (5:23) we completely belong to Him. Nothing defiles the person more than sexual sin (2 Cor. 7:1; 1 Cor. 6:13-20). People who violate their marriage vows sin against God, themselves, and fellow Christians; God will deal with them in truth.

"Vessel" in v. 4 may refer to the believer's body or to the wife (1 Peter 3:7). In either case, these vessels have been purchased by the blood of Christ, sanctified by the Spirit (1 Cor. 6:9-11), and must be used for the glory of God. To despise God's warnings about sexual sin is to grieve the Spirit and invite chastening. Remember David, Samson, Judah, and other Bible personalities who fell into this sin and paid dearly.

II. Walk in Love (4:9-10)

There was no need to write to them about love; he had taught them about this, and God Himself taught them through the Spirit (Rom. 5:5). Love is one of the birthmarks of the believer (1 John 3:14; 1 Peter 1:22; 1 John 4:9-12)."Behold, how they love one another!" exclaimed the lost as they witnessed the fellowship of the early church. But it is not enough that we love only those in our own fellowship; like these people in Thessalonica, we must love all of God's people and also the lost (3:12) more every day.

III. Walk in Honesty (4:11-12)

Now Paul talks about the believer's vocation and his contacts with the unsaved in the world. One of the problems in the Thessalonian church was that some people had misunderstood the promise of Christ's return, quit their jobs, and had become "parasites" who lived off the other Christians. See 2 Thes. 3:5-15 for Paul's admonition. "Study to be quiet" (v. 11) literally means "Be ambitious to be quiet." That is, do not fret and worry and involve yourself in the world's activities. "Attend to your own affairs" and therefore stay out of the affairs of others. It is a sad thing when Christians have nothing to do and become busybodies in other peoples' lives. The Christian who does an honest day's work and who is careful to maintain a good testimony will influence the unsaved (see Col. 3:22-25 and 4:5). Those who do not work, should not eat (2 Thes. 3:10). Let us not practice unscriptural Christian "charity" by taking the Lord's money to support "Christian loafers" and encourage them in their careless way of life.

IV. Walk in Hope (4:13-18)

This is the classic passage on the rapture of the church. Sorrow had come to the lives of these saints, and they were wondering whether their dead fellow Christians would be left behind at the return of Christ. Paul assures them that their dead will be raised first, and that all the saints will be gathered together to meet Christ in the air. Do not confuse the rapture of the church (meeting Christ in the air) with the revelation of the Lord, that time when He comes with His saints to earth to judge sinners and to establish His kingdom (2 Thes. 1:7-12). The rapture (meeting Christ in the air) can take place at any time; but the revelation (returning with Christ) will occur some seven years after the rapture.

Christians are expected to mourn when loved ones die, but they are not to grieve as do the people of the world who have no hope. Certainly Christ expects us to shed tears and feel loneliness (see John 11:33-36) as we go through the valley; but in the midst of our sorrow, there must be the testimony of the living hope we have in Christ (1 Peter 1:3). Note the comforts the believer has in times of sorrow:

A. The comfort that death for the believer is only sleep.

"Sleep in Jesus" in v. 14 is literally "put to sleep through Jesus." Regardless of how a believer dies, Jesus Christ is there to put him to sleep. Of course, the soul goes to be with Christ (Phil. 1:20-24; 2 Cor. 5:6-8); it is the body that sleeps, not the soul. The word "cemetery" means "a sleeping place"; it is the place where the bodies sleep, awaiting the resurrection.

B. The comfort of heavenly reunion.

The hardest thing about death is separation from our loved ones; but when Christ comes, we will be "together with the Lord" forever. The living saints will not precede those who have died; all will be caught up together to meet Christ.

C. The comfort of eternal blessing.

We shall be "forever with the Lord." We shall obtain new bodies (1 John 3:1-3; Phil. 3:20-21). Paul says that the body we place in the cemetery is like a seed awaiting the harvest (1 Cor. 15:35-58). Of course, the body turns to dust, and that dust becomes a part of the earth (Gen. 3:19). The Bible nowhere teaches that God raises and unites every particle of the believer's body. What it does teach is that the resurrection body has identity with the body that was buried. Just as the seed that is planted (and that dies) in the ground has identity and continuity with the seed it produces, so the resurrection body will have identity and continuity with the body that was buried. Resurrection is not reconstruction.

The words "caught up" (v. 17) are full of meaning. They mean: (1) to catch away speedily, for there will be no warning (5:1-10); (2) to seize by force, for Satan will seek to hinder our rapture to heaven; (3) to claim for one's self, just as the Bridegroom claims the bride; (4) to move to a new place; and (5) to rescue from danger, for the church will not go through the Tribulation (1:10; 5:9).

1 THESSALONIANS 5

The final chapter gives a series of admonitions instructing the Christians how to live in the light of Christ's coming. As we read these many exhortations, we see that there were some definite problems in the infant church. Christians were living carelessly; some were not respecting their church leaders; others were abusing the public services; and there was a general need for love and harmony among the saints. These admonitions point out how the local church can live in harmony and purity.

I. Be Watchful (5:1-11)

Paul presents a series of contrasts here between the Christians and the lost:

A. Light/Darkness.

Christ's coming, as far as the world is concerned, will be sudden and unexpected, like a thief in the night; but not so for the believer. We are looking for Him to come. Unbelievers are in the dark: their understanding is darkened (Eph. 4:18; 5:8); they love the darkness (John 3:19-21; Eph. 5:11); they are controlled by the power of darkness (Eph. 6:12); and they are headed for eternal darkness (Matt. 8:12). But the Christian is associated with the light, for God is light, and Christ is the Light of the world (John 8:12). The Christian is a child of light (Eph. 5:8-14), though at one time he was darkness itself. The change that was wrought is described in 2 Cor. 4:1-6; Col. 1:13; and 1 Peter 2:9. Since Christians belong to the day, they should live in the light and be ready for Christ's return.

B. Knowledge/Ignorance.

Satan likes to keep people in the dark (Acts 26:18). Judas was in the dark (John 13:27-30) and so were Ananias and Sapphira (Acts 5). The world is ignorant of God's plans because the world has rejected Christ and the Bible. Read Isa. 8:20 to see why even intelligent world leaders are in the dark when it comes to understanding what is going on in the world. They go by appearances and say, "Where is the promise of His coming?" (see 2 Peter 3) But the Christian who reads his Bible and keeps his eyes open knows the way God is working in this world and is not ignorant.

C. Expectancy/Surprise.

The unsaved world lives in false security, like the people before the flood (Gen. 6) or the citizens of Sodom and Gomorrah (Gen. 18–19). Paul gives two comparisons to Christ's coming: (1) the thief, telling of the surprise and unpreparedness of those affected by it; (2) the woman giving birth, telling of the suddenness and suffering involved. When Christ has taken the church out of the world, the Day of the Lord will begin, a seven-year period of tribulation and suffering for the world. Thus, the Day of the Lord will come to the world as a thief in the night, but will not be so to the believer.

D. Soberness/Drunkenness.

Christians who are looking for Christ to come will stay awake and be alert; they will not become drunken like the people of the world. "Wake" and "sleep" here do not mean "alive" and "dead" as in 4:13-18; they mean respectively "alert" and "careless." Christians should be living clean, dedicated lives when Jesus comes.

II. Be Respectful to Your Leaders (5:12-13)

The church family must have spiritual leadership, and this leadership is vested in the pastor(s) and deacons. The church may establish whatever organizations it pleases (so long as these groups are organized according to biblical guidelines). The pastor, however, must lead the flock as God directs. Certainly he needs, and wants, the prayers and counsel of the people, especially the elected leaders; but all in the church must respect the leadership that God provides. Christians should: (1) accept their leaders (Eph. 4:7-11; 1 Peter 5:1-5); (2) honor their leaders, recognizing the work they do; (3) love their leaders; (4) and follow their leaders (Heb. 13:7-9, 17, 24). Whenever a church is not united, it is often because the pastor will not take the responsibility of leadership, or because the members will not permit him to lead. Keep in mind that leadership is not dictatorship. The leader sets the example, pays the price, and seeks to help others in Christian love. The dictator uses law, not love; he does not lead, he drives; and his motives are selfish, even if he thinks he is working for the good of the church.

III. Be Mindful of One Another (5:14-15)

It is not enough to have church leadership; there must also be partnership, with each member doing his or her share of the work. First Peter 4:7-11 reminds us that each Christian is a steward of a spiritual gift, and that we must use that gift for the good of others and the glory of the Lord. Paul specifies certain kinds of Christians who need special help: (1) The unruly—the careless who will not be ruled, those who are out of line, must be warned. (2) The feebleminded—the fainthearted must be encouraged. (3) The weak—those not mature in the Lord (Rom. 14:1-5) must be supported until they can walk in the Lord. Our attitude toward all people ought to be one of patience and love, never returning evil for evil (Rom. 12:17-21).

IV. Be Thankful (5:16-18)

"Rejoice, pray, and give thanks" sound like ordinary admonitions; but when you add the adverbs, you have a real challenge: "Rejoice evermore; pray without ceasing; in everything give thanks." The Christian who walks with the Lord and keeps in constant communion with Him will see many reasons for rejoicing and thanksgiving all day long.

"Pray without ceasing" does not mean a constant mumbling of prayers (see Matt. 6:7). True prayer is the attitude of the heart, the desire of the heart (Pss. 10:17; 21:2; 37:4; 145:19). When our hearts desire what God desires, we are praying all day long as the Spirit intercedes for us and in us (Rom. 8:26-27).

V. Be Careful in Worship (5:19-21)

"Prophesying" in the early church was the immediate work of the Spirit: the prophet would give the message from God. But Satan is a counterfeiter, so it was necessary to test the messages (see 1 Cor. 12:10; 14:29-33). The danger was that the believers would "go overboard" in emotional abuses or, the other extreme, quench the Spirit by rejecting His revelations. "Prove all things, hold fast that which is good" (v. 21) is the admonition we must heed whenever we hear or read a message from the Word.

VI. Be Faithful in Daily Conduct (5:22-28)

"Appearance of evil" means "every form of evil." Of course, no saint should allow anything in his life that others could misunderstand and criticize. God is faithful to build us up in holiness if we but yield to Him. Prayer, brotherly love, and attention to the Word of God will sanctify us and keep us ready for Christ's return.

2 THESSALONIANS

A Suggested Outline of 2 Thessalonians

Greeting — 1:1-2

I. Encouragement in Suffering (1)

A. Suffering helps us to grow (1:3-5)
B. Suffering prepares us for glory (1:6-10)
C. Suffering glorifies Christ today (1:11-12)

II. Enlightenment about the Day of the Lord (2)

A. The apostasy must take place (2:1-3)
B. The temple must be rebuilt (2:4-5)
C. The Restrainer must be removed (2:6-12)
D. The church must be completed (2:13-17)

III. Establishment in Christian Living (3)

A. Prayer and patience (3:1-5)
B. Working and eating (3:6-13)
C. Hearing and doing (3:14-15)

Farewell — 3:16-18

Comparison of the themes of 1 and 2 Thessalonians

1 Thessalonians	2 Thessalonians
1. The coming of Christ in the air for the church, 4:13-18	1. The coming of Christ to the earth with His church
2. The present age of grace	2. The future day of the Lord
3. The Spirit's working in the church	3. Satan's working in the world ("mystery of iniquity"), 2:7
4. Reminded them of what he had taught	4. Corrected false teachings they had heard

2 THESSALONIANS 1

The church was going through persecution (1:4-7), and some of the believers thought they were already in the Day of the Lord, that time of tribulation in which the whole world will be judged. It is possible that a letter, supposedly from Paul, had come to the church (2:1-2), or that one of the church prophets had given this false message during a public meeting. At any rate, Paul writes to explain God's program for the age and to encourage these suffering Christians to remain true to the Lord. He points out three purposes behind their suffering.

I. Suffering Helps Us to Grow (1:3-5)

"The blood of the martyrs is the seed of the church," wrote the Latin church father Tertullian; and history proves that it is true. A devoted Chinese Christian said, "The suffering in China has multiplied the blessings because it has purified the church." The Thessalonian Christians had a reputation for growing faith, abounding hope, and radiant love (1 Thes. 1:3); and their difficult experiences were causing their faith, hope, and love to grow.

Furthermore, their testimony was growing as well, for all the churches heard about them and their stand for the Lord. Paul was able to glory in them among all the churches. Their steadfast endurance was an encouragement to other believers.

Note too that they were growing in patience (v. 4). "Tribulation produces perseverance" (Rom. 5:3, NKJV). Of course, "perseverance" in the New Testament is not simply "waiting it out"; it is steadfast endurance in the Lord, keeping going when the going is tough. The Christian who prays for more patience must expect more tribulation, for tribulation is the spiritual tool God uses to make us patient.

When suffering comes, it will either make us or break us. If we accept the suffering, yield to God's will, and by faith continue to stand true, then the suffering will cause us to grow. If we resist the suffering, complain to God, and give up in unbelief, then the suffering will break us and weaken our testimony. See 1 Peter 4:12-19.

II. Suffering Prepares Us for Glory (1:6-10)

Paul does not look upon suffering as a burden, but as a blessing, a privilege. Suffering for Christ is a gift (Phil. 1:29). When Paul said that they should be counted "worthy of the kingdom" (v. 5), he is not suggesting that they could earn a place in heaven by their own merit. "Worthy" describes fitness, not merit. God fits us through suffering for the glory that lies ahead. Suffering and glory cannot be separated (Matt. 5:10-12; 1 Peter 4:12-14; 5:1). Our suffering here today is but preparation for the glory yet to be revealed (Rom. 8:18; 2 Cor. 4:16-18).

But steadfastness in suffering is also a testimony to the lost world. It may seem that God is not judging the sins of the world, but this is not true. If we walk in unbelief, we will get discouraged, thinking that God is not vindicating His own (see Ps. 73 and Habakkuk), but God is preparing judgment for the wicked. Knowing this, we can rest in confidence. God will "recompense" judgment; that is, He will mete out to the wicked in the same measure and kind that they have meted out to Christians. Pharaoh drowned the babies of Israel, and God drowned the Egyptian army in the Red Sea. Judas betrayed Jesus to be hanged on a tree, and Judas went out and hanged himself. Saul tried to slay David with a sword, and was slain with a sword himself. Sinners reap what they sow.

When Christ comes to earth with His church, He will judge the wicked who will then be living on earth. They will suffer eternal hell for two reasons: they would not come to know God (willful ignorance, Rom. 1:18-32), and they would not obey God (willful disobedience). God commands sinners to repent (Acts 17:30); rejecting Christ is disobedience. Of course, the world will not be ready for Christ's sudden return in judgment (Rev. 19:11-21) and His coming will catch them unawares. The order of events is: (1) the secret return of Christ in the air for the church, which can happen at any time; (2) the Day of the Lord (1 Thes. 5:1ff); (3) the rise and increase in power of the Man of Sin; (4) the sudden return of Christ to the earth with the church; (5) judgment on sinners and the binding of Satan for 1,000 years (Rev. 19:11–20:3).

III. Suffering Glorifies Christ Today (1:11-12)

Jesus Christ shall be glorified in His saints in that day (v. 10); but believers ought to glorify Him every day that they live. This is the burden of Paul's prayer for the believers: that God might fulfill His purpose in their lives, and that the name of Christ might be glorified through them. Paul's ministry was the Word of God and prayer (see Acts 6:4). He taught the people God's truths, then prayed for them to live out what he had taught them.

Believers can be confident in suffering because God has chosen us and will never forsake us. The good work that God begins, He will complete (Phil. 1:6). If the sinful world seems to be winning the battle today, we can rest in faith, knowing that they will lose the battle tomorrow. Our responsibility is to live worthy of this high calling (v. 11) and to allow God to work out His perfect will in faith and power. Note the "twin truths" in this chapter: faith and love (v. 3); faith and patience (v. 4); faith and power (v. 11).

What should Christians who are in the will of God do when they go through painful testing and trial? They should: (1) thank God for His salvation and that He is with them; (2) surrender to the will of God without complaining; (3) ask God to give wisdom to understand His will; (4) watch for opportunities to witness and glorify God in the situation; (5) wait patiently until God's purposes have been fulfilled. Of course, if we are out of the will of God and trouble comes (and it will!), we must accept His chastening hand.

This first chapter is a great encouragement for the believer in these trying days. The world is going downhill toward hell at breakneck speed. People do not want to hear or heed the Word of God. Faithful Christians are suffering while godless unbelievers prosper. It seems as though God has forsaken His own. Not so, says Paul. The believer can "rest" (v. 7) — and this word means "the relaxation of strain" — knowing that God is at work in the world. One day He will vindicate His own and bring vengeance on the lost.

2 THESSALONIANS 2

Paul comes in this chapter to the heart of his letter, his explanation about the Day of the Lord and the Man of Sin. The Christians were "shaken" instead of established (1 Thes. 3:2, 13) because they had been told (falsely) that the Day of the Lord was already upon them. "At hand" in v. 2 should be "already present." Paul explains that certain events must take place before this day of wrath and judgment can come to the world.

I. The Apostasy Must Take Place (2:1-3)

The word "apostasy" means "a falling away." Here it refers to a falling away from the truth of the Word of God. While there were certainly false teachers in Paul's day, the church at large was united on the truths of the Word of God. If you met another Christian, you knew he believed in the Word of God, the deity of Christ, and the salvation by faith in Christ. This is certainly not true today! We live in a day of "Christian unbelief"; people say they are Christians, yet deny the deity of Christ, the inspiration of the Bible, and so on.

This apostasy, or falling away from the truth, is promised in 1 Tim. 4 and 2 Tim. 3. We are living in apostate days right now, which indicates that the coming of the Lord is near. The professing church (Christendom) has departed from the faith.

II. The Temple Must Be Rebuilt (2:4-5)

Paul promises the rise of a world dictator, the "man of sin . . . son of perdition" (v. 3). He is not talking about a world system, but a person who will head up a world system. This "man of sin" contrasts with Christ, the Savior from sin. He is the son of perdition; Christ is the Son of God. He is the liar; Christ is the Truth. We commonly call this man "the Antichrist," which means both "against Christ" as well as "instead of Christ." This world ruler will be energized by the devil and will unite the nations of Europe in a great federation (the ten horns of Daniel's image, Dan. 7). According to Rev. 17, the Antichrist will cooperate with the apostate world church in his rise to power, and then will destroy this religious system when he doesn't need it anymore.

The program is as follows: (1) the church will be raptured; (2) the Antichrist will begin his rise to power in a peaceful way; (3) he will unite Europe and make a seven-year covenant with Israel to protect it (see Dan. 9); (4) after three and one-half years he will break that covenant and invade Israel; (5) he will abolish all religion and set himself up to be worshiped (Rev. 13); (6) at the end of the seven-year tribulation period (Day of the Lord), Christ will return to earth and destroy the Antichrist and his system. Both the OT and NT predict the return of the Jews to Palestine and the rebuilding of the Jewish temple. When the Antichrist sets himself up in the temple, this will mark the "abomination of desolation" of Dan. 11:31 and Matt. 24:15.

III. The Restrainer Must Be Removed (2:6-12)

Satan's mystery of iniquity is already working in the world, and we can see its godless activities increasing rapidly. What, then, holds back Satan's evil program and the rise of the Antichrist? God has a "restrainer" in the world, which we believe is the Holy Spirit working in and through the church. God has "times and seasons" marked out (1 Thes. 5:1), and even Satan cannot get God off schedule. The One who hinders in v. 7 is the Spirit, and He will continue to hinder Satan's activities until He is taken "out of the midst" when the church is raptured. Of course, the Spirit will still work on earth, since people will believe and be saved after the rapture; but His hindering ministry through the body of Christ will end. This will give Satan free course to fill the cup of iniquity to the full.

Satan will work through the Antichrist in miraculous powers (vv. 9-10), just as the magicians in Egypt imitated Moses' miracles. He will imitate Christ's powers (see Acts 2:22) and get the world to accept and worship him. Men would rather believe a lie than the truth! Of course, true believers who are saved after the rapture will not be deceived; it is the lost who will be deluded and ultimately end up in hell. They will believe the lie, which is worshiping and serving the creature instead of the Creator (Rom. 1:25).

IV. The Church Must Be Completed (2:13-17)

The Day of the Lord applies to the Gentile nations and the Jews, but not to the church. It is a day of wrath, and the church is not destined for wrath (1 Thes. 1:10; 5:9). The purpose of the Tribulation is the punishment of the Gentiles and the purification of the Jewish nation, which by this time has returned to its own land in unbelief. But Antichrist cannot begin his rise to power until Christ has taken the church from the earth. What a contrast between the church and the followers of Antichrist! We have been saved by believing the Truth; they will be damned because they believe a lie. We have believed the good news of the Gospel; they believe the false promises of the devil. We have been chosen for glory; they are destined for hell.

Paul makes a wonderful application: stand fast! Don't be moved by world convulsions, political upheavals, or religious apostasy. All these things must take place, but God is still on the throne. As the end of the age draws near, it will be more and more difficult to live for Christ and serve Him. What should the Christian do? Hold on to the Word of God! Don't listen to the lies of the devil—the teachings of the cults, the sugar-coated promises of false teachers.

Hold to the Word of God! We have in Christ and His Word eternal encouragement and good hope.

We must keep on working. "Every good word and work" (v. 17) is a good motto to follow in these dark days. Keep on giving out the Word; keep on working for Christ. As we win others to Christ, we are building up the body. When the body is completed, it will be caught away to glory. This is what Peter means by "hastening the coming of the day of God" (2 Peter 3:11-12). As long as the church is in the world, Satan's program of wickedness is held back; but once the church is gone, Satan will have more freedom. He will seek to destroy Israel and ruin mankind.

These are great and challenging days. May we be found faithful when He comes!

2 THESSALONIANS 3

The second coming of Christ is more than a doctrine to examine and study; it is a truth to grip our lives and make us better Christians. It is not enough to know about His coming or to believe it; we must practice it in daily life. Unfortunately, some of the believers at Thessalonica were abusing the doctrine of Christ's return. In this final chapter, Paul exhorted them to change their ways. There are three practical admonitions here.

I. Pray and Be Patient (3:1-5)

What a tremendous power the believer has in prayer! Though Satan is at work in the world, we can still pray to God and see Him answer. Paul's request was that they pray for his ministry of the Word. The only way to counteract Satan's lies is to share the truth of the Word of God. The Word is living (Heb. 4:12), and Paul desires to see it "run freely" (v. 1) throughout the world. Where the Word is ignored, Paul yearns to see it glorified. The Word did have free course among the believers at Thessalonica and was being glorified because they received it and believed it (1 Thes. 2:13; 2 Thes. 2:13).

He also prayed that God's servants might be delivered from wicked men. Wherever we take the Gospel, Satan will raise up unreasonable (perverse) and evil men to oppose us (see Acts 18:1-12). These unbelievers oppose the Word itself and even those who would give out the Word! We cannot trust men, but we can trust our faithful God. "He is faithful" (see v. 3) is the watchword of the steadfast Christian.

Believers need to be patient as they pray and give out the Word. God is able to give us this patience as we grow in our love for Christ. The steward who became impatient as he waited for his Lord had trouble with his heart and obedience (Matt. 24:42-51). Paul tells us to love His appearing (2 Tim. 4:8). Where there is love, there will be patience and hope.

II. Work If You Want to Eat (3:6-13)

Some of the believers had misapplied the teaching concerning the return of Christ. "If the Lord is coming back soon," they reasoned, "then we ought to give up our jobs and wait for Him to come!" Down through the ages, fringe groups have made this same mistake. They have left the world, gone off to a mountain, and waited for the Lord to come back, only to return home embarrassed. How foolish people can be when they resist the clear teaching of the Word of God! Paul admonished the true believers to withdraw from these lazy Christians who were disobeying the Word, that the offenders might be ashamed and correct their foolish ways (vv. 6 and 14). The faithful were to treat the offenders as brothers and sisters, not as enemies; but they were not to put up with their sin.

He pointed back to his own teaching and example. While with them, Paul worked with his own hands and supported himself and his co-laborers (see 1 Thes. 2:9-12; Acts 20:33-35). He had repeatedly taught them to work faithfully as Christians and care for their own needs. "If any man does not work, he should not eat!" was the principle Paul followed. Of course, the church cared for those who had honest needs and could not work (see Acts 6; 1 Tim. 5); but the church is not obligated to help those who are able to work but who will not. Those who refuse to work become busybodies; they have time on their hands, and they interfere with other people's business. This creates a bad testimony to the unsaved (see Col. 4:5). The truth of the second coming of Christ ought to impel us to work harder and to be faithful to obey His Word.

When faithful Christians see unfaithful Christians living as they do, it often discourages them. "What's the use!" they say. Paul encourages them, "Be not weary in well-doing! Don't give up!" (v. 13) Let's be found faithful when Jesus comes and we stand before Him.

III. Hear the Word and Do It (3:14-18)

The Word of God is to be heard and obeyed. Those who refuse to obey what Paul has to say were to be marked by the Thessalonian believers and treated accordingly. This action is not official church discipline, such as discussed in 1 Cor. 5, but personal corrective action by individual members of the church. We ought not to encourage laziness. If each Christian would obey the Word of God, the church would be holier, happier, and more effective in witness and service.

One of the strengths of the Thessalonian church was its attitude toward the Word of God. They heard and received the Word, believed it (1 Thes. 1:5-6; 2:13), and shared it with others. But apparently some of the believers were becoming hardened to the Word: they heard it but did not obey it. The evidence of their unbelief and disobedience was seen in the way they lived, and their lives were a disgrace to the church. We must be hearers *and* doers of the Word (James 1:22-27).

Paul's benediction deals with peace and grace. How these believers needed peace! They were experiencing great tribulation; some of their number had died; some were living disorderly lives. We can have peace in our hearts if we surrender to Christ, believe His promises, and look for His return. Nothing will encourage the tested believer like the expectation of Christ's return!

This peace comes from His presence: "The Lord be with you all." This is the God of peace giving us the peace of God (Phil. 4:4-9).

Paul added his personal signature and benediction of grace, which was the way he closed all of his letters, thus guaranteeing their genuineness. Satan has his counterfeits and forgeries, so Paul assured them that this letter was authentic and authoritative. See 1 Cor. 16:21, Gal. 6:11, and Col. 4:18.

1 TIMOTHY

A Suggested Outline of 1 Timothy

I. The Church and Its Message (1)

   A. Teaching sound doctrine (1:1-11)

   B. Preaching a glorious Gospel (1:12-17)

   C. Defending the faith (1:18-20)

II. The Church and Its Members (2–3)

   A. Praying men (2:1-8)

      1. For rulers (2:1-3)

      2. For sinners (2:4-8)

   B. Modest women (2:9-15)

      1. In dress (2:9-10)

      2. In behavior (2:11-15)

   C. Dedicated officers (3:1-13)

      1. Pastors (3:1-7)

      2. Deacons (3:8-13)

   D. Behaving believers (3:14-16)

III. The Church and Its Minister (4)

   A. A good minister (4:1-6)

   B. A godly minister (4:7-12)

   C. A growing minister (4:13-16)

IV. The Church and Its Ministry (5–6)

   A. To older saints (5:1-2)

   B. To widows (5:3-16)

   C. To church leaders (5:17-25)

   D. To servants (slaves) (6:1-2)

   E. To trouble-makers (6:3-5)

   F. To the rich (6:6-19)

   G. To the "educated" (6:20-21)

Introductory Notes to 1 Timothy

I. Background

The Book of Acts closes with Paul a prisoner in Rome (28:30-31). While the NT does not give us a clear picture of Paul's later years, the following chronology is agreed upon by most students: Paul was acquitted before Caesar and forced to leave Rome after his two years of imprisonment. This would be about the spring of A.D. 62. With Luke and Timothy, he visited Ephesus, where he discovered that his prophecy about the "wolves" (Acts 20:29-30) had been fulfilled, for the church at Ephesus had been invaded by false teachers. His warnings in 1 Timothy suggest that this false teaching was similar to the gnosticism he had attacked at Colosse. Paul ministered there himself for a short time, then left to go to Philippi. He left Timothy behind as his special assistant to oversee the Ephesian church and get rid of the false teachers. Their parting was a sorrowful one, according to 2 Tim. 1:4.

II. The Letter

It is likely that Paul was at Colosse, enjoying his promised visit to Philemon, when he wrote this first letter to young Timothy (Phile. 22). Paul was planning to return to Ephesus shortly (1 Tim. 3:14), but matters in the Ephesian church were so urgent that he dared not delay advising his associate. This letter is filled with encouragement for a youthful Christian worker who was facing many difficult problems in a "big city church." We may summarize these problems as follows:

(1) Timothy was a young man seeking to pastor older people (4:12; 5:1-2), and this was not easy to do.

(2) Timothy greatly missed Paul and wanted to quit (1:3; 2 Tim. 1:4).

(3) Timothy was prone to neglect his pastoral duties and his own personal devotional life as a Christian leader (4:11-16).

(4) Timothy had made some hasty decisions, especially about church officers, that had caused some difficulties (5:17-22).

(5) Timothy had a tendency toward asceticism and bodily discipline that was actually hurting him physically (4:7-8, 5:23).

(6) Timothy had admitted to Paul that "youthful temptations" plagued him (2 Tim. 2:22), no surprise in godless Ephesus.

(7) There were false teachers there who needed to be silenced (1:3ff).

(8) Timothy needed counsel on managing the affairs of the church, especially with reference to officers and widows (3:1ff; 5:3ff).

One of the key words in 1 Timothy is "charge," sometimes translated "commandment" (1:3, 5, 18; 4:11; 5:7; 6:13, 17). It was a military term, referring to an order to be passed down the line. God had entrusted the Gospel to Paul (1:11), who had passed it along to Timothy (1:18-19; 6:20). Timothy was "charged" to guard this treasure (2 Tim. 1:13-14) and pass it along to faithful people who would, in turn, entrust it to others (2 Tim. 2:2). Military language is woven throughout both epistles to Timothy: 1:18; 5:14 (where "occasion" means "a base of operations"); 2 Tim. 2:3; 3:6.

The basic theme of 1 Timothy is summarized in 3:15 — that people (not "thou") might know how to conduct themselves as members of the local church. It is a book of "know-how" for the young pastor and the church member. The local church is "the pillar and ground (foundation) of truth," yet people neglect it and abuse it by disobeying the Word of God. As we study 1 Timothy, let us pray that it will make us better Christians and therefore better church members.

1 TIMOTHY 1

Timothy wanted to resign, and Paul's first burden was to encourage him to stay on and finish the task. Almost every Christian worker has wanted to quit at one time or another, but, as Dr. V. Raymond Edman, former president of Wheaton College, used to say, "It is always too soon to quit!" Paul encourages young Timothy in this chapter by reminding him of his position before God and of the fact that God would see him through to victory.

I. God Has Entrusted You with a Ministry (1:1-11)

Timothy was not at Ephesus because Paul put him there. It was *God* who entrusted him with ministry in that important city. Just as God had committed a ministry to Paul's trust (1:11), He had given Timothy a special stewardship, and He expected him to be faithful. "Godly edifying" in v. 4 should read "a stewardship of God." The false teachers at Ephesus were ministering their own program, not a stewardship that God had given them. A steward's first responsibility is to be faithful to his master (1 Cor. 4:1-7). There were false teachers at Ephesus who were trying to make a name for themselves as teachers of the Law but who did not know what they were talking about. They had turned away from the truth of the Word and were listening to fables (myths, v. 4) and endless genealogies, raising more questions than they could answer. What a picture of some teachers today! Their "ministries" do not build up Christians or the local church, but instead foster arguments and divisions. In v. 5, Paul contrasts the false teachers and their ministry with that of the true steward of God's grace. The object of God's steward is to see people love one another with a love that comes from a pure heart, a good conscience, and a sincere faith. But these false teachers were promoting endless divisions and empty talk!

Paul explains to Timothy the significance of the Law. "God did not give the Law to save people," he points out, "but to show people how much they need to be saved." There must be a lawful use of the Law (see Rom. 7:16). In vv. 9-10, Paul lists the sinners who are convicted and condemned by the Law, and if you will compare this list with Ex. 20, you will see that practically all the Ten Commandments are included.

God had entrusted Paul and Timothy with a glorious Gospel, not a system of laws (2 Cor. 3–4). "Sound doctrine" (v. 10) literally means "healthy teaching," that is, teaching that promotes spiritual health. Our word "hygiene" comes from this Gk. word. Note 2 Tim. 1:13 and 4:3, as well as Titus 1:9, 13, and 2:1-2, 8. In 2 Tim. 2:17, Paul warns that false teachings eat "as a gangrene." (Dr. Luke must have appreciated Paul's many references to medical science!)

II. God Will Enable You to Do Your Work (1:12-17)

Paul refers to himself as an example of one whom God enabled, by grace, to serve effectively. The word "ministry" in v. 12 is *diakonia* in the Gk. from which we get our English word "deacon," meaning "a servant."

Timothy was disturbed because he thought he was too young and lacked the necessary qualifications for the ministry. "Look at me!" says the apostle. "I was a blasphemer and murderer before God saved me! If the grace of God can make a missionary out of a murderer, then it can make a success out of you!" Paul was always careful to give God the glory for his life and ministry (1 Cor. 15:10). Anyone who serves the Lord (and all believers ought to be servants) needs to depend on the grace of God. We are saved by grace (Eph. 2:8-9), but we also serve through grace (Rom. 12:3-6). In v. 14, Paul lists the three motivating forces in his life: grace, faith, and love. His love for Christ and for lost sinners constrained him to labor (2 Cor. 5:14ff); his faith in Christ empowered him (Eph. 1:19); and the grace of God worked in his life, enabling him to serve God (Heb. 12:28).

Paul considered his salvation a pattern (example) of what God would do for lost sinners, especially his beloved Israel. Unbelievers today are not saved in just the fashion Paul was, that is, by seeing a light and hearing a voice; but we are saved by grace, through faith, in spite of our sins. The people of Israel will be saved one day in the future as Paul was saved on the Damascus road: they will see Christ, repent, believe, and be changed.

In v. 15, we have the first of several "faithful sayings" that Paul quotes (see 3:1; 4:9; 2 Tim. 2:11; Titus 3:8). These are thought to be sayings of the NT prophets in the early church that summarized important teachings. Early Christians had no written Bible to refer to; they quoted these "sayings" as authoritative statements of the faith.

III. God Has Equipped You for Battle (1:18-20)

The Christian life is not a playground; it is a battleground. Timothy had been enlisted by God as a Christian soldier (2 Tim. 2:3-4). Paul reminds the young pastor of his ordination years ago. Apparently some of the prophets in the local church had been instructed by the Spirit to single Timothy out and ordain him for special service (see Acts 13:1-3; 1 Tim. 4:14; 2 Tim. 1:6). "God would not call you without first equipping you!" encourages Paul. "The fact that His Spirit set His seal upon you is proof that God will see you through the battles ahead." See Phil. 1:6. He was to use the Word of God as a sharp two-edged sword to overcome Satan (Eph. 6:17; Heb. 4:12).

It is not enough, however, to have correct doctrine; the Christian soldier must also have correct living ("faith and a good conscience," v. 19). Paul mentions the conscience several times in his pastoral letters to Timothy and Titus (see 1 Tim. 1:5, 19; 3:9; 4:2; 2 Tim. 1:3; Titus 1:15). The word "conscience" has a Latin origin and means "to know with." Conscience is that inward judge that bears witness of our actions (see Rom. 2:15). It is possible for a believer to maintain orthodox doctrine while living in hidden sin; and this is the way to spiritual shipwreck. To "thrust away" conscience is to open the door to sin and Satan. A "pure conscience" becomes a "defiled conscience" and ultimately could become a "seared conscience" without spiritual sensitivity at all.

Paul named two men in Ephesus who might give Timothy trouble: Hymenaeus (2 Tim. 2:17) and Alexander (2 Tim. 4:14). These two men had been a part of the Ephesian church, and Paul had disciplined them because of their blasphemy, probably teaching false doctrine. The word "learn" in v. 20 means "to learn by discipline," suggesting that Satan would deal with them through adverse circumstances. It was not easy for young Timothy to face these men with God's truth, but he had to do so to preserve the purity and power of the church. There would be less false doctrine today if Christians had withstood false teachers yesterday.

1 TIMOTHY 2

In chapters 2–3, Paul discusses the public ministry of the church and the roles that different members ought to play. Chapter 1 deals with the ministry of the Word, and in this chapter the emphasis is on prayer. The two main ministries of the pastor are the Word of God and prayer (Acts 6:4). It is sad to see churches robbing their pastors of these important ministries by keeping them "busy" promoting a program, pleasing people, and practicing church politics. If the churches would simplify their organization and purify their motives, the pastors would be able to do a spiritual work for the glory of the Lord.

It is important that the church have a balanced ministry of the Word of God and prayer. The Word instructs the church; prayer inspires the church to obey the Word. The church that has an abundance of Bible teaching but little prayer will have "much light, but no heat." It will be orthodox but frozen! The other extreme is the church that has much prayer and religious enthusiasm, but little teaching from the Word; this may produce a group of people with zeal but no knowledge.

I. The Place of Prayer in the Local Church (2:1-8)

A. Its importance.

Paul lists prayer "first of all." The local church does not pray because it is the expected thing to do; it prays because prayer is vital to the life of the local church. The Holy Spirit works in the church through prayer and the Word of God (1 Thes. 2:13; Eph. 3:20-21). The church that prays will have power and will make a lasting impact for Christ. Note how the believers in Acts turned to prayer and overcame their enemies. Paul exhorts us to pray—it is important!

B. Its nature.

The church's praying ought to include: (1) supplications, which means telling God our needs; (2) prayers, meaning worship and adoration; (3) intercessions, which involves requests on the behalf of others; and (4) thanksgiving, or appreciation for what God has done. See Phil. 4:6 and Dan. 6:10-11. We should pray for the church family, of course, but we should not stop there. "All men" (v. 1) need our prayers.

C. Its aims.

Verse 2 suggests that prayer helps to maintain the peace of society. As Christians pray for leaders in government, God overrules and protects His church from wicked men. Verse 3 indicates that, above all else, prayer pleases God and glorifies Christ. If we pray only to have our needs met, we have a low view of prayer. Of course, we ought to pray for the salvation of the lost (vv. 4-7). Christ died for all men, and God would have all men to be saved (see 2 Peter 3:9); therefore, the Spirit directs the believer to pray for lost people.

D. Its conditions.

Verse 8 lays down three conditions for the public praying in the local church: (1) "without wrath" — loving one another; (2) "holy hands," that is, clean, obedient lives; and (3) faith. See Mark 11:20-26. The men are to take the lead in the prayer ministry of the church.

II. The Place of Women in the Local Church (2:9-15)

Christianity, like no other religious faith, elevated the position of women and children. Instead of criticizing Paul for these instructions, women ought to thank God for the blessing the Christian faith has been to women around the world. Paul is emphasizing again the principle of headship (see Eph. 5:22ff; 1 Cor. 11:1-16). The local church that refuses to recognize this principle may create confusion. There is a three-fold headship in the local assembly: (1) the headship of Christ over the body, Col. 1:18; (2) the headship of the pastor over the flock, Acts 20:28; and (3) the headship of the man over the woman, 1 Cor. 11:1-16 and 1 Tim. 2:12.

Paul gives us the characteristics of the ideal Christian woman in the church:

A. Modesty (v. 9).

Paul is not saying that the Christian woman must wear old clothes and be out of style! Rather, he is emphasizing that the inner person is more important than the outer appearance (1 Peter 3:1-6). Modest apparel glorifies Christ; extreme fashions only point to the person and make the Christian look worldly. It is possible for the believer to be modern and still be modest.

B. Purity.

She "professes godliness." Godliness is one of Paul's favorite words; see 2:2, 10; 3:16; 4:7-8; 6:3, 5-6, 11; 2 Tim. 3:5; Titus 1:1. Of course, godliness is simply a shortened form of "god-likeness."

C. Industry.

She practices good works (v. 10). Later in this letter (5:11-14) Paul warns about idle women who wander from house to house and give Satan opportunity to lead them into sin. The best way for a Christian woman to preach is with her life.

D. Humility.

In 1 Cor. 14:34-40, Paul amplifies this commandment. Just as Satan got a footing in Eden through Eve, so he can get a footing in the local church through some sincere, misguided woman. (Misguided men can also be a problem; see 1 Tim. 1:20.) When the local church meets in assembly, the women are instructed to exercise submission. If they have any questions, rather than interrupt the meeting, they should ask their husbands at home. This rule does not prevent a woman from teaching or from leading in ministries assigned by the local assembly.

Paul undergirds this ruling with a solid doctrinal foundation: Adam was created first and had precedence over Eve. (See 1 Cor. 11:8-9.) Headship is written into the very course of nature; when we violate this principle, we invite confusion. The Corinthian church was confused and carnal partly because the women were taking precedence over the men, and neither the men nor the women were submitting to the Word of God.

Paul gives a second reason for this principle: Satan finds it easier to deceive women than men (v. 14, and see 2 Cor. 11:3). Eve was deceived by Satan and sinned. Had Adam been at her side protecting her, she might not have yielded to Satan's lies. Adam sinned with his eyes wide open, choosing rather to be with his wife (now a sinner) than to walk with God.

"Childbearing" in v. 15 probably refers to the curse of Gen. 3:16; in other words, godly women would be delivered in dangerous childbirth. Some take it to mean the birth of Christ, since the original Gk. is "through the childbearing," that is, a very special child. But the first meaning is probably the best; see also 5:14. Mothers-to-be who are in the will of God can claim this promise.

1 TIMOTHY 3

Though the church is an organism, a living and growing body united to Christ, the church is also an organization. In fact, every organism has to be organized or it will die. The human body is a living organism, but it is also a highly organized machine. If the local church is to do its task effectively, it must have leadership, and this implies organization.

I. The New Testament Pastor (3:1-7)

The terms "pastor," "elder," and "bishop" refer to the same office. See Acts 20:17 and 28, and Titus 1:5 and 7. Elder is a translation of the Gk. word *presbuteros* (translated "presbytery" in 4:14). The word simply means an older, mature person. The Jewish elders (Luke 22:66) were the leading adult men, recognized for their maturity. In the early church, pastors were chosen from the mature men of the fellowship. Bishop comes from the Gk. word *episkopos* and means "overseer." The Episcopal church gets its name from this word. The local pastor, then, was an elder in terms of spiritual maturity, and an overseer in terms of ministry. Philippians 1:1 gives the makeup of the NT church: saints, bishops, deacons. It was usual for the churches to have more than one elder or pastor.

A. His personal qualifications (vv. 2-3).

"Blameless" does not mean sinless; rather, it means "without reproach." Literally, the word means "that cannot be laid hold of"; that is, there is nothing in his life that the enemy can lay hold of to hinder the work or ruin the witness. Since moral laxness was a serious problem in those days, the pastor was required to have but one wife; that is, there had to be no question as to his marriage standards. There has been long (and heated) debate over whether Paul meant to attack polygamy (a man having more than one wife at one time) or divorce. "Vigilant" means "temperate," referring to sober judgment and action. "Sober" indicates seriousness of purpose and self-control. "Good behavior" should be translated "orderly"; it suggests a well-ordered life and testimony. He should be a real gentleman. He should love people and enjoy having them in his home. "Apt to teach" ties in with Eph. 4:11, where "pastor and teacher" are one office. Read 1 and 2 Tim. again to see how much Paul says about teaching the Word. While total abstinence is not explicitly demanded in the Bible, sobriety is certainly stressed; modern problems encourage the church to take a stand against alcohol and drunkenness. A "striker" (v. 3) is one who uses physical force to get people to agree with him, and we know that "the wrath of man does not produce the righteousness of God" (James 1:20, NKJV). The pastor must not be money-hungry; he must have patience toward the sheep; he must not be contentious (a brawler, given to arguing); and he must be free from covetousness, putting Christ and the church first in his life.

B. His family qualifications (vv. 4-5).

The pastor should be the head of the household, and he should have his children under control. This does not mean that the pastor's children should not be allowed to be children! It means that they are to respect the Lord and their parents and grow to be examples as all Christians should.

C. His church qualifications (vv. 6-7).

He must not be a new convert; if he is, Satan may puff him up with pride and he will fall into sin. It is dangerous to thrust new converts into Christian leadership. The pastor must have good testimony even among the unsaved ("those who are outside," v. 7), lest his bad reputation tear down the witness of the church. It is tragic when pastors leave behind bad debts and unfulfilled promises. This hurts the testimony of the church in the community.

II. The New Testament Deacon (3:8-13)

"Likewise" indicates that God has equally important standards for the deacon, for he is to work with the pastor in guiding the affairs of the church. "Grave" means "held in high respect." A "double-tongued" person is a tale-bearer, one who says one thing to one person and another thing to another person, trying to court the favor of both. Church leaders must be people who keep their word. The matters of wine and money were discussed in v. 3. There may be the warning in v. 11 against misusing church funds for personal gain. They should be people of clean conscience, living what they profess.

Some translate v. 11 as "deaconesses"; the word is probably "wives." We have no clear evidence in the NT that the early church had deaconesses as well as deacons. In any event, these standards applied also to the deacons' wives. Note that both pastors and deacons are to be proved before given the office, that is, allowed to exercise their gifts in other ministries before being made leaders. The deacon's office is to be used, not just filled. Church officers who are faithful will acquire a good standing (degree) before God and men, and thus are able to further the work of Christ.

III. The New Testament Church (3:14-16)

Much has been written about the "true church" or the "invisible church." Certainly there is such a concept in the Bible, in that all believers belong to Christ and are one in Him. But the primary NT emphasis is on the local church, and the local church is just as much the "true church" as the "mystical body of Christ" that we hear so much about. In the NT, Christians were expected to unite with local assemblies and go to work for God. In these verses, Paul shows the importance of the local church by describing it under several images:

A. The house of God.

That is, the family or household of God on earth. All believers are children of God, and the church is His family. See Gal. 6:10 and Eph. 2:19. Paul wrote this letter to teach people how to behave as members of God's family. If the church is God's family, then certainly it is more important than any other organization on earth.

B. The pillar and ground of truth.

This is architectural language. The church is what holds up God's truth in this world. The word "ground" means "bulwark" or "foundation"; one translator renders it "basement." As the local church is faithful to preserve, preach, and practice the truth, God's work prospers on earth. The unfaithful Christian is weakening the very foundation of God's truth in the world.

C. The body of Christ.

Verse 16 is perhaps an early Christian hymn, memorized by the saints for their worship services. The mystery of godliness is God's hidden program to bring godliness into the world. Of course, Christ is God's great Mystery, and this song exalts Him: His birth; His death and resurrection; His earthly ministry. This is a summary of the Person and work of Christ, and the idea is that the local church now continues the work which He began. The church on earth is the body of Christ on earth (see 1 Cor. 12:12, where Paul is speaking of a local church, not the church universal).

The church is important to God and should be important to us.

1 TIMOTHY 4

This chapter deals with the pastor's spiritual life and labors. It indicates that a true minister will have three qualities. He will be:

I. A Good Minister: Preaching the Word (4:1-6)

A. The danger (vv. 1-3).

The Ephesian church had been warned already about the coming of false doctrines (Acts 20:29-30). Throughout Paul's letters, the Spirit speaks "in stated words" (expressly) that the church will see apostasy, a falling away from the true faith (see 2 Thes. 2). The word "depart" in the Gk. gives us our English word "apostasy." He points out too the cause for the apostasy—not the "growing intelligence of scholars" but the satanic influence of demons so that professed believers deny the basic doctrines of the Bible. The problem is not with the head but with the heart!

What are the marks of these false teachers? For one thing, they preach one thing but practice another. They are such hypocrites that they even "brand" their own consciences by their willful disobedience to God's Word! They read the Word but explain it away through their self-serving lies. They teach a false piety—namely, asceticism, that is, abstaining from marriage and certain foods. There are some so-called "Christian" groups that have never studied Colossians 2 to discover that bodily disciplines do not automatically advance spiritual life.

B. The answer (vv. 4-6).

"The Word of God and prayer" (v. 5) settle the matter. God, in His Word, has declared that all foods are clean (Gen. 1:29-31; 9:3; Mark 7:14-23; 1 Cor. 10:23-26; Acts 10); and through prayer, the Christian thanks God and dedicates the food to His glory (1 Cor. 10:31). The pastor must teach these things to his people, nourishing them and himself on "healthy" (sound) doctrine; see notes on 1:10. A good minister will feed on the Word that he might be able to feed others.

II. A Godly Minister: Practicing the Word (4:7-12)

Just as "healthy" doctrine will promote spiritual health, so the foolish and silly myths of false teachers will produce spiritual sickness. Spiritual food and spiritual exercise are a happy combination! It is suggested that Timothy was leaning toward asceticism, the disciplining of the body; and that Paul is here teaching him to emphasize spiritual disciplines and exercises more than physical. If some Christians would put as much energy and enthusiasm into spiritual things as they do athletics and body-building, how much stronger they and their churches would be! "Bodily exercise profits for a little time," Paul admits, "but spiritual exercise — practicing the Word of God — is profitable for this life and the life to come" (v. 8). See Heb. 4:14.

The Christian, and especially the pastor, must practice the Word of God and be known for godliness (godlikeness). This may mean carrying burdens and bearing suffering (v. 10), but it is worth it. Even young people can be examples of the faith, as Paul admonishes in v. 12: in word, in behavior (conversation), in love, in spirit (enthusiasm), in faith (faithfulness), and purity.

III. The Growing Minister: Progressing in the Word (4:13-16)

"That your progress [pioneer advance] may be evident to all" (NKJV) is the goal Paul sets in v. 15. A growing pastor will produce a growing church, for a man cannot lead others where he has not been himself. How could Timothy, or any believer, for that matter, make progress in the Christian life?

A. The Word of God.

"Give attendance to reading" (v. 13), that is, the public reading of the Word of God in the assembly. Of course, the Word should be explained and applied. It is not enough just to know the facts of the Word; believers must know the doctrines of the Word.

B. Spiritual gifts.

Every Christian has some spiritual gift (Rom. 12:3-8; 1 Cor. 12), and far too often these gifts are neglected instead of exercised by faith. When the elders (presbytery) ordained young Timothy, assisted by Paul (2 Tim. 1:6), God gave Timothy some spiritual gifts to equip him for his ministry. But he had been neglecting these gifts and needed to stir them up in the way that a dying fire has to be stoked. Spiritually speaking, what we do not use, we lose; see Heb. 2:1-3.

C. Dedication.

The original Gk. in v. 15 reads "attend to these things, be in these things." In other words, give yourself to them completely, with no compromise or distraction. Certainly meditation is a part of this, but Paul's commands are much broader. The Christian who is listless about spiritual matters will never make progress.

D. Examination.

"Take heed to yourself" comes first. Examine yourself, find out where you are spiritually and where you are going. "The unexamined life is not worth living," said the ancient philosopher Socrates. It is easy to correct doctrine, but much more challenging to live the doctrine. We will never save others if we lose our own spiritual power.

As you review these verses, you can see that Paul expected Timothy to build the church on the Word—to preach it, teach it, and practice it. The Word was to be his personal food and guide, as well as the food for the church. The pastor who spends time in the Word and in prayer will grow himself and will pastor a growing church.

We might conclude by asking, "How can the church member help his pastor grow?" One of the best ways is to protect his time, so that he has opportunity to study and pray. Every pastor wants to be available when there is a need, but no pastor can afford to waste time on trivial matters. Another way is to pray for him daily. A third suggestion is to pay attention when he preaches. What blessing it is to preach to people who want to listen! How discouraged a pastor can become when church members do not apply themselves to follow the messages from the Word. Finally, the church should provide the means needed to build the work of the church. This means faithful stewardship, bringing tithes and offerings to the Lord. Many a godly pastor cannot accomplish what God wants done because the church is in debt or has a poor financial history. Also, if the church doesn't pay the pastor a living wage, it adds to his burdens and can hinder the work.

1 TIMOTHY 5

These final two chapters deal with the church and its ministry to at least seven kinds of people (see outline on page 617).

I. To Older Saints (5:1-2)

Being a young man, Timothy had to be careful in his relationship to the older believers in the church. The word "elders" here refers to age, not office. The pastor is not to rebuke older saints, but exhort and encourage them. "Look upon them as you would your own parents," Paul advises. (See Titus 2:1-4.) The church needs to recognize the needs and problems of the older believers and seek to help them. "Senior saints" are important to the church, and the younger people of the church need them more than they may realize. See 1 Peter 5:1-7.

II. To Widows (5:3-16)

Read Acts 6, 9:36-43, and James 1:27. The early church cared for needy widows. The word "honor" in v. 3 means "to fix the value," as in our word "honorarium," an amount paid to a speaker for services. Timothy had to be careful not to misuse the church funds by giving money to unworthy widows. In his day, as today, there were deceivers who preyed on people under the masquerade of religion. Such people usually visited churches because they knew that soft-hearted saints would give them a handout "for Jesus' sake."

But note that v. 4 says that the family has the first responsibility of caring for their needy. ("Nephews" ought to be translated "grandchildren" here.) Children and grandchildren are to repay (requite) their parents and grandparents, and not expect the church to put them on charity. Any Christian who does not take care of his own is worse than an unbeliever (v. 8). This is why the pastor and deacons must investigate every case of charity, and why individual church members or church groups ought not to do charitable work without first consulting with the spiritual leaders. Too much of God's money, brought by faithful worshipers, has gone to waste because well-meaning Christians followed their emotions instead of God's Word.

Paul gives the requirements for widows being "enrolled" ("taken into the number," v. 9—their name put on the roll); note vv. 5 and 9-10. See also Luke 2:36-37 for an example of this kind of woman. First, she must be a true widow, without family support or care. She must be a godly woman, given to praying and serving others. (It is likely that these widows who were supported by the church served the church in many ways, perhaps as Dorcas did.) She must be 60 years old or older, and have a good testimony (v. 10), especially in her marriage.

In vv. 11-16, Paul deals with the younger widows and warns Timothy not to enroll them. For one thing, the younger widows would pledge faithfulness to serve Christ and the church ("their first faith" in v. 12 is "their first pledge"), but would then be tempted to start looking for husbands. "They will marry" in v. 11 is "they will to be married," that is, marriage becomes the consuming passion of their lives. Furthermore, having grown cold spiritually, they will stop serving others and will start getting into trouble (v. 13). This will bring reproach on the name of Christ and the witness of the church. Paul's commandment is that the younger widows marry, raise godly families, stay at home, and be careful not to give Satan opportunity for accusation. Verse 16 summarizes the matter; let relatives take care of their own needy family members, so that the church is not burdened (charged).

III. To Church Leaders (5:17-25)

Apparently, Timothy was having trouble with some of his officers. Part of the problem may have stemmed from the fact that he had chosen and ordained some of them too quickly (v. 22). Another factor was that he had misjudged some of them (vv. 24-25) and made some hasty decisions. Pastors make mistakes, even if their hearts are right! But then, officers make mistakes too.

As Paul's personal representative in Ephesus, Timothy was to oversee the work of the various elders in the area. These men were paid by the church, since God's command is that those who teach the Word should live from the Word (1 Cor. 9:1-14). Elders who were faithful to do their work well should receive double pay (honor, referring to money, as in v. 3). Of course, double recognition would not be out of order, either! Paul supports this principle of Christians paying their ministers by quoting Deut. 25:4 and referring to what Christ said in Luke 10:7.

But what about church leaders who cause trouble? First of all, get the facts. If every church would practice 1 Tim. 5:19, we would have fewer church splits. Every accusation must be supported by at least two witnesses. The matter must be given honest appraisal, and there must not be any partiality shown (v. 21). How easy it is for us to judge other believers, or to draw conclusions from a few facts (or rumors)! Where the accusation is found to be true, and the witnesses and facts point to conviction, then the offending officer must be dealt with publicly. The suggestion here is that the offender confess his sins and ask the congregation for forgiveness. If an officer's sin is known by at least two people, you can be sure that others know it too; and public sins demand public confession and restitution.

Many a worldly Christian has fled to v. 23 to support his or her bad habits. While the Bible does not demand total abstinence, it does encourage restraint; in any event, this verse applies to a special situation. To begin with, Paul was urging Timothy to take care of his body; and by no stretch of the imagination can we believe that by drinking alcohol, we will better our bodies. The drinker is often the person with the sickest body. The wine that Paul prescribed was to help Timothy's stomach; it was medicine, not a social beverage. (Some have suggested that Timothy's problems with his church officers had given him ulcers!) It is not wrong for Christians to use available means to help God answer their prayers for healing. Paul prayed for Timothy, but he also suggested a practical remedy for his needs. Perhaps Timothy was being swayed by the false teachers who emphasized bodily discipline and asceticism and this had affected his health.

Church officers and leaders are important, because they help the pastor to carry the load. But the pastor must always be the shepherd of the flock. The best thing a church officer can do is to make it possible for the pastor to exercise his spiritual gifts and ministries without hindrance or distraction. Then the church will prosper.

1 TIMOTHY 6

This chapter continues Paul's explanation of the church's ministry to different groups in the fellowship, particularly those that might cause problems.

I. To Slaves (6:1-2)

Slavery was an integral part of ancient life; it is estimated that there were 60 million slaves in the Roman Empire. Many slaves found Christ, but their masters often remained unbelievers; therefore the Christian slaves might be prone to disobey or claim freedom because they were Christians. Paul urges them to be good testimonies to their unsaved masters that their masters might learn to respect the name of God and His Word. Then again slaves who had believing masters would be tempted to take advantage of them, and this behavior Paul prohibits. See Eph. 6:5ff, Col. 3:22ff, and 1 Peter 2:18-25.

II. To Troublemakers (6:3-5)

"Don't worry about doctrine," some modern preachers say; "the important thing is spiritual unity." Paul refutes that lie in this section: whenever there is disunity in a church, it is because somebody does not really believe and practice the Word of God. Those who were teaching false doctrine and who would not agree to Paul's teachings were to be noted and dealt with.

The apostle clearly pictures these people who cause trouble in the church. They are proud; they want to be "important people" in the church. Yet they are ignorant, "knowing nothing" (v. 4). Furthermore, they are sick; for the word "doting" actually means "diseased, sickly." Having rejected the healthy (sound) doctrine, they have made themselves spiritually sick. Instead of feeding on the truths of God's Word, they feed on empty questions and the meanings of words; and all of this leads to envies, strife, constant turmoil, and not to godliness. These people are "deprived" (destitute) of the truth; their only goal is personal profit. If they can use religion to further their own goals, then that is all that concerns them.

Note that Titus 3:10 commands that a troublemaker ("heretic," meaning one who causes factions and divisions) is not to be permitted membership in the church after he or she has been warned two times. Troublemakers who move from church to church ought not to be received back into the fellowship after the second offense.

III. To the Rich (6:6-19)

The thought of "gain" in v. 5 leads Paul into a discussion of the Christian and wealth. Using godliness to try to secure gain will never bring contentment; but a godly life, which is a contented life, is certainly great gain to a person. How important it is to have the right values!

It is easy to misinterpret vv. 9 and 10. In v. 9, Paul is warning those who *will* to be rich, that is, who set their whole attention on securing wealth. This kind of person is bound to fall into temptations and snares and will eventually sink into destruction. Think of all that Lot lost when he set his eyes on the rich plains of Sodom! Or all that Haman lost (see the Book of Esther) when he set his heart on riches and honor! What does a man need for contentment? Very little: food and raiment and a godly life. Think of the poverty of Christ, yet He made many rich (2 Cor. 8:9).

Verse 10 does not teach that money is the root of all evil, or even that the love of money is the root of all evil; but that the love of money is a root of all kinds of evil. Money itself is not neutral; it is basically defiled. Jesus called money "unrighteous mammon" (Luke 16:9, 11), and Paul called it "filthy lucre"(1 Tim. 3:3, 8; Titus 1:7, 11). Money can be invested for eternity by bringing Christ to lost people, or it can send a man to hell by becoming his god. You find both examples in Luke 16. Every one of the Ten Commandments can be broken because of money. Because of a desire for money, people have denied God, blasphemed His name, stolen, lied, murdered, committed adultery, and so on. A lust for material things makes people wander (err) from the faith, and this leads to shipwreck. They look for pleasure but find pain and sorrows.

Paul then injects a warning to Timothy, because Christian leaders can be led astray by false values and a desire for material gain. Demas forsook Paul because he loved the world (2 Tim. 4:10); Judas sold Christ for thirty pieces of silver. Note that Paul called this youthful pastor a "man of God" (v. 11). What an encouragement! Note too the three exhortations: flee, follow, fight. Flee these things — pride, covetousness, false teachings. Sometimes the finest thing the Christian soldier can do is run. In 2 Tim. 2:22, Paul commands him to "Flee youthful lusts." This is what Joseph did when Potiphar's wife tempted him (Gen. 39). But it is not enough to flee. We must also follow, and we must also fight. Paul points to the wonderful example of Christ when He made His courageous witness before Pilate. "We serve the King of kings!" writes Paul. "Be faithful until He comes. When He comes, He will honor you for your good work."

Verses 17-19 form a positive instruction to the rich, telling them how to use their riches for God's glory. Note that he calls them "rich in this present world." It is possible to be rich in this world but not rich toward God (see Luke 12:13-21). First, these people must be humble, accepting their wealth as a stewardship from God. They should keep their eyes on the Giver and not put their trust in the gifts. God wants His own to enjoy the blessings of life; the word "enjoy" is in the Bible! In Christ, we have "all things to enjoy" and they are given to us "richly"! But these material blessings are not only for enjoyment, they are also for employment — to be used for the glory of God and the winning of souls. Money should be used for good works; it should be shared (communicated); it should be invested in things eternal, laying a good foundation for the time to come. "Treasures in heaven" is the way Jesus put it in Matt. 6.

IV. To the "Educated" (6:20-21)

"Science" in v. 20 means "knowledge," but to Paul it was a false knowledge. He was no doubt referring to the Gnostics (see introduction to Colossians) who claimed to have "full knowledge" about the universe, not too different from some of our philosophers today. These false teachers at Ephesus were disturbing young Timothy with their high-sounding theories and their questions about the Word of God; so Paul warned him not to get involved with this "profane and vain babbling"! The wisdom of this world is foolishness with God (see 1 Cor. 1–2).

What is Timothy's responsibility? To "guard the deposit" that God committed to him through Paul. God had given the Gospel message, the deposit of truth, to Paul (1:11), who had in turn committed it to Timothy (1:18-19). Timothy was to guard it (6:20) and pass it on to others (2 Tim. 2:2). This is the task of the church today; may we be faithful to guard the deposit and pass it on to others!

2 TIMOTHY

A Suggested Outline of 2 Timothy

I. The Pastoral Appeal (1)

    A. The reminder of God's call (1:1-6)

    B. The resource of God's grace (1:7-11)

    C. The reward at God's throne (1:12-18)

II. The Practical Appeal (2)

    A. How to endure suffering (2:1-13)

        1. It is part of your calling (2:1-7)

        2. It is a privilege from Christ (2:8-13)

    B. How to deal with false teachers (2:14-23)

        1. Rightly divide the Word (2:14-15)

        2. Reject lies and fables (2:16-18)

        3. Look for godly living (2:19-23)

    C. How to settle church problems (2:24-26)

III. The Prophetic Appeal (3)

    A. An explanation of the future (3:1-9)

    B. An example from the past (3:10-13)

    C. An exhortation for the present (3:14-17)

IV. The Personal Appeal (4)

    A. Preach the Word! (4:1-4)

    B. Fulfill your ministry! (4:5-8)

    C. Hasten to come to Rome! (4:9-18)

    D. Greet my friends in Christ! (4:19-22)

Introductory Notes to 2 Timothy

I. Background

We have no details of Paul's travels after his release from his first
Roman imprisonment. Titus 3:12 indicates that he visited Nicopolis. He must have departed from there and gone to Troas, where, in
a "quick exit," he had left his cloak, books, and parchments
(2 Tim. 4:13) with his host, Carpus. How or where he was arrested
again, we do not know. We do know that Nero had unleashed a
terrible persecution against the Christians, and that Paul's second
imprisonment was far different from his first (Acts 28). He was now
a hated prisoner in a Roman prison, not an accused man in "his
own hired house" awaiting trial. As we read this final letter from
Paul's heart, we can sense his loneliness and heartache as he faced
his trial and certain martyrdom. "Only Luke is with me," he writes,
as he begs his son in the faith, Timothy, to come to him as quickly
as possible.

If the Alexander mentioned in 2 Tim. 4:14 is the same as the
man in Acts 19:33, then it is possible that Paul's arrest took place
in or near Ephesus. When talking to the Ephesian elders, Paul
mentioned "plottings of the Jews" (Acts 20:19), and it is possible
that Alexander the coppersmith had something to do with these
plots. Some students think that Alexander was associated with the
guild of idol-makers and that he was unhappy at Paul's first escape
from Ephesus.

Timothy was no longer the leader at Ephesus; Tychicus had
been sent to take his place (4:12). Apparently Timothy was doing
work as a traveling minister and evangelist in the area around Ephesus. Paul expected Timothy to come to Rome because he knew
that Timothy would be in Troas (4:13) and Ephesus (1:16-18).
These cities were on the road to Rome.

II. Purpose

The letter is intensely personal. Paul is alone at Rome, awaiting
trial and certain death. He longs to see his son Timothy and to
encourage him to take his place in the ministry of the Gospel. Paul
sees apostasy and defeat all around him. Dr. Sidlow Baxter, in
Explore the Book, points out that the "some" of 1 Timothy has
become "all" in 2 Timothy. "Some have turned aside" (1:6);

"some have made shipwreck" (1:19); "some have turned aside after Satan" (5:15); "some have been led astray" (6:10); "some have erred" (6:21) — this is the theme of his first letter. But in 2 Timothy we read: "all have turned away from me" (1:15); "all forsook me"! (4:16) The churches were turning from the faith, and Paul urged young Timothy to be true to his calling and fulfill his ministry. Woven into the exhortations in this letter are the personal sentiments and concerns of the great apostle. This letter is not a "swan song" of defeat; it is an anthem of victory!

If we follow the chapter divisions in our Bible, we see four appeals from Paul to Timothy to encourage him to be a faithful minister in spite of discouraging conditions. Chapter 1 is the pastoral appeal, in which Paul reminds Timothy of his calling to the ministry and of the responsibilities and privileges that go with it. Chapter 2 is the practical appeal, in which Paul seeks to solve some of the young minister's problems: his persecution for the sake of the Gospel, false teachers, and church difficulties. In chapter 3, Paul uses the prophetic appeal, explaining the course of events and the importance of holding fast to the Word. Finally, chapter 4 gives the personal appeal from the heart of the aged apostle, urging Timothy to remain true because he (Paul) would soon be executed. He did not want Timothy to become another Demas.

2 TIMOTHY 1

As you read Paul's two letters to Timothy, you begin to understand the problems of this young minister. For one thing, he hesitated to face matters squarely and settle them according to the Word of God. There was "fear" (cowardice) in his life, perhaps the fear of man that "brings a snare" (Prov. 29:25). He faced the usual temptations of a young man and certainly did not feel adequate for the task. Paul shared with Timothy five wonderful encouragements to sustain him and help him stay with the task.

I. A Praying Friend (1:1-5)

Paul was facing martyrdom, yet he took time to pray for Timothy! If you will compare 1 Tim. 1:1 with 2 Tim. 1:1, you will see that Paul, facing death, was now thinking about the "promise of life in Christ Jesus"—and what a wonderful promise it is! He assures Timothy of his love and prayers and of his good remembrance of him night and day.

He reminds Timothy that there is much to be thankful for, in spite of the problems he was facing. He reminds him of his godly heritage and of the faith that God has given him, not only for salvation, but also for daily living and Christian service. We do not know if Timothy's loved ones were still living at this time; but if they were, they were certainly bearing him up in prayer. What a blessing it is to have praying friends! What an encouragement it is to pray for others and to help them along in their spiritual lives. See 1 Sam. 12:23.

II. A Wonderful Gift (1:6-7)

One of Timothy's problems was cowardice, a timidity about facing problems and doing God's work. His youthfulness probably contributed to this (1 Tim. 4:12). Paul reminds Timothy that he was neglecting the gift God had given him (1 Tim. 4:14) and that he needed to stir it up, as a man would fan into flame the embers of a dying fire. Paul was not suggesting that Timothy was losing his salvation, for this is impossible, but that he was losing his zeal for the Lord and enthusiasm in the Lord's work.

Paul is writing about the Holy Spirit in v. 7. The Spirit does not generate fear in us (see Rom. 8:15), but rather power, love, and discipline (sound mind, self-control). Every Christian needs all three! The Holy Spirit is the power of our lives (Acts 1:8; Eph. 3:20-21; Phil. 4:13). Paul uses this word "power" in all of his letters except the one to Philemon. The Spirit also gives us love, for the fruit of the Spirit is love (Gal. 5:22). Our love for Christ, for the Word, for other believers, and for the lost, must come from the Spirit (Rom. 5:5). The Spirit also gives us discipline and self-control; as a result we are not easily captured by our feelings or circumstances. When the Spirit is in control, we will experience peace and poise, and fear and cowardice will vanish. Note Acts 4:1-22, especially v. 13.

III. A Holy Calling (1:8-11)

The people at Ephesus knew that Timothy was Paul's friend and co-laborer, but Paul was now a Roman prisoner! "Don't be ashamed of me or of the Gospel!" Paul admonished. "Our suffering is all a part of our heavenly calling as ministers." When Christians suffer, they suffer with Christ (Phil. 3:10). The same power that saves us also strengthens us for the battle. Paul emphasized that our calling is by grace; we do not deserve to be saved. If God permits us to suffer, after giving us such a wonderful salvation, what right have we to complain or quit! "God has a purpose in mind," Paul advised. "Let Him work out that purpose."

God's wonderful purpose in the Gospel was hidden in ages past but now it has been revealed. "Abolished" in v. 10 means "made of no effect, disarmed." God did not eliminate death through the cross, because people still die. But He did disarm death — take the sting out of it — for the believer. Christ has brought life and immortality (the condition of never dying) to light. These doctrines are "in the shadows" in the OT, but we must beware of building a doctrine of immortality, death, or resurrection from OT passages alone. Many false cults use Job, Ecclesiastes, and some of Psalms to defend such strange doctrines as soul-sleep.

IV. A Faithful Savior (1:12-14)

What an encouragement it is to know that Christ is faithful and able to keep His own! "I know whom I have believed!" was Paul's confidence — not "I hope" or "I think." There are two ways of reading v. 12, and perhaps Paul meant both of them. Paul is saying that he knows he can trust Christ to keep him and his soul; but he is also saying that he knows Christ will enable him to keep what

He has committed to him. It is possible to translate it, "He is able to keep that which He has committed to me." Christ had committed the Gospel to Paul (1 Tim. 1:11), and Paul was sure that He would enable him to guard it and keep it safe (1 Tim. 6:20; 2 Tim. 4:7). Review 1 Tim. 1:1-11.

"Form" in v. 13 means "outline." The church had an outline of sound (healthy) doctrine, and to digress from that outline was to sin. Timothy was to hold fast to that basic outline of doctrine through the power of the Spirit (v. 14). Verses 12 and 14 are parallel: Christ in glory is able to keep what we give to Him, and the Spirit on earth helps us to keep what Christ gives to us!

V. A Godly Example (1:15-18)

All in Asia had forsaken Paul (see also 4:16). The two men he names may have been members of the Ephesian church, men whom Timothy would know personally. But there was one man who had remained true—Onesiphorus ("one who brings profit or benefit"). This godly man was probably a deacon at Ephesus, for v. 18 can be translated "and in how many things he fully played the deacon" since the word "minister" can also mean "deacon" in the Gk.

This man came to Rome, sought Paul, and served him without fear or shame. "He was not ashamed of my chain!" (v. 16) What an example for Timothy to follow and for all of us to observe! Here was a deacon in the church showing more zeal, love, and courage than his pastor!

Note that v. 17 says that Onesiphorus *was* in Rome. Apparently he was no longer there and perhaps was on his way back to Ephesus. It may be that he carried this letter to Timothy. At any rate, Paul greets this deacon's household in v. 16. To teach as some have that Onesiphorus was no longer living and that Paul's words in v. 18 constitute a prayer for the dead is to twist the Scriptures. We have no evidence that he was deceased, and certainly Paul never taught believers to pray for the dead.

2 TIMOTHY 2

Paul has reminded Timothy of his pastoral calling. Now Paul deals practically with the local church and the pastor's special responsibilities. He presents several pictures of the local church, showing the various ministries God has for His people and their pastor. The local church is:

I. God's Family (2:1)

"My son" suggests, of course, that Timothy had been born into God's family by faith in Christ. As Paul wrote in 1 Cor. 4:15, he had "begotten" him through the Gospel. In Eph. 2:19, Paul calls the local church the "household of God." The local church is not a sanctified country club; it is the family of God meeting together for fellowship, worship, and service. The only way to enter this family is by being born of the Spirit (John 3:1-6) and the Word (1 Peter 1:23).

II. God's Treasury (2:2)

"Commit" means "deposit" and refers to the treasure of Gospel truth that Paul had committed to Timothy (1 Tim. 6:20) and which God had first committed to Paul (1 Tim. 1:11). This is why Paul calls the local church "the pillar and ground of the truth" in 1 Tim. 3:15. God has deposited with His people the truth of the Word of God. It is our responsibility to guard this treasure and pass it on to others. The task of the local church is not to preserve the truth, as in a museum; but to live it and to teach it to the generations to come. Note that Timothy is to deposit the truth with "faithful men" and not just any believer. How important it is to be faithful to the Word!

III. God's Army (2:3-4)

Timothy's call to service is found in Acts 16:3 — "him would Paul have to go forth with him." The words "go forth" literally mean "to take to the field as a soldier." This was Timothy's enlistment. Every Christian is already a soldier in God's army; it is just that some troops are loyal and some are not. We have been "enrolled" (chosen, v. 4) by Christ, the Captain of our salvation, and we must take our orders from Him.

Christians must learn how to endure hardship for Christ. Timothy was discouraged because of the persecution he was facing, but he should have expected opposition. The Christian life is not a playground; it is a battleground. We do not have the strength ourselves, but by His grace we can endure and stand against the wiles of the devil (Eph. 6:10ff). Furthermore, Christian soldiers must not entangle themselves with the world; their first loyalty is to Christ. Where would an army be if every soldier had part-time work that took him away from his military duties! Our main task is to please Him—not others, not ourselves.

IV. God's Team (2:5)

There are in Paul's letters more than two dozen references to athletics—boxing, wrestling, running, to name a few. The Greeks and Romans were enthusiastic athletes (and spectators), and in this verse, Paul used the Olympic Games as an illustration of the practical life of the believer. No matter how skilled the athletes were, they had to obey the rules of the game. If they won the race but broke the rules, they were disqualified. "Strive for masteries" means "contend in the games." The local church is God's team of runners, racing toward the goal He has set for them (see Phil. 3:12-14). It takes discipline, dedication, and direction for an athlete to be a winner, and it takes these same qualities to produce a winning Christian life. There must be teamwork in the local church. "Labored with me" in Phil. 4:3 literally means "were teammates with me."

V. God's Garden (2:6-7)

"Husbandman" means "farmer," and the picture here is an agricultural one (see 1 Cor. 3:6-9). The church is a garden, and the seed is the Word of God. Various servants plant, water, and harvest the seed in due season. Timothy was not to be discouraged if the harvest failed to come immediately. It takes time, patience, and hard work to develop a fruitful garden. Like the faithful farmer, the pastor should share in the blessings God sends. "In due season we shall reap, if we faint not" (Gal. 6:9).

VI. Christ's Body on Earth (2:8-13)

Paul reminds Timothy that he too was suffering, but that their suffering had a dual blessing in it: they were suffering for and with Christ, and their suffering was for the benefit of the church. Verses 11-13 may have been an early Christian hymn or confession of faith. It emphasizes the believer's oneness with Christ: when He died, we died with Him as members of His body; we arose with Him; we shall reign with Him. Our unbelief will not cancel the faithfulness of God! "Are you not afraid you will slip through His fingers?" an unbeliever asked an old saint. "How can I?" she replied. "I am one of His fingers!"

VII. God's School (2:14-18)

Timothy was being attacked by false teachers, just as the church is attacked today. What are we to do? First, remind the people to stick to essentials and not to argue about empty words and philosophies. Second, be sure to rightly divide the Word, being diligent ("in study") to handle it carefully. "Rightly divide" implies "cutting through" the Word carefully, the way an engineer builds a highway, so that people understand God's program for the ages. Paul warns that false doctrine "eats like a cancer, or ulcer" (v. 17), and that the only remedy is the "healthy doctrine" (sound doctrine) of the Word of God. When you start listening to the old wives' fables or the false teachers, you may become spiritually sick. One lie can grow like a cancerous tumor and eat out the spiritual strength of the Christian or the local church. Every church should be a Bible school, where the Word of God is taught accurately.

VIII. God's House (2:19-26)

Paul describes the local church as a house with a solid foundation and containing vessels of different kinds. The OT Jews often put Bible verses on their houses (see Deut. 11:20), and it was not uncommon for Gentiles to write mottoes on their houses too. God's house has two affirmations on it, one that is God-ward and one that is man-ward (v. 19). God knows His own, and His own ought to be known to others by their godly lives. Each Christian is a vessel in the great house, but some vessels are defiled and cannot be used. Timothy is warned to purge (cleanse) himself from the dishonorable vessels, lest they defile him. This is the biblical doctrine of separation (2 Cor. 6:14–7:1). Believers should be set-apart vessels unto honor, suitable ("meet") for Christ's use. Fleeing youthful lusts, and following that which is spiritual, would help Timothy be a prepared vessel that Christ could use for His glory.

Verses 23-26 explain how to deal with problems in God's house ("household") so that there might not be strife and contention.

2 TIMOTHY 3

Paul now looks down through the years and with the eyes of the prophet tells us what to expect. This chapter is his prophetic appeal to Timothy, his charge in the light of the future of the church.

I. An Explanation of the Future (3:1-9)

"The last days" is a period of time that actually began with the life and ministry of Christ on earth (Heb. 1:1-2). However, the NT indicates that "the last days" refers particularly to the state of the church before the coming of Christ. These shall be "perilous" times, that is, "difficult, hard to deal with." This is the same word used in Matt. 8:28 to describe the Gadarene demoniac. Because people will believe the "doctrines of demons" (1 Tim. 4:1ff), this world will become a "demonic graveyard" just as in Gadara. We are in those days now!

Self-love will be the hallmark of the last days. This self-love will lead to a grasping attitude and a boastful spirit. "Boasters" really means "swaggerers." True affection will almost disappear; unnatural affection will prevail. "Incontinent" means "intemperate"; "fierce" means "savage," and savage conduct is certainly evident today. "Heady" means "reckless"; and we surely live in a reckless age, whether you look at the speed of travel, the waste of money, or the carelessness of human lives.

Verses 5-8 indicate that there will be plenty of religion in the last days, but it will be a mere imitation, a form of godliness without the life-changing power of God. The departing from the faith that Paul predicted in 2 Thes. 2 is upon us today, yet there is still plenty of religion! The Bible continues to be a national best-seller, yet the crime rate increases and problems multiply. True Christians are in the minority. These false teachers of Paul's day preyed especially upon women who were loaded with sins and led astray by their lusts, women who were "ever learning" but who never really came to an understanding of the truth.

Paul compared the apostate teachers to the Egyptian magicians Jannes and Jambres, who opposed Moses by imitating what he did (Ex. 7:11ff). Satan is an imitator, and his imitation gospel and church will spread in the last days. But just as Moses overcame these imitators by the power of God coming in great judgment, so

Christ will ultimately overcome these latter-day deceivers. "From such turn away!" warns Paul (v. 5). Timothy was not to get involved with Christ-denying deceivers, even if it meant being branded as a "crank."

II. An Example from the Past (3:10-13)

If Jannes and Jambres were ministers of Satan's work, then Paul is our best example of a worker for the Lord. He hid nothing. See Acts 20:17ff. Paul names the cities in the area near Timothy's home, because Timothy would be familiar with them. Timothy knew Paul's doctrine (teaching); his manner of life (conduct); the purpose that motivated his life (see Acts 20:24; 2 Tim. 4:7); the faith that sustained him in trial; the long-suffering, love, and endurance that he showed, even when persecuted; and the wonderful way God took care of him through it all. Paul had been a divine object lesson to young Timothy, and we ought to be examples to others.

Persecution is not something that Christians should deliberately encourage, but if they live godly lives, persecution will come automatically (see 1 Peter 4:12-19). "Yes, and all who desire to live godly" (NKJV) is the best translation of v. 12. When our will is dedicated to God, then Satan will attack us. You can be sure that during these last days, it will be more and more difficult to live for Christ. As never before, we need Christians who will, like Paul, live for Christ completely.

III. An Exhortation for the Present (3:14-17)

Since these satanic seducers are going to continue, what should the Christian do? Continue to be faithful to the Word of God. The only answer to Satan's lies is God's truth. If every local church would get back to the Word of God, and if every pastor and Sunday School teacher would teach the Word of God, Satan's disciples would be defeated.

Timothy's relationship to the Bible is outlined in these verses. It began when he was a child and learned the OT Scriptures from his mother and grandmother. They did not merely teach him the facts of the Bible; they gave him assurance and spiritual understanding. Timothy knew for himself the truth of the Word; he did not depend on others to defend the Word for him. This Word imparted faith to him (Rom. 10:17), and this faith in Christ brought salvation.

Verses 16-17 are a great testimony to the divine origin and character of the Bible. Some say, "The Bible only contains the word of God," or "The Bible is inspired the way Shakespeare is inspired." But Paul would not agree with these statements. The Bible is the inspired Word of God. The word "inspired" means "God-breathed—filled with the breath of God." The Spirit of God enabled men of God to write the Word of God (see 2 Peter 1:20-21), for the Spirit of God is the "breath" of God (John 3:1-8; Ezek. 37:1-14). While men like Shakespeare may have had literary inspiration of a high quality, they did not write the very words of God. "All Scripture" means that every word of God is inspired.

What is the purpose of the Bible? Of course, salvation is the first purpose (v. 15), but Christian living is also included. The Word is profitable for teaching (doctrine), conviction (reproof), setting right (correction), and discipline (instruction). It enables the child of God to become a man or woman of God, matured in the things of the Lord. "Perfect" (v. 17) does not mean sinless; it means "mature." And "thoroughly furnished" means "fully equipped" (vv. 16-17). So, the Bible transforms the child of v. 15 into a mature person in Christ; it equips the saints to be servants. It is fine for Christians to take study courses and learn methods of ministry, but the best way for them to equip themselves to serve God is to study and practice the Word of God. Study books tell us how, but the Bible gives us the motivation and power to live what we learn.

It is interesting to compare the uses of the Bible with the order of the epistles: doctrine—Romans; reproof—1 and 2 Corinthians; correction—Galatians; instruction in righteousness—Ephesians and Colossians.

The great need among churches and Christians today is to return to the Bible. If the churches do not get back to God's Word, the satanic deceivers will take over and millions of lost sinners will go to hell because they were led astray by religious lies.

2 TIMOTHY 4

This chapter records the final message from the inspired pen of Paul. Shortly after dictating these words, Paul was martyred for the cause of Christ. It is no surprise, then, that we find in this chapter an intense personal appeal for Timothy's faithfulness to the Lord and to his beloved Paul. There are four "charges" or admonitions in this chapter that should be heeded by all believers.

I. Preach the Word! (4:1-4)

Paul closed the previous chapter by exhorting Timothy to continue in the Word in his own personal life; now he exhorts him to share that Word with others. We must first receive before we can transmit. So important was the preaching of the Word to Paul and to the ministry of the church that he gave Timothy a charge — a "military command" — to keep on preaching the Word. And Paul called upon Christ to witness his charge to Timothy, reminding Timothy that Christ would one day return and test his ministry.

"Preach the Word" (v. 2) implies knowing the Word, rightly dividing it and making it understandable and applicable to the lives of the people. The great Bible expositor G. Campbell Morgan once said, "Our first business is to impart knowledge, and then our purpose must be to lead those whom we teach to obedience." He also said, "Preaching is not the proclamation of a theory, or the discussion of a doubt. . . . Preaching is the proclamation of the Word, the truth as the truth has been revealed."

"Be instant" means "be ready, be urgent"; and this should be the minister's attitude whether service is convenient or inconvenient. Compare v. 2 with 3:16-17 and you will see that the preacher's duties parallel the purposes for which the Word was given. The minister of the Word does not reprove, rebuke (warn), and exhort with his own words, but with the inspired Word of God.

Why must we Christians proclaim the Word of God? "Because the time will come" (v. 3) when people will not want the Word of God — and that time is upon us! Many church attenders do not want "healthy" (sound) doctrine; instead, they want religious entertainment from Christian performers who will tickle their ears. We have a love for novelty in the churches today. Too often the person who simply opens the Bible and teaches it is ignored, while the shallow religious entertainer becomes a celebrity. Verse 4 indicates that "itching ears" soon become "deaf ears" as people turn away from the truth and believe man-made fables.

II. Fulfill Your Ministry! (4:5-8)

Paul was about to finish his course, but Timothy's life and ministry still lay before him. "Make full proof" means "fulfill, accomplish the purpose." How wonderful it is that God has a specific ministry for each of His children (Eph. 2:10). Our task is to find His will and do it as long as we live. This involves watching, enduring, and working.

Paul's argument is clear: he is now about to leave the scene, and somebody must take his place. Young people in our churches need to be reminded that they are the future in the church. Paul declares, "I am ready to be poured out like a drink-offering, and the time is at hand for loosing the anchor and setting sail, for taking down the tent and moving on" (literal translation). Paul has no regrets as he faces eternity: he had been a good soldier, a faithful runner, a faithful steward of the treasure of the Gospel. He looked forward to receiving his reward from the Lord. What was it that kept Paul going during more than thirty years of toil and suffering? He loved Christ's appearing! "The love of Christ constrains us!" (2 Cor. 5:14, NKJV) And all the saints who love His appearing will also be faithful, as Paul was, to serve Him now, and will, with Paul, receive their reward.

Next to losing one's soul and going to hell, the greatest tragedy of life would be to come to the brink of eternity and discover we had missed God's will and wasted our lives on fruitless, transient things.

III. Come Quickly to Rome! (4:9-18)

Why was Timothy to hurry? Demas had forsaken Paul (Col. 4:14; Phile. 24); Crescens and Titus were away ministering; Tychicus had been sent to Ephesus; and only Dr. Luke was with him. As he waited patiently for the Lord to call him home, Paul yearned for the Christian companionship of his son in the faith. In v. 21 Paul urged him to "come before winter" because the shipping season would soon end; it was likely that Paul would be dead if Timothy waited too long.

We first met Dr. Luke in Acts 16:10. It was at this point that Luke joined Paul's party. He was a Gentile and was the author of the Gospel of Luke and the Book of Acts. Luke is mentioned with Demas in Col. 4:14 and Phile. 24, and the contrast is clear: Demas was unfaithful while Luke was faithful to Christ and Paul.

John Mark had been rejected by Paul in Acts 15:37ff but now was accepted. Mark had proved himself in his ministry with Barnabas. Paul was willing to forgive and forget, the mark of a great man.

The word "profitable" in 4:11 is the same as "meet" in 2:21. Mark proved himself "suitable" for the Master's use.

Paul asked for the cloak he had left at Troas; winter was coming, and he would need it in his Roman prison. The "books" were probably some of his own writings; the "parchments" would be his copies of the OT Scriptures. While awaiting trial, Paul would spend his time studying the Word. What an example to follow!

He warned Timothy about Alexander (1 Tim. 1:20; Acts 19:33), who withstood his words (see 3:8). At Paul's first defense (answer), no believer stood with him; but the Lord was still with him, and that is all that mattered! This had always been his encouragement in difficult times (Acts 18:7-11; 23:11; 27:19-25).

IV. Greet My Friends! (4:19-22)

Though facing certain death, Paul still thought about others. How like Christ when He was hanging on the cross. Paul fulfilled the pastoral requirement given in Titus 1:8—he was "a lover of good men." We have met Priscilla (Prisca) and Aquila before (see Acts 18:2, 18, etc.). For Erastus, see Acts 19:22; Trophimus is mentioned in Acts 20:4 and 21:29. The fact that Paul did not heal Trophimus indicates that not all saints are to be healed and that the absence of healing does not necessarily prove a lack of spirituality.

"Grace be with you!" says Paul, and closes his part of the NT writings. "Grace" was the key word in his ministry. May it be the key word in our lives as well.

TITUS

A Suggested Outline of Titus

I. Personal Greeting (1:1-4)

II. Church Organization (1:5-16)
  A. Qualifications of elders (1:5-9)
  B. Characteristics of false teachers (1:10-16)

III. Christian Obligation (2–3:11)
  A. Aged saints (2:1-3)
  B. Young men and women (2:4-8)
  C. Servants (2:9-15)
  D. Citizens (3:1-11)

IV. Closing Admonitions (3:12-15)

Introductory Notes to Titus

I. The Man

Titus was a Greek believer (Gal. 2:3), won to Christ through Paul's ministry (Titus 1:4). We know little about his background; he is not once mentioned in Acts. It is likely he was a convert from heathenism whom the apostle enlisted for service. He assisted in taking the offering for the saints (2 Cor. 2:1-9; 7:8-12; 12:18); and he met Paul at Troas with the report of the Corinthian situation (see 2 Cor. 2:12-13; 7:5-16). Titus carried 2 Corinthians back for Paul (2 Cor. 8:16-24). Titus was Paul's helper, left at Crete to organize the church (Titus 1:5) until Paul could send Tychicus or Artemas to take over (Titus 3:12). Titus was at Rome during Paul's second imprisonment, from whence he traveled to Dalmatia on a mission for the apostle (2 Tim. 4:10). Paul's estimate of Titus is given in 2 Cor. 8:23.

II. The Letter

Paul's haste in leaving Titus at Crete made it necessary for him to write to encourage and instruct this dedicated co-laborer. The Cretians were not the easiest people to work with, as Titus 1:12-13 points out. We do not know who started the church at Crete, but this much we know: the organization of the church and the lives of the members had both fallen into disrepute. It is likely that the church suffered from two sources: (1) visiting Judaizers who mixed law and grace, and (2) ignorant Christians who abused the grace of God and turned it into license. Paul had several purposes in mind when he wrote this letter: (1) to remind Titus of his work of organizing the church and appointing elders; (2) to warn him about false teachers; (3) to encourage him in pastoring the different kinds of people in the church; (4) to emphasize the true meaning of grace in the life of the Christian; (5) to explain how to deal with troublemakers in the church.

III. The Emphasis

Several words are repeated in this brief letter, helping us to understand the burden that was on Paul's heart. Notice that there is a major emphasis on good works (1:16; 2:7, 14; 3:1, 5, 8, 14). Saved by grace means saved unto good works. Christian doctrine and Christian living are to be sound (1:9, 13; 2:1-2, 8). There ought to be a life of godliness (1:1; 2:12), not worldliness. God's grace leads a person to live a godly life (1:4; 2:11ff; 3:7, 15). If you want a key verse for the book, it is probably 3:8: "those who have believed in God should be careful to maintain good works" (NKJV).

TITUS 1

Paul opened his letter with several admonitions for Titus to heed in order that he might fulfill his ministry.

I. He Was to Proclaim the Word (1:1-4)

This formal greeting is more than the opening part of the letter. It is a statement of the place of the Word of God in the life of the local church. Paul was a servant and apostle according to the faith of the church (God's elect, chosen ones). His ministry was not apart from the church but tied directly to it. This "faith" is what Jude calls "the faith which was once delivered unto the saints" (Jude 3). It is that deposit of truth that God gave to Paul (1 Tim. 1:11), and which Paul in turn had given to Titus and Timothy.

One of the problems in Crete was an abuse of the grace of God. "God has saved us by grace," these people argued, "so we are free to sin." Paul answers this teaching from the start by defining the faith as the "truth which is after godliness." Godliness is a favorite word with Paul (1 Tim. 2:2; 3:16; 4:7-8; 6:3, 5, 6, 11; 2 Tim. 3:5). It means practical holiness in one's daily life (see Titus 1:16 for the contrast). Later, in Titus 2:11-15, Paul explains that grace saves us and also disciplines us to live dedicated lives. The person who uses the doctrine of grace to excuse sins either is not saved or does not understand what grace really means.

The message of grace also points ahead to the blessed hope of Christ's return; see 2:13. Here, then, is the message Titus was to preach: God's grace to save sinners and sanctify believers; the holy life that follows true faith in Christ; and the daily expectation of Christ's return. God's wonderful program of salvation was marked out before the world began, but now it has been revealed through preaching (the proclamation of the Gospel). Never minimize the place of preaching in the local church.

II. He Was to Organize the Church (1:5-9)

We do not know who founded the church in Crete, but we do know that Paul left Titus there to organize it and remedy the weaknesses that existed. There was definite opposition to Titus' ministry, and there is the suggestion that he wanted to resign. "But that is why I left you there," Paul writes. "If there were no problems to solve, the church would not need you!" As long as Christians are in this body of flesh, there will be problems in our churches. When these problems arise, the answer is not to hide them, or for officers to resign and find a new church. The answer is to face them honestly and prayerfully and settle them according to the Word of God. "Set in order" in v. 5 is a medical term meaning "to set a broken bone, or straighten a crooked limb." The church is a body, and the pastor must occasionally be a "spiritual physician" and set some bones.

Titus was not to select the elders (i.e., bishops, v. 7—two names for the same office); he was to ordain those whom the churches had chosen. "In every city" in v. 5 indicates that the Gospel had spread from place to place, which is as it should be. These qualifications for elders are parallel to those given in 1 Tim. 3. "Faithful children" in v. 6 means "believing children." For "riot" see Luke 15:13. The bishop is a steward of God's blessings, both material and spiritual; see 1 Cor. 4:1-2. He is to hold fast the "faithful word," and this brings to mind Paul's "faithful words" in 1 Tim. 1:15; 4:9; 2 Tim. 2:11; and Titus 3:8. The pastor must know the Word for two reasons: (1) to be able to minister to the saints and (2) to be able to refute the false teachers. "Gainsayers" (v. 9) means "those who say against, those who contradict."

III. He Was to Refute the False Teachers (1:10-16)

Wherever Christ sows the good seed (believers), Satan follows with counterfeit seed and false teachers. There was, in Crete, a group of people who contradicted the teachings of Paul and taught instead Jewish fables (legalism) and the commandments of men (traditionalism). We must constantly beware of false teachings. "Those of the circumcision" (v. 10) had battled Paul from Jerusalem to Rome, and they are still opposing the truth. When we mix Law with grace, we end up with false doctrine. Paul describes these teachers as empty talkers, deceivers, and unruly.

Paul even quoted a famous poet, Epimenides, who described the Cretians as liars, ferocious beasts, and "idle gluttons"—not a beautiful description! In fact, the people of Paul's day invented a new word out of the name "Cretan" that meant "to lie, to speak like a Cretian." Of course, Paul is not suggesting that all Cretians were lazy gluttons and liars. Doubtless there were many people, both within and outside of the churches, who lived decent lives.

Dietary laws and asceticism were key doctrines to false teachers, and Paul attacked these people in v. 15. It is unfortunate that v. 15

has been so grossly abused by misinformed Christians. Some Christians use it to support their own sinful practices, saying, "To the pure, all things are pure—so what I am doing is not wrong." Paul had nothing of this sort in mind when he dictated these words. He was dealing with the problem of clean and unclean foods, as he had in 1 Tim. 4:2-5. He is teaching that the believer who knows the Word of God receives all foods as clean; the unbeliever (and the false teacher) has a defiled mind and conscience and therefore sees nothing as pure. In fact, instead of the impure foods defiling the heretic, he defiles the food! Moral purity is not a matter of diets; it is a matter of a clean heart and a good conscience. Jesus taught this in Matt. 6:22-23; see also Rom. 14:14.

How was Titus to treat these false teachers? Was he to unite with them and try to see their point of view? No! He was to stop their mouths (v. 11) and rebuke them sharply (v. 13). After all, their teachings were upsetting (subverting) entire families (v. 11). And their motive was simply to gain money ("filthy lucre"); they did not wish to honor the Lord. Verse 16 sums up the situation: these false teachers professed one thing and practiced another; they denied Christ by their works; they were abominable and disobedient; they would never pass the test (i.e., they were reprobates).

We have false teachers attacking the church today. It is one thing for people to hold to a false doctrine because of ignorance, and quite another for them to hold it and teach it as God's truth. Ignorant people should be pitied and patiently taught the truth; deliberate false teachers should be rebuked and rejected. Once the church compromises on the truth, the truth will be swallowed up in lies.

Note the emphasis here on "sound doctrine" (v. 9) and "sound faith" (v. 13). This is the "healthy" doctrine we read of in Paul's letters to Timothy. False doctrines lead only to spiritual sickness in the body of Christ.

TITUS 2

If Titus had spent all his time refuting the false teachers, he would have neglected other matters that are necessary for a healthy church. It is important that the pastor have a balanced ministry, teaching and exhorting the saints as well as refuting the enemies of the truth. In this chapter, Paul deals with three groups of people in the church and exhorts Titus to remind them of their obligations in the Lord.

I. The Aged Saints (2:1-3)

The church at Crete may have been the result of Peter's ministry at Pentecost (Acts 2:11), in which case there would have been older saints in the fellowship. It is a blessed thing when the local church family has in its number those aged pilgrims who have long walked with the Lord. They are indeed privileged to live such long lives, and with this privilege comes a serious responsibility.

The aged men are to be sober (vigilant), grave (serious, easy to respect), temperate (self-controlled), and sound (healthy) in the faith. Spiritual health is more important than physical health. Their love and patience should be an example to all; how difficult it is for some "senior saints" to be patient with the younger generation!

The aged women were to be reverent in their behavior, not gossips or drunkards. They had the wonderful opportunity of teaching the younger women in the church, both by precept and example. It is possible that Paul may have had in mind some of the widows who were supported by the church and expected to minister to its members.

II. The Young Men and Women (2:4-8)

Paul speaks of the young women first, encouraging them to listen to the older women and learn from them how to be godly wives and mothers. Here we have a description of what God expects of the young Christian wife. She should be sober, taking a serious attitude toward marriage and the home. No younger woman who does not want to be a serious wife and mother ought to marry. The home is not a playground. Love is vital to a happy home, so Paul reminds these women to love both their husbands and their children. Read Eph. 5:22-23 for the details.

The Christian wife must have careful conduct, being discreet and chaste. "Keepers at home" (v. 5) literally is "home-workers" or "homemakers." She should be faithful at home and not put outside interests ahead of her husband and her children. Why? "That the Word of God be not blasphemed." It is tragic when a Christian home is a poor testimony for Christ because of disobedient and careless wives and husbands whose values are confused. The husband or wife who neglects the home is worse than an unbeliever.

Since Titus was a young man himself, Paul used him as an example of what young men in the church ought to be like: "Be a pattern of good works that all may follow" (v. 7). Be clean, be sincere, be serious; these statements summarize Paul's admonition. In v. 8, he reminds Titus that he must be careful in his speech lest the enemy find something to criticize.

III. The Servants (2:9-15)

We have met this group before in 1 Timothy as well as in Ephesians and Colossians. Paul had a heart for the slaves and was anxious that their daily lives honor Christ. Their first responsibility was obedience; they were not to "talk back" (same Gk. word as "gainsayers" in v. 9). A submissive will and a controlled tongue can be a wonderful testimony for Christ. Servants should seek to please their masters and not do only what they require of them. Going the "extra mile" helps prove to people the reality of salvation.

"Purloining" in v. 10 means "stealing." Since they had no wages, slaves were often tempted to steal from their masters, and such theft would be easy since masters often left their possessions in the management of their servants. "Good faith" means "honesty, faithfulness." Paul gives slaves a higher motive for honest service in v. 10—"that they may adorn the doctrine of God." That is, that they might, in their lives, "beautify the Bible," making it attractive to the unbelievers.

The grace of God was an abused doctrine in Crete, so Paul paused to undergird his admonitions with a doctrinal foundation. There are some who would turn grace into license, teaching that Christians can live in sin since they are no longer under Law. Of course, the believer is not under Law but under grace; but grace brings an even greater responsibility. How can the Christian deliberately sin against the grace and kindness of God? Paul presents the three tenses of the Christian life:

Past: "The grace of God that brings salvation has appeared to all men" (v. 11)

Present: "teaching us" (v. 12)

Future: "looking for the blessed hope" (v. 13)

In other words, God's grace not only redeems us, but it also reforms us and rewards us. "Teaching" in v. 12 in the Gk. is the word for training or disciplining. We are disciplined by grace. Believers who honestly understand the grace of God will not want to live in sin. They will turn from ungodliness and worldly lusts; they will live serious, clean, dedicated lives in this present world.

There is no greater incentive for Christian living than the second coming of Jesus Christ. "Looking for that blessed (happy) hope and the appearing of the glory of our great God" is the more accurate translation of v. 13. God's glory dwelt here on earth in the person of Christ (John 1:14), but went back to heaven when He ascended (Acts 1:9). His glory now abides in the believer (1 Cor. 6:19-20). When Christ returns, we shall see His glory and share His glory (John 17:22-24). Paul speaks of "Christ in you, the hope of glory" (Col. 1:27).

Jesus gave Himself for us; the least we can do is give ourselves to Him and live Christ-honoring lives until He comes. "Redeem" means to purchase out of slavery. We are His "peculiar people"; that is, we are His special treasure, His personal and beloved possession (see Ex. 19:5; 1 Peter 2:9). "Peculiar" does not mean "odd"; it means purchased and possessed by Christ. We are a purchased people, a purified people, and a practicing people, "zealous of good works." Trace the theme of "good works" in Paul's letter to Titus and you will see how important it is.

There are two "poles" to the Christian life: we look back to the cross (v. 14) and ahead to the coming of Christ (v. 13). These two poles help keep us steady in our Christian walk. These themes are written into Paul's description of the Lord's Supper (1 Cor. 11) where we are to remember His death "till He comes."

TITUS 3

This chapter continues Paul's exhortation to Titus concerning the ministry of the local churches. He has discussed the aged saints, young men and women, and servants. Now he deals with two additional classes of people:

I. Civil Rulers (3:1-7)

Christians ought to be good citizens. True, our "citizenship is in heaven" (Phil. 3:20), but while we are here on earth, we ought to apply our Christian faith in practical daily life. The church is not to get involved in party politics, but certainly Christian people should seek to apply Christian principles to the affairs of city and nation (Rom. 13; 1 Peter 3:8-17).

Even if the believer cannot honor the personal conduct of a ruler, he must honor the office and the laws of the land. Of course, if the laws contradict the Word, the Christian's first allegiance is to God (Acts 4:19; 5:29). "Ready to every good work" (v. 1) suggests that Christians ought to support that which is good in the program of the government. Certainly many of the great humanitarian reforms of the past have been led by men of Christian principles, and we ought not to be mere spectators when it is possible for us to do good. Christians are the salt of the earth and the light of the world; therefore we must involve ourselves in the good causes of government, provided we do not compromise our convictions or hinder the work of the Lord.

Some Christians think they will accomplish their purposes by arguments, and in v. 2 Paul warns against spreading lies with evil intent and starting fights. "The wrath of man does not produce the righteousness of God" (James 1:20, NKJV). Gentleness and meekness can be stronger than even political power. Christians depend on different weapons as they fight sin (2 Cor. 10:1-6). The believer knows how to trust God to fight his battles after he has done all he can (Rom. 12:17-21). Meekness is not weakness; rather, it is power under control. Jesus was meek (Matt. 11:29), yet He knew how to exercise power.

In vv. 3-7, Paul reminded these believers of the motive for honest living: the grace of God. The emphasis of this letter is that God's grace not only saves us, but it also controls our daily lives and makes us more like Christ. "Remember your old life, before you were saved," Paul wrote. "This will help you understand your unsaved friends better and have pity upon them." We have been saved by God's "kindness and love." God hates the sins listed in v. 3, but He loves the sinners. Through Christ's death on the cross, God has been reconciled to the world (2 Cor. 5:14-21) and is thus able to save all who will come to Him by faith. The Gk. word for "love" in v. 4 is similar to our word "philanthropy." It is God's gracious and giving attitude toward undeserving sinners. This news of God's love "appeared" in Christ, His Person and work, His teachings, and most of all, His death and resurrection.

Paul makes it clear that our salvation is not by works, although it results in good works (v. 8, and see Eph. 2:8-10). The "washing" (v. 5) has nothing to do with baptism; in the Gk. this word means "laver" and refers to the OT implement used in the tabernacle. He uses the same word in Eph. 5:26, where the washing is accomplished by the Word. Throughout the Bible, water for washing is likened to the Word of God (John 15:3; Ps. 119:9; and Eph. 5:26). In other words, v. 5 describes the two agents of our new birth (regeneration): the Word of God and the Spirit of God (John 3:5). See also 1 Peter 1:23 and James 1:18. The Spirit has been "poured out" upon all believers, and the tense of the verb here indicates that this action occurred once and for all, that is, at the pouring out of the Spirit in His baptism of believers at Pentecost. The believer is justified by grace and is an heir of God. What a blessed position we have in Christ. This wonderful salvation ought to motivate us to be better citizens, that the lost around us might see Christ in us and want to know Him.

II. Heretics (3:8-11)

The word "heretic" comes from a word meaning "to choose" and suggests a person who causes divisions in the church because he forces people to choose: "Are you for me or for the pastor?" Galatians 5:20 lists "heresy" (forming of parties, divisions) as a work of the flesh; it was prevalent in the carnal church at Corinth (1 Cor. 11:19). These church troublemakers loved to argue about words and genealogies, which suggests that they had a Judaizing background and tried to build novel doctrines on OT ideas. Such unprofitable and empty discussions are to be avoided; they will never convince the enemy and only divide the church.

How was Titus to handle these problem people? For one thing, he had to avoid arguing with them. Then, if they persisted in causing strife even after two admonitions (and this implies public warnings), they were to be dismissed from the fellowship. Church members who cause divisions and then take their membership to another church should be allowed to go. If they come back but manifest a repentant spirit, they should be warned and received. If they cause trouble again, they may be granted the right to transfer a second time; but if they attempt to return again, they must not be received into the fellowship. Some sympathizing but untaught saints might say, "But perhaps they have reformed this time." Paul points out in v. 11 that such people will not reform; they are "turned inside out" (subverted) and in a state of constant sin; that is, they are beyond remedy. Our local churches would have fewer divisions if pastors and officers would observe this important principle.

Paul closed his brief letter with information about the travels of his associates in the Lord's work. He informs Titus that "reinforcements are coming" to assist him in the difficult ministry on Crete. Either Artemas or Tychicus would replace him so that he might join Paul at Nicopolis; but meanwhile, Titus was to stay on the job until someone arrived to continue the work. It is well to keep in mind that God does not destroy one ministry to build up another one. When He moves a servant, He has a replacement ready to step in. If no replacement is ready, it might be an indication that it is not time to move.

It seems that Zenas and Apollos were the ones who delivered this letter to Titus. Paul advised Titus to assist them as they continued their journey, which was probably a special mission for Paul. Christians ought to help one another as they go about in His service; see 1 Cor. 16:6, 11 and Rom. 15:24. We must take care not to assist those who teach false doctrine, however (2 John 9-11).

Verse 14 was Paul's reminder that the local Christians ought to assist Titus in his work and in his ministry of helping others on their way. The pastor and the people should share in this ministry of hospitality and encouragement. "Being fruitful in every good work" (Col. 1:10) should describe all Christians and not the pastor and officers only.

He closed with his apostolic greeting, linking love with faith. "Grace be with you all" marks the letter as genuinely from Paul (2 Thes. 3:17).

PHILEMON

A Suggested Outline of Philemon

Introductory Notes to Philemon

I. The Man

Philemon was a Christian of Colosse (Phile. 2; see also Col. 4:9 and 16-17). It is possible that his son, Archippus, pastored the church at Laodicea (Col. 4:16-17); there was an assembly in Philemon's house too (v. 2). Philemon had been won to Christ through Paul's ministry (v. 19), possibly at Ephesus, since Paul had not visited Colosse personally.

II. The Letter

Onesimus was one of Philemon's slaves (v. 16) who had robbed his master and fled to Rome. By the providential leading of the Lord, this runaway slave met Paul, who led him to Christ. Legally, Philemon could have had his slave put to death for breaking the law, but Paul stepped in to intercede for the new Christian and to save his life. This brief letter speaks volumes to us, since it demonstrates in a vivid way the heart of the great apostle. His purposes for writing were: (1) to inform Philemon that his slave was not only safe but saved; (2) to ask Philemon to forgive Onesimus; (3) to request of Philemon that he prepare a room for Paul, who expected to be released shortly.

Of course, the main lesson of the letter is its picture of Christ as the Redeemer of lost sinners. Just as Paul was willing to pay the price to save disobedient Onesimus, so Christ paid the price on the cross for His wayward children. "Receive him as you would receive me," Paul wrote, reminding us that we are "accepted in the Beloved" (Eph. 1:6; 2 Cor. 5:21). The Christian will never enter heaven on his or her own merits. When the believer stands before the Father, Christ will have to say, "Receive him as Myself!" Thank God we have been covered by His righteousness!

III. Slavery

We need to remember that slavery was an accepted institution in the Roman Empire. Romans and Greeks brought multitudes of slaves (old and young) home from their wars, and the buying and selling of slaves was a daily part of life. Paul had a tender interest in slaves (1 Cor. 7:20-24; Col. 3:22–4:1; Eph. 6:5-9), encouraging them to be the best Christians possible and to win their freedom lawfully if they could. We do not read that Paul specifically attacked the institution of slavery; the Gospel itself, preached and lived in the early church, ultimately destroyed this social problem. Paul's letter to Philemon is a classic example of how Christ changes a home and society by changing lives. It was not that Paul avoided the problem of slavery; rather, he realized the true solution would be found as men and women gave their hearts to Christ.

PHILEMON

I. Greeting

Paul's greeting in vv. 1-3 identifies him as a prisoner, a theme he repeats in vv. 7, 13, 22, and 23. Perhaps he wants to remind Philemon of the price he himself was paying, suggesting that anything Philemon might do for Onesimus would be insignificant in comparison. Of course, Paul was the prisoner of Christ, not of Rome, and he was not ashamed of his chains. Paul accomplished more from his Roman prison than we do as free citizens!

Apphia is called "beloved" or literally "the sister." She was most certainly the wife of Philemon and the mother of Archippus (Col. 4:17). She would without doubt be concerned about Onesimus and would be playing an important role in the ministry of their "house" church.

II. Paul's Appreciation of Philemon (vv. 4-7)

A Spirit-led man will certainly be gracious and tactful, and Paul illustrates this attitude in his approach to the problem of the runaway slave. Instead of immediately pleading for the man's life, Paul first expressed sincere appreciation for his friend Philemon. This was not empty flattery; it was sincere Christian appreciation, "the love of God shed abroad" in Paul's heart.

Philemon sounds like the kind of man any of us would want to have as a friend. He was a man of love and faith (see Titus 3:15); after all, a love for the brethren is the best evidence of faith in Christ. Note in v. 5 the two-fold outreach of Philemon's life: upward to Christ and outward to others. See Gal. 5:6.

Philemon did not keep his faith to himself; he shared it (communicated) with others. Paul had been praying for Philemon, that his faith might "go to work" (be effectual) and be a blessing to others. Verse 7 indicates that Philemon was a "refreshing Christian" and the kind of man others appreciated. Philemon was about to face a serious test of his faith and love as he learned about the conversion of his slave, Onesimus.

III. Paul's Appeal for Onesimus (vv. 8-17)

Paul might have used his apostolic authority and commanded Philemon to forgive and receive Onesimus, but this would not have been right. For one thing, it would not help Philemon grow in grace or gain a real blessing from the experience. Law is a much weaker motivation than love, and Paul wanted Philemon to broaden his spiritual understanding. This is why Paul uses the word "beseech" (v. 9).

Paul's appeal is based on several factors. For one thing, he appeals to Philemon's Christian love, a love which he had already praised (v. 5). Then Paul called the disobedient slave his own son in the faith, reminding Philemon that Onesimus was now a brother in Christ. The play on words in v. 11 is based on the meaning of the name "Onesimus," which means "profitable." In other words, Onesimus had already proved himself to be profitable to Paul's Christian service in Rome. He was now the slave of Jesus Christ! Paul would have kept Onesimus as one of his own fellow laborers (v. 1), but he wanted to do nothing without his friend's knowledge and consent.

The doctrine of the believer's identification with Christ is beautifully portrayed here. "Receive him, that is, mine own heart" was Paul's plea. Onesimus was so a part of Paul that it pained Paul even to send him back home! Verse 17 is what Jesus Christ says of every true believer, "Receive him as Myself!" We are "accepted in the Beloved" (Eph. 1:6). Onesimus was not returning home the same old person. He had a completely new standing before his master: he was now a brother beloved, identified with Paul, and therefore accepted. This is what the Bible means by justification: we are in Christ and therefore accepted before God.

IV. Paul's Assurance of Payment (vv. 18-25)

But what about the Roman law? What about the money that Onesimus took? How could Philemon forgive if there was to be no restitution? This kind of forgiveness would only make him the accessory of a criminal. "I will repay!" promises the aged apostle. "Put that on my account."

Again, this is a touching picture of Calvary. Christ found us as runaway slaves, law-breakers, rebels, but He forgave us and identified us with Himself. He went to the cross and paid the debt for us. This is the doctrine of imputation. "To impute" means "to put to one's account." Our sins were put to Christ's account, and His righteousness was put to our account when we believed on Him. What marvelous grace! "Blessed is the man to whom the Lord does not impute iniquity" (Ps. 32:2; Rom. 4:1-8). Our sins were put on His account, even though He committed no sin (2 Cor. 5:21). Our sins were laid on Christ, and His robe of righteousness was imputed to us.

The Christian needs to keep in mind the distinction between "accepted in Christ" and "acceptable to Christ." The one who has trusted Christ for salvation is forever accepted in Christ and can never be rejected by the Father. Whenever believers sin, they are accepted, but their actions are not acceptable. It is necessary to confess that sin and receive Christ's cleansing (1 John 1:9). Because we are accepted in Him, we have sonship; as we live lives acceptable to Him, we have fellowship.

Verse 19 illustrates the common form of an "IOU" back in Paul's day. Paul was actually taking Onesimus' debt upon himself.

Paul closed with personal greetings to Philemon and his household, reminding his friends of the many obligations they had to him. In fact, they owed their very salvation to Paul. The apostle was sure that Philemon would go "the extra mile" and do even more than he had requested. It is touching to read Paul's request for their prayers and for a place to stay when he was released from prison. How wonderful to have Christian friends who are concerned with the physical and spiritual needs of others.

This brief letter is priceless for what it reveals about the heart of Paul. It also illustrates what Christ has done for the believer. The two phrases that summarize the letter are: "receive him as myself" (v. 17) (our identification with Christ) and "put that on my account" (v. 19) (imputation—our sins laid on Christ).

HEBREWS

A Suggested Outline of Hebrews

I. A Superior Person: Christ (1–6)

   A. Christ compared to the prophets (1:1-3)

   B. Christ compared to the angels (1:4–2:18)

   C. Exhortation: Let us not drift from the Word (2:1-4)

   D. Christ compared to Moses (3:1–4:13)

   E. Exhortation: Let us not doubt the Word (3:7–4:13)

   F. Christ compared to Aaron (4:14–6:20)

   G. Exhortation: Let us not grow dull toward the Word (5:11–6:20)

II. A Superior Priesthood: Christ and Melchizedek (7–10)

   A. A better order: Melchizedek, not Aaron (7)

   B. A better covenant: new, not old (8)

   C. A better sanctuary: heavenly, not earthly (9)

   D. A better sacrifice: God's Son, not animals (10)

   E. Exhortation: Let us not despise the Word (10:26-39)

III. A Superior Principle: Faith (11–13)

   A. The examples of faith (11)

   B. The endurance of faith (12:1-13)

   C. Exhortation: A warning against disobeying the Word (12:14-19)

   D. The evidences of faith (13)

Introductory Notes to the Hebrew Epistle

The Epistle to the Hebrews presents several interesting problems to the student. Here is a book that begins like a sermon, yet ends like a letter (13:22-25). No author's name is attached to it, nor is its destination clearly given. Certain passages in this book have been wrongly used to upset Christians; we should remember that the epistle was originally given to exhort and encourage God's people. It is important to study Hebrews in the light of all the Word of God, and not as an isolated book.

I. The Message

The main message of Hebrews is summarized in 6:1: "let us go on unto perfection [spiritual maturity]." The people to whom Hebrews was addressed were not growing spiritually (5:11-14) and were in a state of second childhood. God had spoken in the Word, but they were not faithful to obey Him. They were neglecting God's instruction and drifting away from His blessing. The writer seeks to encourage them to move ahead in their spiritual lives by showing them that in Christ they have the "better" blessings. He is the "author and perfecter [finisher] of our faith" (12:2). The book presents the Christian faith and life as superior to Judaism or any other religious system. Christ is the superior Person (1–6); His Priesthood is superior to that of Aaron (7–10); and the principle of faith is superior to that of law (11–13).

II. The Writer

Since no name is attached to the book, students have been discussing for centuries who the author is. The earliest traditions point to Paul. Others have suggested Apollos, Luke, Philip the Evangelist, Mark, and even Priscilla and Aquila! The writer is obviously a Jew, since he identifies himself with his Jewish readers (1:2; 2:1, 3; 3:1; 4:1; etc.). He also identifies himself with Timothy (13:23), which certainly Paul could do. The closing benediction of grace is typical of Paul (see 2 Thes. 3:17-18). The writer has been in prison (10:34; 13:19). The matter seems to be settled by 2 Peter 3:15-18, where Peter clearly states that Paul had written to the same people Peter wrote to, the Jews of the dispersion (1 Peter 1:1; 2 Peter 3:1). Furthermore, Peter calls Paul's letter Scripture. Now, if Paul wrote an inspired letter to the Jews scattered abroad, and that letter has been lost, then a part of God's inspired, eternal Word has been destroyed; and this is impossible. The only writing in Scripture that is addressed to Jews and is not credited to another author is Hebrews. Conclusion: Paul must have written Hebrews. Those who argue that the style and vocabulary are not typical of Paul must bear in mind that writers are free to adapt their style and vocabulary to their readers and topics.

III. The "Warnings"

Even Peter informs us that some people had taken Hebrews and misinterpreted the "hard things" to their own destruction (2 Peter 3:16). This is because they wrest the Scriptures, or twist passages out of context, perverting the letter to say what it does not really mean. We must be careful to interpret Hebrews in the light of the entire Word of God. The five exhortations (see 13:22) are placed in our outline so that you may be able to see clearly the development of the book. We believe that these exhortations are written to believers, since the writer identifies himself with the people he addresses: "We ought to give heed . . . "; "how shall we escape . . . "; "let us therefore fear . . . "; etc. To say that 6:4-5 describes people who were "almost" saved is to abuse these verses' meaning. Some Christians have so misunderstood the grace of God and the precious doctrine of eternal security that they forget that God also chastens His people when they sin. We should approach Hebrews as a letter written to believers who were in danger of lapsing into a carnal state of spiritual immaturity because of their wrong attitude toward the Word of God. Such disobedience, Paul warned, might lead them to the chastening hand of God and loss of rewards at the judgment seat of Christ (see 10:35-36; 11:26). Hebrews does not warn believers that their sins will condemn them, since no true Christian can ever be eternally lost.

IV. Key Words

The key words are "better" (1:4; 6:9; 7:7, 19, 22; 8:6; 9:23; 10:34; 11:16, 35, 40; 12:24) and "perfect" (2:10; 5:9, 14; 6:1; 7:11, 19, 28; 9:9, 11; 10:1, 14; 11:40; 12:2, 23).

HEBREWS 1

"God has spoken!" This is the great message of Hebrews. "God has spoken"—so take heed how you respond to His Word. After all, the way we respond to the Word of God is the way we respond to the Son of God, for He is the Living Word. In this first chapter we see Christ's superiority over the prophets and the angels.

I. Christ Is Better Than the Prophets (1:1-3)

A. In His Person.

Christ is the Son of God; the prophets were merely men who were called to be servants. Christ made the worlds (or "framed the ages"), and it is He who upholds the worlds. His Word has power. He spoke the worlds into being, and now His Word controls and sustains our world. Christ is also the Heir of all things. "All things were made by Him and for Him" (Col. 1:16). He is God's sacrifice for the sins of the world. He "purged our sins" by His death on the cross. Now He is seated in glory, as God's King-Priest. His work on earth is completed; He has sat down.

B. In His message.

God's revelations in old times were given "in many portions and in many ways." No prophet received the complete revelation. God spoke through visions, dreams, symbols, and events, as well as through human lips. These revelations pointed to Christ, and He is the final revelation from God. Christ is God's "last Word" to the world. All of OT revelation led up to Christ, God's final and full revelation. Anyone today who boasts of having a "new revelation from God" is deceived. God is not giving revelations today; He is illuminating His once-for-all revelation in Christ.

II. Christ Is Better Than the Angels (1:4-14)

Angels played a vital role in the Jewish religion. The Law was given through the ministry of angels, according to Gal. 3:19, Acts 7:53, and Deut. 33:2 (*saints* means "holy ones, angels"). If the Jews paid attention to the Law, given through angels, then they ought to give greater heed to the message given by Christ, who is greater than the angels. The author cites seven OT quotations to show Christ's superiority to the angels.

A. *Verses 4-5 quote Ps. 2:7 and 2 Sam. 7:14.*

As the Heir of all things, Christ has a greater inheritance and thus a greater name. In Ps. 2:7, God the Father calls Christ "My Son," a title He would not give to angels. (In the OT, the angels collectively are termed "sons of God," but this title is not bestowed on them individually.) Psalm 2:7 refers to Christ's resurrection, not His birth at Bethlehem (see Acts 13:33). Christ was "begotten" from the virgin tomb when He was raised from the dead. Colossians 1:18 calls Him "the first-born from the dead." The second quotation refers to Solomon; read all of 2 Sam. 7 carefully, for the "house" of David comes up again in Hebrews. David wanted to build a house for God, but God decreed that Solomon would do the work. God promised David that He would be a Father to Solomon; and Heb. 1:5 applies this promise to Christ, who is "greater than Solomon" (Matt. 12:42).

B. *Verse 6 quotes Ps. 97:7 (or perhaps Deut. 32:43 in the Greek version, called the Septuagint).*

This quotation refers to the return of Christ to the earth ("And again, when He brings . . . "). Just as the angels worshiped Him at His first coming (Luke 2:8-14), they will worship Him when He returns to reign. Christ is greater than the angels.

C. *Verse 7 quotes Ps. 104:4.*

The angels are spirits, created by God to be servants. The next quotation shows that Christ is not a servant but a Sovereign.

D. *Verses 8-9 quote Ps. 45:6-7.*

Psalm 45 is a marriage psalm, picturing Christ and Israel. God clearly states that Christ has a throne, and the Father calls the Son "God." Those who deny the deity of Christ twist these verses to try to prove their point. One version even says, "Thy throne is God. . . ." No, these verses boldly announce the deity of Christ; He is God.

E. *Verses 10-12 quote Ps. 102:25-27.*

Here, again, Jesus is called "Lord." He is from the beginning the Creator of the universe. Like a worn-out garment, creation will decay and fall to pieces, but Christ will never change. He is "the same, yesterday, today, and forever." Angels are created beings; Christ is the eternal Son.

F. Verse 13 quotes Ps. 110:1.

This is the key psalm in Hebrews, for Ps. 110:4 declares the priesthood of Christ after the order of Melchizedek. Christ is now seated at God's right hand, a Priest-King. Peter quotes this same passage in Acts 2:34. Christ's enemies have not yet bowed before Him, but they will one of these days.

Verse 14 summarizes the place of the angels: they are ministering spirits, not enthroned sons; and their work is to minister to us who are heirs with Christ in His wonderful salvation.

As you review these quotations, you can see the majesty and glory of the Son of God. As v. 4 states, Christ has a more excellent name than the angels because through His suffering and death He acquired a greater inheritance. In His character, work, and ministry Christ stands supreme. Though His glorious kingdom is not seen on earth today, He has still been enthroned as King and will return one day to establish righteousness on this earth.

HEBREWS 2

This chapter continues the argument that Christ is superior to the angels. The writer interrupted the argument for an exhortation, the first of five in the book (see Hebrews outline).

I. An Exhortation (2:1-4)

Since the Word spoken by angels was steadfast, then certainly the Word spoken by God's Son would also be steadfast! If in the OT days God dealt with those who disobeyed His Word, then surely He would deal with those who ignored or rejected His Word as given by His Son in the last days!

The danger here is one of drifting through neglect: "lest at any time we should drift from them" is the best translation of v. 1. Note that v. 3 does not say, "How shall sinners escape if they reject" but "How shall we [believers] escape if we neglect. . . ." Spiritual deterioration begins when Christians start to neglect this great salvation. From the admonitions in 10:19-25, it seems that these Jews were guilty of neglecting prayer and united fellowship with God's people. Note 1 Tim. 4:14.

The word *disobedience* literally means "unwillingness to hear." Saints who will not hear and heed the Word of God are disobedient and will not escape the chastening hand of God. After all, God confirmed His Word through "signs, miracles, and powers" (v. 4, and see Acts 2:22 and 43); this Word is not to be treated lightly! In fact, the word *neglect* is translated "made light of" in Matt. 22:5.

II. An Explanation (2:5-18)

The writer's argument in chapter 1 that Jesus is better than the angels has raised a new question: "How could Jesus be better when He had a human body? Are not the angels better than He because they had no human bodies to limit them?" This question is answered with an explanation of why Jesus took upon Himself a body of flesh.

A. To be the Last Adam (vv. 5-13).

Nowhere in the Bible does God promise the angels that they will rule in the world to come. God gave Adam the rule over all the earth (Gen. 1:26-31). The writer quotes Ps. 8:4-6 in which God's blessing is repeated from Genesis. God made man a little lower than the angels or, literally, "for a little while lower than God." The suggestion seems to be that Adam and Eve were in a period of probation. They were not created to remain less than God, and had they refused to sin, they would have ultimately shared God's glory in a wonderful way. Satan knew that they would be lower than God only "for a little while," so he hurried and promised them glory ahead of time. Sin came into the human race and robbed Adam of his earthly dominion. He ceased being a king and became a slave. That is why v. 8 says, "But now, we see not yet all things put under him [man]."

What do we see? "We see Jesus!" He is the Last Adam who, by His death and resurrection, undid all the ruin Adam caused when he disobeyed God. For a little while, Christ was lower than the angels, even to the depths of Calvary (Phil. 2:1-12). Christ had to have a body of flesh in order to die for the sins of the world. Men crowned Him with thorns on earth, but now He has been crowned with glory and honor; see 2 Peter 1:17. There is now a new family in the world: Christ is bringing many sons to glory. Adam, through his sin, plunged his descendants into sin and death; Christ now changes Adam's children into the children of God. He is the "Pioneer" (captain) of our salvation, the one who blazes the trail that we might follow. We are His brethren, for we are all of one family, having become partakers of His divine nature and set apart unto God through His death (10:10). Verse 22 of Psalm 22, that Calvary Psalm, is quoted here, speaking of Christ's resurrection. Isaiah 8:17-18 is also quoted.

Isaiah's two sons were signs to the nation: Shear-jashub (Isa. 7:3) means "a remnant shall return"; and Maher-shalal-hash-baz (Isa. 8:1) means "haste-spoil-hurry-prey." In other words, in the Prophet Isaiah's day there was a faithful remnant that was saved when the nation was judged. These people were "Isaiah's children," so to speak. Likewise, Christ has a family of believers, a remnant among the Jews and Gentiles; they too will be delivered from the wrath to come.

B. To defeat the devil (vv. 14-16).

Death and the fear of death were the consequences of Adam's sin (Gen. 2:17; 3:10). The fear of death has been Satan's strongest weapon. Satan does not have "the power of death" absolutely, since, as we see in Job's case, Satan could do nothing without God's permission (Job 1–2). The word for power in v. 14 means "might" rather than "authority." Satan has might over sinners and darkness (Luke 22:53), but Christ has delivered saints from the power of darkness (Col. 1:12-13). Satan seized this "might of death" to get control over God's creatures; but by His death on the cross, Christ "made inoperative" (destroyed) this power and thus delivered those who were in bondage because of the fear of death. Christ had to have a human body in order to die and thus defeat Satan. See also 1 John 3:8. In v. 16 the writer makes it clear that Christ did not take on Himself the nature of angels, but rather the seed of Abraham. In other words, Christ did not become an angel; He became a man, a Jew. He did not die for angels; He died for humans. Fallen angels can never be saved, but fallen men and women can be saved!

C. To become a sympathetic priest (vv. 17-18).

This is the third reason Christ took on Himself a human body. God knew that His children would need a sympathetic priest to help them in their weaknesses. He permitted His Son to suffer; and through this suffering, He equipped Him for His priestly ministry (v. 10). Christ's person needed no perfecting, since He is God; but as the God-Man, He endured suffering to prepare Himself to meet our needs. He was made flesh at Bethlehem (John 1:14); He was "made like unto His brethren" during His earthly life; and He was "made sin" at the cross (2 Cor. 5:21). Now He is a merciful and faithful High Priest; we can depend on Him! He is able to succor us when we come to Him for aid. The word *succor* means "to run when called for" and was used of physicians. Christ runs to our aid when we call Him!

This section completes the argument for the superiority of Christ over the angels. The writer has shown that Christ is superior in His person and work and in the name the Father has given Him "above every name." The conclusion is clear: since Christ is superior, we must heed His Word and obey it. We must beware of drifting through neglect.

HEBREWS 3

We move now into the third argument for the superiority of Christ: Christ is better than Moses. Of course, Moses was the great hero of the Jewish nation, and for Paul to prove Christ's superiority over Moses was tantamount to proving the superiority of the Christian faith over Judaism. How could these people go back to Judaism when what Christ offered was so much greater than what Moses could offer?

I. Christ Is Greater in His Office (3:1-2)

Moses was primarily a prophet (Deut. 18:15-19; Acts 3:22), although he did exercise the functions of a priest (Ps. 99:6), and even a king (Deut. 33:4-7). However, Moses was called of God, while Christ was sent by God. Christ is the "Apostle" or "The Sent One" (see John 3:17; 5:36-38; 6:57; 17:3, 8, 21, 23, 25). Christ is also the High Priest, an office that Moses never occupied. Furthermore, Christ's ministry has to do with the "heavenly calling" and not only the earthly calling of Israel. Moses ministered to an earthly people whose calling and promises were primarily earthly; Christ is the Apostle and High Priest of a heavenly people who are strangers and pilgrims on this earth. We might also add that Moses was a prophet of law, while Christ is the Apostle of grace (John 1:17). Moses sinned, while Christ lived a sinless life. No wonder we are told in v. 1 to "consider" or "observe attentively" Jesus Christ!

II. Christ Is Greater in His Ministry (3:3-6)

God states that Moses was faithful (Num. 12:7) as was Christ (3:2), but their ministries part at this point. Moses was a servant; Christ is the Son. Moses served in the house, while Christ is Lord over the house. "The house" means, of course, the household of God, not the temple or the tabernacle. Moses was a servant in Israel, God's OT household; Christ is a Son over God's household, which, today, is the church (Heb. 3:6 and 10:21; also 1 Peter 2:5; 4:17; Eph. 2:19). For an example of the word "house" meaning "people" see 2 Sam. 7:11, where God promised to "build David a house," that is, establish his family and his throne forever.

While Israel was God's earthly household and the church His heavenly household, we need to keep in mind that God's household is always marked by faith. People in OT times were saved by faith just as people are today. It is this continuity of faith that tied together the people of God under both covenants. This is why Gal. 3:7 calls true believers "children of Abraham," for he is the "father of the believing."

Two other matters remain in this contrast between Moses and Christ:

A. Moses was a servant while Christ is the Son.

This statement suggests that the OT ministry was one of bondage and servitude, while Christ's ministry under the New Covenant is one of liberty and joy. The OT Law is termed "a yoke of bondage" (Gal. 2:4; 5:1, and see Acts 15:10). The blessed privileges of sonship that we enjoy in God's household of faith were unknown under the Old Covenant.

B. Moses ministered using symbols, while Christ is the fulfillment of these things.

See 3:5 — "those things which were to be spoken after. . . . " In Christ we have the true light shining; in Moses, we are in the shadows. For his readers to go back to Judaism meant to exchange fulfillment for types and shadows!

III. Christ Is Greater in the Rest He Gives (3:7-19)

The word "rest" is used twelve times in chapter 4 but not always with the same meaning. We will study this word in detail in the next chapter, but we must introduce the basic ideas at this point.

The writer uses the nation of Israel as an illustration of spiritual truth (see also 1 Cor. 10:1-13). The Jews were in bondage in Egypt, just as sinners are in bondage in the world. God redeemed Israel by the blood of the lamb, just as He redeems us through the blood of Christ. God promised the Jews a land of blessing, and He has promised to His own a life of blessing, a spiritual inheritance in Christ. But this blessing could come only to those who separated themselves from the world and followed God by faith. So, God took Israel through the Red Sea (separation from Egypt, the world) and led them to the border of Canaan. Deuteronomy 1:2 informs us that this was an eleven-day journey. But at this point, Israel rebelled in unbelief and refused to believe God (Num. 14). Because of this, God judged the entire congregation, excepting Joshua and Caleb, who trusted God and opposed the vote of the people. The Jews had to wander in the wilderness for forty years, a year for each day the spies were in the land. The nation did not enter into the promised rest (Deut. 12:9; see Josh. 1:13-15).

It is here that the writer warns his readers. They had been redeemed by the blood of Christ and set free from the world. Now, like Israel, they had been tempted to go back. To do so meant not entering into the life of fullness and blessing that God had promised them. There are, in chapters 3 and 4, three different rests, all of which are related in God's plan: (1) the rest of salvation (4:3, 10); (2) the rest of victory in the midst of trials, symbolized by the Promised Land of Canaan (4:11); (3) the future eternal rest, the heavenly rest (4:9). We will study these distinctions in detail in the next chapter. The exhortation here is for the people of God to trust Him in spite of difficulties, as did Joshua and Caleb, and move into the promised rest. Please keep in mind that Canaan is not a picture of heaven; it is a symbol of the life of blessing and battles, progress and victory, that we have in Christ as we yield to Him and trust Him. It is that present rest that we have even in the midst of trials and testings. This rest neither Moses nor Joshua could give.

The writer quotes Ps. 95 and reminds the readers of Israel's hardness of heart. You will want to read Ex. 17 as well to see how Israel provoked and tested God when the going got tough. Believers do this today when trials and testings come! And here we have the basic theme of Hebrews: Let us go on to maturity, overcoming the enemy and claiming our inheritance in Christ. Let us cross Jordan (die to the old life, Rom. 6) and claim the present inheritance God has planned for us (Eph. 2:10).

Can this warning in v. 12 apply to believers? Certainly! Unbelief is a besetting sin among Christians, and this unbelief comes from an evil heart that neglects the Word. It is one thing to trust God for salvation, and quite another to surrender our wills and lives to Him for daily guidance and service. Many Christians are still "wandering in the wilderness" of defeat and unbelief; they have been delivered from Egypt, but they have never crossed into Canaan to claim their inheritance in Christ. The Jews were bought by the blood and covered by the cloud, yet most of them died in the wilderness! Is this a matter of "losing salvation"? Of course not! It is a matter of losing one's life of victory and blessing through lack of trust in God. And what causes this evil heart of unbelief? (1) Not hearing God's voice, vv. 7 and 15; and (2) allowing ourselves to be deceived by sin, v. 13.

How important it is to hear the Word of God! If we fail here, we then start to drift from the Word (2:1-4) and then doubt the Word (3:18-19). We refuse the exhortations of those who want to help us (3:13) and go on in stubborn disobedience until we become dull toward the Word (5:11–6:20).

Sin in the life of the believer is deceptive. It begins small, but gradually grows larger. Doubting God in one point can lead to an evil heart of unbelief. Those who press on and hold fast their confidence prove that they are truly saved (3:6, 14) and by doing so avoid God's chastening—and possibly (as with Israel) judgment in this life. Unbelief is a serious thing!

HEBREWS 4

This chapter continues the theme of rest that was begun in 3:11. The word "rest" is used in five different senses in this section: (1) God's Sabbath rest of Gen. 2:2 and Heb. 4:4, 10; (2) Canaan, the rest for Israel after wandering for forty years (3:11, etc.); (3) the believer's present salvation rest in Christ (4:3, 10); (4) the over-comer's present rest of victory (4:11); and (5) the future eternal rest in heaven (4:9). God's Sabbath rest is a type of our present rest of salvation, following the finished work of Christ on the cross. It is also a picture of the "eternal Sabbath" of glory. Israel's Canaan rest is similar to the life of victory and blessing we gain as we walk by faith and claim our inheritance in Christ. There are in this chapter four exhortations relating to the life of rest.

I. Let Us Therefore Fear (4:1-8)

God promised rest to the people of Israel, but they failed to enter that rest because of disobedience stemming from unbelief. God has promised a rest for His own today—peace in the midst of trial, victory in spite of seeming impossible problems. This "life of rest" in our spiritual Canaan is called "going on unto perfection (maturity)" in 6:1; "the full assurance of hope" in 6:11; "inheriting the promises" in 6:12. Keep in mind that the readers of Hebrews were going through a time of testing (10:32-39; 12:3-14; 13:13) and were tempted, like Israel of old, to "go back" into the old life. God had promised them a rest of victory, yet they were in danger of falling short of it. God had given them the Word, but they would not "mix it with faith" (4:2) and apply it to their own lives. Again, see the importance of the Word of God in the life of the believer.

The writer's argument runs like this: God has promised a rest to His people (v. 1), but Israel failed to enter that rest (4:6). His promise still stands, because Joshua (v. 8) did not give them this spiritual rest, even though he did lead them into national rest (see Josh. 23:1). Otherwise, David would never have spoken about this rest centuries later in Ps. 95. Conclusion: "There remains therefore a rest for the people of God" (v. 9, NKJV). He relates this rest to God's Sabbath rest (vv. 4, 10); that is, it is a rest of satisfaction, not a rest after exhaustion. God was not tired after creating the worlds; the "rest" of Gen. 2:2 speaks of completion and satisfaction. It is a "Sabbath of the soul." This is the "rest of faith" that Jesus promises in Matt. 11:28-30. The "rest" of Matt. 11:28 is salvation, and it is a gift that we receive by faith. The rest of 11:30 is what we find day by day as we take His yoke and surrender. "Let us therefore fear" (v. 1) is God's warning, for many of His children have failed to enter into this life of rest and victory.

II. Let Us Therefore Labor (4:9-12)

"Labor" here means "give diligence"—let us give diligence to enter into this rest. To "give diligence" is just the opposite of "drifting" (2:1-3). Nobody ever matured in the Christian life by being careless or lazy. Read carefully 2 Peter 1:4-12 and 3:11-18, where Peter three times exhorts believers to be diligent. If we are not diligent, we will repeat the failure of Israel and fail to enter the promised rest and inheritance. (Note, again, that this is not salvation, but victory in the Christian life.)

What is the secret of entering into this rest? The Word of God. Hebrews 4:12 is the answer to every spiritual condition; if we allow the Word to judge us and expose our hearts, then we will not fail to inherit the blessing. Israel rebelled at the Word and would not "hear His voice" (Ps. 95); therefore, they wandered in defeat for forty years. God's Word is a sword (see Rev. 1:16; 2:12-16; 19:13; Eph. 6:17). It pierces the heart (see Acts 5:33 and 7:54, where Israel again refused to yield to the Word). Too many believers fail to hear and heed God's Word and thus rob themselves of blessing. It takes diligence to mature spiritually, and so a believer needs to apply God's Word faithfully.

III. Let Us Hold Fast Our Profession (4:14)

Verse 14 does not say, "Let us hold fast our salvation." The word "profession" here is really "confession — to say the same thing" (3:1; 10:23; 11:13). "Confession" has to do with the believer's testimony of his faith in Christ and his faithfulness to live for Christ and gain the promised blessing. Read 10:34-35. The Jews who wandered in the wilderness had lost their confession even though they were still under the cloud and redeemed from Egypt. What a poor testimony they were of the power of God! God brought them out, but they would not trust Him to bring them in! Their unbelief had robbed them of God's blessing.

This explains why these Jewish readers are reminded of the great "giants of faith" named in chapter 11. All of these people faced difficulties and trials, yet they overcame and maintained a good confession. Hebrews 11:13 states that all of these people "confessed" (same word as 4:14) that they were "strangers and pilgrims on the earth." Before he was taken to heaven, Enoch had a good testimony (11:5). At the end of the chapter, the writer sums it all up by saying, "And these all, having obtained a good report [witness]" (11:39). Where there is faith, there is a good testimony (11:2); where there is unbelief, there is no testimony.

Where does faith come from? "So then faith comes by hearing, and hearing by the Word of God" (Rom. 10:17, NKJV). Israel in the OT would not hear the Word, and therefore these people had no faith. "Today, when you hear His voice . . . " is the warning repeated in 3:7, 15, and 4:7. Christians who hear and heed the Word of God will maintain good confessions and will not lose their testimony before the world.

IV. Let Us Come to the Throne of Grace (4:15-16)

These verses offer proof that the believer cannot lose his salvation. We have a High Priest who knows our temptations and weaknesses, who endured testings that we must endure. When times of testing come, we need but turn to the throne of grace for the help Christ alone can give. The writer will elaborate on this theme in the later chapters, but he puts this exhortation here lest his readers become discouraged and say, "It is impossible for us to go on! We simply do not have what it takes!" Of course we don't! No believer has strength enough to cross Jordan and conquer the enemy! But we have a great High Priest who has mercy and "grace to help in the nick of time!" (That is the literal meaning of v. 16.)

Why does the writer refer to a "throne" at this point? The reference is to Ex. 25:17-22, the golden mercy seat. The ark of the covenant was a wooden chest covered with gold. On top of the ark, Moses put a golden "mercy seat" with a cherub at each end. This mercy seat was God's throne, where He sat in glory and ruled the nation of Israel. But the OT mercy seat was not a throne of grace, since the nation was under a yoke of legal bondage. "The law was given by Moses, but grace and truth came by Jesus Christ" (John 1:17). Christ is our Mercy Seat ("propitiation" in 1 John 2:2). When we come to Him, we come to a throne of grace, not a throne of judgment; and He meets us, talks to us, and strengthens us.

Read this chapter again, and you will see that it is not warning us against losing our salvation. Rather, it is encouraging us to live in the Word and in prayer, and to let Christ take us into our spiritual Canaan where we will find rest and blessing. Spiritual progress is the result of spiritual discipline.

HEBREWS 5

In the first two chapters, the writer has shown that Christ is greater than the prophets and the angels; in chapters 3–4, he has shown that Christ is even greater than Moses. Now he points to Aaron, Israel's first high priest, and proves that Christ is a greater priest than Aaron. If his readers were to abandon Christ for Judaism, they would be exchanging a great High Priest for a lesser high priest. The writer shows that Christ is superior to Aaron in at least three ways.

I. Christ Has a Greater Ordination (5:1, 4-6)

Aaron was taken from among men and elevated to the position of high priest. He passed this honor along to his eldest son, and thus the line continued. Aaron belonged to the tribe of Levi; this tribe was set aside to be the priestly tribe for the nation of Israel.

But Christ's ordination was greater. For one thing, He is not merely man; He is God in the flesh, the Son of God and the Son of Man. He did not selfishly take this honor of the priesthood for Himself. The sons of Korah tried to do this (Num. 16) and died for their sin. No, God Himself ordained His Son. Here the writer quotes from Ps. 110:4, in which the Father ordains the Son into the eternal priestly ministry. He ties this verse to the quotation from Ps. 2:7 in v. 5 because the priestly ministry of Christ is related to His resurrection, and it is the resurrection of Christ that is involved in Ps. 2:7 (Acts 13:33).

The priesthood of Melchizedek is the main theme of Hebrews 7–10, so we need not enter into the details now. You will want to read Gen. 14:17-20 for the background. The whole argument of Heb. 7–10 is that Christ is a greater high priest because His priesthood is of a greater order—it belongs to Melchizedek, not Aaron. The name "Melchizedek" means "king of righteousness"; he was also priest of Salem, which means "peace." Aaron was never a priest-king; but Jesus is both Priest and King. He is a Priest seated on a throne! And His ministry is of peace, the "rest" that was discussed in chapters 3–4.

Christ came from Judah, the kingly tribe, and not from Levi, the priestly tribe. Melchizedek suddenly appears in Gen. 14 and then drops out of the story; there is no listing of his beginning or ending. Thus, he is compared to Christ's eternal Sonship, for He too is "without beginning and ending." Aaron died and had to be replaced; Christ will never die—His priesthood is forever. Aaron was priest over an earthly household, while Christ is Priest over a heavenly people.

II. Christ Has a Greater Sympathy (5:2-3, 7-8)

Not only must the high priest be chosen of God; he must also be sympathetic with the people and be able to help them. Of course, Aaron himself was a mere man and would know personally the weaknesses of his people. In fact, he had to offer sacrifices for himself and his family.

But Christ is better able to enter into the needs and problems of God's people. In vv. 7-8 we are told of the "training" Christ received as He endured suffering while here on earth. Keep in mind that, as God, Christ needed nothing; but as the Man who would one day become High Priest, it was necessary for Him to experience trials and suffering, a theme discussed in 2:10-11. The Jews might look down upon Christ and question His deity because of the suffering He endured. These sufferings, however, are the very mark of His deity. God was preparing His Son to be the sympathetic High Priest of His people. Verse 7 refers to His prayers in Gethsemane (Matt. 26:36-46). Note that Christ did not pray to be saved "from death" but "out of death." He did not pray for the Father to rescue Him from the cross, but to raise Him from the tomb. And this prayer was answered. Certainly Christ was willing and ready to face the cross and to drink of the cup God had poured for Him (John 12:23-34).

Someone may ask, "But can the Son of God really know our trials better than another man would, such as Aaron?" Yes! To begin with, Christ was perfect and experienced each trial totally. He was tested to the full, tasting every temptation men and Satan had to offer. This means that He went beyond anything any mortal man could endure, since most of us give in before a test really gets difficult. A bridge that has endured fifty tons of weight has experienced more testing than one that has felt but two tons.

III. Christ Offered a Greater Sacrifice (5:3, 9-14)

Aaron's main ministry was to offer sacrifices for the nation, especially on the Day of Atonement (Lev. 16). The priests and Levites would minister to the people during the year, but everyone looked to the high priest on the Day of Atonement, for he alone could enter into the holiest with the blood. First of all, though, he had to offer sacrifices for himself.

Not so with Jesus Christ! Being the sinless Lamb of God, He needed no sacrifices for sin. And the sacrifice He did offer for the people was not that of an animal, but Himself. Moreover, He did not have to repeat this sacrifice; He needed to offer Himself but once, and the matter was settled. How much greater He is than Aaron and his successors! Christ is the "Author of eternal salvation" (v. 9); Aaron could never do this. The blood of bulls and goats only covered sins; Christ's blood took away sin once and for all.

The writer now wanted to enter into a deeper study of the heavenly priesthood of Christ, but he found himself in difficulty. The problem was not that he was a dull preacher or writer, but that he had dull hearers. He wanted to go from milk (the basic things of the Christian life, listed in 6:1-2) to meat (the heavenly priesthood of Christ); but he could not do it unless his readers woke up and grew up. How many Christians there are who live on milk—they recognize the ABCs of the Gospel and Christ's mission on earth—but gain no nourishment from the meat, those things that Christ is now doing in heaven. They know Christ as Savior, but they do not understand what He can do for them as High Priest.

These people had been saved long enough for them to be teaching others, yet they had lapsed into a spiritual "second childhood." Somebody had to teach them again the things they had forgotten. They were "inexperienced" in the Word ("unskillful" in v. 13). We see again the vital role of the Word of God! Our relationship to the Word of God determines our spiritual maturity. These people had drifted from the Word (2:1-3), doubted the Word (chaps. 3-4), and became dull toward the Word. They had not mixed the Word with faith (4:2) and practiced it in their daily lives (5:14). They had not "exercised their spiritual faculties" (5:14) and therefore were growing dull and ineffective in their spiritual lives. Instead of going forward (6:1), they were going backward.

Growing in grace depends on growing in knowledge (2 Peter 3:18). The more we know about ourselves and Christ, the better we are able to move forward spiritually. Where are you in your spiritual growth? Are you a babe, still living on milk, wandering in the wilderness of unbelief? Or are you maturing, feeding on the meat of the Word and making it a habit to practice the Word of God?

HEBREWS 6

No chapter in the Bible has disturbed people more than has Heb. 6. It is unfortunate that even sincere believers have "fallen out" over the doctrine of "falling away"! Scholars have offered several interpretations of this passage: (1) it describes the sin of apostasy, which means Christians can lose their salvation; (2) it deals with people who were "almost saved" but then backed away from trusting Christ; (3) it describes a sin possible only to Jews living while the Jewish temple was still standing; (4) it presents a "hypothetical case" or illustration that could not really happen. While I respect the views of others, I must reject those ideas just listed. I feel that Heb. 6 (like the rest of the book) was written to believers, but this chapter does not describe a sin that results in a believer "losing salvation." If we keep the total context of the book in mind, and if we pay close attention to the words used, we will discover that the main lessons of the chapter are ones of repentance and assurance.

I. An Appeal (6:1-3)

The writer has severely scolded his readers because of their spiritual dullness (5:11-14); now he urges them to go on to maturity ("perfection"). This, of course, is the main theme of the book. The word "perfection" (maturity) is the same word used in the Parable of the Sower in Luke 8:14 ("and bring no fruit to perfection"). This image ties in later with the illustration of the field in Heb. 6:7-8. The appeal "Let us go on" is literally, "Let us be borne, or carried, on." It is the same word translated "upholding" in 1:3. In other words, the writer is not talking about self-effort; he is appealing to the readers to yield themselves to the power of God, the same power that upholds the whole universe. How can we fall when God is holding us?

Instead of going ahead, however, these believing Jews were tempted to lay again "a foundation" that is described in vv. 2-3. The six items in this foundation do not refer to the Christian faith as such, but rather to the basic doctrines of Judaism. Facing the fires of persecution, these Hebrew Christians were tempted to "fall by the wayside" by forsaking their confession of Christ (4:14 and 10:23). They had already slipped back into "babyhood" (5:11-14); now they were prone to go back to Judaism, thus laying again the foundation that had prepared the way for Christ and the full light of Christianity. They had repented from dead works, referring to works under the law (9:14). They had shown faith toward God. They believed the doctrine of washings (not baptism, but the Levitical washings; see Mark 7:4-5 and Heb. 9:10). Laying on of hands refers to the Day of Atonement, Lev. 16:21; and every true Jew held to a future resurrection and judgment (see Acts 24:14-15). If they did not move forward, they would be moving backward, which meant forsaking the substance of Christianity for shadows of Judaism.

II. An Argument (6:4-8)

Note from the beginning that the issue here is repentance, not salvation: "For it is impossible . . . to renew them unto repentance" (vv. 4, 6). If this passage is talking about salvation, then it is teaching that a believer who "loses salvation" cannot regain it. This means that salvation depends partly on our own works and, once we lose salvation, we can never get it back again.

But the subject of the chapter is repentance—the believer's attitude toward the Word of God. Verses 4-5 describe real Christians (see 10:32 as well as 2:9, 14), and v. 9 indicates that the writer believed they were truly saved. We do not have "almost saved" people here, but real believers.

The two key words in v. 6 are "fall away" and "crucify." "Fall away" is not the Gk. word *apostasia*, from which we get the English word "apostasy." It is *parapipto*, which means "to fall beside, to turn aside, to wander." It is similar to the word for "trespass," as found in Gal. 6:1 ("if a man be overtaken in a fault [trespass]"). So, v. 6 describes believers who have experienced the spiritual blessings of God but who fall by the side or trespass because of unbelief. Having done this, they are in danger of divine chastening (see Heb. 12:5-13) and of becoming castaways (1 Cor. 9:24-27), which results in loss of reward and divine disapproval, but not loss of salvation. The phrase "seeing they crucify" (v. 6) should be translated "while they are crucifying." In other words, Heb. 6:4-6 does not teach that sinning saints cannot be brought to repentance, but that they cannot be brought to repentance while they continue to sin and put Christ to shame. Believers who continue in sin prove that they have not repented; Samson and Saul are cases in point. Hebrews 12:14-17 cites the case of Esau as well.

The illustration of the field in vv. 7-8 relates this truth to the image of the testing fires of God, a truth given in 1 Cor. 3:10-15 as well as Heb. 12:28-29. God saved us to bear fruit; our lives will one day be tested; what we do that is not approved will be burned. Note that the field is not burned, but rather the fruit. The believer is saved "yet so as by fire" (1 Cor. 3:15). So, the whole message of this difficult passage is this: Christians can go backward in their spiritual lives and bring shame to Christ. While they are living in sin, they cannot be brought to repentance, and they are in danger of divine chastening. If they persist, their lives will bear no lasting fruit, and they will "suffer loss" at the judgment seat of Christ.

And, lest we use "grace" as an excuse for sin, Heb. 10:30 reminds believers: "The Lord shall judge His people."

III. An Assurance (6:9-20)

The writer closes with as solid a passage on eternal security as we will find anywhere in the Bible. He points, first of all, to their own lives (vv. 10-12) and reminds them that they had given every evidence of being true Christians. We find faith, hope, and love described in these three verses, and these traits are the characteristics of true believers (1 Thes. 1:3; Rom. 5:1-5). But he cautions them in v. 12 not to be "dull of hearing" (or "slothful," same word as in 5:11). God has given His promises; they need only exercise faith and patience to receive the blessing.

He then uses Abraham as an illustration of patient faith. Certainly Abraham sinned—and even repeated one sin twice!—yet God kept His promises to him. After all, the covenants of God do not depend on the faith of the saints for their certainty; they depend only on the faithfulness of God. God verified the promise of Gen. 22:16-17 by swearing by Himself—and that settled it! Abraham did not receive the promised blessing because of his own goodness or obedience, but because of the faithfulness of God. Abraham experienced many trials and testings (as did the original readers of Hebrews), but God saw him through.

In v. 17, the writer says that God did all this for Abraham that the "heirs" might know the dependability of God's counsel and promise. Who are these heirs? According to v. 18, all true believers are heirs, for we are Abraham's children by faith (see Gal. 3). So, there are "two immutable things" that give us assurance: God's promises (for God cannot lie) and God's oath (for God cannot change). The unchanging Word of God and the unchanging Person of God are all we need to assure us that we are saved and kept for eternity. We have a "hope" to anchor our souls, and this "hope" is Christ Himself (7:19-20; 1 Tim. 1:1). How can we "drift" spiritually (2:1-3) when in Christ we are anchored to heaven itself? We have a sure and steadfast anchor; and we have a "Forerunner" (Christ) who has opened the way for us and will see to it that we one day shall join Him in glory. Instead of frightening saints into thinking they are lost, this wonderful chapter warns against unbelief and an unrepentant heart and also assures us that we are anchored in eternity.

HEBREWS 7

This chapter introduces us to the major second section of Hebrews (see outline). It is the writer's purpose in this section to show that the priesthood of Christ is better than that of Aaron's (whose successors were at that time ministering on earth, 8:4) because His priesthood is of a superior order (chap. 7). It is ministered under a superior covenant (chap. 8), in a superior sanctuary (chap. 9), because of a superior sacrifice (chap. 10).

The key figure in chapter 7 is that mysterious king-priest, Melchizedek, who appears but twice in the entire OT (Gen. 14:17-20 and Ps. 110:4). The writer presents three telling arguments to prove the superiority of Melchizedek over Aaron.

I. The Historical Argument: Melchizedek and Abraham (7:1-10)

First, the writer identifies Melchizedek as a type of Christ (vv. 3, 15). He was both king and priest, and so is Jesus. No priest in Aaron's line ever sat on a throne. In fact, the Aaronic priests did not sit down at all (spiritually speaking), for their work was never done. There were no chairs in the tabernacle or temple! See Heb. 10:11-14. Furthermore, Melchizedek was king of Salem, which means "peace"; and Jesus is our King of Peace, our Prince of Peace. The name "Melchizedek" means "king of righteousness," a name which certainly applies to Christ, God's Righteous King. So, in his name and his offices, Melchizedek is a beautiful likeness of Christ.

But Melchizedek also resembles Christ in his origin. The Bible contains no record of his birth or his death. Of course, this does not mean that Melchizedek had no parents or that he never died. It simply means that the OT record is silent on these matters. Thus Melchizedek, like Christ, is "without beginning of days or end of life"—his priesthood is eternal. His priesthood did not depend on earthly successors, while the Aaronic priests had to defend their office by family records (see Neh. 7:64). Every high priest that descended from Aaron died, but Christ, like Melchizedek, holds His priesthood permanently (vv. 8, 16, 24-25).

Having identified Christ with the order of Melchizedek, the writer now explains that Melchizedek is superior to Aaron, for Aaron paid tithes to Melchizedek while yet unborn in the loins of Abraham. And when Melchizedek blessed Abraham, he was blessing the house of Levi as well; and certainly "the lesser is blessed by the better" (v. 7). On earth, in the Jewish temple, the priests received tithes; but in Genesis 14, the priests (in Abraham's loins) gave tithes to Melchizedek. This event clearly showed the inferiority of the Aaronic priesthood.

II. The Doctrinal Argument: Christ and Aaron (7:11-25)

Having clearly established the historical foundations for the superiority of Melchizedek over Aaron, the writer now shows that Melchizedek is also superior from a doctrinal point of view. Here he uses the quotation from Ps. 110:4 as the basis for the argument, and he presents three facts:

A. Aaron was replaced by Melchizedek (vv. 11-19).

When God said to Christ in Ps. 110:4, "Thou art a priest forever after the order of Melchizedek," He was actually setting aside the Levitical priesthood founded in Aaron. It is impossible for two divine priesthoods to operate side by side. The fact that God established the new order proves that the old order of Aaron was weak and ineffective; and it also meant that the Law under which Aaron functioned was likewise set aside: "The Law made nothing perfect" (v. 19). Consequently, the priesthood made nothing perfect (v. 11), and the sacrifices these men offered made nothing perfect (10:1). Of course, the Hebrew word for *perfect* means "having a perfect standing before God" and has nothing to do with sinlessness. Aaron was made priest by a carnal commandment, but Christ's priesthood functions "after the power of an endless life" (v. 16) because, unlike Aaron, Christ will never die.

B. Aaron was not ordained by an oath (vv. 20-22).

While God acknowledged Aaron and his successors in the elaborate ceremonies described in Ex. 28–30, we have no record of a divine oath that sealed their priesthood. In fact, God would not seal their order with an oath because He knew that their work would one day come to an end. But when He ordained Christ to be a priest, He confirmed it with an unchanging oath.

C. Aaron and his successors died, but Christ lives forever (vv. 23-24).

The Law was holy and good, but it was limited by the frailties of the flesh. Aaron died; his sons after him also died. The priesthood was as good as the man, and the man did not last forever. But Christ lives to die no more! He has an unchanging priesthood because He lives by the power of an endless life. He "continues forever" to make intercession for God's people and thus is able to save them (God's people) "to the uttermost." We often apply v. 25 to the lost, but its main application is to the saved, those for whom Christ intercedes daily. Yes, He saves from the uttermost, and any sinner can be forgiven. But the point here is that those whom He saved are saved forever, for eternity!

III. The Practical Argument: Christ and the Believer (7:26-28)

"Such a high priest was fitting for us" (v. 26, NKJV) — that is, suits us, meets our needs. No descendant of Aaron could fit the description given of Christ in these verses. These men were not "holy, harmless, undefiled." Aaron made a golden calf and led Israel into idolatry! And Eli's sons were guilty of gluttony and immorality (1 Sam. 2:12ff). But we have a perfect High Priest: He is holier and higher than any priest on earth, for He is ministering in the heavenly tabernacle in the very presence of God.

Aaron and his sons had to offer daily sacrifices, for themselves first, and then for the people. Christ is sinless; He needs no sacrifices. And the one sacrifice that He offered settled the problem of sin for all eternity. Furthermore, He offered *Himself*, not the blood of bulls and goats, as the sacrifice.

It is easy to see, then, that the order of Melchizedek is superior to the order of Aaron. This point has been proved historically, for Abraham honored Melchizedek above Levi; it has been proved doctrinally, for Ps. 110:4 definitely states that God created a new order of priesthood in the Law; and it has been proved practically, for no man could ever qualify to be High Priest except Jesus Christ. There is no need for us to look beyond Christ — He is all that we need.

HEBREWS 8

Having proved that Christ's heavenly priesthood is of a better order, the writer now shows that this priesthood is ministered through a better covenant. The Levitical priests ministered according to the Old Covenant that God had made with Israel at Sinai. The very fact that God calls it an "Old Covenant" by introducing a "New Covenant" proves that the old Levitical priesthood has been done away by the cross. To prevent his readers from going back to Aaron and the Old Covenant, the writer in chapter 8 proves the superiority of the New Covenant. In what ways, then, is the New Covenant better than the Old?

I. The New Covenant's Superior Priest (8:1)

Verse 1 is the "summing up" of the previous arguments. "We have such an high priest" (as described in 7:26-28), a high priest already proved to be superior to Aaron. Christ, our High Priest, has sat down, since His work of redemption is finished. No priest of Aaron's line ever sat down. Neither did any Levitical priest ever sit down on a throne. Christ is our King-Priest in heaven; and because He is a better High Priest, He mediates for us a better covenant. Certainly He would not minister an Old Covenant from heaven; a new High Priest demands a new and better covenant.

II. The New Covenant's Superior Place (8:2-5)

Since Jesus came from the tribe of Judah, not Levi, He would not have been considered to minister as a priest. We find Christ in the courts of the temple while on earth, but never in the holy place or in the holy of holies. But this only proves the superiority of the New Covenant: it is ministered from heaven and not from earth.

The writer adds another argument: the original; the earthly tabernacle (and temple) were but copies of the heavenly tabernacle. Moses copied the tabernacle from the pattern God revealed to him on the mount (Ex. 25:9, 40). The Jews revered their temple and its furnishings and ceremonies; yet these things were merely shadows of the reality in heaven. To go back to the Old Covenant meant forsaking the realities of heaven for earthly imitations. How much greater it is to have a heavenly high priest ministering in a heavenly sanctuary.

III. The New Covenant's Superior Promises (8:6-13)

This passage contains the key argument of this chapter: the promises of the New Covenant are far better than those of the Old

Covenant. Consequently, the priesthood of Christ, which is based on better promises, must be itself a better priesthood—and it is. First, read Jer. 31:31-34 and then note what these better promises are:

A. The promise of grace (vv. 6-9).

Six times in vv. 8-13 God says "I will." This is grace! The Old Covenant was a yoke of bondage, demanding perfect obedience. But the New Covenant emphasizes what God will do for His people, not what they must do for Him. Note that God does not find fault with the Old Covenant, but with the people themselves. The Law is spiritual, but men are carnal, "sold under sin," says Rom. 7:14; and Rom. 8:3 makes it clear that the Law was "weak through the flesh." In other words, the failure of Israel could not be blamed on any weakness in the Old Covenant, but on the weakness of human nature. It is here, then, that grace steps in; what the Law could not do because of man's weakness, God accomplished through the Cross.

B. The promise of an inner change (v. 10).

Read Jer. 31:31 for the promise of the New Covenant, and note that it involves an inner change of the heart. Read 2 Cor. 3 for additional light on this wonderful topic. The Old Covenant was written with the finger of God on tablets of stone, but the New Covenant is written by the Spirit on the human heart and mind. An external law can never change a person; it must become a part of the inner life if it is to change our behavior. See Deut. 6:6-9. This is the meaning of Rom. 8:4—"That the righteousness of the law might be fulfilled in us." This is accomplished, of course, by the Holy Spirit, who enables us to obey God's Word.

C. The promise of unlimited blessing (v. 11).

The day will come when there will be no need for personal witnessing, for all people will know the Lord. Of course, the ultimate fulfillment of this promise awaits the establishing of the kingdom. "All shall know Me" (v. 11) parallels the repeated promise of the OT that "the earth shall be filled with the knowledge of God" (Isa. 11:9), Gentiles and Jews alike.

D. The promise of sins forgiven (v. 12).

Read Heb. 10 and you will see that, under the Old Covenant, there

698

was a remembrance made of sins but no remission of sins. The blood of bulls and of goats could cover sins, but only the blood of the Lamb of God could "take away the sins of the world" (John 1:29). What a wonderful promise the New Covenant gives to the burdened sinner: his sins will be forgiven and forgotten forever!

E. The promise of eternal blessing (v. 13).

The very fact that God calls it a "New Covenant" means that the Old Covenant is obsolete and will pass away. About the time Hebrews was being written, the Roman legions were being readied for their invasion of Palestine, which occurred in A.D. 70. The phrase "ready to vanish away" indicates that but a brief time would elapse before the temple would be leveled and the priestly activities cease. But the New Covenant, like the priesthood of Christ, would endure forever.

When did this New Covenant come into being? Luke 22:20ff and 1 Cor. 11:23-26 make it clear that the New Covenant was established by the shedding of Christ's blood on the cross. According to Heb. 12:24, Christ is today the Mediator of the New Covenant.

But Jer. 31:31ff states that God promised this New Covenant to the Jews. What right do we have to apply it to the church? The answer lies in the dispensational character of the Book of Acts. We recall that Acts 1–7 is God's offer of the kingdom to the Jews. When the Holy Spirit came to the believers at Pentecost, the New Covenant was in force. Had the nation repented and received Christ as Messiah, all of the blessings and promises of the New Covenant would have followed. But Israel refused the message and resisted the Spirit, and thus the nation was set aside. It is at this point that God brought the Gentiles into the New Covenant and formed the church out of believing Jews and Gentiles. So, we today in the body of Christ share in the New Covenant; but the nation of Israel at some future date will enjoy these same blessings when it "looks upon Him whom they have pierced" and the kingdom is established (Zech. 12:10).

HEBREWS 9

We have seen that Christ's priesthood is better than Aaron's because it belongs to a better order, that of Melchizedek (chap. 7) and because it is administered under a better covenant, namely the

New Covenant (chap. 8). Here in chapter 9 we will see that Christ's priesthood is superior because it is administered from a better sanctuary.

I. The Inferior Sanctuary Under the Old Covenant (9:1-10)

The writer gives five reasons why the Old Covenant sanctuary was inferior:

A. It was on earth (v. 1).

The word "worldly" means "of this world, on the earth." God gave Moses the pattern from heaven, but Moses built the tabernacle (and Solomon the temple) on earth and of earthly materials. The sanctuary was divinely appointed, and the services were carried on under God's direction. Still, everything was on the earth. As we shall see in the latter part of this chapter, the new sanctuary is heavenly.

B. It was but a shadow of things to come (vv. 2-5).

Here the writer describes the arrangement and furnishings of the OT tabernacle. Note that "the first" in vv. 2 and 6 means "the first section of the tabernacle," the holy place. "The second tabernacle" of v. 7 does not refer to a second tabernacle built after the first one that Moses made; it means the second division of the tabernacle—the holy of holies. The brazen altar and the laver stood in the outer court. The first veil (note v. 3) hung between this outer court and the holy place. In the holy place stood the candlestick, the table of bread, and the incense altar. Behind the second veil was the holy of holies, into which only the high priest could go, and then only on the annual Day of Atonement (Lev. 16). In the holy of holies stood the ark of the covenant. All these things pointed to Christ and were shadows of the great spiritual realities that God would give in the New Covenant.

C. It was inaccessible to the people (vv. 6-7).

Only the priests could minister in the court and the holy place, and only the high priest could enter the holy of holies. As we shall see, the heavenly sanctuary is open to all of God's people.

D. It was temporary (v. 8).

The veil between men and God reminded the people that the way into God's presence had not yet been opened. Verse 9 says that while the veil remained, there would still be two parts to the tabernacle—a symbol (figure, parable) of the relationship between Israel and God. When Christ died, the veil was torn and the need for an earthly sanctuary was abolished.

E. It was ineffective for changing hearts (vv. 9-10).

Day after day, the priests offered the same sacrifices. The blood covered sin but never washed it away. Nor could the blood of animals change the hearts and consciences of the worshipers. These were "carnal ordinances," that is, ceremonies that dealt with the externals, not the inner person. They were temporary acts, awaiting the full revelation of the grace of God in Jesus Christ at the cross.

II. The Superior Sanctuary Under the New Covenant (9:11-28)

At v. 11 the picture changes, and the writer explains why the New Covenant sanctuary is superior to the Old and why Christ's priesthood is superior to Aaron's.

A. It is a heavenly sanctuary (v. 11).

Christ is a high priest of good things "that have come to pass." His heavenly sanctuary is greater and more perfect because it was not made with human hands. The word "building" ought to read "creation"; it is not of this creation because it is of the new creation. The earthly tabernacle belonged to the Old Covenant, the old creation, but Christ's sanctuary is of the New Covenant, the new creation. See also v. 24.

B. It is effective for changing lives (vv. 12-23).

What a contrast! The high priest took another creature's blood into the holy of holies many times during his life; but Jesus took His own blood into God's presence once for all. The OT sacrifices brought about ceremonial cleansing for the body (v. 13) but could never reach into the heart and conscience. But the blood of Christ, shed once and for all, purges the conscience and gives the believer an unchanging and perfect standing before God. All Jewish ceremonies were but "dead works" in comparison to the living relationship with God under the New Covenant.

Verses 15-23 use the illustration of a testament or will. A person makes a will and determines how to distribute the estate. But the inheritance goes to no one until the person dies. Christ had an eternal inheritance to give to His church, and this inheritance is spelled out in the New Covenant, Christ's "last will and testament." For the will to take effect, He had to die. But the amazing thing is this: Christ died to make the will effective, and then came back from the dead to administer His estate personally! Even the first covenant, under Moses, was sealed with blood (Ex. 24:6-8). When the earthly sanctuary was erected, it was also dedicated with blood. But this blood of animals could only bring about ceremonial purity, not inward cleansing.

Verse 23 suggests that Christ's death even purified the heavenly things. These things may be the heavenly people of God (see 12:22ff; Eph. 2:22) who have been purified by Christ's blood; or, it may suggest that the presence of Satan in heaven (Rev. 12:3ff) demanded a special cleansing of the heavenly sanctuary.

C. It is the fulfillment and not the shadow (v. 24).

The Aaronic priests ministered in a tabernacle that was temporary; it pointed to a Christ yet to come. Christ is not ministering in a man-made tabernacle full of earthly imitations; He is ministering in a heavenly sanctuary that is the fulfillment of these OT practices. The high priest sprinkled blood on the mercy seat for the people, but Christ represents us in the very presence of God. What a tragedy it is when people cling to religious ceremonies that please the senses and fail to lay hold, by faith, of the great heavenly ministry of Christ.

D. It is based on a completed sacrifice (vv. 25-28).

The superiority of Christ's sacrifice is the theme of chapter 10, but it is also mentioned here. The priest's work was never done because the sacrifices were never final. Christ's death was final. He appeared "at the climax of the ages" to put away sin, not merely cover it. The veil has been rent and the way opened into the presence of God. Christ appears in heaven for us; we can come into the presence of God. The OT Jew did not have access to God's immediate presence; he would not have dared to enter the holy of holies. But because of Christ's completed work on the cross ("It is finished!"), we have an open path to God through Him.

Note that the word "appear" is used three times in vv. 24-28.

We see Christ's past appearance, which put away sin (v. 26), His present appearance in heaven for us (v. 24), and His future appearance to take us to glory (v. 28). When the high priest disappeared into the tabernacle on the Day of Atonement, the people waited outside expectantly for him to reappear. Perhaps God would refuse the blood and kill the high priest. What joy there was when he came out again! And what joy we will have when our High Priest appears to take us to our eternal holy of holies, to live with Him forever!

HEBREWS 10

This chapter closes the section on "the Superior Priesthood" (7–10) by explaining that the priesthood of Jesus Christ is based on a superior sacrifice—the sacrifice of Christ Himself. The writer gives three reasons why Christ's sacrifice is superior to those described in the OT.

I. Christ's Sacrifice Takes Away Sin (10:1-10)

A. The OT sacrifices were ineffective (vv. 1-4).

For one thing, they belonged to the age of types and shadows, and therefore could never change the heart. They were repeated "year by year" (v. 1) and "day by day" (v. 11), thus proving that they could not do away with sin. Otherwise the high priest and his helpers would not have had to repeat these actions. As Heb. 9:10-14 explained, the OT rituals dealt only with external things and ceremonial uncleanness. Sacrifices produced a "remembrance of sins" but not a remission of sins (see 9:22). In the Lord's Supper, we remember Christ, not our sins (1 Cor. 11:24; Luke 22:19), because He has forgotten our sins (8:12).

B. Christ's sacrifice is effective (vv. 5-20).

Here he quotes Ps. 40:6-8. The Holy Spirit has changed "My ears have You opened" to "a body You have prepared for Me" (NKJV). The reference may be to Ex. 21:1-6. In the year of release, the Jew was required to set his Hebrew servants free. But if a servant loved his master and wanted to remain with him, he was marked by placing a hole through his ear lobe. From that moment on, his body belonged to his master for life. When Christ came into the world, the Spirit prepared for Him a body, and He was completely dedicated to and dependent on His Father's will. That body would be sacrificed on the cross for the sins of the world. Passages such as Ps. 51:10 and 16, 1 Sam. 15:22, and Isa. 1:11ff make it clear that God saw no finished salvation in the blood of animals; He wanted the believer's heart. In vv. 8-9, he uses the words of Christ to show that God, through Christ, set aside the first covenant with its animal sacrifices and established a New Covenant in His own blood. By Christ's surrender to the will of God, we have been set apart for Him (sanctified) once and for all.

II. Christ's Sacrifice Need Never Be Repeated (10:11-18)

Note the contrasts: the OT priest stands daily, but Christ has sat down; the OT priest offered the same sacrifices often; Christ offered one sacrifice (Himself) once. By one offering God has given a right standing, that is perfected, forever to those who have been set apart through faith in Christ. (In v. 10, we are sanctified once for all; in v. 14 we are being sanctified daily. This is positional and progressive sanctification.) The OT sacrifices produced a remembrance of sins, but Christ's sacrifice makes possible remission of sins (v. 18). *Remission* means "sending away." Our sins have been pardoned and sent away forever (Ps. 103:12; Micah 7:19). On the annual Day of Atonement (Lev. 16), the high priest confessed the sins of the nation over the head of the scapegoat, and then the goat was led off to be lost in the wilderness. This is what Christ did with our sins. There is no more suffering for sin because there is no more remembrance of sin. The Holy Spirit witnesses in our hearts, and we have the blessing of that promised New Covenant (vv. 14-17; Jer. 31:33ff).

III. Christ's Sacrifice Opens the Way to God (10:19-39)

A. Explanation (vv. 19-21).

The writer reviews the blessings that believers have because of Christ's once-for-all death. Because we have a perfect standing in Christ, we can have boldness (literally "freedom of speech") to come into His presence. No veil stands now between us and God. That tabernacle veil symbolized Christ's human body, for it covered the glory of God (John 1:14). When His body was offered, the veil was torn. We have a new way based on the New Covenant; we have a way to life, because we have a living high priest (7:25). The house of God (the church) has a great high priest in glory.

B. Invitation (vv. 22-25).

There are three "let us" statements here (see 6:1 also): (1) "Let us draw near" instead of drifting away; (2) "Let us hold fast" our confession (testimony) of faith (or hope, as in some translations), not wavering because of trials; (3) "Let us consider" other believers and, by our example, encourage them to be true to Christ. If we provoke each other at all, it should be unto love (see 1 Cor. 13:5). The boldness we have in heaven ought to lead to spiritual growth and dedication on earth. It seems that these believers, because of trials, were neglecting Christian fellowship and the mutual encouragement that believers need from each other. Since Christ is our high priest, and we are a kingdom of priests (1 Peter 2:9), we ought to assemble together for common worship, teaching, and service. The OT Jew could not enter the tabernacle, and the high priest could not enter the holy of holies whenever he pleased. But, through Christ's sacrifice, we have a living way into heaven. We can come to God at any time. Do we take advantage of this privilege?

C. Exhortation (vv. 26-39).

This is the fourth of the five exhortations (see outline). It warns against willful sin. Please remember that this exhortation is to believers, not unsaved people, and that it is related to the previous three exhortations. Careless Christians start to drift through neglect; then they doubt the Word; then they grow dull toward the Word; and the next step is deliberately sinning and despising their spiritual heritage. Note the important facts about this particular sin. It is not one sin committed once; "sin willfully" in v. 26 should read "willingly go on sinning." It is the same continuous tense of the verb as in 1 John 3:4-10 — "Whosoever continually and habitually sins is not born of God." So, this passage is not dealing with an "unpardonable sin"; it is talking about an attitude toward the Word that God calls willful rebellion. There were no sacrifices in the OT for deliberate, presumptuous sins (see Ex. 21:14; Num. 15:30). Sins of ignorance (Lev. 4) and of sudden passion were covered; but willful sins merited only punishment.

Verse 29 reminds us that our salvation (and the shed blood that purchased it) are held in high regard by God. The Father values His Son; the Son shed His blood; the Spirit applies the merits of the cross to the believer. For us to sin willfully is to sin against the Father and the Son and the Spirit. The writer quotes Deut. 32:35-36 to show that God, in the OT, saw to it that His people (not unbelievers) reaped what they sowed and were judged when they disobeyed willfully. The fact that they were His covenant people made their obligations that much greater (Amos 3:2). God judges His people; see Rom. 2:16; 1 Cor. 11:31-32; and 1 Peter 1:17. Of course, this is not eternal judgment, but rather His chastening in this life and the loss of reward in the next. Note vv. 34-35, where the writer emphasizes reward for faithfulness, not salvation. See also 1 Cor. 3:14-15, 5:5, 9:27, and 11:30.

In vv. 32-39 (as in 6:9-12), he gives a wonderful assurance to these believers that their lives had proven they were truly born again. They were among those who had put faith in Christ (Hab. 2:3-4) and therefore could not "draw back" as those did who were not truly saved (1 John 2:19). Their destiny is perfection, not perdition, because they have Christ in their hearts and look for His return.

HEBREWS 11

This chapter illustrates the lesson of 10:32-39 and shows that throughout history, men and women have done the impossible by faith. "The just shall live by faith" states 10:38. This chapter proves that faith can conquer in any circumstances.

I. Faith Described (11:1-3)

True biblical faith is not an emotional kind of wishful thinking; it is an inner conviction based on the Word of God (Rom. 10:17). In v. 1 the word *substance* means "assurance" and *evidence* means "proof." So, when the Holy Spirit gives us faith through the Word, the very presence of that faith in our hearts is all the assurance and evidence we need! Dr. J. Oswald Sanders says, "Faith enables the believing soul to treat the future as present and the invisible as seen." Through faith, we can see what others cannot see (note vv. 1, 3, 7, 13, and 27). When there is true faith in the heart, God bears witness to that heart by His Spirit (note vv. 2, 4-5, and 39). By faith, Noah saw coming judgment, Abraham saw a future city, Joseph saw the Exodus from Egypt, and Moses saw God.

Faith accomplishes things because there is power in the Word of God, as illustrated by the Creation in v. 3. God spoke, and it was done! God still speaks to us. When we believe what He says, the power of the Word accomplishes things in our lives. The same Word that acted in the old creation acts in the new creation.

II. Faith Demonstrated (11:4-40)

A. Abel (v. 4; Gen. 4:3ff).

God asked for a blood sacrifice (Heb. 9:22), and Abel had faith in His word. Cain did not show faith, however, and was rejected. God witnessed to Abel's faith by accepting his sacrifice; and by this witness, Abel still speaks to us.

B. Enoch (vv. 5-6; Gen. 5:21-24).

In a wicked age, Enoch lived a dedicated life; he did this by trusting God's Word. See Jude 14ff. He believed that God would reward him for his faith, and God did so by taking him to heaven so that he did not die. The reward of faith is important in Hebrews (10:35; 11:26; 12:11).

C. Noah (v. 7; Gen. 6–9).

No one had seen or anticipated judgment through a flood; Noah saw it by faith. Faith leads to works. Noah's attitude and actions condemned the unbelieving, wicked world around him.

D. Abraham (vv. 8-19; Gen. 12–25).

Here we have the great "father of the believing" who is one of the OT's, greatest examples of faith. Abraham believed God when he did not know where (vv. 8-10), when he did not know how (vv. 11-12), when he did not know when (vv. 13-16), and when he did not know why (vv. 17-19). It was faith in God's Word that made him leave his home, live as a pilgrim, and follow wherever God led. Faith gave Abraham and Sarah power to have a child when they were "as good as dead." Abraham and his pilgrim descendants did not turn back, as the Hebrew leaders were tempted to do, but kept their eyes on God and pressed on to victory (vv. 13-16; 10:38-39).

E. Isaac (v. 20; Gen. 27).

He believed the Word passed on to him from Abraham and conferred the blessing on Jacob.

F. Jacob (v. 21; Gen. 48).

In spite of his failures, Jacob had faith in God's Word and blessed Ephraim and Manasseh before he died.

G. Joseph (v. 22; Gen. 50:24ff; Ex. 13:19; Josh. 24:32).

Joseph knew that Israel would one day be delivered from Egypt, for this is what God promised Abraham (Gen. 15:13-16). It is amazing that Joseph had any faith at all, after going through so many trials and after living in pagan Egypt most of his life.

H. Moses (vv. 23-29; Ex. 1–15).

Moses' parents had faith to hide Moses since God had told them (in some way) that he was a special child (Acts 7:20). Moses' own faith led him to refuse position in Egypt and to identify with Israel. Again, he saw the reward of faith (v. 26) as opposed to the pleasures of sin for a season. Faith in the Word led to the Passover deliverance (how the Egyptians must have scoffed at the blood on the doors!) and the crossing of the Red Sea.

I. Joshua (v. 30; Josh. 1–6).

God promised to deliver Jericho to Joshua, and faith in that promise led to victory. Israel marched around the city for seven days and must have looked foolish to Jericho's citizens, but the Jews' faith was rewarded.

J. Rahab (v. 31; Josh. 2; 6:22-27).

Her confession of faith is in Josh. 2:11. Her faith led to works (James 2:25) when she risked her life to save the spies. Though a harlot, she was saved by faith and was even brought into the human ancestry of Christ (Matt. 1:5). Her faith was contagious because she also won her family (Josh. 6:23).

K. "Others" (vv. 32-40).

Some people are named, others are not. All these men and women, nevertheless, are among the giants of the faith. The writer sees the entire OT history as a record of victories of faith. Some victories were public and miraculous, such as deliverance from death; others were private and rather ordinary, such as "out of weakness were made strong . . . " and "wrought righteousness." Some were delivered by faith; others did not escape, but were, by faith, given grace to bear suffering. The unbelieving world looked upon these believers as refuse, "cranks," and "pests." God, though, says of them, "Of whom the world was not worthy" (v. 38). Each of them received from God that witness of faith (v. 39).

Though faith enabled these people to receive promises (plural), they did not receive the promise (v. 39); but now, in Christ, that promise has been fulfilled. Note v. 13 as well as 1 Peter 1:11-12. Verse 40 indicates that God's plan for these OT saints also includes NT Christians who today share in that New Covenant through Christ. That "better thing" has been described in Hebrews—the better priest, sacrifice, sanctuary, and covenant. In a very real sense, Christians today are heirs of the promise (6:17-18) through faith in Christ, since all of our spiritual blessings are the results of the promises God made to Abraham and David (Rom. 11:13-29). Of course, though these promises are now fulfilled spiritually in Christ (Gal. 3), they will also literally be fulfilled in Israel during the "age to come" (Heb. 2:5-9).

The lessons of this chapter are many, but perhaps it would be helpful to mention just a few. (1) God works through faith and faith alone. Exercising faith is the only way to please Him and receive His blessing. (2) Faith is a gift from God through the Word and the Spirit. It is not something we "work up" ourselves. (3) Faith is always tested; at times it seems that trusting God is foolish, but faith always conquers in the end.

HEBREWS 12

The key word in this chapter is "endure"; it is found in vv. 1 (translated "patience"), 2-3, 7, and 20. The word means "to bear up under trial, to continue when the going is tough." These Christians were going through a time of testing (10:32-39) and were tempted to give up (12:3). None of their number had yet been called to die for Christ (12:4), but the situation was not getting any easier. To encourage their trust in Christ, the writer reminded them (note v. 5) of three encouragements that would help keep them going and growing.

I. The Example of the Son of God (12:1-4)

In chapter 11, his readers looked back and saw how the great saints of the OT won the race of life through faith. Now the writer urges them to "look away to Jesus" and have their faith and hope strengthened. The picture here is of an arena; the spectators are the heroes of faith listed in the previous chapter; the runners are the believers going through trials. (This image does not necessarily imply that people in heaven watch us or know what is going on here on earth. It is an illustration, not a revelation.) If the Christians are to win the race, they must get rid of the weights and sins that make it hard for them to run. Most of all, they must keep their eyes on Christ as the goal! Compare Phil. 3:12-16. Christ has already run this race of faith and conquered for us! He is the Author (Pioneer, Trailblazer) and Finisher of our faith; He is Alpha and Omega, the Beginning and the End. What He starts, He finishes; He can see us through to victory.

Our Lord went through many trials while on earth. What was it that helped take Him through to victory? "The joy that was set before Him" (v. 2). This was His goal—the joy of presenting His church before the Father in heaven one day (Jude 24). Note also John 15:11, 16:20-24, and 17:13. His battle against sin took Him to the cross and cost Him His life. Most of us will not run on that course; it will probably be our task to live for Him, not die for Him. "Consider Him!" "Look unto Jesus!" These words are the secret of encouragement and strength when the race gets difficult. We need to get our eyes off of ourselves, other people, and circumstances and get our eyes on Christ alone.

II. The Assurance of the Love of God (12:5-13)

These Christians had forgotten the basic truths of the Word (5:12); and v. 5 tells us they had even forgotten what God says about chastening. The writer quoted Prov. 3:11ff and reminded them that suffering in the life of a Christian is not punishment, but chastening. This word "chastening" literally means "child-training, discipline." They were spiritual babes; one way God had of maturing them was to put them through trials. Punishment is the work of a judge; chastening is the work of a father. Punishment is handed out to uphold the law; chastening is given out as a proof of love, for the bettering of the child. Too often we rebel at God's loving hand of chastening; instead, we ought to submit and grow. Satan tells us that our trials are proof that God does not love us; but God's Word says that sufferings are the best proof that He does love us!

When suffering comes to believers, they can respond in several ways. They can resist the circumstances and fight the will of God, growing bitter instead of better. "Why does this have to happen to me? God doesn't care anymore! It doesn't pay to be a Christian!" This attitude will only produce sorrow and bitterness of soul. The writer argues, "We have had earthly fathers who chastened us, and we respected them. Should we not respect our Heavenly Father who loves us and desires to bring us to maturity?" After all, the best proof we are God's children, and not illegitimate children, is that God disciplines us. The suggestion is made in v. 9 that if we do not submit ourselves to God, we may die. God will not have rebellious children and may take their lives if He must.

Then too the Christian may give up and quit. This is the wrong attitude (see vv. 3, 12-13). God's chastening is meant to help us grow, not to beat us down. The correct attitude is that we endure by faith (v. 7), allowing God to work out His perfect plan. It is that blessed "afterward" of v. 11 that keeps us going! Chastening is for our profit that we might be sharers of His holiness, and our submission brings the most glory to His name.

III. The Power of the Grace of God (12:14-29)

This is the fifth of the exhortations in Hebrews, and the key thought is grace (see vv. 15, 28). The contrast is made between Moses and Christ, Sinai and Mt. Zion, the Old Covenant and the New Covenant. When the Law was given at Sinai, fear and terror ruled, and the mountain was covered with smoke and fire. When God spoke, the people trembled. But today, we have a spiritual experience greater than that of Israel's at Sinai, for we have a heavenly priest, a heavenly home, a heavenly fellowship, and a voice speaking from on high that gives a message of grace and love.

The description in vv. 22-24 is of the New Covenant blessings in Christ. Mt. Zion is the heavenly city (13:14; Gal. 4:26), in contrast to earthly Jerusalem, which was about to be destroyed. There are three groups of people in the heavenly city: (1) the host of angels, who minister to the saints; (2) the church of the firstborn (see 1:6); and (3) the OT saints. "Made perfect" (v. 23) does not mean that believers in glory are now in their perfect resurrection bodies. It refers, rather, to the OT saints who have now a perfect standing before God because of the death and resurrection of Christ (10:14; 11:40). Anyone who believes God's Word (as did the OT saints) goes to heaven; but the perfection of God's work did not come until Christ's death on the cross.

At the top of this list is Jesus, the Mediator of the New Covenant. How could these people go back to an earthly city (about to be destroyed) and an earthly temple (which would also be destroyed), earthly priests and earthly sacrifices? The blood of Christ has taken care of everything! Abel's blood cried out from the earth for vengeance (Gen. 4:10), but Christ's blood speaks from heaven for salvation and forgiveness. This is grace! Christ is a minister of grace. The New Covenant is a covenant of grace. God's grace does not fail, though we may fail of His grace (v. 15) because we fail to appropriate it. Esau is the illustration of one who despised spiritual things and lost the blessing. ("Profane" means "outside the temple" or "worldly, common.") Esau failed of the grace of God because he would not repent (note 6:6).

"God is shaking things!" is the theme of the closing verses. None of us likes to have things shaken; we enjoy stability and security. But God was shaking already the Jewish economy and was about to destroy the temple in Jerusalem. The material things would have to go so that the spiritual realities might take their place. God was building a new temple, His church; and the old temple would have to be removed. The writer quotes Haggai 2:6 to show that one day God will shake the world itself and usher in a new heaven and earth.

"Wherefore" (v. 28) introduces the practical application: "Let us have grace." How do we receive grace? At the throne of grace, where our eternal High Priest intercedes for us. We must serve God, not old laws and customs. We are part of a kingdom that will never be shaken or removed. We are building our lives on the eternal, unchanging spiritual realities that we have in Christ. Therefore, let us serve God with reverence. Let us heed His Word and not refuse to listen, for in His Word is the grace and life that we need. The admonition of v. 25 does not regard our eternal destiny. As with the other exhortations of Hebrews, it deals with God's chastening in this life, and not judgment in the next.

HEBREWS 13

Here we have the final appeals of this epistle. The writer has explained the doctrinal truths; now he closes with practical admonitions for all believers. Their enemies were saying, "If you stay true to Christ, you will lose everything—your friends, your material goods, your religious heritage in the temple, sacrifices, and priesthood!" But here, the writer points out that the believer loses nothing by trusting Christ. By faith, Christians turn their backs on the "religious systems" of this world (in this case Judaism) and fix their eyes and hearts on the true spiritual worship of God in Christ. Note in this chapter the spiritual blessings Christians have, though they may lose everything in this world.

I. A Spiritual Fellowship of Love (13:1-4)

Love for God's people is one of the marks of a true believer in Christ (John 13:35; 1 John 3:16; 1 Thes. 4:9, etc.). Christians are hated by the world (John 15:17-27) and need the mutual love of the saints for encouragement and strength. This love is expressed in practical ways, such as sympathizing with those in trials (v. 3, see 1 Cor. 12:26) and being hospitable. He refers to the visits of angels in the OT, to Abraham (Gen. 18), Gideon (Jud. 6:11ff), and Manoah (Jud. 13). Of course, true Christian love ought to be seen first in the home and family, so he warns about sexual sins that can destroy marriage. In this day when marriage vows are taken so lightly, we need to remember that God judges all immoral people, whether believers or unbelievers.

II. Spiritual Treasures (13:5-6)

It cost something to be a Christian in the first century. These people had suffered the plundering of their goods (10:34) and were paying a price for their testimony. How easy it is for Christians to be covetous and desire the things of the world (1 Tim. 6:6ff and Luke 12:15). "Be content!" is easy to read but difficult to practice. True contentment never comes from possessing many things; it comes when we rest our lives wholly on Christ. The writer quotes the OT promise that God gave to Moses (Deut. 31:6-8) and Joshua (Josh. 1:5) and applies it to God's people today. Since Christ is always with us, we have all that we need! We need never desire any material thing (Phil. 4:19); we need never fear the attacks of people. Christ is our Helper; we need never fear (Ps. 118:6). When the children of God are in the will of God, obeying the Word of God, they will never lack anything and can never be harmed. This is a promise that we can count on.

III. Spiritual Food in the Word (13:7-10)

There are three commandments in this chapter that refer to the local church and the place of the pastor and people:

A. *"Remember them which have the rule over you" (v. 7).*

He is probably referring to pastors who had led them but were now gone. Perhaps they had been martyred. "Have the rule" means "to lead"; the pastor is expected to be the spiritual leader of the flock. How does he lead? Through the Word of God, which is the spiritual food for God's sheep. The believers are to follow the example of their faith, but the leaders are expected to point to Christ. Verses 7-8 should read: " . . . considering the end (purpose) of their behavior, which is Jesus Christ. . . . " Pastors come and go, but Christ remains the same.

B. *"Obey them that have the rule over you" (v. 17).*

Christians are to submit to the Word of God as taught and lived by their spiritual leaders. It is a solemn thing to be a pastor entrusted with the watch for souls. The pastor must give an account of his ministry to the Lord; if his flock has disobeyed the Word, the sorrow will be theirs, not his. How important it is to respect pastoral leadership and submit to the Word of God.

C. *"Salute them that rule over you" (v. 24).*

The people should communicate with their leaders and be on "speaking terms" with them. It is a tragedy when Christians become angry and refuse to talk with their pastor. This is disobedience to the Word of God.

Believers who do not feed on the Word will feed on "strange doctrines" (v. 9) and become "spiritually sick." The only way to grow to maturity and be established is through the Word of God (Eph. 4:14ff, and see Heb. 5:11-14). Our hearts are established by grace, not by law or earthly religious systems. The Christian's "altar" is Christ, the once-for-all sacrifice for sin; we feed on Him as we feed on His Word. Just as the OT priests ate the meat and grain from the sacrifices, so we feed on Christ, the living sacrifice.

IV. Spiritual Sacrifices (13:11-16)

In turning to Christ, these Hebrews lost the temple and its priesthood and sacrifices; but they gained in Christ far more than they lost. Christ rejected the temple and called it "a den of thieves"; and He rejected the city of Jerusalem by being crucified outside the gate (John 19:20). The writer compares Christ's death to the burning of the sacrifices on the day of atonement (Lev. 16:27), since both suffered "outside the camp." The readers were being tempted to go back to Judaism. "No," admonishes the writer. "Instead of going back, go outside the camp and bear reproach with Christ!" You may summarize the two-fold message of Hebrews in the phrases "within the veil" (fellowship with Christ) and "without the camp" (witness for Christ). Believers look to no earthly city; they have a heavenly city awaiting them, as did the heroes of faith of old (v. 14; Heb. 11:10; 12:27).

As a kingdom of priests, Christians are to offer spiritual sacrifices (1 Peter 2:5). A spiritual sacrifice is something done or given in the name of Christ and for His glory. In v. 15, he states that praise is such a sacrifice; see Eph. 5:18-19, Pss. 27:6 and 69:30-31. Good works and sharing material blessings are also spiritual sacrifices (v. 16). Other spiritual sacrifices include the believer's body (Rom. 12:1-2); offerings (Phil. 4:18); prayer (Ps. 141:2); a broken heart (Ps. 51:17); and souls won to Christ (Rom. 15:16).

V. Spiritual Power (13:17-24)

The benediction of vv. 20-21 explains how the Christian is enabled to live for Christ in this wicked world: Christ works in us from His throne in heaven. There are three separate titles given to Christ, the Shepherd: (1) the Good Shepherd, who dies for the sheep — John 10:11 and Ps. 22; (2) the Great Shepherd, who perfects the sheep — Heb. 13:20-21 and Ps. 23; and (3) the Chief Shepherd, who will come for the sheep — 1 Peter 5:4 and Ps. 24. Our High Priest is our Shepherd and Helper; He works in us and gives us the grace and power to live for Him and serve Him.

"Make you perfect" is the theme of Hebrews; "let us go on unto perfection [maturity]" (6:1). Maturity does not come through our striving in our own strength; it comes as we allow Christ to work in us through the Word of God. This parallels Phil. 2:12-16 and Eph. 3:20-21. God cannot work through us until first He works in us, and He works in us through His Word (1 Thes. 2:13).

The closing greetings show the love that bound believers together in the early church. The closing benediction of grace identifies Paul as the writer (compare 2 Thes. 3:17-18).

JAMES

A Suggested Outline of James

I. The Perfect Believer and Suffering (1)
   A. The perfect work: God's purpose (1:1-12)
   B. The perfect gift: God's goodness (1:13-20)
   C. The perfect law: God's Word (1:21-27)

II. The Perfect Believer and Service (2)
   A. Faith proved by love (2:1-13)
   B. Faith proved by works (2:14-26)

III. The Perfect Believer and Speech (3)
   A. The exhortation (3:1-2)
   B. The illustrations (3:3-12)
   C. The application: true wisdom (3:13-18)

IV. The Perfect Believer and Separation (4)
   A. The enemies we must fight (4:1-7)
      1. The flesh (vv. 1-3)
      2. The world (vv. 4-5)
      3. The devil (vv. 6-7)
   B. The admonitions we must heed (4:8-17)
      1. Warning against pride (vv. 8-10)
      2. Warning against criticism (vv. 11-12)
      3. Warning against self-confidence (vv. 13-17)

V. The Perfect Believer and the Second Coming (5)
   A. Patient when wronged (5:1-11)
   B. Pure in speech (5:12)
   C. Prayerful in trials (5:13-18)
   D. Persistent in soul-winning (5:19-20)

Introductory Notes to James

I. The Writer

Three men in the NT are named James: (1) the son of Zebedee and brother of John (Mark 1:19); (2) the son of Alphaeus, one of the apostles (Matt. 10:3); and (3) the brother of our Lord (Matt. 13:55). It is likely that James, the brother of our Lord, wrote this epistle. During Christ's ministry, James and his brothers were unbelievers (Mark 3:21 and John 7:1-10). James was given a special resurrection visit by the Lord (1 Cor. 15:7) which undoubtedly brought him to salvation. We see him with the believers in the Upper Room (Acts 1:14). After Peter moved off the scene as leader in the Jerusalem church (Acts 12:17), James took his place. It was James who directed the conference of Acts 15 and who handed down the final decision. In Gal. 2:9-10, Paul acknowledged the leadership of James, but in Gal. 2:11-14, he seems to criticize James for his legalistic influence. Acts 21:17-26 bears out the fact that James leaned heavily toward the Jewish law.

II. The Letter

This Jewish emphasis is seen clearly in the Epistle of James. James addressed the letter to Jewish Christians (1:1-2) who are "scattered abroad" in the Dispersion. See also 1 Peter 1:1 and John 7:35. The Dispersion was composed of Jews who had left Palestine but kept in contact with their "fatherland," returning home for the feasts when possible. Note in Acts 2 that there were multitudes of devout Jews in Jerusalem from other nations of the world. Some of these Jewish communities were the results of Israel's various persecutions and deportations. Others were formed voluntarily for business reasons. Of course, Acts 11:19 informs us that many Christian Jews were scattered abroad because of the persecution in Jerusalem. These Jews would maintain separate communities and continue their way of life in these foreign lands. It was to Christian Jews scattered in the Roman Empire (possibly Syria in particular) that James addressed his letter. It was written about A.D. 50.

The Jewish emphasis in James is seen in several ways. For one thing, "assembly" in 2:2 is the word for "synagogue" (although the word "church" is used in 5:14). Christ's name is mentioned twice (1:1 and 2:1). The illustrations are all from the OT, or from nature.

There are strong parallels between James and the Sermon on the Mount, which was Christ's spiritual explanation of the Law. There are also many parallels between James and 1 Peter (which was also written to Jews of the Dispersion). These Christian Jews were true believers, but they still maintained their Jewish ways in their Jewish communities. They were born again (1:18) and expected the coming of the Lord (5:7). Do not expect to find in this epistle the well-developed doctrines of the church that we find in Paul's letters. The temple was still standing; many Jewish synagogues were Christian synagogues; and the full understanding of "the one body" had not yet dawned upon all the believers.

III. Basic Theme

Woven throughout the letter are two themes: persecution from outside the fellowship, and problems within the fellowship. The believers were experiencing trials, and James sought to encourage them. But there were also divisions and sins within the assembly, and James sought to help them confess and forsake their sins. One of the key thoughts is perfection or spiritual maturity (see outline). These people needed to grow up in the Lord, and their various trials could help to mature them if they would obey God.

IV. James and Paul

There are no conflicts between James and Paul on the matter of justification by faith. James could not be contradicting Galatians because Galatians had not yet been written! Paul explains that sinners are justified by faith (Rom. 3–4); James explains that a person's faith is dead unless it is proved by works. We are not saved by works, but the faith that saves us leads to good works. Paul wrote about our standing before God; James wrote about our witness before the world.

JAMES 1

One of the best tests of Christian maturity is tribulation. When God's people go through personal trials, they discover what kind of faith they really possess. Trials not only reveal our faith; they also develop our faith and Christian character. The Jews to whom James was writing were experiencing trials, and he wanted to encourage them. The strange thing is that James tells them to rejoice! The word "greeting" in v. 1 can mean "rejoice!" How is the Christian able to have joy in the midst of troubles? James gives the answer in this first chapter by showing the certainties Christians have in times of tribulation.

I. We Can Be Sure of the Purpose of God (1:1-12)

The experiences that come to the children of God are not by accident (Rom. 8:28). We have a loving Heavenly Father who controls the affairs of this world and who has a purpose behind each event. Christians should expect trials to come; James does not say "if" but "when." (The Gk. word for "temptation" in 1:2 means "testings or trials"; while the Gk. word for "tempt" in 1:13 means "solicitation to do evil.") What is God's purpose in trials? It is the perfection of Christian character in His children. He wants His children to be mature (perfect), and maturity is developed only in the laboratory of life. Trials can produce patience (see Rom. 5:3), which means "endurance"; and endurance in turn leads the believer into deeper maturity in Christ. God put young Joseph through thirteen years of testing that He might make a king out of him. Peter spent three years in the school of testing to be changed from sand to rock! Paul went through many testings, and each one helped to mature his character. Of course, it takes faith on the part of the Christian to trust God during testings, but knowing that God has a divine purpose in mind helps us to yield to Him.

In vv. 5-8 James deals with this matter of faith, as expressed in prayer. We do not always understand God's purposes, and often Satan tempts us to ask, "Does God really care?" This is where prayer comes in: we can ask our Father for wisdom, and He will give it to us. But we must not be double-minded. The word suggests hesitation, doubting; it literally means "two-souled." Double-minded Christians are not stable during trials. Their emotions and their decisions waver. One minute they trust God; the next minute, they doubt God. Faith in God during trials will always lead to stability; see 1 Peter 5:10.

Both rich and poor worshiped in the assemblies to which James wrote (2:1-9; 5:1), and James pointed out that trials benefit both groups. Trials remind the poor that they are rich in the Lord and therefore can lose nothing; trials remind the rich that they dare not live for riches or trust in them. Verse 12 is a wonderful beatitude and promise for us to claim in times of testing and trial.

II. We Can Be Sure of the Goodness of God (1:13-20)

Many people seem to have the idea that because God is good, He should not allow His people to suffer or be tempted. They forget that God wants His children to grow up and experience new blessings of His grace; and one way they can mature is by going through trials and temptations. In this passage, James emphasizes the goodness of God and warns Christians about rebelling against God in times of trial (1:13, 20).

First, he makes a careful distinction between trials and temptations. God sends trials to bring out the best in us (see Abraham, Gen. 22:1), but Satan sends temptations to bring out the worst in us. Believers should not say that God tempts them, because temptations to sin arise from our very nature. He describes the "birth" of sin: enticement from without generates lust within; lust conceives and gives birth to sin; and sin brings death! The words "drawn away" and "entice" (v. 14) are hunting terms; they form an image of a hunter or a fisherman using bait to lure the prey.

Then, James reminds these believers that God gives only good gifts, and that good gifts come down from heaven. God is light; His goodness does not flicker like some faraway star. We are God's children. He begat us through His Word, and we are the firstfruits of His creatures, the "sample" of what is to follow at Christ's coming (Rom. 8:23). Therefore, Christians should not be swift to speak and complain when trials come. Rather, they should be swift to hear the Word, trust it, and obey it. After all, God works out His will in our lives when we are patient, not when we are angry.

III. We Can Be Sure of the Word of God (1:21-27)

The phrase "swift to hear" (v. 19) reminds us of how the Christian should hear and obey God's Word, the theme of this section. James uses an illustration from agriculture in v. 21 when he talks about "firstfruits" and "the implanted [engrafted] Word." James may be referring to the Parable of the Sower (Matt. 13:1-9, 18-23) in which the heart is compared to soil and the Word to seed. If believers are going to receive the Word and get strength from it in trials, then they must pull out the weeds! "Superfluity of naughtiness" can be translated "rank growth of wickedness"—weeds! The soil of the heart must be prepared to receive the Word. If we have unconfessed sin in our hearts, and bitterness against God because of our trials, then we cannot receive the Word and be blessed by it.

In vv. 22-25, James changes the picture and compares the Word to a mirror (glass). The Word of God reveals what we are on the inside, just as a mirror reveals how we appear on the outside. When Christians look into the Word, they see themselves as God sees them and thus are able to examine their hearts and confess their sins. But it is not enough merely to look into the Word and read it; we must obey what we read. A person who merely hears the Word but does not obey it is like a man who glances casually into the mirror, sees that his face is dirty, and goes on his way without doing anything about it. Such a man thinks he has bettered himself spiritually when he has actually harmed himself.

Verse 25 tells us we must gaze carefully (not glance casually) into the Word, study it, and through it see ourselves. We must then obey what the Word says. If we do, we will be happy (blessed). It is not reading the Bible that makes a person happy; it is obeying what it says. He calls the Word "the perfect law of liberty" because obedience to the Word produces spiritual liberty (John 8:30-32). Living the Christian life is not bondage, it is wonderful liberty!

Verses 22-25 speak of the private life of believers as they look into the Word; vv. 26-27 describe their public life, their practice of the Word. The Gk. word for "religious" (v. 26) means "the outward practice of religion." The Bible nowhere calls the Christian faith "a religion"; it is a miracle, a new birth, a divine life. "If any man imagines himself to be religious," says James, "then let him prove it by the life he lives." What are the characteristics of pure religion? They are: (1) self-control—a bridled tongue (see 3:2); (2) love for others; and (3) a clean life. The word "visit" (v. 27) means "care for"; it suggests sacrificial care for those who are in need. True religion is not a matter of forms and ceremonies; it is a matter of a controlled tongue, sacrificial service, and a clean heart.

James uses the word "perfect" several times in this chapter. In vv. 1-2 we have God's perfect work; in vv. 13-20, God's perfect gift;

and in vv. 21-27, God's perfect law. God's perfect work is His purpose to mature us; His perfect gift is His goodness to us in times of testing; and His perfect law is the Word that strengthens and sustains us.

JAMES 2

In Gal. 5:6, Paul describes the Christian life as "faith working through love" (NKJV). These two aspects of faith are discussed in this chapter. The basic idea is that true Bible faith is not dead; it reveals itself in love (vv. 1-13) and in works (vv. 14-26). Too many people have an intellectual belief in Christ, but not a heart belief. They have faith in the facts of historic Christianity, but not saving faith in Christ personally.

I. Faith Is Proved by Love (2:1-13)

"Have not" (v. 1) really means "practice not." We are not simply to have faith; we are to practice it in our daily lives. We must not believe in "God" in a vague, general way as many church members do (and even Satan — v. 19); we must have a personal faith in Jesus Christ specifically. It is not a "hope-so" faith in God that saves the soul; it is a definite commitment to the Son of God, Jesus Christ. Here Christ is called "the Glory" (omit the words "the Lord of"), since He is the very glory of God (Heb. 1:3). To the Jews reading this letter, "the Glory" would identify Christ with the Shekinah Glory of the OT, the glory of God that dwelt in the tabernacle and the temple. That Glory now dwells in the believer and in the church (Col. 1:27; 3:4; Rom. 8:30; John 17:22).

How do we show love to others? By accepting them for what they are and seeing them as persons for whom Christ died. We are not to judge others or condemn them. Preferring the rich to the poor is a terrible sin, for Christ became poor that we might be rich in Him. See Rom. 2:11 and 1 Tim. 5:21. James states boldly that when a poor man comes into the Christian assembly (here the word is "synagogue"), he is to be received in love and shown just as much grace as a rich man. Man may look on the outward appearance; God sees the heart (1 Sam. 16:7). The "gold-ringed man" (suggesting that he is wearing many "flashy" rings) is no better in God's sight than the man in humble ("vile") clothing. Some Jews loved places of honor (Luke 14:7-11) and the admiration of great men (Matt. 23:5-12). Unfortunately, many Christians do too!

What is so sinful about showing respect to wealthy persons? For one thing, it makes us judges, and only God can honestly judge a person (v. 4). The word "partial" here means "divided" and takes us back to the double-minded person of 1:8. This kind of judging shows false values (vv. 5-6), for Christ clearly stated that the poor would inherit the kingdom (see Luke 6:20; Matt. 5:3). James reminds them that the rich oppress the saints and even drag them into court! By refusing to receive the poor, these believers have dishonored the poor whom God loves (see Prov. 14:31).

In v. 7, James reminds them that the rich even blaspheme the name of Christ "which is called upon you" (referring probably to their baptism; Matt. 28:19-20). Furthermore, the "royal law" for the believer is the law of love. He quotes Lev. 19:18, 34; but he is also referring to Christ's words in Matt. 22:34-40. See also Rom. 13:8-10 and Gal. 5:14. It is a sin to show favoritism to persons; to break one commandment is to be guilty of breaking the whole law! The same God gave all the commandments, and all must be obeyed and practiced. Of course, James is not putting the Christian back under the Mosaic law; he is referring to the moral law which still abides under the New Covenant. We are to speak and act as those who will be judged, not by the law of Moses, but by the more severe "law of liberty," the law of love written in our hearts by the Holy Spirit.

II. Faith Is Proved by Works (2:14-26)

James in these verses is not contradicting Paul. Paul, in Rom. 4:1-5 and Gal. 3, is explaining how the sinner is justified, given a right standing before God; James, on the other hand, is writing about how the saved person proves that salvation before others. People have no right to believe that we are saved if they do not see a change in our lives. A sinner is saved by faith, without works (Eph. 2:8-9), but true saving faith leads to works (Eph. 2:10). Being a Christian is not a matter of what we say with the lips; it involves what we do with the life. (Note that the statement in v. 14, "Can faith save him?" ought to read, "Can that kind of faith save him?" referring to the first sentence in the verse.)

We do not show our faith in Christ only by great deeds of achievement, such as those listed in Heb. 11, but by the things we say and do, day by day. Read 1 John 3:16-18 along with vv. 14-16. Faith that does not lead to works is dead faith (vv. 17, 26), not living faith. There is a challenge in v. 18: "Show me your faith without your works!" This is impossible to do! The only way faith can be expressed in the Christian's life is by practical loving obedience to the Word of God. Even the devil has dead faith! (v. 19) Read Matt. 8:29 and Acts 16:17 to see how the demons acknowledge Christ. Still, this kind of faith will not save them.

James reaches back into the OT for two examples of faith that lead to works. The first is Abraham (Gen. 22:1-19). Abraham was anxious to have a son, and God promised one to him. Abraham believed God's promise, and this faith gave to him the righteousness he needed for salvation (Gen. 15:1-6; Rom. 4:1-5). God had promised Abraham that through Isaac, he would have children more numerous than the sand of the sea and the stars of the heavens. Then God asked Abraham to sacrifice that son Isaac on the altar! Abraham had faith in God, and therefore was not afraid to obey Him. Hebrews 11:17-19 indicates that Abraham believed that God could even raise Isaac from the dead! In short, Abraham proved his faith by his works. His obedience to the Word was evidence of his faith in the Word. His faith was made perfect (brought to maturity) in his act of obedience. See 2 Chron. 20:7 and Isa. 41:8 for "the friend of God."

James' second illustration is Rahab (Josh. 2; 6:17-27). This woman was a sinner, yet her name is listed in the family of Christ! (Matt. 1:5) Hebrews 11:31 indicates that she was a woman of faith. She lived in the condemned city of Jericho, and she heard that God had judged the enemies of Israel. She believed the report she heard about God (Josh. 2:10-11), for "faith comes by hearing" (Rom. 10:17, NKJV). Note that she also had assurance (Josh. 2:9, 21). Keep in mind that Rahab was a believer in the God of Israel before the two spies came to her house. It was her reception and protection of the two spies that proved her faith in God. She risked her own life to identify herself with Israel. Because of her faith, proved by her works, she and her family (who also believed) were delivered from the judgment that came to all the people in Jericho.

Verse 24 summarizes the entire matter: faith that does not lead to works is not saving faith. Sad to say, there are multitudes of professing Christians and church members who have this "dead faith." They profess faith with their lips (v. 14), but their lives deny what they profess. This is the same truth Paul explained when writing to Titus. "They profess that they know God, but in works they deny Him" (Titus 1:16). Real Christians are "a peculiar people, zealous of good works" (Titus 2:14). This is why Paul warns, "Examine yourselves as to whether you are in the faith; prove yourselves" (2 Cor. 13:5, NKJV). This does not mean that a true Christian never sins (1 John 1:5-10). But it does mean that a true Christian does not make sinning the habit of his or her life. A true Christian bears fruit for God's glory and walks so as to please God.

The whole matter of faith and works is summed up in Eph. 2:8-10 (NKJV): (1) the work God does for us (salvation) — "For by grace you have been saved . . . not of works"; (2) the work God does in us (sanctification) — "For we are His workmanship"; (3) the work God does through us (service) — "created . . . for good works."

JAMES 3

We can identify mature Christians by their attitude toward suffering (chap. 1) and by their obedience to the Word of God (chap. 2). Now James tells us that a Christian's speech is another test of maturity. We read and hear many words every day and forget what a wonderful thing a word is! When God gave us the faculty of speech, He gave us a tool to build with; but it can also become a weapon of destruction.

I. The Exhortation (3:1-2)

Apparently there was a rivalry in the assemblies over who would teach, for James warns them, "Let not many of you become teachers!" The reason? Those who teach will be judged more strictly than those who listen. It is a sad thing when immature Christians try to become teachers before they are ready. They think they have attained a great place of honor, when they have really asked for a more severe judgment from God!

James is quick to agree that all of us stumble in many ways, especially in what we say. In fact, the person who is able to control the tongue proves that he or she has control over the whole body. Read 1:26 again, and note also the many references to the tongue in the Book of Proverbs. Peter is a good illustration of this truth. In the Gospels, while an immature disciple, he often lost control of his tongue and had to be either reproved or taught by the Lord. But after Pentecost, his spiritual discipline was evident by his controlled speech.

II. The Illustrations (3:3-12)

James used three paired illustrations to portray the power of the tongue.

A. Power to direct—the bit and rudder (vv. 3-4).

The word "helm" in v. 4 is "rudder," the part of the ship that steers it through the water. We often think that our words are unimportant, but the wrong word can direct the listener into the wrong paths. An idle word, a questionable story, a half-truth, or a deliberate lie could change the course of a life and lead it to destruction. On the other hand, the right word, used by the Spirit, could direct a soul out of sin and into salvation. Just as the horse needs a guide, and the rudder needs a pilot, so our tongues need the Lord to control them.

B. Power to destroy—the fire and animal (vv. 5-8).

The size of a thing does not determine its value or power. The tongue is a little member in the body, but it can cause great destruction. How the tongue loves to boast! (Of course, what the tongue says comes from the heart: Matt. 12:34-35.) "How great a forest a little fire kindles!" (v. 5) Each year, many thousands of acres of timber are lost because of careless campers or smokers.

A little flame can set a whole forest on fire. The tongue is a flame: it can, through lies and gossip and heated words, set a whole family or church on fire. See Prov. 16:27. And the "soot" from the fire can defile everybody involved. When the Spirit came at Pentecost, there were tongues of fire from heaven to enable the Christians to witness; but it is also possible for the tongue to be "set on fire from hell" (v. 6). James also compares the tongue to a fierce and poisonous beast that cannot be tamed. No *man* can tame the tongue; only God can control it through His Spirit. The tongue is restless, unruly (that is, it cannot be ruled). What poison it can spread! A spiritual tongue is medicine (Prov. 12:18).

C. Power to delight—the fountain and tree (vv. 9-12).

It is impossible for a fountain to produce both fresh water and salt;

and it is impossible for a tongue to speak both blessing and cursing. How often we "bless God" in our praying and singing, and then "curse men" in our anger and impatience! See Prov. 18:4. Christians must allow the Spirit to give forth the "living waters" of the Word through their tongues. There is something wrong with the heart when the tongue is inconsistent. Likewise, a tree cannot bear two kinds of fruit. See Prov. 13:2 and 18:20-21. The "fruit of the lips" (see Heb. 13:15) ought always to be spiritual.

After considering these six examples, believers must realize that they cannot permit Satan to use their tongues. The wrong word at the wrong time could break a heart or lead a person astray. We need to make Ps. 141:1-4 our constant prayer.

III. The Application (3:13-18)

One of the key themes in the Book of James is wisdom, or practical living directed by the Word of God (see 1:5). It is tragic when Christians lack practical wisdom to direct their affairs, both personally and in the church. Far too many people have the idea that to be "spiritual" means to be impractical — and nothing is farther from the truth! When the Holy Spirit guides us, He uses our minds, and He expects us to get the facts and weigh issues in the light of the Word of God. James indicates that there are two sources of wisdom and that the believer needs to be discerning. The tongue of the believer can be filled with true wisdom from above or the false wisdom from below.

A. False wisdom from below (vv. 14-16).

When we have bitterness and envy in our hearts, our tongues will express these things. It matters not how spiritual our teaching might be: if the tongue is not controlled by the Spirit from a loving heart, then we are imparting false wisdom. To their shame, Christians often believe this false wisdom and even glory in it! They know this "wisdom" contradicts the Bible, so they lie even against the truth of God's Word! False wisdom belongs to the world (earthly), the flesh (sensual), and the devil (devilish) — the three great enemies of the believer (Eph. 2:1-3). You can always tell when a church or a family follows false wisdom: you will find jealousy, division, and confusion. Instead of humbly depending on the Spirit and the Word, they look to the world for ideas and to the flesh for strength, and by so doing play right into the hands of the devil.

B. *True wisdom from above (vv. 17-18).*

Truly wise believers do not need to advertise the fact that they are wise; you will see it expressed in their daily life (edifying conversation and good behavior) and attitude (meekness). Knowledge puffs up (1 Cor. 8:1), but spiritual wisdom humbles us and keeps us from being arrogant. While the false wisdom has its origin in the world, the flesh, and the devil, the true wisdom "comes down from above" (see 1:17). It comes from God, by the Spirit; it is not invented by the mind of man.

This true wisdom is pure; there is no error in the Word of God. It is peaceable: it leads to peace and harmony, not discord (see 4:1-10). Man's method for attaining peace is to sacrifice purity for the sake of harmony, but God does not work that way. Where people bow to the pure Word of God, there will always be peace.

The wisdom from above is also gentle; gentleness includes patience and forbearance. When the flesh controls the tongue, it unleashes a flood of words without self-control or a willingness to listen to others. "A fool vents all his feelings," says Prov. 29:11 (NKJV). The wise person uses gentleness and persuasion with patience; he or she does not threaten or accuse. "Easy to be intreated" (v. 17) suggests a willingness to yield, or to be reasonable. Wise people are full of mercy, not quick to judge or condemn; their lives are full of good fruits. There is no wavering ("partiality," 1:6 and 2:4); though they are willing to yield, they are not willing to compromise with the truth. Finally, true wisdom will not allow for hypocrisy; the truth is spoken and is backed with a true motive.

JAMES 4

This chapter makes it clear that there were carnal divisions and disputes among these believers. One cause was the selfish desire of many to be teachers (3:1), but the basic cause was disobedience. There was a lack of true separation in the lives of the people. It is tragic when brethren dwell together in discord instead of unity (Ps. 133). "Can two walk together except they be agreed?" (Amos 3:3)

I. The Enemies We Must Face (4:1-7)

We noted in 3:15 that the Christian battles the world, the flesh, and the devil. You find this same listing in Eph. 2:1-3, where the life of the unsaved sinner is described. The unsaved person lives for the world and the flesh and is controlled by the devil. Those who trust Christ receive the Holy Spirit within and have a new nature. Still, they will battle these enemies.

A. The flesh (vv. 1-3).

The word "lusts" does not necessarily mean sensual passions. It simply means desires. These desires are at work in the members of the body, and they excite the flesh and create problems. Please keep in mind that the body itself is not sinful; it is the fallen nature that would control the body that is sinful. The flesh is human nature apart from God, just as the world is human society apart from God. This is why Rom. 6 exhorts us to yield the members of our bodies to the Spirit: see also the emphasis in Rom. 8 and Gal. 5. Note also what James says in 1:5 about our desires.

In v. 2 James describes these believers' sinful actions: they desire, they kill to obtain (see Gal. 5:15), and they do not stop to pray about their desires. And, when they do pray, they pray selfishly that they might enlarge their pleasures, not glorify God. The flesh can even encourage a person to pray! Of course, when a believer is at war with himself, it is not likely that he can have peace with others.

B. The world (vv. 4-5).

Spiritual adultery is being married to Christ (Rom. 7:4) yet loving the world (2 Cor. 11:2-3). In the OT, God called Israel's idolatry "adultery" because the idols had robbed Him of the people's devotion. How can Christians have friendship with the world when they have been called out of the world? (John 15:18-19) We have been crucified to the world, and the world to us (Gal. 6:14). There are four dangerous steps that take the believer into a wrong relationship with the world: (1) friendship with world, James 4:4; (2) being soiled by the world, James 1:27; (3) love with the world, 1 John 2:15-17; (4) conformity to the world, Rom. 12:1-2. The result is that the compromising believer is judged with the world (1 Cor. 11:32). Lot illustrates this folly; see Gen. 13:10-13 and chapter 19. Believers who are friends of the world are at enmity with God. They grieve the Spirit, who jealously yearns for their love.

C. The devil (vv. 6-7).

Christians who live for the world and the flesh become proud, and the devil takes advantage of this situation, for pride is one of his chief tools. God wants to give us more grace — more than anything Satan can give! The Christian must use the Word to resist Satan (Luke 4:1-13), and this the Spirit will enable him to do. But God cannot help the Christian who is proud, who refuses to repent of sin and humble himself. Grace is for the lowly, not the lofty. We must first submit to God; then we can effectively resist the devil.

It is important that Christians examine themselves to see if any of these enemies are defeating them.

II. The Exhortations We Must Heed (4:8-17)

James turns now to three important warnings and calls Christians to repent of their sins. Unless individuals in the church are right with God, there can be no peace.

A. *Warning against pride (vv. 8-10).*

Wars and fighting originate in pride; the wise Christian sows seed of peace (3:13-18). Pride puts us at a distance from God; pride defiles our hearts and our works. It is the sin of double-mindedness again, and this is basically lack of surrender. "Purify your hearts" (v. 8) carries the idea of having a chaste and faithful heart, not loving the world or grieving the Spirit. These believers were living in pleasure, surrounded with laughter and worldly joy. They needed to be sober and serious, putting sin out of their lives. James promises that if they humble themselves, God will lift them up. See Matt. 23:12, Luke 14:11, 1 Peter 5:6, and Prov. 29:23.

B. *Warning against criticism (vv. 11-12).*

When people are worldly minded and proud, they are often quick to criticize others. The conflicts among these Christians had their origin in their judging and speaking evil of one another. Here is the tongue again! (1:19-20, 26, and 3:5-6) How many churches have been divided and disgraced by hateful, critical tongues! The Bible teaches us that we must have Christian discernment (1 Thes. 5:21-22; 1 John 4:1-6), but this does not mean that we can judge the hearts and motives of others. In Matt. 7:1-5, Jesus teaches that believers have the right to help others conquer their sins, but they must first judge their own sinfulness. If I have a plank in my eye, what right do I have to criticize the man who has a speck of dust in his eye? And I cannot see clearly enough to help him until I first take care of my own needs. When we judge other Christians without love and mercy, we are making ourselves lawgivers; and God is the only Lawgiver. If all of us would devote ourselves to obeying the Word and not investigating to see how well others obey it, our churches would have harmony and peace. James suggests in v. 12 that the only one with the right to judge is the one with the power to punish — namely, God.

C. Warning against arrogant self-confidence (vv. 13-17).

Pride, criticism, and self-confidence go together. Humble people pray for God to help disobedient Christians, and they try to love them back to fellowship with Christ. The humble know how to say "If the Lord wills" as they make their plans day by day. But these believers were boasting of their plans and anticipated success. They would go to the big city, set up business, and come back wealthy! He warns them that this carnal boasting and self-confidence is dangerous. To begin with, we know nothing about tomorrow; only God knows. The person who boasts about tomorrow is claiming to be God! Furthermore, life itself is uncertain — a cloud that quickly comes and goes (Job 7:7; Ps. 102:3). We do not even know when life will end, so how can we be so confident? We ought to say, "If the Lord wills, we shall live. . . ." Every believer needs to keep before his or her eyes an awareness of the brevity of life. "So teach us to number our days, that we may apply our hearts unto wisdom" (Ps. 90:12). Boasting about an unknown future is sin. Yet so many people make their plans without praying or seeking the mind of God. They live like the worldly sinner who thinks he has security for the future, but discovers he has lost everything (Luke 12:15-21).

Verse 17 sums up the chapter and points out that we can sin by neglect as well as by deliberate action. It is not simply what we do, but also what we do not do, that is sinful. This is why the Puritans used to talk about "sins of commission" and "sins of omission." Life is so brief that we cannot afford to waste it. We must make our lives count for Christ before He returns.

JAMES 5

There are several miscellaneous matters in this last chapter, but the key thought seems to be that of the second coming of Christ

(vv. 7-9). When Christians honestly look for the return of Christ, the evidences of this hope show up in their lives.

I. They Are Patient When Wronged (5:1-11)

In those days a great gulf existed between the rich and poor; the "middle class" as we know it today was not a major presence in society. It appears that the Gospel appealed to the poor masses, while the rich rejected Christ (with some exceptions) and oppressed the Christian poor.

A. The sins of the rich (vv. 1-6).

James lists several sins and shows that the rich were only preparing themselves for coming judgment. First, he names hoarding (vv. 1-3). He proclaims that the rich had amassed their wealth only to have it fade away. Their gold, silver, and garments (see Matt. 6:19-20) would only rust and be eaten away. Their very riches, by fading away, bore witness against their present selfishness and would testify against them again at the judgment. They had heaped up treasures but forgot that the "last day" was upon them and that judgment was coming. James may have been referring to the impending fall of Jerusalem. The second sin he names is stealing wages (v. 4); these rich people had held back the honest wages of the poor (see Lev. 19:13). They used fraud to steal these wages, and their sins would find them out! We often hear the phrase "Money talks!" In this case, the stolen wages cried out to God for justice, and the needy workers cried out to God too. "Lord of Sabaoth" (v. 4) means "Lord of the armies" and is the "battle name" of God. See Isa. 1:9 and Rom. 9:29. God would come with His armies and judge these thieves! The third sin named is extravagant living (v. 5). Certainly God wants us to enjoy the blessings of life (see 1 Tim. 6:17), but He does not want such a life to be wasteful and luxurious while robbing others in need. These men were living in needless luxury and were spending wantonly, using money that was not rightfully theirs. James compares them to senseless cattle who feed themselves without restraint, little realizing that they are only being fattened up for the slaughter! See Amos 4:1-3. The final sin is injustice (v. 6). The rich took advantage of their power to abuse and kill the poor. These Christians did not resist; they left their case in the hands of the Righteous Judge (Rom. 12:17-21).

B. The patience of the poor (vv. 7-11).

James encourages these suffering Christians to get their eyes on the promise of Christ's coming. The word "patient" (v. 8) does not mean that they were to sit idly by, doing nothing. Rather, the word carries the idea of endurance, bearing the burdens and fighting the battles until the Lord comes. He uses several illustrations to hammer home this lesson of patience. (1) The farmer (vv. 7-8). The farmer plants the seed and prepares the soil but does not reap a crop immediately. God sends the rains to water the soil, and then comes the harvest. (The early rain came in October and November and the latter rain in April and May.) Even so, the Christian must be patient, knowing that "in due season we shall reap, if we faint not" (Gal. 6:9). (2) The judge (v. 9). Apparently their trials had made some of the Christians critical, and complainers emerged in the church. James reminds them that they are not to judge; Christ, the Judge, is at the door! He hears what is said, and He will come quickly and make things right. Murmuring and complaining is a serious sin among God's people. If we would all remember that Christ is coming, we would not complain and criticize so much. (3) The prophets (vv. 10-11). James refers these Christians to the OT believers, who suffered under the hands of sinners yet left their trials with God and won the victory. Job is the classic example. God had a wonderful purpose and result in mind when He permitted Job to be tried, even though Job did not understand what God was doing. Regardless of what trials may come to our lives, we know that God is full of love and mercy and that all things work together for good.

II. They Are Pure in Speech (5:12)

James is not forbidding legal oaths, for even Jesus took an oath at His trial (Matt. 26:63-64). He is telling us to have such honest speech that we need not "back up" our promises with oaths. The rich men did not keep their promises; but the Christian must always keep his word, even if it hurts him or her personally.

III. They Are Prayerful in Trials (5:13-18)

The Bible nowhere promises that Christians will have an easy life, but the Bible does tell us what to do when trials come. Some Christians will be afflicted, that is, go through a trial specifically planned by God. What should they do? Pray! James does not promise that God will remove the affliction, but he does suggest that God will give the grace necessary to endure it. See 2 Cor. 12. Other Christians will have sickness, and the suggestion in v. 15 is that this sickness is the result of sin (see 1 Cor. 11:30). What should they do? Call the leaders of the church and ask for prayer. This is not a church ritual to prepare a person for death, because James says that it results in the healing of the person's body. The word "anoint" (v. 14) is the common word for "massage"; it is used in Mark 16:1, where the women wanted to prepare the body of Christ for burial. Oil was a common medicine in that day; physicians often anointed the sick with oil (Luke 10:34). The picture here is of saints not only praying for one another but also using the means God has supplied for their health. In v. 16 James summarizes the lesson: Christians are to confess their sins (when they have sinned against each other) and pray for each other.

James believed in prayer. In fact, tradition tells us that he spent so much time in prayer that his knees became hard and calloused. God works effectually through prayer, but that prayer must come from a clean, dedicated heart. James uses Elijah as the example of the power of prayer; see 1 Kings 17ff. "Like passions" (v. 17) means "with a nature like other men"; see Acts 14:15. It was not Elijah's natural gifts that made him a great man of prayer; it was his dedication and faith.

IV. They Are Persistent in Soul-Winning (5:19-20)

We can be so wrapped up in our own trials that we forget the needs of the lost and of believers who have strayed. The basic meaning of these verses is that saints should seek to bring wandering brethren back to the Lord. "Convert" simply means "to turn back again" (Luke 22:32). How easy it is for a saint to be seduced (to err) from the truth. Disobedient Christians are in danger of serious discipline, and even death (1 Cor. 11:30). In love, we should seek them out and help restore them (Gal. 6:1). When we do, we are rescuing them from death (the discipline of God) and, in love, we see their sins covered (see 1 Peter 4:8).

But we may apply these verses to the lost as well. As we see the return of Christ approaching, how much we need to dedicate ourselves to witnessing! The Christian who really believes in the return of Christ cannot help but want to win others.

1 AND 2 PETER

A Suggested Outline of 1 Peter

Greeting (1:1-2)

I. God's Grace in Salvation (1:3–2:10)

    A. Living in hope (1:3-12)
    B. Living in holiness (1:13-21)
    C. Living in harmony (1:22–2:10)

II. God's Grace in Submission (2:11–3:12)

    A. Submission to authorities (2:11-17)
    B. Submission to masters (2:18-25)
    C. Submission in the home (3:1-7)
    D. Submission in the church (3:8-12)

III. God's Grace in Suffering (3:13–5:11)

    A. Make Christ Lord of your life (3:13-22)
    B. Have Christ's attitude (4:1-11)
    C. Glorify Christ's name (4:12-19)
    D. Look for Christ's return (5:1-6)
    E. Depend on Christ's grace (5:7-11)

Farewell (5:12-14)

A Suggested Outline of 2 Peter

I. Explanation: The Knowledge of Christ (1)

    A. The gift of this knowledge (1:1-4)
    B. The growth in knowledge (1:5-11)
    C. The grounds for knowledge (1:12-21)

II. Examination: The False Teachers (2)

    A. Their condemnation (2:1-9)
    B. Their character (2:10-17)
    C. Their claims (2:18-22)

III. Exhortation: The True Christian (3)

    A. Beloved . . . be mindful (3:1-7)
    B. Beloved . . . be not ignorant (3:8-10)
    C. Beloved . . . be diligent (3:11-14)
    D. Beloved . . . beware (3:15-18)

Introductory Notes to 1 and 2 Peter

I. Author

The Apostle Peter is the author of the two letters that bear his name. In writing these letters, Peter was continuing to fulfill the commandment Christ gave him to "feed" the sheep and the lambs (John 21:15-17). The "Babylon" of 1 Peter 5:13 is probably Rome (see Rev. 17:5, 18), where Peter had gone shortly before his death to minister to the suffering churches (2 Peter 1:12-15). There is no scriptural or historical evidence that Peter founded the church at Rome and served as its "bishop" for twenty-five years, as tradition claims. There were several congregations in Rome when Paul wrote Romans (see especially Rom. 16, in which several "household groups" are mentioned). Paul himself would never have gone to Rome to minister had Peter been there first. Paul's policy was to go places where no other apostles had gone (Rom. 15:20).

II. Situation

Nero began a terrible persecution of Christians in October, A.D. 64. It was most severe in Rome itself, where Nero even burned Christians alive to illuminate his gardens at night. Some students believe that Paul was released in the spring of 64 and traveled to Spain (Rom. 15:28), leaving Peter to minister to the believers in the city. Silas and Mark are mentioned with Peter (1 Peter 5:12-13), so Paul must have left them and journeyed to Spain with other companions. Nero burned Rome in July and started his persecution of the church in October.

Peter knew that the "fiery trial" (4:12ff) would spread from Rome to the Roman provinces, and he wanted to encourage the saints there. Paul was not on hand to do it, so Peter wrote these two letters, inspired by the Spirit, to the churches Paul had founded in Asia Minor (1 Peter 1:1 and 2 Peter 3:1). These believers had already been faced with local, personal persecutions (1 Peter 1:6-7; 3:13-17), but Peter wanted them to be ready for the severe trials now on the way (4:12ff; 5:9-10).

A careful reading of 1 Peter and Ephesians (which was also written to saints in Asia Minor) shows more than one hundred parallels in teaching and wording! It is as though the Spirit is telling us that Peter and Paul agree on spiritual truths; in fact, Peter himself points to the writings of Paul (2 Peter 3:15-16, which may refer to Hebrews). Compare the two doxologies (Eph. 1:3 and 1 Peter 1:3), for example. Here are some other parallels: 1 Peter 1:12 / Eph. 3:5, 10; 1 Peter 2:2 / Eph. 4:13, 15; 1 Peter 4:10 / Eph. 4:7, 11; 1 Peter 4:11 / Eph. 3:6, 21.

III. Theme

The major theme of 1 Peter is grace (5:12); in fact, the word "grace" is used in every chapter: 1:2, 10, 13; 2:19-20 (where "thankworthy" and "acceptable" can also be translated "grace" in the original Gk.); 3:7; 4:10; 5:5, 10, 12. Peter's aim is to testify of the sufficiency of God's grace. After writing the first letter, Peter was arrested and tried; and he wrote his second letter as he awaited execution (2 Peter 1:13-21). The theme of the second letter is assurance that comes from knowledge. Peter saw the danger of false doctrine in the church and warned the believers to beware (3:17). In other words, the two letters together emphasize the perils facing the church: Satan can come as a lion to devour with persecution (1 Peter) or as a serpent to deceive with false doctrine (2 Peter). Satan is a liar and a murderer (John 8:44-45). The Christian can depend on God's grace to see him through the fiery trials; and his knowledge of the truth will conquer the false teachers that will arise in the church (2 Peter 2). These two words summarize the two letters: 1 Peter—grace; 2 Peter—knowledge. Peter urges us to grow both in grace and in knowledge (2 Peter 3:18).

1 PETER 1

The greeting in vv. 1-2 identifies the writer as Peter, an apostle (one sent with a commission). He claims no other title for himself, either here or in 5:1ff. His readers are "strangers," that is, "resident aliens" in a foreign land. This was true politically, for they were Jews away from their fatherland; but it was also true spiritually, for their citizenship was in heaven (Phil. 3:20). "Scattered" means "dispersed" as a farmer scatters seed. Believers are God's seed (Matt. 13:38), and He plants them where He will. Sometimes He uses persecution to scatter the seed (Acts 8:1; 11:19ff). Verse 2 outlines the plan of salvation: we are chosen by the Father, set apart unto faith by the Spirit, and cleansed by the blood of Christ. The Father chose you in Christ before the foundation of the world (Eph. 1:4); the Son saved you when He died for you; but it took your surrendering to the Spirit to seal the transaction.

Peter now describes the lives believers ought to live in this hostile world:

I. Live in Hope (1:3-12)

The unsaved person is "without hope" (Eph. 2:12); yet the believer has a living hope because he has a living Savior. Christ is our Hope (1 Tim. 1:1), and we look for His soon-expected return. The Christian does not work for this hope; it is a part of his spiritual birthright. We are born again (John 3:5) into this living hope.

This hope is not only a living hope; it is a lasting hope (vv. 4-5). It is reserved in heaven, where it cannot decay ("incorruptible"), be defiled, or lose its beauty and delight. But not only is the hope reserved; the believer too is kept (guarded as by a soldier) by the Lord! We are kept by God's power because of the faith we have placed in Him. Eternal security is not based on the faith of men, but on the faithfulness of God. The believer is saved; he is being saved daily (through sanctification); and he will be saved completely when Christ returns (Rom. 8:15-25). The end (completion, perfection) of our faith will be the complete salvation of the believer (v. 9), who will inherit a new body.

However, until Christ returns, the believer must go through testing. A faith that cannot be tested cannot be trusted. Our suffering is but "for a season" as the Lord sees it ("if need be"—v. 6); but the glory will be forever. Verse 7 compares the trial of our faith to the testing of gold. The word "trial" means "approval." The comparison suggested by Dr. Kenneth Wuest is that of a prospector bringing ore in to be tested. The assayer gives him a certificate stating that the ore contains gold. The certificate is the approval of the ore, and this paper is worth much more than the little sample of ore that was tested. In the same way our faith is tested, a "sample" at a time; and the approval of our faith means that there are more riches to follow. The suffering we endure here will result in more glory when Christ comes. Knowing this, we love Him the more.

In vv. 10-12, Peter reminds us that the OT prophets spoke of this salvation we enjoy. They did not, however, fully understand the time or circumstances in which it would appear. They saw the cross and the kingdom, but they did not anticipate the "valley" in between, this present age of the church.

II. Live in Holiness (1:13-21)

The blessed hope ought to make us live holy lives (1 John 3:1-3). We must "gather our thoughts" and not let them fly loose (see Ex. 12:11). Another motive for separated living is the commandment of the Word (Lev. 11:44; 19:2; 20:7). "Holy" does not mean sinless perfection, which is a condition impossible in this life anyway (1 John 1:8-10). It means set apart, separated unto God. If we are God's children, then we ought to be like our Father.

A third motive for holy living is the judgment of God (v. 17). God chastens His children today and tests their works at the Judgment Seat of Christ (1 Cor. 3:1ff). He has no "favorites" but treats all of His children alike.

Verses 18-21 give a fourth motive for dedicated living: the price Christ paid on the cross. Before we were saved, our lives were empty and meaningless ("vain"—v. 18); but now they are full and happy through Him. Our salvation was not purchased with money; it took the blood of Jesus Christ, the spotless Lamb of God (John 1:29). His death was planned by God ages before we ever were born; yet, God in His grace included us in that plan! How grateful we should be, and what better way is there for us to show our gratitude than to surrender our all to Him (1 Cor. 6:15-20).

III. Live in Harmony (1:22-25)

Salvation gives us a living hope, a desire for a holy life, and a wonderful fellowship with the people of God. The Spirit of God loved us and brought us to Christ; this same Spirit has planted within us a love for the people of God (Rom. 5:5, and see 1 John 3:16ff). Peter uses two words for "love" in v. 22: one means brotherly love and the other divine love (*agape*). The Christian possesses brotherly love; but he needs to exert spiritual energy and love others the way God loves him. Even unsaved people can show brotherly love; it takes a Christian, controlled by the Spirit, to show *agape* love.

Peter likes this phrase "born again"; he uses it in 1:3 and 1:23. We are born again through God's mercy unto a living hope, and we are born again by the Word of God unto love for the people of God. He compares the Word to seed, as Jesus does in the Parable of the Sower (Matt. 13:1-9, 18-23). Like a seed, the Word is small and seemingly insignificant, but it has life and power within. The Word must be planted to do any good; but when it is planted in the heart, it produces fruit. God's Word is eternal, and the fruit it produces is eternal; but the things of the flesh do not last. Peter refers in vv. 24-25 to Isa. 40:6-8. Whatever we do in obedience to the Word of God will last forever! But whatever we do in the energy of the flesh will look beautiful for a time, but will then die.

Christian harmony is a blessing to the Lord, the church, and the believers themselves (Ps. 133). If every believer is obeying the Word and practicing love, there will be harmony.

1 PETER 2

The "wherefore" of v. 1 connects this section with the theme of 1:23, "being born again." The key thought of 2:1–3:7 is submission (2:13, 18; 3:1, 5).

I. Our Heavenly Privileges (2:1-10)

A. Children in God's family (vv. 1-3).

The phrase "newborn babes" is the same as that used for the infant Jesus in Luke 2:16. The new believer is a babe in need of milk (1 Cor. 3:1-3; Heb. 5:13-14). In fact, one of the evidences of spiritual life is a hunger for spiritual food, the Word of God. We must not remain babes in Christ. But just as the baby has a great appetite, so we should have a similar desire for God's Word. As we grow in the Lord, we include meat and bread in our spiritual diet

(Matt. 4:4). We become "young men" and "fathers" in the family (1 John 2:12-14). Our food must be the unadulterated Word, not one mixed with human philosophies or doctrines (2 Cor. 2:17). Once we have tasted the Lord's blessing (Ps. 34:8), we want to put away the old sins of the flesh—malice, deceit, hypocrisies, envies, etc.—and cultivate an appetite for God's truth.

B. Stones in God's temple (vv. 4-8).

Peter never claimed to be "the rock" on which the church is built (Matt. 16:18); he states clearly that Christ is the Stone (v. 4). Christ was rejected of men, but chosen of God. Read carefully Matt. 21:33-46, Isa. 28:16, Acts 4:11, and Ps. 118:22-23. Believers are living stones built on the Living Stone (1:3), comprising a spiritual temple for God's glory (Eph. 2:19-22). We are also priests in this temple, offering up spiritual sacrifices through Christ (see Heb. 13:15-16). Christ, the Stone, is rejected of men; but whoever believes on Him will not be ashamed. Unbelievers stumble over this Stone and will one day be crushed by it; but to us, He is precious.

C. Citizens in the new nation (vv. 9-10).

The church is "the people of God," His holy nation, His "Israel" (see Ex. 19:6; Gal. 6:16). This fact does not mean that the OT promises will not be literally fulfilled for the Jews in the kingdom, but rather that the church today is to God what Israel was to Him under the Old Covenant, in a spiritual sense. Since Christ is our King-Priest, we are a royal priesthood. "Peculiar" (v. 9) means "for one's own possession" (Eph. 1:14). What a privilege it is to be a child of God and have citizenship in heaven (Phil. 3:10).

II. Our Earthly Responsibilities (2:11-25)

A. Submission to ordinances (vv. 11-17).

As pilgrims and strangers (aliens and exiles), we might not think we have any responsibilities toward human government, but Peter tells us we have an even greater obligation to obey the laws. The unsaved world watches the Christian; therefore, we must abstain from sins by the power of the Spirit. Our behavior ("conversation"—v. 12) must be honest (seemly, suitable), for this is the only way to silence their evil talk. Verse 12 teaches that our good works can help lead the lost to Christ, and they will praise God on the day that He visits and saves them. Though we may not respect the men and women who hold office, we must respect the offices and obey the laws. Yes, the Christian is free, but his freedom is not license (Gal. 5:18). Read Rom. 13 for Paul's counsel on this matter.

B. Servants and masters (vv. 18-25).

Peter speaks here to household slaves who were saved and members of local assemblies. See Eph. 6:5-8 and Col. 3:22. It is interesting that neither Peter nor Paul attacked slavery as an institution. Rather, they encouraged slaves to be devoted Christians and to obtain their liberty if they could.

Servants must show submission and reverence to their masters, even if these masters are unreasonable and hard to get along with. This same principle applies to workers today. Unsaved supervisors often try to "lord it over" Christian employees or persecute them in different ways. The easiest thing to do is to fight back, but this is the wrong approach. Peter explains that anybody, saved or lost, can and should bear it if he is being punished for his faults. Only a Christian can do good and "take it" if he suffers wrongfully. Note that important word "wrongfully," for Peter is not telling us to look for excuses to suffer. He is talking about suffering for the name of Christ (see Matt. 5:9-12), suffering when we have done no wrong but have let our lights shine. The Gk. word for "thankworthy" and "acceptable" in vv. 19-20 is actually the same one used for "grace." What grace is shown if we endure suffering for our faults? It takes real grace to endure when you do good but are treated badly anyway. See Luke 6:32-36.

Peter gives "conscience toward God" (v. 19) as one reason why Christians suffer wrongfully. In v. 21 he gives a second reason: Christians have been called to suffer. We should not expect our lives to be a bed of roses, nor should we be surprised when trials come (4:12ff). Jesus promised that His followers would be persecuted for His name's sake.

Peter then points to Christ as our example in suffering. He is not teaching that we are saved by following Christ. The sinner is dead, and a dead person cannot follow anybody! In His sufferings on earth, Christ is our example of how to endure and glorify God. Peter was a witness of Christ's sufferings (5:1); he knew that his Lord had done no sin and that He was condemned wrongfully. In word, attitude, and deed, our Lord set a perfect example for us to follow. He did not argue; He did not fight back; He did not revile

His accusers after they had reviled Him. He simply committed Himself to His Father and left the outcome with Him. Since He lives in us (Gal. 2:20), He can enable us to act as He acted when the world persecutes us.

Again, Peter takes us to the cross (vv. 24-25), reminding us that Christ died for us and that we died with Him (Rom. 6). Our identification with Christ in death (2:24) and resurrection (1:3) makes it possible for us to live a righteous life. We have been healed of the malady of sin by His sacrifice on the cross. Verse 24 refers to the healing of the soul in the forgiveness of sins.

The picture of the shepherd and sheep (v. 25) would mean much to Peter, since he had heard Jesus teach about the Good Shepherd (John 10) and since Christ had commanded him to tend His sheep (John 21). The lost sinner is a straying sheep (Isa. 53:6; Luke 15:3-7); but Christ, the Shepherd, seeks him out and saves him. The word "bishop" (v. 25) means "overseer"; Christ saves us, then watches over us to guard us from evil.

Peter has filled this chapter with striking images of the believer. We are babes feeding on His Word; stones in the temple; priests at the altar; a chosen generation; a purchased people; a holy nation; the people of God; strangers and pilgrims; disciples following the example of the Lord; and sheep cared for by the shepherd. The Christian life is so rich and full that it takes these comparisons and many more to show how wonderful it is.

1 PETER 3

Peter continues the theme of submission (3:1, 5, 22) and shows that Christians must be subject in three areas of life.

I. Submission in the Home (3:1-7)

A. The unsaved husband.

Peter here refers to a divided home. Since being married, the wife has come to trust Christ but the husband is not a believer. Peter describes how the wife can win her unsaved husband to the Lord.

B. The Christian wife.

She must be subject to her husband and show him honor and respect (Eph. 5:22; Col. 3:18). She must not nag or preach but live such a devoted life that her husband may be won to Christ "without a word," that is, apart from preaching and pleading. Unsaved loved ones watch our lives; if we point to Christ, we can win them.

Her behavior must be pure (chaste), and her attention must be drawn to the inner person and not to outward appearance. Peter is not forbidding women from wearing jewelry; what he is forbidding is going to worldly extremes just to be "fashionable." See 1 Tim. 2:9-12. "Plaiting the hair" (v. 3) means weaving the hair into conspicuous fashions, intertwining gold decorations, and so on. "Apparel" (v. 3) refers to decorative clothes in particular, those "extravagant extras" that call attention to themselves. Christian women can be attractive without being worldly. In fact, the outlandish fashions sported by much of the world would embarrass the devoted Christian woman and make it difficult for her to witness.

True beauty comes from within (v. 4). Peter used Sarah, Abraham's wife, as his example. She was a beautiful woman, for several kings tried to take her from her husband; yet she was devoted to the Lord and to her husband in the Lord. Gen. 18:12 states that she even called Abraham my "lord-master." She was not a slave, of course; rather, she was expressing her submission based on love. When a Christian is devoted to the Lord and to her husband, she need never fear what might happen, for God will rule and overrule. (The word "amazement" in v. 6 means "terror.") Of course, a Christian woman must never marry a man who is not worthy of her love and respect.

C. Living as a Christian husband.

"Likewise" (v. 7) indicates a similar attitude of love and respect on the part of the husband. Marriage is a partnership. Husbands must not remain ignorant but should grow in knowledge of the Lord and of the other partner. The husband must give honor to the wife. They are heirs together of the grace of life, suggesting that children are an inheritance of the Lord. If there is something wrong between Christian mates, their prayers will be hindered; trouble in the home will result. Peter assumes that they do not simply live together; they also pray together!

II. Submission under Suffering (3:8-14)

Verse 8 describes the mutual love of Christians in the church; contrast it with the turmoil found in James 4. In vv. 9-14, Peter deals with the Christian who suffers in the world. This is the day-by-day suffering that we endure, not the "fiery trial" of special suffering that appears later (4:12ff). How should Christians act when persecuted by the world?

A. They must be a blessing (v. 9).

Read Luke 6:22-28. We conquer hate by showing love. The best way to meet the slanderer and persecutor is with patience and grace. Let God do the rest!

B. They must keep clean (vv. 10-11).

He refers to Ps. 34:12-16. "He who wills to love life" is the best translation of v. 10. "Eschew" means "avoid," and "ensue" means "strive after."

C. They must remember that God is watching (vv. 12-14).

God sees the problems and He hears our cries. He knows how to deal with those who persecute us for His sake. Rather than complain, we should rejoice that we are suffering for His sake (Matt. 5:11-12; Acts 5:41).

III. Subjection to Christ (3:15-22)

"Sanctify Christ as Lord" is the best translation of v. 15. Put Him on the throne of your heart. If He controls our lives, then we will always have an answer when people ask about the hope we have in Him (Mark 13:11). A surrendered heart and a good conscience will together give peace when people accuse us falsely.

Sinners may accuse us, but God knows the heart; and we fear God, not men (Isa. 8:12-13). Again, Peter reminds them of the sufferings of Christ, that He was falsely accused yet left the matter with His Father.

The mystery of the "spirits in prison" (vv. 19-20) has perplexed students for years and not all interpreters agree on its meaning. Just keep in mind the main lesson of this passage: Christ suffered wrongly, but God honored Him and gave Him glory (v. 22). The rest of this passage describes mainly the good conscience of the believer toward God. As for the problems raised by other parts of the passage, several explanations have been given. Some suggest that Christ gave the dead in hell a second chance to be saved, but this is contrary to what is taught in the rest of the Bible. Others suggest that Peter is only saying that the same Holy Spirit who raised Christ from the dead (v. 18) preached through Noah, and that Christ, between His death and resurrection, visited the spirits of these lost people in prison (the world of the dead) and announced His victory. Why Jesus visited these men and not others is not explained.

One good explanation, however, is that the "spirits in prison" are the fallen angels of Gen. 6 who consorted with the daughters of men, "going after strange flesh" as Jude 6-7 explains it. The word "prison" in 3:19 refers to the place of judgment mentioned in 2 Peter 2:4, "chains of darkness." It was this violation of God's order that helped bring on the Flood, which explains why Peter mentions Noah. Note too that Peter's theme is the subjection of angels to Christ (v. 22). These fallen angels were not subject to Him, and therefore they were judged.

Between His death and resurrection, Christ visited these angels in prison and announced His victory over Satan. The word "preached" in 3:19 means "to announce" and not "to preach the Gospel." Jesus announced their doom and His victory over all angels and authorities. It is likely that at this time Christ "led captivity captive" (Eph. 4:8), rescued godly souls dwelling in Hades (see Luke 16:19-31), and took them to heaven. There is not one hint here of anybody having a second chance to be saved after death.

Peter then ties Noah to the subject of baptism. The flood was actually a global baptism of water; the world is now being reserved for a global baptism of fire (2 Peter 3:5-7). Peter does not say that baptism saves us or that water washes away sins. In fact, he makes it clear that baptism cannot put away the filth of the flesh. Submission to the Lord in baptism is an inward matter, the answer of a good conscience toward God. Baptism is a picture of death, burial, and resurrection. Christ's baptism in water by John the Baptist was a symbol of His baptism of suffering on the cross (Luke 3:21-22; 12:50). Christ Himself pointed to Jonah as the sign of His death, burial, and resurrection. The water that buried the wicked world bore Noah to safety. The water did not save him; the ark did. In this way Noah anticipates Christ's death, burial, and resurrection. Note too that Noah sent out a dove; and when Christ was baptized, a dove lit upon Him.

This is a complex passage, so keep the main lessons in mind: (1) Christ is Lord of all, and we must submit to Him; (2) a good conscience makes us strong in testing; (3) Christian baptism, pictured by the flood, illustrates death, burial, and resurrection but does not save the soul. Baptism is important because it indicates our submission to the Lord.

1 PETER 4

Chapters 4 and 5 deal with God's grace in suffering. Peter has already touched upon the everyday suffering that the Christian faces (e.g., reproach, accusations); but now he tells his readers that a "fiery trial" of official persecution is about to come upon them. In this chapter, he gives three wonderful and blessed benefits that can come to Christians when they go through suffering in the will of God.

I. Suffering Purifies the Saint (4:1-6)

When life is easy, we drift into carelessness and sin; but suffering changes our values and goals. The "fiery trial" is a furnace that purifies the gold and allows God to remove the dross (Ps. 66:10). Here is what suffering does for us:

A. It identifies us with Christ (v. 1).

He suffered for us that He might save us from sin. As we suffer for Him—and with Him—we learn to hate sin and love Him more. Peter encourages them to have "the mind of Christ" and to realize that their identification with Christ means victory over sin. This is Peter's version of Romans 6.

B. It reminds us that life is short (vv. 2-3).

We take life for granted until we have to suffer, and then our values change. How foolish for the Christian to waste "the rest of the time" by running with the world and sinning! There is a better way. Rather than live in the will of sinful men, we must live in the will of God.

C. It points ahead to God's judgment (vv. 4-6).

A Christian lives either according to the judgment of men or by the judgment of God. The world thinks it is strange that we no longer join them in sin, and they speak evil of us. But their evil-speaking does not upset us; God will judge them someday. They will give account to Him! Verse 6 may be paraphrased this way: "There are people now dead physically, but alive with God in the spirit, who were judged by the world. But they heard the Gospel before they died and they believed. They suffered and died because of their faith—but they are living with God! It is better to suffer for Christ and go to be with God than to follow the world and be lost." There is no connection between 4:6 and 3:19-20, nor is there any suggestion of a second chance for the lost after death.

It is important that Christians "arm themselves" with the same attitude toward the world, sin, and suffering that Jesus had while on earth. If we face suffering without a spiritual attitude, suffering will embitter us rather than purify us.

II. Suffering Unifies the Church (4:7-11)

Peter repeats the exhortation, "Be sober—serious-minded!" (See 1:13 and 5:8.) He reminds them that Christ is coming soon (5:4) and that, in the midst of suffering, saints have responsibilities to one another. Prayer is one of them; so is fervent love; the word "fervent" here means "stretched out." Christian love never reaches a breaking point! It is bad enough when the world accuses the saints; the saints ought not to accuse one another. Love will help cover the sins of the saints. Love does not cleanse sin, but it does cover sin in that we do not go around talking about other people's sins.

Peter exhorts these Christians to open their homes as well as their hearts. Christian hospitality is a forgotten blessing in the modern church, and we need to restore it.

Finally, Christians need to serve the Lord in spite of persecution, ministering their gifts as good stewards of God's many-sided (manifold) grace. "Manifold" also means "many-colored, variegated." God's grace can meet any need or match any "color" that might come to life! God gives us the gifts and the strength to use all things for His glory.

III. Suffering Glorifies the Lord (4:12-19)

A. Expect trials (v. 12).

Trials are not strangers to the Christian life; they are to be expected. Trials that are part of the will of God are not warnings that we are disobeying Him; they are God's tools for perfecting His own.

B. Rejoice in trials (vv. 13-14).

When trials come, we are suffering for His sake and sharing suffering with Him. See Phil. 1:29 and 3:10. The suffering we endure now is but a prelude to the glory that we will share at His coming. Furthermore, the Spirit of God "rests with refreshing power" (literal translation of v. 14) upon the suffering believer. When the three Hebrew children went into the fiery furnace, they had faith that God could deliver them (Dan. 3:19-30). He not only delivered them, but He walked with them.

C. Do not be ashamed in trials (vv. 15-16).

Roman law required each citizen to pledge his loyalty to the emperor. Once a year, the citizen would put a pinch of incense on the proper altar and say, "Caesar is Lord!" But the Christian confesses that "Jesus Christ is Lord!" (See 3:15.) Believers refused to bow before Caesar. Sometimes the Roman official would write the name of Christ on the ground or on a wall and ask the Christian to spit on it. If the Christian refused, he or she would be arrested, tried, and perhaps killed. By bearing the name of Christ (Christian), they were put to shame before their friends. But what a glorious name to bear! It is a name higher than any other.

D. Witness in trials (vv. 17-18).

If God sends trials to the church now, this is evidence that He will someday judge the lost. We have our trials now and our glory later; the lost have their glory now and their suffering later. The only heaven the lost sinner will know is on earth today! God begins His judgment at His house (the church); see Ezek. 9:6. If persecution for the name of Christ is but the beginning of trials, then what will happen when it comes time for the lost to be judged? The righteous (believers) are saved "with difficulty" (v. 18); what hope is there for the ungodly? See Prov. 11:31.

E. Commit yourself to God (v. 19).

The word for "commit" used here is a banking term; it refers to the act of leaving an amount on deposit for safekeeping. It ties in beautifully with the "gold" illustration in 1:7. God sends the fiery trial to burn away the dross, and we commit ourselves to Him for safekeeping, knowing that He cannot fail us. We can be sure that God will "pay interest" on our deposit. But note that we commit ourselves in doing good; that is, we commit ourselves to God as we obey His Word. This is a daily and hourly surrender, living to please Him and serving others.

Christians will go through fiery trials before Christ returns. The world situation will not get better. Attitudes toward Christians will not improve. The world has always hated the name of Christ and will continue to hate it. If we identify ourselves with the name of Christ, the world will hate us (John 15:18-21). If we compromise, we will escape persecution, but we will also miss the blessing and glory of sharing Christ's sufferings.

1 PETER 5

As he closes this letter of encouragement, Peter gives three exhortations to the saints. We see in this chapter several references to Peter's experiences in the Gospels as he walked with Christ. Peter witnessed Christ's sufferings (v. 1); he was commissioned to care for the sheep (v. 2, and see John 21:15-17); he saw Christ clothe Himself as a servant and humbly wash the disciples' feet (v. 5, and see John 13); and Peter knew what it was to be unprepared when Satan was on the prowl (v. 8, and see Mark 14:37). It is as though the Spirit of God searched Peter's memory and used these past experiences to testify to the saints (see v. 12). Peter discovered that God's grace was adequate for him, and he wanted the church to know that God's grace would sustain them as well.

I. Be Faithful (5:1-4)

The exhortation is addressed primarily to the pastors. The words "pastor" (shepherd), "bishop" (overseer), and "elder" (mature leader) all refer to the same office (Acts 20:17, 28; 1 Tim. 3:2; Titus 1:5-7). Peter did not put himself above others; rather, he called himself a "fellow elder" and deliberately included himself among the church leaders he was exhorting. There was a time when Peter would have worried about his position in the kingdom, but that time was past. Peter knew that the pastors would go through greater suffering as leaders of the people, so he encouraged them in two ways: (1) he reminded them that Christ had suffered for them and would sustain them; and (2) he reminded them that glory always follows suffering if we submit to the Lord. The two themes of suffering and glory are interwoven in 1 Peter.

A. Their ministry: "Shepherd the flock!"

Pastors' duties included feeding, leading, encouraging, discipling, guarding. The shepherd is to take the oversight and be the leader. Where would the flock be if the sheep led the shepherd or if every sheep were given his or her own way?

B. Their motive: "Not constraint, but consent."

The shepherd must serve the Lord with a willing heart because he loves Christ and the flock, and not simply because he has a job to do. He must never serve for "shameful gain" (v. 2), whether it be money, prestige, power, or promotion. He must be eager to work (of a ready mind), not listless or lazy.

C. Their manner: Leadership does not mean dictatorship.

Pastors are overseers, not overlords! "God's heritage" literally means "the portion assigned to you." All believers in a given locality are part of the church, but there are little flocks here and there under the direction of different elders. Nowhere is it suggested in the NT that all the churches in a town unite to form one church. There can be spiritual unity without organizational uniformity. Pastors should be examples, for, after all, the best way to get people to follow is to set the pace yourself! The pastor does not demand respect; he commands it by the godly life he lives and by his sacrificial service.

D. Their reward: In the future, not today.

There would be glory in heaven. Each undershepherd must submit to the Chief Shepherd, Jesus Christ. It is more important to please and glorify Him than anyone else.

II. Be Humble (5:5-7)

Verse 5 refers literally to the young people of the church, but we may apply it to all members as they follow their spiritual leaders (Heb. 13:17). Peter refers here to that evening in the Upper Room when Jesus washed the disciples' feet. To be "clothed with humility" (v. 5) means to be controlled by a humble spirit, to be a servant. God resists arrogant, self-seeking persons but gives grace to the humble (Prov. 3:34; James 4:6). "Be humbled under the mighty hand of God!" he exhorts. "Allow this time of suffering to bring you low before Him, and then He will exalt you when He sees you are ready." The wonderful promise "He cares for you" (NKJV) reminds us of the night in the boat when the disciples asked Jesus, "Do You not care that we are perishing?" (see Mark 4:38, NKJV) Of course, Jesus cares! Satan would have these Christians believe that their "fiery trial" was an evidence of God's indifference; but Peter reminds them that they may "cast the whole of their care" (v. 7) once and for all upon Christ.

III. Be Watchful (5:8-11)

Who better than Peter would know about the prowlings of Satan! Several times Jesus warned Peter that Satan was after him, but he failed to heed the warning. Too many Christians have "gone to sleep," opening the way for Satan to work (Matt. 13:25, 39).

Satan is an "adversary," which means "one who accuses at court." The word "devil" means "a slanderer." Satan accuses us before God (Job 1–2; Zech. 3:1-5; Rev. 12:10), and he uses the lips of unsaved people to accuse us falsely (1 Peter 2:12; 3:16; 4:4, 14). Satan comes either as a serpent to deceive (Gen. 3) or as a lion to devour. He is a liar and a murderer (John 8:44).

What can Christians do to defeat Satan? (1) Be alert! We must keep our eyes open and not relax our guard. When David relaxed and left the battle, he fell into sin (2 Sam. 11). When Peter felt self-confident, he went to sleep and fell into Satan's trap. (2) Resist! This word calls to mind an army, standing together to oppose the enemy. Christians must be united against Satan (Phil. 1:27-30). If there is a break in the ranks, Satan has an opportunity to attack. (3) Believe! We resist him in the faith, that is, trusting in the victory of Christ. Satan uses lies as his chief weapon, and the believer must counteract Satan's lies with God's truth. Jesus used the sword of the Spirit in the wilderness (Matt. 4). (4) Remember! Remember that other Christians are going through the same trials and that you are not alone. If Satan can get us to feel that we are alone, that God has singled us out, then he will discourage and defeat us.

Peter's theme has been grace (5:12), so he closes by reminding the saints that their God is the God of all grace! The Christian goes "from grace to grace" (John 1:16). The Christian life begins with saving grace (Eph. 2:8-10). It continues with serving grace (1 Cor. 15:9-10); then sanctifying grace (Rom. 5:17; 6:17). God also gives sacrificing grace (2 Cor. 8:1-9), singing grace (Col. 3:16), speaking grace (Col. 4:6), strengthening grace (2 Tim. 2:1), and suffering grace (2 Cor. 12:9). "He gives more grace" (James 4:6, NKJV).

Verse 10 indicates that grace is provided through the disciplines of life. God allows us to suffer that He might be able to shed His grace upon us. When we suffer, we come to the end of ourselves and learn to lean on Him. Grace is supplied only to those who sense their need for Him. First we suffer; then, as we suffer, He equips us, confirms us, and puts a foundation under us. The words "make you perfect" (v. 10) are used in Matt. 4:21 and carry the image of mending a net. The Gk. word means "to equip for service." Suffering not only helps the believer grow, but it also equips him for future service. Sometimes the best way God has of "mending our nets" is to put us through suffering.

In his conclusion (5:12-14), Peter indicates that Silas and Mark are with him. Silas was one of Paul's associates (Acts 15:22ff); but if, as we have surmised, Paul was not in Rome, it would be expected that Peter and Silas would work together. John Mark's presence indicates that the "old disagreement" involving Barnabas, Mark, and Silas was forgiven and forgotten. "Babylon" (v. 13) probably is a code name for Rome; although, some students think that Peter was writing from ancient Babylon.

2 PETER 1

The key word in 2 Peter is "knowledge," and the danger Peter writes about is false teaching. In 1 Peter, Satan is described as a roaring lion, for Peter's theme is the fiery persecution that was about to come to the saints. But in 2 Peter, Satan is a serpent seeking to deceive (see John 8:44-45). False teaching from within the church is far more dangerous than persecution from without (see Acts 20:28-32). Persecution has always cleansed and strengthened the church; false teaching weakens the church and ruins its testimony. The only weapon to fight false teaching and the devil's lies is the Word of God, which is why Peter emphasizes spiritual knowledge.

I. The Gift of Knowledge (1:1-4)

Salvation is a personal experience; one comes to know Jesus Christ through faith. Note Christ's definition of salvation in John 17:3. It is not enough simply to know about Christ; we must know Him personally (Phil. 3:10). When we put our faith in Him, He gives us His righteousness (2 Cor. 5:21), and He becomes our Savior. It is a personal experience.

Peter emphasizes the Word of God in this letter. God has given us His Word, this "precious faith" and the "precious promises" of God, that we might live godly lives. As he penned these words, Peter must have thought of his testimony in John 6:68—"Lord, to whom shall we go? You have the words of eternal life!" (NKJV) In the Bible, we have all that we need for life and godliness. While the writings of teachers and preachers can help us better understand the Bible, only the Bible can impart life to our souls.

Note the definition of a Christian in v. 4—"partaker of the divine nature." The Christian has been born into God's family and has God's nature within. People who try to live "like Christ" on the outside, but lack this divine nature on the inside, are deceived and defeated. Contrast 2 Peter 2:20-22, where we find a description of false Christians: (1) They have escaped the pollutions of the world, not the corruptions; that is, they have been washed on the outside, and have not been changed on the inside. (2) They have a "head knowledge" of Christ and not a heart faith. (3) They are not truly saved, for they go back to the old life after professing faith for awhile. These false Christians are "dogs" and "pigs" that have been washed (reformed), but they have never received the new nature.

II. The Growth in Knowledge (1:5-11)

"And beside this" (v. 5) indicates that there is something beyond the new birth; there is growth. It is not enough to be born into God's family; we must also grow spiritually. This demands diligence and earnestness; a lazy, careless Christian does not grow. Peter then lists the spiritual characteristics that ought to be seen in the believer's life. He is not suggesting that we "add" these virtues the way we add beads to a string. Rather, each virtue helps us develop the next one. They are like the sections of a telescope: one leads into the other.

We add to faith (saving faith) virtue, or praise. We have been saved to advertise God's virtues (1 Peter 2:9). The only way to prove our faith is by living a life of virtue. We add to virtue knowledge, or moral discernment. Christians must be able to discern right from wrong. After knowledge comes temperance, or self-control. Self-control leads to patience, or endurance. This is the "staying power" of the Christian in times of trial. We add to patience godliness; see v. 3. This word means "right worship" or a dependence on God that reveals itself in a devoted life. Brotherly kindness is the next virtue, meaning a love for the people of God. The final virtue Peter names is charity, or love, which "wraps" all the virtues together into one.

You can usually tell when Christians are not growing, for they have these three characteristics: (1) They are barren, or idle; that is, they will not work for Christ. (2) They are unfruitful; that is, their meager knowledge of Christ does not produce fruit in their lives. (3) They are blind, lacking spiritual insight, spiritually "nearsighted." Behind this lack of spiritual development is a poor memory, forgetting what God has done for them through Christ. Yet Peter himself had once been forgetful; "And Peter remembered the word of the Lord" (Luke 22:61). So, for the second time, Peter says, "Be diligent!" Be sure you are saved! The Christian does not save himself or keep himself saved; but it is his responsibility to be sure he has the marks of a true believer (1 Thes. 1:4-5). This will assure us a "richly supplied entrance" (v. 11) into God's kingdom; this is far better than being saved "so as by fire" (1 Cor. 3:15).

III. The Ground of Knowledge (1:12-21)

"But how can we be sure that this message is the true Word of God?" Peter answers this question by referring to his experience with Christ on the Mount of Transfiguration (Matt. 17:1-13; Luke 9:27-36). Peter knew that he would not be in the body (his tabernacle) very long; see John 21:18. The word "decease" (v. 15) is actually "exodus"; it is the same word used of Christ's death (Luke 9:31). When Christians die, it is not the end; rather, it is a triumphant exodus from this world into the next.

The Gospel message is not a fable that men devised to deceive others. It is based on the historical truth of the death, burial, and resurrection of Christ. Peter refers to the return of Christ in glory, an event that was foreshadowed in the Transfiguration. On the mountain, Christ revealed His glory, as He will when He returns to earth. Moses and Elijah were there, representing believers who died (Moses) and believers who were caught away at the rapture without dying (Elijah). See 1 Thes. 4:13-18. The disciples represent the believing Jews who will see Christ's glory when He returns.

Keep in mind that Peter's ministry had been primarily to Israel (Gal. 2:7-8), while Paul's had been to the Gentiles. The question had been raised, "What about God's promises to the Jews of a glorious kingdom on earth?" The Word of prophecy has not been abandoned; instead, it has been made more sure. Peter is saying, "We have Christ's Transfiguration to assure us that the kingdom will come; but we also have the sure Word of prophecy that has been verified by the Transfiguration." Christians are not to "spiritualize" the OT prophecies and apply them to the church. We must interpret them literally, just as we do the NT Word, because God will fulfill them one day.

Peter compares the prophetic Word to a light shining in a dark (squalid) place. The world, to him, is a dark and murky dungeon. The Word of God is the only dependable light we have in this world. We must heed this Word and not lean on the ideas of men. One day soon, Christ, the Day Star, will arise and take His people home. To the church, Christ is the Day Star that appears when things are the darkest, just before the dawn. To Israel, Christ is the Sun of Righteousness who comes with judgment and healing (Mal. 4).

Verses 20-21 do not teach that it is wrong for Christians to read and interpret the Bible; the Word was given to us to be read, obeyed, and passed on to others. "Private" (v. 20) means "by itself." No passage of Scripture is to be interpreted "by itself," that is, apart from the rest of the Word of God or apart from the Holy Spirit who gave it. Prophecy did not come by the will of men, so it cannot be interpreted by the natural mind. The Spirit gave the Word, and the Spirit must teach us the Word (1 Cor. 2:9-16; John 14:26; 16:13-14).

We thank God that our Bible is sure! We can trust it because God gave it to us.

2 PETER 2

This is a complex chapter, and we should compare it to Jude's epistle where some of these same phrases are used. The danger of false teachers is so great that the Holy Spirit used both Peter and Jude to warn us, so we had better pay attention.

Please keep in mind that a false teacher is not a person who teaches false doctrine out of ignorance. In Acts 18:24-28, Apollos taught mistakenly the message and the baptism of John, but he was not a false teacher. Many of the great leaders of the church in centuries past have held interpretations of minor matters that we may not believe are biblical; still, we cannot call them false teachers. False teachers are professed believers who know the truth but who deliberately teach lies in the hope of promoting themselves and getting financial gain from their followers (2:3, 14). They are able to live in sin to please themselves (2:10, 13-14, 18-19). They use deceptive means (2:1, 3) and twist the Word of God to suit their fancies.

I. Their Condemnation (2:1-9)

Peter opens this section by declaring that false teachers are bound to appear but will ultimately be condemned by God. Verse 1 summarizes the methods of the false teachers: (1) they appear among the people as members of the church; (2) they work secretly, under cover of hypocrisy, pretending to be what they are not; (3) they bring in their false teachings alongside the true doctrine, and then replace the truth with their lies; (4) their lives deny what their lips teach. In other words, "heresy" is not simply false doctrine; it is false living based on false doctrine. "Wolves in sheep's clothing" is the way our Lord pictured them (Matt. 7:15; and see 2 Cor. 4:1-2; 11:13). Unfortunately, the false teaching will be more popular than the true way (v. 2); but then, Jesus said that the leaven of false doctrine would permeate the whole lump (Matt. 13:33). People will choose to follow the false teachers because they exalt themselves rather than Christ, and many people love to worship popular and successful people. Also, the false way makes it easy to live in sin while pretending to practice a religious life.

"Feigned words" in 2:3 means "counterfeit words" or "manufactured, fabricated words." The Gk. word is *plastos,* from which we get the English word "plastic." These false teachers depart from the Spirit-given words of the Bible (1 Cor. 2:9-16) and manufacture their own words to fit their own doctrines. They take familiar Bible words and manufacture new meanings for them. They use our vocabulary but empty these words of spiritual meaning. It is not what a teacher says, but what he or she means, that counts.

These false teachers will be destroyed, and Peter cites three OT

examples to prove it: the angels that sinned and are now imprisoned in Tartarus (which is the meaning of the word translated
"hell"); the world before the flood; and the cities of Sodom and
Gomorrah. In each of these cases, the persons involved had a form
of religion but not the true faith that empowers the life (2 Tim.
3:5). Before Christ comes back, there will be a great deal of "religion" in the world, but it will not be true faith in Him. Peter also
points out that God is able to preserve and deliver His true saints,
as He did with Noah and his ɟamily, and Lot. Noah is a symbol of
the believing Jews who will be preserved through the Tribulation;
Lot stands for the church saints who will be "caught away" before
the destruction begins. These false teachers may seem to be successful and protected, but one of these days God will destroy them.

II. Their Character (2:10-16)

A. Pride (vv. 10-11).

They despise any kind of dominion or authority. God has established the "dominions" in this world—human government, headship in the home, leadership in the church, and so on. But false
teachers want to run things their own way and reject God's order.
Even the angels do not despise God-given authorities; see Jude 8-9.

B. Ignorance (v. 12).

The false teachers are willfully blind to what the Bible teaches (see
2 Peter 3:5). They call evangelical Christians "uneducated" and
biblical theology "old-fashioned"!

C. Lust (vv. 13-14).

Wrong doctrine and wrong living go together. False teachers live in
luxury and "beguile" (catch with bait) unstable people who are
enticed into their teachings. It is tragic the way the name of Christ
has been disgraced (v. 2) by "religious leaders" who live in sin
while attempting to help others find the Lord.

D. Covetousness (vv. 15-16).

Verse 3 points out that false teachers use counterfeit words to
exploit the people; and v. 18 says they use "great swelling words."
Unfortunately, there are many unstable people who delight in following these religious "windbags," not realizing that these teachers
are picking their pockets while they poison their lives. Peter cites

Balaam as an example (Num. 22–25). He was a prophet who used his gifts to make money and lead Israel into sin.

III. Their Claims (2:17-22)

They promise their followers satisfaction but do not quench their spiritual thirst. How useless are wells without water! These teachers, with their great swelling words (religious propaganda), give the appearance of being truthful and helpful, but they turn out to be clouds driven by the wind—beautiful, but of no help to thirsty people. Millions today are following false religions that promise help but can give none.

False teachers promise liberty but lead people into bondage. Peter uses a bit of sarcasm here; how can people who are slaves of sin themselves ever set anybody else free! In v. 12, he called these teachers "brute beasts"; and now he clearly names them as pigs and dogs! Please keep in mind that Peter in vv. 20-21 is not talking about somebody "losing salvation," for that would contradict what he wrote in 1 Peter 1:3-5. In 1 Peter 2:25, Peter compares Christians to sheep, not to dogs or pigs. The Christian has received the new nature (2 Peter 1:4) and has been set free from the corruption of the world. You do not have to worry about a sheep eating vomit or wallowing in filth, because a sheep is a clean animal.

Peter is describing false Christians, people who merely wash off the pollutants on the outside (this is "religious" reformation), but never receive the new nature on the inside. You can wash a dog or a pig, but the animal does not change its basic nature. These people knew the way of righteousness and had a knowledge of Christ's work, but they did not personally receive Him into their hearts. Their outward pollution was washed away, but the inward corruption was still there. These "professors but not possessors" seemed to experience salvation, but in due time they drifted back to the life that suited their nature. Dogs go back to the vomit; pigs go back to the mire. See Prov. 26:11.

We live in a day of false teachers. We may detect them by their exaltation of themselves instead of Christ; their counterfeit talk and "great swelling words"; their emphasis on making money; their great claims that they can change people; and their hidden lives of lust and sin. For the time being we cannot stop them except by teaching the Word sincerely, but one day God will expose them and judge them.

2 PETER 3

This chapter reveals Peter as the loving pastor, caring for his lambs and sheep. He uses the word "beloved" four times and each time gives a solemn admonition.

I. Beloved . . . Be Mindful! (3:1-7)

"Remembrance" has been a key theme in this letter (see 1:12-15). Peter himself had been guilty of forgetting (Luke 22:61), so his admonition was meaningful. He wanted them to have "sincere" minds; that is, minds not confused by the false doctrines named in chapter 2. He points them back to the OT prophets and the NT apostles — the entire Word of God. See 1:19-21.

The doctrine Peter is defending is the return of Christ to the earth to set up His kingdom, and then, after 1,000 years, to usher in the new heavens and earth. Peter is not referring to the rapture of the church, that is, the secret return of Christ in the air (1 Thes. 4:13-18). Of course, the world scoffs at the idea of the return of Christ (Jude 18) and cannot see that all of history is moving in that direction. "All things continue as they were" is the argument we hear from the world's thinkers. "God is not going to break into history and interrupt the progress of time!"

But Peter cites OT examples to prove that God does break into history. He begins with the created world in Gen. 1 (v. 5), made by the Word of God. He then introduces the Flood (Gen. 6) and the world that was judged by God (v. 6). Verse 7 indicates that the world now "is stored with fire" and already prepared for judgment. This may suggest the release of atomic power. If we relate v. 6 to the Flood, we have the same argument: God does judge sin at a time when men are confident that nothing is going to happen.

II. Beloved . . . Be Not Ignorant! (3:8-11)

People view history in terms of days and years, but to God, time is always present tense. A thousand years are but a day to Him (Ps. 90:4). But God will not be tardy (slack); when the right time arrives, He will act and fulfill His Word. Why is He delaying His judgment, the awful Day of the Lord? Because He wants sinners to come to Christ and be saved from the coming wrath.

"The Day of the Lord" is that period of judgment also known as the Great Tribulation. It will come upon the whole earth after the church has been raptured to heaven (Rev. 3:10; 1 Thes. 5:8-9). A thief comes suddenly, when he is least expected (Matt. 24:43; Luke 12:39; 1 Thes. 5:2; Rev. 3:3; 16:15). When the world says "peace and safety," then judgment will fall (1 Thes. 5:3). God's people will not be caught unprepared when Christ comes to take them to heaven, but the world will be surprised by the judgments that follow.

III. Beloved . . . Be Diligent! (3:11-14)

This is the third time Peter has mentioned diligence (1:5, 10). In these last days, believers must be on guard. In view of what God has planned for this world, how should Christians live?

We are not looking for peace or hope in this world. We are looking for the new heavens and the new earth that God creates and over which Jesus Christ will reign (Rev. 21:1ff). This blessed assurance helps us to keep clean and to be faithful to do our work until Jesus comes.

IV. Beloved . . . Beware! (3:15-18)

Peter explains the seeming delay in God's program and refers us to Paul's letters for the details. Note that Peter calls Paul's letters "Scripture." Why has Jesus not returned to establish His kingdom? Because He is today building His church, a thing not mentioned in the OT Scripture prophecies. This delay means salvation for believing Jews and Gentiles. Those who do not understand God's program twist the Scriptures and mix OT prophecy with church truth, ending up with confusion.

How do we keep from falling? By growing and building ourselves up in the Lord (Jude 24-25). "Baby Christians" who will not feed on the Word (1 Peter 2:2) and grow in the Lord are unstable. In this wicked world, Christians must take time to feed on the Word, pray, and exercise their spiritual muscles.

The theme of 1 Peter was grace; the theme of 2 Peter was knowledge; Peter sums up both books by admonishing us to grow in grace and in knowledge. This knowledge is not merely that of the Bible; it is knowledge of Christ through the Bible. We must come to know Him better (Phil. 3:10). It is possible, unfortunately, to grow in knowledge (have Bible truth in our heads) and never grow in grace (show Bible truth in our lives). Peter wants us to have balanced lives: we should learn *and* live the Word.

1 JOHN

A Suggested Outline of 1 John

Introduction: The reality of Jesus Christ (1:1-4)

I. The Tests of Fellowship: God is Light (1:5–2:29)

   A. The test of obedience (1:5–2:6)
   B. The test of love (2:7-17)
   C. The test of truth (2:18-29)

II. The Tests of Sonship: God Is Love (3–5)

   A. The test of obedience (3:1-24)
   B. The test of love (4:1-21)
   C. The test of truth (5:1-21)

First John is built around the repetition of the three main themes: light vs. darkness, love vs. hatred, and truth vs. error. These three "strands" weave in and out of the letter, making it difficult to construct a simple outline. The above outline is based on the main lessons of each section, although the careful student will see that the three themes intermingle. In these days when many Christians think they have fellowship with God but do not, and when many religious people think they are true sons of God but are not, it is important that we apply these tests and examine our own lives carefully.

Introductory Notes to 1 John

I. Author

The Spirit used the Apostle John to give us the Gospel of John, three epistles, and the Book of the Revelation. These three works complement each other and give to us a full picture of the Christian life.

The Gospel of John	The Epistles of John	The Revelation of John
Emphasis on salvation	Emphasis on sanctification	Emphasis on glorification
Past history	Present experience	Future hope
Christ died for us	Christ lives in us	Christ comes for us
The Word made flesh	The Word made real in us	The Word conquering

II. Aim

John stated five purposes for the writing of his first epistle:

A. That we might have fellowship (1:3).

"Fellowship" is the key theme of the first two chapters (see 1:3, 6-7). Fellowship has to do with our communion with Christ, not our union with Christ, which is sonship. Our daily fellowship changes; our sonship remains the same.

B. That we might have joy (1:4).

The word "joy" is used only here, but the blessing of joy is seen throughout the entire letter. Joy is the result of a close fellowship with Christ.

C. That we might not sin (2:1-2).

The penalty of sin is taken care of when the sinner trusts Christ, but the power of sin over the daily life is another matter. First John explains how we may have victory over sin and how to get forgiveness when we do sin.

D. That we might overcome error (2:26).

John was facing the false teaching of his day just as we face false teachers today (2 Peter 2). The false teachers in John's day were claiming: (1) that matter was evil, therefore Christ did not come in the flesh; (2) that Christ only appeared to be a real man; (3) that knowledge of truth is more important than living the truth; and (4) that only a "spiritual few" could understand spiritual truths. As you read 1 John, you will see that John emphasizes: (1) that matter is not evil, but man's nature is sinful; (2) that Jesus Christ had a real body and experienced a real death; (3) that it is not enough "to say" what we believe, we must practice it; and (4) all Christians have an unction from God and can know His truth.

E. That we might have assurance (5:13).

In his Gospel, John tells us how to be saved (John 20:31), but in this epistle, he tells us how to be sure we are saved. The letter is a series of "tests" that Christians may use to examine their fellowship (chaps. 1–2) and their sonship (chaps. 3–5). Note that the emphasis in chapters 3–5 is on being born of God (3:9; 4:7; 5:1, 4, 18).

III. Analysis

Study the suggested outline and you will see that the letter falls into two divisions: chapters 1–2 emphasize fellowship, and chapters 3–5 emphasize sonship. In each of these sections, John gives three basic "tests": obedience (walking in the light), love (walking in love), and truth (walking in the truth). In other words, I can know I am in fellowship with God through Christ if I have no known sin in my life, if I have love for Him and His people, and if I believe and practice the truth and not some satanic lie. Furthermore, I can know that I am a son of God in the same way: if I am obeying His Word; if I have love for Him and His people; and if I believe and live the truth. John asks us to apply these tests, that we might enjoy the Christian life to the fullest.

IV. Study

I recommend that you also read 1 John in a modern translation, preferably *The New Testament*, translated by Charles Williams (Moody Press). The Gk. verbs are important in this letter, and the *Authorized Version* sometimes does not bring their meaning out in their fullest. First John 3:9, to be discussed later, is a case in point.

1 JOHN 1–2

These two chapters deal with fellowship, and in them, John gives us the three tests of true fellowship. Note the contrast between saying and doing: "If we say . . . " (1:6, 8, 10; 2:4, 6). Too many times we are better at the "talk" than we are at the "walk"! In 1:1-4, John introduces his theme: Christ the Word who has revealed the Father. (See 1:1-14.) He explains that when Christ was here on earth, He was a real Person, not a phantom, and that He had a real body (Luke 24:39). The false teachers of John's day were denying that Jesus had come in the flesh. If we do not have a real Christ, how can we have real forgiveness of sin? John is being a witness by telling what he had seen and heard (Acts 4:20). He explains that Christ was manifested to reveal God and to make possible our fellowship with Him. See also 3:5, 8, and 4:9 for other reasons why Christ came.

I. The Test of Obedience (1:5–2:6)

John introduces us to the image of light (John 1:4). God is light, and Satan is the prince of darkness (Luke 22:53). To obey Him is to walk in the light; to disobey is to walk in darkness. Keep in mind that fellowship is a matter of light and darkness; sonship is a matter of life and death (3:4; 5:11-12). John points out that it is possible for people to say they are in the light, yet actually live in darkness. Note the four "liars" here: (1) lying about fellowship, 1:6-7; (2) lying about our nature, saying that we have no sin, 1:8; (3) lying about our deeds, saying that we have not sinned, 1:10; and (4) lying about our obedience, saying that we have kept His commandments when we have not, 2:4-6.

Christians do sin, but this does not mean they must be saved all over again. Sin in the life of the believer breaks the fellowship but does not destroy the sonship. A true Christian is always accepted even if he is not acceptable. How does God provide for the sins of the saints? Through the heavenly ministry of Christ. We are saved from the penalty of sin by His death (Rom. 5:6-9), and we are saved daily from the power of sin by His life (Rom. 5:10). The word "advocate" means "one who pleads a case" and is the same Gk. word as "Comforter" in John 14:16. The Holy Spirit represents Christ to us on earth, and the Son represents us to God in heaven. His wounds testify that He died for us, and therefore God can forgive when we confess our sins. Read carefully Rom. 8:31-34. The word "confess" means "to say the same thing." To confess sin means to say the same thing about it that God says. Keep in mind that Christians do not have to do penance, make sacrifices, or punish themselves when they have sinned. Every sin has already been taken care of at the cross. Does this give us license to sin? Of course not! The Christian who truly understands God's provision for a life of holiness does not want to deliberately disobey God.

II. The Test of Love (2:7-17)

A. The new commandment (vv. 7-11).

See John 13:34. When we are in fellowship with God, walking in the light, we also walk in love. It is a basic spiritual principle that when Christians are out of fellowship with God, they cannot get along with God's people. We are all members of God's family, so we ought to love one another. This was even an "old commandment" back in the days of Moses (Lev. 19:18).

B. The new family (vv. 12-14).

Like a loving father, John calls the saints "little children"; all of God's children have been forgiven. But we ought to grow in the Lord, becoming strong young men and women in the faith and ultimately spiritual "fathers and mothers."

C. The new danger (vv. 15-17).

There is conflict between love for the Father and love for the world. By "the world" John means all that belongs to this life that is opposed to Christ. It is Satan's system, society opposed to God and taking the place of God. If we love the world, we lose the love of the Father and cease to do His will. Anything in our lives that dulls our love for spiritual things or that makes it easy for us to sin is worldly and must be put away. John mentions three specific problems: the desires of the flesh, the desires of the eyes, and the pride of life. Is this not what the people of the world live for? But living for the world means losing everything in time, because the world is passing away. Lot suffered such loss. But if we live for God, we will abide forever.

There can be no true fellowship without love. Unless we love God and God's children, we cannot walk in the light and fellowship with God.

III. The Test of Truth (2:18-29)

God reveals Himself to us in His Word, which is the Truth (John 17:17); thus we cannot believe lies and have fellowship with God. John warns about the anti-Christian teachers already in the world, and he tells us how to recognize them: (1) they have left the fellowship of the truth, v. 19; (2) they deny that Jesus Christ is the Son of God come in the flesh, v. 22; (3) they try to seduce believers, v. 26. John agrees with what Peter describes (2 Peter 2): that these false teachers once were in the church, but then departed from the truth they professed to believe.

Here is where the Holy Spirit comes in: He is our heavenly unction (anointing) who teaches us the truth. The Spirit of God uses the inspired Word of God to communicate God's truth to us. "You know all things" in v. 20 (NKJV) should read "and you all know." Verse 27 should not be taken to mean that Christians have no need for pastors and teachers, otherwise Eph. 4:8-16 would not be in the NT. Rather, he is saying that believers must be Spirit-taught personally through the Word and should not always depend on human teachers. The Christian in fellowship with God will read and understand the Bible and be taught by the Spirit.

In vv. 28-29, John suggests (as Peter also taught) that false doctrine and false living go together. If we believe the truth with our hearts and commit ourselves to it, then we will live holy lives before men. Of course, one of the greatest incentives to holy living is the imminent coming of Jesus Christ. How tragic that some Christians who have not been abiding (fellowshipping) with Christ will be ashamed when He returns.

While there are many details in these chapters that we have had to overlook, the main lesson is clear: If Christians desire to have fellowship with Christ, they must obey the Word, love God's people, and believe the truth. Whenever sin enters, the Christian must immediately confess it and claim God's forgiveness. We must spend time in the Word, learning the truth and letting the truth take hold of the inner person. Or, to look at it negatively, the Christian who deliberately disobeys the Word, neglects the Word, and who cannot get along with God's people is out of fellowship with God and in the dark. It is not enough to talk about the Christian life; we must practice it.

"Propitiation" (2:2 and 4:10) has to do with the meaning of Christ's death from God's perspective. Christ's death brought forgiveness; but before God could forgive a guilty sinner, His justice had to be satisfied. This is where propitiation comes in. The word carries the idea of satisfying God's holiness through the death of a substitute. It does not mean that God was so angry that Christ had to die to make Him love sinners. Christ's death met the demands of God's law and thus broke down the barrier between men and God, making it possible for God to take away sin. The word "mercy seat" in Heb. 9:5 is equivalent to "propitiation." See Ex. 25:17-22. The blood on the mercy seat covered the broken law and made it possible for God to deal with Israel.

1 JOHN 3

We move now into the second half of the letter, which deals with sonship. The word "fellowship" is not found in this section at all. Instead, John emphasizes being "born of God" (see 3:9; 4:7; 5:4). This passage ties in with John 3 and emphasizes the theme "God is love" (4:8, 16). In this chapter, John states that a true child of God will prove his spiritual birth by being obedient to God's Word. He gives five motives for obedience:

I. God's Wonderful Love (3:1)

"Behold, what foreign-kind of love" is literally what John writes. Paul had this idea in mind when he wrote Rom. 5:6-10. Love is the greatest motive in the world, and if we understand God's love, we will obey His Word. "If you love me, keep My commandments" (John 14:15). Of course, the world has no understanding of this love, and the world hates us. But the world does not know Christ, so it cannot know Christ's own.

II. Christ's Promised Return (3:2-3)

What we are now is wonderful; but what we shall be is even more wonderful! "We shall be like Him." This means inheriting a glorified body like His body (Phil. 3:20-21) and sharing in His eternal glory (John 17:24). But the saint who really expects Christ to return will obey His Word and keep his life clean. We shall see Him "as He is," but we must also "walk as He walked" (see 2:6) and "be righteous even as He is" (3:7). Saints are expected to purify themselves, that is, keep their hearts clean (2 Cor. 7:1).

III. Christ's Death on the Cross (3:4-8)

John gives several reasons why Christ was made manifest: (1) to reveal the Father and enable us to fellowship with Him, 1:2-3; (2) to take away our sins, 3:4-5; (3) to destroy (annul) the works of the devil, 3:8; and (4) to reveal God's love and bestow God's life, 4:9. The fact that sin resulted in Christ's suffering and death ought to be reason enough for the Christian to hate sin and flee from it. John defines sin as transgressing the law. The Christian who abides in Christ (this is the fellowship of chaps. 1–2) will not deliberately break God's law. Every Christian sins, perhaps without knowing it (Ps. 19:12); but no true Christian will deliberately and repeatedly defy God's Word and disobey Him. Verse 6 ought to read, "Whosoever abides in Him does not habitually sin." Ephesians 2:1-3 makes it clear that the unsaved sin constantly because they live in the flesh and for the devil. But the Christian has a new nature within and is no longer Satan's slave.

IV. The New Nature Within (3:9-18)

The key thought of chapters 3–5 is "sonship," which results in a new nature within the believer. God does not destroy or eradicate the old nature; rather, He implants a new nature that gives the believer a desire for spiritual things. Verse 9 should say, "Whosoever is born of God does not habitually, deliberately sin; for he has the seed of the new nature within." This new nature cannot sin. Of course, believers who yield to the old nature will stumble and fall. See Gal. 6:1-2.

John contrasts the children of God and the children of the devil, using Cain and Abel as examples. Abel had faith and was accepted; Cain tried to be saved by works but was not accepted (Gen. 4). Cain was a liar and a murderer, like the devil (John 8:44); he murdered his brother, then lied about it to God. Genesis 3:15 states that Satan's seed (children) will oppose God's seed. Note Matt. 3:7 and 23:33. This will finally culminate in Christ's battle with the Antichrist in the last days. But please note that Satan's children are "religious." Cain worshiped at an altar, and the Pharisees were the most religious people of their day. Not religion, but a true love for God and God's children, should be the test of our devotion to God. True Christians do not hate and murder; instead, they show love and try to help others. The new nature that is implanted at the new birth is responsible for this change.

V. The Witness of the Spirit (3:19-24)

True Christianity is a matter of the heart, not the tongue. We have the witness of the Spirit in our hearts that we are God's children (Rom. 8:14-16). Of course, v. 19 should be tied in with 2:28. When Christ returns, the believers with assurance in their hearts will not be ashamed.

Christians need to cultivate assurance. "Make your calling and election sure" is what Peter wrote (2 Peter 1:10). Verse 19 assures us that as we sincerely love the brethren, we belong to the truth and are saved (see also 3:14). Unsaved people may like some Christians because of their personable qualities, but only a born-again Christian loves even a total stranger when he or she discovers the stranger is a Christian. This is the message of Rom. 5:5. Sadly, our hearts (consciences) do condemn us because we know we have not always loved the brethren as we should. But John helps us by pointing away from our feelings to the God who knows us. Thank God salvation and assurance are not based on the feelings of the heart!

Verse 21 promises that the Christian with an assured heart can pray with boldness (confidence). If there is sin in our hearts, then we cannot pray with confidence (Ps. 66:18-19). But the Holy Spirit within convicts me of this sin, and I may confess it and get back into fellowship with the Father. What a tremendous revelation: whenever a Christian is out of fellowship with another Christian, he or she cannot pray as one should. Read 1 Peter 3:1-7 to see how this applies in the Christian home. The secret of answered prayer is obeying God and seeking to please Him. By doing so we abide in Him, and when we abide in Him, we may pray with power (John 15:7).

Faith and love go together (v. 23). If we trust God, we love one another. We love the saints because we are all one in Christ and because we seek to please the Father. How happy earthly parents are when their children love one another! The indwelling Holy Spirit yearns to unite all believers in a wonderful fellowship of love, the kind of spiritual unity Christ prayed for in John 17:20-21.

God abides in us by His Spirit; we ought to abide in Him by yielding to the Spirit and obeying the Word. People who claim to be born of God, but who repeatedly disobey the Word and have no desire to please God, ought to examine themselves to see if they are really born of God.

1 JOHN 4

You have noticed that John repeats himself. The themes of light, love, and truth are interwoven throughout this brief letter. Chapter 4 states that those who are born of God prove it by their love. In this chapter, John uses the same motives for love as he did for obedience in chapter 3. True believers will have love for one another for these reasons.

I. We Have a New Nature (4:1-8)

John begins with a warning about the false spirits in the world. Keep in mind that the NT was not yet completed and what had been written was not widely known; until the completion of the NT, the local churches depended on the ministry of people with spiritual gifts to teach them truth. How could a believer know when a preacher was from God and that his message could be trusted? (See 1 Thes. 5:19-21.) After all, Satan is an imitator. John states that the false spirits will not confess that Jesus is the Christ (see 1 Cor. 12:3). The false cults today deny the deity of Christ and make Him a mere man or an inspired teacher. But the Christian has the Spirit within, the new nature, and this gives overcoming power.

There are two spirits in the world today: God's Spirit of Truth, who speaks through the inspired Word, and Satan's spirit of error that teaches lies (1 Tim. 4:1ff). Teachers sent by God will speak from God, and God's children will recognize them. Satan's workers will speak from and depend on worldly wisdom (1 Cor. 1:7–2:16). The true sheep recognize the voice of the Shepherd (John 10:1-5, 27-28). True sheep also recognize and love one another. Satan is a divider and destroyer; Christ unites people in love.

II. Christ Died for Us (4:9-11)

The world does not really believe that God is love. They look at the awful ravages of sin in the world and say, "How can a God of love permit these things to happen?" But people need never doubt God's love: He proved His love at the cross. Christ died that we might live "through" Him (1 John 4:9), "for" Him (2 Cor. 5:15), and "with" Him (1 Thes. 5:9-10). The logic is clear: "If God so loved us, we ought also to love one another." We should love each other in the same measure and manner as God loves us.

The cross is a plus sign; it reconciles sinners to God and people to one another. If two Christians do not love one another, they have taken their eyes from the cross.

III. The Spirit Witnesses to Us (4:12-16)

People cannot see God, but they can see God's children revealing Him in their love for one another and for those in need. This love is not something that we work up; it is the work of the Spirit within (Rom. 5:5). God's love flows from us as we yield to the Spirit. Christians do not love each other because of their good qualities, but in spite of their bad qualities. As we abide in His love, we have no difficulty loving other Christians.

IV. Christ Is Coming for Us (4:17-18)

Christians who obey God have boldness with God now (3:21-22); and Christians who love one another will have confidence when Christ returns. Some, however, will be ashamed at His coming (2:28). Christians will have to get along with each other in heaven, so why not begin by loving one another down here? Where there is true love for God and His people, there need be no fear of future judgment. God may have to chasten us in love during this life, but we need not fear to face Him when He returns. We may be ashamed, but we need not be afraid.

Verse 17 should read, "Herein is love made perfect with us." God's love has been manifested "toward" us (4:1), "in" us (4:12), and also "with" us. This is a life and a church fellowship saturated with the love of God. This kind of love seeks to please the Father and has no interest in the world. We need not fear the day of judgment, because the Spirit's witness of love proves that we are His children and that we will never face condemnation. Note the astounding statement at the end of v. 17—"as He is (now in heaven), so are we (now on earth)." He is in heaven representing us before the Father, and we are on earth representing Him before sinful men. As long as He is there in heaven, we have nothing to fear. Do we do as good a job here on earth as He does in glory?

God never meant for people to live in terror. There was no fear on earth until Satan and sin entered the world (Gen. 3:10). Adam and Eve were afraid and hid. Judgment is coming, and anyone who has never trusted Christ ought to be afraid. But Christians need never be afraid to meet their Lord (2 Tim. 1:7; Rom. 8:15).

V. God Loves Us (4:19-21)

The theme of God's love began chapter 3, and here it closes the chapter: "We love, because He first loved us." By nature, we know little about love (Titus 3:3-6); God had to show it to us on the cross (Rom. 5:8) and plant it in our hearts (Rom. 5:5). Note 1 John 4:10. "There is none who seeks after God," says Rom. 3:11 (NKJV), so God came seeking man (Gen. 3:8; Luke 19:10).

John shows the contradiction between saying we love God while hating other Christians. How can we love God in heaven when we do not love God's children here on earth? John uses the term "brethren" or "brother" seventeen times in his letter, referring, of course, to all of God's children, male and female. Christians are expected to love each other because they have experienced the love of God in their own hearts.

God commands us to love one another; see 3:11; John 13:34-35; John 15:17; Col. 1:4. It is too bad that our hearts are so cold that He must keep reminding us of this obligation.

Keep in mind that Christian love does not mean we must agree with everything a brother or sister thinks or does. We may not like some of their personal characteristics. But, because they are in Christ, we love them for Jesus' sake. Read James 4 to see what happens when selfishness reigns instead of love.

1 JOHN 5

We come now to the third test of sonship, the test of truth. "We know" is the key phrase here (vv. 2, 15, 18-20). There are several certainties found in this chapter.

I. We Know What a Christian Is (5:1-5)

Most people in the world do not know what a Christian is or how they can become Christians. They trust in religious works and good intentions, depending on the energy of the flesh. God says that a Christian is someone who has been born again. It is faith in the finished work of Christ that makes a child of disobedience into a child of God (see John 1:12-13; James 1:18; 1 Peter 1:3). John uses the phrase "born of God" seven times in his first epistle and describes the "birthmarks of believers": (1) they practice righteousness, 2:29; (2) they do not practice sin, 3:9; (3) they love other Christians, 4:7; (4) they overcome the world, 5:4; and (5) they keep themselves from Satan, 5:18.

Again, John emphasizes love, obedience, and truth as the tests of true sonship. If we have God as our Father and love Him, then surely we will also love His other children. This love will lead to obedience (see John 14:21 and 15:10). Where there is love, there is a willingness to serve and please others. God's commands are not irksome to us because we love Him. There is a law in every city that parents must take care of their children, or else be put in jail. Is it a burden for parents to work and sacrifice to care for their children? Or do they care for them only because they fear this law? Neither is true! They obey the law because they love their children. The Christian who complains that God's Word is a burden does not know the meaning of love. See Matt. 11:28-30.

Christians are not to love the world, belong to the world, or yield to the world. They are overcomers, overcoming the world, the devil (2:13-14), and the false teachers (4:4). They overcome by faith in God's Word, not by their own power or wisdom.

II. We Know Who Jesus Is (5:6-13)

Sinners must believe that Jesus is the Christ and that He died for their sins before they can be saved and born into God's family. Verse 5 stresses the Person of Christ, and vv. 6-7 His work on the cross. There are several suggested explanations of the phrase "water and blood." We may relate it to John 19:34-35, where John saw the blood and water come out of Christ's wounded side, thus proving that He had really died. Or, it may be that John had the false teachers in mind. Some of them taught that Jesus was a mere man, but that "the Christ" came upon Jesus at the baptism, then left Him when He died on the cross. This would mean that we have no Savior at all. No, said John, our Savior Jesus Christ was declared to be the Son of God at His baptism (Matt. 3:17), and proved to be the Son of God at the cross (John 8:28; 12:28-33). Of course, the symbolism reminds us of the brazen altar (blood) and the laver (water of the Word) in the OT tabernacle. The Spirit bears witness that Jesus is the Christ through the written Word of God.

The entire Godhead agrees that Jesus is the Christ; and on earth, the Spirit, the Word (water), and the cross (blood) bear the same witness. God is witnessing to the world that this is His Son—yet people will not believe. They receive the witness of men, but reject the witness of God. But when we reject this witness, we make God a liar. All God asks is that we trust His Word. We can rely on the inner witness of the Spirit (v. 10, see Rom. 8:16) as He uses the Word. Verses 11-13 summarize as clearly as possible the assurance we have in Christ. Eternal life is in Christ: God has witnessed to this. If we believe God's witness, then we have this life within us. Christian assurance is not a matter of "working up" a religious emotion; it is simply a matter of taking God at His Word.

III. We Know How to Pray with Confidence (5:14-17)

It has well been said that prayer is not a way of overcoming God's reluctance but laying hold of His willingness. If we know God's will, we can pray with boldness. This is "praying in the Spirit" (Jude 20), allowing the Spirit to give us the inward witness of God's will, supported by the witness of God's Word. See 3:22. John mentions praying specifically for another believer who has sinned in a way that might result in death (1 Cor. 11:30). This "sin unto death" is not some "unpardonable sin" that a believer unwittingly falls into, but a deliberate sin in defiance of the Word of God (Heb. 12:9), something that other believers can see and recognize as rebellion. Jeremiah was told not to pray for the rebellious Jews (7:16; 11:14; 14:11; and see Ezek. 14:14, 20). When we show true repentance and confession, the Father is quick to forgive and cleanse (1 John 1:9–2:2).

True prayer is much more than saying words to God. It involves searching the Word, letting the Spirit search the things of God (Rom. 8:26-28), and yielding to God's will as we share our requests with Him. There is a price to pay in this kind of praying, but it is worth it.

IV. We Know How a Christian Acts (5:18-19)

The Gk. verb in v. 18 means "does not practice sin." Christians do not keep themselves saved, but they do keep themselves out of the snares of the devil. "Keep yourselves in the love of God" (Jude 21). "He that is begotten of God" may refer to Jesus Christ, the only begotten Son, or to the believer; perhaps both are true. We must yield to Christ in order to have victory; but we fight "from" victory as well as "for" victory.

God's people must keep their eyes wide open because the whole world "lies in the lap" of the wicked one. Satan is the god of this age and the prince of darkness. He has blinded millions of people spiritually and has kept them in bondage.

V. We Know the Truth (5:20-21)

The Spirit and the Word always agree, for "the Spirit is truth" (5:6) and God's Word is truth (John 17:17). The witness of the Spirit within the heart will never contradict the words of the Spirit in the Bible. The false teachers John was opposing taught that one had to belong to a special "inner circle" before one could understand spiritual knowledge, but John affirms that any true believer can know God's truth.

The true God is opposed to the false gods, the idols. An idol is man's conception of god. God made man is His image; now men make gods in their own image! Read Rom. 1:21ff. Note that John affirms that Jesus Christ is the true God!

Obedience, love, and truth are the key thoughts in this epistle. They are the evidence of salvation and the essentials of fellowship, the secret of true and abiding life.

2 JOHN

The aged John wrote this brief personal letter to an esteemed woman in a local church. Verses 2-3 are introductory and describe the woman as one who is known and loved for her practice of the truth (the Word of God). Note that truth and love go together; Christians cannot have fellowship where there is false doctrine. John next deals with two specific matters.

I. Practicing the Truth (vv. 4-6)

Note the repetition of the word "walk." The truth is not something we simply study or believe; it is a motivating force in our lives. It is not enough to know the truth; we must show it through our actions wherever we are. John rejoiced because he was certain this lady's children were walking in the truth—the equivalent of "walking in the light," which the apostle discussed in 1 John 1.

Christian love is not an emotion that we work up; it is simple obedience to the Word of God. Children love their parents by obeying them. "If you love Me, keep My commandments" (John 14:15, NKJV). How sad it is when Christians claim to love the Bible but hate the brethren. While saints may differ in their interpretations of certain passages in the Word, they must all agree on loving one another. Where there is a sincere love for the Bible, there will be a love for God's people. Loving the truth and loving the brethren cannot be separated.

II. Protecting the Truth (vv. 7-11)

A. Those who deceive (v. 7).

Here John is referring to the false teachers mentioned in his first epistle. He reminds us that the test of a teacher is what he or she believes about Jesus Christ. If this teacher denies that Jesus Christ came in the flesh, then he or she is false and from the Antichrist. While the one great "Man of Sin" (or Antichrist) will be revealed at the end of the age (1 Thes. 2), the spirit of Antichrist is already in the world (1 John 4:3).

B. Those who destroy (v. 8).

Here John warns us not to destroy the things that have been wrought in Christ. The easiest way to get detoured from your

Christian walk and to lose all the spiritual ground you have gained is to get involved with false doctrine. Satan is a destroyer, and he uses lies to rob saints of their blessings.

C. Those who depart (v. 9).

The word "transgress" here means "go beyond." That is, these false teachers are not content to stay within the limits of the Word of God. They are "progressive" and "modern," preferring to go beyond the Bible and "improve on" what God has written. This is the wrong kind of progress! While Christians are to progress in their walk, they must never go beyond the limits of the Bible. We are to "abide" in the doctrine, affirming the fundamentals of the Word of God.

John warns us not to entertain these false teachers in our homes or even to greet them. Any aid that we give to false teachers is a share in their evil deeds. Find out what people believe before you let them in your home or give them donations. Check with your pastor if you have any questions.

3 JOHN

Third John was written to a member of a local church that was beset with problems. In the letter, John discusses three men.

I. Gaius: A Prosperous Christian (vv. 1-8)

How we thank God for church members like Gaius. John uses the word "beloved" four times when referring to him (vv. 1-2, 5, 11). Verse 2 suggests that Gaius may not have been in good health or that he was just recovering from an illness. But this we know: he had a healthy spiritual life. Whatever the condition of the outer man, the inner man was prospering.

Gaius was the kind of Christian others enjoyed talking about. The brethren (probably traveling evangelists and missionaries) had met Gaius and been entertained in his home. They reported that Gaius was walking in the truth and faithfully trying to help the different Christian workers who came his way. Keep in mind that there were no hotels in John's day, only inns that were uncomfortable and often dangerous. Traveling evangelists depended on the saints for food and lodging. Gaius was the kind of Christian who loved to entertain the saints and "bring them forward" as they went from place to place.

Why did Gaius help the saints? Because he loved them, for one thing, and because he wanted to share in their ministries and further the truth. A man might not be a preacher himself, but he can help others to preach.

II. Diotrephes: A Proud Christian (vv. 9-10)

This is the kind of church member we can do without. He wanted to be the "boss" of the church; he loved to have preeminence and be first in everything. Colossians 1:18 says that Christ alone deserves preeminence. "He must increase, I must decrease," is the way John the Baptist put it (John 3:30).

How did this member act? Well, for one thing, he refused to acknowledge the leadership of John. Whenever a church member wants position and prestige, he or she usually attacks the pastor either privately or openly. Usually they start a "whispering campaign" and try to undermine the pastor's character and ministry. Like Absalom in the OT, they "hint" that the present leadership is not efficient (2 Sam. 15:1-6), and that they could handle things better. Hebrews 13:7, 17 settle this matter once and for all.

Diotrephes told lies about John. "Prating" in v. 10 means "to bring false charges" and is similar to "tattlers" in 1 Tim. 5:13. If church members would remember that they are to listen to no accusations against their pastor without witnesses present, this would help to solve the gossip problem (1 Tim. 5:19).

He also refused to help the brethren, and even went so far as to domineer the church and throw some of them out. The NT teaches that in some cases of discipline, members are to be dismissed, but Diotrephes dismissed people without giving them opportunity to defend themselves or be heard by the congregation. Note 1 Peter 5:3.

It is this kind of member that destroys churches. Eager for power and authority, they trample on the truth, ignore the Bible, grieve the Spirit, and scatter the flock.

III. Demetrius: A Pleasant Christian (vv. 11-12)

How refreshing to turn from Diotrephes to Demetrius! He was the kind of person others could follow ("mimic"). He had a good report from the saints and from the Word itself. You could test his life by the Bible, and it passed the test.

Churches today need more members like Gaius and Demetrius, saints who love the Bible, the church family, and lost souls. We can do without those like Diotrephes!

JUDE

The writer was the half brother of Christ, called "Judas" in Mark 6:3. The resurrected Christ was seen by James, another half brother (1 Cor. 15:7), so undoubtedly both James and Judas became believers about the same time. Christ's brethren are mentioned in Acts 1:13-14 as sharing in the prayer meeting before Pentecost. Note that Jude does not boast of his human relationship to Christ. He prefers to call himself a "bond-slave of Jesus Christ" and a brother of James. Though in his letter Jude speaks of judgment, he is careful to point out that the true believer is kept in Christ (vv. 1, 24). We do not keep ourselves saved, but we should keep ourselves in the love of God by obeying His Word (v. 21).

I. The Aim of the Letter (vv. 3-4)

Jude started to write a message on "salvation," but was led by the Spirit to abandon his theme and warn the believers of the false teachers now in the church. You will note that many verses in Jude parallel 2 Peter 2. Jude was written later, for Peter prophesied that these false teachers would come (2 Peter 2:1; 3:3), and Jude says that they are now here and at work. He reminds us that Peter has already announced their condemnation. He identifies these false teachers as the same people Peter described: they creep in secretly, bring false doctrine, and live in sin. "Turning the grace of God into lasciviousness" (v. 4) means they told people that grace permitted them to live as they pleased. See Rom. 6:1ff.

How are Christians to react to this danger? "Contend earnestly for the faith!" (v. 3) is Jude's command. We are to defend God's truth and the body of doctrine the NT calls "the faith." We are to be soldiers who hold the fort at any cost.

II. The Argument (vv. 5-16)

Jude's theme in this section is the condemnation of these false teachers and those who follow them. He cites seven OT examples to prove his point:

A. Israel (v. 5).

God delivered Israel from Egypt and its plagues, but afterward had to destroy unbelievers. Jude makes it clear that these men are not believers; v. 19 states that they do not have the Spirit. Merely being "in the church" is no evidence of salvation. Many Jews were "in the nation" yet destroyed because of their sin.

B. Fallen angels (v. 6).

See 2 Peter 2:4. Jude seems to be referring to the angels who consorted with the daughters of men in Gen. 6. This was Satan's scheme to corrupt the human race and thus prevent the birth of the promised Seed (Gen. 3:15). These angels who defied God were judged and imprisoned in Tartarus, a special part of hell.

C. Sodom and Gomorrah (v. 7).

The phrase "in like manner" suggests that the sins of these cities parallel the fornication of the angels of v. 6. Second Peter 2:6-8 discusses these wicked cities. Jude says that the judgment of these cities is an illustration of hell.

D. Michael and Moses (vv. 8-10).

Michael the archangel is the special angel for Israel (Dan. 12:1). The reference here seems to be to the burial of Moses (Deut. 34:6). God will bring Moses back as one of the witnesses to the Jews during the Tribulation period (Rev. 11), but Satan tried to secure the body. Jude's point is that the archangel did not rebuke Satan, for this takes more authority than Michael really had. The angel allowed God to do the rebuking. These false teachers, in their pride, despise authority and speak evil of holy things in their sin and ignorance.

E. Cain (v. 11).

This example takes us back to Gen. 4, where Cain appears at the altar without a blood sacrifice. The way of Cain is the way of man-made religion, rejecting the revelation of God and the blood of the Savior. See 1 John 3:11-12; Heb. 11:4.

F. Balaam (v. 11).

See 2 Peter 2:15-16. The error of Balaam involved leading others into sin for personal gain. Balaam knew the truth but deliberately led Israel into sin that he might make money. See Num. 22–25, especially 25:1-9.

G. Korah (v. 11).

Read Num. 16. Korah and his followers rejected the divine authority given to Moses and tried to assume power for themselves. False teachers promote themselves and override the authority of God's servants. They will be judged, as were Korah and his followers.

In vv. 12-13, Jude describes these false teachers in vivid terms; read these verses in a modern translation for an accurate description. Of what value are clouds without water, trees without fruit, and stars that wander and so give no help to the traveler? He closes his argument by quoting Enoch who, at the beginning of history, prophesied of their doom. Note the repetition of the word "ungodly" in these verses.

III. The Admonition (vv. 17-25)

How are Christians to act in the light of this situation? First, they are to remember the Word (see 2 Peter 3). Christ promised that mockers would come, and now they had appeared. The growth of apostasy is more evidence of Satan's determination to block the truth of the Word of God. Further, Christians are to grow spiritually, building themselves up in the Lord. They do this by praying in the Spirit (as the Spirit leads, see Rom. 8:26-27), obeying the Word and thus abiding in God's love, and watching for Christ's return. What a combination for a victorious Christian life: praying, learning and living the Bible, and expecting Christ's return.

How are Christians to act toward those who are following these false teachers? "Make a difference" (v. 22) is his admonition. In other words, treat each situation individually. Some persons need to be shown pity; others can be saved and snatched out of the fire. Some may be too far gone to help. Jude warns us that, as we seek to help others, we must take care not to be defiled by them ourselves. The OT priest was not to get his garments defiled, and NT Christians (who are also priests) must keep themselves unspotted from the world (James 1:27).

Jude closes with a wonderful benediction, emphasizing the power of Christ to keep His own. Christians do not keep themselves saved; Christ keeps them to the very end. Verse 1 says that we are "kept for Jesus Christ," indicating that the Father has a personal interest in our preservation. Verse 24 states that we are "kept by Jesus Christ." What more security could the Christian desire?

Hebrews 12:2 says that Christ endured the cross "because of the joy that was set before Him." Jude tells us what that joy was: the privilege of presenting His church before the Father in glory. The

Bridegroom will one day present His bride faultless in glory. What a day that will be!

As you read this epistle, you cannot help but realize that Christians must defend the faith and oppose false teachers. Christ is guarding us, but He wants us to guard the deposit He has left in our hands (2 Tim. 1:13-14; 1 Tim. 6:20). There is awful doom awaiting those who reject Christ and teach Satan's lies. Some we might be able to save; others we can only pity. May God help us to be faithful until He comes!

REVELATION

A Suggested Outline of Revelation

Key verse (1:19)

I. The Things Which Thou Hast Seen (1)

  A. John's vision of the glorified Christ as King-Priest

II. The Things Which Are (2–3)

  A. The seven churches reveal the condition of God's people

III. The Things Which Shall Be Hereafter (4–22)

  A. The rapture of the church (4–5)
    1. John is caught up
    2. The Lamb takes His throne
  B. The tribulation of seven years (6–19)
    1. First half of the Tribulation (6–9)
    2. Middle of the Tribulation (10–14)
    3. Last half of the Tribulation (15–19)
  C. The millennial kingdom of Christ (20)
  D. The new heavens and earth (21–22)

Introductory Notes to Revelation

I. Background

The Apostle John took over the pastoral work in Ephesus about A.D. 70, including the churches in the surrounding area, the "seven churches of Asia Minor" of Rev. 2–3. The Roman Emperor Nero had persecuted Christians in Rome, but the "fiery trial" that Peter had promised (1 Peter 4:12ff) had not yet begun. But when Domitian became emperor (A.D. 81–96), the persecution was intensified. Domitian was as cold-blooded a murderer as you will ever meet in the pages of history. He promoted "emperor worship" and began his announcements, "Our Lord and God Domitian commands. . . ." Everyone who spoke to him had to address him, "Lord and God." He was bitter in his treatment of both Jews and Christians, and it was at his behest that John was exiled to the Isle of Patmos, a rocky island ten miles long and six miles wide, in the Aegean Sea. Rome had a penal camp there where the prisoners labored in the mines. It was here in this isolated spot that John received the visions that make up Revelation. He wrote it about A.D. 95.

II. Character

Revelation is a unique book with characteristics that must be noted. John's text is:

A. Prophetic.

It is a book of prophecy (1:3; 10:11; 19:10; 22:7, 10, 18-19).

B. Christ-centered.

It is the revelation of Jesus Christ, not simply a prophetic program. In chapter 1, He is the Risen Priest-King; in chapters 2–3, He examines the churches; in chapters 4–5, He receives worship and praise and the title-deed to creation; in chapters 6–19, He judges the world and returns in glory; and in chapters 20–22, He reigns in glory and power.

C. Open.

The word "revelation" means literally "unveiling." Daniel was told to seal his book (Dan. 12:4), but John to "seal it not" (22:10). Instead of being a collection of puzzling prophecies, Revelation is a reasonable, orderly unveiling of Christ and His final victory over Satan, sin, and the world-system.

D. Symbolic.

"He sent and signified it" (1:1) suggests that the book uses signs and symbols to convey its message. Some are explained (1:20; 4:5), some are unexplained (4:4; 11:3), and some are explained by referring to OT parallels (2:7, 17, 27-28). This spiritual symbolism would be clear to the Christians receiving the book but would make no sense to their Roman persecutors. Keep in mind that symbols speak of reality. A flag, for example, stands for the existence of a nation. The picture of Christ in 1:12-16 is not literal, but each of these symbols conveys a spiritual truth about Him.

E. Based on the OT.

It is impossible to understand this book without referring to the OT Scriptures. Out of the 404 verses in Revelation, 278 contain references to the OT. It is calculated that there are over 500 references or allusions to the OT in Revelation, with Psalms, Daniel, Zechariah, Genesis, Isaiah, Jeremiah, Ezekiel, and Joel being referred to most often.

F. Numerical.

There is a series of "sevens" in the book: seven churches, seals, trumpets, vials, lampstands, etc. The number three and one half also shows up often (11:2-3; 12:6; 13:5). We also find the 144,000 (a multiple of twelve) sealed Israelites, twelve stars (12:1), twelve gates (21:12), and twelve foundations (21:14).

G. Universal.

Revelation focuses on the whole world. John sees nations, peoples, masses of humanity (see 10:11, 11:9, 17:15, etc.). This book describes God's judgment of the world and His creation of a new world for His people.

H. Majestic.

This is the "book of the throne," for from chapter 4 to the end, we read about the King and His rule. The word "throne" is used forty-four times; "king," "kingdom," or "rule" about thirty-seven times; "power" and "authority" some forty times. We see Christ as the Sovereign of the universe, ruling from the heavenly throne.

I. *Sympathetic.*

Throughout the book we see the sufferings of God's people and the compassion of heaven for the people of God on earth. John is in exile (1:9); Antipas is martyred (2:13); the church in Smyrna will face imprisonment (2:10); souls under the altar cry for God's avenging judgment (6:9-10); the hour of trial is coming (3:10); the great harlot has drunk the blood of the saints (17:6; 18:24; 19:2). Yet God will judge the world and save His people.

J. *Climactic.*

Revelation is the climax of the Bible and shows the fulfillment of the plan and purpose of God for the universe.

III. Interpretation

Good and godly students differ on the meaning of the details of the book. Four broad interpretations have been suggested:

A. *Preterist* (from the Latin word *preter*, meaning "past").

This approach states that everything in the book took place in the first century. John deals, they say, with the war between the church and Rome. He wrote the saints to comfort and encourage them in their time of persecution. But, John states seven times that he is writing *prophecy.* Certainly the book had a special value to those enduring Roman persecution, but its value did not cease with the close of the Apostolic Age.

B. *Historical.*

Interpreters in this camp claim to see the fulfillment of church history in the symbols of Revelation. They believe that the book outlines the course of history from apostolic times to the end of the age. They search history books to find events that parallel those in Revelation, but sometimes the results are disastrous. One interpreter sees Luther and the Reformation in a symbol that, to another student, stands for the invention of the printing press! Of what value would Revelation be to the believers in John's day if all it did was foretell world history? And of what value would it be to us today?

C. *Spiritual.*

These students abandon the idea of prophecy completely and use

Revelation as a symbolical presentation of the conflict between Christ and Satan, good and evil. They reject the idea that John writes about actual events; they claim he is dealing only with basic spiritual principles. But, again, John tells us he is writing *prophecy*. While we recognize that Revelation does contain many basic spiritual principles in symbolic form, we must also admit that the book deals with real events that will one day take place in the world.

D. Futurist.

This school emphasizes that Revelation is prophecy; chapters 6 through 22 describe a scenario of events that will transpire on earth and in heaven after the church is raptured. While such students gladly recognize the spiritual lessons of the book, they also recognize that it talks about actual events that will be fulfilled one day. If Revelation is not to be interpreted as prophecy, then God has not given the church a book in the NT to explain the future of the world, the course of events, the victory of the church, the judgment of sin, and the fulfillment of the promises and prophecies found in the OT. This is unthinkable. No, Revelation is that book; and the student who reverently approaches this book as a prophecy of events that will occur after the church is caught away will be rewarded for his or her labors.

IV. Genesis and Revelation — Complementary Books

Genesis	Revelation
Creation of the heavens and earth (chaps. 1–2)	Creation of the new heavens and earth (chaps. 21–22)
The first Adam reigning on earth (1:26)	The Last Adam reigning in glory (21:5)
Night and seas created (1:5, 10)	No more night; no more sea (21:1, 25)
A bride brought to Adam (2:18-25)	The Bride prepared for Christ (19:7ff)
A tree of life in Eden (2:9; 3:22)	A tree of life in the new creation (22:2)
Death and a curse (3:14, 17-19)	No more curse; no more death or tears (22:3)
Conflict between Christ and Satan (3:15)	Satan's final doom (20:10)

Man driven from God's face (3:23; 4:16)	Men see His face in glory (22:4)
Believers looking for a city (Heb. 11:13-16)	The holy city presented in glory (21:10)
"Where is the Lamb?" (22:7)	The Lamb reigns (22:3)
Satan utters the first lie (3:1)	Nothing that makes a lie enters the city (21:27)

Revelation, then, outlines God's program for human history. What began ages ago in the first creation will ultimately be completed in the new creation. This is the "book with a blessing" (1:3, and see the six other "blessings" in 14:13; 16:15; 19:9; 20:6; 22:7, 14). It shows us that "history is His story"—that human affairs are in the hands of our victorious Christ. As we study this book, we should be encouraged, inspired to serve, and enabled to live clean lives, that we might be ready when He returns.

REVELATION 1

God the Father gave the contents of the book to Christ, who gave it to His angel to give to the Apostle John. "His angel" may be translated "His messenger," since the Gk. word *aggelos* (angel) means "messenger" (22:16). "Signified" indicates that the book uses signs or symbols to convey spiritual truth. John actually saw the contents of the book unfold before his eyes. Physically, he was on the isle of Patmos (1:9), but God transported him to heaven (4:1), to the wilderness (17:3), and to a mountain (21:10) that he might witness these events and record them for us.

There is a blessing for the one who reads this book aloud and for those who hear it with attentive hearts. But v. 3 indicates that Revelation is not a book to study with idle curiosity; these words must be "kept," that is, obeyed and practiced.

The phrases "at hand" (v. 3) and "shortly come to pass" (v. 1) do not mean that these prophecies were to be fulfilled right away in John's day. Rather, they indicate how swiftly time will transpire when they are fulfilled. Today, long-suffering God is waiting to give sinners a chance to repent. But when the time comes for these judgments to fall, there will be no delay.

I. The Christ John Knew (1:4-8)

John sends greetings to the churches in Asia Minor as he was commanded to do (v. 11). He reviews the wonder of the Godhead, naming each of the Persons of the Trinity:

A. The Father.

"Him which is, which was, and which is to come" (v. 4), that is, the eternal God. See 1:8 and 4:8. God stands above history; He is not limited by time.

B. The Spirit.

"Seven" is the number of completion and stands for the fullness of the Spirit. In 4:5, we see that the seven-fold Spirit is symbolized by seven lamps; and in 5:6, by seven eyes. Christ has the seven-fold Spirit (3:1); the Spirit points to Christ.

C. The Son.

Christ is presented in His three-fold Person as Prophet (faithful witness), Priest (first begotten of the dead, that is, highest of those raised from the dead), and King (prince of the kings of the earth). Then, John praises God for the three-fold work that Christ accomplished on the cross: He loved us, washed us (or freed us) from our sins, and made us a kingdom of priests. The dominion we lost in Adam we have regained in Christ.

Verse 7 is the first of seven references in Revelation to the return of Christ (2:25; 3:3, 11; 22:7, 12, 29). This return is public (Dan. 7:13; Acts 1:8ff) and should not be confused with the rapture of the church, which is secret (1 Thes. 4:13ff). The Gentiles will mourn because of Him, and the Jews will see Him whom they pierced (Zech. 12:10-12; see Matt. 24:27-30).

II. The Christ John Heard (1:9-11)

John was an exile on an island located about seventy miles from Ephesus, where he had pastored the Asian churches. In Mark 10:35-45, James and John asked for thrones; yet in later years, both were given tribulation. James was slain (Acts 12), and John suffered exile. He was exiled because of the Word of God which he had preached. It is interesting that John mentions the sea twenty-five times in this book. "On the isle . . . in the Spirit" (vv. 9-10): what a wonderful situation! Our geographical location ought never to rob us of spiritual blessings.

John heard the voice of Christ as a trumpet. Trumpets are important in Revelation; in 4:1, the trumpet calls John up to heaven, a picture of the rapture; and in 8:2ff, trumpets signal that the wrath of God will be poured out on the world. In the OT, the Jews used trumpets to gather the assembly, to announce war, or to proclaim special days (Num. 10). God's trumpet will call the church home (1 Thes. 4:16), gather Israel (Matt. 24:31), and announce war on the world (Rev. 8:2ff). The voice told John to write this book and send it to the churches from which he had been separated. There were more than seven churches in this area, but Christ chose these churches to represent the spiritual needs of His people.

III. The Christ John Saw (1:12-20)

John could no longer "know Christ according to the flesh" (2 Cor. 5:16, NKJV); He is now the risen, exalted King-Priest. John saw the glorified Christ standing in the midst of the seven lampstands, which symbolized the seven churches (1:20). God's people are the light of the world; the church does not create the light, but merely holds it and lets it shine. We do not see one gigantic lamp; rather, we have seven separate lampstands.

Use your cross references to study the symbols that here stand for the glorified Christ. His garments are those of a Priest-King. The white hair speaks of His eternalness (Dan. 7:9). His eyes see all, and they judge what they see (Dan. 10:6; Heb. 4:12; Rev. 19:12). In the midst of the churches, Christ sees what is going on, and He judges. The feet of brass speak of judgment; the brazen altar was the place where sin was judged. His voice — "as the sound of many waters" — suggests two things: (1) the power of His Word, like the sea; and (2) all the "streams" of divine revelation converging in Christ. See Ps. 29 and Ezek. 43:2.

He holds seven stars in His hand, and these stars are the messengers (or pastors) of the seven churches. It is possible that messengers came to John from these churches and received this Book of Revelation from him personally. The stars are the messengers (1:20); Christ holds His servants in His hands. See Dan. 12:3. The sword from His mouth is His Word that judges; see Isa. 11:4, 49:2 and also Rev. 2:12, 16, and 19:19-21. The shining of His face as the sun speaks of His glory; see Mal. 4:2. In 22:16, He is the bright and morning star, for He will appear for His church when the hour is the darkest, just before the wrath of God breaks on the horizon.

When Christ was on earth, John lay on His bosom (John 13:23); but now he falls at His feet (Dan. 8:17, and see Rev. 22:8). Saints today need to avoid becoming too "familiar" with Christ in their speech and attitudes, for He deserves all honor and praise. Christ assures John and calms his fears. Christ is first and last (1:8; 22:13), so we need not fear. He has the keys of Hades (not "hell"), the realm of the dead. Hades will one day empty out the souls of the lost (20:13-14).

Christ outlines the Book of Revelation for us in 1:19 (see the outline). To follow any other approach is to presume that we know more about this book than Christ does.

In chapters 2–3, Christ deals with the seven churches. As He stands in their midst, He examines their spiritual condition with His eyes of fire. He is doing this today. It matters not what men or denominations think of a church; what does Christ think of it? We should note that the different elements of the description of Christ in vv. 13-16 are repeated in the letters to the seven churches. That attribute of Christ that applied to the particular needs of the church is emphasized in the message. The danger to the churches is that Christ would remove their testimony (2:5). He would rather have a city in the darkness than to have a lampstand out of His divine will.

Much of the symbolism of this chapter will be repeated later in the book. It cannot be emphasized too much that you trace your cross references as you study.

IV. The Seven Churches of Asia Minor

If Rev. 1:19 is the inspired outline of the book, then Rev. 2–3 deals with "the things which are." In other words, Christ selected seven churches out of many in Asia Minor in order to get across His specific message. Certainly there were sins in the other churches, but the matters discussed in these seven churches cover all possible circumstances. Christ selected these seven churches to illustrate the spiritual conditions possible in the churches until He returns.

Some students believe these churches also illustrate the "prophetic history" of the church from apostolic times until the end of the age: Ephesus was the church of apostolic times, starting to lose that first love for Christ; Smyrna was the persecuted church of the first centuries (c. A.D. 100–300); Pergamos was the church joined to Rome, the state church; Thyatira represented the dominance of Roman Catholicism; Sardis symbolized the Reformation church; Philadelphia ("brotherly love") the missionary church of the last days; and Laodicea was the lukewarm, apostate church of the last days. However, keep in mind that all of the conditions named were present in the churches at that one time, and they are present with us today. Furthermore, if this sequence is a "prophetic history" of the church, then Jesus could not return for His people until the era of the Laodicean church; and this would make His imminent return impossible. While the seven churches may illustrate the general development of the church through the ages, that was not the main purpose of these seven letters.

Note that a special word is spoken to the "overcomers" in each church (2:7, 11, 17, 26; 3:5, 12, 21). These "overcomers" are not the "super-saints" in each church, a special group that will receive special privileges from Christ, but the true believers in each of these churches. We dare not assume that every member of every local church in every period of history is a true child of God. Those who truly belong to Christ are "overcomers" (1 John 5:4-5). In every period of history, there have been true saints in the professing church (often called "the invisible church"). Christ speaks a special word of encouragement to them, and certainly we may apply these words to ourselves today.

Note too that Satan is mentioned in connection with four churches: (1) he causes the persecution at Smyrna, 2:9; (2) he has his throne ("seat") at Pergamos, 2:13; (3) he teaches his "deep doctrines" at Thyatira, 2:24; and (4) he uses his "synagogue" of false Christians to oppose the soul-winning efforts at Philadelphia, 3:9.

Christ points out several dangers in these churches:

A. The Nicolaitanes (2:6, 15).

The name "Nicolaus" means "conquer the people" and suggests a separation of clergy and laity in the churches. This sin began as "deeds" in Ephesus (v. 6) but became a doctrine in Pergamos. So it goes: deceivers introduce false activities into the church, and before long these activities are accepted and encouraged.

B. Satan's synagogue (2:9; 3:9).

This refers probably to assemblies of people who claim to be believers but are really children of the devil (John 8:44). The word "synagogue" simply means "to bring together"; it is an assembly of religious people. Satan, then, has a church!

C. The doctrine of Balaam (2:14).

Read Num. 22–25. Balaam led Israel into sin by telling them that because they were God's covenant people, they could mix with the heathen and not be judged. Balaam could not curse them, but he could tempt them with sins of the flesh. This doctrine, then, is the idea that the church can be married to the world and still serve God.

D. Jezebel (2:20).

Read 1 Kings 16 through 2 Kings 10. Jezebel was the heathen wife of King Ahab, a woman who led Israel into Baal worship. She seduced Israel with her false teaching.

V. The Personal Message

Note the spiritual problems in these churches and what Jesus instructed them to do if they were to have His blessing:

A. *Ephesus.*

Busy working for the Lord, but no sincere love for Him. Program without passion. This is the busy church with the great statistics, but one drifting away from heartfelt devotion to Christ.

B. *Smyrna.*

This church gets no criticism from the Lord, but a danger is still present. This was a poor and suffering church. How easy it would have been to compromise, become rich, and escape persecution. How discouraged they might have been because they were not as "rich" as the Laodicean church.

C. *Pergamos.*

This church had members who held the false doctrine that it was easy to profess Christ while living in sin at the same time. Also, the people were under the heavy hand of spiritual dictators who promoted themselves, not the Lord.

D. *Thyatira.*

This woman was out of place in teaching doctrine; her doctrine led the people into sin. We must maintain God's order in the local church (1 Tim. 2:11-15).

E. *Sardis.*

Reputation without life. Her best days were behind her. This is the "has-been" church, a great name in the past, but no ministry today. It is ready to die, but it can receive new life if it will but strengthen what it has.

F. *Philadelphia.*

The church before the open door, taking the Gospel to the world. This is the church that holds the Word and honors Christ's name. But Satan's synagogue is not far away, and there is always the danger of compromise.

G. *Laodicea.*

The lukewarm, apostate church, with a big budget and no blessing. This is the church that is materially rich and spiritually poor. And the tragedy is, the people do not know how poor and miserable they really are! Christ stands outside the church, calling for even one believer to yield to Him.

REVELATION 2

I. Ephesus: The Backsliding Church (2:1-7)

The hands and feet of the exalted Christ are emphasized here: He holds the stars (the messengers of the churches), and He walks in judgment among the churches (lampstands). He begins with Ephesus, the city closest to Patmos. It was a great commercial center. The emperor had made Ephesus a free city; it had the title "Supreme Metropolis of Asia." Most important was the great temple of Diana, one of the seven wonders of the ancient world. It was 425 feet long, 220 feet wide, and 60 feet high, with great folding doors and 127 marble pillars, some of them covered with gold. The worship of Diana was "religious immorality" at its worst. Read Acts 19–20.

The church at Ephesus had works, labor, and patience—but no love for Christ. In contrast, the Thessalonians were commended for their "work of faith, labor of love, and patience of hope" (1 Thes. 1:3). It is not "what" we do for Christ, but the motive behind it, the incentive, that counts. Ephesus had a busy church with high spiritual standards. They could not bear "worthless [evil] people" and would not listen to false teachers. The work had been difficult, but they had not fainted. In every way, it was a successful church from the human point of view. Some of today's busy churches with their full calendars and weary workers would fit the description.

But the Man in the midst of the churches saw what was missing: they had left (not "lost") their first love (Jer. 2:2). The local church is espoused to Christ (2 Cor. 11:2), but there is always the danger of that love growing cold. Like Martha, we can be so busy working for Christ that we have no time to love Him (Luke 10:38-42). Christ is more concerned about what we do with Him than for Him. Labor is no substitute for love. To the public, the Ephesian church was successful; to Christ, it had fallen.

His counsel to them is in these words: "remember, repent, repeat the first works" (v. 5). If we get back to our first love, we will repeat the first works, those labors of love that marked our first meeting with Christ. If the church does not get its heart back in the right condition, the lampstand will be removed. The local church is to shine as a light in the world. Without true love for Christ, its light will go out.

He commends them for hating the deeds of the Nicolaitans.

The Gk. name "Nicolaus" means "to conquer the people." It refers to the development of a priestly caste (clergy) in the church that throws aside the common believers. While there must be pastoral leadership in the church, there must not be a distinct "clergy" and "laity" in which the former lords it over the latter.

II. Smyrna: The Suffering Church (2:8-11)

Note how each description of Christ goes back to the picture in 1:13-16, and how each one meets the special need of that church. Smyrna was the persecuted church, so Christ reminds them of His own suffering, death, and resurrection (2:8). Smyrna means "bitter" and is related to the word "myrrh." One thinks of fragrance released because of crushing persecution. The church has always been the purest and the most fragrant when it was going through times of suffering.

Christ offers no criticism of this church. The saints were faithful in spite of suffering. They thought they were poor, but were rich—in contrast to Laodicea, which thought it was rich and was poor (3:17). The saints were being blasphemed (slandered) by false Christians (of the synagogue of Satan, John 8:44; Phil. 3:2). Satan is behind all persecution, even that which is done in the name of religion. Christ promises them that more persecution is coming; the "ten days" (v. 10) may refer to the ten great persecutions in the early centuries of the church. Satan came as a lion, seeking to devour (1 Peter 5:8), but the persecution only made the church stronger.

The enemy may kill the body, but the saint need never fear the second death, which is hell (20:14; 21:8). Those who are born twice will die only once. Those born only once will die twice.

III. Pergamos: The Worldly Church (2:12-17)

Pergamos means "married," and this church was wedded to some doctrines and practices that were wrong. Three serious problems existed at Pergamos:

A. Satan's throne (v. 13).

This passage refers to the "mystery cults" of Babylon that set up their headquarters in Pergamos. It also includes the emperor worship that played a key role in this heathen city.

B. The doctrine of Balaam (v. 14; see also Num. 22–25).

Balaam was a hireling prophet who led the people of Israel into sin in return for the wealth and prestige he received. He encouraged Israel to worship heathen idols and indulge in fornication. At Pergamos the church was wedded to the world in order to get worldly advantages.

C. The doctrine of the Nicolaitanes (v. 15, see also v. 6).

What began as "deeds" in one church is now a settled doctrine in another. We now have this church divided into "priests" and "people."

IV. Thyatira: The Unrepentant Church (2:18-29)

The eyes of fire and feet of brass come to see and to judge, but this wicked church will not repent. The church had works, service, and patience, but it was filled with sin. Here we have Jezebel, the only woman mentioned in the seven letters, referring to wicked Queen Jezebel, wife of Ahab (1 Kings 16–2 Kings 10). She was a heathen woman, daughter of a priest of Baal; and she promoted Baal worship in Israel. She was guilty of whoredom and witchcraft (2 Kings 9:22) as well as idolatry, murder, deceit, and priestcraft. And the church at Thyatira was following her example and leadership!

Note that this false prophetess in the church was using false teaching to seduce (deceive) God's people. She gave them license to sin (see 2 Peter 2 and Jude). The tragedy is that she would not repent, even though God gave her the opportunity. It is never too late for a church to repent and return to the Lord, but we must beware lest we miss our God-given opportunities.

REVELATION 3

I. Sardis: The Dying Church (3:1-6)

Sardis was a church with works but not much life. It once had a reputation for being alive, but it was dead. What a graphic description of some historic ministries today! G. Campbell Morgan called it "reputation without reality."

Christ warns the saints: (1) Be watchful, be alert; (2) strengthen the few things you do have; (3) remember the Word you have received and heard; (4) hold fast and be ready when I come.

Verse 5 has bothered people, for it seems to suggest that unfaithful Christians will have their names taken out of the book of life. The "book of life" contains the names of all those who are born. Those who reject Christ have their names blotted out of the book, for they are dead. True believers have their names recorded in the Lamb's Book of Life (13:8; 21:27). Those who do not have their names in the latter book of life will go to hell (20:15). A person may have his or her name on a church roll, but not be saved. What surprises there will be when "the books are opened"! (20:12) Churches today can have "living" names and yet be dead.

II. Philadelphia: The Serving Church (3:7-13)

The name means "brotherly love," so immediately we know we are dealing with saved people who love each other and the Lord. This church represents the missionary church of the last days. With the exception of occasional mission ventures, the churches of the Middle Ages did little to spread the Gospel to other lands. They spent more time fighting religious wars and playing politics with the civil rulers. Churches may not be large or strong (v. 8), but they can have the faith and love to go through the doors of service that Christ has opened with His key. "Key of David" (v. 7) refers to His authority as the Son of David; see Isa. 22:22, where a key is a symbol of authority. Around the world, doors are always opening or closing, so it is important that the church be alert and ready to take advantage of the opportunities God presents. When Christ opens or shuts a door, nobody can interfere.

This church has opposition from the false church (synagogue of Satan), the counterfeits. These false brethren claim to be the church and oppose the ministry of God's people, but Christ promises to bring them to their knees. The false church has popularity, influence, and money, but it must one day bow before the few saints of God who take the truth to the world.

Verse 10 is one of the strongest declarations that the church will not go through the Tribulation. True believers today are a part of the Philadelphia church and will not enter into that seven years of awful judgment on earth. See also 1 Thes. 5:8-9. The very text of Revelation is another proof, for there is no mention of the church until 22:16. The prayer of 22:20 would be impossible to pray if we had to wait for the Tribulation to come before we would be raptured.

III. Laodicea: The Apostate Church (3:14-22)

The name "Laodicea" means "the rule of the people" and suggests a democratic church that no longer follows spiritual leaders or the authority of the Word of God. The church is lukewarm, a condition that comes from mixing hot and cold. It is a church with truth that has been diluted with error. The tragedy is that this church is "rich" and knows not that it is poor, pitiful, blind, and naked. What a picture of the apostate church of today, with its prestige, wealth, and political power, yet all the while spiritually poor.

The city of Laodicea was known for its wool, wealth, and medicine, so Christ used those images in v. 18. He wanted to give them the true riches of the Word of God, the garments of grace, and the ability to see spiritual things. There was something wrong with their values, their vesture, and their vision. If they would not repent, He would chasten them in love.

Verse 20 is often used as a Gospel invitation, and this application is fine. But the basic interpretation is that Christ stands outside the door of the lukewarm church. This church has wealth and power, but no Christ. He is even willing to come into the life of one person, if that person will but invite Him. How tragic that a church can become so lukewarm and proud that Christ has to leave and stand outside. They are totally indifferent toward Christ. He is left outside their plans and programs, and their hearts.

Just as these churches existed in John's day, so they all exist today. We have busy churches that have left their first love (Ephesus) that often end up as churches that are lukewarm toward Christ (Laodicea). False doctrine begins in a small way, but then it grows and infects the whole assembly. Yet, there is a remnant of true believers (the overcomers) in each church who are responsible to be faithful to Christ until He returns.

It has been pointed out by Bible students that the promises to the overcomers in these chapters resemble OT history: the tree of life in Eden, 2:7; man cast out of the Garden to die, 2:11; the manna of the wilderness, 2:17; the kingdom age of Israel, 2:26-27; the priestly ministry, 3:5; the temple, 3:12; and the glorious throne of Solomon, 3:21. It is as though Christ gathered up the history of Israel and applied it to His people today.

Note, finally, the importance of the Word of God to the churches. Seven times Christ calls the churches to hear what the Spirit is saying. When churches stop listening to the voice of the

Spirit through the Word and start listening to the voices of false teachers, they begin to turn away from the truth. We must not deny the faith (2:23), even if it costs us our lives. We must keep His Word (3:8, 10) and not deny His name. Apart from the Word of God, there is no life or hope for the churches.

REVELATION 4

The key word in this chapter is "throne"; it is used twelve times. In fact, the word is used forty-six times in the entire book. The Book of Revelation makes it clear that it is the throne of God that rules the universe, not the thrones of men. See Ps. 103:19.

I. The Summons from the Throne (4:1)

This is a vivid picture of the rapture of the church. Remember that Rev. 1:19 is the divinely given outline of the book; so we are now about to see "the things which must be hereafter." Everything from 4:1 on is prophecy. The fact that John is "caught up" at this point is another evidence that the church will not go through the Tribulation. Note how his experience resembles the rapture: (1) heaven is opened to receive God's child; (2) there is a voice like a trumpet, 1 Thes. 4:16; 1 Cor. 15:52; (3) it is a sudden event; (4) it comes at the end of the "church age" (chaps. 2–3); (5) it introduces John to the throne room of heaven; (6) it signals the beginning of God's judgment on the world. We might note the different doors in Revelation: (1) the door of service, 3:8; (2) the door closed against Christ, 3:20; (3) the door into heaven, 4:1; and (4) the door out from heaven, 19:11.

II. The Glory of the Throne (4:2-3)

The person on the throne is God the Father, since the Spirit is represented by the lamps before the throne (4:5), and the Son comes to the throne in 5:6. John uses precious gems to symbolize the glory of the Father. Jasper is a clear stone, speaking of God's purity; sardine is red, speaking of God's wrath and judgment; and the emerald is green, a color associated with grace and mercy. All of these stones were found on the beautiful breastplate of the High Priest (Ex. 28:17-21).

Around the throne was an emerald-colored rainbow. This takes us back to Gen. 9:11-17, when God made His covenant with man-kind and nature not to destroy the world again with water. The rainbow speaks of God's promise and His covenant of mercy. Even though the throne of God is about to send forth awful judgment on mankind, in His wrath God will still remember mercy (see Hab. 3:2). In Rev. 10:1 we see Christ wearing the rainbow over His head, for it is through Christ that grace and mercy have come to the world. Noah saw only an arc in the sky, while John saw the complete rainbow all around the throne. What we see of God's mercy is incomplete today, for we "see through a glass darkly" (1 Cor. 13:12); but when we get to heaven, we will see the whole pattern.

III. The Elders Around the Throne (4:4)

These elders cannot be angels, for several reasons: (1) we never see angels on thrones; (2) we never see angels with crowns; (3) in 7:11, the elders are distinguished from the angels; (4) in 5:8-10, the elders sing a hymn of praise, and we have no record that angels ever sing; (5) in their song, they claim to have been redeemed, something an angel could not say; (6) in 5:12, the angels say, while in 5:9 the elders sing; (7) the angels are never numbered, Heb. 12:22; (8) the name "elder" signifies maturity, while angels are timeless beings.

Twenty-four priests served in the OT temple (1 Chron. 24:3-5, 18, and Luke 1:5-9). It seems likely that these twenty-four elders signify the saints raptured and reigning with Christ in glory. When Daniel saw the thrones "set up" (Dan. 7:9; not "cast down"), they were empty; but John sees the thrones filled, for now God's people have been called home. We are kings and priests with Him (1:6).

IV. The Judgments Out of the Throne (4:5a)

Verse 5 describes not a throne of grace, but a throne of judgment. Thunder and lightning are warnings that the storm is coming! God thundered at Sinai when He gave the Law (Ex. 19:16), and He will thunder again to judge those who have broken His Law (see Ps. 29 and Ps. 77:18). God warned Egypt in this way (Ex. 9:23-28), and He will also warn this wicked world. See Ps. 9:7.

V. The Objects Before the Throne (4:5b-11)

A. The lamps.

These are symbols of the Holy Spirit (1:4), who is the Spirit of burning (Isa. 4:4). Christ has the fullness of the Spirit, for seven is the number of fullness (3:1). During this age of grace, the Spirit is pictured as a dove of peace (John 1:29-34); but after the church is taken away, the Spirit will minister a judgment of fire.

B. The sea of glass.

We have here a heavenly temple, similar to the OT temple (see 11:19 and Heb. 9:23). The seven lamps correspond to the seven-branched lampstand; the sea of glass to the laver; and the throne to the ark of the covenant where God reigned in glory. Revelation 6:9-11 indicates that there is an altar of sacrifice in heaven, and 8:3-5 that there is an incense alter. The twenty-four elders would correspond to the priests in the temple, and the living creatures to the cherubim embroidered on the veil. For the laver (or "sea") in the temple, see 1 Kings 7:23-27. The heavenly sea pictures God's holiness; the fire, His judgment on sin because He is holy.

C. The living creatures.

"Beasts" means "living creatures." Four is the number of the earth, so we have here God's covenant with creation. Read Gen. 9:8-13 and you will see that God has made His covenant with mankind, fowls, cattle, and the wild beasts; and each of these is represented by a face on the living creatures. God gave man dominion over creation, but this rule was lost through sin (Gen. 1:28-31; Ps. 8). However, in Christ, that dominion will be regained when the kingdom is established; see Isa. 11:6-8 and 65:25. The presence of the four creatures (symbolizing creation) before God's throne teaches us that He is in control of creation, and that He will keep His promise to one day deliver creation from the bondage of sin (Rom. 8:19-24).

These four living creatures are a combination of the seraphim of Isa. 6 and the creatures of Ezek. 1 and 10. These creatures are not named. In Rev. 4:7, each creature had four faces, corresponding to the four of Ezekiel's vision. These creatures before the throne praise God and give glory and honor to Him. Psalm 148 shows how all creation praises God; what a tragedy that a sinful world refuses to praise Him.

The elders join in this praise and cast their crowns before the throne. These crowns symbolize their rewards for service while on earth. When we get to heaven, we will realize in a new way that all praise belongs to God and to God alone. Verse 11 is the first of several doxologies in Revelation. Here the heavenly beings praise God because He is the Creator of all things. In Rev. 5:9-10, the beasts and elders join to praise God for His redemption through Christ's blood; for even creation is redeemed through the cross. In Rev. 11:16-19, heaven praises God because He is the judge who will justly punish the world for its sins.

The stage is now set: the church has been taken to heaven; the Lord is on the throne; all of heaven praises Him and awaits the outpouring of His wrath. It is interesting to note that the name of God used here is "Lord God Almighty" (4:8). History tells us that this was the official title used by Emperor Domitian, who was responsible for the persecutions that sent John to Patmos. Men and women may honor themselves, but the day will come when everybody — great and small — will acknowledge that Jesus Christ is Lord of all.

REVELATION 5

I. The Sealed Book (5:1-5)

The word "book" (v. 1) refers to a scroll; bound books did not exist in those days. These scrolls were made of rushes that grew along the rivers and were very costly. This particular scroll is Christ's title deed to creation. A Roman will was sealed with seven seals; this scroll is the will, or testament, giving Christ the right to claim creation by virtue of His sacrifice (v. 9). A will could be opened only by the heir, and Christ is the "heir of all things" (Heb. 1:2). Some students think that the scroll contains the judgments of chapters 6–9. The fact that the scroll is written on both sides shows that nothing more can be added to it; the destiny of the sinful world is determined.

To understand this scene, we must consider the Hebrew system of owning land. If a man became poor and had to sell his land, or himself, he could be redeemed by a kinsman. The story of Ruth is based on this law; see also Jer. 32:6-15 and Lev. 25:23-25. This redeemer had to be a near relative who was willing and able to purchase the property and set the kinsman free. All of creation has been under bondage to sin, Satan, and death; but now Christ, our Kinsman-Redeemer, is going to set creation free.

God makes it clear that only Christ can redeem. No saint in

glory, no person on earth, no soul in the underworld of death, could take that book. No one was worthy. John wept for several reasons: (1) he yearned to see creation set free from bondage; (2) he wanted the promise of 4:1 to be fulfilled; (3) he knew that the OT promises to Israel could never be fulfilled unless the scroll could be opened. John was sharing in the "groaning" of Rom. 8:22-23. The angel dried his tears by pointing to Christ. The "Lion" (v. 5) takes us back to Gen. 49:8-10 and speaks of Christ's royalty in the family of David. The "Root of David" speaks of His deity, the One through whom David came (Isa. 11:1, 10). Christ is worthy to open the book because He has "prevailed," which means "to overcome" (2:7, 11, 17, 26, etc.), "conquer" (6:2), or "win the victory" (15:2). The Lamb has taken the victory! (17:14)

II. The Slain Lamb (5:6-10)

John looked for a lion, but he saw a Lamb. In the two names Lion and Lamb we have the two-fold emphasis of OT prophecy: as the Lion, Christ conquers and reigns; as the Lamb, He dies for the sins of the world. We cannot separate the suffering and glory (Luke 24:26; 1 Peter 1:11), the crown and the cross. It is worthy of note that Christ is called "the Lamb" twenty-eight times in Revelation. In fact, the whole Bible could be summarized by tracing the theme of "the lamb." Isaac asked, "Where is the lamb?" in Gen. 22:7; and John the Baptist answered, "Behold the Lamb of God!" (John 1:29) Now John writes, "Worthy is the Lamb!" See also Ex. 12 and Isa. 53.

The word "slain" literally means "cut in the throat for a sacrifice." Christ was not merely killed; He was offered as a sacrifice. His death and resurrection are proof that He is worthy to be the heir of creation, worthy to take the book and open the seals. When Christ takes the book, the elders (representing the glorified church) sing His praises and magnify His death for the redemption of a lost creation. Heaven sings about the cross. The vials of incense typify the prayers of God's people (Ps. 141:2; Luke 1:10). This does not mean that Christians on earth can access believers now in heaven. It is a symbolic reminder that God remembers the prayers of His people, "Thy kingdom come" (see Matt. 6:10). Note in 6:9-11 and 8:1-6 that God will one day answer the prayers of His people who have suffered persecution and trial because of their faith. For hundreds of years, God's people have been praying for the return of Christ and the righting of wrongs in the world; one day God will answer those prayers. "We shall reign on earth" (v. 10) is their expectation. This is another proof that Christ will one day reign over a literal kingdom on earth. See 20:4.

III. The Shouting Hosts (5:11-14)

The elders sing, but the angelic creatures "say with a loud voice." There is no evidence in the Bible that angels sing. Job 38:7 states that, at Creation, the "sons of God [angels] shouted for joy." The "Christmas angels" of Luke 2:13-14 praised God by "saying," not singing. The multitudes of angels in heaven joined their voices in a great shout of praise when the Lamb took the scroll, but they did not sing. Singing is a privilege reserved for the saints of God who have experienced the joy of salvation. There are many things angels can do that saints cannot; but an angel cannot experience salvation, nor can he sing with the saints the praises of the Lamb. On the number of the angels, see Dan. 7:10.

Christ alone is worthy of praise. It is interesting to contrast this doxology with the earthly life of Christ. His enemies said He was worthy of death (John 19:7), but the angels say He is worthy of praise. Men accused Him of working by the power of Satan (Matt. 12:24), but the angels say He is worthy of power. He became poor for our sakes (2 Cor. 8:9), but He deserves all riches. "The preaching of the cross is foolishness" to sinful man (1 Cor. 1:18), but it is wisdom to the angels. On earth, Jesus was "crucified in weakness" (2 Cor. 13:4), but in heaven He is lauded for His power. Dishonored on earth, He is honored in glory. Made a curse on the cross, He is today both the recipient and bestower of blessing.

After the angels completed their praise, all of creation joined to honor the Lord Jesus Christ. "Every creature" suggests that all creation anticipates the redemption that will come when Christ finally overcomes the enemy and establishes His kingdom.

Compare v. 13 with Phil. 2:10-11 and Col. 1:20. All creation praises God the Father and God the Son; see John 5:23. Many people say, "I worship God, but not Jesus Christ." To ignore Christ is to insult the Father. In heaven, every angel and every raptured saint will honor the Father and the Son and praise them.

Christ is about to open the sealed book and release judgment on the world. Keep in mind the dual purpose of the Tribulation: (1) to punish the nations for their sins, especially the way they have treated Israel, and (2) to purge Israel and prepare a believing remnant to receive Christ when He comes in glory (Rev. 19:11). The inhabitants of the earth are ignorant of this glorious scene in heaven. As in the days of Noah and Lot, they go on their way, eating and drinking and ignoring God's warnings. Then the Lamb will begin to open the book, and judgment will fall. How important it is for you to be saved *now*, while there is still opportunity!

REVELATION 6

John now begins to describe the first half of Daniel's 70th week (Dan. 9:27), that seven-year period of tribulation. The Lamb has taken the sealed book (His title deed to creation); He is about to open the seals and declare war on the godless world. With the opening of each seal in heaven, an important event will take place on earth. Be sure to compare these seals with what Christ taught about the end times in Matt. 24.

I. The First Seal: Antichrist Rises to Power (6:1-2)

With the opening of the first four seals, one of the four living creatures before the throne (4:6-11) calls for the rider and horse to "Come!" The first horse is white, and his rider is given a bow and a crown. Do not confuse this scene with that described in Rev. 19:11, where we see Christ riding in conquest. No, the rider here is Antichrist, the false Christ, beginning his conquest on earth. The fact that he has a bow, but no arrows, indicates that he conquers the nations peacefully. After the church has been raptured, the way will be opened for Antichrist to move in triumph (2 Thes. 2). There will be a false peace temporarily, for he will unite Europe and make his pact with the Jews (1 Thes. 5:2-3). This passage parallels Matt. 24:5 and fulfills Christ's prophecy in John 5:43.

II. The Second Seal: War (6:3-4)

This worldwide peace will not last long, for while men are saying "Peace and safety," terrible wars will break loose. This parallels Matt. 24:6-7. Red is a color associated with terror and carnage. In Revelation we have the red horse of war (6:3-4), the red dragon (12:3), and the red beast (17:3). Note that God gives Antichrist authority to take peace from the earth; this is all a part of the divine plan. Antichrist exchanges his arrowless bow for a great sword, and men begin to kill each other. This indicates clearly that methods of international agreement and diplomacy will not bring lasting peace.

III. The Third Seal: Famine (6:5-6)

Famine and war often go together; see Matt. 24:7. The color black makes one think of famine; see Jer. 14:1-2 and Lam. 5:10. The rider (still Antichrist) holds a pair of balances, indicating that his government has established control of food. A measure of wheat was about a quart; and a penny was a day's wages for a worker. In other words, food will be so scarce it will take a person all day to earn enough wages for just a quart of grain! But note that there is no scarcity of oil and wine for the rich. The rich get richer and enjoy their luxuries, while the poor get poorer and can hardly get enough to eat. This indicates that all man-made schemes to give people even the necessities of life will fail. It is worth noting that grain, oil, and wine were the key products of Israel (Hosea 2:8). Since Antichrist has made his covenant with Israel, he would want to protect its resources.

IV. The Fourth Seal: Death (6:7-8)

The word "pale" suggests a leprous color (Lev. 13:49, "greenish"). Death rides this horse, and "Hades" (not hell) rides with him. Death claims the body, Hades the soul. God gives them authority to kill one-fourth of the earth's population! Four methods are used: the sword (violence and war); hunger (famine); death, or pestilence (disease accompanies war and famine); and beasts (nature takes over when civilization falls apart). Read Ezek. 14:21 for a parallel. Even the wild beasts will be hungry and attack humans! What terrible judgments await the Christ-rejecting world after the church is taken to heaven! See Matt. 24:7.

V. The Fifth Seal: The Martyrs (6:9-11)

The OT priest poured the blood of the sacrifice under the brazen altar (Lev. 4:7); and since the blood speaks of the life (or soul, Lev. 17:11), we witness here the souls of the martyrs under the heavenly altar. Their murderers had not yet been avenged. These martyred saints pray for vengeance; see Ps. 74:9-19, 79:5, and 94:3-4. It is true that saints in this age are told to pray for those who persecute them, and this is what Christ, Stephen, and Paul did (Luke 23:34; Acts 7:60; 2 Tim. 4:16). But this period will be a time of judgment, when God will be answering the prayers of His people for deliverance and vengeance. After all, God is judging the world when they pray; so they are praying in the will of God. This parallels Matt. 24:9. God promises them that He will answer their prayers; but first, more of their brethren will be slain. We see other saints slain in 12:11, 14:13, and 20:4-5. Among the slain will be Moses and Elijah, God's two witnesses, who even then were ministering on earth (11:1-7). Revelation 20:4 indicates that these Tribulation martyrs will be resurrected to reign during the Millennium.

VI. The Sixth Seal: World Chaos (6:12-17)

This passage parallels Luke 21:25-26; see also Joel 2:30-31, 3:15 and Isa. 13:9-10, 34:2-4. Three earthquakes are mentioned in Revelation (6:12; 11:13; 16:18-19). There is no doubt that these are literal earthquakes, but along with them will be disturbances on earth and in the heavens that will frighten great and small. Some students think that these verses describe the results of atomic warfare, with the sun and moon blacked out, great land masses moved, and people hiding in holes in the ground to escape atomic radiation. This may be so; but we need to note that the people are hiding from Christ and His wrath in particular, not from some manmade catastrophe.

Verse 15 is a vivid description of what life will be like during the first three and one-half years of tribulation. For one thing, kingdoms will be revived. Today, the movement is toward nationalism and democracy; but this trend will change. See 16:12-14. Antichrist will rule over "the United States of Europe," the revived Roman Empire, with a number of petty kings following him (17:12-14). Another characteristic of Tribulation days is militarism; there will be "chief captains." This is a Roman title meaning "military tribunes" and is completely in keeping with the revived Roman Empire of Antichrist. Slavery ("bondmen") will be present; see 18:13, where "slaves and the souls of men" are included in the merchandise of Babylon. Great wealth will coexist with great poverty, and this redistribution of wealth will wreck the economies of nations. It seems, then, that the judgment of the sixth seal involves literal physical destruction in the heavens and on earth, as well as a shaking of the economic and political systems of nations. All of this will make it easier for Antichrist to extend his rule.

The peoples of the earth will know then that Christ is sending judgment, but they will not receive Him! They would rather hide in the rocks than in the Rock. The first three and one-half years of the Tribulation are mere preparation for the last three and one-half years, and this latter period is known as "the wrath of God" (see 11:18; 12:12; 14:10; 18:3; etc.). There is a pause, however, between the sixth and seventh seals (as there is also between the sixth and seventh trumpets, 10:1–11:13) for us to see the two great groups of redeemed who will be saved during the Tribulation period.

In summary, note that Antichrist begins his career as a peaceful political conqueror, but then resorts to war and economic controls to dominate other nations. The world will accept his false peace because it has rejected the Prince of Peace, Jesus Christ.

REVELATION 7

There is a pause between the opening of the sixth and seventh seals; judgment halts for a brief time while God seals 144,000 Jews who will carry His message to the ends of the earth. We are not specifically told that these Jews will be God's ambassadors, but we assume that this is why He seals them. We have seen that the day of God's wrath is about to come (6:15-17); so God brings a lull in the storm and extends His mercy to Jew and Gentile alike. We see here two groups of redeemed people:

I. The Sealed Jews (7:1-8)

The winds of heaven speak of God's judgment, and the judgments here are specifically on the earth, sea, and green vegetation. It may be that these four angels holding the four winds are also the angels who blow the first four trumpets, for the judgments are similar (see 8:6-12). The angel from the east holds the seal of God. A seal signifies possession and protection; note 9:4. Today, the Christian is sealed by the Holy Spirit (Eph. 1:13-14). This sealing happens the instant the sinner trusts Christ, and it assures the believer of eternal life and an inheritance in heaven. The sealing angel commands the angels of the winds to hold back their judgment until His servants have been sealed and thus protected from the judgment to come. For a parallel scene, see Ezek. 9. Remember too that Christ taught that the angels of God would have a part in gathering His elect (Matt. 24:31). Along with the angels of the winds, we have also the angels of fire (14:18) and of water (16:5). These angels are God's special ministers who supervise the activities of nature.

These sealed servants are all Jews: there are 12,000 each from twelve tribes of Israel. It is unfortunate that some well-meaning Christians have taught that the 144,000 are symbolic of the church (the new Israel), because the church is no longer on earth at this point in history. The 144,000 are true Jews who will be alive on earth at this time. They will probably be won to Christ through the ministries of Moses and Elijah, the two witnesses who will preach during the first three and one-half years of the Tribulation (see 11:1-12). These Jews will probably be God's chosen missionaries — 144,000 "Apostle Pauls" who carry the Gospel to all nations! This event will fulfill Christ's prophecy of Matt. 24:14; the result will be the salvation of a multitude of Gentiles (7:9ff). When you think of the multitudes that Paul won during his ministry, you can begin to imagine what 144,000 such missionaries would do!

The tribe of Dan is missing from this list, and the tribe of Manasseh takes its place. The reasons seem to be: (1) Dan led Israel into idolatry, Jud. 18:30; 1 Kings 12:28-30; (2) therefore God promised to blot out the name of the idolater, Deut. 29:18-21.

II. The Saved Gentiles (7:9-17)

The Jews were numbered, but this multitude could not be numbered. These Gentiles are the fruit of the labors of the 144,000, and they come from every nation under heaven. They are not a part of the church, since we see them *before* the throne, and not *on* thrones, as are the elders. Verse 14 makes it clear that they come (not "came") out of the Great Tribulation. Here John sees them standing before the heavenly throne, praising God and the Lamb. Their "palms" suggest the Feast of Tabernacles in the OT (Lev. 23:40-43), the event at which Israel rejoiced at the blessings of the Lord. They are dressed in white robes, which indicates their righteousness through the Lamb. Verse 14 says that these Gentiles were saved by faith in Christ, for this is the only way anyone can be saved.

Verses 15-17 lists the trials that these Gentiles endured on earth.

They had been hungry and thirsty, for they were likely victims of the scarcity of food and pure water. They had no refuge from the heat of the day. They suffered tears and testings. It is likely that these Gentiles belong to the "sheep" of Matt. 25:31-46, the Gentiles who loved the Jews and befriended them during the Tribulation. These believers refused to receive the mark of the Beast (13:16-18) and thus were not able to buy or sell. Their friendship with the hated and persecuted Jews would incur the wrath of the rulers. Of course, they would also have to endure the terrible judgments of the Tribulation: the rationing of food, 13:17; water turned to blood, 16:4; and scorching heat, 16:8-9.

Note that the 144,000 survive the Tribulation, while multitudes of believing Gentiles will give their lives during this awful time. (Remember the souls under the altar in 6:9-11.) God will reward these Gentile believers and will give them glory for their suffering. Many students believe that the promises of vv. 14-17 will be fulfilled in the millennial kingdom rather than in heaven. Revelation 20:4 indicates a special resurrection for these Tribulation martyrs and promises that they will live and reign during the kingdom age. However, we have good reason to apply vv. 14-17 to the blessed state of the saints of God now in glory.

In summary, we note that Israel has returned to its ancient land in unbelief. The temple worship has begun. Antichrist is ruling over the United States of Europe, and the world is convulsed with war, famine, and political and economic chaos. The two witnesses (Moses and Elijah) are preaching in Israel, and God has sealed a remnant within the nation—144,000 Jews—to be His witnesses among the Gentiles. Of course, their ministry will suffer persecution, and many of them will be arrested (Matt. 25:36). But their Gentile converts will assist them and, because of their testimony, many Gentiles will lay down their lives for the Gospel.

Some students believe that 2 Thes. 2:11-14 teaches that people who willfully reject the Gospel during this age of grace cannot be saved after the church is removed from the earth. They argue that people would not believe the truth, but instead will believe a lie. Those left behind heard the Word and understood it, yet willingly refused it. However, a multitude of Gentiles will believe the Gospel after the church is gone, and they will be willing to lay down their lives for Christ. Yes, people will be saved during the Tribulation, but they will pay a severe price. How much wiser it is to receive Christ today!

We may outline the chapter as follows:

Group #1 (7:1-8)	Group #2 (7:9-17)
1. Jews	1. Gentiles
2. A group of 144,000	2. Multitude no man could number
3. Sealed and protected	3. Not sealed; many will die
4. Seen witnessing on earth	4. Seen worshiping in heaven
5. Enter into the kingdom	5. Share in the kingdom

REVELATION 8

The opening of the seventh seal introduces the next series of judgments, the seven trumpets. In the OT, trumpets were used to announce war (Num. 10:5-9), move the camp (Num. 8), announce the feasts (Num. 10:10), and bring judgment (Josh. 6:13ff). The trumpet sound is a symbol of power and authority (Ex. 19:16). Note that there is a parallel between the seven trumpets and the seven vials of chapters 15–16:

The trumpets	Recipient of Judgment	The vials
8:1-7	The earth	16:1-2
8:8-9	The sea	16:3
8:10-11	The rivers	16:4-7
8:12-13	The heavens	16:8-9
9:1-2	Mankind	16:10-11
9:13-21	Army/Euphrates	16:12-16
11:15-19	Nations in wrath	16:17-21

It would seem that the seven vials are an intensified judgment that follow the trumpet judgments. The trumpets belong in the first three and one-half years, while the vials are poured out during the last three and one-half years, the period called "the wrath of God" (14:10; 15:7).

I. The Preparation in Heaven (8:1-6)

A. Silence (v. 1).

This is the lull before the storm; see Zech. 2:13; Hab. 2:20; Isa. 41:1; and Zeph. 1:7, 14-18. In 7:10-12, we have a great expression of praise from the heavenly hosts; here we have breathless silence in heaven as judgment is about to fall.

B. Supplication (vv. 2-6).

We noted in chapter 4 that there is a heavenly sanctuary, and here we have the altar of incense, symbolic of prayer. See Lev. 16:12 and Ps. 141:2. This angel may be Christ, the Heavenly Priest. The "prayers of the saints" are not prayers given through the saints in glory. In 5:3, no man was found worthy to open the book save Jesus Christ; so why should we pray through any other name? These prayers are the prayers of God's people, "Thy kingdom come!" This incense especially represents the cries of the martyrs (6:9-11; 20:4). Many of the prayers of vengeance in the Psalms will be used rightfully by God's people during those days of intense suffering. The fire from the altar cast upon the earth speaks of the wrath of God about to be poured out on unbelievers. Compare v. 5 with 4:5, 11:19, and 16:18, and you will see that the thunderings always give warning that the storm is coming. The seven angels stand poised for action, then sound their trumpets one by one.

II. The Desolation on the Earth (8:7-11)

The first judgment parallels the seventh plague of Egypt (Ex. 9:18-26). Egypt was the center of a godless world system, so it is logical that the plagues in Moses' day would be repeated on a worldwide scale during the Tribulation. Hailstorms can do terrible damage, but when fire is mixed with hail, the possibilities of desolation are staggering. One-third of the trees and green grass will be destroyed by this first trumpet of judgment. There are thirteen references to "the third part" in Rev. 8–9. Some students believe this refers only to the area covered by the revived Roman Empire, ruled over by the Antichrist.

The second trumpet affects the sea, turning one-third of it into blood and killing one-third of its creatures, as well as destroying one-third of the ships. This event parallels the first plague in Egypt (Ex. 7:19-21). The burning object that fell was not a literal mountain; it was "something like" a great mountain. "The sea" here may mean only the Mediterranean; but it is likely that all the seas on the globe are involved.

The third trumpet affects the rivers, making their waters bitter. The great star of v. 10 is known only to God, who calls the stars by their names (Job 9:9-10). Jeremiah prophesied that one day Israel would have to drink the bitter waters (Jer. 9:14-15). It seems that this bitterness will continue until the establishment of the millennial kingdom, for in Ezek. 47:6-9, it is prophesied that the healing waters will overcome the bitter effects of the Tribulation judgments.

Are these judgments to be understood literally? We think so. If God could send these same judgments to Egypt in Moses' day, what is to prevent Him from sending them upon the whole world? We can only imagine the tremendous economic consequences from the loss of farm and pasture land and from the pollution of pure water. Mankind has never appreciated the blessings of God's goodness in nature. Yet, even when He takes away some of those blessings, sinners will still not repent (9:20-21).

III. The Agitation in the Sky (8:12)

The fourth angel sounds and brings about tremendous calamities in the skies, for one-third of the light of the heavenly bodies is blacked out! This is the fulfillment of a prophecy by Christ in Luke 21:25-28 (see also Amos 8:9). It is interesting to note that God brought the heavenly bodies into being on the fourth day of Creation; when the fourth trumpet sounds, He will darken them.

What will the consequences be? For one thing, terror will fill the earth. Mankind has always feared signs in the skies. This terror, however, will not bring men to repentance. The first judgment will devastate vegetable life, and shortened days will rob plants of sunlight. Jesus said that the shortening of days during the Tribulation would mean the saving of lives (Matt. 24:22). However, it is easy to imagine the sin, crime, and terror that will rule the streets when darkness comes early in the day, and when night is darker than ever. "Everyone practicing evil hates the light," says John 3:19-20. This crime wave will be one such as humanity has never seen before.

IV. The Proclamation from the Angel (8:13)

This angel is a literal messenger from God, giving warning to the world that the next three judgments would be even worse! We would think that men would heed God's call and repent, but such is not the case.

The phrase "inhabiters of the earth" is found also in 3:10, 6:10,

11:10, 13:8, 13:14, 14:6, and 17:8. It refers not to those who live "on" the earth, but those who live "for" the earth. They are "earthlings"—people who reject heaven and its Christ for the comforts of this world. They are perfectly described in Phil. 3:18-20. They are described in Exodus as the "mixed multitude" that lusted after the foods of Egypt and refused the manna from heaven. Such people will go through tribulation (Rev. 3:10) and will be responsible for the killing of God's saints (Rev. 6:10). They will rejoice when God's two witnesses are slain (11:10); but note the contrast in 12:12, where heaven rejoices at Satan's expulsion! Revelation 13:8 makes it clear that these earth-dwellers will worship the Beast, which means they will reject Christ completely. Having rejected the Truth, they will believe the lie.

Every soul must answer: Is my citizenship in heaven, or do I belong only to this world?

REVELATION 9

The well-known Bible scholar and Revelation expert Dr. Wilbur M. Smith writes: "It is probable that, apart from the exact identification of Babylon in chapters 17 and 18, the meaning of the two judgments in this chapter represents the most difficult major problem in the Revelation." The angel in 8:13 promised three "woes" upon the earth, and these are sent with the sounding of the fifth (9:1-12), sixth (9:13-21), and seventh (11:15-19) trumpets. Review the suggested outline of Revelation and you will see that we are now approaching the middle of the Tribulation, at which time several critical events will take place.

I. The Army of Hell Released (9:1-12)

A. The star (vv. 1, 11).

John did not see the star fall; v. 1 should read, " . . . and I saw a star having fallen . . . " (at some time in the past). It is likely that this star refers to Satan. He is called "Lucifer," which means "brightness" or "morning star." Isaiah 14:12ff describes the fall of Satan in the dateless past, and Ezek. 28:11-19 completes the picture. Note also Luke 10:18. God gives Satan the "key to the abyss." This bottomless pit is not Hades or hell; rather, it is a prison somewhere in the underworld, where demons are confined by God. (Read Luke 8:26-36 to see how the demons dread being sent into the pit.) In 1:18 we read that Christ holds all the keys; Satan must get his authority from Christ. This fallen star (Satan) is also described as a destroyer in v. 11. He is king over the demons of hell.

B. The smoke (v. 2).

The smoke itself is not the demonic creatures, for v. 3 makes it clear that the creatures come out of the smoke. The underworld is a place of darkness and fire; it is here compared to a great furnace. People who joke about hell little realize how ignorant they are of its torments. This awful darkness reminds us of the plague in Egypt (Ex. 10:21-29) when the darkness could be felt. Satan is the prince of darkness. It is worth noting that this "bottomless pit" will release the Beast one day (11:7; 17:8) and that the devil will one day be cast into it (20:1-3).

C. The scorpion-like creatures (vv. 3-10).

Scorpions are native to the Holy Land, with some species growing to six inches in length. Their main weapon is the sting at the end of their tails, and they are used in the Bible as a symbol of painful judgment (Deut. 28:38, 42; 1 Kings 12:11-14). These hellish creatures from the smoke are also compared to the locust, since plagues of locusts were common scourges in Israel (see Joel 2). That these are not literal locusts is clear from the warning in v. 4 (see 8:7), and from the fact that they have a king (v. 11, see Prov. 30:27). They are forbidden to torment the sealed Jews (7:1-3); their time is limited to five months. Their purpose is to torment, not to kill. In fact, people will want to die, but God will not permit it (see Jer. 8:3). It is likely that these are demonic creatures, released from the pit to torment men. This judgment parallels the eighth plague of Egypt (Ex. 10:3-20). The fact that the creatures have characteristics of beasts (horses, v. 7), men, and wild animals (v. 8) suggests that Satan is imitating the heavenly creatures of 4:7.

This is the first woe, and what a time of torture the population of the earth will endure! How much better it is to know Christ today and escape the wrath to come!

II. The Angels at the River Released (9:13-21)

This is the second of the three "woes" promised in 8:13. The voice comes from the altar of incense because the prayers of the saints have gone up to God, asking Him to avenge their blood (6:9-11; 8:3). In 7:1-3 we saw four angels restrained by command; here we see four angels (undoubtedly fallen angels) commanded to be released. The Euphrates River has always held a notable place in history. It flowed from Eden, where history began; and it will figure in the events that will be the climax to history (16:12ff). Babylon was situated on the Euphrates (Rev. 17–18). These four angels are prepared for "the hour, day, month, and year" on God's schedule; and it is their task to slay one-third of the earth's population. In 6:8 we read that one-fourth of the people were slain, leaving three-fourths for the judgments to come; after these angels had destroyed another third, one-half of the world's population had been killed.

Once released, these angels bring into battle armies of horsemen totaling 200 million soldiers! This satanic cavalry is not like any other army either in appearance or in the weapons it uses. Fire, brimstone, and smoke are their chief weapons; they also have serpent-like tails. This is not another description of the army discussed in vv. 1-12, since that army is forbidden to kill. This army is commissioned to slay one-third of humankind. This is one way God will answer the prayers of the martyrs in 6:9-11.

One would think that multitudes of people would repent of their sins and turn to Christ; but such is not the case. Those who (in God's mercy) are spared will only continue in their awful sins. The goodness of God in sparing them did not lead them to repentance (Rom. 2:4-6); therefore, they will have to endure greater judgments in the days to come, and ultimately the lake of fire.

Verses 20-21 give us a vivid picture of what life will be like after the church is taken to heaven. There will be widespread idolatry. Of course, idol worship is demon worship (1 Cor. 10:16-22). Satan has always wanted mankind to worship him (Matt. 4:8-10), and now he will receive that worship. Wherever you find idolatry, you will find ignorance and immorality; v. 21 tells us of the awful sins and crimes that will occur in those days. The word "sorceries" is *pharmakeia* in the Gk., the root for the English words "pharmacist" and "pharmaceutical." It means "having to do with drugs." This same word is translated "witchcraft" in Gal. 5:20 and "sorcerers" in 21:8 and 22:15. See also 18:23. The fact that sorcerers use drugs and potions in their devilish activities shows the connection between these words. John suggests that there will be a revival of witchcraft and an increase in the use of drugs in the latter days. Several organizations of witches exist worldwide, and spiritism is on the increase. As for the increase in the use of drugs, we need only read today's newspapers!

How does this chapter fit into the whole scheme of Revelation? It is likely that this huge army of 200 million horsemen will appear just before the middle of the Tribulation. The Beast is already the head of the revived Roman Empire, co-operating with the "world church" and the United Nations. God permits Satan to muster this huge army, possibly from Russia. We do know from Ezek. 38–39 that Russia will invade Palestine about the middle of the Tribulation period. It will try to conquer Israel, but the Beast will deliver the Jews and fulfill the seven-year covenant that he made to protect them. Ezekiel makes it clear that God judges Russia and sends the army home in defeat. Once in the Holy Land, the Beast will break his covenant, move into the temple, and begin to assume worldwide powers. Revelation 11:1-2 indicates that the Gentiles are in possession of the rebuilt temple in Jerusalem; and the rest of the chapter indicates that the Beast slays the witnesses who have been preaching for the first three and one-half years of the Tribulation. This huge army (v. 16) is not the Russian army that invades Israel, but the blowing of this sixth trumpet indicates the rise of military conquests and points to the Battle of Gog and Magog that will take place at this point. Review the prophetic timetable given in the introductory notes.

REVELATION 10

This chapter introduces us to the middle of the Tribulation period (see the outline). According to Dan. 9:27, this is the time the Beast breaks his covenant with Israel and reveals himself in his satanic fury. Note also that the two witnesses minister during the first three and one-half years (11:3); the Jewish remnant is protected by God during the last three and one-half years (12:6, 14); the Beast has world-wide authority the last three and one-half years (13:5); Satan is cast to earth for three and one-half years of awful persecution against believers (12:12); and Jerusalem is trodden down by the Gentiles for three and one-half years (11:2). We note a parenthesis between the sixth and seventh trumpets (10:1–11:14). The seventh trumpet will introduce the seven vials of the wrath of God, and the last three and one-half years of tribulation ("the wrath of God") will get underway.

I. The Appearance of the Angel (10:1-4)

This heavenly messenger is most likely Jesus Christ, the Angel of the Lord. John had seen a "strong angel" back in 5:2; now he sees "another mighty angel." The symbols used here take us back to the description of the glorified Christ given in 1:12-16. The cloud and rainbow refer to 1:16; the feet of fire to 1:15; the face as the sun to 1:16. The voice like the lion certainly refers to 5:5; see also Hosea 11:10 and Joel 3:16. This is not a voice of gracious invitation; it is a voice announcing that judgment is coming. Perhaps the best evidence that this angel is Christ is in 11:3, where He says, "I will give power unto My two witnesses." So, here is Christ, the Angel of the Lord, coming to announce that God is about to work speedily and finish His purposes on the earth.

The little book (v. 2) is in contrast to the large scroll of 5:1. This scroll is open; the one in 5:1 is sealed. We see from vv. 9-11 that this is a book of prophecy; v. 7 makes it clear that the contents of the book were declared by the prophets. Since the OT prophets did not speak of church truths, these prophecies must relate to Israel, the Jews, and Jerusalem; this theme is exactly what we find in chapters 11 and following. Perhaps this little book is the sealed message of Dan. 12:4, 9; it is now opened to be fulfilled.

The Lord claims, as it were, all of the earth and seas by standing on the land and the sea. Read Josh. 1:1-3. We do not know what He said, nor what the thunders uttered (see 1 Sam. 7:10 and Ps. 29). It is useless to speculate. John is told to seal up (not reveal) the words of the thunders, the only revelation in this book that is sealed. This vision of Christ makes it clear that He is in control, and that He will fulfill God's purpose and claim His inheritance.

II. The Announcement from the Angel (10:5-7)

This solemn scene begins as Christ lifts His hand and affirms that there will be delay (not "time") no longer. The souls under the altar had asked, "How long?" (6:10-11), and the answer is now given: there is to be delay no longer! Scoffers ask today, "Where is the promise of His coming? Why isn't God doing something?" (2 Peter 3) This present period of delay is the sinner's opportunity for salvation! Christ states that in the days of the seventh trumpet sound (11:15-19), God will finish His program. The term "mystery" (v. 7) means a hidden truth from God. Mortal man cannot understand why sin and suffering are in the world, and why honest saints suffer while the rebellious sinners go free. We can be sure God will straighten these things out and complete His program. Note 11:18 especially—and take comfort!

Some think that the "mystery of God" is contained in the contents of the little book. Perhaps it is. This much we know: God is in control of history and will ultimately see to it that right triumphs over wrong.

III. The Appropriation of the Book (10:8-11)

It is not enough for John to see this book in Christ's hand, or even to know what it contains. He must appropriate it, make it a part of the inner person. Read Ezek. 2–3 and Jer. 15:16 for similar events. The Word of God is our food (Matt. 4:4; Ps. 119:103); we must take it in and assimilate it before it can do us any good. It is good to read the Bible and study it; but we also need to memorize the Word and digest it inwardly through the power of the Spirit.

The eating of the little book had a two-fold effect on John: it was sweet to his taste, but bitter in his stomach, much like the effect of the two-edged sword of the Word (Heb. 4:12). We enjoy the blessings of the Word, but we must also feel the burdens of the Word. John was blessed to know that God would fulfill His promises; but he felt bitterness as he realized the sufferings that would take place during the next three and one-half years of tribulation.

This digesting of the Word prepared John for his continued ministry as a prophet. What a lesson for us as witnesses! How tragic it is when we try to serve the Lord and speak for Him, without first taking time to appropriate His Word. Only that which is a part of our inner selves can ever be shared with others. How important it is for the saint to take time daily to read the Word and absorb it.

The word "before" in v. 11 should read "concerning"; John would prophesy concerning many peoples, nations, tongues, and kings. We see the nations of the world referred to often in the next section of Revelation, for Satan will be stirring them up and getting them ready for the campaign of Armageddon (16:12-14).

REVELATION 11

In chapters 11–12, we are definitely on Jewish ground. We see the Jewish temple (11:1-2), Jerusalem (11:8), the ark (11:19), the ruling Christ (12:5), Michael (12:7), and Satan's persecution of the Jews (12:17). If we spiritualize this passage and apply any of it to the church, we will be in serious trouble. At this point, we are at the middle of the Tribulation.

I. The Ministry of the Two Witnesses (11:1-14)

A. The period of their ministry (vv. 1-4).

By now the Jewish temple has been rebuilt, and the nation (though in unbelief) is worshiping Jehovah again. It seems likely that the two witnesses will minister during the first half of the Tribulation, preaching to the Jews and having access to the temple. At the middle of the Tribulation, Antichrist will break his covenant with Israel and take possession of the temple area (2 Thes. 2; Dan. 9:27; Matt. 24:15). He will set himself up as god, thus bringing about the "abomination of desolation" that both Daniel and Christ predicted. We see the temple overrun by the Gentiles for three and one-half years. God asks John to measure the temple area, a symbolic action that goes back to Ezek. 40–41 and Zech. 2. To measure something means to claim it. Though the forces of Satan have taken over the Jewish temple, Christ will claim it again and restore it to His people. Note the allusion in v. 4 to Zech. 4–5 concerning Zerubbabel and Joshua, the high priest. These two men were God's servants for reclaiming and rebuilding the temple and the nation after the Babylonian Captivity, a time of national troubles.

B. The purpose of their ministry (vv. 5-6).

They will display God's power to unbelieving Jews and Gentiles, and many will be saved through their witness. They are called prophets (vv. 6, 10) as well as witnesses. They will announce to the world the great events to come and will incur the wrath of the Beast and his people. Because of the miracles they perform, these men have been identified with Moses and Elijah. Moses turned water into blood in Egypt, and Elijah prayed for drought and for rain, and also brought fire down from heaven. Malachi 4:5-6 promises that Elijah will come to minister again. However, some believe the two witnesses are Enoch and Elijah, since neither of these men died, but were both taken to heaven alive.

C. The persecution in their ministry (vv. 7-10).

Sinful men have never wanted to hear or obey God's Word (cf.

9:20-21). These two witnesses will be divinely protected until their work is finished; then God will allow the Beast to oppose them and slay them. Certainly Antichrist could not take possession of the temple unless these two prophets were out of the way. The citizens of Jerusalem will not even give them proper burial (see Ps. 79), and the whole world will see their bodies and rejoice. This period of three and one-half days will be a "satanic Christmas" celebration. People will host parties and exchange gifts and rejoice that their tormentors are dead.

D. The panic following their ministry (vv. 11-14).

God raises them from the dead! Think of the fear that will come to hearts around the world as people see two dead men come to life on the streets of Jerusalem! And then the two men will be caught up to heaven as their enemies stand and watch! Then will come an earthquake that will destroy one-tenth of the city and kill 7,000 people. What a day that will be!

II. The Testimony of the Seventh Trumpet (11:15-19)

We have been waiting since chapter 8 for this "third woe" that was promised. The seventh angel sounds the trumpet, and great voices from heaven announce that the kingdom (not kingdoms, for now the Beast has a united kingdom, 17:13) of this world is in Christ's power. Christ does not gain control of the world until 19:11ff, so this is a declaration of events to come. In this section, we also have the anticipation of heaven as the elders look ahead to see what will happen. How wonderful it is to have the vantage of heaven, and not of earth! All that happens from this point on leads up to the Son of God taking the reins of government and conquering His enemies.

This prophecy is followed by praise, as the elders glorify Christ for His power. This is the third of the heavenly praises. In 4:10-11, they praised Him as Creator; in 5:8-10, they praised Him as Redeemer; and here, they praise Him as the King and Judge. The prayers of the martyrs will now be answered (6:9-11), as well as the prayers of God's people, "Thy kingdom come!"

Verse 18 outlines what will happen in the last three and one-half years of the Tribulation period:

A. National and international hostility.

"The nations (Gentiles) were angry!" Read Pss. 2, 83, and Joel

3:9-13. This means that the nations will show their hatred for Christ and His people and that persecution will increase. Of course, Satan is on the scene (see 12:12ff), making a special effort to destroy the Jews. He has sought to destroy God's people ever since Cain killed Abel (1 John 3:10-13).

B. Resurrection.

The Tribulation martyrs will be raised (20:4) as well as the wicked dead (20:2ff). Daniel 12:1-3 seems to indicate that the OT saints will be raised after the Tribulation.

C. Judgment.

The saints will have their works judged, and the wicked will be judged and condemned for their sins. It will be a time of reward for the saints and of wrath for the sinners. Note that the lost are described as "them which destroy the earth." Satan is the Destroyer (9:11), and all who follow him share in his program of destruction. God commanded man to care for the earth and use its resources for his good and God's glory; but Satan has led men into destroying the earth and using its resources selfishly for evil.

The final three and one-half years of the Tribulation will climax the program of God. There will be delay no longer (10:6). The chapter begins with the temple on earth, and closes with the temple in heaven. We have again the evidences of the coming storm: lightnings, thunderings, voices. We saw this in 4:5 coming from the throne; in 8:5, coming from the incense altar; and now coming from the holy of holies in the temple. Some believe that the ark here is the literal ark from the OT temple, which vanished after the Captivity. But this is not likely, since none of the other temple furnishings in heaven have an earthly origin. The ark is the symbol of God's presence and God's covenant. It is called "the ark of the covenant." On earth, Israel is going through intense suffering, and God is reassuring them of His government and His care. There were thunderings and signs when the Law was given at Sinai; there are thunderings now as God is about to judge the world for breaking His Law.

"Thy wrath is come!" is the statement of v. 18, and this judgment will be fulfilled in chapters 15–16 when God pours out the vials of His wrath. The first three and one-half years are a period of tribulation, but the last three and one-half years are known as "the wrath of God" (14:10; 14:19; 15:7; 16:1).

REVELATION 12

The theme of this chapter is conflict, with the forces of Satan opposing the people of God. These visions outline in an amazing way the major themes of the Bible.

I. The Wonders in Heaven (12:1-6)

A. The Woman.

Some students want us to believe that this is Mary, the mother of our Lord, but vv. 6 and 13-17 make this impossible. Genesis 37:9 indicates that the woman represents the nation of Israel. Verse 5 informs us that the woman gives birth to Christ, and this symbolism points again to Israel (Rom. 1:3; 9:4-5). In the OT, Israel is pictured as a woman and mother (Isa. 54:5; Jer. 3:6-10). The woman is in travail, and the Child that is born is Christ (v. 5 with Ps. 2:9; Micah 5:2-3; Rev. 19:14ff). There is a gap of at least thirty-three years between the first and second sentences in v. 5, and between vv. 5 and 6 we have the entire church age.

B. The Dragon.

This is Satan (v. 9); and the heads, horns, and crowns refer us to 13:1 and 17:3, where the Beast (Antichrist) is described. Please keep in mind that the Beast is present from the outset as the leader of the federated nations of Europe, but he will not openly be revealed as Satan's "superman" until the middle of the Tribulation period. Verse 4 relates to Isa. 14:12ff, when Satan revolted against God and drew some of the angels down with him. See Job 38:7 and Jude 6.

Satan has always been a murderer (John 8:44), and now he seeks to destroy Christ. During OT days, Satan did all he could to keep the Savior from being born; when Jesus was born, Satan tried to kill Him (Matt. 2:16ff). During His earthly life, Christ was attacked by Satan in various ways, culminating in the cross. Satan also attacks the Jews. The 144,000 will be protected because they are sealed by God, but the other Jews will also be cared for by God. Perhaps the "they" in v. 6 refers to the Gentiles who care for the Jews at that time (Matt. 25:31-46).

Jesus told the believing Jews to flee when the Antichrist was revealed (Matt. 24:15-21). Note the parenthetical admonition in Matt. 24:15 that refers to the "reading" of the Word. Jewish believers during the middle of the Tribulation will read Matt. 24:15-21 and know what to do.

II. The War in Heaven (12:7-12)

The first two chapters of Job make it clear that Satan now has access to heaven, and Zech. 3 reveals that Satan accuses the saints before the throne of God. In the middle of the Tribulation, Satan will be cast out of heaven to the earth. Michael is the archangel assigned to protect Israel (Dan. 10:13, 21; 12:1; Jude 9). His name means "who is like God?" Satan said, "I will be like the Most High!" but God defeated him; and now Satan is cast from heaven. Verse 9 describes him as the serpent, which takes us back to Gen. 3; the word "devil" means "accuser," which ties in with v. 10 and with Zech. 3; and "Satan" means "adversary." What an enemy Satan is! In heaven, Satan had been accusing the saints; but the saints had overcome him with three weapons: (1) the blood, which cleanses us of all sin, 1 John 1:9–2:2; (2) the Word, which assures us of forgiveness and is the sword of the Spirit; and (3) their surrender, for they would rather die than obey Satan. There is joy in heaven because Satan is defeated; but there will be woe on earth! Satan's time is short (three and one-half years); then he will be cast into the bottomless pit (20:1-3).

III. The Wrath on Earth (12:13-16)

The great dragon comes down in great wrath. Since he can no longer accuse the saints before God in heaven, he will persecute them on earth. The liar becomes the lion. He focuses his attacks on Israel primarily. Anti-Semitism (persecution of the Jews) is satanic in origin. Egypt persecuted the Jews; so did Babylon. In modern days, Germany slaughtered millions of Jews in the Second World War. God judged all of these nations. Satan could not kill the woman's Son, so now he tries to exterminate her seed, the believing remnant of Israel.

God protects the Jewish remnant (v. 14). When God led Israel out of Egypt, it was "on eagle's wings" (Ex. 19:4). God cared for them in the wilderness as a mother eagle would her brood (Deut. 32:11-12). Their return from Babylonian Captivity would be "on wings as eagles" (Isa. 40:31). God takes His believing remnant to a special place of protection (v. 6) where Satan cannot penetrate.

Satan then uses "water as a flood" to try to exterminate the Jews

(v. 15), which probably symbolizes Gentile persecution. Read carefully Ps. 124. This psalm will certainly be sung by the Jews of the Tribulation when God delivers them from Satan's attacks. Read also Isa. 26:20–27:13 for another parallel passage. Daniel 11:41 indicates that, when the Beast (inspired by Satan) begins his persecution of the Jews in the middle of the Tribulation, the Jews will flee to places of refuge in Edom, Moab, and Ammon. This area has been excavated by archeologists; they have found cities carved out of the rocks, perfect places of refuge for Israel. The fleeing Jews of Matt. 24:16-21 will find safety and peace there during the last three and one-half years, the period called "the Great Tribulation."

A dual war is now going on: God is warring against the unbelieving world, and Satan (through the Beast) is making war on the saints (13:7). What a time of turmoil and trouble it will be! No wonder Jesus said, "Except those days should be shortened, there should no flesh be saved" (Matt. 24:22). For the "elect's sake" (the believing Jews), the days are limited.

There are several practical lessons to be learned from this chapter. (1) Satan is at war with the saints, and we can overcome him only through faith in the Word of God. (2) Satan is the accuser of the brethren. The sins of the saints give Satan all the evidence he needs before God's throne. Thank God we have our Advocate in Christ! (1 John 1:9–2:2) When we confess our sins, Christ cleanses us, and Satan is silenced! (3) Let us not be found accusing the saints, for if we are, then we are on Satan's side and not the Lord's. "Love covers a multitude of sins." (4) We must never be guilty of anti-Semitism. The Jews are God's elect people, and were it not for Israel, we would have no Savior or Bible. We must love Israel, pray for its peace, and seek to win our Jewish friends to Christ. The nation of Israel may not always be right politically, but they are God's people and have an important task to fulfill in this world. We must pray for the peace of Jerusalem.

REVELATION 13

This chapter introduces us to the two beasts. Keep in mind that the term "beast" does not mean that these persons are animals. They are persons that act like animals instead of humans. These verses present the "satanic trinity" — Satan, the Beast (Antichrist), and the False Prophet.

I. Antichrist: The Beast from the Sea (13:1-10)

Verse 1 can read, "And he [Satan, 12:17] stood upon the sand of the sea." The sea symbolizes the nations (17:15), as does the sand of the sea (20:8). Satan calls out his "superman" from the nations and reveals his true character to the world. Up until now, the Antichrist has been operating peacefully as the friend of Israel. He made a covenant with the Jews three and one-half years before (Dan. 9:27), promising them the protection of the federation of Europe that he controls. But now this world ruler is to be revealed in his true satanic character. (For the heads, horns, and crowns, see 17:10-12.)

Three animals are used to describe the Beast, resembling Daniel's prophecy in Dan. 7. Please read the chapter carefully. The four beasts picture four successive empires: Babylon (the lion), Media-Persia (the bear), Greece (the leopard), and the kingdom of Antichrist (the dreadful fourth Beast). The "little horn" of Dan. 7:8 is the Beast of Rev. 13, the Antichrist. Note that John saw the animals in reverse, since he was looking back; Daniel was looking ahead. In other words, the kingdom of the Beast will be a continuation of these kingdoms, a revival of the Roman Empire.

Who is the Beast? Bible students have differed in their interpretation of the symbols in Rev. 13 and 17. It is important to note that three times we are told of his wound (13:3, 12, 14). This might suggest that the Beast will be slain and raised from the dead. In 11:7 and 17:8, we are told that the Beast ascends out of the pit, which certainly suggests a resurrection. Some think he will be Judas, raised from the dead. Both the Beast and Judas are called "the son of perdition" (John 17:12; 2 Thes. 2:3); Judas is called "a devil" in John 6:70. Whoever he might be, the Beast is Satan's superman, his counterfeit Christ. The whole world will admire the Beast and worship Satan (v. 4), something Satan has always craved.

Up to this point, the Beast has been head of the federation of Europe, working in close co-operation with the world church (Rev. 17). He will pretend to be obedient to this apostate religious system and will use it to further his own conquests. About the middle of the Tribulation, Egypt and Russia will invade Palestine (Ezek. 37–38), forcing the Beast to protect the Jews. When the Beast gets to Israel, he will find that God has defeated Russia; and the Beast will decide to conquer Israel. He will at this point destroy the apostate church (the harlot of Rev. 17) and set himself up as the ruler and god of the world. Satan will give him power to do wonders; 2 Thes. 2 states that God will allow "strong delusion" to come upon the unbelieving world. People would not accept Christ, who is the Truth, but they will receive Antichrist, "The Lie." The Beast will blaspheme the church in heaven and persecute the believing Jewish remnant on earth. As we saw in Rev. 11, at this point he will also slay the two witnesses, whose bodies will be raised from the dead after three and one-half days.

II. The False Prophet: The Beast from the Land (13:11-18)

We see a satanic trinity (vv. 19-20). Satan counterfeits the Father; the Beast is the imitation Son and Savior; and the False Prophet counterfeits the Spirit. This second beast comes from "the land," which probably means Israel. He is likely to be a Jew. We find in Dan. 9:26 that Antichrist will have Roman citizenship; but, like Paul, he could be a Roman Jew. However, Antichrist will need an associate to help him win the world. This associate will be the False Prophet. He has "horns like a lamb," suggesting peace and friendliness, but there are no crowns (authority) on the horns. Satan gives him the same power as the first beast, but his task is to glorify the Beast and get the world to follow and worship him. Read Dan. 3 for a similar situation.

The False Prophet will duplicate the miracles of the two witnesses by making fire come from heaven (11:5; 13:13). This event will fulfill Paul's prophecy of 2 Thes. 2:9 and Christ's prophecy in Matt. 24:24.

The False Prophet is the one who orders the image of the Beast made. This is the "abomination of desolation" found in Matt. 24:15, Dan. 11:45, and 2 Thes. 2:4. The Beast will have his image set up in the restored Jewish temple in Jerusalem at this time. This image will come to life! It will speak and greatly amaze the world. Both the Beast and his image will speak "great things" and utter blasphemies against heaven.

Worldwide worship is not the only goal of the False Prophet. He will also establish worldwide economic controls. Just as the 144,000 have the Father's mark on their foreheads (14:1), so the followers of the Beast will have his mark on their foreheads or on their right hand. This mark will enable them to buy and sell. Those who do not follow the Beast and who do not have his mark (his name) will suffer greatly; see 20:4. Satan will now have what he has always wanted: the world will be worshiping him, and he will be in complete control of all the kingdoms of the world. The only "fly in the ointment" is that Christ is reigning in heaven, and His kingdom will one day be established on earth. Satan will vent his fury upon the saints of God on earth since he cannot touch Christ and the saints in heaven.

Verses 17-18 have caused a great deal of speculation: what is the meaning of the number of the Beast, 666? It is interesting to note that the first six Roman numerals add up to 666 (I = 1; V = 5; X = 10; L = 50; C = 100; and D = 500). This suggests, of course, the revival of the Roman Empire, but it does not tell us anything about the Beast. Both Nebuchadnezzar's image and the giant Goliath are identified with the number 6 (Dan. 3:1 and 1 Sam. 17:4-7), indicating that the Beast will be a "superman" in the eyes of the world. We do know that, in both Hebrew and Greek, numbers are made from letters, as in Roman numerals. The numerical value of "Jesus" in Greek is 888. However, it is futile to juggle letters and numbers to try to discover the name of the world ruler.

Six is the number of man. Man was created on the sixth day, and was given six days for labor. The total hours of the day are a multiple of six ($4 \times 6 = 24$); so are the number of months ($2 \times 6 = 12$) and the number of minutes ($6 \times 10 = 60$). The Hebrew OT uses four different words for "man," and the Greek NT uses two, a total of six. There are six different names for both the serpent and the lion in the OT; both are symbols of Satan. History tells us that the number "six" was used in the secret mystery religions of the East. It seems, then, that the Antichrist's number "666" represents the highest man can become apart from Christ. He is Satan's "superman," his false Christ. Seven is the number of perfection, and this Satan cannot reach.

REVELATION 14

God gives us a summary in this chapter, a "panoramic view" of the events that lie ahead in Revelation.

I. The Establishing of the Kingdom (14:1-5)

There is disagreement whether this Mt. Zion is a heavenly landmark (see Heb. 12:22-23), or the literal Mt. Zion on earth. It seems likely that we have an earthly scene, a picture of the coming kingdom. For one thing, John hears "a voice from heaven" in v. 2, which suggests he is on earth. The "new song" suggests that there is a new experience; they have gone through the Tribulation and are now reigning with Christ. But, even if this is a heavenly scene, it anticipates the coming kingdom on earth. Verse 3 indicates that the church (elders) will reign with Christ on earth.

The character of the 144,000 is now described. The terms "not defiled with women" and "virgins" (v. 4) are to be taken in a spiritual sense, not physical. The sin of the earth-dwellers in that day will be spiritual fornication (14:8; see James 4:4 and Ex. 34:15). Marked with their Father's name, and not the name of the Beast, these believing Jews will be spiritually separated and dedicated wholly to Christ. Instead of worshiping the Beast, they follow the Lamb. They will become the nucleus of the Jewish kingdom, the "firstfruits" of the harvest to follow.

II. The Pouring Out of the Vials of Wrath (14:6-13)

Each angel has a special announcement:

A. The everlasting Gospel (vv. 6-7).

Today, God uses people to give His message; but in that last period of judgment, He will use angels as well. "The everlasting Gospel" presents God as the Creator, not the Savior, and warns that judgment is coming. It calls men to fear God and give glory to Him, not to the Beast and Satan. The suggestion is that all who will honor God will be saved. Sad to say, men worship and serve the creature, not the Creator (Rom. 1:25). This is God's final call to a world deluded by Satan.

B. The fall of Babylon (v. 8).

This event will be described in chapters 17 and 18, although the event is anticipated here and also in 16:18-19. Babylon here refers to the apostate religious political system headed up by the Beast in conjunction with the apostate world church. Read Rev. 17–18 to see the fulfillment of this prophecy; study also Jer. 50:14, 15, 38, and 51:7-8.

C. The final judgments (vv. 9-13).

In the seven vials of judgment we have the pouring out of the wrath of God (Rev. 15–18). It will be "without mixture"; that is, there will be no grace or mercy mingled with His wrath (Hab. 3:2). This angel warns the world that all who wear the mark of the Beast will suffer eternal torments without rest or relief. There is a striking contrast in the destinies of the followers of the Beast and the followers of the Lamb; the believers will rest from their labors and be blessed. It is better to reign with Christ 1,000 years than with Antichrist for three and one-half years! This is why v. 12 calls for "endurance" on the part of the saints who must go through trials; see Luke 21:19.

While v. 13 refers strictly to the tribulation saints, we certainly may apply it to believers today. The world looks upon death as a curse, and for the unsaved man, it is a curse; but for the Christian, it is a blessing. The Christian who dies experiences rest and reward; the unbeliever, however, experiences eternal torment and loss of everything.

III. The Fighting of the Battle of Armageddon (14:14-20)

John sees Christ on a white cloud, coming with a sickle to reap the harvest of the earth. It is a picture of judgment. When He came in the flesh, He came as a sower of the seed; but people rejected the seed of the Word (Matt. 13:3-23). Instead, they received Satan's lies. Now Christ must come as a Reaper, bringing judgment to the world. "The harvest of the earth is ripe!" calls the second angel. God knows just when to judge; He patiently waits for the seeds of iniquity to come to fruition (James 1:14-15; Gen. 15:16). This is an anticipation of the battle of Armageddon (see Joel 3:11-16).

At this point, we should review the events leading up to Armageddon. During the first half of the Tribulation, when the Beast was working with the Jews, Russia and Egypt attacked Israel. The Beast was forced to go to Palestine to keep his covenant with the Jews. God defeated Russia, the Beast defeated Egypt; both enemies are sent home in utter defeat. Then the Beast sets himself up as the world ruler and deity, reigning from Jerusalem. However, Russia and her allies plan rebellion against the Beast. After Babylon is destroyed, the enemies of the Beast have their opportunity to attack. During the final three and one-half years of the Tribulation, armies will move toward Palestine (see 16:13-16) to fight the Beast. Dr. Dwight Pentecost suggests that the word "battle" ought to be "campaign"; see Rev. 16:14. In other words, the "battle of

Armageddon" is not a single battle so much as a military movement that climaxes with the armies of the world facing each other at Megiddo. Revelation 19:17-21 indicates that the sign of the Son of Man will appear at that time, and these armies will unite to fight Christ instead of fighting each other.

The picture in vv. 17-18 is that of a man cutting clusters of grapes off a vine. The wicked world-system is "the vine of the earth" (v. 18), while Christ is the True Vine (John 15). Israel was planted in this world to be God's holy vine, to bear fruit for His glory (Isa. 5:1-7; Ps. 80:8-16). Sad to say, Israel bore bitter fruit. In fact, Israel rejected its true Messiah and accepted the false Christ, and had to suffer the bitter consequences. Read Isa. 66:1-6 and Joel 3 for additional material on this final battle.

Verse 20 presents a terrifying picture: the blood will run for 200 miles out of the city of Jerusalem, and be as deep as the distance from the horses' bridles to the ground! This is the winepress of God's wrath (19:15). See Isa. 63:1-6.

We have, then, in this chapter a prophetic summary of the events to follow. There are some very practical lessons for us to learn from this chapter: (1) God will establish His kingdom on earth in spite of Satan's opposition. The OT promises will be fulfilled literally, Israel will have her promised kingdom. (2) Those who reject the Gospel of the grace of God today will face awful judgment tomorrow. It is better to die for Christ's sake and have eternal glory than to live for the devil and suffer eternally. (3) The nations of the world are today taking the path to Armageddon. We see the rise of Europe and Egypt, and of the Asian nations. We see also the coming federation of Europe. But man's final war against God will end a dismal failure for Satan and his allies!

REVELATION 15

Before the seals were opened, we were shown the scene in heaven (chaps. 4–5), and there was a similar vision before the trumpets were sounded (8:1-6). John gazes upon two scenes:

I. The Victors and Their Song (15:1-4)

We have met these saints before; they are the believers of the tribulation period who refused to bow their knees to the Beast and, as a result, lost their lives for the sake of Christ (12:11; 13:7-10). John sees them as victors, standing by the heavenly sea. We think immediately of Israel in Ex. 15, where God had delivered the people victoriously from the bondage of Egypt. Please note that the "sea of glass" now has fire mingled in it; in 4:6, this crystal sea was clear. The fire reminds us that the wrath of God is now about to be revealed (Heb. 12:29).

These saints were slain for their faith, yet John says that they "have the victory" over the Beast! They would not wear his mark or worship his image, and so lost their lives; but in losing their lives for Christ's sake, they found them again! Even if the Christian dies in his witness, he is the victor, not the loser. Here again we see these saints singing by the heavenly sea; in 20:4, we see their dead bodies raised so that the company might reign with Christ during the Millennium. If we suffer with Christ, we shall reign with Him (2 Tim. 2:12).

In 14:3, the 144,000 sang a new song that nobody else could sing; but here we have the Song of Moses and of the Lamb. The Song of Moses is probably Israel's song of victory at the Red Sea in Ex. 15, although some students believe that this song echoes Moses' final words in Deut. 31–32. I prefer the former. Note that the refrain, "The Lord is my strength and song, and He is become my salvation" (Ex. 15:2) is repeated in Ps. 118:14 and Isa. 12:2. In each case, there is a deliverance for Israel. The Jews sang the Song of Moses when they were delivered from Egypt, but they also sang it when they returned to their land after the Captivity, for Ps. 118 was very likely written after the return from Babylon. Isaiah 12 looks forward to the time when Israel will be regathered from the nations of the world and returned to her land; so in each case, the song celebrates Israel's deliverance from the enemy. In Ex. 15, God's people stood by an earthly sea; but here it is a heavenly sea. In Exodus, they had been delivered by the blood of the Passover lamb; and here they overcame the Beast "by the blood of the Lamb" (12:11). Note that they sing not only the song of Moses, but also the song of the Lamb. "The Lamb" is the title of Christ most repeated in Revelation; it is used at least twenty-eight times. We have here a wonderful union of OT and NT, of Moses and the Lamb. God's Law is being vindicated; God's grace is at work. The Old and New Covenants are being fulfilled as Christ judges the nations and prepares to reign.

Check these references in Psalms and you will see the origin of the song given in vv. 3-4: 90:1-2; 92:5; 145:17; 86:9; 98:2; 111:9. "King of saints" in v. 3 ought to read "King of the ages" or "King of the nations." To the church, Christ is the Bridegroom, the Head of the body, the Priest-King like Melchizedek.

II. The Vials and Their Significance (15:5-8)

Verse 1 indicates that the angels with the seven vials (bowls) carry the seven last plagues. You will recall that in 10:7, Christ had announced that, with the pouring out of these vials, the "mystery of God" would be completed and there would be no more delay. In these seven last judgments, God will complete His wrath. Satan at this time is pouring out terrible wrath upon believers, the Jews especially (12:12ff); but God will have the last word.

Once again, the temple of heaven is opened; see 11:19. The earthly temple has been taken over by the Beast (13:13ff; 2 Thes. 2:3-4), but the Beast cannot touch the heavenly temple. All he can do is blaspheme it (13:6). The opening of the temple is another reminder that God will keep His covenant with His people, Israel. Many of the believing Jews have fled to Edom, Moab, and Ammon, where God will protect them. Others will die for their faith, along with many Gentiles.

Seven angels come out of the temple. Seven is the number of completion, and with seven angels delivering these vials of wrath, God's judgments are completed on earth. The angels come out of the holy of holies, where the ark and the tables of the law are kept. The wicked world has defied and disobeyed God's Law, but now judgment is coming. The robes of these angels signify holiness and royalty. The white linen reminds us of the dress of the OT priests; the golden girdle speaks of the king. This is another reminder that the saints of God are "kings and priests" (Rev. 1:6), a royal priesthood. Their dress also takes us back to the description of Christ in 1:13; for He is the High Priest after the order of Melchizedek.

One of the living creatures delivers the bowls of wrath to the angels. All of nature (symbolized by these four creatures) will taste of the wrath of God.

The heavenly temple is now filled with smoke from the glory of God. When the OT tabernacle was dedicated, God's glory filled the tent (Ex. 40:34-35), as it did when the OT temple was dedicated (2 Chron. 7:1-4). During these events no smoke mingled with the glory. Here, however, we have smoke, usually a symbol of judgment

(9:2). When the Prophet Isaiah saw the glory of God, the whole house was filled with the smoke (Isa. 6:4). This was because Isaiah's message was one of judgment as well as mercy. John states that nobody in heaven was allowed into the temple until the bowls of wrath had been poured out. No saint or angel could go into the temple to intercede for the nations of the world. The nations were "beyond intercession"; God's long-suffering had come to the end, and His judgment was about to fall.

Students of prophecy are not agreed on the chronological arrangement of the seals, trumpets, and vials. Many students believe that these three sets of judgments follow after each other: the seventh seal leads into the trumpets, and the seventh trumpet leads into the vials, like three parts of a telescope. But if this is so, then the seven trumpets and seven vials are actually contained in the seventh seal. This might suggest that the seven seals are actually opened throughout the entire seven years of tribulation, with the trumpets and vials coming in quick succession at the end. In his excellent commentary on Revelation, William R. Newell contends that the first six seals will be broken during the first three and one-half years, and that the seventh seal (which includes the trumpets and vials) covers the last three and one-half years.

REVELATION 16

Review the outline of Revelation 8 to see the parallel between the trumpet judgments and the vial judgments. In each case, the judgment affects the same things, but the vial judgments are more severe. It seems too that the vial judgments occur in quick succession, aimed especially at the Beast and his satanic kingdom. These afflictions prepare the way for Armageddon and the return of Christ to earth to claim His kingdom.

I. Grievous Sores (16:1-2)

This passage reminds us of the sixth plague of Egypt (Ex. 9:9), when boils broke out on the Egyptians. The word "noisome" (v. 2) comes from an Old English word (similar to "annoy") that means "troublesome, vexing." God promised to send Israel this plague if they rebelled against Him (Deut. 28:27, 35); and no doubt the unbelieving Jews will suffer along with the unbelieving Gentiles.

Note that these sores still trouble the world when the fifth vial is poured out (v. 11). The affliction did not soften their hearts; men still blasphemed God and refused to bow before Him.

II. Water to Blood (16:3-7)

Two of the vials are poured out in these verses. The second angel turns the sea to blood, and the third vial turns the fountains and rivers to blood. Again, we are reminded of the first plague of Egypt (Ex. 7:18; Ps. 105:29), as well as the second trumpet (8:8ff). However, during the trumpet judgment, only a third of the sea became blood; here we see the entire water system of the world polluted! The angel of the waters (see 7:1-2 and 14:18) praises God for this judgment and explains that it is a fair one. The people of the earth have shed blood, so they must drink blood. We see this law operating throughout the Bible. Pharaoh drowned Hebrew boys, so his army was drowned in the Red Sea. In the Book of Esther, Haman built a gallows to hang Mordecai, and Haman and his sons were hanged on it instead! Note that in v. 7, the souls under the altar are now satisfied; God had answered their prayers and vindicated them (6:9).

III. Scorching and Darkness (16:8-11)

The judgments from the fourth and fifth angels involve the heavens. The fourth angel causes the sun to scorch men. This is a sharp contrast with the trumpet judgment in 8:12, where a part of the sun was darkened. In this case, God allows the sun to burn men, to give them, as it were, a foretaste of hell. This is the day Malachi promised would "burn as an oven" (Mal. 4:1-2). Did sinners repent? No! Such is the hardness of the human heart!

The fifth angel brings darkness. It is possible that this darkness covered only the immediate kingdom of the Beast, where his throne (seat) was located. This darkness parallels the ninth plague of Egypt (Ex. 10:21-23). Satan is the prince of darkness, so it is only right that darkness should invade his kingdom. Joel 2:1-2 declares that the day of the Lord would be a time of darkness. See also Christ's prophecy in Mark 13:24. Imagine the agony of men with sores that will not heal, having to endure their pain in the darkness! This is another foretaste of hell. Still, they will not repent. As William Newell says, "Men who will not be won by grace will never be won at all."

IV. Gathering of the Armies (16:12-16)

When God delivered Israel from Egypt, He dried up the Red Sea to let the nation out. Here He dries up part of the Euphrates to allow the armies of the kings of the east to meet with the armies of the nations of the world at Armageddon. The word "battle" in v. 14 is better translated "campaign." You will recall that Russia and her allies invaded Palestine about the middle of the Tribulation (battle of Gog and Magog, Ezek. 38–39) and were judged by the Lord. This left the Beast in complete control of the world-system, ruling from Jerusalem. But Russia, the kings of the east, and Egypt join forces to battle the armies of the Beast at Armageddon. The word "Armageddon" means "mountain of Megiddo." This area has long been recognized as one of the world's greatest battlefields; and it is here that the battle will be fought between Christ and Antichrist.

How are these armies gathered? The satanic trinity uses demons to assemble them (vv. 13-14). These are not literal frogs, of course; frogs are symbols of the demonic means Satan will use to assemble the largest army in the history of the world in his fight against the Lord. (See 1 Tim. 4:1; Ex. 8:5-7; 1 Kings 22:20-38.) The armies will gather to attack Jerusalem; but then the sign of the Son of Man will appear (Matt. 24:29-30) and the armies will unite to fight against Christ. The result is disclosed in Rev. 19:11-21. Read also: Joel 3:9-14, Zeph. 3:8, Zech. 12, and Isa. 24:1-8.

Verse 15 is a promise to the saints on earth at that time. First Thessalonians 5:2 makes it clear that the church will not be caught "in the dark." Read Rev. 18:4 and you will see that in this warning Christ is asking His people to keep themselves from the world and the defilement of the satanic system. Keep your garments clean (2 Cor. 7:1). This is a good warning to saints today.

V. The Mystery of God Finished (16:17-21)

In 10:6-7, God promised that "the mystery of God" would be finished when the seventh angel poured out his vial; now we see this fulfilled. The events described in this section look forward to the fall of Babylon and the return of Christ to reign. What occurs in the next chapters (chaps. 17–19) is included in this seventh vial.

Why did the angel pour his vial out in the air? Because this is the realm assigned to Satan, "the prince of the power of the air" (Eph. 2:2). The judgments thus far have touched the world of nature and of mankind, but not the "mastermind" behind it all—Satan. However, from this point on, Christ will deal with Satan's religious system (chap. 17), his political system (chap. 18), his armies (chap. 19), and the old serpent himself (20:1-3). When the seventh vial is emptied out, the throne and the temple of heaven unite in saying, "It is done!" The mystery of God is finished! The souls under the altar must no longer ask, "How long?" This announcement reminds us of Christ's words on the cross, "It is finished!" When the new heavens and earth are ushered in, God will again say, "It is done!" (Rev. 21:6)

The earthquake divides Jerusalem (see 11:8) into three parts; see Zech. 14:4. But this is not the only city to be judged; other great cities of the earth fall, and the great Babylon comes up for judgment. Babylon in Rev. 17 is the apostate church of the last days; Babylon of Rev. 18 is the political-economic system of the Beast.

The hail (v. 16) reminds us of the seventh plague (Ex. 9:22-26). Imagine hailstones that weigh 125 pounds, which is what a talent of silver weighed in John's day. Leviticus 24:16 states that the blasphemer should be stoned to death, so the men of the earth who continued to blaspheme God get what they deserve (vv. 9, 11, 21).

REVELATION 17

Chapters 17 and 18 introduce us to Babylon, which typifies the last great world system before the return of Christ. In chapter 17, the emphasis is on the religious aspect of the system, while in chapter 18, the commercial aspect is stressed. Religious Babylon will be overthrown by the Beast (17:16-18), while commercial Babylon will be destroyed by God.

I. The Invitation (17:1-2)

Since the seven vials (chap. 16) brought about the climax of God's wrath on the world, including the fall of Babylon (16:17-21), one of those angels invites John to go to the wilderness to see "the great whore," the apostate world-system. It has been pointed out that there are four women in Revelation: (1) Jezebel, symbolizing apostasy creeping into the church, 2:20; (2) Israel, 12:1; (3) the harlot, the final apostate world-system, chapter 17; and (4) the bride, the church, 19:7.

II. The Explanation (17:3-18)

There are several symbols involved in this description, but the angel explains them to us. If we accept the interpretation of God's Word, we will have little trouble understanding what the chapter teaches.

A. *The woman.*

Verse 18 makes it clear that she is a city, and in John's day, she was reigning over the kings of the earth. The seven heads of v. 3 are identified as seven mountains in v. 9. There seems to be little doubt that the city is Rome. It is situated on seven hills; when Revelation was written, Rome was reigning over the kings of the earth.

B. *The Beast.*

This is the same Beast we met in chapter 13, the Antichrist. Verse 8 indicates that this world ruler will come out of the bottomless pit, suggesting that he was raised from the dead. "Perdition" links him with Judas (John 17:12; 2 Thes. 2:3); and for this reason, some students believe that Antichrist will be Judas raised from the dead. The Beast is scarlet-colored, linking him with the dragon, Satan (12:3). The fact that the Beast has seven heads and ten horns also identifies him with Satan (see 12:3 and 13:1). Verse 10 tells us that the seven heads are seven kings (as well as seven mountains); and v. 12 explains that the ten horns are ten more kings. So, the Beast resembles the kingdom of Antichrist as well as his own person. The "seven kings" of v. 10 could also be translated "seven kingdoms." In other words, the kingdom of the Beast will be the seventh world kingdom, the one that "has not yet come."

C. *The seven heads.*

We have already seen that these heads represent seven mountains (v. 9) and seven kings or kingdoms (v. 10). The five kingdoms that had fallen were Egypt, Assyria, Babylon, Persia, and Greece. The kingdom "that is" would be Rome in John's day; the one yet to come, the seventh, would be the kingdom of the Beast. If we compare the seven heads to specific kings, then the five who were fallen (of Roman rulers) would be Julius Caesar, Tiberius, Caligula, Claudius, and Nero. The "one that is" would be Domitian; the one yet to come, the Beast, the king of the revived Roman Empire.

D. The ten horns.

Verse 12 explains that these are ten more kings. They parallel the ten toes of Daniel's image in Dan. 2:36-45, the revived Roman Empire. In John's day, these kings had not yet received their power; it is reserved for the last days when the federation of Europe, headed by the Beast, comes to power. Note that these ten kings willingly give support to the Beast in his battle against Christ and the saints; and that, with the help of the Beast, they will destroy the great harlot.

E. The waters.

The waters on which the harlot is seated are the peoples of the world (v. 15). She will have influence over the whole world, politically, economically and, most of all, religiously.

III. The Application

The harlot represents the apostate world church of the latter days, centered in Rome. The name "Babylon" takes us back to Gen. 10:1-11 and 11:1-9, where the first organized rebellion against God took place. The name "Babel" means "confusion" and stands for apostate religion. The Babylonian system has been guilty of persecuting true believers ever since Cain killed Abel. All anti-Christian sects (even those that call themselves "Christian") that have killed God's servants are a part of this abominable system.

In the last days, one world church will be formed. This world church (the harlot) will be involved in the political and economic affairs of the world and, with the help of the Beast, will become a great power. The world church will "ride into power" on the back of the Beast, that is, with the help of Satan and the United States of Europe.

The Beast will get the support of the ten kings as he rides to victory (Rev. 6:1-2). A union will exist between the nations of Europe, the Beast, and the world church. The scene in chapter 17 takes place during the first half of the Tribulation. Note that the Beast has not yet been revealed in his true satanic character.

During the middle of the Tribulation, the Beast will want to have all power and worship for himself (chap. 13). This means he must get rid of the harlot, because she represents the worship of God, if even in an apostate way. Verse 16 indicates that the federated nations of Europe will turn against the world church and destroy her, fulfilling the prophecy of Rev. 2:20-23. Once the harlot is out of the way, the Beast will declare himself to be a god and demand the worship of the nations.

The apostate church is called a "harlot," while the true church is pictured as a pure bride. The harlot is in the wilderness; the bride is in heaven. The harlot is adorned by Satan (17:4), while the bride is adorned by Christ (19:8). The harlot is judged forever; the bride reigns forever. The harlot is stained with the blood of the martyrs; the bride is redeemed by the blood of the Lamb.

It behooves dedicated Christians to separate themselves from Satan's false church and to identify with those who are true to Christ and the Word of God. The false church may appear to be successful for a season, but her doom is fixed.

REVELATION 18

Here we read of commercial Babylon, which represents the great global system of the latter days. Of course, religious Babylon (the apostate church) will have a great part to play in the economics of the nations. When this religious system collapses, it will be the beginning of the end for the Beast's entire empire, although he will have three and one-half years yet to reign. It is comforting to read 17:17 and realize that all of these things fulfill the Word of God! Note in this chapter four different voices:

I. The Voice of Judgment (18:1-3)

This angel announces the fall of Babylon, an event that has already been announced (14:8 and 16:19). The repetition of "is fallen, is fallen" suggests the dual judgment of the two chapters (on religious and commercial Babylon), as well as the statement in v. 6 that she would receive double for her sins. This "great city" (v. 10), the center of the world economic system, will finally get what it deserves from the hand of God. It has become a habitation of demons (see Eph. 2:22, where the church is a habitation of the Spirit), and a haven for foul spirits (see 16:13-14). Satan is often pictured as a bird (Matt. 13:4, 19, 31-32). Verse 3 indicates that Babylon influenced the nations of the earth the way wine influences drunkards. But this city made them rich, which was all that mattered to them.

II. The Voice of Separation (18:4-8)

Some of God's people are in this city, and God wants them to come out for two reasons: (1) the city will be destroyed and He wants them saved; (2) the city is satanic and He does not want them defiled. "Come out!" has always been God's call to His people, for salvation means separation from the world unto the Lord (2 Cor. 6:14ff). The world glorifies itself (v. 7); the Christian seeks to glorify God. The world lives for the "delicious pleasures of sin," while the Christian lives for the pleasures of Christ. Look at Babylon's pride in v. 7: "I sit a queen . . . and shall see no sorrow!" But v. 8 indicates that in one day she will exchange her joys for sorrow, her riches for famine! There is a lesson here for God's people today: "Do not share in other people's sins" (see 1 Tim. 5:22; also Jer. 51:9).

III. The Voice of Mourning (18:9-19)

We see two groups lamenting the fall of Babylon: the kings of the earth (vv. 9-10), and the merchants of the earth (vv. 11-19). They had "committed fornication" with Babylon by rejecting the true God and going after idols, money in particular. They sold their souls for wealth. Their luxurious living was now at an end. Note the repetition of "Alas, alas!" in vv. 10, 16, and 19. Babylon is judged in one day (v. 8) and one hour (vv. 10, 19).

Why do the merchants and kings lament? Because their merchandise is now gone. Verses 12-13 indicate the vast wealth of the mercantile system, including "slaves and the souls of men." Slavery will increase in the last days, for Satan has always wanted to enslave the souls and bodies of humans. The rich will get richer, the poor will get poorer. Both luxuries and necessities will be destroyed when God judges Babylon. Shipping will be destroyed and the shipping industry brought to ruin. The world's peoples depend on this economic system to care for them, protect them, and satisfy them; but ultimately it will fail them.

IV. The Voice of Rejoicing (18:20-24)

The men of the earth never have the same viewpoint as the people of God. When Satan was cast out of heaven, heaven rejoiced but the earth mourned (12:10-12). Now that Babylon has been destroyed, heaven rejoices but earth laments.

The main reason for heaven's rejoicing is that God has avenged the blood of the martyrs. The Babylonian system is satanic and from the very beginning (Gen. 4) has been responsible for the martyrdom of God's faithful people. The souls under the altar in Rev. 6:9-11 had asked, "How long, O Lord?" Now their prayer is answered: God has avenged their blood. See Rom. 12:19.

The casting down of the millstone indicates the suddenness of God's judgment on the empire of the Beast. Some students see in this millstone the return of Christ, the Smiting Stone, as pictured in Dan. 2:34-35, 44-45. Just when the world thinks it is performing beautifully, Christ will return to destroy its works.

Note the repeated "no more" statements in this chapter, and read Jer. 25:9-11. When God says "No more!" there is nothing man can do to change it. Read Jer. 51 also.

We have seen, then, the destruction of the Beast's economic and religious empire. All that remains is for Christ to destroy his armies, and this we see in chapter 19.

REVELATION 19

These verses present the climax of God's wrath as Jesus Christ comes to destroy the armies of the nations of the world.

I. The Anthems of Joy in Heaven (19:1-10)

A great heavenly multitude proclaims four "Hallelujah choruses" here in anticipation of Christ's return to earth. The word "hallelujah" (in the Gk. "alleluia") means "Praise Jehovah" and is a familiar OT word. Why does heaven rejoice?

A. Because sin has been judged (vv. 1-4).

In chapter 18, the merchants of earth and the kings lamented because of the fall of Babylon; but here, heaven is rejoicing. Babylon was the source of all religious deception and confusion; Babylon has caused the death of multitudes of God's saints; and now Babylon has been destroyed. In fact, the fall of Babylon merits three "Alleluias" from heaven!

B. Because God is reigning (vv. 5-6).

It seems that all of heaven's voices unite to praise God because He is God, and because He is on the throne. "Omnipotent" means "all powerful." It is this theme that Handel uses in his magnificent "Hallelujah Chorus." How we ought to praise God because He is on the throne!

C. Because the marriage of the Lamb is come (vv. 7-10).

The words "is come" (v. 7) may be translated "has been completed." The bride is now the wife (v. 7), and the marriage supper is now to be served. It is interesting that this is the marriage supper of the Lamb, and not of "the King" or "the Lord." The one title that Christ wants emphasized for all eternity is "the Lamb," for it speaks of His love for the church and the price He paid to purchase it. Of course, the church has to "make herself ready" for this supper. This cleansing was done at the judgment seat of Christ, when all the "spots and wrinkles" were taken away (Eph. 5:25-27). The bride goes to heaven by God's grace, and not by good works. But once in heaven, believers will be judged at Christ's judgment seat for their faithfulness in life and in service. Verse 8 states that the wife will wear "the righteousness of the saints"; that is, "the righteous deeds of the saints." Christ will reward us according to our faithfulness, and the rewards we receive will make up the "wedding gown." Dr. Lehman Strauss writes, "Has it ever occurred to you . . . that at the marriage of the Bride to the Lamb, each of us will be wearing the wedding garment of our own making?" What a solemn thought!

II. The Armies of Jesus Christ from Heaven (19:11-16)

In 4:1, heaven opens to let the church in; but here, heaven opens to let Christ and His armies ride forth in victory. At His trial, Christ said that the Father could send legions of angels to deliver Him; and here the Lord rides forth with the armies of glory: the OT saints, the church, and the angels (Matt. 25:31; 1 Thes. 3:13). In 6:1, the Antichrist had ridden on a white horse, imitating Christ, but here the "Faithful and True" (v. 11) rides forth to judge and make war (Ps. 45).

This description of Christ is thrilling! He is no longer on a humble donkey, but on a fiery white charger. His eyes are not filled with tears as when He beheld Jerusalem; nor is He wearing a mocking crown of thorns. Instead of being stripped by His enemies, He wears a garment dipped in blood, signifying judgment and victory. When on earth, He was abandoned by His followers; but here the armies of heaven follow Him in conquest. His mouth does not speak "words of grace" (Luke 4:22), but rather the Word of victory and justice. See Isa. 11:4. He comes to rule with a rod of iron (Ps. 2). He comes not to bear the wrath of God on the cross, but to tread the winepress of God's wrath at the Battle of Armageddon. He is King of Kings and Lord of Lords!

Keep in mind that the armies of the east have gathered in Palestine to oppose the Beast and his armies. But they will see the sign of the Son of Man in the heavens, and all unite to oppose Christ. Read again Rev. 16:12-16 and 14:14-20.

III. The Announcement of Judgment on Earth (19:17-21)

Two suppers are seen in this chapter: the marriage supper of the Lamb (v. 9) and the supper of the great God, Armageddon. The first is a time of blessing and joy; the second is a time of judgment and sorrow. All of human history is moving rapidly toward Armageddon.

The angel announces that the armies of earth will lose the battle. In fact, there will not be much of a battle, for Christ will destroy His enemies instantly (2 Thes. 1). Note the repetition of the word "flesh" in this section, signifying that man is only flesh and can never successfully fight against God. "Flesh" has been the source of trouble since the fall of Adam. Flesh does not change; God has condemned flesh; flesh can never please God. How foolish for flesh to fight against Christ! Even "kings, captains, and mighty men" (v. 18) are no match for the King of Kings.

Who are the armies gathered together against Christ? These are the armies of the ten-kingdom federation of Europe, as well as the forces of the kings of the east, Egypt, and Russia. They gather on the Plain of Esdraelon in Palestine, an area that Napoleon called the most natural battlefield in the world. The name "Armageddon" means "Mount of Megiddo."

Christ destroys the armies with the Word, the sword that comes from His mouth (Heb. 4:12). Men would not bow to His Word and receive the Gospel; now they must be slain by that same Word. The followers of the Beast are "marked men"; the mark of the Beast on their bodies seals them for certain judgment. Christ not only destroys the armies of the Beast, but He also captures the Beast and False Prophet and casts them alive into hell. He also takes Satan and casts him into the bottomless pit (20:1-3).

The OT prophets wrote about this great battle. See Isa. 63, Zech. 14, and Joel 2–3.

REVELATION 20

This is the "thousand years" chapter (mentioned six times here), which describes the Millennium. The word "millennium" means "thousand years" in Latin. Some sincere Bible students deny that there will be a literal thousand-year reign of Christ on earth. They prefer to "spiritualize" the OT kingdom prophecies and apply them to the church today. But I believe that there will be a literal thousand-year kingdom on earth for several reasons: (1) To fulfill the OT promises to Israel, Luke 1:30-33; (2) To give a public display of Christ's glory to the nations of earth; (3) To answer the saints' prayer of "Thy kingdom come"; (4) To fulfill the promises to the church that saints will reign with Christ; (5) To bring about the complete redemption of nature as promised in Rom. 8:19-22; (6) To give mankind one final trial under the sovereign rule of Christ.

I. Before the Millennium (20:1-5)

The Battle of Armageddon is now over, and the Beast and False Prophet have been cast into hell. Christ now lays hold of that old serpent, Satan, and casts him into the bottomless pit. Some of Satan's followers are already chained (2 Peter 2:4; Jude 6), but now the "old serpent" himself is imprisoned. The Beast came out of the bottomless pit (17:8) and was cast into hell; but Satan's final judgment is not yet come.

After Satan is cast down, there is a resurrection of the Tribulation saints who gave their lives in faithful service to Christ. From the description in Dan. 12:1-3, it seems that the OT saints are also raised at this point. Not being members of the body of Christ, the church, they are not necessarily raised with the saints at the rapture. At this point, then, all saved people have been raised to reign with Christ. This is known as the first resurrection. It extends from the rapture of the church (1 Thes. 4:13ff) to the resurrection of the saints described in Rev. 20:4. All who are raised in the first resurrection are saved people; they will not experience the second death, which is hell. See John 5:24-29.

The OT saints believed in a resurrection of the dead, but they knew nothing of the "out-resurrection from among the dead" taught in the NT (see Mark 9:9-10, where "rising from the dead" means literally "the out-resurrection from among the dead"). The Bible makes no mention of "the general resurrection." The saved are all raised (at different times) in the first resurrection; the lost are raised at the second resurrection. A period of 1,000 years will elapse between the first and second resurrections.

Thrones are prepared, and the purified nation of Israel, the church, and the Tribulation saints reign with Christ. Matthew 25:31-46 makes it clear that the living Gentiles will be judged before the Millennium begins. Believing Gentiles (sheep) will have proved their faith by loving and helping the believing Jews ("my brethren"). The saved Gentiles will enter into the joy of the kingdom that God promised for His people Israel.

II. During the Millennium (20:6)

The millennial kingdom will be the divine rule of heaven upon earth. Christ will rule with a rod of iron, permitting no injustice or sin. Jerusalem will be the center of the kingdom (Isa. 2:1-4), and the disciples will reign with Christ (Matt. 19:28). Israel will be in its land, sharing the glory of Christ, its rightful King. There will be peace on earth among men and animals (Isa. 11:7-9 and 54:13-14). Each person will be suited to his or her best job, and perfect efficiency and joy will fill the earth. Of course, since these human beings on earth are still human (apart from the church and resurrected saints, who have glorified bodies), children will be born with sinful natures. At the close of the Millennium, many people will still give only outward obedience to Christ but will not submit to Him from the heart. One of the main purposes of the Millennium is to prove conclusively that mankind cannot be changed, even under a perfect rule in a perfect environment. For, at the end of the thousand years, Satan will be able to muster a huge army to rebel against Christ! If people are not changed by the grace of God, nothing else will change them.

The saints will reign with Christ as kings and priests, and will serve Him in various capacities during the Millennium. Our faithfulness to Him today will determine the extent of our glorious responsibilities during the kingdom age (Matt. 25:14-30; Luke 19:11-27).

III. After the Millennium (20:7-15)

A. The final battle (vv. 7-10).

Satan is loosed at the end of the thousand years, and he gathers a huge army to fight Christ. This rebellion proves that a rule of perfect law cannot change the human heart; sinners would rather follow Satan. This is not the battle of Gog and Magog, for that battle takes place about the end of the first half of the Tribulation (Ezek. 38–39) and results in the Beast defeating both Russia and Egypt. Rather, this battle involves perhaps Russia (Gog and Magog) as the leading force, now that the Beast and the False Prophet are suffering eternal punishment. These armies will attack the millennial Jerusalem, but fire from heaven will devour them. Satan will be captured and consigned eternally to the lake of fire. Note that the Beast and False Prophet are still suffering in hell a thousand years after being taken! There is no way to get out of hell once you are there. It is a place of eternal torment.

B. The final judgment (vv. 11-15).

John now sees a throne of judgment. It is great, because all of the sinners of history will stand before it. It is white because it represents the unchanging holiness of God; He is not a respecter of persons. Heaven and earth flee away; there is no place for the lost sinner to hide! The Judge on the throne is Jesus Christ (John 5:22-23). Today He is the Savior of the world; on that day, He will be the righteous Judge.

There is a resurrection. Death gives up the bodies of lost sinners; Hades (not "hell" as in v. 13) gives up the soul. This brief moment when the body and soul of the lost sinner are joined before Christ's judgment throne is the only relief from punishment these sinners will know before being cast into hell! All lost sinners will be there: small and great, rich and poor; there will be no escape (Heb. 9:27).

What books are involved in this final judgment? The Bible will be there, according to John 12:48. The very Word that sinners hear and reject today will judge them on the last day. There is the Book of Life, containing the names of the saints. If a person's name is not found in the Book of Life, he or she is cast into hell (v. 15). Also present is the book containing the deeds people have done. God is a Righteous Judge; He keeps a record of their deeds and will punish each one justly. Certainly those who knew the truth and deliberately disobeyed it will be punished with greater severity than those who did not know the truth. Hell will have degrees of punishment in the same way that heaven has degrees of reward (Matt. 11:20-24). Good works will not save sinners, but God will judge their works fairly and give them a just punishment in hell.

There will be no opportunity for sinners to argue their case. When the books are opened and the facts revealed, they will stand speechless before Christ (Rom. 3:19). God will not weigh the good against the bad; He will pronounce every lost sinner condemned. All those who share in the second resurrection must face the second death—eternal hell.

Satan and sin have been judged; human rebellion has been put down; now God can usher in the new heavens and earth—eternal bliss for the people of God!

REVELATION 21–22

The theme of these two chapters is stated in 21:5: "Behold, I make all things new!" While it would be interesting and edifying to go into the many details of these chapters, we will have to confine ourselves to the main lessons. Note the "new things" that will be a part of the believer's eternal home.

I. The New Heaven and Earth (21:1-2)

The Gk. word for "new" means "new in character" rather than "new in time," and this suggests that God will renovate the old heaven and earth and remove all that is sinful and destructive. Note 2 Peter 3:7-10, where we are told that a fiery judgment brings about this renewal of the old creation. "Passed away" does not mean "destroyed." The fact that there is "no more sea" is significant, since John was exiled on an island and separated from those he loved. Two-thirds of the globe today is water; so that in the new creation, God will have devised a whole new system for watering the earth.

II. The New People of God (21:3-8)

What wonderful changes there will be when we enter eternity! God will dwell personally with His people in a glorious and intimate way. There will be no more tears, death, or sorrow. All of these came into the world through sin (Gen. 3), but now the curse is removed (22:3). God's "It is done!" parallels Christ's "It is finished!" (John 19:30) The same Lord who started creation will also finish it; He is Alpha and Omega (the first and last letters of the Gk. alphabet). But v. 8 solemnly declares some people will not enter this new creation. They are the fearful, or the cowards who would not confess Christ; those who would not believe in Christ; those who "went along with the crowd" and practiced sin. Note that God puts "cowards" at the head of the list! When people are afraid to take a stand for Christ, they are liable to commit any kind of sin as a result.

III. The New Jerusalem (21:9-27)

Verse 2 suggests that this heavenly city will hover over the earth during the Millennium, and then descend when the new creation is ushered in. The city is identified with God's people; she is looked upon as a bride. You will recall that the Babylonian system of chapter 17 was pictured as a harlot. After all, a city is not its buildings; it is the people who live in it. In Gen. 4:17, rebellious Cain went out from God's presence and built a city; but believing Abraham "looked for a city . . . whose builder was God" (Heb. 11:10). The new Jerusalem is that city. Note that the city unites God's people of the OT and the NT, Israel and the church. The tribes of Israel are named on the gates, and the twelve apostles are named on the foundation stones. (On the apostles, see Eph. 2:20 and Matt. 19:28.) The dimensions and descriptions of the city stagger our imagination. "Foursquare" means "equal on all sides"; which may mean the city is a perfect cube, a "holy of holies" radiant with the presence of God. Or, it could be a pyramid. In either case, the city measures about 1,500 miles each way, or two-thirds the size of the United States! The beautiful colors of the gems (vv. 18-20) suggests the "manifold (many-colored) grace of God" in 1 Peter 4:10. Consult your Bible dictionary for the colors of these jewels.

Several things are missing from the city: a temple, natural light, and night. Since God dwells personally with His people, no temple is necessary. His glory replaces the glory of the sun, moon, and stars. Night in the Bible symbolizes death, sin, sorrow; these things are banished from the city forever. The gates will never be shut, so God's people will have access to the city from every part of His renewed universe! This new earth will have nations (v. 24, see also 22:2). All the glory of these nations will be brought to God, where it belongs.

IV. The New Paradise (22:1-5)

In this new creation, God reverses all the tragedies that sin brought to the original creation. The old heaven and earth were plunged into judgment; this new heaven and earth glisten with perfection. Eden had an earthly river (Gen. 2:10-14); but here we have a wonderful heavenly river. The tree of life in Eden was guarded after man sinned (Gen. 3:24); but here the heavenly tree of life is available to God's people. The curse was pronounced in Gen. 3:14-17; but now there is no more curse. Adam and Eve were forced to leave the original paradise and labor for their daily bread; but here men serve God and see His face in perfect fellowship. When the first man and woman sinned, they became slaves and lost their kingship; but v. 5 indicates that this kingship will be regained, and we shall reign with Christ forever!

The present creation is not God's final product. It is groaning and travailing under the bondage of sin (Rom. 8:18-23). But one day, God will usher in His new creation, and we will enjoy perfect liberty and fullness of life forever.

V. The Final Message (22:6-21)

Three times at the close of this book Christ says, "I am coming quickly!" (vv. 7, 12, 20). The word "quickly" suggests "swiftly." It means that when these great events start to occur, there will be no delay. We do not know when Christ will appear, and it behooves us to be ready.

In Dan. 12:4, the prophet was told to seal up the book; John, on the other hand, was commanded not to seal the book because "the time is at hand" (v. 10). Daniel's words would not be fulfilled for many years; John's prophecy would come to pass shortly. Verse 11 is not an enticement for sinners to remain unchanged; otherwise the invitation in v. 17 would be a mockery. Instead, v. 11 is warning us that continued sin defines character and determines destiny. "The wicked shall do wickedly," says Dan. 12:10. When Christ comes, our true character will be revealed. Another lesson of this verse is that people make their own decisions; God does not force them to be either wicked or righteous. Compare 22:15 with 21:8.

The final verses of this book present a plea, a prayer, and a promise. In vv. 7 and 12, the Lord has said, "I come quickly!" In v. 17, the Spirit and the bride say "Come!" to the Lord Jesus. The Spirit prays through the church for the return of the Savior. The lost soul is invited to "Come, drink of the water of life!" The last prayer of the Bible is that of the Holy Spirit through John saying, "Even so come, Lord Jesus!" This ought to be our daily prayer also.

Verses 18-19 are a warning against tampering with God's Word. Satan loves for men to add to the Word or take from the Word, but to do so is to invite judgment. Note Deut. 4:2 and Prov. 30:5-6. In John's day, books were copied by hand, and the copyist might have been tempted to edit or emend the material. Even today, people add their theories and traditions to God's Word or strike from it whatever does not fit into their scheme of theology. John's warning applied specifically to the Book of Revelation, but certainly it includes all of the Word of God.

Thus ends the last book of the Bible, the book of the last things. We can end these study notes in no better way than to echo the prayer of the Spirit, "Even so come, Lord Jesus!"